ACCESS
PARIS

Orientation	4

P9-CEZ-823

The Islands: Ile de la Cité and Ile St-Louis	18
The Latin Quarter	36
St-Germain	62
Eiffel Tower/Invalides	96
Les Halles, Marais, and The Bastille	126
Louvre and The Champs-Elysées	168
St-Honoré	198
Montmartre	230
Additional Highlights	244
Day Trips	252
History	257
Index	260

ACCESS®PRESS does not solicit individuals, organizations, or businesses for inclusion in our books, nor do we accept payment for inclusion. We welcome, however, information from our readers, including comments, criticisms, and suggestions for new listings. Send all correspondence to: ACCESS®PRESS, 10 East 53rd Street, Fifth Floor, New York, NY 10022

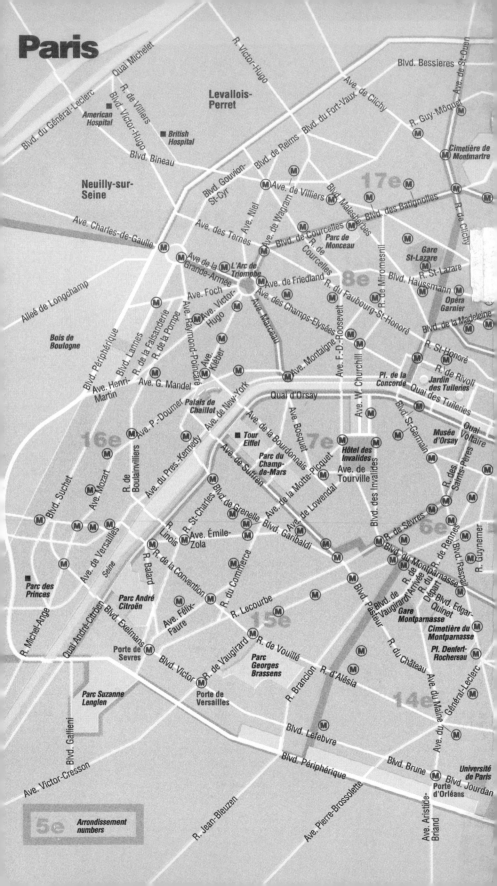

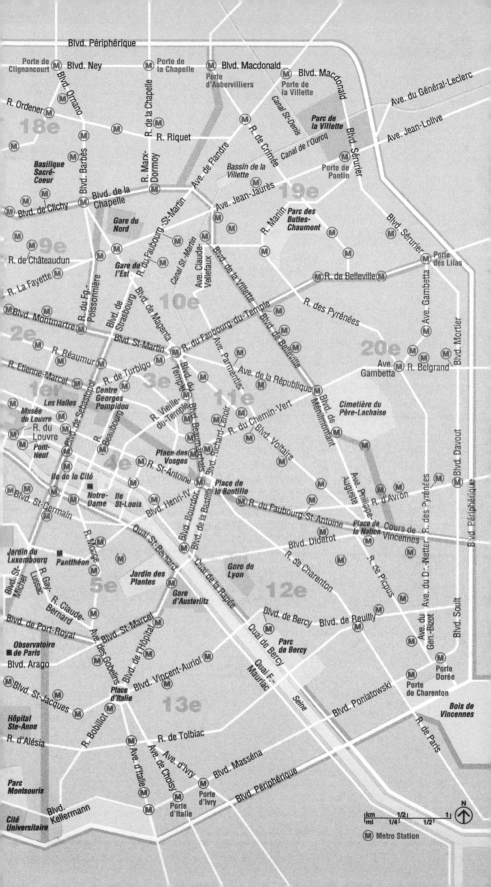

Orientation

"Paris is the greatest temple ever built to material joys and the lust of the eyes," wrote novelist Henry James. Indeed, the richness and variety of France's capital elevates even the necessities of life to works of art. Parisians seem to perform such everyday routines as eating and dressing with vitality and flair. The streets themselves are museums lined with splendid architecture and historic monuments, making even the simple act of walking through the city one of life's greatest pleasures.

Paris is located in the north-central part of France in the **Ile-de-France** region, in the **Seine** river valley. Covering only 105 square kilometers (41 square miles) and populated by over 2 million people, it is France's largest city and the densest of all European capitals. It is roughly circular in shape and bounded by the **Boulevard Périphérique**, a ring road on the site of mid–19th-century fortifications that once defined the city limits.

Cutting across the whole map is a seven-mile stretch of the Seine River that separates Paris into two distinct areas, the northern **Rive Droite (Right Bank)** and the southern **Rive Gauche (Left Bank).** The Seine unites rather than divides the city; Paris is linked by no fewer than 26 bridges in the city center alone. The quays are lined with fine apartment and town houses, *bouquinistes* (booksellers) and street artists, such world-class museums as the **Musée du Louvre** and the **Musée d'Orsay**, and dazzling monuments, including the **Tour Eiffel** and the **Cathédrale de Notre-Dame.** The Seine is alive with commercial barges and *bateaux mouches* (small passenger steamers) taking sightseers up- and downriver to enjoy the panoramas, and the riverbanks are animated with people promenading along their course.

Each of the city's 20 arrondissements (quarters) boasts its own distinct character, so Paris feels less like a monstrous metropolis and more like a score of small towns. Travel from the villagelike atmosphere of **Montmartre**, the **Latin Quarter**, or the **Marais** to the grandeur of the **Avenue des Champs-Elysées** and the **Hôtel des Invalides;** from the haute-couture shopping areas along the **Rue du Faubourg-St-Honoré** and the **Boulevard St-Germain** to the trendy regions around the **Bastille** and **Les Halles;** and to the two islands that form the physical and spiritual heart of the city, the **Ile de la Cité** and the **Ile St-Louis.** In Paris the past is ever present, and a stroll through the city of today is also a journey back in time.

Paris is an ancient city, more than 2,000 years old. Begun as a village named Lutetia and inhabited by a tribe called the Parisii, it was subsequently settled by the Romans and then became the capital city of the kingdom of the Franks. Under Charlemagne the capital of France was moved to Aix-la-Chapelle, but Paris regained its capital status in 987 under Hugh Capet, the first of the Capetian line of kings. During the Middle Ages the city was an intellectual and religious center, but it lapsed into chaos during the Hundred Years' War with England (1337-1453), a period that also saw outbreaks of the bubonic plague.

The city again flourished during the Renaissance and saw significant expansion and development under the Bourbon kings of the 17th and 18th centuries. Although Louis XIV moved the court to **Versailles** in the late 17th century, Paris enjoyed great wealth and power during his reign, known as *Le Grand Siècle* (the Great Century). Under Louis XV Paris emerged as a center for culture and ideas, the arts flourished, and such intellectuals as Voltaire, Rousseau, Diderot, and Montesquieu were renowned throughout Europe. At the end of the 18th century, however, the extravagances of Louis XVI and his court led to the French Revolution and the bloodbath known as the Reign of Terror.

The instability following the Revolution allowed General Napoléon Bonaparte to seize control of the French government, and by 1804 he had proclaimed himself Emperor of France and set about making Paris the most magnificent city in the world. After Napoléon's defeat at Waterloo and subsequent exile, the Bourbon monarchy took one last gasp; then Napoléon's nephew assumed power, declaring himself Napoléon III in 1851. Like his uncle, he undertook a vast urbanization program. Unfortunately, however, he also embroiled the country in a succession of wars, culminating in the 1870 Franco-Prussian War, during which Paris suffered under siege and famine. The insurrection that followed France's capitulation to Prussia in 1871 saw violent massacres in Paris.

By the end of the 19th century, Paris had recovered and was once again a driving force in Western culture. This optimistic period, known as the Belle Epoque (Beautiful Age), was captured in the work of the Impressionist painters. In the early part of this century, Paris became a mecca for intellectuals, artists, and philosophers, including Henri Matisse, Pablo Picasso, Georges Braque, Man Ray, Marcel Duchamp, James Joyce, Gertrude Stein, Ernest Hemingway, F. Scott Fitzgerald, Samuel Beckett, Simone de Beauvoir, and Jean-Paul Sartre. After being occupied by the Germans, the city emerged from World War II with relatively little damage to its buildings and monuments. In the 1950s, 1960s, and 1970s, Paris saw the construction of numerous modern buildings, and, more recently, the *grands projets* of the late Socialist president François Mitterrand.

Paris continues to evolve into the 21st century as one of Europe's most modern cities; yet it is at the same time an ancient city, with reminders of its remarkable history evident at every turn. The artistic and cultural capital of a unified Europe, the Paris of today offers a wealth of beauty and experiences. Few visitors fail to succumb to the splendor of this city, made even more appealing by the Parisian's love of grace, beauty, and fine living.

Louvre Pyramid

How To Read This Guide

PARIS ACCESS® is arranged so you can see at a glance where you are and what is around you. The numbers next to the entries in the following chapters correspond to the numbers on the maps.

Restaurants/Clubs: Red   **Hotels:** Blue

Shops/🍴 Outdoors: Green   **Sights/Culture:** Black

Rating the Restaurants and Hotels

The restaurant star ratings take into account the quality, service, atmosphere, and uniqueness of the restaurant. An expensive restaurant doesn't necessarily ensure an enjoyable evening; however, a small, relatively unknown spot could have good food, professional service, and a lovely atmosphere. Therefore, on a purely subjective basis, stars are used to judge the overall dining value (see the star ratings at right). Keep in mind that chefs and owners often change, which sometimes drastically affects the quality of a restaurant. The ratings in this guidebook are based on information available at press time.

The price ratings, as categorized at right, apply to restaurants and hotels. These figures describe general price-range relationships among other restaurants and hotels in the area. The restaurant price ratings are based on the average cost of a three-course meal for one person, excluding tax and tip. Hotel price ratings reflect the base price of a standard room for two people for one night during the peak season.

Restaurants

★	Good
★★	Very Good
★★★	Excellent
★★★★	An Extraordinary Experience
$	The Price Is Right (less than $25)
$$	Reasonable ($25-$70)
$$$	Expensive ($70-$120)
$$$$	Big Bucks ($120 and up)

Hotels

$	The Price Is Right (less than $75)
$$	Reasonable ($75-$150)
$$$	Expensive ($150-$300)
$$$$	Big Bucks ($300 and up)

At press time, the exchange rate was about 5.65 francs to $1 US.

Map Key

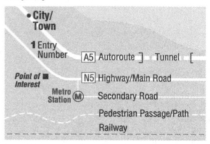

- City/Town
- **1** Entry Number
- Point of Interest ■
- Metro Station Ⓜ
- A5 Autoroute ⌐ Tunnel [
- N5 Highway/Main Road
- Secondary Road
- Pedestrian Passage/Path
- Railway

All numbers in the Paris area are preceded by the code 01. (Numbers in the northwest are preceded by 02; in the northeast, 03; in the southeast and Corsica, 04; and in the southwest, 05). To call Paris from the US, dial 011.33.1, followed by the eight-digit phone number. To call Paris from elsewhere in France, dial 01, then the eight-digit number.

Getting to Paris

Airports

Roissy–Charles-de-Gaulle Airport

Twenty kilometers (12 miles) north of Paris, **Roissy–Charles-de-Gaulle Airport** is the busier of Paris's two airfields. It consists of two separate terminals: **Roissy I** handles all foreign carriers, and **Roissy II** services **Air France** only. Both have tourist information and money-exchange facilities, and a shuttle bus connects the two terminals.

Airport Services

Airport Emergencies/Security	01.48.62.31.22
Business Service Center	01.48.62.33.06
Currency Exchange	01.48.62.38.28
Customs	01.48.62.35.35
Immigration	01.48.62.31.22

Flight Information	01.48.62.22.80

Lost and Found

Roissy I	01.48.62.13.34
Roissy II	01.48.64.25.94

Medical Emergencies

Roissy I	01.48.62.28.00
Roissy II	01.48.62.53.32
Parking	01.48.62.12.83

Traveler's Aid (for people with disabilities)
....................01.48.62.59.00

Airlines

Air France	08.02.80.28.02, 800/237.2747
Lufthansa	01.42.65.37.35, 800/645.3880
Northwest	01.42.66.90.00, 800/447.4747
TWA	01.49.19.20.00, 01.40.69.70.00, 800/892.4141
United	01.41.40.30.30, 800/241.6522

Getting to and from Roissy–Charles-de-Gaulle Airport

Barring any major traffic snarls, the trip to **Roissy–Charles-de-Gaulle Airport** from the center of Paris by airport minibus, bus, car, or taxi should take about 45 minutes. The suburban **RER (Réseau Express Régional)** trains also provide 45-minute service, except during peak commuting hours when there may be significant delays. To play it safe, allow twice that time to get to the airport.

By Airport Minibus

Several minibus services provide daily transportation to and from the airports. The shuttle services don't charge for baggage (as do taxis), and unlike other buses, passengers are delivered to their door. Some leading services are: **Airport Shuttle** (01.45.38.55.72; fax 01.43.21.35.67; ashuttle@club-internet.fr); **ParisShuttle** (01.43.90.91.91; fax 01.43.90.91.10; Parishuttl@aol.com); and **Paris Airports Service** (01.49.62.78.78; fax 01.49.62.78.79; pas@magic.fr).

By Bus

An **Air France** bus (01.41.56.89.00) travels between the airport and **Place Charles-de-Gaulle** (the **Arc de Triomphe**) at Avenue Carnot and **Place de la Porte-Maillot** opposite the **Méridien Etoile Hotel** (both stops on the métro line **Grande Arche de La Défense/Château de Vincennes**). Buses leave daily every 20 minutes from 6AM to 11PM. Another **Air France** bus runs between the airport and the **Gare Montparnasse** train station, with a stop at **Gare de Lyon**. Buses leave daily every 30 minutes from 6:30AM to 9PM. The **Roissybus** (01.48.04.18.24) is operated by **Réseau Autonome du Transport Parisien (RATP),** the public mass transit system, and runs between the airport and the **Place de l'Opéra** opposite the **American Express office** at 5 Rue Scribe. Buses leave daily every 15 minutes from 5:45AM to 11PM.

By Car

From the airport, take **Autoroute A1** south to **Porte de la Chapelle** in the north of Paris, or **Highways N17 and N2** south straight to **Porte de la Villette** in the northeast of Paris. From Paris, take Autoroute A1 north from Porte de la Chapelle or Highway N2 north from Porte de la Villette to the airport. Shuttle service is offered from the parking lots to the terminals daily every eight minutes from 4:30AM to 1AM.

Rental Cars

The following rental car companies have counters at **Roissy–Charles-de-Gaulle Airport;** all are open Monday through Friday from 6AM to midnight.

Avis

    Roissy I 01.48.62.34.34

    Roissy II 01.48.62.59.59, 800/331.1084

Europcar

    Roissy I 01.48.62.33.33

    Roissy II.........01.48.62.56.47, 800/CAR.EUROPE

Hertz

    Roissy I 01.48.64.29.00

    Roissy II 01.48.62.58.58, 800/227.3876

By Limousine

To arrive in (or depart from) Paris in expensive style, hire a chauffeur-driven private car, minibus, or stretch limousine. The trip from the airport into town (or vice versa) costs 700 to 900 francs for a private car, 1,100 to 1,200 francs for a limo (rates are slightly higher for night service).

The following limousine companies offer round-the-clock service to the airport:

American Limousines (stretch limos)

    ....01.39.35.09.99

Avis Chauffeurs 01.45.54.33.65, 800/331.1084

Biribin et Guarniéri 01.43.48.65.65

Martin Didier 01.45.54.71.07

Massey...01.43.80.51.89

Prestige Limousines 01.42.50.81.81

By Taxi

There are a number of taxi stands at the airport. A ride downtown will cost between 200 and 350 francs depending on traffic and destination. There is a baggage charge of 10 francs per suitcase. Rates increase by 30 percent between 7PM and 6AM.

By Train

The **RER B** (08.36.68.77.14) train runs between **Roissy–Charles-de-Gaulle Airport** and the **Gare du Nord, Châtelet–Les Halles,** and **Luxembourg** stations. Trains leave daily about every 15 minutes from 5:30AM to midnight; the trip from the airport to **Châtelet–Les Halles** takes about 45 minutes.

Orly Airport

Orly Airport, located 13 kilometers (8 miles) south of Paris, has 2 terminals: **Orly Sud** (south) handles both trans-Atlantic and European flights, and **Orly Ouest** (west) handles mostly domestic flights. Both have tourist information and money-exchange facilities, and there is frequent transportation service into the city. A free shuttle bus connects both terminals.

Airport Services

Airport Emergencies/Security 01.49.75.43.04

Currency Exchange............................01.49.75.59.29

Customs..01.49.75.40.80

Immigration/Border Police 01.49.75.43.04

Information 01.49.75.15.15

Lost and Found, Orly Sud 01.49.75.34.10

Lost and Found, Orly Ouest 01.49.75.42.34

Medical Emergencies 01.49.75.45.12

Parking...01.49.75.56.50

Airlines

American 08.01.87.28.72, 800/433.7300

Continental 01.42.99.09.09, 800/231.0856

Delta.........................01.47.68.92.92, 800/221.1212

US Airways 01.49.10.29.00, 800/428.4322

Getting to and from Orly Airport

Like **Roissy–Charles-de-Gaulle Airport, Orly** is about a 45-minute trip from the center of Paris by bus, car, taxi, or train. But allow double that time in case there are traffic tie-ups or other delays.

By Airport Minibus

See **Roissy–Charles-de-Gaulle Airport** above (page 7) for a list of companies that provide door-to-door minibus service. The rates are the same for both airports.

By Bus

The **Air France** bus service (01.41.56.78.00) provides transportation between **Orly** and the **Air France** offices in **Montparnasse** (25 Blvd de Vaugirard, between Pl Raoul-Dautry and Blvd Pasteur) or the **Air France Terminal at Invalides** (Gare des Invalides, 2 Rue Robert-Esnault-Pelterie, at Quai d'Orsay). Departures are daily every 12 minutes from 5AM to 11PM. **RATP**'s **Orlybus** (08.36.68.41.14) travels between the airport and **Place Denfert-Rochereau.** Buses leave daily about every 15 minutes from 6AM until 11PM. The trip takes 30 minutes.

By Car

From the airport, take **Highway N7** north to **Porte d'Italie** in the south of Paris. From Porte d'Italie, take N7 south to **Orly.** The **P1** parking lot is closest to the **Orly Sud** terminal and the **P0** lot is closest to **Orly Ouest.** Free shuttle service operates daily every seven minutes between 5AM and 12:15AM from the **P4** through **P7** parking lots, which are farther away from the terminals.

Rental Cars

The following rental car companies have counters at **Orly Airport;** they usually are open Monday through Friday from 6AM to midnight.

Avis 01.49.75.44.97, 800/331.1084

Budget 01.49.75.76.00, 800/527.0700

Europcar 01.49.75.47.48, 800/CAR.EUROPE

Hertz..........................01.49.75.84.84, 800/654.3001

By Limousine

See **Roissy–Charles-de-Gaulle Airport** above (page 7) for a list of companies that offer chauffeur-driven private-car and stretch-limousine service to and from both airports. The trip from **Orly** into town (or vice versa) will cost 600 to 800 francs for a private car, and 900 to 1,200 francs for a limo (rates are slightly higher for night service).

By Taxi

There are a number of taxi stands at **Orly.** A ride into Paris will cost between 100 and 150 francs. Rates increase by 30 percent between 7PM and 6AM.

By Train

The **RER Orly C Line** (08.36.68.77.14) is linked to **Orly Airport** by shuttle bus; it connects with the **Gare d'Austerlitz, St-Michel–Notre-Dame,** and **Invalides** stations. Trains leave approximately every 15 minutes from 5:30AM to 11PM. The trip takes 50 minutes.

Orly is also connected to the **RER B Line,** the métro, and train stations by the **Orlyval** monorail service from **Antony** station; the combined monorail/train trip takes about 30 to 45 minutes. The monorail operates Monday through Friday from 6AM to 11:30PM, and Saturday and Sunday from 6AM to 11PM.

Bus Station (Long-Distance)

Buses arriving from other European cities disembark at the **Gare Routière Internationale** (Ave Général-de-Gaulle and Autoroute 3) in the eastern suburb of **Bagnolet.** The métro connection to the city center is via the **Gallieni** station. For bus information, call **Eurolines** (08.36.69.52.52).

Train Station (Long-Distance)

In Paris you can't simply jump into a taxi and cry *"A la gare!"* (To the station!). Paris has six train stations, each offering service to different regions of France and Europe: **Gare d'Austerlitz** (53 Quai d'Austerlitz, between Blvd Vincent-Auriol and Pl Valhubert), for southwest France, Spain, and Portugal; **Gare de l'Est** (Pl du 11-Novembre-1918, between Rues du Faubourg-St-Martin and d'Alsace) for eastern France, Luxembourg, Switzerland, southern Germany, Austria, and Hungary; **Gare de Lyon** (20 Blvd Diderot, at Rue de Chalon) for south and southeastern France, Switzerland, Italy, and Greece; **Gare Montparnasse** (17 Blvd de Vaugirard, between Pl Raoul-Dautry and Blvd Pasteur) for western France (including Versailles), Chartres, and Brittany; **Gare St-Lazare** (20 Rue de Rome, between Pl Gabriel-Péri and Rue de Vienne) for northwest France, Normandy, and Le Havre; and **Gare du Nord** (18 Rue de Dunkerque, between Rues du Faubourg-St-Denis and de Maubeuge) for northern France, Belgium, the Netherlands, Scandinavia, Poland, Russia, northern Germany, and Britain, including the **Eurostar** trains, which travel between London and Paris via the **Channel Tunnel** in three hours.

Two types of train serve each station: *grandes lignes* for long-distance travel, and *banlieue lignes,* for riding to the suburbs. Before boarding either type of train, you must *composter* (punch) your ticket in one of the orange machines in the station; if you fail to do this, the conductor might charge you the price of another ticket.

When reserving a ticket be sure to request either a *fumeur* or *non-fumeur* (smoking or nonsmoking) car. Reserved seats are available in both first and second class. First-class tickets are approximately 40 percent more expensive; the extra bucks buy you a slightly more comfortable seat, a less crowded car, and a fancier dining car.

Trains are operated by **Société Nationale de Chemin de Fer (SNCF).** For reservations and information, call 08.36.35.35.39 for the **Eurostar,** 08.36.35.35.35 for the *grandes lignes,* and 01.53.90.20.20 for the *banlieue lignes.*

Getting Around Paris

The quickest and easiest ways of getting around Paris are by métro, taxi, and often your own two feet.

Bicycles

Two wheels can be more fun—albeit more hazardous—than four. Bicycle lanes are now a permanent fixture along a number of major arteries in central Paris, and the *quais* (embankments) along the Seine in the center of the city are closed to automobile traffic on Sunday morning and afternoon. From March through October, the **RATP** (08.36.68.77.14) rents bikes at five **Roue Libre** (Free Wheel) centers—**Square de la Tour-St-Jacques** (Métro: Châtelet), **Bois de Boulogne** (Métros: Ranelagh, La Muette), **Bois de Vincennes** (Métro: Porte Dorée), **Eiffel Tower** (RER: Champ de Mars–Tour Eiffel), and **St-Germain-en-Laye** (RER: St-Germain-en-Laye)—for biking on your own or with guided multilingual tours.

Energetic and adventurous visitors can also rent bicycles from **Paris Vélo** (2 Rue du Fer-à-Moulin, at Rue Geoffroy-St-Hilaire, 01.43.37.59.22), **La Maison du Vélo** (11 Rue Fénelon, between Rues d'Abbeville and de Belzunce, 01.42.81.24.72), or **Paris à Vélo C'est Sympa** (37 Blvd Bourdon, between Rue de la Cerisaie and Blvd Henri-IV, 01.48.87.00.01).

Paris is surrounded with beautiful, flat countryside that's perfect for bicycling. If you're planning day trips outside Paris—to **Chantilly, Fontainebleau,** or **Versailles,** for example—it might be a good idea to wait until you get to your destination and rent a bike for the day at the local train station. The **RER** stations in **Noisiel-le-Luzard, Vincennes, St-Germain-en-Laye, Courcelle Vallée de Chevreuse,** and **Vallée de la Marne** all have bikes for rent.

For general cycling information, contact the **Fédération Française de Cyclotourisme** (8 Rue Jean-Marie-Jégo, between Rues de la Butte-aux-Cailles and Samson, 01.44.16.88.88; fax 01.44.16.88.98).

Boats

The **Batobus,** operated by **Compagnie des Batobus** (01.44.11.33.99), is a boat service that runs up and down the Seine from mid-April to mid-October. The circuit covers six stops: **Port de la Bourdonnais** (near the **Tour Eiffel**), **Porte de Solférino** (near the **Musée d'Orsay**), **Quai Malaquais** (opposite the **Louvre**), **Quai de Montebello** (near **Notre-Dame**), **Quai du Louvre** (near the **Louvre**), **Quai de l'Hôtel-de-Ville** (near the **Hôtel de Ville**).

Buses

Riding the métro may be the quickest and easiest way to get around town, but buses are a far more pleasant means of transportation in Paris. The tourist office on the Champs-Elysées has selected more than a dozen get-acquainted bus routes for tourists, and it provides maps and trilingual (English, German, and Italian) commentary on the sights along the way. The *No. 24* bus, for example, makes a marvelous circuit of Paris. It crosses the Seine four times; passes **Place de la Concorde,** the **Assemblée Nationale,** the **Louvre, Pont-Neuf, Notre-Dame,** Ile St-Louis, and **Place St-Michel;** goes down Boulevard St-Germain; and finally turns back past the **Jardin des Plantes** and the **Musée d'Orsay**—all for just a few francs.

The *Nos. 30, 48, 82,* and *95* routes are equally enjoyable. Maps of the bus system and schedules are posted on the walls of bus shelters.

Bus service is limited in the evening and on Sunday. The standard fare is one métro ticket; an additional ticket will be needed for transfers to another bus. Buy a bus ticket at any métro station, or on the bus. Be sure to punch your ticket in the machine beside the driver when you board and hold onto your punched ticket throughout the trip; occasionally a *contrôleur* in a blue uniform boards the bus to check them. Those without punched tickets receive heavy fines. Travelers who have multiride public transport passes, such as *Le Paris Visite* or the *Carte Orange* should show them to the driver, but not have them punched. For discount ticket and pass information, see "Métro" below.

Driving

Those planning on driving in Paris stand forewarned: The most civilized Parisian becomes a homicidal maniac on the road. Rush hour is Monday through Friday from 8 to 10AM and 5 to 8PM. Conditions are also rough on Sunday nights between 5 and 9PM, when weekend travelers are heading back into the city.

If you dare to drive, the main car-rental agencies are: **Avis** (5 Rue Bixio, at Ave de Ségur, 01.44.18.10.50; 60 Rue de Ponthieu, between Rues La Boétie and de Berri, 01.43.59.03.35); **Hertz** (92 Rue St-Lazare, between Pl d'Estienne-d'Orves and Rue d'Amsterdam, 01.42.80.35.45; Gare des Invalides, 2 Rue Robert-Esnault-Pelterie, at Quai d'Orsay, 01.45.51.20.37); and **Europcar** (48 Rue de Berri, between Rue du Faubourg-St-Honoré and Blvd Haussmann, 01.53.93.73.40). These companies also have offices at **Roissy–Charles-de-Gaulle** and **Orly Airports.** **Europcar** offers a nonresident discount, but you must make your reservations 24 hours before arriving in France, and there is a minimum rental period of 3 days and a maximum of 99 days. When renting a car, be sure to take the rental company's insurance if your auto insurance doesn't cover you. If your credit card company offers coverage, check before leaving home to be sure that it is valid in Europe.

Métro

It's one of the oldest—and best—subway systems in Europe. The first line, designed by engineer Fulgence Bienvenue, opened on 19 July 1900 between **Porte Maillot** and **Vincennes.** In the early 1900s, the station entrances were Art Nouveau masterpieces designed by Hector Guimard. These days, the symbol of the system is the aqua-and-brown ticket of the **RATP.**

The first new métro line since 1935 opened in October 1998. Called *Météor* (or *No. 14*), it runs from **Bibliothèque Nationale de France, Site François Mitterand/Tolbiac** to the **Madeleine.**

Nearly 120 miles of rail snake beneath the streets of Paris, connecting about 300 stations. Aboveground, you're never very far away from a métro stop, and for the cost of a single ticket you can ride all day anywhere within the system, which operates between 5AM and about 12:45AM (each train pulls into its final destination at 1:15AM). Hang onto your ticket:

9

occasionally a team of *contrôleurs* in olive brown uniforms boards the train to check them.

Getting lost in Paris takes some effort. Métro maps (see inside back cover) are everywhere—inside and outside the stations. And the métro lines are named for the stations at which they end. Simply follow the signs for the terminus in the direction you are headed. If, for example, you want to go from the **Louvre** to **Concorde,** take the line marked **Direction La Défense.** To transfer from one line to another, look for an orange-and-white *correspondance* sign on the station platform. Each station has a map of the neighborhood surrounding it, so you can get your bearings before you emerge aboveground.

To use the métro, slip the magnetized ticket into the slot by the turnstile, retrieve it when it pops up, and pass through. Remember that when getting on and off the métro you must open the car door yourself; it closes automatically behind you.

When purchasing tickets, it's less expensive to buy a *carnet* (book) of 10, which cuts the price of a single ticket by a third. Also available are tourist passes, which are valid for both the métro and the bus. *Le Paris Visite* passes are usable for one, two, three, and five days of unlimited travel in the metropolis of Paris and the suburbs (the price increases the farther you go), and include reductions on admission to numerous places of interest. The *Carte Orange* offers a week or month of travel privileges in Paris and the suburbs (again the card costs more for longer distances), and requires a photograph.

A métro ticket also allows you to use the **RER** rail system (an express métro) within Paris, but study its route before you board because it is primarily a suburban line, and the stops within the city are few and far between. Always hang onto your tickets; you may need them to get in and out of the station. Call 08.36.68.77.14 for métro information.

Parking

If you think driving in Paris is tough, wait until you try to park your car. If you are lucky enough to find a legal spot on the street, you can leave your car there as long as you keep feeding the meter, in effect Monday through Saturday from 9AM to 7PM except holidays (August is considered a holiday in certain quarters of Paris). If your car is towed, be prepared to pay a very hefty fine and spend the better part of a day trying to resolve the problem and recover the vehicle. The easiest option is an underground parking lot. There are many throughout the city; look for the "Parking" signs or the big letter "P."

Taxis

Most of the time, Paris's 15,000 cabs are lined up at *têtes de station* (stands with blue-and-white *Taxi* signs) throughout the city. Hailing a cab in the street is not a very rewarding experience; if you try it, look for a taxi with a bright roof light (a dim light means it's occupied). Even then drivers may not pick you up, because if you're not going in their direction, *tant pis* (tough luck). Either way, fake some knowledge of

the city and tell the driver the main street or métro station closest to your destination; given that guidance she or he is less likely to take you out of your way. Taxis usually aren't expensive, but the rates increase between 10PM and 6:30AM, on Sunday, and if you're picked up at a train station, hotel, or outside the city. If you need to be somewhere at a specific time (including the airport), call ahead for a taxi; the meter starts running the moment the driver receives the call, but the dispatcher will tell you how long it will take for the cab to arrive (it's usually less than 10 minutes). Tip the driver 10 to 15 percent. Some cab companies include **Taxis Bleus** (01.49.36.10.10), **Taxis G-7** (01.47.39.47.39), and **Alpha Taxis** (01.46.85.85.85).

Tours

To observe the city through the windows of a climate-controlled, double-decker tour bus, climb aboard one of the sleek coaches of **Cityrama** (4 Pl des Pyramides, between Rues de Rivoli and des Pyramides, 01.44.55.61.00) or **Paris Vision** (214 Rue de Rivoli, between Rues St-Roch and d'Alger, 01.42.60.30.01). Both companies offer tours (in several languages) past all the main attractions, as well as separate excursions to Versailles, Giverny, **Malmaison,** Chantilly, **Chartres,** Fontainebleau and **Barbizon,** the **Loire Valley,** Mont St-Michel, and the **Normandy landing beaches.** They also run "Paris by Night" tours to the **Moulin Rouge** and the **Lido** and to X-rated hot spots (for adults only).

The jaunty red double-deckers of **Parisbus** (01.42.30.55.50) offer "Paris en toute liberté" (Paris at your leisure). The buses stop at nine main spots of tourist interest, and passengers can get on and off as they please. Tickets are valid for two days, and the commentary is in French and English.

On a late summer afternoon, nothing could be better than spending an hour touring the Seine river in a *bateau mouche,* especially if you take along some creamy goat cheese, a fresh baguette, and a bottle of cool St-Joseph. Take a seat at the rear of the boat out of range of the irritating tape-recorded commentary, then put your feet up and watch the sun set over the City of Light. For a more luxurious trip, book one of the expensive candlelit dinner cruises. Tours lasting between one and three hours (the longer excursions feature lunch or dinner) are available from **Bateaux Mouches** (Pont de l'Alma and Pl de l'Alma, 01.42.25.96.10), **Bateaux Parisiens** (Port de La Bourdonnais, just northeast of Pont d'Iéna, 01.44.11.33.44), **Vedettes de Paris** (Port de Suffren, between Ponts de Bir-Hakeim and d'Iéna, 01.44.18.19.50), and **Vedettes du Pont-Neuf** (Sq du Vert-Galant, 01.53.00.98.98). The boats operated by **Vedettes du Pont-Neuf** tend to be smaller and have live guides rather than recorded commentary.

Tours of the **Canal St-Martin** are offered by **Paris Canal** (01.42.40.96.97) daily from April through November; on Sunday January through March and December. The offbeat three-hour cruises run between the **Musée d'Orsay** and the **Parc de la**

Villette, pass through a milelong subterranean tunnel under the **Place de la Bastille** and **Boulevard Richard-Lenoir,** and encounter nine locks and two turning bridges en route. Reservations are required.

Paris Walking Tours (01.48.09.21.40; fax 01.42.43.75.51; ParisWalking@compuserve.com) offers walks through virtually every district in Paris, with lively and informative commentary in English by Peter and Oriel Caine, a British couple who created this service in 1994. Some of the most popular of the 70 walks they have designed are the Historic Marais, Hemingway's Paris, the Opéra, Montmartre, and the Sewers of Paris. There is at least one walk daily, each lasts an average of 90 minutes.

ACCESSPress—the authors of this guidebook—now offer *ACCESSWalks,* a three-hour series of walking tours on audiotape that take you through Paris's prime neighborhoods at a pace that can be set by the switching of the ON/OFF button of a cassette player. Available in the travel section of bookstores, the lively narrative covers the city's history, architecture, great restaurants and shops, with a host of little-known tidbits thrown in for good measure.

For serious shoppers who want the inside scoop on where and what to buy, **Shopping Plus** (99-103 Rue de Sevres, between Rues St-Placide and St-Romain, 01.47.53.91.17; fax 01.44.l8.96.68) offers half-day walking tours with bilingual guides focusing on a theme and a place, such as haute couture in the **Triangle d'Or** (bounded by Aves des Champs-Elysées, Montaigne, and George-V) on the Right Bank, antiques in the Marais, or home decoration in the Left Bank. In a daylong tour, "French for a Day," participants go to an outdoor food market, and then to a two-hour class at the **Toque d'Or** cooking school where your culinary efforts are savored. The afternoon brings visits to fashion boutiques, art galleries, antiques and home decoration shops of the Left Bank, and a stop for tea at a suitably chic spot. Lunch with wine and afternoon tea are included. Tours can also be custom-tailored for individuals or small groups.

For an exciting audiovisual tour of Paris, **Paristoric** (11 *bis* Rue Scribe, at Rue Auber, 01.42.66.62.06; fax 01.42.66.62.16) presents a wide-screen journey through space and time, covering Paris's two-millennialong evolution from the pre-Roman settlement of Lutetia to today's capital of glamour and *grands projets.* This splendid show focuses on Paris's architecture and style of life as they have developed over the ages—Roman, Medieval, Renaissance, Enlightenment, Revolution and Empire, Belle Epoque, and 20th century—with poetic, informative commentary available in English and 11 other languages, and magnificent music by Lully, Offenbach, Debussy, Ravel, Edith Piaf, and others. The 45-minute program is a fine introduction to the many architectural styles visitors will encounter as they explore the city. The show is presented daily every hour on the hour from 9AM to 8PM April through October; daily from 9AM to 6PM November through March.

Walking

Whether by promenading along the broad boulevards or threading your way through intimate medieval neighborhoods, the best way to discover Paris and its environs is by foot. Strolling yields the joy of discovering the little things—the grace notes, embellishments, and architectural details that define the feel and texture of Paris. But walking can be a somewhat perilous proposition: On the street you're fair game for distracted drivers and reckless in-line skaters, and on the sidewalk you're likely to tread on what dogs have left behind.

FYI

Accommodations

Hotel reservations are essential in Paris not only in the summer months but also during the heavy convention and trade-show months of March and October. Keep in mind that hotel rates rise regularly and renovations often prompt hotels to raise their prices, so it is always sensible to call in advance to check rates. If you do arrive without accommodations, contact the **Office de Tourisme de Paris** (see "Visitors' Information Centers," page 16). The tourist office also offers a free brochure charting room availability throughout the year.

For those looking for an alternative to the traditional hotel room, the **Organisation pour le Tourisme Universitaire** (OTU; 01.40.29.12.12; otuvoyages@terranet.fr) maintains more than 700 clean, safe, inexpensive beds in youth centers throughout the Paris area. Reservations must be made in person, and those 35 years of age and under have priority. Rooms generally sleep one to eight people, and bathrooms are shared. The centers in the Marais quarter, housed in 17th-century mansions, are the most desirable.

There are three **OTU** offices in central Paris: **OTU Beaubourg** (119 Rue St-Martin, between Rues Aubry-le-Boucher and Rambuteau, 01.42.72.72.09), the largest; **OTU Port Royal** (39 Ave Georges-Bernanos, between Blvds de Port-Royal and St-Michel, 01.44.41.38.50); and **OTU Jussieu** (2 Rue Malus, at Rue de la Clef, 01.43.36.80.27). To secure a room, get to one of the offices by 9AM, when they open.

Those wishing to rent an apartment can contact **Paris-Accueil Locaflat** (63 Ave de La Motte-Piquet, 75015 Paris, 01.40.56.99.50). **The French Experience** (370 Lexington Ave, New York, NY 10017, 212/986.1115; info@frenchexperience.com) also arranges bed-and-breakfast accommodations, as well as apartment and country cottage rentals and hotel reservations.

Addresses

Parisian addresses include a street name and a number, *plus* which of the 20 arrondissements it is in. For instance, an address in the Latin Quarter (fifth arrondissement) might be "23 Quai St-Bernard, 5eme, or 75005 Paris" (the small "eme" is the French equivalent of an English "th"), while an address in

Les Halles (first arrondissement) would read "6 Rue Coquillière, 1er, or 75001 Paris" ("er" standing in for the English "st").

Cafes

As noble a French institution as the **Académie Française,** cafes serve sandwiches, simple meals, and a variety of beverages throughout the day. If *un café* (a demitasse of espresso) is too potent for you in the morning, try a *café crème* (a large cup of coffee with hot, frothy milk); in the afternoon you might switch to *vin rouge* (red wine), *un demi* (a 25-centiliter draft beer), or a *citron pressé* (fresh lemonade). Drinks are cheaper at the *zinc* (bar), and coffee can be more expensive after 10PM, but by then you'll probably have moved on to Cognac, Armagnac, or perhaps Calvados.

Climate

Chances are that fabled Paris in the springtime will be soggy. The city logs more rainy days a year than London, so bring an umbrella or trench coat. Winters are cold and damp, and summers can be as cool and dry as the martinis at the **Ritz Bar.** The average temperature ranges from 38 degrees F in January to 75 degrees in July. August, when most Parisians leave the city, can be very hot, with temperatures rising well up into the 80s during a *canicule* (heat wave). May and September are the best times for finding decent weather and fewer tourists.

Months	Average Temperature (°F)
December-February	46
March-May	58
June-August	76
September-November	61

Drinking

The legal drinking age is 18. Bars typically stay open until 2 or 4AM. As in most cities, drunk driving is a serious problem, so police often stop erratic drivers for a breath test. If they fail it, the penalties are severe: a heavy fine that must be paid on the spot, a possible stay in jail, and possible loss of a driver's license.

Embassies and Consulates

American Embassy (2 Ave Gabriel, at Rue Boissy-d'Anglas, 01.43.12.22.22)

American Consulate (2 Rue St-Florentin, at Rue de Rivoli, 01.43.22.23.47)

Australian Embassy (4 Rue Jean-Rey, at Quai Branly, 01.40.59.33.00)

British Embassy (35 Rue du Faubourg-St-Honoré, between Rues Boissy-d'Anglas and de l'Elysée, 01.44.51.31.00)

British Consulate (18 *bis* Rue d'Anjou, at Rue de Surène, 01.44.51.31.00)

Canadian Embassy/Consulate (35 Ave Montaigne, between Rues François-1er and Clément-Marot, 01.44.43.29.00)

Entertainment

Paris is one of the world's greatest cities for all kinds of entertainment—opera, ballet, classical music in churches and concert halls, films, jazz and blues, theater and floor shows, and discotheques and rock clubs. For up-to-date listings on all musical and theatrical events, movies, and art exhibits, check out the publications *Pariscope* and *L'Officiel des Spectacles,* both of which come out every Wednesday.

Parisians are film fanatics. Each week more than 300 films are shown in the city, and all are listed along with their show times in *Pariscope* and *L'Officiel des Spectacles.* The *v.o. (version originale)* after a film title means the movie is being shown in its original language with French subtitles; *v.f. (version française)* means it's dubbed in French. If you arrive in time for the *séance* (previews), you'll see the ads, which are often risqué, usually silly, and sometimes brilliantly imaginative.

Ticket prices for movies are uniformly reduced by 30 percent on Monday.

Health and Medical Care

For round-the-clock medical house calls, call **SOS Médecins** (01.47.07.77.77). The **American Hospital** is just outside Paris (63 Blvd Victor-Hugo, between Blvds du Château and de la Saussaye, Neuilly-sur-Seine, 01.47.47.70.15); most of the physicians there speak English. An English-language crisis line (operated 3-11PM) can be reached by dialing 01.47.23.80.80.

In Paris, all pharmacies are marked by a neon green cross on the front of the building. When the cross is lit, it means the pharmacy is open for business. Many pharmacists speak English, and you can be sure of getting English prescriptions translated and filled with equivalent medicines at the following places: **British and American Pharmacy** (1 Rue Auber, at Pl de l'Opéra, 01.47.42.49.40), **Pharmacie Anglaise** (130 Rue La Boétie, at Ave des Champs-Elysées, 01.43.59.22.52), **Pharmacie Dhéry** (84 Ave des Champs-Elysées, between Rues La Boétie and de Berri, 01.45.62.02.41), and **Pharmacie Swann** (6 Rue de Castiglione, between Rues de Rivoli and du Mont-Thabor, 01.42.60.72.96).

Holidays

On the following *jours feriés* (national holidays) most shops and businesses, including banks, are closed, while many museums and restaurants stay open. Buses don't run, but the métro remains operational.

Jour de l'An (New Year's Day), 1 January

Pâques (Easter), 23 April 2000, 15 April 2001

Lundi de Pâques (Easter Monday), 24 April 2000, 16 April 2001

Fête du Travail (Labor Day/May Day), 1 May

Fête de la Victoire (VE—Victory in Europe—Day), 8 May

Lundi de Pencôte (Pentecost Monday), mid- to late May

Fête de l'Ascension (Ascension Day), 1 June 2000, 24 May 2001

Fête Nationale/Jour de la Bastille (Bastille Day), 14 July

Fête de l'Assomption (Assumption Day), 15 August

Toussaint (All Saints' Day), 1 November

Armistice (Armistice Day), 11 November

Noël (Christmas), 25 December

Hours

Shops are usually open Monday through Saturday from 10AM to 7PM, but many observe the tradition of closing on Monday, and some still close for lunch (noon-2PM). Some larger department stores stay open one night a week, usually Thursday; they also offer additional hours during busy holiday seasons. The **Virgin Megastore** on the Champs-Elysées and a number of boutiques in the Marais district have pioneered business hours on Sunday, but they are exceptions. Other than the morning food markets and the flea markets, Sunday shopping is not commonplace in Paris.

Most Parisian museums are open from 10AM to 6PM; many stay open until 10PM one night a week. Museums are open on Sunday, but many are *fermé* (closed) on either Monday or Tuesday. Restaurants generally are open from noon to 2PM and 7 to 10:30PM. Cafes open early in the morning and often stay open late in the evening.

While August is still the *fermeture annuelle*, when many Parisians flee the city on vacation and leave countless shops and restaurants closed in their wake, more and more stores and restaurants are staying open during this time. Annual closing times may vary from one year to the next.

Opening and closing times for shops, attractions, cafes, etc., are listed by day(s) if the normal hours described above apply. In all other cases, specific hours will be given (e.g., 6AM-2PM, daily 24 hours, noon-5PM).

Laundry

Self-serve *laveries* (Laundromats) are peppered throughout the city. Try the **Dorvag** (25 Rue des Rosiers, between Rues des Ecouffes and Vieille-du-Temple, 01.48.87.37.33); **Laverie Self-Service Monge** (113 Rue Monge, between Ave des Gobelins and Rue Censier, 01.47.07.68.44); or **Laverie du Marché St-Honoré** (24 Pl du Marché-St-Honoré, between Rues du Marché-St-Honoré and Gomboust, 01.42.61.04.49). Most are open Monday through Saturday, 8AM to 8PM.

Money

Although the Euro became the official money of France and the 10 other original members of the European Currency Union on 1 January 1999, the French franc (abbreviated F) will remain the country's currency until 2002, when Euro bank notes will replace the member nations' national currencies. The franc is divided into 100 centimes. There are 500F, 200F, 100F, 50F, and 20F bills, and 20F, 10F, 5F, 2F, 1F, 50-centime, 20-centime, 10-centime, and 5-centime coins.

Banks are generally open Monday through Friday from 9AM to 4:30PM, but they close at midday the day before a holiday. They will display a sign reading *"change"* if they exchange foreign currency. The exchange window of **American Express** (11 Rue Scribe, at Rue Auber, 01.47.77.77.07) is open on Saturday, and there are exchange booths open daily at **Beaubourg,** Les Halles, on the **Rue de Rivoli** opposite the **Tuileries** gardens, and other spots frequented by tourists. If you're stuck with dollars and the banks are closed, you can change money at these train stations: **Gare d'Austerlitz** (until 8PM), **Gare de l'Est** (until 7PM), **Gare St-Lazare** (until 7PM), and **Gare de Lyon** (until 11PM). (For train station locations, see page 8.)

Credit cards (especially VISA) are in wider use here than elsewhere in Europe. Automatic teller machines (ATMs) are common; check with your bank or credit card company about using cash machines in Paris.

Museums

Most Parisian museums stay open late one night a week and are open on Sunday, but many are closed on either Monday or Tuesday. If you're planning on serious museum hopping, buy a *Carte Musées*, a pass that allows admission to 70 Parisian museums and monuments without waiting in line. Available in one-, three-, and five-day variations, they are sold in major métro stations, at most of the participating attractions, and at the **Office de Tourisme de Paris** (see below). Admission to the **Louvre** is free the first Sunday of every month.

Personal Safety

Paris is a fairly safe city, and visitors generally need only to concern themselves with pickpockets, who prey on tourists. Crowded cars on such large métro lines as **Grande Arche de La Défense/Château de Vincennes** are these thieves' natural habitat. In general, be aware of your surroundings. Watch your money pouch, keep the clasp of your purse against your body, and don't put your wallet in your back pocket, especially if it bulges. Beware of bands of children—sometimes they possess a sleight of hand Fagin would have envied. Don't wear jewelry in crowded places (like on the métro or at Montmartre) and don't leave possessions unattended.

France maintains a strong police and military presence at borders, airports, and railway stations after experiencing some terrorist bombings in the not-too-distant past. Additionally, police officers and heavily armed soldiers patrol the main Paris subway stations and other potential targets, such as the **Arc de Triomphe** and the **Eiffel Tower,** and trash cans are no longer in métro stations.

Travelers are advised to carry their passports with them in the unlikely event of being stopped by police for an identity check. French law requires everyone to carry proof of identity.

Post Offices

Post offices are marked **PTT** and are open Monday through Friday from 8AM to 7PM and Saturday 8AM to noon. The main post office (52 Rue du Louvre, at Rue Etienne-Marcel, 01.40.28.20.00) is open 24 hours a day. If you want to buy stamps, make sure you're in the correct line and not wasting your time queuing up at the window where Parisians pay their gas and telephone bills. Stamps are also sold at *tabacs* (tobacco shops), hotels, and some newsstands.

Publications

The English-language *International Herald Tribune* (a felicitous child of the *Washington Post* and *The New York Times*) will keep you abreast of world events and Parisian happenings. It appears at newsstands every morning except Sunday. The main French dailies in Paris are *Libération* and *Le Figaro* in the morning and *Le Monde* in the afternoon.

For weekly listings of exhibitions, movies, concerts, plays, discos, and restaurants, pick up a copy of *Pariscope* or *L'Officiel des Spectacles*, which both come out on Wednesday. They are sold at newsstands, and although they're written in French, they are possible to decipher even if you do not speak the language. *Pariscope* includes a guide in English published by *Time Out,* highlighting restaurants and giving the entertainment schedules for the week. The magazine *e.m@le is a free weekly (in French) for gays and lesbians, with an extensive list of bars, clubs, restaurants, businesses, organizations, and special events. It is available at the* **Centre Gai et Lesbien** *(3 Rue Keller, between Rues de Charonne and de la Roquette, 01.43.57.21.47; fax 01.43.57.27.93) and most gay bars and restaurants.*

The Paris Free Voice, an English-language monthly, has good, brightly written articles about current cultural goings-on, restaurant and wine bar reviews, and tips on living in Paris. It is distributed free in all English-language bookshops and at its offices in the **American Church** building (65 Quai d'Orsay, between Rues Surcouf and Jean-Nicot).

Metric Conversions

France uses the metric system. Equivalents are the following:

one kilometer = .6214 miles

one meter = 3 feet, 3.37 inches

one centimeter = .394 inches

one square meter = 10.76 square feet

one hectare = 2.471 acres

one liter = 1 liquid quart, .1134 pints

one liter = .2642 gallons

one kilogram = 2.20 pounds

one degree celsius = 1.8 degrees Fahrenheit

Rest Rooms

You can usually walk into any cafe and use the toilet. Such a facility may be a hole or a throne, with or without toilet paper. Your alternative is using the beige automatic toilets in the streets. For a two-franc piece, these clever contraptions automatically let you in and out and disinfect themselves between visits. Warning: Don't let young children into the automatic toilets alone; they may not be strong enough to push open the doors to get out.

Restaurants

The French generally lunch between noon and 2PM, and dine between 7:30 and 10PM. To eat at a particularly prestigious restaurant, such as **Taillevent, Lucas Carton,** or **Alain Ducasse,** you may have to book reservations months in advance, but in most cases advance notice of one week, or even a day or two, should suffice. In less expensive restaurants, reservations are not usually necessary. In many dining spots you may either order à la carte or choose a less expensive prix-fixe menu, which often includes the day's special. The fancier restaurants usually offer a *dégustation* (sampler) of the chef's specialties. If the wine list puzzles you, ask the waiter or the sommelier for advice; remember, the quality of the wine does not necessarily increase with the price. A 15-percent service charge is always included in the bill. Restaurants are normally open only at lunchtime and dinnertime.

The term "bistro" (sometimes spelled *bistrot*) usually refers to small, quaint, family-run restaurants serving modestly priced traditional French cooking, though in recent years several top chefs have opened chic little bistro spin-offs of their famous and far more expensive restaurants. They are generally open for lunch and dinner. A *brasserie* is literally a brewery, and these lively Alsatian-style eateries feature draft beer, Reisling and Gewürztraminer wines, *choucroute* (sauerkraut) with boiled ham, pork, and sausages, along with a goodly array of traditional French dishes, and usually a fresh seafood bar. Brasseries serve meals all day long without interruption and generally stay open later than restaurants or bistros.

Shopping

Haute couture, jewelry, perfume, and gourmet delights are all here. The big department stores are mostly located near **Boulevard Haussmann** and the **Opéra** district. The most chic boutiques are located in the 6th, 7th, 8th, and 16th arrondissements.

Big department stores include **Galeries Lafayette** (40 Blvd Haussmann, between Rues de la Chaussée-d'Antin and de Mogador, 01.42.82.34.56, **Au Printemps** (64 Blvd Haussmann, between Rues de Caumartin and du Havre, 01.42.82.50.00), **La Samaritaine** (19 Rue de la Monnaie, between Pl de l'Ecole and Rue de Rivoli, 01.40.41.20.20), **Le Bazar de l'Hôtel de Ville (BHV,** 52 Rue de Rivoli, at Rue des Archives, 01.42.74.90.00), and **Le Bon Marché** (main store, 22 Rue de Sèvres, at Rue du Bac, 01.44.39.80.00). Also worth a visit are such major shopping centers as **Porte Maillot** (Pl de la Porte-Maillot, 01.45.74.29.09), **Forum des Halles** (1 Rue

Pierre-Lescot, at Rue Berger, 01.44.76.96.56), the glass-roofed **Galerie Vivienne** behind the **Bibliothèque Nationale de France, Site Richelieu** (01.42.60.08.23), **Carrousel du Louvre** (99 Rue de Rivoli, between Rue de l'Amiral-de-Coligny and Ave du Général-Lemonnier, 01.46.92.47.47), and the posh **Passy Plaza** (53 Rue de Passy, at Pl de Passy, 01.40.50.09.07). **Maine Montparnasse** (Pl du 18-Juin-1940 and Rue de l'Arrivée) is a large shopping area with several big stores.

The most elegant designer boutiques for fashion, shoes, and leather goods, are to be found along **Rue du Faubourg-St-Honoré**, in the Triangle d'Or, and in recent years, **St-Germain-des-Prés** on the Left Bank. Many of the best (and most expensive) antiques dealers are located in **Le Carré Rive Gauche**, an association of more than 100 antiques shops in the area bordered by Rues des Sts-Pères, du Bac, and de l'Université and Quai Voltaire. Another important concentration of prestigious antiques dealers is at **Le Louvre des Antiquaires**, an association of 240 shops in a grand old building at 2 Place du Palais-Royal, just across Rue de Rivoli from the **Louvre**.

Antiques and curio collectors also should explore such flea markets as **Marché de Puces de Montreuil** on the eastern edge of Paris, especially good for secondhand clothing; **Marché aux Puces de Vanves** on the southern edge of the city, for furniture and bric-a-brac; and the largest and best known, **Marché aux Puces de St-Ouen** (more commonly called the **Puces de Clignancourt**; Ave Michelet and Rue des Rosiers, St Ouen), which offers an admirable array of antiques. The **Marché Biron** is one of the best of the smaller markets that make up the **Puces de Clignancourt**; it is especially good for fine crystal, china, and furniture. Most of the flea markets are held on the weekend year-round, no matter the weather.

Smoking

French law prohibits smoking in the métro and requires that all restaurants provide separate smoking and nonsmoking areas. However, most smokers still consider it only a politeness, certainly not a mandate, to refrain from smoking in no-smoking zones.

Street Plan

At first glance, Paris's broad expanse looks like one great tangle of medieval streets. Don't be dismayed, however, for there's logic in the layout that, once grasped, makes Paris as easy to navigate as your average college campus. The reference points provided by the major monuments (**Eiffel Tower, Panthéon, Arc de Triomphe**, etc.) and the Seine make locating yourself and your destination surprisingly easy. The series of axes that cut through the city also is a splendid means of orientation. The most obvious axis runs in a straight line from **La Défense** in the west, eastward through the **Arc de Triomphe**, and down the Champs-Elysées to the **Louvre**. The city is subdivided into 20 arrondissements, or quarters. Starting from the first arrondissement (the area around the **Louvre**), they spiral outward clockwise like the compartments of a snail's shell to the city limits.

While this overall understanding of Paris's layout is helpful, it won't change the fact that the streets are labyrinthine. For navigating the city's streets, Parisians carry a map of the métro in their heads and a *Paris par Arrondissement* guide in their pockets. Sold at most Parisian newsstands and bookshops, and at some travel bookstores in the US, this little book lists every street in Paris, with indexed references to maps of each of the city's 20 arrondissements (indicating the nearest métro station).

Taxes

Included in the purchase price of many items is a 20.6 percent VAT (value-added tax). Non-EEC tourists are entitled to VAT refunds on items that they take out of France; a minimum purchase of 1,200 francs per store is required. To get a refund, ask for the VAT refund forms when you make your purchase and be prepared to produce the items and the forms at the airport *détaxe* (refund) desk. The most convenient way of getting the refund is to charge the purchase to a credit card and get a credit for the tax refund applied to your credit card account.

Telephones

Phone booths adorn half the street corners in Paris, but it's a minor miracle to find one that works. Most operate only with *télécartes*, special phone cards that are sold at post offices and *tabacs*. To use phones in cafes, you may have to purchase a *jeton* (phone token) at the bar.

Telephone calls made from hotels are expensive; if making a long-distance call, it is worth having a phone card. Direct-dial to the US can be made by dialing 001, followed by your area code and number. Phone rates are much cheaper after 10PM than in the daytime.

Tickets

"Everything that exists elsewhere exists in Paris," said Victor Hugo in *Les Misérables*. So it goes for the array of entertainment options available to both the spectator and the participant in this city. For a daily recording (in English) of exhibitions and concerts, call 01.49.52.53.56.

There is a kiosk at the **Place de la Madeleine** that sells half-price tickets to about 120 different events in Paris—including plays, concerts, ballets, and operas—on the day of the performance.

Time Zone

France is one hour ahead of Greenwich Mean Time (GMT); throughout most of the year, when it's 9PM in Paris it's 8PM in London, 3PM in New York, and noon in Los Angeles. However, Europe starts and ends *l'heure d'été* (daylight saving time) several weeks before North America, so from about the end of March to the end of April France is seven hours ahead of New York, and from the end of September to the end of October it is five hours ahead.

Tipping

Since a 15-percent service charge is added to restaurant bills in Paris and throughout France, a supplementary tip is not necessary. However, you may leave an additional 5 percent for *service extraordinaire*. Tip cab drivers 10 to 15 percent of the fare. It is not customary, but certainly much appreciated, to tip hotel porters and maids (10 francs per bag for the former; 10 francs a day for the latter).

Visitors' Information Centers

The **Office de Tourisme de Paris** (127 Ave des Champs-Elysées, between Rues Galilée and de Presbourg, information about exhibitions and help with hotel reservations in French and English 08.36.68.31.12; fax 01.49.52.53.00) is the home of the city's official tourist bureau, where you can find free maps and sight-seeing information; it's open daily except 1 May. From May through September, another tourist office operates daily at the **Eiffel Tower** (01.45.51.22.15). A smaller *Bureau d'Accueil,* open Monday through Saturday from 8AM to 8PM, is located in the **Gare de Lyon** (01.43.43.33.24) train station.

L'Espace Tourisme du Carrousel du Louvre (Carrousel du Louvre, 99 Rue de Rivoli, between Rue de l'Amiral-de-Coligny and Ave du Général-Lemonnier, 08.03.03.19.98) offers tourist information about the Ile de France, the region surrounding Paris, which includes Versailles, Fontainebleau, and Chartres. It is open Monday, and Wednesday through Sunday.

Phone Book

Emergencies

Ambulance	15
Burn Center	01.42.34.17.58
Crisis Line (English-language, 3-11PM)	01.47.23.80.80

Dental Emergency (SOS Dentaire)	01.43.37.51.00
Doctor (SOS Médecins)	01.43.07.77.77
Fire	18
Hospitals	
American Hospital	01.47.47.70.15
British Hospital	01.46.39.22.22
Pharmacy (British and American)	01.47.42.49.40
Poison Center	01.40.05.48.48
Police (emergency)	17
Police (nonemergency)	01.53.73.53.73
Roadside Emergency (Automobile Club de l'Ile-de-France)	01.40.55.83.00

Visitors' Information

AIDS Hotline	01.44.93.16.69
American Youth Hostels	01.43.61.08.75
Métro	08.36.68.77.14
Road Conditions	
Paris	01.48.99.33.33
all regions	08.36.68.20.00
Time	36.99
Tourist Information	08.36.68.31.12
Weather	08.36.68.00.00

Fêtes et Foires (Festivals and Fairs)

Paris has a full calendar of special events, celebrations, and trade expositions throughout the year that attract Parisians and visitors alike. For additional details on the events listed, consult the **Office de Tourisme** (127 Ave des Champs-Elysées, between Rues Galilée and de Presbourg, 08.36.68.31.12), which publishes a free annual calendar of events, or the weekly listings in *Pariscope* and *L'Officiel des Spectacles* (available at newsstands).

January

Fashion Shows The haute-couture summer season kicks off this month with much fanfare. Many of the shows are held in the **Carrousel du Louvre**. For more information, call 01.43.16.47.47.

Fête des Rois (Feast of the Kings) Called the **Feast of the Epiphany** in English-speaking countries, this religious holiday, which falls on 6 January but is celebrated the first Sunday of the month, commemorates the visit to the infant Jesus by three kings. It is also an excuse for a tasty treat: a round, buttery, almond-paste cake called a *galette des rois.* Inside the cake is hidden a tiny charm, and whoever finds it gets to be king or queen for the day, donning the crown that comes with the cake. The cakes are sold all month long.

February

Tournoi des Cinq Nations (Five Nations Trophy) The **Stade de France** in the north suburbs is the setting for this international rugby tournament held mid-month. For more information, call 01.53.21.15.15.

March

Salon International d'Agriculture This is a vast farming fair featuring the animals and products of French and foreign *agriculteurs* and a sampling of regional food and wine. It's held the first week of the month at **Paris Expo,** at the **Porte de Versailles.** For more information, call 01.41.69.20.20.

Foire du Trône The largest fair and carnival in France takes place from the last week of March until the end of May in the **Bois de Vincennes.** For more information, call 01.43.43.92.92.

April

Paris Marathon Held during the first week of the month, this race starts from the **Place de la Concorde** and ends on **Avenue Foch.** The best place to catch a glimpse of the runners is along the **Avenue des Champs-Elysées.** For more information, call 01.53.17.03.10.

Salon de la Jeune Peinture The work of young contemporary artists is exhibited at the **Grand**

Palais for two weeks in mid-month. For more information, call 01.44.13.17.17.

Shakespeare Garden Festival In a small open-air theater in the **Bois de Boulogne,** set in a garden blooming with flora, classic plays are performed from the end of April until the beginning of October. There are occasional English-language performances. For more information, call 01.42.71.44.06.

May

May Day On the French **Labor Day** (1 May), most shops and museums are closed and trade unions and left-wing parties organize marches. Bouquets of *muguet* (lily of the valley) are sold all over Paris.

French Open This tennis tournament, held in the **Stade Roland Garros** is the Wimbledon of France. Advance tickets can be purchased starting in January (write to Stade Roland Garros, 2 Ave Gordon-Bennett, 75016 Paris, 01.47.43.48.00); they're also available one week before the tournament at the stadium.

June

Fête du Cinéma For three days cinema-lovers get to watch as many films as they want in any movie theater in Paris for 10 francs per ticket, after paying full price for the first movie and receiving a cinema "passport."

International Rose Competition at Bagatelle Prizes are given on 21 June, but the public can view the competitors in the **Bois de Boulogne**'s **Jardins de Bagatelle** from 22 June through the end of September. For more information, call 01.40.67.97.00.

Gay Pride Parade The largest gay and lesbian parade in France takes place on one of the last Saturdays of the month. For more information, call 01.43.57.21.47.

Garçons de Café Hundreds of cafe servers run around the city, each carrying a tray with a bottle and glass; any spillage or breakage disqualifies the entrant. The race takes place at the end of the month. For more information, call 08.36.68.31.12.

Tour de France After pedaling for 3 weeks and 3,835 kilometers (2,301 miles), cyclists in the world's most famous bicycle race complete the last leg on the streets of Paris and arrive at the finish line on the Champs-Elysées. For more information, call 01.49.35.69.00.

July

Fashion Shows Winter haute-couture collections are launched in the **Carrousel du Louvre.** For more information, call 01.43.16.47.47.

Bastille Day The French national holiday (14 July) celebrates the 1789 storming of the **Bastille** prison by the masses with a military parade down the Champs-Elysées and a fireworks show at the **Palais de Chaillot.**

August

Fête de L'Assomption (Feast of the Assumption) The 15 August procession in front of **Notre-Dame** and the accompanying Mass are memorable experiences.

September

FIAC (Foire Internationale d'Art Contemporain) From 15 to 20 September, gallery owners gather in the large exhibition space of **Paris Expo** to show artists' work. For more information, call 08.36.68.00.51.

Les Journées du Patrimoine (Patrimony Days). On the third Saturday and Sunday of the month, 300 historic buildings and sites that are usually closed to the public are open free of charge, giving history and architecture buffs the chance to explore private houses, *hôtels particuliers,* and other historic structures. For more information, call 08.36.68.31.12.

October

Fêtes des Vendanges à Montmartre (Wine Harvest Festival) The only vineyard left in Paris is no bigger than a baseball diamond and produces 500 bottles of Clos Montmartre every year. On the first Saturday of the month, the basement of the 18th arrondissement *mairie* (town hall) becomes a winery, and festivals and parades liven the tiny crooked streets of **Montmartre.** For more information, call 01.42.52.42.00.

Prix de l'Arc de Triomphe This event marks the opening of the horse-racing season and is attended by the fashionable Chanel-suit, Hermès-scarf, and Gucci-bag crowd. The races take place during the first Sunday of the month at the **Hippodrome de Longchamp** in the **Bois de Boulogne.** For more information, call 01.44.30.75.00.

November

Armistice Day In a somber ceremony in remembrance of those who died in the two world wars, the French president lays wreaths at the **Tomb of the Unknown Soldier** under the **Arc de Triomphe** on 11 November.

Beaujolais Nouveau Day Posters proclaiming that the "*Beaujolais Nouveau est arrivé*" announce the day (the third Thursday of the month) that the first wine of the Beaujolais vintage, pressed and drunk without the aging process, arrives in Paris. Cafes, wine bars, bistros, and wine shops, all join together in a country-wide wine-tasting party. Beaujolais Nouveau is never a sophisticated wine but, depending on the year, it can be pleasantly light and fruity or have less pleasing banana or bubblegum undertones.

December

La Crèche de Notre-Dame A life-size Nativity scene stands under a large tent in the square in front of **Notre-Dame** from early December through early January. Proceeds go to the **Notre-Dame Foundation** for restoration of the cathedral. For more information, call 01.56.56.44.22.

Christmas Eve Mass Both **Notre-Dame** and **St-Eustache** have memorable Masses, which include impressive organ music on Christmas Eve (24 December). The holiday services draw ample crowds.

The Islands: Ile de la Cité and Ile St-Louis

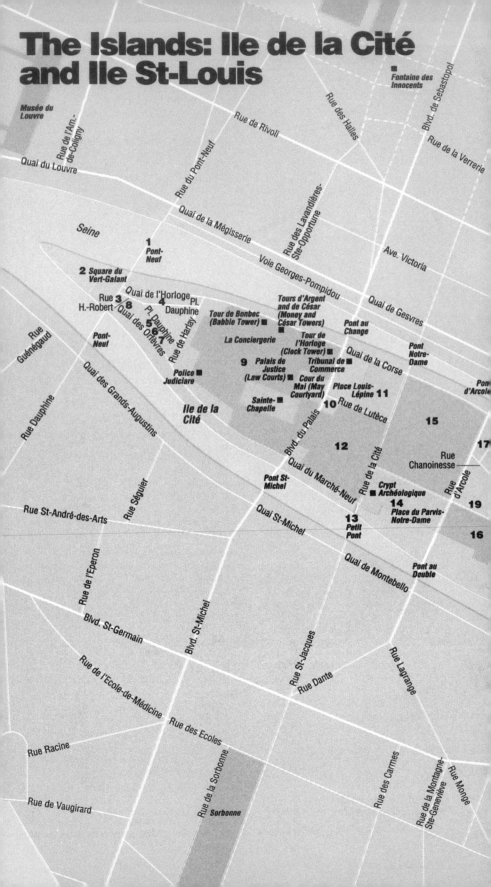

Fontaine des Innocents

Musée du Louvre

Rue de Rivoli

Rue des Halles

Blvd. de Sébastopol

Rue de la Verrerie

Rue de l'Am.-de-Coligny

Quai du Louvre

Rue du Pont-Neuf

Quai de la Mégisserie

Rue des Lavandières-Ste-Opportune

Voie Georges-Pompidou

Ave. Victoria

Seine

1 Pont-Neuf

2 Square du Vert-Galant

Quai de l'Horloge

Pl. Dauphine

Rue 3 8 4
H.-Robert

Pl. Dauphine

5 6 7

Quai des Orfèvres

Rue de Harlay

Quai de Gesvres

Tours d'Argent and de César (Money and César Towers)

Tour de Bonbec (Babble Tower)

La Conciergerie

Pont au Change

Rue Guénégaud

Pont-Neuf

Tour de l'Horloge (Clock Tower)

Pont Notre-Dame

Quai de la Corse

9 Palais de Justice (Law Courts)

Tribunal de Commerce

Pont d'Arcole

Police Judiciare

Quai des Grands-Augustins

Rue Dauphine

Cour du Mai (May Courtyard)

Place Louis-Lépine 11

Ile de la Cité

Sainte-Chapelle

10 Rue de Lutèce

15

Blvd. du Palais

12

Rue de la Cité

17

Rue Chanoinesse

Rue Séguier

Pont St-Michel

Quai du Marché-Neuf

Rue d'Arcole

Rue St-André-des-Arts

Crypt Archéologique

19

Quai St-Michel

14 Place du Parvis-Notre-Dame

Rue de l'Eperon

13 Petit Pont

16

Blvd. St-Germain

Blvd. St-Michel

Quai de Montebello

Pont au Double

Rue de l'Ecole-de-Médecine

Rue St-Jacques

Rue Lagrange

Rue Racine

Rue des Ecoles

Rue Dante

Rue des Carmes

Rue Monge

Rue de la Sorbonne

Rue de la Montagne-Ste-Geneviève

Rue de Vaugirard

Sorbonne

The Islands: Ile de la Cité and Ile St-Louis

At the heart of Paris are two islands: the sloop-shaped Ile de la Cité, which cradles the **Cathédrale de Notre-Dame de Paris** in its stern, and Ile St-Louis, which follows in the wake. Although the islands have no grand hotels, banks, major restaurants, theaters, or designer shops, they do possess two gems of Gothic architecture (**Notre-Dame** and **Sainte-Chapelle**), a world-famous prison, an elegant 17th-century subdivision, some of the city's most beautiful private mansions, the nation's law courts and police headquarters, an Art Nouveau métro station, a flower and bird market, 15 bridges, and one too many souvenir shops selling miniature Napoléon busts and "I Love Paris" bumper stickers.

The following sites serve as an introduction to the islands. If you happen to tour this area on a Sunday, additional attractions include **Notre-Dame**'s morning Mass (10:30AM) and late-afternoon organ concerts, and the bird market at **Place Louis-Lépine.** If visiting the Ile St-Louis galleries and boutiques and the **Palais de Justice** is more your style, a weekday would be a better time to drop by. You might begin with a stop at a pastry shop to purchase croissants and brioches in time for a boat trip up the **Seine** (tour boats leave from the **Pont-Neuf**). Then, after stopping at the flower market and **Notre-Dame,** have lunch at a tea salon on Ile St-Louis before strolling down to look at the exterior of the 17th-century **Hôtel de Lauzun.** Top off your day with a candlelit concert in **Sainte-Chapelle**, followed by dinner at the exceedingly fancy **L'Orangerie** or the more plebeian, all-you-can-eat **Nos Ancêtres les Gaulois.**

Ile de la Cité

The birthplace of Paris, the Cité (as the island is called) was founded by the Parisii in the third century BC and overtaken by the Romans in 52 BC. It survived attacks by Germans and barbarians, floods, and famine, but succumbed to a Frenchman, Baron Georges-Eugène Haussmann, Napoléon III's prefect (1853-70). Baron Haussmann ordered the Cité's "hygienizing," in the process destroying 90 streets and most of its medieval and Louis XIII homes. In their place, he constructed four architecturally dull buildings (**Hôtel-Dieu Hospital,** the **Préfecture de Police,** the **Tribunal de Commerce,** and the **Palais de Justice**) and increased by six times the size of the square in front of **Notre-Dame.**

1 Pont-Neuf Despite its name (New Bridge), Paris's most famous bridge is also its oldest. Completed in 1607, it was the city's original pedestrian bridge as well as the first in Paris to be constructed without houses on top of it. Crossing the Seine at the river's widest point, it's also the city's grandest bridge; designed by **Androuet du Cerceau,** it features 12 broad arches and a series of turrets for street vendors, jugglers, and acrobats. It was completed under the popular Henri IV (Henri of Navarre), who inaugurated the bridge by galloping his charger across it. The bronze equestrian statue of *Henricus Magnus* (Henri the Magnificent, as the king was also called) at the bridge's center is an 1818 replacement; the original, erected two centuries earlier by the king's wife, Marie de Médicis, was melted down to make cannons during the Revolution. The cornices overlooking the river have a carved frieze of grimacing caricatures, perhaps of King Henri's ministers and courtiers.

The bridge became such a well-traveled thoroughfare that, legend held, it was impossible to cross without encountering a monk, a prostitute, and a white horse. One of the most notorious Pont-Neuf charlatans was the Great Jean Thomas, who in 1715 set up a stall on the bridge to peddle bottles of an odorous elixir called Solar Balm. As part of an inventive advertising campaign, he hawked his wares dressed in a scarlet suit, a hat of peacock feathers, and a string of human teeth hung around his neck. The bridge has been sketched by J.M.W. Turner among others, rhapsodized by poets such as Victor Hugo and Jean Loiret, and (in 1985) wrapped by Bulgarian artist Christo in acres of beige canvas and more than seven miles of rope.
♦ Métro: Pont Neuf

2 Square du Vert-Galant Borrowing Henri IV's nickname (which translates roughly as "Gay Old Dog" or "Old Flirt"), this cobblestoned spit of land may be reached by steps behind the king's statue in the middle of Pont-Neuf. Lush with chestnut trees and a haunt of anglers by day and of lovers on warm summer nights, the square affords the best fish-eye view of Paris. Departing from here are one-hour boat tours of the Seine offered by **Les Vedettes du Pont-Neuf** (01.53.00.98.98). The tours leave daily every 30 minutes from 10AM to noon and from 1:30 to 6:30PM. "Lights of Paris" one-hour boat tours with a commentary in English, departing from 9 to 10:30PM, are offered daily from May to 15 October; Friday through Sunday January through April and 15 October through December. ♦ Métro: Pont Neuf

TAVERNE HENRY IV

3 Taverne Henry IV ★★$ Named after the king in bronze across the street, this reasonably priced bistro serves delicious charcuterie, regional cheeses, and goose rillettes and is well stocked with Bordeaux and Burgundy wines. ♦ M-F lunch and dinner; Sa lunch; closed 15 August to 15 September. No credit cards accepted. 13 Pl du Pont-Neuf (at Rue Henri-Robert). 01.43.54.27.90. Métro: Pont Neuf

4 Place Dauphine Once the royal garden, this tranquil triangle of stone and redbrick town houses dates from 1607 and takes its name from Henri IV's son, the princely dauphin who became Louis XIII. The square was one of Henri IV's first city-planning projects in the 17th century and regrettably lost its third side with the expansion of the **Palais de Justice.** Surrealist poet André Breton (1896-1966) called it "one of the most secluded places I know." ♦ Métro: Pont Neuf

4 La Rose de France ★★$$ This tiny restaurant with an outdoor terrace specializes in tasty *côtelettes d'agneau* (lamb chops with *herbes de Provence*), mussels in vermouth, and *filet de boeuf en croûte* (tenderloin of beef in a pastry crust). ♦ M-F lunch and dinner; closed the last three weeks of August and Christmas through New Year's Day. 24 Pl Dauphine (between Rues de Harlay and Henri-Robert). 01.43.54.10.12. Métro: Pont Neuf

5 Hôtel Henri IV $ The wallpaper is peeling, the rooms are tiny, and the showers and bathrooms are in the hall, but that's a minor price to pay for a room with a view of one of the prettiest squares in Paris and a daily rate that's less than the cost of a decent bottle of wine. There are only 22 rooms at this very popular hostelry, so reserve well in advance. There's no restaurant. ♦ No credit cards accepted. 25 Pl Dauphine (between Rues de Harlay and Henri-Robert). 01.43.54.44.53. Métro: Pont Neuf

6 Le Caveau du Palais ★★$$ Charming and comfortable, this restaurant (illustrated above) is wedged between the Place Dauphine and the Quai des Orfèvres. Sample the salad of lamb sweetbreads in a raspberry vinegar, *filet de boeuf à la moutarde de Meaux* (tenderloin of beef with mustard sauce), grilled grouper with basil, and *fondant au chocolat.* Dine inside under the exposed wood beams in winter, on the terrace facing Place Dauphine in summer. ♦ M-Sa lunch and dinner. 19 Pl Dauphine (between Rues de Harlay and Henri-Robert). 01.43.26.04.28. Métro: Pont Neuf

Ile de la Cité

The Building Baron

More than any other individual in Paris's long history, Baron Georges Eugène Haussmann, Napoléon III's powerful public works czar from 1852 to 1870, is responsible for the way the city looks and functions today. When he started, Paris was a dense mass of overcrowded, grown-together villages with tangled webs of dark, narrow, and winding medieval streets. When he finished, it was the bright, unified, and modern City of Light we know today.

The transformation was astonishing. But to achieve it he made himself the most hated man in Paris. "The Vulture," as he became known, condemned and demolished the dwellings of hundreds of thousands of people to cut his wide, tree-lined avenues through the heart of their ancient neighborhoods. When he began reworking the **Ile de la Cité**, for example, 25,000 people lived in its teeming, insalubrious medieval streets. When he finished cutting the **Boulevard du Palais** through the island and building the sprawling **Palais de Justice**, the **Hôtel-Dieu** hospital, and other public buildings that cover it today, less than 1,000 residents were left.

The suppression of civic uprisings was an important motive of the wily baron's grand design. His broad new avenues made it difficult for malcontents to erect barricades, as they had in 1830 and 1848, when revolutionaries succeeded in overthrowing the government, and the long straight thoroughfares offered Napoléon III's army clear fields of fire against any potential mob. Haussmann's redevelopment also divided rich from poor. Before, the moneyed citizen and the local tradespeople lived side by side in their mansions or humble dwellings. Afterwards, skyrocketing real estate values drove the poor to the city's fringes.

Beside the vast network of avenues and traffic circles that he created, this supremely willful bureaucrat developed Paris's sewer system with more than 1,300 miles of tunnels; its gas street lights and domestic gas lines; its reservoirs and running water; most of the railway stations; the huge central food market of **Les Halles;** the **Opéra de Paris;** and the **Ecole des Beaux Arts.** He also doubled the land surface of Paris by annexing the then-peripheral villages around it, such as **Belleville** and **Montmartre** (which he proceeded to populate with former residents of buildings he tore down); built the imaginative urban parks of **Monceau, Buttes-Chaumont,** and **Montsouris;** and added the **Bois de Boulogne** and the **Bois de Vincennes,** Paris's only two large parks, located at opposite ends of the city.

L'Avenue de l'Opera

Many men made huge fortunes from Haussman's grand projects, but the baron himself refused to take what would have been easy pickings. When this scrupulously upright man from a strict Alsatian Protestant upbringing was finally forced from office, he retired to the country on a modest civil servant's pension and had to sell his autobiography to make ends meet.

To get an idea of what Paris looked like before the baron came along, take a stroll through the narrow, winding streets of the **Marais** or Montmartre that he didn't have time to straighten out. Then take a stroll up **Avenue de l'Opéra** to the **Place de l'Opéra** to get the full flavor of Haussmann's City of Light.

---

6 Le Bar du Caveau ★$ Managed by **Le Caveau du Palais** next door, this wine bar serves light meals: charcuterie, country cheese, and a variety of Bordeaux and Beaujolais. ◆ Daily breakfast, lunch, and snacks until 8PM. 19 Pl Dauphine (between Rues de Harlay and Henri-Robert). 01.43.54.45.95. Métro: Pont Neuf

Two unwritten rules of etiquette when dining at someone's home in France: Arrive 10-20 minutes late for a dinner party, but on time for lunch.

Restaurant PAUL

7 Restaurant Paul ★★$$ Long marble tables set with cloth napkins as big as dish towels dominate this spot. Try the lobster salad with curry sauce, the *mignon de veau en papillote* (veal tenderloin steaks baked in parchment), and, for dessert, the *baba au rhum flambé* with red currant jam. During the summer months don't miss the wild strawberries. ◆ Daily lunch and dinner April through September; M lunch, Tu-Su lunch and dinner October through March. 15 Pl

Dauphine (between Rues de Harlay and Henri-Robert) and 52 Quai des Orfèvres (between Rue de Harlay and Pl du Pont-Neuf). 01.43.54.21.48. Métro: Pont Neuf

8 Quai des Orfèvres (Goldsmiths Quay)
This is the Scotland Yard of Paris, home of the city's detective force, the *police judiciare* or "PJ." Perhaps the most famous member of the PJ is Inspector Maigret, the protagonist of the detective stories by the late Georges Simenon. ♦ Métros: Cité, St-Michel

On Quai des Orfèvres:

Au Rendez-Vous des Camionneurs ★$$
Owner-chef Alain Haye creates simple but tasty fare at this cozy restaurant. Start with his *poelon de moules et de crevettes à la fondue de poireaux* (mussels and shrimp with minced leeks and cream) or *émincé de haddock à la sauce Coulibiac* (smoked minced haddock with cream-and-lemon sauce). Follow with *oeufs pochés à la confiture d'oignons* (poached eggs with onion chutney) or *blanquette de veau* (veal with béchamel sauce and mushrooms). Desserts are especially good—the *truffé au chocolat* and *charlotte aux fraises* (trifle with strawberries) should satisfy any sweet tooth. ♦ Daily lunch and dinner. No. 72 (between Rue de Harlay and Pl du Pont-Neuf). 01.43.54.88.74

9 Palais de la Cité This massive interlocking series of structures has been occupied by the French government since 52 BC, first as the palace of Roman prefects, later as the Gothic palace of the first 12 kings of France. In the 13th century it was the residence of St. Louis (Louis IX), who lived in the upper chambers (now the **First Civil Court**). The king meted out justice beneath a tree in the courtyard. All that remains of the original palace is the breathtaking **Sainte-Chapelle** and the gloomy **Conciergerie,** one of history's most hideous and brutal prisons (see below for details on both places). Most of the original site was covered by the **Palais de Justice,** which was built after the great fire of 1776. ♦ Bounded by Blvd du Palais and Rue de Harlay, and Quais des Orfèvres and de l'Horloge. Métro: Cité

Within the Palais de la Cité:

Tours de Bonbec, d'Argent, and de César (Babble, Money, and César Towers) Along the Quai de l'Horloge side of the old palace is a set of round, imposing towers. The first is **Tour de Bonbec,** nicknamed the "babbler" because it was used as a torture chamber during the Reign of Terror, a period of brutal purges following the Revolution. Next are the **Tour d'Argent** (where the royal treasure was once kept) and the **Tour de César,** two steepled gate towers beside the entrance to the **Conciergerie.** The tower interiors are not open to the public. ♦ Quai de l'Horloge (between Blvd du Palais and Rue de Harlay)

La Conciergerie After the bloody mob revolt led by Etienne Marcel in 1358, young King Charles V moved the royal residence to the Marais but left behind the royal dungeon and Supreme Court in the charge of the king's caretaker, known as the *Comte des Cierges* (Count of Candles) or *Concierge.*

Among the dungeon's long list of former residents are such notorious criminals as Ravaillac, the fanatic who murdered popular Henri IV and was imprisoned and tortured here before his execution. During the Revolution, the Tribunal commandeered the palace and administered its own ruthless form of justice. The **Conciergerie** became the antechamber to the guillotine during the Reign of Terror between January 1793 and July 1794. About 2,600 Parisians were condemned to death, among them Charlotte Corday, who had stabbed Marat in his bath, and, perhaps the best-remembered inmate, Marie Antoinette, the Austrian queen who had reputedly scoffed at the starving French masses with the phrase "Let them eat cake." Shortly after the Tribunal executed her husband, King Louis XVI, she was held here in a tiny cell from August until October 1793, when she was delivered to the guillotine. Royalty were not the only victims during this tumultuous time; no one in a position of authority was safe. Revolutionary Danton, who had ordered the execution of 22 people, was in turn condemned to death by citizen Robespierre, who later was sent to the guillotine by a panel of judges, the Thermidor Convention. At the end of the Terror, the Tribunal's own public prosecutor, Fouquier-Tinville, was dragged off to the gallows shouting "I am the ax! You don't execute the ax!"

Put yourself in the shoes of Marie Antoinette as she walked down the prison's Rue de Paris (which during the Terror led to the quarters of an executioner known as *Monsieur de Paris*). She was jailed in dank cell **No. VI;** in the cell next door, both Danton and Robespierre were held on death row, and, in the adjoining chapel, the 22 condemned Girondins heard Mass before their execution. All these rooms, as well as the *salle de la dernière toilette,* from which prisoners were led to the block, have been restored to their original state.

On your way out, duck into the magnificent medieval vaults of the four-aisled **Salle des Gens d'Armes** (Hall of the Men-at-Arms), frequently used these days for classical concerts, theater performances, and wine tastings. The spiral staircase at the far end of the hall is worth a peek. Also be sure to stroll through the 14th-century kitchen that served some 3,000 guests and had large walk-in ovens. The souvenir shop near the exit sells replicas of Revolutionary playing cards that replace kings, queens, and jacks with humbly clothed men and women personifying common virtues such as Industry and Justice. The original deck (1793) by Jaume and Dugorc is kept in the **Bibliothèque Nationale.** ♦ Admission. Daily. Tours in English: 11AM, 3PM. 1 Quai de l'Horloge (between Blvd du Palais and Rue de Harlay). 01.53.73.78.50

Tour de l'Horloge (Clock Tower) This tower was the site of the city's first public clock (1334). Today's more Baroque version is set in a constellation of golden fleurs-de-lis and flanked by angels, rams, and royal shields. Until the French Revolution, the clock signaled royal births and deaths by pealing nonstop for three days. ♦ Quai de l'Horloge and Blvd du Palais

Palais de Justice (Law Courts) Behind the lusciously gilded Louis XVI railing and portal gates on the Boulevard du Palais is the main entrance to the **Palais de Justice** and the **Cour du Mai** (May Courtyard). The courtyard was the last stop for the condemned before they left by wooden carts, or tumbrils, for the gallows in the Place de la Concorde. Look above the door at the top of the marble steps for the words *Liberté, Egalité, Fraternité.*

On the right in the lobby (**Salle des Pas-Perdus,** literally "Room of the Wasted Steps") is an amusing statue of Berryer, a 19th-century barrister. To his right sits a sculpted muse with her foot on a turtle, a jab at the speed of the legal process. Behind the door to the left is the gorgeous blue-and-gold **Première Chambre,** also known as the "Chambre Dorée" (Gilded Chamber), where the Revolutionary Tribunal sat on 6 April 1793 and sentenced Queen Marie Antoinette to death.

In the "cathedral of chicanery," as Balzac called the Law Courts, a thicket of police, public *écrivains* (letter writers), and prisoners used to gather while hawkers sold newspapers and rented black judicial robes. Today, the lobby is still a chaos of black-robed barristers, plaintiffs, and judges dashing about. If you'd like to see a French Perry Mason putting *liberté, égalité,* and *fraternité* into action, visit on a weekday, when courtroom proceedings (except the juvenile court) are in session. ♦ M-Sa. 2 Blvd du Palais (between Quais des Orfèvres and de l'Horloge). 01.44.32.50.00. Métro: Cité

Within the Palais de Justice:

Sainte-Chapelle After **Notre-Dame,** this is the city's most significant medieval monument. St. Louis (Louis IX, 1214-70), France's only canonized king, erected this Gothic jewel of a chapel in 1248 to enshrine the relics he bought from Venetian merchants during his first crusade. His purchases included Christ's Crown of Thorns, two pieces of the True Cross, a nail from the cross, the Roman soldier's lance that pierced Christ's side, and several drops of Christ's blood. For the relics, he paid 35,000 livres in gold, a sum far in excess of what it cost to construct this building.

Sainte-Chapelle (the name means "holy chapel") was built in fewer than five years and is thought to have been designed by **Pierre de Montreuil.** It soars 67 feet without the aid of flying buttresses, a daring architectural feat in those days. In medieval times the chapel was connected to the palace of Louis IX, but today it's hidden away in a side courtyard. The interior has two tiers—the royal family worshipped upstairs in the light and airy **Chapelle Haute,** out of view of the court members who prayed on the somber ground floor.

SAINTE-CHAPELLE

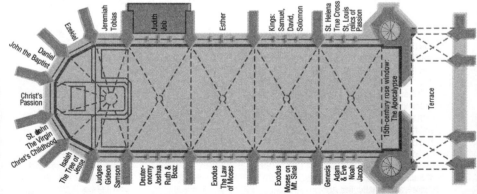

Sainte-Chapelle

The chapel suffered considerable damage during the Revolution, when the gold reliquary was melted down and the structure was put to use as a flour warehouse. In the 19th century the chapel was thoroughly made over by **Eugène-Emmanuel Viollet-le-Duc** (1814-79), one of the Baron Haussmann–hired architects who also restored **Notre-Dame** and cathedrals at Amiens and St-Denis. **Louis Charles Auguste Steinheil,** a compatriot of Balzac and Baudelaire, restored the windows. Of the 12 apostle statues, only 1 (the bearded apostle 5th down on the left side) is original. Portions of the damaged originals are on exhibit in the **Musée de Cluny.** The chapel's spectacular windows (see diagram opposite) are older than **Notre-Dame's** and comprise the largest expanse of stained glass in the world—1,500 square yards, enough to cover 3 basketball courts. Created in an age of mass illiteracy, this pictorial Bible consists of 1,134 scenes. Start at the lower-left panel of each window and read from left to right, row by row from bottom to top. The narrative begins with Genesis and continues through the Crucifixion (illustrated in the choir apse), with scenes and figures from both the Old and New Testaments interspersed throughout. The concluding windows (on the left side of the church as you face the entrance to the Chapelle Haute) depict Louis IX's acquisition of the holy relics, the construction of the chapel, and, finally, the Apocalypse. Notice

that a liberated Louis IX devoted entire windows to two women of the Old Testament, Judith and Esther.

Because the windows are backlit by the sun, different ones are more brightly illuminated at different times of day; you have to get up early to catch the Battle of Jericho and must come after lunch for David and Goliath. If the flies on Pharaoh's face interest you, bring your opera glasses, because many of the panels, particularly the highest ones, are nearly impossible to decipher with the naked eye. Anyone who identifies even a few Bible characters in a short visit is doing well. A while back, a Belgian Benedictine monk arrived here with his Bible and a pair of binoculars; it took him two full weeks, gazing every day from dawn to dusk, to complete the cycle.

For an initial visit, the best approach is to set aside your guidebook and gaze upward. Note how the thick, predominantly red and blue dyed glass of the 15 main windows contrasts sharply with the green and yellow hues of the flamboyant rose window (restored by Charles VIII in 1485). Imagine yourself among the royal family in the 13th century watching as Louis IX mounted the stairs to the gold reliquary to display the sacred Crown of Thorns. (The crown now resides in **Notre-Dame** and is exhibited only on Good Friday.) In addition to its visual splendors, **Sainte-Chapelle** is renowned for its acoustics; Couperin played the organ here in the 17th century. Nowadays, rather expensive evening concerts of classical music are held here every evening from 15 March through October. ◆ Admission. 01.53.73.78.61; concerts 01.44.07.12.38

⚖ **BRASSERIE DES DEUX PALAIS**

10 Brasserie des Deux Palais ★$
This corner cafe with 1920s-style mirrored columns serves omelettes, good coffee, and hot lunch specials. ◆ Daily breakfast, lunch, and dinner. 3 Blvd du Palais (at Rue de Lutèce). 01.43.54.20.86. Métro: Cité

11 Place Louis-Lépine Named after a Belle Epoque police chief remembered for having armed Parisian *gendarmes* with whistles and truncheons, this square is a charming urban Eden surrounded by the grim walls of **Hôtel-Dieu Hospital,** the **Préfecture de Police,** and the **Tribunal de Commerce.** One of the largest flower markets in Paris blooms here year-round with everything from chrysanthemums to lemon trees. On Sunday, the square is transformed into a bird market selling cages, seed, and a palette of colorful canaries, finches, and parrots. ◆ Métro: Cité

25

On Place Louis-Lépine:

Cité Métro Station This is one of the original 141 Art Nouveau "dragonfly" métro station entrances designed by **Hector Guimard** in 1900.

12 Préfecture de Police A bunker of a building, this structure is the headquarters of the fictional Inspector Clouseau of *Pink Panther* fame and the very real Paris police. On 19 August 1944, during the liberation of Paris, about a thousand Paris police officers revolted against the German occupation, barricaded themselves inside, hoisted the tricolor to a rousing chorus of the *Marseillaise,* and held off Nazi tanks and artillery for four days until the Allies arrived. In the ensuing battle 280 died, and buildings around **Notre-Dame**'s parvis are still pockmarked with bullet holes. ♦ 1 Rue de la Cité (between Quai du Marché-Neuf and Rue de Lutèce). Métros: Cité, St-Michel

13 Petit Pont The "Little Bridge" was first built in 1185 by Bishop Maurice de Sully, who also oversaw the construction of **Notre-Dame.** In the Middle Ages, minstrels were allowed to cross the bridge without paying the toll. A 19th-century version now stands in the place where the original one stood. ♦ Métros: Cité, St-Michel

14 Place du Parvis-Notre-Dame In the Middle Ages, when miracle plays were performed, the square in front of **Notre-Dame** represented *paradis,* or paradise, a name contracted over the centuries to "parvis." Critics of Baron Haussmann, who enlarged the parvis sixfold in the 19th century, called it the "paved prairie." ♦ Métros: Cité, St-Michel

Beneath the Place du Parvis-Notre-Dame:

Crypte Archéologique (Archaeological Crypt) In 1965, while excavating for an underground parking lot, city workers unearthed Gallo-Roman and medieval ruins, now preserved in this slightly eerie but intelligently designed archaeological site/museum beneath the Place du Parvis-Notre-Dame. The crypt, designed by **André Hermant,** is worth a quick visit, if only to see the museum's interesting scale models of Paris, which show its evolution from a Celtic settlement during the Second Iron Age to a Roman city in 50 BC. Notice that the Romans, in anticipation of another barbarian invasion, reinforced the original ramparts with a second wall. This is one of the city's most accessible museums, with information in English and French. ♦ Admission. Daily. 01.43.29.83.51

On the Place du Parvis-Notre-Dame:

Rue de Venise Paris in the Middle Ages was a snarl of narrow horse paths. Marked in the pavement of the parvis in front of the cathedral is the former position of this one-yard-wide medieval alley, no doubt once the narrowest street in Paris.

14 Statue de Charlemagne On the south side of the parvis rests a bronze statue, created in 1882, of Charlemagne, the Frank who was crowned the first Holy Roman Emperor in AD 800. The center of Charlemagne's empire was at Aix-la-Chapelle; under Charlemagne and his successors, Paris was merely a provincial town. (If you happen to be looking for public toilets, follow the tail of Charlemagne's prancing horse; it points west to nearby stairs leading underground.)

Notre-Dame

14 Point Zéro All distances in France are measured from this brass compass star *(Point Zéro des Routes de France)* fixed in the pavement in front of **Notre-Dame.** Throughout France, highway signs tell you how far away you are (in kilometers) from Paris.

15 Hôtel-Dieu Hospital Behind the double row of chestnut trees along the north end of the parvis is "God's Hostel," founded by St. Landry, Bishop of Paris. The original hospital building was erected here in AD 651. In 1400, this became the site of the oldest known cabaret in Paris, **La Pomme de Pin;** it was frequented by Rabelais, Villon, Molière, and Racine. The present hospital building was built here in the mid-19th century by Baron Haussmann as part of his urbanization project; in the latter part of that century it was an important training facility for US doctors. ◆ Pl du Parvis-Notre-Dame (between Rues d'Arcole and de la Cité). Métros: Cité, St-Michel

16 Cathédrale de Notre-Dame de Paris (Cathedral of Our Lady of Paris)
"The cathedral of **Notre-Dame**," wrote e. e. cummings, "does not budge an inch for all the idiocies of this world." For six centuries, this world-famous masterpiece of the Middle Ages has endured as a sonnet in stone, harmonizing mass and elegance, asymmetry and perfection. Among its architectural triumphs are the Gothic ribbed vaulting and the flying buttresses, which opened up the church by permitting the erection of higher, more slender walls pierced by glorious stained glass.

In 1163 no less a personage than Pope Alexander III laid the cathedral's foundation stone, and the final masterful touches were not completed until 1345—more than two centuries later. (**Sainte-Chapelle,** by comparison, was erected in five years.) The design followed the sketches executed in 1159 by Bishop Maurice de Sully and was

implemented by architects **Pierre de Montreuil** who was responsible for **Notre-Dame**'s south transept, and **Jean de Chelles,** as well as generations of anonymous workers.

To tour the cathedral is to stroll through French history. On this site the Romans built a temple in antiquity to Jupiter and the emperor Tiberius. In the cathedral during the Middle Ages, the homeless slept and were fed; trade unions met; passion plays were performed; and merchants from the Orient sold everything from ostrich eggs to elephant tusks. During the 12th century the cathedral's adjoining school became an intellectual center known throughout Europe; it eventually gave birth to the **Sorbonne.** During the Revolution the cathedral was rechristened the "Temple of Reason"; shortly thereafter, it was auctioned off to a demolition contractor for scrap building material. Though never demolished, **Notre-Dame** was in shambles in 1804 when Napoléon Bonaparte called Pope Pius VII from Rome to officiate at his coronation, which was held before the cathedral's high altar. After the anointing, Napoléon defiantly snatched the crown from the pontiff and crowned himself emperor, a dramatic scene captured by Jacques-Louis David in his famous painting, which hangs in the **Louvre.**

West Facade At the base of the west facade, which is topped by two 69-meter (226-foot) towers, are 3 famous portals. The ones on the left and right honor the Virgin Mary and her mother, St. Anne, respectively; the one in the center depicts the Last Judgment. Royalty also managed to get into the picture; in the tympanum of the portal to St. Anne, a kneeling King Louis VII (far right) dedicates the cathedral with Bishop Sully (on the left with a crook in his hand), as the bishop's faithful secretary takes notes straddling a Gothic stool. The presence of Barbedor, the scribe, represents one of the first times an intellectual was honored in a cathedral facade.

On 22 April 1769, kilometer zero for France was fixed in front of Notre-Dame Cathedral. The location was originally marked by a triangular post, but was replaced by a star embedded in the pavement in 1924.

"Of course they came to France a great many to paint pictures and naturally they could not do that at home, or to write they could not do that at home either, they could be dentists at home."

Gertrude Stein

Restaurants/Clubs: Red **Hotels:** Blue
Shops/ 🌳 **Outdoors:** Green **Sights/Culture:** Black

Above the three portals is the **Gallery of Kings**, **Eugène-Emmanuel Viollet-le-Duc's** 19th-century replicas of medieval masterpieces, which were once painted in vibrant yellow, cobalt, and scarlet. The 28 kings represent the kings of Judea and Israel, thought by the Catholic Church to be the ancestors of Christ. In 1793 Revolutionaries mistook them for the kings of France and toppled and decapitated them. Fortunately, an educator spirited away the heads and buried them in his yard at 20 Rue de la Chaussée-d'Antin, near the present site of the **Opéra Garnier.** They languished there until 1977, when they were unearthed during excavations for a bank vault and put on exhibit at the **Musée de Cluny.**

North and South Towers Enter the **North Tower** from a separate entrance at its foot. At the end of a spiraling 255-step climb you will find not Victor Hugo's tormented hunchback, Quasimodo, but an equally unsettling sight: **Viollet-le-Duc's** stone bestiary of gargoyles, gremlins, and demons. It was believed that the gargoyles kept evil spirits from the cathedral; a number of them also serve as downspouts, squirting rain from their mouths—an entertaining sight during spring showers. The 90-meter (297-foot) spire was added during the heavy-handed Gothic Revival restoration of 1860. **Viollet-le-Duc** placed a statue of himself alongside the copper apostles and evangelists. The apostles stand on the cathedral roof looking outward, blessing the city, but the architect looks upward, admiring his work. For a bird's-eye view of the **Viollet-le-Duc** statue, the celebrated flying buttresses, and the splendid chain of bridges over the Atlantic-bound Seine, climb the last 125 steps to the top of the **South Tower.** The tower also houses the cathedral's famous 13-ton **Emmanuel Bell,** tolled on solemn occasions.

Interior A recent clean-up of the cathedral's interior has made it much brighter and easier to see its splendors. One of them is the massive organ. It is France's largest, a masterwork installed in the mid-19th century by Aristide Cavaillé-Coll. Following in the tradition of François Couperin, César Auguste Franck, and Olivier Messiaen, all of whom performed here, some of Europe's greatest organists offer free recitals every Sunday afternoon. These concerts, as well as the candlelit Easter vigil and Christmas Eve Mass, draw ample crowds, as does the deeply moving cathedral service held each 11 November, when the Royal British Legion honors British and Commonwealth soldiers who died on French soil during World War I. The cathedral's seating capacity is nearly 10,000.

Mays Paintings During the Middle Ages, the *Orfèvrerie* (the gold workers' union) presented paintings to the cathedral each May. The paintings, called *Mays,* were originally hung between the church pillars; today, they are displayed in the side chapels. Among them are works by Charles Le Brun (1619-90) and Eustache Le Sueur (1616-55).

Windows New windows were installed in the cathedral's clerestory after World War II, but not because of damage caused by the Germans. In the 18th century Louis XV declared stained glass déclassé and destroyed the Gothic glass in the upper-level nave windows, replacing it with clear glass (the rest of the stained-glass windows were left intact). The change gave the interior a bright, Protestant appearance. It was not until after the war that contemporary glass replicas of the original upper-nave Gothic windows were installed. Of **Notre-Dame**'s three famous rose windows (north, south, and west), only the north has the original 13th-century glass. The south and west rose windows glow most brilliantly at twilight, while the north window is best viewed in morning light. The stained-glass windows of the 13th and 14th century are thick, with small images and a predominance of deep reds, blues, and purples (the colors are actually dyed into the glass). Over the centuries, it became possible to make thinner glass. Images became larger and were hand-painted on the glass surface, and ways of making brighter greens and yellows were discovered. These developments are evident in the differences between the original windows and the modern replicas.

Wood Sculpture One of the cathedral's most charming decorations is the 14th-century Gothic relief on the north side of the chancel that depicts the life of Christ from the Nativity to the Last Supper.

The new altar (in front of the old altar) reflects the liturgical changes in the 1960s that allowed the priest to say Mass facing the congregation instead of turning his back. In addition, Mass is now said in French instead of Latin (although the cathedral's echoing acoustics sometimes make it hard to figure out what language is being spoken). ♦ 6 Pl du Parvis-Notre-Dame and Rue du Cloître-Notre-Dame. 01.42.34.56.10, 01.44.32.16.70 for tour information. Métros: Cité, St-Michel

17 Rue de la Colombe This medieval street was cut along the former site of the old Roman wall, which protected Paris against barbarian invasions. ♦ Métros: Cité, Hôtel de Ville

On Rue de la Colombe:

No. 4 Originally a 13th-century tavern and later a famous cabaret in the 1950s, this building was until the mid-1990s the home of **La Colombe** restaurant, which was classified as a French historic landmark and, according to *Le Figaro* magazine, is the most photographed house in Paris. Today the faded sign proclaiming the former restaurant's landmark status and the sculpted doves over the door (*la colombe* is French for "the dove") are the only reminders of the home-style menu of *confit de canard* (duck confit) and *foie gras de maison* that were dished up at this old tourist favorite, which was closed and boarded up at press time.

Paris Seen from on High

Among the most treasured mental snapshots visitors take home from Paris are the panoramas of the city viewed from observation decks and restaurants in the sky. While the **Eiffel Tower** is the best known, it is far from the only place from which to see the City of Light from up high. Here are the top spots—some cost a bundle, others not a sou.

Left Bank

La Tour d'Argent The spectacular penthouse panorama of **Notre-Dame's** flying buttresses and the barges passing on the **Seine** have helped make this one of the city's most famous gourmet restaurants. It's also among the most expensive.

Le Ziryab This North African restaurant on the top floor of the **L'Institut du Monde Arabe** has an even better river view than **Tour d'Argent.**

Tour Eiffel One of the most-visited venues in Paris is the tower's third-level observation deck at 899 feet. (In 1998, more than six million people took the elevator up—the most on record to date.) The ride all the way to the top is always exciting, but for a view that's worth the hefty entrance fee, be sure to come on a clear day, and an hour before sundown for the best light. Ambitious folks can also make the climb up 1,652 steps to the top. The tower also supports two high-angle eating places. The glamorous gastronomic **Le Jules Verne** restaurant on the second level is the loftier at 377 feet, but the amusing and far lower-price **Altitude 95** on the first level at 187 feet above the ground is high enough for a grand view.

Tour Montparnasse The vista from the 59th floor of this sinister black glass monolith at Place Raoul-Dautry (between Rue du Départ and Blvd de Vaugirard) dominating the hill of **Montparnasse** takes in the **Eiffel Tower,** all of central Paris, and the hill of **Montmartre** beyond.

Ile de la Cité

Notre Dame Cathedral It's a 380-step hike up to the bell tower, but for those who are in shape it's well worth it for a Quasimodo-eye view of Paris.

Right Bank

Arc de Triomphe Peruse the *étoile* (star) formed by the dozen wide, tree-lined avenues that lead to the arch's traffic circle from the rooftop deck of Napoléon's grandest monument.

Centre Georges Pompidou The fifth-floor observation balcony offers dramatic views of Notre-Dame's towers and roof, the **Panthéon,** the **Tour St-Jacques,** the nave of **St-Eustache** church, and Montmartre. It's free.

Grand Arche de la Défense The rooftop platform of this huge open glass and marble cube offers a wonderful panorama of the straight line of monuments and avenues extending from the **Pyramid** of the **Louvre** through the middle of the **Tuileries Gardens** and the **Place de la Concorde,** up the **Champs-Elysées,** through the **Arc de Triomphe,** and on to the **Grande Arche de La Défense**—a distance of 4.5 miles.

Magasin II (Store II) of the **La Samaritaine** department store on the Seine has superb vistas from three different levels. Two reasons to come here: the view of the **Eiffel Tower,** and the lack of an entrance fee. There is a 360° panorama of all of Paris from the rooftop observation platform (take the elevator to the 10th floor and climb the circular staircase to the upper deck). The open-air cafeteria on the 10th floor offers a fine Seine and Left Bank view, as does the smashing Hilton McConnico–designed **Toupary** restaurant on the 5th floor.

Maison Blanche This spectacular gourmet restaurant high atop the **Théâtre des Champs-Elysées** presents a dazzling vista of the **Eiffel Tower** across the Seine—either through a vast expanse of windows or from the outdoor terrace in good weather. The view is particularly stunning at night, when the tower glows with golden light. The restaurant is expensive.

Montmartre Atop the city's highest natural feature (423 feet above sea level), the **Butte de Montmartre,** the heart of Paris lies at your feet from the terrace in front of the **Sacré-Coeur** basilica. All this magnificent view costs is the effort to hike up there. The lovely seventh-floor terrace restaurant of the **Terrass Hôtel** offers the same grand panorama of the city.

18 9-11 Quai aux Fleurs The sculpted heads on the facade of this 19th-century building commemorate two of history's most famous lovers, Héloïse and Abélard, who today cast plaintive glances at couples strolling arm-in-arm along the Quai aux Fleurs (where, by the way, no flowers are sold). In 1118 Pierre Abélard (1079-1142), an iconoclastic theologian who helped found the **University of Paris,** fell in love with one of his students. She was Héloïse (1101-64), the brilliant niece of Fulbert, the foul-tempered canon of **Notre-Dame.** "Under the guise of study, we gave ourselves to love," wrote Abélard. ". . . We exchanged more kisses than sentences." The passionate affair was brought to an abrupt, brutal, and tragic end by Fulbert, whose thugs emasculated Abélard. Héloïse and Abélard lived on, cloistered separately for many years, but were buried side-by-side in **Père-Lachaise Cemetery.** ♦ 9-11 Quai aux Fleurs (at Rue des Chantres). Métros: Cité, Hôtel de Ville

Le Vieux Bistro

19 Le Vieux Bistro ★★$$ Far removed from the traffic and crush of tourists is this quiet, charming restaurant featuring the cuisine of Lyons. The *civet de canard* (duck stew) and the Burgundy sausage are both delicious choices. ♦ Daily lunch and dinner. Reservations recommended. 14 Rue du Cloître-Notre-Dame (between Rues Massillon and d'Arcole). 01.43.54.18.95. Métro: Cité

20 Square Jean-XXIII Cherry trees blossom here in the spring, lime trees provide shade in the summer, and the chestnut leaves are heaped ankle-deep in autumn. **Notre-Dame**'s west face is towering but flat compared to the south and east sides, shored by dramatic flying buttresses that loom above this park. Here is a place to pause and feed the birds or to perch on a wooden bench during one of the occasional outdoor concerts given by a local police officers' orchestra. ♦ Quai de l'Archevêché and Rue du Cloître-Notre-Dame. Métros: Cité, Maubert-Mutualité

21 Mémorial de la Déportation (Deportation Memorial) Designed by **G.H. Pingusson** in 1962, this structure commemorates the 200,000 people, most of them Jewish, who were deported from France and died during the Holocaust. Some 30,000 people from Paris alone were sent to Nazi death camps during World War II. Reflecting the Jewish tradition of paying homage to the dead by placing a stone on the grave, the memorial is constructed around a tunnel of 200,000 quartz pebbles. It also contains small tombs with earth from each of the concentration camps.

Visitors descend a narrow stair to an open space where they can look out at water through iron-barred windows. From there they pass through a door to a low, enclosed room where they can look through other barred windows into the tunnel of pebbles. The visitor here feels trapped visually and psychologically by the low ceiling and iron bars. Stark and simple, the memorial is one of city's most moving monuments. ♦ Free. Daily. Sq de l'Ile-de-France. Métros: Cité, Maubert-Mutualité

22 Pont St-Louis Step lightly; this pedestrian bridge is the ninth on a site that has had a shaky history. The first bridge linking Ile de la Cité and Ile St-Louis was erected in 1634 by developer Jean-Christophe Marie; it crumbled on opening day, drowning 20 people. But that wasn't the worst of Marie's bridge disasters: his Pont-Marie, built the following year, later collapsed during a flood, killing 121 people. ♦ Métros: Cité, Pont Marie

Ile St-Louis

A world apart from the rest of Paris, this once-bucolic cow pasture and site of sword duels is jammed today with grand 17th-century town houses (which with few exceptions are closed to the public) and fashionable shops. Ile St-Louis is named after Louis IX, the saintly French king who recited his breviary here among the cows. Voltaire considered this island the "second best" location in the world (his first choice was the straits of the Bosporus separating Europe from Asia).

People have only lived here for 300 years, yet the island is the oldest fully preserved section of the French capital, bisected by a single commercial street. When Henri IV decided to "urbanize" the pastoral Ile St-Louis for his courtiers as an extension of Place des Vosges, he hired developer Jean-Christophe Marie. Between 1614 and 1630, Marie laid out one of the city's first real estate developments with straight streets on a grid, an avant-garde idea in an age when streets followed meandering medieval cow paths.

Ile St-Louis is an isolated village with no subway stop, four small hotels, and a baker whose ovens are fueled with wood. *Louisiens* (as island residents are called) are a proud, independent breed who don't always take kindly to interlopers (Ile St-Louis was the first quarter in Paris to chase out the Nazis during the Liberation). The list of former island residents includes Apollinaire, Balzac, Voltaire, Zola, Baudelaire, Cézanne, Courbet, Daumier, Delacroix, Colette, George Sand, and Georges Pompidou. When *Louisiens* leave the island, they say they are going "to Paris" or "to the continent" or "to the mainland," a voyage that's less than the length of a football field. Many of the elder residents have not been off the island in years, and up until the 1970s there was so little traffic here on Sunday that the islanders played *boules* (boccie) in the streets.

Soon after **Berthillon** opened its doors here in 1954, ice cream became the rage of Paris and the island was rediscovered. Along with the notoriety came the inevitable chic tea salons and hordes of tourists. Nonetheless, Ile St-Louis retains its own distinctive identity and charm and remains one of the most exclusive addresses in the city.

La Brasserie de l'Isle Saint-Louis

23 La Brasserie de l'Isle Saint-Louis ★★ $$ This Alsatian brasserie/tavern comes complete with the regional mascot—a stork perched on the old wooden bar. The bird, of course, is stuffed, and soon so are the neighborhood habitués who sit elbow-to-elbow dining on sausage, sauerkraut, ham knuckles, blueberry tarts, and *chopes* (steins) of Mutzia beer. The 1913 silver-plated espresso machine is a museum piece. The servers are paragons of patience and good cheer when talking to foreigners. ♦ M-Tu, Th-Su lunch and dinner until 1:30AM; closed in August. 55 Quai de Bourbon (at Rue St-Louis-en-l'Ile). 01.43.54.02.59. Métro: Pont Marie

24 Le Flore en l'Ile ★★$ A three-star view of the **Panthéon** on the Left Bank and the flying buttresses of **Notre-Dame** are just two of the draws of this Viennese-style tearoom. Other highlights here include music by Mozart, good breakfasts, a hearty onion soup, traditional plats du jour, and delicious fruit tarts. ♦ Daily breakfast, lunch, and dinner until 2AM. 42 Quai d'Orléans (at Rue Jean-du-Bellay). 01.43.29.88.27. Métro: Pont Marie

La Chaumière en l'Ile

24 La Chaumière en l'Ile ★$$ Enjoy such traditional French dishes as onion soup, foie gras, roast salmon, and cod with red peppers in a rustic setting of stone walls and oak beams. Desserts—including the chocolate cake and fresh fruit salads—are just as satisfying. ♦ Daily lunch and dinner. 4 Rue Jean-du-Bellay (at Rue St-Louis-en-l'Ile). 01.43.54.27.34. Métro: Pont Marie

25 La Maison Lafitte *Magret de canard* (duck fillet), *confit d'oie* (goose confit), foie gras, and other gourmet by-products of force-fed fowl are preserved, packaged, and ready to be taken home in your suitcase. ♦ Tu-Sa. 8 Rue Jean-du-Bellay (between Rue St-Louis-en-l'Ile and Quai de Bourbon). 01.43.26.08.63. Métro: Pont Marie

26 Alain Carion You'll find minerals, geodes, meteorites, and minuscule fossilized black nautiluses fashioned into earrings at this rock collector's paradise. ♦ Tu-Sa. 92 Rue St-Louis-en-l'Ile (between Rues Le Regrattier and Jean-du-Bellay). 01.43.26.01.16. Métro: Pont Marie

26 Au Lys d'Argent ★$ For light fare that is also light on your pocketbook, pop into Lucy Rouffet's cheerful, mirrored *glacier-crêperie-salon de thé*. In addition to 24 crepes, 25 kinds of tea, and the mouthwatering array of ice cream and pastries, copious salads and omelettes, and a daily big brunch are offered. ♦ M, W-Su noon-10:30PM. 90 Rue St-Louis-en-l'Ile (between Rues Le Regrattier and Jean-du-Bellay). 01.46.33.56.13. Métro: Pont Marie

27 Hôtel St-Louis $$ The cousin of **Hôtel de Lutèce** and **Hôtel des Deux-Iles** (see below for both), this 21-room hostelry has exposed wooden beams, Louis XIII furniture, thick carpeting, and modern bathrooms, but *petits* bedrooms. Fifth-floor rooms have a view of the rooftops. There's no restaurant. ♦ 75 Rue St-Louis-en-l'Ile (at Rue Boutarel). 01.46.34.04.80; fax 01.46.34.02.13; www.paris-hotel.tm.fr. Métro: Pont Marie

27 Le Monde des Chimères ★★$$ This stone-and-beam bistro is a strong favorite of Ile St-Louis natives. Among the specialties of chef Cécille Ibane are 40-garlic chicken, *brandade de morue* (codfish puréed with olive oil, garlic, and milk), and duck with apples. ♦ Tu-Sa lunch and dinner. 69 Rue St-Louis-en-l'Ile (between Rues Le Regrattier and Boutarel). 01.43.54.45.27. Métro: Pont Marie

28 Hôtel de Lutèce $$$ Named after the first Roman settlement in Paris, this restored 17th-century town house is now a hotel offering 23 comfortable rooms. The small breakfast room opens onto a flowered atrium. Ask for one of the brighter rooms on the top floor; they offer exquisite views of the island's rooftops and the dome of the **Panthéon** across the river. ♦ 65 Rue St-Louis-en-l'Ile (between Rues Le Regrattier and Boutarel). 01.43.26.23.52; fax 01.43.29.60.25. Métro: Pont Marie

29 Aux Anysetiers du Roy ★$$ Originally called **Au Petit Bacchus** (the scorched remains of a 300-year-old effigy of the god of drink and revelry slouch above the entrance), this tavern used to serve the gamblers and jocks who frequented the ancient *jeu de paume* (tennis) court across the street at **No. 54**. The chef recommends the foie gras, *magret de canard au miel et aux raisins* (duck breast with honey and grapes), and the *profiteroles au chocolat.* Don't leave without washing your hands in the 17th-century pewter bathroom sink upstairs. ♦ Daily lunch and dinner. Reservations recommended. 61 Rue St-Louis-en-l'Ile (at Rue Le Regrattier). 01.40.46.87.85. Métro: Pont Marie

29 Hôtel des Deux-Iles $$$ An abundance of fresh flowers adorns this 17th-century mansion-turned-hotel. The hotel bar, which has a fireplace, and the Renaissance-style ceramic tiles in the bathrooms are adequate compensation for the 17 smallish Provence-inspired rooms. There's no restaurant. ♦ 59 Rue St-Louis-en-l'Ile (between Rues Budé and Le Regrattier). 01.43.26.13.35; fax 01.43.29.60.25. Métro: Pont Marie

29 Pylones The fanciful rubber jewelry and accessories displayed here sell as briskly as hot chestnuts on a winter afternoon. In lieu of that Boucheron diamond bracelet, wouldn't you rather be wearing a fanciful cactus, fish skeleton, monkey, or maybe the Pyramids of Giza on your wrist? Other novelties include children's bibs and rubber suspenders, plus whimsical alligator knives, Flintstone chess sets, and New Wave eggcups. ♦ Daily. 57 Rue St-Louis-en-l'Ile (between Rues Budé and Le Regrattier). 01.46.34.05.02. Métro: Pont Marie

30 Hôtel Chenizot This former residence of the city's archbishops was also the home of Theresa Cabarrus, a noblewoman of insatiable sexual appetite. She offered herself to drawing-room Revolutionaries and as a result of this gesture was dubbed *Notre Dame de Thermidor.* While the plaster cornucopia and ferns in the first courtyard date from an 18th-century restoration, the mythological sea god over the front door and the sundial in the damp rear courtyard are original 17th-century decorations. This is now an apartment building with a restaurant and shop on the ground floor (see below). ♦ 51 Rue St-Louis-en-l'Ile (between Rues Budé and Le Regrattier). Métro: Pont Marie

Within Hôtel Chenizot:

LA CASTAFIORE

Spécialités Italiennes

La Castafiore ★★★$$ In 1988 a North American and an Englishman left the advertising business to open Ile St-Louis's only Italian restaurant. The result was this dining spot with terra-cotta walls, white tablecloths, and a warm ambience in which to enjoy *tagliatelles aux cèpes* (pasta with mushrooms) or saltimbocca. Don't pass up the homemade tiramisù or the naughty *Coupe Amarena* (ice cream with chestnut purée and warm chocolate sauce) for dessert. ♦ Daily lunch and dinner. Reservations recommended. 01.43.54.78.62

L'Epicerie French gourmands will feel right at home in this tiny shop packed to the rafters with delicacies to do penance for. Champagne mustard, *terrine de canard lapin* (duck casserole), fois gras, homemade wild strawberry jam, and beautifully wrapped bonbons are but a few of the treats. ♦ Daily 10:30AM-9PM. 01.43.25.20.14

31 Rue de la Femme Sans Teste (Street of the Headless Woman) Shortly after the Revolution, the Rue Le Regrattier (named in the 17th century for an entrepreneur in the island development consortium) was dubbed the "Street of the Headless Woman" (in old French, *tête* was spelled with an *s*) after a decapitated statue at the corner of Rue Le Regrattier and Quai de Bourbon. "Headless woman" is a misnomer, however; the robed stone figure, severed at the torso, is believed to be St. Nicholas, the patron saint of boatmen. His statue stands at the top of the stairs that once led down to the ferry. ♦ Rue Le Regrattier. Métro: Pont Marie

31 6 Rue Le Regrattier Jeanne Duval, the voluptuous West Indian mistress of Charles-Pierre Baudelaire who was known as the "Black Venus," lived here. It's still a private residence. ♦ Between Quai d'Orléans and Rue St-Louis-en-l'Ile. Métro: Pont Marie

32 18-20 Quai d'Orléans Columnist Walter Lippmann lived here in 1938. It remains a private residence. ♦ Between Rues Budé and Le Regrattier. Métro: Pont Marie

33 10 Quai d'Orléans James Jones, the author of *From Here to Eternity,* resided here with his family 1958-75 and entertained such famous writers and artists as Henry Miller, Alexander Calder, William Styron, Sylvia Beach, and James Baldwin. This is still a residential building. ♦ At Rue Budé. Métro: Pont Marie

34 Musée Adam Mickiewicz The life and times of exiled Mickiewicz, the "Byron of Poland," as well as the poet's relationships with great Romantic French authors and musicians, are brought to life on the second floor of this library and museum. The private library, established in 1852, contains some 200,000 volumes as well as copies of nearly every Polish newspaper published in the 19th century. In the **Chopin Room** on the first floor are composer Frédéric Chopin's frayed armchair, his hand-penned mazurka scores, a death mask, and the world's only daguerreotype of the young pianist. ♦ Admission. Tu-F 2-6PM; Sa 10AM-1PM. Guided tours: Th 2-5PM on the hour. 6 Quai d'Orléans (between Rues des Deux-Ponts and Budé). 01.43.54.35.61. Métro: Pont Marie

34 Isami ★★$$ Small, simple, and casual, the only Japanese restaurant on the island specializes in sushi and sashimi, but also serves such dishes as oyster salad with vinegar and steamed *daurade* (sea bream). ♦ Tu-Sa lunch and dinner; Su dinner. 4 Quai d'Orléans (between Rues des Deux-Ponts and Budé). 01.40.46.06.97. Métro: Pont Marie

35 Nos Ancêtres les Gaulois ★$$ Tackily decorated with sheepskins, battered shields, and mounted heads of wild boars (in sunglasses) to loosely evoke the Middle Ages, this cavernous, all-you-can-eat establishment seats 240 people. Earthy do-it-yourself salads, greasy sausage platters, grilled meat, chocolate mousse, and barely drinkable red wine are perennial hits with starving students and rowdy German tour groups. It's always crowded; arrive early and avoid Saturday nights, when the ambience is raucous, bordering on Neanderthal. ♦ M-Sa dinner until 1AM; Su lunch and dinner until 1AM. Reservations required. 39 Rue St-Louis-en-l'Ile (between Rues des Deux-Ponts and Budé). 01.46.33.66.12. Métro: Pont Marie

36 Hôtel du Jeu de Paume $$$ Deftly fashioned around a royal tennis court dating from 1624 (*jeu de paume* is the medieval precursor of the game now played at Wimbledon and Flushing Meadow), this refined 32-room hotel was opened in the 1980s. There's no restaurant. ♦ 54 Rue St-Louis-en-l'Ile (between Rues des Deux-Ponts and Le Regrattier). 01.43.26.14.18; fax 01.40.46.02.76; www.jeudepaumehotel.com. Métro: Pont Marie

37 3 Quai de Bourbon Explaining the plainness of the facade of this real-estate agency is a story in itself. The sumptuous Empire-style windows and storefront that once adorned the building were purchased by J. Pierpont Morgan and in 1926 moved to the Metropolitan Museum of Art in New York. They now serve as the entrance to the museum's Wrightsman Galleries, which house a superb collection of Louis XVI furniture and porcelain. ♦ Between Rues des Deux-Ponts and Le Regrattier. Métro: Pont Marie

37 Boulangerie Rioux Old-fashioned bread is baked in a *four chauffé au bois* (wood-burning oven) at this traditional bakery. ♦ M-W, Sa-Su. 35 Rue des Deux-Ponts (between Rue St-Louis-en-l'Ile and Quai de Bourbon). 01.43.54.57.59. Métro: Pont Marie

37 Les Fous de l'Ile ★★$ Fresh-cut flowers on the bar and brass candlesticks on old wooden bistro tables, combined with wacky monthly art exhibitions, and music from Paganini to Pearl Jam make this converted *épicerie* (grocery shop) the island's most relaxing and hip restaurant/cafe. At lunch, famished students arrive for the warm goat cheese salad, *tagliatelles au saumon fumé* (pasta and smoked salmon) with caviar, steak with roquefort sauce, and cheesecake. ♦ Tu-Sa lunch and dinner; Su brunch and dinner. 33 Rue des Deux-Ponts (between Rue St-Louis-en-l'Ile and Quai de Bourbon). 01.43.25.76.67. Métro: Pont Marie

38 Berthillon This Ile St-Louis landmark is so popular that around Christmas police officers direct the flow of Parisians queuing up for what is undeniably the best ice cream and sorbet in Paris. Its position as the city's preeminent ice cream shop is so secure that it has the nerve to close two days a week, on school holidays, and for six weeks in summer, the prime ice-cream–eating season. Women in pink aprons scoop up more than 70 flavors, all made without a single artificial ingredient. Sample the exotic fruit flavors in season: rhubarb, black currant, fig, kumquat, and fresh melon. ♦ W-Su; closed school holidays and mid-July through August. 31 Rue St-Louis-en-l'Ile (between Rues Poulletier and des Deux-Ponts). 01.43.54.31.61. Métro: Pont Marie

39 Au Gourmet de l'Isle ★★$$ Famous for its *andouillette* (sausage with tripe)—a nice dish if you can stomach it—this bargain bistro is a bustling place. Other less challenging specialties: artichoke hearts and pork in red wine sauce, fruit tarts, and Auvergne wines. ♦ W-Su lunch and dinner. Reservations recommended for dinner. 42 Rue St-Louis-en-l'Ile (between Rues Poulletier and des Deux-Ponts). 01.43.26.79.27. Métro: Pont Marie

---

Approximately 1.6 million motor vehicles enter Paris every day from the suburbs.

Restaurants/Clubs: Red   **Hotels:** Blue
Shops/ 🌳 Outdoors: Green   **Sights/Culture:** Black

40 L'Auberge de la Reine Blanche ★$$
Named for the mother of the island's patron, St. Louis, this pretty pale apricot dining room offers dependable French classics: *canard* (duck) *à l'orange*, coq au vin, and *boeuf bourguignon*. Catch the cute dollhouse furniture displayed on the walls. ♦ M-Tu, F-Su lunch and dinner; W-Th dinner. Reservations recommended. 30 Rue St-Louis-en-l'Ile (between Rues Pelletier and des Deux-Ponts). 01.46.33.07.87. Métro: Pont Marie

40 L'Orangerie ★★$$$ A mini **Maxim's**, with 18th-century decor and background harpsichord music, this restaurant specializes in elegant late suppers. The ribs of beef, leg of lamb (cooked over a wood fire), rich Bordeaux reds, and sophisticated ambience cause Rolls-Royce traffic jams out front. Actor Jean-Claude Brialy is the owner. ♦ Daily dinner; closed in August. Reservations required. 28 Rue St-Louis-en-l'Ile (between Rues Pelletier and des Deux-Ponts). 01.46.33.93.98. Métro: Pont Marie

 Librairie Ulysse

40 Librairie Ulysse In 1971 the free-spirited Catherine Domain opened this vest-pocket shop specializing in travel books. She has crammed in, higgledy-piggledy, 20,000 French and English titles on everything from trekking in the Himalayas to canoeing in South America, a large collection of maps, and, of course, many books on Paris and France. ♦ Tu-Sa 2-8PM. 26 Rue St-Louis-en-l'Ile (between Rues Pelletier and des Deux-Ponts). 01.43.25.17.35; fax 01.43.29.52.10. Métro: Pont Marie

la Charlotte de l'isle

40 La Charlotte de l'Isle ★★$ For a diabolically delicious treat, order *gâteau du diable* (devil's cake), half-moon cookies, or witch's brooms (chocolate-dipped orange rinds) at this little-known tea salon. Sylvie Langlet, the hospitable, kimono-clad owner, seems strangely obsessed with Halloween but swears she has yet to turn a customer into a toad. Sip freshly brewed Chinese tea at one of four tiny tables nestled in the back room or three in the front among the clutter of puppets, dried-flower bouquets, and an old stereo playing Poulenc. Poetry readings, puppet shows, and piano concerts are regular events here. ♦ Tea: Th-Su noon-8PM. Poetry readings: Tu 8:30PM. Puppet shows: W 2PM by reservation. Piano concerts: F 6-8PM. Closed July through August. 24 Rue St-Louis-en-l'Ile (between Rues Pelletier and des Deux-Ponts). 01.43.54.25.83. Métro: Pont Marie

41 St-Louis-en-l'Ile Popular for weddings and candlelit concerts, this Jesuit Baroque–style church was built in 1726; it follows plans created by island resident **Louis Le Vau**, the great French architect who designed portions of the **Louvre** and **Versailles.** Inside is a statue of St. Louis in chain mail and crusader's sword, and next to the tomb of a Polish freedom fighter with a daunting name (Damaiowicestrzembosz) is a 1926 plaque that bears the inscription: "In grateful memory of St. Louis in whose honor the City of St. Louis, Missouri, USA, is named." The church was vandalized during the Revolution. For example, the empty-handed carved cherubs over the massive wooden west portal once held the king's fleur-de-lis. The only reason the statues of Saint Geneviève and the Virgin Mary survived the Revolution is that they were disguised as the goddesses of Reason and Freedom. Evening concerts are held here frequently. ♦ 3 Rue Pelletier (at Rue St-Louis-en-l'Ile). 01.46.34.11.60. Métro: Pont Marie

42 Flood Marker Written on the wall along Quai de Béthune are the words *Crue Janvier 1910* and a line marking the astounding level, or *crue*, the Seine reached during the *inondation* (flood) of January 1910, when many streets became canals and rowboats were the preferred form of transportation. ♦ Quai de Béthune (between Ponts de Sully and de la Tournelle). Métro: Pont Marie

43 24 Quai de Béthune In 1935 Helena Rubinstein demolished one of the island's finest town houses (constructed in 1642) and built an Art Deco structure in its place. She reigned from the new building's rooftop apartment. This remains a residential building. ♦ At Rue Pelletier. Métro: Pont Marie

44 **Square Barye** At the eastern tip of Ile St-Louis, this pocket park is all that remains of the terraced gardens of Duc de Bretonvillier. You might glimpse sunbathers or witness a schoolboys' fishing competition here on the cobblestone quay. ♦ Métros: Pont Marie, Sully-Morland

45 5 Rue St-Louis-en-l'Ile The expatriate literary agent William Aspenwall Bradley, who represented such authors as Thornton Wilder, Edith Wharton, Katherine Anne Porter, and

John Dos Passos, lived in this apartment building. Bradley was the one who closed the deal for publication of the *Autobiography of Alice B. Toklas* by Gertrude Stein. ♦ Between Quai d'Anjou and Rue de Bretonvilliers. Métros: Pont Marie, Sully-Morland

46 Hôtel Lambert Probably the most opulent of 17th-century private residences in Paris, this frescoed and pilastered *hôtel particulier* was designed by **Louis Le Vau** in 1640 for Lambert the Rich. Its lavish gilded ceilings by Charles Le Brun predate and rival his **Great Hall of Mirrors** at **Versailles.** After the 1830-31 insurrection, Polish prince Adam Czartoryski fled to France, married King Louis-Phillipe's granddaughter, and bought the **Hôtel Lambert** for his personal residence. Over the years, Czartoryski's home served as a salon for expatriate Polish royalty and intelligentsia, as well as a rehearsal hall for Frédéric Chopin. Later it functioned as a girls' finishing school and a safe house for Allied fighter pilots who had been shot down in France. Voltaire briefly nested here with his lover, the Marquise de Châtelet, while writing the *Henriade.* Since 1972 the house has belonged to the Rothschilds. Behind the locked gate is a horseshoe-shaped courtyard and the famous **Galerie d'Hercule,** containing the Eustache Le Sueur frescoes and Jacques Rousseau trompe l'oeil landscape paintings. The building is open to the public only on rare occasions. ♦ 2 Rue St-Louis-en-l'Ile (between Quai d'Anjou and Rue Poulletier). Métros: Pont Marie, Sully-Morland

47 9 Quai d'Anjou The 19th-century illustrator and satirist Honoré Daumier lived in this apartment building off and on for 17 years in the company of such distinguished islanders as poet Charles Baudelaire and fellow artist Ferdinand Delacroix. It was on the Ile St-Louis that Daumier sketched his mordant portrayals of life and politics and painted masterpieces such as *La Blanchisseuse* (The Washer Woman), which hangs in the **Louvre.** ♦ Between Rues St-Louis-en-l'Ile and Poulletier. Métros: Pont Marie, Sully-Morland

48 Hôtel de Lauzun **Louis Le Vau** built this mansion in 1656 for a corrupt French army caterer, Charles Gruyn des Bordes, who was arrested soon afterward. That is why the building is named for its second tenant, the dandy Duke of Lauzun. The roll call of residents and visitors to the **Hôtel de Lauzun** includes Rilke, Wagner, Daumier, Delacroix, and **Louis Charles Auguste Steinheil** (who restored the **Sainte-Chapelle** windows). In 1834 Baudelaire gathered his bohemian "hashish club" in an upstairs room and conducted the hallucinatory research for his book *Les Paradis Artificiels.* Some of the gaudiest suites in all of Paris are the **Chambres de Parade** (parade rooms), which are cluttered with golden nymphs, cut-velvet walls, trompe l'oeil murals, and allegorical figures. In 1928 the city bought and restored it as a residence for visiting heads of state. ♦ Tours one Tuesday per month, by appointment only; reserve a least a year in advance. 17 Quai d'Anjou (between Rues St-Louis-en-l'Ile and Poulletier). 01.42.76.57.99. Métros: Pont Marie, Sully-Morland

49 29 Quai d'Anjou In 1922, with a hand-printing press, North American William Bird established his Three Mountains Press in this building. Under the editorial aegis of Ezra Pound, it published Ernest Hemingway and Ford Madox Ford. ♦ Between Rues Poulletier and des Deux-Ponts. Métro: Pont Marie

50 37 Quai d'Anjou When he arrived in France in 1921 after the acceptance of his first major novel, *Three Soldiers,* John Dos Passos rented a room in this apartment building. ♦ Between Rues Poulletier and des Deux-Ponts. Métro: Pont Marie

51 Pont-Marie King Louis XIII laid the first stone of this bridge, which was completed in 1635. Twenty-three years later, a spring thaw caused a flood that partially destroyed the bridge; 22 of the 4-story houses above the structure fell into the Seine, drowning 121 residents and shopkeepers. The bridge is not named after Marie de Médicis, Henri IV's widow, who commissioned the work, but after Jean-Christophe Marie, the contractor hired to develop Ile St-Louis and the *quais.* ♦ Métro: Pont Marie

Bests

Joseph Smallhoover
Attorney, Donhort Price & Rhoads

Taking the sun in the **Luxembourg Gardens.**

Strolling through the **Tuileries Gardens.**

Visiting the statue of the *Virgin Mary* at **Notre-Dame.**

In-line skating on Sunday mornings—when it is not raining.

Paris public transportation strikes are a hoot!

Angelina's cocoa on a wet damp winter Saturday!

Dining in restaurants the tourists don't know about yet.

Pretending not to speak English to impolite Yankee tourists.

Helping lost tourists who are smart enough to try a few words of French, no matter how badly they speak.

The little wreath-laying parades at the **L'Arc de Triomphe** on Saturday and Sunday at 6PM.

Doing the marketing just about anywhere.

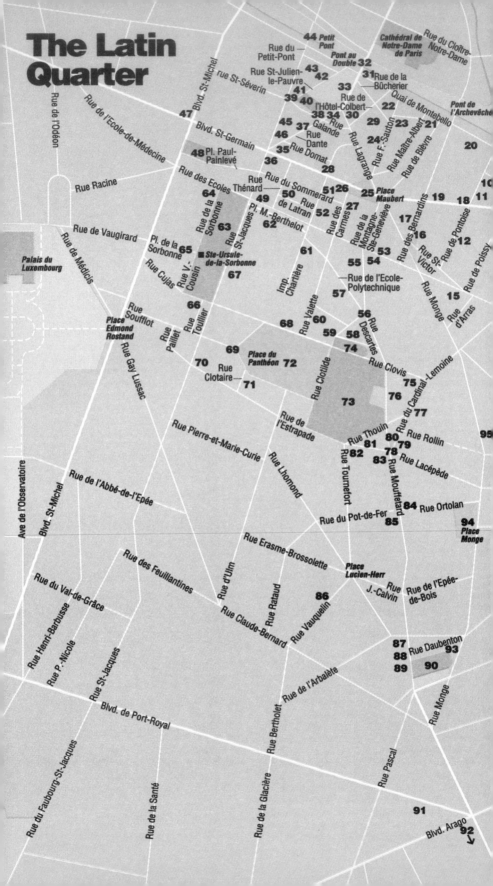

The Latin Quarter

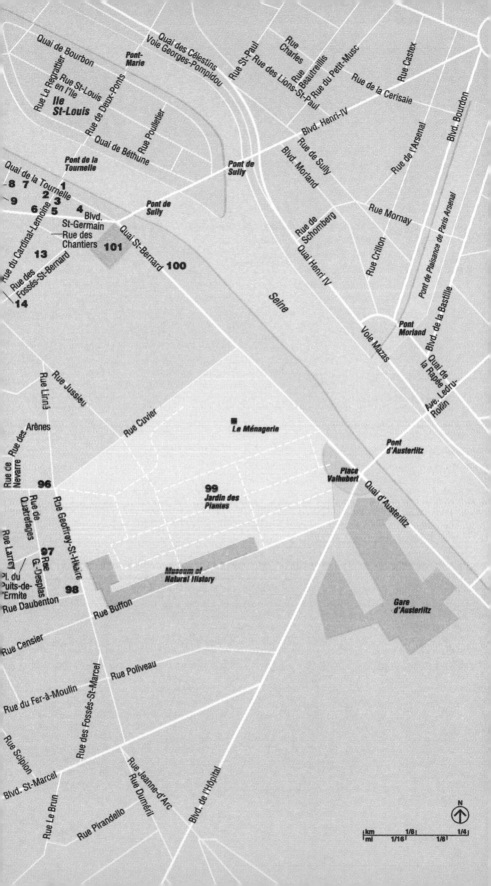

The Latin Quarter

Home to Roman Paris, the **Sorbonne**, and the bohemian quarter, the Latin Quarter is a cultural mecca. The Henri Murger novel *Scènes de la Vie de Bohème,* which became the Puccini opera *La Bohème,* was set in this district. Verlaine and Descartes lived here, and today old bookshops, student cafes, publishing houses, jazz clubs, and, more recently, expensive boutiques, grace the streets of the Latin Quarter. For seven centuries, this was a city within a city, inhabited by Latin-speaking scholars who were exempt from civil law and recognized no authority other than the pope. Latin, which hasn't been spoken here since the Revolution, has been replaced on the streets of the Left Bank by the Moroccan, Greek, and Vietnamese of immigrant families selling couscous, souvlaki, and imperial rolls to supplement the basic bohemian diet of coffee and cheap cigarettes.

This overview of the Latin Quarter begins at the **Pont de la Tournelle,** in front of the famed penthouse restaurant **La Tour d'Argent.** From here you can browse the bookstalls along the **Seine** and enjoy a splendid view of **Notre-Dame**'s flying buttresses. Next come two funny, offbeat museums—the **Musée des Hôpitaux de Paris–Assistance Publique** (Museum of Public Health and Welfare) and the **Musée des Collections Historiques de la Préfecture de Police** (Police Museum); and then the **Rue des Ecoles,** which leads to the **Sorbonne** and the **Collège de France,** for centuries the most celebrated seats of learning in Europe. At the end of the street are the **Roman Baths** adjoining the extraordinary medieval **Musée de Cluny.** As you climb **Montagne Ste-Geneviève,** named after the patron saint of Paris, you'll pass King Philippe Auguste's 13th-century city wall; **Le Raccard** restaurant, a landmark for fondue lovers; and the **Panthéon,** a Classical monument and the final resting place of Voltaire, Rousseau, and Victor Hugo.

At the **Place de la Contrescarpe,** visitors can embark on a detour that passes a Roman arena and a Moorish mosque en route to the zoo and botanical gardens—a nice spot for a picnic lunch purchased in the **Place Monge** market or along **Rue Mouffetard.** On this medieval market street frequented this century by the likes of young Ernest Hemingway, you can meander past stalls selling everything from tropical mangoes to African monkey bread, and then end up at **Gobelins,** the old royal weaving mills, for an afternoon tour.

For a quick bite while sight-seeing, stop at one of the many inexpensive Vietnamese or Greek shish kebab restaurants along Mouffetard near **Gobelins.** To find the Latin Quarter's fancier restaurants, including **La Tour d'Argent,** head toward the Rue des Ecoles and the Seine. The area's nightspots, including **Paradis Latin** and **Les Trois Maillets,** are also located here and are an appropriate way to end a day spent in the bohemian Latin Quarter.

---

1 Statue de Ste-Geneviève On the Pont de la Tournelle, one of the Seine's newest bridges (1928) and the fifth in a long line that dates back to 1369, is a missilelike statue of the city's patron saint. Apparently ready for a heavenly liftoff, the angular obelisk of Saint Geneviève by Landowski turns her back on **Notre-Dame** and faces upriver, guarding the city as her spirit has done since 450. In that year, the prayers of the then 27-year-old nun were credited with halting Attila the Hun's advance on Paris, after his army of barbarians had just sacked Cologne and brutalized 10,000 of its maidens.

In 473, while the city was under siege by the Franks, Geneviève courageously smuggled 11 boatloads of food through enemy lines to feed starving Parisians. She lived on **Montagne Ste-Geneviève** until the age of 89. Like France's other virgin saint, Joan of Arc, Geneviève was eventually consigned to flames, but not until 1,281 years after her death. The fanatic anticlerics of the Revolution burned her remains and cast the ashes into the river. ◆ Pont de la Tournelle and Quai de la Tournelle. Métros: Cardinal Lemoine, Pont Marie

2 Les Comptoirs de la Tour d'Argent If you want to take one of the **Tour d'Argent**

restaurant's trademark blue-and-white Limoges plates home as a souvenir, walk across the street to the gourmet boutique of Claude Terrail, the enterprising restaurateur who has become the Pierre Cardin of French cuisine. Here, instead of dinner for $180, you can buy a menu for $20, fresh *foie gras de canard* (duck liver pâté) to go, or an entire **Tour d'Argent** place setting, including fluted Champagne glass, coffee spoon, and ashtray. Also on sale are such items as Dijon mustard and wine. ♦ Tu-Su until midnight. 2 Rue du Cardinal-Lemoine (at Quai de la Tournelle). 01.46.33.45.58. Métros: Cardinal Lemoine, Maubert-Mutualité

3 La Tour d'Argent ★★★★$$$$ This may no longer be the top restaurant in Paris, but its penthouse panorama of **Notre-Dame**'s flying buttresses and the barges passing on the Seine have helped make it the city's most famous and spectacular eating establishment, and one of its most expensive. The renowned dining spot stands on the site of the **Café Anglais**, which opened in 1582. The cafe was mentioned by Mme. de Sévigné in her famous letters and provided the setting for a Dumas novel; it is also said to be where the fork was first used in Paris. On the ground floor of the restaurant is a table set with the silver, crystal, and china used at a dinner here on 7 June 1867 that was attended by Czar Alexander II, the Czarevitch, Wilhelm I, and Bismarck.

Touches of class are found throughout the establishment, from the Grand Siècle–style elevator to the traditional blue cornflower in the jacket lapel of restaurant owner and dandy Claude Terrail. The kitchen's pièce de résistance is pressed duck flambé, first served in 1890 to Edward VII, then Prince of Wales. The kitchen keeps a running tally of the number of ducklings pressed, and each order arrives at the table with a numbered card. (Almost 900,000 ducklings later, the dish is still a hit.) Other recommended dishes include *filet de sole Cardinal* (with crayfish), flambéed peaches, and bittersweet chocolate cake. The wine list draws from the 300,000 bottles in the vaulted cellars underground. Diners can tour the cellars after dessert and watch Terrail's little sound-and-light show while sipping a vintage liqueur. Tables in the rooftop dining room must be reserved far in advance; ask for one by the picture window. Bear in mind, however, that lunch is half the price of dinner and midday is when Parisians eat out. The restaurant is popular with North American and Japanese tourists, and at dinnertime the waiters may be the only French speakers in the place. ♦ Tu-Su lunch and dinner.

Reservations required. 15-17 Quai de la Tournelle (between Blvd St-Germain and Rue du Cardinal-Lemoine). 01.43.54.23.31. Métros: Cardinal Lemoine, Maubert-Mutualité

3 La Rôtisserie du Beaujolais ★★$$ Owned by Claude Terrail of the pricey **Tour d'Argent** next door (see above) and managed by Alain Robert, this boisterous bistro serves Lyonnais specialties and rotisserie-roasted meat. Try the coq au vin and the *canette rôtie* (roast duck, which comes from the same farm that supplies **La Tour d'Argent** with its birds). Drink in the warm, jolly atmosphere along with a bottle of Moulin-à-Vent, the richest of the Beaujolais, while you consider Terrail's philosophy: "Simple things are what people want, even those in fur coats." ♦ Tu-Su lunch and dinner. 19 Quai de la Tournelle (at Rue du Cardinal-Lemoine). 01.43.54.17.47. Métros: Cardinal Lemoine, Maubert-Mutualité

4 Le Rallye ★$ Locals lunch on sandwiches and the plat du jour here, but when an earthy crowd takes over at night, the cafe comes to resemble an Amsterdam bar. Just down the street but a world away in spirit from **La Tour d'Argent**, it has a collection of Tintin cartoon memorabilia on display, a friendly boxer named Figaro underfoot, and music ranging from opera to The Clash. ♦ Cafe: daily breakfast and lunch. Bar: daily 7AM-2AM. 11 Quai de la Tournelle (between Blvd St-Germain and Rue du Cardinal-Lemoine). 01.43.54.29.65. Métros: Cardinal Lemoine, Maubert-Mutualité

5 L'Atlas ★★$$ Chef El Jaziri Binjamin likens himself to a culinary ambassador promoting unique dishes from his native Morocco. The tasty *tajines* (stews) include lamb with forest mushrooms and lustily spiced fish with saffron. The elegant *couscous de L'Atlas*, with veal, meatballs, and lamb, is another fine main course. Have sweet mint tea with orange blossom nectar to end the meal on a soothing note. ♦ Daily lunch and dinner. 12 Blvd St-Germain (at Rue du Cardinal-Lemoine). 01.46.33.86.98, 01.44.07.23.66. Métros: Cardinal Lemoine, Maubert-Mutualité

Parlez-Vous Français?

The French take great pride in their culture and their language. If you attempt to speak their language, no matter how poorly, they will take it as a compliment. Don't be put off if they respond to you in English, however—be glad. It will be that much easier to understand one another. Here are some phrases that will enable you to start communicating *en français*. When there is both a masculine and a feminine spelling, the feminine is in parentheses. *Bon voyage!* (Have a good trip!)

Hello, Good-bye, and Other Basics

Hello/Good morning/ Good afternoon	*Bonjour*
Good evening	*Bonsoir*
How are you?	*Comment allez-vous?*
Good-bye	*Au revoir*
Yes	*Oui*
No	*Non*
Please	*S'il vous plaît*
Thank you	*Merci*
You're welcome	*De rien* or *Je vous en prie*
Excuse me	*Excusez-moi* or *Pardon*
I don't speak French	*Je ne parle pas français*
Do you speak English?	*Parlez-vous anglais?*
I don't understand	*Je ne comprends pas*
Do you understand?	*Comprenez-vous?*
More slowly, please	*Plus lentement, s'il vous plaît*
I don't know	*Je ne sais pas*
My name is . . .	*Je m'appelle . . .*
What is your name?	*Comment vous appelez-vous?*
miss	*mademoiselle*
madame, ma'am	*madame*
mister, sir	*monsieur*
good	*bon(ne)*
bad	*mauvais(e)*
open	*ouvert(e)*
closed	*fermé(e)*
entrance	*entrée*
exit	*sortie*
push	*poussez*
pull	*tirez*
today	*aujourd'hui*
tomorrow	*demain*
yesterday	*hier*
week	*semaine*
month	*mois*
year	*an*

Hotel Talk

I have a reservation	*J'ai une réservation.*
I would like to reserve . . .	*Je voudrais réserver . . .*
a double room	*une chambre pour deux personnes*
with (private) bath	*avec une salle de bain (privée)*
with air-conditioning	*avec la climatisation*
Are taxes included?	*Est-ce que les taxes sont comprises?*
Is breakfast included?	*Est-ce que le petit déjeuner est compris?*
Do you accept traveler's checks?	*Prenez-vous des chèques de voyage?*
Do you accept credit cards?	*Prenez-vous des cartes de crédit?*

Restaurant Repartee

Waiter!	*Monsieur!*
I would like . . .	*Je voudrais . . .*
a menu	*la carte*
a glass of	*un verre de*
a bottle of	*une bouteille de*
The check, please	*L'addition, s'il vous plaît*
Is the service charge (tip) included?	*Est-ce que le service est compris?*
I think there is an error in the bill	*Je crois qu'il y a une erreur avec l'addition.*
lunch	*déjeuner*
dinner	*dîner*
tip	*service, pourboire*
bread	*pain*
butter	*beurre*
pepper	*poivre*
salt	*sel*
sugar	*sucre*
soup	*soupe*
salad	*salade*
vegetables	*légumes*
cheese	*fromage*
eggs	*oeufs*
beef	*boeuf*
chicken	*poulet*
veal	*veau*
fish	*poisson*
seafood	*fruits de mer*
pork	*porc*
ham	*jambon*
chop	*côtelette*
dessert	*dessert*

As You Like It

cold	*froid(e)*
hot	*chaud(e)*
sweet	*sucré(e)*
dry	*sec (sèche)*
broiled, roasted	*rôti(e)*
baked	*au four*

boiled	*bouilli(e)*	one-way ticket	*aller-simple*
fried	*frit(e)*	round-trip ticket	*aller-retour*
raw	*cru(e)*	first class	*première classe*
rare	*saignant(e)*	second class	*seconde classe* or
well done	*bien cuit(e)*		*deuxième*
spicy	*épicé(e)*	smoking	*fumeur*

Thirsty No More

		no smoking	*non-fumeur*
water	*l'eau*	Does this train	*Est-ce que ce train*
coffee	*café, express*	go to . . . ?	*s'arrête à . . . ?*
coffee with steamed milk	*café au lait*	Where is/are . . . ?	*Où est . . . ?/Où sont . . . ?*
tea	*thé*	How far is it	*Quelle est la distance*
beer	*bière*	from here to . . .	*entre ici et . . . ?*

rosé wine	*vin rosé*
red wine	*vin rouge*
white wine	*vin blanc*

The Bare Necessities

		aspirin	*aspirines*
		barbershop, beauty shop	*coiffeur, salon de beauté*
milk	*lait*	condom	*préservatif*
mineral water	*l'eau minérale*	dry cleaner	*teinturerie*
carbonated	*gazeuse*	laundromat, laundry	*blanchisserie*
not carbonated	*non-gazeuse*	letter	*lettre*
orange juice	*jus d'orange*	post office	*bureau de poste*
ice	*glaçons*	postage stamp	*timbre*
without ice	*sans glaçons*	postcard	*carte postale*

Sizing It Up

		sanitary napkins	*serviettes hygiéniques*
How much does this cost?	*Combien coûte-il?*	shampoo	*shampooing*
inexpensive	*bon marché*	shaving cream	*lotion à raser*
expensive	*cher (chère)*	soap	*savon*
large	*grand(e)*	tampons	*tampons périodiques*
small	*petit(e)*	tissues	*mouchoirs en papier*
long	*long(ue)*	toilet paper	*papier hygiénique*
short	*court(e)*	toothpaste	*dentifrice*
old	*vieux (vieille)*	Where is the bathroom/	*Où est la salle de bains?/*
new	*nouveau (nouvelle)*	toilet?	*Où sont les toilettes?*
used	*d'occasion*	Men's room	*WC pour hommes*
a little	*un peu*	Women's room	*WC pour dames*
a lot	*beaucoup*		

On the Move

Days of the Week

		Monday	*lundi*
		Tuesday	*mardi*
north	*nord*	Wednesday	*mercredi*
south	*sud*	Thursday	*jeudi*
east	*est*	Friday	*vendredi*
west	*ouest*	Saturday	*samedi*
right	*droite*	Sunday	*dimanche*

left	*gauche*
highway	*autoroute*

Numbers

		zero	*zéro*
street	*rue*	one	*un*
gas station	*station-service*	two	*deux*
here	*ici*	three	*trois*
there	*là*	four	*quatre*
bus stop	*l'arrêt de bus*	five	*cinq*
bus station	*gare routière*	six	*six*
train station	*gare*	seven	*sept*
subway	*métro*	eight	*huit*
airport	*aéroport*	nine	*neuf*
road map	*carte routière*	ten	*dix*

Chez René

6 **Chez René** ★$$ An authentic bistro with amusing waiters, this eatery offers tasty daily Lyonnais specials that range from Monday's pot-au-feu to Friday's *blanquette de veau* (veal with béchamel sauce and mushrooms). Also on the menu are cucumbers and cream, country sausages, mutton with white beans, entrecôte, and, in autumn, *pleurottes Provençales* (fresh wild mushrooms baked with garlic). ♦ M-F lunch and dinner; Sa dinner; closed in August. Reservations recommended. 14 Blvd St-Germain (at Rue du Cardinal-Lemoine). 01.43.54.30.23. Métros: Cardinal Lemoine, Maubert-Mutualité

Campagne et Provence
Restaurant

7 **Campagne et Provence** ★★★$$ Patrick Jeffroy's classy little restaurant is a treat to behold. Here chef Olivier Ferrel prepares a palette of dishes with flavors ranging from soothing to robust. Choose from the fresh cod with aïoli or saddle of roast lamb with coriander and polenta. Those who habitually abstain from dessert may be tempted by the apricot and black chocolate *nougatine* (nougat) or the superb *crème brûlée* with fennel and preserved fruits. ♦ M dinner; Tu-F lunch and dinner; Sa dinner. 25 Quai de la Tournelle (between Rues du Cardinal-Lemoine and de Poissy). 01.43.54.05.17. Métro: Maubert-Mutualité

VIVARIO
MICHEL HILAIRE

8 **Vivario** ★★$$ This small, lively neighborhood restaurant is serious about the quality of Corsican meals it serves. Its menu changes daily to make the most of what's fresh, but it always includes delicious pasta dishes. ♦ M, Sa dinner; Tu-F lunch and dinner; closed mid-August to mid-September and Christmas. 6 Rue Cochin (between Rues de Poissy and de Pontoise). 01.43.25.08.19. Métro: Maubert-Mutualité

9 **Boulangerie Beauvallet Julien** Modesty may prevent M. Ousbih and his family from putting their bakery's name in the window, but they won't divulge the recipe that results in the best baguettes in the Latin Quarter. Thin, crusty, with the tang of sourdough, one of these baguettes is the perfect base for building a picnic to take down to the quay. Fresh loaves come out of the oven at 7AM, 11AM, and 1PM. ♦ M-Tu, Th-Su; closed in August. 6 Rue de Poissy (at Rue Cochin). 01.43.26.94.24. Métro: Maubert-Mutualité

10 **Chez Toutoune** ★★$$ Colette Toutoune and Christophe Darney offer fine home-style Provençal cuisine with a Southern accent and at old-fashioned prices. The five-course menu chalked on the blackboard in the cozy dining room changes daily, but you can count on hot and cold soups, *caviar d'aubergine* (eggplant puree), roast lamb with thyme, iced nougat, and creamy brie. ♦ M dinner; Tu-Su lunch and dinner. Reservations recommended for dinner. 5 Rue de Pontoise (at Rue Cochin). 01.43.26.56.81. Métro: Maubert-Mutualité

11 **La Marée Verte** ★★★$$ A nautical decor of marine blue with yellow accents and prints of grand old ocean liners on the walls make for a charming setting in which to enjoy the ever-popular and impeccably fresh fish platter of salmon, cod, scallops, and scorpion fish; skate wings with *tapenade* (Provençal olive paste) and capers; or roast duckling with blueberries. The restaurant is also known for its exhilarating foie gras, fine vegetarian platters, *café glacé* that is the soul of coffee in ice, and a good and very affordable wine list. Besides superb food and wine and reasonable prices, the warm, serene ambience created by owners Hélène and Julvic Thomas has kept this restaurant a favorite of neighborhood regulars, figures from the worlds of politics (the late President Mitterand dined here often), show business personalities, and foreigners in Paris for more than 20 years. The Thomases admit to a particular *faible* (soft spot) for North Americans—there's even a perfect translation of the menu items from French to English, a rarity in a French restaurant. ♦ M dinner; Tu-Sa lunch and dinner. Reservations recommended. 9 Rue de Pontoise (between Blvd St-Germain and Rue Cochin). 01.43.25.89.41. Métro: Maubert-Mutualité

12 **Club Quartier Latin** The pretty indoor pool at this athletic club is one of the few in Paris where lap swimming is the norm and lane markers are respected. Downstairs are four squash courts, a Jacuzzi, saunas, dance classes, a lounge, and a snack bar where salads, steaks, and fruit juices are served. Day passes are available. ♦ M-F 9AM-11:30PM; Sa-Su. 19 Rue de Pontoise (between Rue St-Victor and Blvd St-Germain). 01.55.42.77.88. Métros: Cardinal Lemoine, Maubert-Mutualité

Restaurants/Clubs: Red   Hotels: Blue
Shops/ Outdoors: Green   Sights/Culture: Black

13 Moissonnier ★★★$$ Earthenware bowls spilling over with lyonnaise salads, friendly waiters, generous charcuterie, and a homey setting have earned this Left Bank establishment a loyal clientele. Specialties include kidneys with mustard, tripe baked with onions and white wine, creamy au gratin potatoes, and delicious Beaujolais. ♦ Tu-Sa lunch and dinner; Su lunch; closed in August. 28 Rue des Fossés-St-Bernard (between Rues des Chantiers and des Ecoles). 01.43.29.87.65. Métros: Jussieu, Cardinal Lemoine

14 Le Paradis Latin Sidney Israël's glittering nightclub stages one of the city's top floor shows. The food is not the main focus here, but the dinner, the *spectacle,* and **Gustave Eiffel's** magnificent 1889 theater—a national landmark—make for a memorable evening out. It's also possible to see the show without dining. ♦ Cover. M-Tu, Th-Su dinner 8PM. Show: M-Tu, Th-Su 9:30PM (arrive 30 minutes in advance). Reservations required. 28 Rue du Cardinal-Lemoine (between Rue des Ecoles and Blvd St-Germain). 01.43.25.28.28. Métro: Cardinal Lemoine

Familia Hôtel

15 Familia Hôtel $$ In this well-named hotel, amiable owner-managers Eric Gaucheron and his parents, Bernard and Colette, make their guests feel right at home. The 30 rooms in this century-old, Haussmann-style building combine modern conveniences (up-to-date bathrooms, cable TV, and soundproofing) and old-fashioned charm. Nineteen guest rooms are decorated with frescos of Paris, and many are furnished with antiques. Eight rooms have balconies, and the five on the upper two floors have views of **Notre-Dame.** There's no restaurant. ♦ 11 Rue des Ecoles (between Rues d'Arras and Monge). 01.43.54.55.27; fax 01.43.29.61.77. Métro: Cardinal Lemoine

16 St-Nicolas-du-Chardonnet Built in 1709, this church was originally a 13th-century chapel standing in a field of *chardons* (thistles). Later redesigned by Charles Le Brun, it now houses the Le Brun family chapel, along with Charles Le Brun's painting *The Martyrdom of Saint John.* The beautiful wood carving over the side door on the Rue des Bernardins is also his work. This also happens to be one of the most conservative churches in Paris: Mass is still said entirely in Latin. ♦ Sq de la Mutualité and Rue des Bernardins. Métros: Cardinal Lemoine, Maubert-Mutualité

17 Les Deux Tisserins Marie-Claude Leblois's little toy shop, crammed with some of the most unusual playthings in Paris, is a veritable wonderland of rocking horses, marionette theaters, finger puppets, mobiles, sailboats, wooden trains, spinning tops, stuffed animals, dolls, and music boxes. Lebois's famous line of children's clothing includes gaily patterned flannel pajamas, hooded jackets, and cotton dresses; her monogrammed *sacs à dos* (backpacks) have been favorites of Parisian children for years. ♦ Tu-Sa. 36 Rue des Bernardins (between Rue Monge and Blvd St-Germain). 01.46.33.88.68. Métro: Maubert-Mutualité

18 Diptyque Run by English and French artists who met while studying at the **Ecole des Beaux-Arts** after World War II, this tiny corner shop specializes in elegant antique bead necklaces, rose-petal sachets, perfumed soaps, eau de toilette, and candles scented like the forest floor on a damp May morning. ♦ Tu-Sa. 34 Blvd St-Germain (at Rue de Pontoise). 01.43.26.45.27. Métro: Maubert-Mutualité

18 H.G. Thomas The boutique of Hervé Gerald Thomas features such *très chic* gifts as Italian luggage, handsome Grus watches from Barcelona, miniature modern furniture from the Vitra Design Museum, and cutlery from Pott in Germany. The inventory ranges from designer ballpoints to Flex pliable plastic vases. And the chicest note of all: Most everything here comes in black. ♦ Tu-Sa 10AM-8PM. 36 Blvd St-Germain (between Rues de Pontoise and des Bernardins). 01.46.33.57.50. Métro: Maubert-Mutualité

Au Pactole

19 Au Pactole ★★$$ The delicacies of chef Van Santen encompass a carpaccio of Granny Smith apples with fresh herb goat cheese, *pavé de lieu jaune rôti sur la peau* (pollack roasted on its skin), and roast chicken from Bresse. Steak *tartare* (ground raw beef, capers, raw egg, mustard, Tabasco, catsup, chives, and spices), a specialty of the house, is prepared at tableside. The formal dining room, decorated in soft peach tones, provides a refined backdrop. ♦ M-F lunch and dinner; Sa dinner. Reservations recommended. 44 Blvd St-Germain (between Rues de Pontoise and des Bernardins). 01.43.26.92.28. Métro: Maubert-Mutualité

20 Musée des Hôpitaux de Paris–Assistance Publique (Museum of Public Health and Welfare) Tucked away in this 17th-century mansion, which was converted into the central pharmacy for the city's hospitals after the Revolution, is one of Paris's most offbeat yet entertaining museums. Unknown to most Parisians (and visitors), this repository of French medical history contains an extraordinary collection of old ceramic apothecary jars, Roman medicine vials, hospital rosters, pewter syringes, copper basins, blocks of marble that were pulverized to powder baby bottoms, and a model of a quasi–night-deposit box that 19th-century nuns invented for abandoned babies. ♦ Admission. Tu-Sa; closed in August and on holidays. 47 Quai de la Tournelle (between Rues de Pontoise and des Bernardins). 01.40.27.50.05. Métro: Maubert-Mutualité

20 45 Quai de la Tournelle Shortly after being discharged from the American Ambulance Corps in the spring of 1919, John Dos Passos sublet a playwright's apartment here and began what would become his first successful novel, *Three Soldiers.* It remains a residential building. ♦ Between Rues de Pontoise and des Bernardins. Métro: Maubert-Mutualité

A Festival of Food in Paris's Markets

Paris's open-air food emporia feature not only fresh, colorful, and attractively displayed products, but a glimpse into France's cuisine culture. This is reflected, for example, in the exchange between locals doing *les courses* (daily shopping) and the merchants, which can be as droll as a comedy sketch or as intense as a game of high-stakes poker. But however it appears, the interaction is always profoundly serious, as *fromagers* (cheese merchants), *vergers* (fruit and vegetable sellers), *bouchers* (butchers), *poissonniers* (fishmongers), and other vendors take pride in their products, and buyers in their choices. And since food plays a significant role in daily French life, shopping is as important as the preparation and consumption of the final dish.

Three types of markets exist in Paris: *rues commerçantes* (market streets with permanent shops and open stalls in front of them, open Tuesday through Sunday), *marchés couverts* (covered market pavilions with permanent stands, open Tuesday through Saturday), and *marchés volants* ("flying" markets, open two or three days a week at a particular location, with the merchants moving to another location the next day). The following is a birds-eye view of Paris's outdoor markets.

The best *rues commerçantes* include **Rue Cler** (between Ave de La Motte-Picquet and Rue de Grenelle)—a wide, relaxed cobblestone street in the classy seventh arrondissement with high-quality shops; **Rue de Buci** (at Rue de Seine)—colorful and centrally located in **St-Germain-des-Près**, but quite expensive; **Rue Mouffetard** (between Rues Censier and de l'Epée-de-Bois)—on a hill in the **Latin Quarter,** and nearly as colorful today as in Hemingway's descriptions of the street in the 1920s; **Rue Montorgueil**—the last remnant of the huge old **Les Halles** market, a six-block stretch of first-rate shops on an attractive street still patronized by some of the top chefs in Paris; **Marché Aligre** (Rue d'Aligre and Pl d'Aligre, Bastille, open in the morning only)—a big, bustling popular market square with outdoor food stalls, an open-air clothing section, a covered food pavilion, and one of the liveliest wine bars in town, **Le Baron Rouge** (open in the morning only); and **Rue Lepic** (between Blvd de Clichy and Rue des Abbesses)—a run-down, but atmospheric few blocks of an old market street meandering up the hill of Montmartre.

In the great days of **Les Halles,** when Zola dubbed it "the belly of Paris," the huge 19th-century cast-iron and glass pavilions by Baltard housed a veritable circus of food selling. In contrast, today's covered markets are rather sedate affairs. The emporium in the recently renovated **Marché St-Germain** (Rues Mabillon and Lobineau) is neat, well-stocked, and pleasant, but smallish and not very lively. The pavilion of the **Marché Aligre** (see above) is the best bet these days for an animated covered marketplace.

There are colorful "flying markets" at **Place Monge** in the Latin Quarter on Wednesday, Friday, and Sunday morning; **Raspail** (Blvd Raspail, between Rues de Rennes and du Cherche-Midi) on Tuesday and Friday (a **Marché Biologique**—organic food market—is also held here on Sunday mornings); and **Richard Lenoir** (Blvd Richard-Lenoir, between Pl de la Bastille and Rue St-Sabin) on Thursday and on Sunday morning. **Richard Lenoir** becomes a regular street fair on Sunday mornings when two women in long black dresses and red feather boas belt out old French chansons to the tune of a hand-crank organ, a pitch man mesmerizes his listeners with a rapid-fire patter about a hand-operated food processor, a Django Reinhardt–style band plays 1930s swing music, and political activists pass out leaflets denouncing the National Front. It's all a slice of French life every bit as flavorful as the comestibles on display.

21 Jean-Pierre Stella Legions of lead soldiers stand at attention in this little shop on the quay. Military medals, Napoleonic helmets, and vintage weaponry are also sold. ♦ M-Sa 2-4PM, and by appointment in the mornings; closed mid-July through August. 67 Quai de la Tournelle (between Rues de Bièvre and Maître-Albert). 01.46.33.40.50. Métro: Maubert-Mutualité

22 Galerie Urubamba Traditional indigenous art and culture from the Americas—weavings, masks, headdresses, and more—is the specialty of this gallery/folk art shop. A bookshop affords visitors a selection of over 2,000 titles and catalogs. The gallery also organizes language and fabric-weaving classes. ♦ Tu-Sa 2-7:30PM. 4 Rue de la Bûcherie (between Rues du Haut-Pavé and de l'Hôtel-Colbert). 01.43.54.08.24. Métro: Maubert-Mutualité

23 Patchworks du Rouvray Like the Galerie Urubamba across the square, this quilt emporium is run by a North American woman. Diane de Obaldia's shop is named after a 14th-century farmhouse near Chartres, where she started her business. Today she sells traditional patchwork quilts of the 1930s. She also offers many quilting classes (in French and English) and 1,500 varieties of cotton fabric for inspired quilters. ♦ M-Sa. 1 Rue Frédéric-Sauton (between Rues Maître-Albert and des Grands-Degrés). 01.43.25.00.45. Métro: Maubert-Mutualité

24 Chieng-Mai ★★$$ An excellent Thai restaurant, this eatery serves beef satay, squid and mint salad, spicy pork brochette, and, for dessert, grilled flan with coconut milk. The pineapple salad is divine. Red is the predominant color in the two warm and inviting dining rooms. ♦ Daily lunch and dinner. Reservations required. 12 Rue Frédéric-Sauton (between Rues Lagrange and de la Bûcherie). 01.43.25.45.45. Métro: Maubert-Mutualité

25 Place Maubert The name "Maubert" is probably a contraction of Maître (Master) Albert, who was a Dominican teacher at the **University of Paris** in the Middle Ages. For centuries, this wide spot in the road was a crime-ridden skid row, a resort for tramps drinking *gros rouge* (cheap red wine), and the site of public executions. Here, in 1546, during the reign of François I, printer and humanist philosopher Etienne Dolet was burned at the stake as a heretic; his own books were used to kindle the fire. In addition to serving as an execution ground, from the Middle Ages hence this crossroads has been a bustling open-air market. ♦ Market: Tu, Th, Sa 7AM-1PM. Métro: Maubert-Mutualité

26 Than Binh This little Vietnamese grocery store supplies the many Southeast Asian restaurants and families clustered around Place Maubert. The exotic spices and bewildering assortment of food (rice steamed in banana leaves, tapioca in grape leaves, shrimp muffins) will transport you to the Mekong Delta. ♦ M-Sa. 29 Pl Maubert (at Blvd St-Germain). 01.40.46.06.15. Métro: Maubert-Mutualité

27 Musée des Collections Historiques de la Préfecture de Police (Police Museum) This fascinating, often grisly little collection surveys the city's most notorious crimes, from the 16th century to the present. Exhibits include a graphic representation of the 1563 punishment accorded the Duc de Guise's murderer (quartering by four horses); orders for the arrest of Dr. Guillotin in 1795; an account of Charlotte Corday's murder of Marat in his bath; a book stained with blood from the 1932 assassination of French President Paul Doumer; and Verlaine's statement of his attempted murder of fellow poet Rimbaud. Among the more ingenious weapons on display are a strangling cord made of twisted paper and a knife concealed in a lady's fan. There's also a guillotine blade used during the Revolution. ♦ Free. M-Sa. 1 *bis* Rue des Carmes (between Rue des Ecoles and Pl Maubert). 01.44.41.52.50. Métro: Maubert-Mutualité

28 Rue des Anglais In medieval times this street was a favorite haunt of English students attending the **Sorbonne.** ♦ Métro: Maubert-Mutualité

29 Colbert $$$ From 9 of the 36 comfortable rooms in this former 17th-century residence, you can contemplate **Notre-Dame** while having breakfast in bed. All the guest rooms were renovated after Groupe Astotel purchased the property in 1997—some in traditional French style, some contemporary—and now have modern bathrooms, air-conditioning, and satellite TV. The place has an interesting history: parts of the building date back to 1500, and an animal hospital sponsored by the Duke of Windsor once stood on the site of the present courtyard garden. There's no restaurant. ♦ 7 Rue de l'Hôtel-Colbert (at Rue de la Bûcherie). 01.40.46.79.50; fax 01.43.25.80.19; www.astotel.fr. Métro: Maubert-Mutualité

"The sidewalk cafe was still one of the best places for me to meet people. It was not only a fresh air experience, but I always found someone willing to listen to my story. I never varied the telling of it. I told how I had turned my back on millions of dollars in Hollywood to become a struggling writer in Paris. Even the hookers who sat at café tables were taken with my tale."

Art Buchwald, *I'll Always Have Paris*, 1996

30 Les Bouchons de François Clerc ★★★
$$ François Clerc sells the well-selected wines and Champagnes in his cellar at cost in his restaurant. Take advantage of the deal and try a bottle of 1990 Château Batailley or 1993 Château Trotteveille for about 70 percent of what you'd pay anywhere else. The wine prices are only one reason to rush to this dining spot: The wood-beamed dining room is sophisticated and cozy, the homemade bread is warm and crusty, the waiters are young and bubbly, and the four-course prix-fixe menu features such original dishes as *croustillant de rouget* (a light, red mullet cake), *tournedos Rossini* (a sublime version of the classic made with tuna steak instead of the traditional beef), and braised pigeon with cèpes. This place is popular, so book well in advance. ♦ M-F lunch and dinner; Sa dinner. Reservations required. 12 Rue de l'Hôtel-Colbert (between Rues Lagrange and de la Bûcherie). 01.43.54.15.34. Métro: Maubert-Mutualité

MICHAEL STORRINGS

31 Quai de Montebello Booksellers The *bouquinistes* who work in the shadow of **Notre-Dame** practice one of the city's oldest trades, selling old Daumier prints, volumes on everything from Balzac to bebop, and the occasional naughty postcard out of their green boxes on the quay (see illustration above). These famous, free-spirited cowboys of the book business open and close their sidewalk stalls when they please and sell only what interests them. ♦ Daily, depending on the weather. Quai de Montebello (between Pont de l'Archevêché and Petit Pont). Métros: Maubert-Mutualité, St-Michel

32 Pont au Double The name derives from the fact that this was the only bridge in Paris whose toll was two sous instead of one.
♦ Métros: Maubert-Mutualité, St-Michel

33 Square René-Viviani In this lovely little park stands what is reputed to be the oldest tree in Paris. This false acacia *(Robinia pseudoacacia)* leans on concrete crutches, infirm but erect, and blooms every spring. Not bad for a sprout that crossed the ocean from Guyana to be planted in 1680 by Jean Robin. Sit for a moment on one of the park benches and notice the pieces of worn and broken statuary surrounding you; they were once part of **Notre-Dame.** ♦ Métros: Maubert-Mutualité, St-Michel

34 Rue du Fouarre Seated on *fouarres* (bundles of straw), undergraduates in the Middle Ages attended open-air lectures presented in this alley by rowdy intellectuals, notorious throughout Europe. In an attempt to ease tensions in 1358, Charles V chained the street at both ends and closed it at night. During his visit to Paris in 1304, even Dante harkened to the scholars here and later made reference in his writing to this *vico degli strami* (the road of straws). ♦ Métro: Maubert-Mutualité

On Rue du Fouarre:

La Fourmi Ailée ★★$ On a chilly day come to this charming tearoom and women's bookstore and order a hot goat cheese salad, sit back in a caned bentwood chair by the fireplace, and peruse a book by Simone de Beauvoir. Come for brunch on Sunday. ♦ Daily noon-1:30AM. No. 29. 01.43.29.40.99

35 A l'Imagerie The largest old print and poster shop in Paris specializes in original Art Deco, Art Nouveau, and late 19th-century Japanese prints and stamps. ♦ M-Sa. 9 Rue Dante (at Rue Domat). 01.43.25.18.66. Métros: Cluny–La Sorbonne, Maubert-Mutualité

36 Album From Action comics to Zot, Donald Duck to Dick Tracy, this *bande dessinée* (comic strip) shop specializes in new and vintage North American comic books. For the seriocomic art collector, there are oil paintings of Batman and portraits and statues of Mr. Spock. ♦ M-Sa. 67 Blvd St-Germain (at Rue St-Jacques). 01.53.10.00.60. Métros: Cluny–La Sorbonne, Maubert-Mutualité

Geneviève Baudon
LIBRAIRIE GOURMANDE

37 Librairie Gourmande The celebrated *bouquiniste* Mme. Baudon moved to this shop from her stall on the quay where she sells books on food and wine from the 17th century to the present. ♦ Daily. 4 Rue Dante (between Blvd St-Germain and Rue Galande). 01.43.54.37.27. Métros: Maubert-Mutualité, St-Michel

38 Rue Galande The beginning of the old Roman road to Lyon, this meandering street was named in 1202 after a family who lived nearby. It was one of the fancier neighborhoods in 17th-century Paris. ♦ Métro: Maubert-Mutualité

38 Studio Galande Catch one of the cinema's weekend showings of *The Rocky Horror Picture Show.* Watching funkily costumed French college students enjoying their umpteenth viewing of this crazy cult film—singing, dancing, and shouting at the on-screen characters—is guaranteed to have you in stitches. Outside the theater, glance up at the 14th-century stone relief of St. Julien crossing the Seine, which originally stood over the portal of nearby **St-Julien-le-Pauvre** church (see below). ♦ 42 Rue Galande (between Rues du Fouarre and St-Julien-le-Pauvre). 01.43.26.94.08. Métro: Maubert-Mutualité

39 Les Trois Maillets The "Three Mallets" began in the 13th century as a tavern that served the stonemasons constructing **Notre-Dame.** Some 700 years later it was transformed into a postwar jazz club first frequented by North American GIs. Entertainment now includes belly dancing and rap, and it has one of the best piano bars in Paris. ♦ Cover. Daily 6PM–6AM; live music from 11PM. 56 Rue Galande (at Rue du Petit-Pont). 01.43.54.00.79

40 St-Julien-le-Pauvre Named in honor of St. Julian the Poor, a martyred third-century bishop who gave all his money to the penniless, this church, an odd, graceless amalgam of Romanesque and Gothic architecture, has no bell tower, transepts, or organ, and squats on a small square lined with acacia trees. With its iron-caged well in front, it looks more like a humble country church than a Parisian monument. Founded in 1165 (and restored in 1250 and 1651), this is one of several structures that claim the title of oldest church in Paris. Although the construction of **Notre-Dame** began two years earlier, **St-Julien-le-Pauvre** was completed first, and while **St-Germain-des-Prés** is older, it originally stood outside the city walls and therefore was not, strictly speaking, a Parisian church.

In the 12th century, when renegade theologian Pierre Abélard quit **Notre-Dame,** he took more than 3,000 students along with him and established a new university here. The church thus became the seat and meeting place of the new **University of Paris.** In 1524, students critical of a new rector ransacked and nearly destroyed the church. After the Revolution, **St-Julien-le-Pauvre** was used variously as a salt storehouse, wool market, and flour granary. Since 1889 it has belonged to the Greek Orthodox church. The enormous stone slab beside the well came from the fourth-century Roman highway that became Rue St-Jacques. ♦ 1 Rue St-Julien-le-Pauvre (at Sq René-Viviani). 01.43.54.52.16. Métros: Maubert-Mutualité, St-Michel, Cité

41 Rue St-Julien-le-Pauvre The magnificent gate at **No. 14** marks the 17th-century home of the governor of the old **Petit-Châtelet** prison. Also don't miss the house of the dwindling windows at **No. 10;** they start with the largest ones on the ground floor and shrink all the way up to the maids' rooms in the attic. ♦ Métros: Maubert-Mutualité, St-Michel, Cité

41 The Tea Caddy ★$ Looking like a prim and proper English great-aunt's library, with dark wood paneling and thick-paned windows, this is the place for afternoon tea and crumpets. Light meals of quiche, salads, and omelettes are also served. ♦ M-Tu, Th-Su lunch and afternoon tea. No credit cards accepted. 14 Rue St-Julien-le-Pauvre (between Rues Galande and de la Bûcherie). 01.43.54.15.56. Métros: Maubert-Mutualité, St-Michel, Cité

42 Esmeralda $$ This atmospheric 19-room hotel is a favorite with traveling writers and professors. The garrulous owner, artist Michèle Bruel, seems to have stepped right out of the last century. Some of the guest rooms have views of **Notre-Dame.** There is no restaurant. ♦ No credit cards accepted. 4 Rue St-Julien-le-Pauvre (between Rues Galande and de la Bûcherie). 01.43.54.19.20; fax 01.40.51.00.68. Métros: Maubert-Mutualité, St-Michel, Cité

43 Rue de la Bûcherie A *bûcherie* is a woodshed, and this part of the quay is where firewood-laden barges dropped their cargo. ♦ Between Rues St-Julien-le-Pauvre and du Petit-Pont. Métros: Maubert-Mutualité, St-Michel, Cité

On Rue de la Bûcherie:

Shakespeare and Company Octogenarian George Bates Whitman—who was raised in China, speaks five languages, and claims the poet Walt as a distant forebear—has run this charitable bookstore/inn for authors, vagabond intellectuals, and literature professors since the early 1950s. Spiritual heir to Sylvia Beach, whose famous Paris bookstore of the same name on the Rue de l'Odéon supplied Hemingway with free reading material and was the only house that would publish Joyce's *Ulysses,* Whitman bought part of her collection and borrowed the name **Shakespeare and Company.** He even named his daughter Sylvia Beach Whitman. Throughout the years, Whitman's chaotic stacks, which defy the Dewey decimal or any other system of categorization, have been frequented by the likes of Lawrence Durrell, Henry Miller, J.P. Donleavy, and Beat poet Lawrence Ferlinghetti. Whitman is usually here in the late afternoon; while you're browsing he may offer you a cup of tea and, if you happen to be penniless and show promise as a writer, may invite you to spend a night in the **Writer's Room** or to bed down on the floor of his upstairs library. To the left of the bookshop, which has one of the world's most eclectic bulletin boards, Whitman keeps his own private collection. Each book purchased in the shop is stamped with an inscription that reads: Shakespeare and Co. Kilometer Zero Paris. ♦ Shop: daily noon–midnight. Tea parties: Su 4PM. Poetry readings: M 8PM. No. 37. 01.43.26.96.50

La Bûcherie ★★★$$$ Bernard Bosque's menu, featuring cabbage leaves stuffed with langoustines, ocean salmon with chives, and wild duck and oysters, hasn't changed in years and neither has the popularity of this restaurant. In summer, reserve a table on the terrace overlooking **Notre-Dame,** and in winter try to get a table near the crackling fireplace. Expect a crowd, and at all costs avoid sitting behind the chimney, where famished customers can go unnoticed for days. Bosque has hosted Jacqueline Kennedy Onassis, François Mitterand, and many other illustrious figures in his dining room. ♦ Daily lunch and dinner. Reservations recommended. No. 41. 01.43.54.78.06

44 Petit Pont Bishop Maurice de Sully was responsible for the construction of this little bridge, built in 1185 and rebuilt in the 19th century. Formerly located at the end of the bridge was the **Petit-Châtelet** fortress and prison, a more diminutive version of the **Grand Châtelet** on the Right Bank. ♦ Métros: St-Michel, Cité

45 Rue St-Jacques The city's oldest street originated as a Roman road. A thousand years later, it was named after St-Jacques (St. James), whose body is believed to have miraculously appeared in Spain in the ninth century. Paris was the principal starting point of a thousand-mile pilgrimage to Santiago de Compostela in Spain, where the saint's body was buried. In medieval times, pilgrims wearing scallop shells (the symbol of St. James) would set off down this street. The delicious contents of such shells are now served throughout Paris as *coquilles St-Jacques.* ♦ Métros: St-Michel, Cluny–La Sorbonne, Maubert-Mutualité

45 Mirama ★★$ With glazed, roasted ducks hanging in the window and a cauldron whose contents bubble mysteriously just inside the door, this informal Chinese restaurant at first seems suspect. Yet it's crowded all day long, and deservedly so: The ingredients are fresh and the price is right. Try the noodle soup with shrimp dumplings, sweet-and-sour chicken, crispy mixed vegetables, pork ribs in black bean sauce, and, of course, the *canard laqué* you saw on the way in. ♦ Daily lunch and dinner. 17 Rue St-Jacques (between Blvd St-Germain and Rue Galande). 01.43.29.66.58. Métros: Maubert-Mutualité, St-Michel

46 27 Rue St-Jacques More than a hundred sundials can be found in Paris, but few were created by artists of worldwide repute. Surrealist Salvador Dalí designed this *cadran solaire* for friends whose furniture store was located here. The timepiece's completion in 1968 was televised, with Dalí mounting a cherry picker to carve his signature into the still-wet cement. Set on the south face of the building, the sundial depicts a female face in the form of a *coquille St-Jacques* (scallop shell). ♦ Between Blvd St-Germain and Rue Galande. Métros: Maubert-Mutualité, St-Michel

46 Le Bar à Huitres ★★$$ This seafood restaurant has the best and least expensive shellfish served in the city. Fresh oysters and scallops arrive daily from the Normandy and Brittany coasts to become components in sumptuous platters of mollusks and crustaceans. Fish specialties include monkfish curry in winter and roast turbot with wine and butter sauce in summer. Served with velvety *beurre blanc* for dipping, the grilled lobster is heavenly. The bar outside sells oysters and such for takeout, making this place truly a paradise for shellfish lovers. ♦ Daily lunch and dinner until 2AM. 33 Rue St-Jacques (between Blvd St-Germain and Rue Galande). 01.44.07.27.37. Métros: Maubert-Mutualité, St-Michel. Also at: 112 Blvd du Montparnasse

* (at Blvd Raspail). 01.43.20.71.01. Métro: Vavin; 33 Blvd Beaumarchais (at Rue du Pas-de-la-Mule). 01.48.87.98.92. Métros: Bastille, Chemin Vert

Café de Cluny

47 Café de Cluny ★$ Set at one of the Latin Quarter's busiest corners, this sprawling cafe founded in 1869 commands a front-row seat on the boulevards St-Michel and St-Germain. Upstairs in the quiet, plush booths, **Sorbonne** professors take their morning coffee or have a dish of ice cream with their graduate students in the afternoon. ♦ Daily breakfast, lunch, and dinner until 2AM. 102 Blvd St-Germain (at Blvd St-Michel). 01.43.26.98.40. Métro: Cluny–La Sorbonne

48 Hôtel de Cluny, Musée de Cluny (Musée National du Moyen-Age), and Palais des Thermes Constructed by the abbots of Cluny in 1330 and rebuilt in 1510, this magnificent mansion is one of the oldest private residences in Paris. It straddles the ruins of second-century **Roman Baths** and contains one of the world's finest collections of French medieval art, including the beautiful *Lady and the Unicorn* tapestries.

The baths date from Marcus Aurellus (reigned AD 161-80); Julian the Apostate, proclaimed Roman Emperor in 360, lived in the adjoining palace. The baths and palace were sacked during numerous barbarian invasions, and in 1340 Pierre de Châlus, abbot of Cluny, the wealthy Benedictine abbey in Burgundy, bought the ruins and erected the **Hôtel de Cluny** as a pied-à-terre for the abbots when they visited Paris. Shortly after the Revolution, the *hôtel* was occupied by a cooper, a laundress, French navy astronomers, and a surgeon who used the chapel for his dissections. Among the mansion's tenants in 1833 was Alexandre du Sommerard, an art collector who had specialized in Gothic and Renaissance art. When he died in 1842, the state bought the building as well as du Sommerard's collection and appointed his son Edmond as the first curator of the **Musée de Cluny,** also known as the **Musée National du Moyen-Age** (National Museum of the Middle Ages).

As you enter the museum courtyard by the Rue du Sommerard, notice the polygonal stair tower sprinkled with carved shells *(coquilles St-Jacques),* the symbol of the patron saint of Jacques d'Amboise, the abbot of Jumièges, who between 1485 and 1510 rebuilt the *hôtel* in its present Flamboyant Gothic style. The first rooms of the museum are replete with delicate ivory carvings, embroidered Egyptian silks, and Flemish tapestries of gentlemen

setting off for the hunt. ♦ Admission. M, W-Su. 6 Pl Paul-Painlevé (at Rue du Sommerard). 01.53.73.78.00. Métro: Cluny–La Sorbonne

Within the Hôtel de Cluny, Musée de Cluny, and Palais des Thermes:

Notre-Dame Gallery In this stark white room are the sculpted stone heads (1210-30) of 21 noseless but nevertheless majestic monarchs. They represent the kings of Judea and Israel, who, according to St. Matthew's genealogy, were ancestors of Christ. Like most men too closely associated with religion and royalty at the time of the Revolution, they lost their heads. But theirs was a case of mistaken identity. The full-length statues of the kings were originally enshrined in the **Gallery of Kings** on **Notre-Dame's** west facade, but they were beheaded in 1793 by an angry mob who assumed they depicted the kings of France. The statues have stood decapitated since that time, and for nearly two centuries the heads were considered lost. But in 1977, during excavations for a new bank in the **Hôtel Moreau** near the **Opéra,** they were unearthed; the discovery is considered one of the 20th century's major archaeological finds.

Roman Baths The towering roof of the *frigidarium* (cold bath) is the largest Roman vault in all of France. The ceiling has survived 18 centuries of wear and tear, even withstanding being topped with 8 feet of topsoil and an abbot's apple orchard and kitchen garden. The ship prows decorating the base of the groined vaulting are the building signatures of the powerful Boatmen's Guild of Paris. Nearby is the *Boatmen's Pillar,* one of the oldest pieces of sculpture in Paris. It was dedicated to the god Jupiter by the Boatmen's Guild during the reign of Roman emperor Tiberius (AD 14-37) and was later discovered beneath **Notre-Dame.**

Treasury Upstairs, above the baths, is a dazzling display of Gallic, Barbarian, and Merovingian jewelry, including six gold Visigoth crowns, two 13th-century gold double crosses, and the sublimely delicate 14th-century *Golden Rose* that was presented to the Bishop of Basel by Pope Clement V.

Stained Glass Among the medieval stained-glass windows in the upstairs corridor are religious scenes from **Sainte-Chapelle** and the **Basilique de St-Denis.** Take a close look; in the actual churches—even with a strong pair of opera glasses and a craned neck—you won't get this good a view. Three large windows and the surrounding stonework come from the church of **St-Jean-de-Latran,** demolished in 1859 to make way for the Rue des Ecoles built between the **Cluny** and the **Sorbonne.**

Abbots' Chapel One of the few surviving interior details of the original mansion, this chapel was the abbots' oratory and is an architectural masterpiece. The elaborate vaulting sprouts palmlike from a single slender pillar. In a room near the chapel is a 1383 eagle lectern and a 12th-century gilt copper altar table.

Tapestries Saving the best for last, enter the rotunda on the top floor, dimly lit to protect the world-famous *Lady and the Unicorn* tapestry series. In 1844, quite by accident, writer George Sand discovered the tapestries hanging at the **Château de Boussac;** supposedly they were a wedding present in the 15th century from magistrate Jean Le Viste to his bride (the Le Viste coat of arms appears in each panel). The artist, who remains unknown, is thought to have designed the similar set of six tapestries that is now hanging in the Cloisters museum in New York City. The delicate tapestries allegorically depict the five senses. In the one representing sight, for instance, the noble unicorn gazes into the mirror of a bejeweled blond woman. In the mysterious sixth tapestry, the woman's tent is emblazoned with the words "A Mon Seul Désir" (To My Only Desire), thought to represent mastery of all five senses. Notice that the woman on the red *millefleur* (literally, one thousand flowers) background changes from one sumptuous gown to another in a veritable fashion show as you progress around the room.

49 Rue des Ecoles This street name celebrates the presence of all the academic institutions and universities hereabouts. ♦ Métros: Cluny–La Sorbonne, Maubert-Mutualité, Cardinal Lemoine

AU VIEUX CAMPEUR

49 Au Vieux Campeur France's best mountain-climbing outfitters this side of Chamonix carry pitons, ice axes, alpine sleeping bags, and giant spools of brightly colored climbing rope for your next ascent of Everest or the **Eiffel Tower.** Even if a bivouac at a wine bar atop the Montagne Ste-Geneviève's slopes is more your style, pause on the sidewalk and watch France's next generation of rock climbers testing new equipment, rappelling down an indoor version of what looks like the Eiger's North Face. This is one of a chain of nine stores on the Left Bank. ♦ M-Tu, Th-Sa 10:30AM-7:30PM; W

10:30AM-9PM. 48 Rue des Ecoles (between Rues Thénard and St-Jacques). 01.53.10.48.48. Métros: Cluny–La Sorbonne, Maubert-Mutualité. Also at: Numerous locations throughout the city

HOTEL
du
COLLÈGE DE FRANCE

50 Hôtel du Collège de France $$ Some of the 6th-floor rooms of this quiet, simple-but-comfortable 29-room bed-and-breakfast inn offer a glimpse of the **Notre-Dame** towers. There's no restaurant. ♦ 7 Rue Thénard (between Rues de Latran and du Sommerard). 01.43.26.78.36; fax 01.46.34.58.29. Métro: Maubert-Mutualité

51 Club Jean de Beauvais Work off those gourmet French meals at this classy health club, where visitors to Paris are welcome to sign up for daily or weekly memberships. The good-looking staff offer advice and support while members huff and puff through their cardiovascular circuits and weight-training programs. Classes in aerobics, stretching, toning, and yoga are given daily. Somehow, the modern exercise equipment is right at home amidst the beautifully renovated stone walls and wood-beamed ceilings of the 17th-century salons. This is where Jodie Foster exercises when she is in Paris. ♦ Daily. 5 Rue Jean-de-Beauvais (between Rue du Sommerard and Blvd St-Germain). 01.46.33.16.80. Métro: Maubert-Mutualité

52 Eglise Roumaine (Romanian Church)/Beauvais College Chapel One of the Sorbonne's first college chapels, this structure was built in 1380. The restored sanctuary has been used since 1882 by the Romanian Orthodox Church. ♦ 9 *bis* Rue Jean-de-Beauvais (between Rues des Ecoles and du Sommerard). 01.43.54.67.47. Métro: Maubert-Mutualité

53 Da Capo Charles Recht runs this postage stamp–size shop dealing in 78-rpm records, old sheet music, and opera programs. ♦ Tu-Sa noon-6:30PM; closed in August. 14 Rue des Ecoles (between Rues des Bernardins and de la Montagne-Ste-Geneviève). 01.43.54.75.47. Métros: Maubert-Mutualité, Cardinal Lemoine

54 Librairie Présence Africaine Need a few Wolof lessons before visiting Gambia? Looking for a Senegalese cookbook? Want to hear a black gospel concert on the Left Bank? This African bookstore includes a Third World periodical section and a bulletin board. ♦ M-Sa. 25 *bis* Rue des Ecoles (between Rues des Bernardins and de la Montagne-Ste-Geneviève). 01.43.54.15.88. Métros: Maubert-Mutualité, Cardinal Lemoine

55 Montagne Ste-Geneviève The central point of the old **University of Paris**, this French Parnassus is named after one of Paris's two patron saints (St. Denis is her male counterpart). It is admittedly steep, but to call any of the city's seven hills a mountain is certainly an example of Roman grandiloquence. The summit of Ste-Geneviève is gracefully crowned with the **Panthéon** (see below), whose columned dome dominates the Left Bank. This is a vicinity rich in intellectual history: Here was the convent where St. Thomas Aquinas wrote his *Summa Theologica*, upon which the orthodox philosophy of Catholicism is based; here both St. Ignatius Loyola and Calvin studied; here Marat drew up his pamphlets; and here Pascal died a stone's throw from the place where Verlaine was to pass away many generations later. The hill counts among its educational institutions the world-famous **Sorbonne**, the **Collège de France**, prestigious medical and law schools, and three large secondary schools, and was at one time the site of the **Ecole Polytechnique**, the French equivalent of MIT. In 1804 the Rue de la Montagne-Ste-Geneviève was the scene of a plot to murder Napoléon Bonaparte. ♦ Métros: Maubert-Mutualité, Cardinal Lemoine

55 Shobudo Europe's oldest judo school is set in a tranquil 17th-century courtyard. If you don't have time for a self-defense class, you can fake it by buying a black belt and the latest kung fu paraphernalia in the **Budo Store** on the second floor. Or walk to the end of the courtyard, turn left, and squeeze into the spectators' gallery to watch a few bouts of *ken jitsu*, a Japanese martial art predating the shoguns. The judo school is in a building that was once part of the **Hostel of the 33** (named for the number of years Christ lived), established by monk Claude Bernard as a dormitory for theology students. ♦ M-Sa 9AM-10PM. 34 Rue de la Montagne-Ste-

Geneviève (between Rues de l'Ecole-Polytechnique and des Ecoles). 01.44.41.63.20. Métro: Maubert-Mutualité

56 La Nef Parisienne Affixed on this small square, as on city schools and other public structures throughout Paris, is the image of a sailing vessel known as *La Nef Parisienne*. The image has been Paris's coat of arms since 1260, when St. Louis appointed the Boatmen's Guild to administer the affairs of the city. *Fluctuat nec mergitur* (float never sink) is the city motto. In addition to adorning buildings, the coat of arms is embossed on everything from the mayor's stationery to police officers' badges. ♦ Rues Descartes, de la Montagne-Ste-Geneviève, and de l'Ecole-Polytechnique. Métros: Cardinal Lemoine, Maubert-Mutualité

57 Ecole Polytechnique These massive buildings once housed the French MIT. The school was founded as an army-run engineering school by Gaspard Monge, the mathematician who accompanied Napoléon to Egypt, and its best-known graduates are car designer André Citroën and former French president Valéry Giscard d'Estaing. Its annual grand ball at the **Opéra** is also fairly famous. In 1976 the prestigious university moved to the suburbs; the buildings here are now used for scientific research. ♦ Rue de l'Ecole-Polytechnique (between Rues de la Montagne-Ste-Geneviève and Valette). Métros: Cardinal Lemoine, Maubert-Mutualité

58 51 Rue de la Montagne-Ste-Geneviève The Irish author James Joyce shared a flat here with French writer Valéry Larbaud. It's still a residential building. ♦ Between Rues St-Etienne-du-Mont and Descartes. Métro: Cardinal Lemoine

59 Crocojazz This cubbyhole of a record shop resounds with the music of Art Blakey, Miles Davis, Louis Armstrong, and Coleman Hawkins. Jack Daniels whiskey bottles on the wall, the occasional country twang of Hank Thompson and Ricky Skaggs, and the worn Levi's and ersatz cowboy boots of the French clientele round out the ambience here. ♦ Tu-Sa. 64 Rue de la Montagne-Ste-Geneviève (at Pl Ste-Geneviève). 01.46.34.78.38. Métro: Cardinal Lemoine

60 Le Raccard ★★$$ The Swiss chalet decor may be heavy-handed, but the all-you-can-eat raclette is as authentic and delicious as it comes. In winter, fondues made with gruyère or vacherin are served. ♦ Tu-Su dinner; closed in August. Reservations recommended. 19 Rue Laplace (between Rues de la Montagne-Ste-Geneviève and Valette). 01.43.54.83.75. Métro: Cardinal Lemoine

---

Restaurants/Clubs: Red **Hotels:** Blue
Shops/♥ Outdoors: Green **Sights/Culture:** Black

61 Le Coupe-Chou ★$$ This seductive inn with an impressive fireplace occupies the site of a 16th-century barbershop whose proprietor slit the throats of his customers and then gave their bodies to a butcher to be made into pâté. If you can cast that grisly chapter from your mind, you will probably enjoy this attractive dining spot, which serves *escalopes de saumon á la crème d'estragon* (salmon with tarragon cream sauce), lamb with mint, *magret de canard* (duck fillet) with peaches, and *mille-feuilles maison* (homemade puff pastries), a specialty—though you may want to skip the pâté. ♦ M-Sa lunch and dinner; Su dinner. Reservations recommended. 11 Rue de Lanneau (at Impasse Chartière). 01.46.33.68.69. Métro: Maubert-Mutualité

62 Collège de France First called the **Collège des Trois-Langues** (Three Languages College) because Hebrew and Greek were taught here as well as Latin, this institution, founded by François I in 1529, counts among its famous faculty Frédéric Joliot-Curie (son-in-law of Marie and Pierre Curie), who split the uranium atom; the physicist André-Marie Ampère, after whom a unit of measuring electric current is named; poet Paul Valéry; and the more contemporary scholars Roland Barthes, Michel Foucault, and Claude Lévi-Strauss. ♦ 11 Pl Marcelin-Berthelot (between Rues Jean-de-Beauvais and St-Jacques). 01.44.27.12.11. Métro: Maubert-Mutualité

MICHAEL STORRINGS

Cardinal Richelieu

63 Sorbonne France's most famous university began in 1253 as humble lodgings for 16 theology students. In medieval times, the university was not a mass of edifices, pedants, and bureaucrats; it was a loose assembly of soapbox academics giving street-corner lectures to students who boarded at inns throughout Paris. However, by the end of the 13th century, when the **Sorbonne** became the administrative headquarters for the **University of Paris,** there were 15,000 undergraduates studying in the city. St. Thomas Aquinas and Roger Bacon were among the **Sorbonne**'s great teachers; St. Ignatius Loyola, Dante, Erasmus, and John Calvin were students here. As the **Sorbonne** grew in size and power, it frequently contradicted the authority of the French throne. During the Hundred Years' War (1337-1453), the university had the audacity to side with England against France. It recognized Henry V as king of France and cravenly sent one of its best prosecutors to Rouen to try Joan of Arc.

In 1642 Cardinal Richelieu (pictured in the left column) was elected grand master of the Sorbonne; he commissioned architect **Jacques Lemercier** to restore the dilapidated college buildings and erect a Jesuit-style church. During the Revolution the university closed down and remained empty until 1806, when Napoléon headquartered his **Académie de Paris** here. Following the May 1968 student-worker demonstration, the state unceremoniously rechristened the **Sorbonne** "Paris University IV," tossing it into the archipelago of institutions of higher learning scattered about the city.

Don't be shy about wandering down the university's long stone corridors or visiting the lecture halls, including the **Amphithéâtre Descartes** and the **Salle Doctorat.** (Unfortunately, the ornate **Grand Amphithéâtre** with its famous Puvis de Chavannes fresco is strictly reserved for ceremonies of state.) If you decide to enroll in a four-month crash course in French (as hundreds of North Americans do every year), you will come to know the dusty domed ceiling and stiff wooden benches of the **Amphithéâtre Richelieu** intimately. For an admission application, contact: Cours de Civilisation Française de la Sorbonne, Galerie Richelieu, 45-47 Rue des Ecoles, 75005 Paris. ♦ 45-47 Rue des Ecoles (between Rues St-Jacques and de la Sorbonne). 01.40.46.22.11. Métro: Cluny–La Sorbonne

Within the Sorbonne:

Ste-Ursule-de-la-Sorbonne Nothing of Cardinal Richelieu's **Sorbonne** remains save **Jacques Lemercier**'s chapel (1642), which was the first completely Roman-style building in 17th-century Paris. Richelieu is buried here. Above François Girardon's beautiful white marble tomb (1694), which depicts a half-recumbent Richelieu, his red cardinal's hat still hangs by a few slender threads from the ceiling. According to tradition, the hat will remain there until Richelieu's soul is freed from purgatory, at which time the threads will rot and the hat will drop. ♦ The chapel is closed to the public except during special exhibitions of stained glass, tapestry, and old manuscripts. Church services are held in the chapel on 21 October (the feast day of St. Ursula) and 4 December (the anniversary of Richelieu's death). Pl de la Sorbonne and Rue de la Sorbonne. 01.40.46.20.52

64 Brasserie Balzar ★★$$ Camus and Sartre had their last argument at this eatery, and James Thurber, Elliot Paul, William Shirer, and the old *Chicago Tribune* crowd gathered here for the beer and *choucroute* (sauerkraut) *garni*. The faithful clientele, old wood paneling and mirrors, and waiters in long white aprons create an ambiance that makes this one of the best brasseries in Paris. Getting a table for lunch is not difficult; dinner, however, is a different story. At night, especially after the theater, the vinyl banquettes are jammed with university professors, actors, editors, journalists, and aspiring poets dining on hearty fare such as *cervelas rémoulade* (sausage with mustard and herb dressing), cassoulet, and calf's liver, all washed down with a bottle of Bordeaux. It's worth a visit even if you only stop for a kir or coffee on the terrace.

When brasserie mogul Jean-Paul Bucher's Groupe Flo restaurant chain purchased this place in 1998, alarmed regulars banded together as "Les Amis du Balzar" to pressure him not to make any changes in the restaurant's staff, cuisine, or traditions. Bucher met with them and promised to comply. At press time, things were status quo, but Les Amis were keeping their eagle eyes out for any alteration that could possibly disrupt the unique spirit of the place. ♦ Daily breakfast, lunch, and dinner. Reservations recommended. 49 Rue des Ecoles (at Rue de la Sorbonne). 01.43.54.13.67. Métro: Cluny–La Sorbonne

65 Place de la Sorbonne This square, lined with cafes and lime trees, was a focal point of the student-worker protest of 1968. That year, on 10 and 11 May, police and students clashed violently, resulting in the injury of 400 participants and the arrest of hundreds of others. In the square stands a graffiti-marred statue of Auguste Comte (1798-1857), who was fired from his job as examiner in mathematics at the prestigious **Ecole Polytechnique** for his revolutionary ideas. Comte is best remembered as the founder of Positivism, a philosophy that strongly influenced John Stuart Mill. ♦ Métro: Cluny–La Sorbonne

On Place de la Sorbonne:

SELECT HOTEL

Select Hôtel $$$ Basic, comfortable, and conveniently located, this 68-room hotel is an ideal base for exploring the Latin Quarter. In 1937, 25-year-old Eric Sevareid checked into a 50-cents-a-night room here and headed off to work for the *Paris Herald*, soon accomplishing such feats as an interview with Gertrude Stein. There's no restaurant. ♦ No. 1 (at Rue Victor-Cousin). 01.46.34.14.80; fax 01.46.34.51.79; Select.Hotel@wanadoo.fr

CHEZ PENTO
Le Restaurant des Illustrateurs

66 Chez Pento ★★$$ Professors from the **Sorbonne** and nearby *lycées* frequent this 1930s-style bistro at midday, drawn by its reasonably priced lunch menu. At dinnertime, a less homogeneous crowd of Parisians settles into the faux-leather banquettes, choosing among such entrées as *magret de canard au vinaigre de cassis* (breast of duck with black currant vinegar) and quail with grapes in rum sauce. The *mousse de banane sur coulis de fruit rouge* (banana mousse with red fruit sauce) is a divine dessert. ♦ M-F lunch and dinner; Sa dinner. 9 Rue Cujas (at Rue Toullier). 01.43.26.81.54. RER: Luxembourg

67 Lycée Louis Le Grand Founded in 1550, this 1,500-student state-run high school numbers among its former pupils Molière, Voltaire, Robespierre, Hugo, Baudelaire, Pompidou, Giscard d'Estaing, Chirac, and Senghor (the ex-president of Senegal). It's closed to the public. ♦ 123 Rue St-Jacques (between Rue Cujas and Pl Marcelin-Berthelot). Métro: Cluny–La Sorbonne

68 Bibliothèque Ste-Geneviève This library, constructed in 1850 on the Place du Panthéon, occupies the site of the old **Collège Montaigu** where Erasmus, Calvin, and St. Ignatius Loyola studied. Architect **Henri Labrouste**'s revolutionary use of steel-frame-and-masonry construction (further elaborated in his other library, the **Bibliothèque Nationale,** which was finished in 1868) makes this building one of the most important 19th-century forerunners of modern architecture. While you may peek inside, the library itself is restricted to visitors with valid readers' cards except during limited touring hours. ♦ Tours: M-Sa 9-10AM by appointment only. Pl du Panthéon (between Rues Valette and Cujas). 01.44.41.97.97. Métro: Cardinal Lemoine

69 Rue Soufflot Looking down this street (named for the architect of the **Panthéon**), you will see two matching buildings: the **City Hall** of the fifth arrondissement to the left and the **University of Paris Faculty of Law** building to the right, with the **Luxembourg Gardens** and **Eiffel Tower** in the distance.

Eighteen feet below Rue Soufflot lie the remains of a Roman forum, discovered by 19th-century archaeologists; the ruins are not open to the public. ♦ Métros: Cardinal Lemoine, Maubert-Mutualité

On Rue Soufflot:

LES ∞ FONTAINES

Les Fontaines ★$$ This bustling bistro may look as if it lost its soul somewhere in all the cigarette smoke, but it serves surprisingly good, hearty fare for quite reasonable prices. Main courses include gigot (leg of lamb), sweetbread with mushrooms, venison with pepper sauce, and fillet of bass cooked in fifteen spices. Skip dessert. ♦ M-Sa lunch and dinner. No. 9 (at Rue Paillet). 01.43.26.42.80

70 Perraudin ★★$

Popular among **Sorbonne** students and their profs (come early to be assured a table), this bargain canteen has the archetypal bistro decor (lace curtains, red-and-white-checkered tablecloths, and Art Deco tile floors). On the menu is a panoply of *cuisine bourgeoise:* lamb and kidney beans, beef stew, au gratin potatoes, and rough red wines. ♦ M-F lunch and dinner; Sa dinner; closed the last two weeks of August. 157 Rue St-Jacques (between Rues des Fossés-St-Jacques and Soufflot). 01.46.33.15.75. RER: Luxembourg

---

"I got the impulse for doing things my way in Paris."

Alexander Calder

James Baldwin called Paris "the city where everyone loses his head, and his morals, lives through at least one *histoire d'amour* (love story), ceases quite to arrive anywhere on time, and thumbs his nose at the puritans—the city, in brief, where all become drunken on the fine old air of freedom."

71 Hôtel des Grands Hommes $$$ Comfortable and right in the heart of the Latin Quarter, this serene 32-room hotel boasts views of the **Panthéon** and the spire of **Notre-Dame** from some of its top-floor rooms. Surrealism may have had its start at this hotel, as André Breton and Philippe Soupault invented automatic writing here in 1919. There's no restaurant. ♦ 17 Pl du Panthéon (between Rues d'Ulm and Clotaire). 01.46.34.19.60; fax 01.43.26.67.32. Métro: Cardinal Lemoine

72 Panthéon When Louis XV recovered from gout at Metz in 1744, he vowed, in gratitude, to build a great temple honoring Saint Geneviève. The architect, **Jacques-Germain Soufflot,** chose to construct a Classical edifice based on the form of a Greek cross (339 feet long and 253 feet wide). **Soufflot,** who had been inspired by his trips to Italy, intended his building to resemble the Pantheon in Rome; however, the Paris version's lofty 52-pillar dome and handsome Corinthian colonnade wound up being much more reminiscent of St. Paul's Cathedral in London. Finished in 1850 by **Guillaume Rondelet,** one of **Soufflot's** students, the building was secularized into the **Temple of Fame,** a necropolis for the distinguished atheists of France. In its rather depressing crypt lie Voltaire, Rousseau, Victor Hugo (whose coffin passed a ceremonial night under the **Arc de Triomphe** and was carried here in the hearse of the poor), Gambetta, Emile Zola, Louis Braille (the 19th-century Frenchman who, blinded at age three, went on to invent the system of embossed dots that enables the sightless to read), Jean Jaurès (the celebrated leftist politician and orator who was assassinated in 1914), and Jean Moulin (the Resistance leader in World War II who was tortured to death during the Occupation). After the Revolution, the building's 42 tall windows were walled up, and today the monument looms over the square like a prison, grandiose and austere. ♦ Admission. Daily. Pl du Panthéon. 01.44.32.18.00. Métros: Cardinal Lemoine, Maubert-Mutualité

73 Lycée Henri IV Dating from Napoleonic times, this is one of the city's most prestigious high schools; Jean-Paul Sartre, the French novelist and playwright who refused the Nobel Prize for Literature in 1964, taught here. The school's most notable architectural feature is the **Tour de Clovis,** a Gothic belfry. The tower is all that remains of the **Abbaye Ste-Geneviève,** built by King Clovis after he was converted to Christianity by his wife, Clotilde of Burgundy, and Saint Geneviève herself. St. Thomas Aquinas (1225-74) taught at the abbey. The school is closed to the public. ♦ 23 Rue Clovis (at Rue Clotilde). Métro: Cardinal Lemoine

74 St-Etienne-du-Mont The combination of a Gothic rose window, triple Classical pediments, a medieval-style belfry, and a Renaissance dome in this church (see picture below) defies the laws of architectural purity. Its low-hanging chandeliers are a menace to anyone over six feet tall. And it must be the only church in Paris that closes for lunch. But *mon Dieu,* it's beautiful! Completed in 1626, the church is home to two graceful 16th-century spiral staircases, an extraordinary wooden pulpit (1650) shouldered by a grimacing Samson, and the only rood screen left in Paris, as well as the tombs of Pascal, Racine, and Marat. The church surrounds a shrine to Saint Geneviève, which Paris fathers have visited the first Sunday of each year for centuries. During the annual pilgrimage on 3 January 1857, while bowing to bless a child, Monseigneur Sibour, Archbishop of Paris, was stabbed to death by an unfrocked priest named Verger, who apparently objected to the ban on marriage that compelled priestly celibacy. A marker at the rear of the center aisle indicates the spot where the murder was committed. ◆ Pl Ste-Geneviève (between Rues Clovis and St-Etienne-du-Mont). 01.43.54.11.79. Métro: Cardinal Lemoine

75 Rue Clovis This short street is named after Clovis (AD 466-511), king of the Franks, who defeated the Romans at Soissons, ending the Roman Empire's dominion of Gaul and founding France. The narrow sidewalk on the south side of the street (near **No. 5**) is practically blocked by the ivy-draped ruins of King Philippe Auguste's fortified wall. It was originally 33 feet high, with a pathway on top, and was patrolled by city sentries (during the 19th century, a bronze regiment of these sentries was enshrined on the roof of the **City Hall** in the Place de l'Hôtel-de-Ville). Construction of the wall started in 1190, and it marked the city limits of Paris until the 17th century. The wall was pulled down when Louis XIV left Paris for **Versailles.** At the bottom of the hill at **No. 67** Rue du Cardinal-Lemoine is the house where Pascal died in 1662. ◆ Métro: Cardinal Lemoine

76 Rue Descartes This street carries the name of French mathematician and philosopher René "I-think-therefore-I-am" Descartes (1596-1650). He lived on Montagne Ste-Geneviève from 1613 to 1619 and again in 1625, but it is doubtful he ever lived on this street, which was then known as Rue des Bordels (street of brothels). Descartes emigrated to Sweden, where he died in the arms of Queen Christina. ◆ Métro: Cardinal Lemoine

On Rue Descartes:

No. 39 A plaque below the awning marks the house where poet Paul Verlaine (1844-96) died. Later there was a hotel at this same address; in 1922 Ernest Hemingway rented a room in the hostelry, which he later described in *A Moveable Feast.* It's now an apartment building with restaurants on the ground floor. ◆ Between Rues Thouin and Clovis

No. 47 At the end of the passageway through this historic 17th-century, half-timbered Norman-style house is a section of King Philippe Auguste's medieval city wall. Visitors may enter the passageway to see the wall. ◆ Between Rues Thouin and Clovis

St-Etienne-du-Mont

MICHAEL STORRINGS

77 Hôtel des Grandes Ecoles $$ Entering the courtyard here is like stepping into an Impressionist painting. This homey, family-run establishment comprises three ivy-covered houses set in a lush garden. Each of the 51 delightful rooms is decorated differently; ask for one with a garden view. On cool mornings, enjoy your croissants and *café au lait* in the charming lace-curtained breakfast room; in summer, you can eat amid the trees and flowers. (There's no restaurant.) Guests return year after year, so make reservations well in advance. Note: Reservations are taken from 2PM to 6PM only. ♦ 75 Rue du Cardinal-Lemoine (between Rues Rollin and Monge). 01.43.26.79.23; fax 01.43.25.28.15. Métros: Cardinal Lemoine, Place Monge

78 Place de la Contrescarpe In the Middle Ages, this dark, dangerous neighborhood lay outside King Philippe Auguste's city wall, beyond the moat, on the counter-escarpment. Since the days of Hemingway's *A Moveable Feast,* the public urinals and bus stop have disappeared, but a certain seediness remains. In winter, the local *clochards* (street people) still huddle over the heating duct and live off spoils from the markets and spare change from tourists. On summer weekends, harmless bikers in black leather congregate here. ♦ Métro: Place Monge

79 1 Place de la Contrescarpe The name **Maison de la Pomme de Pin** (Pine Cone Cabaret) is carved into the wall above the *boucherie* (butcher's shop) at this address. It marks the site of an old cafe frequented by satirist François Rabelais (1494-1553), author of *Pantagruel* and *Gargantua.* ♦ At Rue du Cardinal-Lemoine. Métro: Place Monge

80 La Chope ★$ Once a Hemingway haunt, this cafe is crowded with stout butchers drinking Calvados and students from the **Lycée Henri IV.** The bill of fare runs from chef's salads to banana splits. ♦ Daily breakfast, lunch, and dinner until 2AM. 2 Pl de la Contrescarpe (at Rue du Cardinal-Lemoine). 01.43.26.51.26. Métro: Place Monge

81 La Truffière ★★$$ Rich specialties from Périgord—the very antithesis of nouvelle cuisine—are served at this rustic eatery: black truffles, foie gras, and generous portions of goose and duck prepared in every conceivable fashion. Have an aperitif near the fireplace in the sitting room before proceeding to dinner. ♦ Tu-Su lunch and dinner. Reservations required. 4 Rue Blainville (between Rues Mouffetard and Tournefort). 01.46.33.29.82. Métros: Cardinal Lemoine, Place Monge

82 9 Rue Blainville The first public library in Paris was once housed in this building. ♦ At Rue Tournefort. Métro: Place Monge

83 Rue Mouffetard Leading out of the Place de la Contrescarpe is the 13th-century Rue Mouffetard. As you descend the narrow street, let your imagination take you back to the time when it was the main Roman road to the southeast, Lyon, and Italy. During the 12th century the area near the Bièvre River was filled with the country homes of rich Parisians. Within four centuries the Bièvre became a foul-smelling stream polluted by the animal wastes and dyes dumped by tanners, skinners, and the Flemish tapestry weavers from the **Gobelins** factory. In 1910 the river was covered over and incorporated into the sewer system.

Some guess that the name "Mouffetard" comes from *mouffette,* French for skunk; more likely it is a corruption of the Roman name of the hill it traverses, Mont Cétar. Prior to the Revolution the poor of Paris lived here in utter wretchedness. The unadorned mansard-roofed 17th-century houses that still line the street were built for ordinary folk. In the 1600s one French writer said more money could be found in one single house of the Faubourg St-Honoré than in all of those combined on the Rue Mouffetard.

Today, this thoroughfare is much beloved by gourmets and gourmands. The upper half of the street is filled with restaurants, many Greek, while a bustling pedestrian street market has convened at the bottom of the hill ever since 1350. The outdoor market section (see page 57) runs from Rue de l'Epée-de-Bois to Rue Censier, with the liveliest area near Rue Censier. ♦ Métros: Place Monge, Censier-Daubenton

83 12 Rue Mouffetard Above this charcuterie is an astounding painting that looks more suited to early Atlanta than Paris. *Le Nègre Joyeux* (The Happy Negro) portrays a stereotyped grinning black servant in striped pants serving tea to his mistress. ♦ At Rue Blainville. Métro: Place Monge

84 51-55 Rue Mouffetard In 1938 workers discovered 3,351 coins of 22-karat gold weighing 16.3 grams each and bearing the image of Louis XV hidden inside the wall here. The buried treasure, according to an accompanying note, belonged to Louis Nivelle, the royal counselor who mysteriously disappeared in 1757. ♦ At Rue Ortolan. Métro: Place Monge

85 Fontaine du Pot-de-Fer What appears to be an Italianate roadside dungeon is actually a restored historic monument. Behind this wall is one of the 14 fountains constructed in 1624 at the behest of Marie de Médicis. The fountain was designed to handle the overflow from the Gallo-Roman aqueduct that she had refurbished to supply water for her new palace in the **Luxembourg Gardens.** ♦ 60 Rue Mouffetard (at Rue du Pot-de-Fer). Métro: Place Monge

85 Chaussures Georges This dinky hundred-year-old shoe store run by a garrulous Armenian named Georges supplies the neighborhood butchers, fishmongers, and masons with their rubber boots and wool-lined French and Swedish sabots. These are shoes for function, not fantasy, proclaims Georges, who keeps all his footwear in 19th-century boxes with pewter handles. He also sells plain espadrilles—the real ones from the French Basque country, not Chinese imitations. ♦ Tu-Sa; Su 9:30AM-12:30PM. 64 Rue Mouffetard (between Rues Jean-Calvin and Pot-de-Fer). 01.47.07.16.66. Métro: Place Monge

86 10 Rue Vauquelin Working in a ramshackle ground-floor laboratory here at the **Sorbonne School of Physics and Chemistry** (which is now housed in a shiny new redbrick-and-glass building), Marie Curie and her husband, Pierre, discovered radium on 26 December 1898. The discovery of radioactivity not only earned them a Nobel prize in 1903 (the first of two for Marie) but triggered a fundamental rethinking of theoretical physics. A few months after their achievements, the quantum theory was published. ♦ Between Rue Claude-Bernard and Pl Lucien-Herr. Métro: Censier-Daubenton

87 Rue Mouffetard Market Among the gastronomic items purveyed at this outdoor market are mangoes, blood oranges, horse meat, wild boar, sea urchins, Colombian coffee, and hundreds of marvelously smelly cheeses. Take a self-guided tour: Just follow your nose. Be sure to go down the Rue Daubenton and Passage Passé-Simple to visit the flower shops and the stalls specializing in Auvergnat sausage. As you wander, remember the two cardinal rules of marketing in Paris: First, don't touch the produce; and second, the vendor, not the customer, is always right. ♦ Tu-Sa; Su 9AM-1PM, 4-7:30PM. Rue Mouffetard (between Rues Censier and de l'Epée-de-Bois). Métro: Censier-Daubenton

87 Le Mouffetard ★★$ The croissants, brioches, and fruit tarts are made fresh daily by the friendly Chartrain family, owners of the best cafe on the street. It's noisy, always crowded with vendors and students, and in winter the windows steam up, thanks to the animated conversation. ♦ Tu-Su breakfast, lunch, and dinner to 8:30PM; closed in July. 116 Rue Mouffetard (at Rue de l'Arbalète). 01.43.31.42.50. Métro: Censier-Daubenton

88 A la Bonne Source This bas-relief of two boys drawing water, whose title means "At the Good Spring," dates from the time of Henri IV (1589-1610). It's the oldest house sign on the street. ♦ 122 Rue Mouffetard (between Rues Edouard-Quénu and de l'Arbalète). Métro: Censier-Daubenton

89 Facchetti & Co. Charcuterie Fine Although it's a first-rate gourmet Italian delicatessen, the main reason for stopping here is not to buy pasta and parmesan but to admire the bucolic outdoor mural of peasants at work below a pair of stags and wild boars. ♦ Tu-Sa 8AM-1PM, 4-8PM; Su 8AM-2PM. 134 Rue Mouffetard (between Rues Edouard-Quénu and de l'Arbalète). 01.43.31.40.00. Métro: Censier-Daubenton

90 St-Médard Built in 1773, this rustic village church is an architectural conglomeration of Flamboyant Gothic and Renaissance styles and has a story for every predilection. French literature majors may remember this as the church in which Jean Valjean accidentally encounters Javert in Victor Hugo's *Les Misérables.* Trade unionists point out that the church was turned into the **Temple of Labor** during the Revolution. Art historians will recall the notorious painting of Saint Geneviève, which for centuries was erroneously ascribed to Watteau. And the occultists in the crowd will appreciate a most famous corpse buried here, that of a church deacon named François Paris, a saintly young Jansenist who died in 1727. Rumors of miraculous cures drew huge crowds of hysterical convulsionaries to his grave within two years of his death. (The frenzied gatherings were finally outlawed by Louis XV in 1732, but Paris's tomb remains beneath the unmarked stones of what is now the **Chapel of the Virgin.**) The majority of the church's construction was financed by fines imposed on Protestants; the money ran out while the vaulted ceiling was being installed, so it was completed in wood. At least that's how the story goes. ♦ 141 Rue Mouffetard (at Sq St-Médard). 01.44.08.87.00. Métro: Censier-Daubenton

Au Petit Marguery

91 Au Petit Marguery ★★$$ This lively 1900s-style neighborhood bistro presents such hearty dishes as *cassolette de gros escargots de Bourgogne* (Burgundy snails in ramekin) and venison (in season). ♦ Tu-Sa lunch and dinner; closed in August. Reservations recommended. 9 Blvd de Port-Royal (between Blvd Arago and Rue Pascal). 01.43.31.58.59. Métro: Les Gobelins

92 Manufacture des Gobelins (Gobelins Tapestry Factory) The factory, the avenue, and the neighborhood all take their name from the brothers Jean and Philibert Gobelin, who in the 15th century established their famous dye works along the stinking Bièvre River. Although the name "Gobelins" has become synonymous with tapestry, the two brothers never wove a thread. Their claim to fame in the tapestry world was making a special scarlet dye. In 1662 Jean-Baptiste Colbert, Louis XIV's famous minister, persuaded the king to take over the Gobelins property. There, under the management of court painter Charles Le Brun, Colbert assembled a crafts colony of about 250 Flemish weavers. His goal was twofold: to compete with Flanders's tapestry industry and to cover the vast expanse of walls in the Sun King's sumptuous palace at **Versailles.** (Within Gobelins's first courtyard stands a marble 1907 statue of Le Brun by Cardier, followed in the next courtyard by an 1894 statue of his boss, Colbert, by Aube.) In time, the tapestry factory became so celebrated that Marie Antoinette and Louis XVI (in 1790) and the pope (in 1895) paid personal visits to the humble workshops.

Today scores of weavers at the factory manufacture tapestries using ancient techniques, working on century-old wooden looms. Using wools from a palette of 14,920 colors, weavers may spend 2 to 4 years completing woven panels, the designs of which are based on modern paintings by artists such as Matisse, Picasso, and Miró. Three days a week, the state-owned mills offer 75-minute guided tours of the tapestry factory and the allied **Savonnerie** (carpet) and **Beauvais** (horizontal loom weaving) workshops, a treat for anyone interested in weaving and crafts. You can visit the studios where weavers, trained from the age of 16, work quietly, occasionally glancing up at mirrors before them to view the reverse side of the tapestry. If you can't get to the factory, you can see Gobelins tapestries hanging at **Versailles** as well as other places reserved for the privileged: the **Paris Opéra,** the **National Library,** the **Elysée Palace,** and the **Luxembourg Palace.** ♦ Admission. Tours: Tu-Th 2:45PM. To arrange group tours, call Caisse Nationale des Monuments Historiques at 01.44.61.21.69. 42 Ave des Gobelins (between Rue de Croulebarbe and Blvd Arago). 01.44.08.52.00. Métro: Les Gobelins

92 Mobilier National (National Storehouse) What institution is as supersecret as the French CIA, answers directly to the president, and is littered with Napoléon-era love seats and andirons? Answer: the **Mobilier National,** France's national attic. This singular government entity was created in 1667 by Colbert as a royal storehouse when he was transforming the **Gobelins Tapestry Factory.** It is the state's interior decorator, responsible for furnishing government ministries and embassies with everything from inkwells to curtains. The institution, which at one time also kept the crown jewels, is quartered within the **Gobelins** complex in an unremarkable redbrick structure designed by **Auguste Perret.** In 1964 André Malraux, then Minister of Culture, offered studio space in the storehouse to contemporary French furniture designers who would be willing to create and sell their prototypes to French manufacturers. Thus, the **Mobilier National** takes credit for the boldly modern furniture used in former president Georges Pompidou's office at he **Elysée Palace.** You can pass by this warehouse on the **Gobelins** tour, but it's off-limits to the public. ♦ Rue Berbier-du-Mets (between Rues de Croulebarbe and Emile-Deslandres). Métro: Les Gobelins

93 La Tuile à Loup Run by the affable Marie-France and Michel Joblin, this crowded shop specializes in French regional arts and crafts. The shelves are stocked with earthenware dishes, hand-carved wooden bowls, toys by well-known French artist Roland Roure, and a vast selection of books on French folklore, rural architecture, and ecology. ♦ M by appointment only; Tu-Sa. 35 Rue Daubenton (between Rues Monge and Mouffetard). 01.47.07.28.90. Métro: Censier-Daubenton

94 Place Monge This square is named for the mathematician Gaspard Monge (1746-1818), who in 1794 founded the prestigious **Ecole Polytechnique.** Near the bustling small farmers' market is the old barracks of the Garde Républicaine, whose famous horse guards parade up the Champs-Elysées on Bastille Day, 14 July. ♦ Market: W, F, Su 7AM-1PM. Métro: Place Monge

95 Arènes de Lutèce (Roman Arena) After the **Roman Baths** at the **Musée de Cluny** (see page 49), this first-century amphitheater is the city's most important Roman ruin. Accidentally discovered (and partially destroyed) in 1869, the 325-by-425-foot oval once seated 15,000 spectators. With its surrounding gardens and benches, the arena provides an island of tranquillity for young parents pushing strollers and old men playing *boules* (boccie); in summer, campy medieval jousts take place here. It's a nice spot for a picnic lunch of sourdough rye bread and charcuterie from the Place Monge market. ♦ Pl Emile-Mâle and Rue de Navarre. Métro: Place Monge

96 Hôtel Jardin des Plantes $$ Guests of this tranquil 33-room hotel in a quiet neighborhood can enjoy breakfast surrounded by flowers on the rooftop terrace. Many of the rooms have views of the magnificent botanical garden nearby. It's a member of the Timotel chain. ♦ 5 Rue Linné (between Rues Lacépède and des Arènes). 01.47.07.06.20; fax 01.47.07.62.74; www.timhotel.fr. Métro: Place Monge

97 La Mosquée de Paris This Moorish ensemble of soaring minarets, pink marble fountains, and crescent moons is the oldest mosque in France. In gratitude for North African support during World War I, France gave the French Arab community the funds to build the mosque. It was constructed in 1926 by Arab artisans and three French architects. Arabs from the poor Belleville and Barbès quarters gather at this enclave of Islam to read the Koran at the **Institut Musulman.** During Ramadan, hundreds of people kneel facing Mecca and pray to Allah on a sea of Persian carpets spread beneath the mosque's delicately carved dome. Nearby, behind a dark curtain, the women intone their prayers. While unfortunately brief, the guided tour of the building, central courtyard, and Moorish garden offers a worthwhile introduction to Islam. You may leave feeling as though you've passed the time in Riyadh or Istanbul. ♦ Admission. M-Th, Sa-Su. Pl du Puits-de-l'Ermite and Rue Georges-Desplas. 01.45.35.97.33/34/35. Métro: Place Monge

RESTAURANT • SALON DE THÉ • HAMMAM • SOUK

LA MOSQUÉE
de

98 Le Restaurant de la Mosquée ★$ Flaky Moroccan pastries, sweet mint tea, and Turkish coffee are served during the summer on a white patio shaded by leafy fig trees. In winter, warm up with tea in a quiet lounge adjoining the *hammam* (Turkish steam bath). No alcohol is served. ♦ Daily breakfast, lunch, and dinner until 10PM; closed in August. 2 Rue Daubenton (at Rue Geoffroy-St-Hilaire). 01.43.31.38.20. Métros: Censier-Daubenton, Place Monge

99 Jardin des Plantes It was begun in 1626 by Louis XIII as a royal medicinal herb garden planted on an old rubbish heap. Today the 74-acre botanical garden hosts a floral orgy of peonies, irises, roses, geraniums, and dahlias from April through October. The garden, surrounded by streets named after great French naturalists and botanists (Jussieu, Geoffroy St-Hilaire, and Buffon), contains a pedestal inscribed to the French scientist Lamarck, the author of the doctrine of evolution (tough luck, Charles Darwin), and another honoring Chevreul, the director of the **Gobelins** dye factory who lived to 103 and whose color-spectrum research informed the Impressionist painters.

Within the park is France's oldest public zoo, **Le Ménagerie,** which has a rather pathetic history. Established shortly after the Revolution to display survivors from the **Royal Menagerie** at **Versailles** (one hartebeest, one zebra, one rhinoceros, and a sheepdog), it was originally called the **People's Democratic Zoo.** In 1795 the first elephants arrived, in 1805 the bear pit opened, and in 1827 an Egyptian prince contributed a giraffe. The zoo grew in size and popularity until the Siege of Paris in 1870 and 1871, when the poor beasts were eaten. For several weeks, it is said, the privileged of Paris dined on elephant steaks the size of manhole covers. The zoo has never recovered from the slaughter, and conditions remain on the shabby side (animals are still jailed in Second Empire pavilions, and rumors of stray cats being fed to snakes and reptiles proliferate). Children still seem to love it, though.

Legend holds that the park's famous Cedar of Lebanon, now 40 feet in circumference, traveled in 1735 as a seedling in the hat of naturalist Bernard de Jussieu, who had carefully preserved it during confinement as a prisoner of war. But in truth, it was given to him after his release.

The park's **Museum of Natural History** has five departments (Paleontology, Paleobotany, Mineralogy, Entomology, and Zoology) and it possesses one of the world's richest mineral collections and some of the oldest fossilized insects on earth. The **Grande Galerie** houses a superb display on the evolution of life. Highlights include a giant whale skeleton, stuffed African Savannah animals, and an extinct and endangered species exhibit. ♦ Admission to zoo and museum. Garden and zoo: daily. Museums and greenhouses: M, W-Su. Bounded by Pl Valhubert, Quai St-Bernard, and Rues Geoffroy-St-Hilaire, Buffon, and Cuvier. 01.40.79.30.00. Métros: Gare d'Austerlitz, Jussieu, Place Monge

---

Restaurants/Clubs: Red   Hotels: Blue
Shops/♥ Outdoors: Green   Sights/Culture: Black

The City of Light on the Big Screen

With its dramatic buildings, beautiful boulevards, and enduring air of romance, mystery, and sophistication, Paris has an undeniable star quality. It's little wonder, then, that the city has been the setting for scores of films from the early days of the motion-picture industry to the present. The following are some of the movies in which Paris plays a featured role.

A Bout de Souffle (Breathless; 1959) One of the first and most influential of the French New Wave films, directed by Jean-Luc Godard, tells the story of a young car thief who kills a policeman and goes on the run with his American girlfriend. This classic stars Jean-Paul Belmondo and Jean Seberg.

An American in Paris (1951) Directed by Vincente Minnelli and featuring music by George Gershwin, this enthusiastic MGM musical stars Gene Kelly and Leslie Caron. The sets of the fabulous ballet sequence are inspired by famous French paintings.

Belle de Jour (1967) In this surreal Luis Buñuel classic, Catherine Deneuve plays a bored *haute-bourgeoisie* Paris housewife with disturbing sexual fantasies who goes to work in a high-class brothel.

Camille (1937) Based on the play by Alexandre Dumas *fils,* this classic MGM flick starring Greta Garbo shows Belle Epoque Paris through the misty eyes of Hollywood when a fatally ill courtesan falls for an innocent young man (Robert Taylor) who loves her.

Casque d'Or (1952) Simone Signoret, Serge Reggiani, and Claude Dauphin are featured in this beautiful and tragic romance, set in the Paris slums of 1898.

Charade (1963) The city becomes the perfect setting for Audrey Hepburn and Cary Grant to fall in love in this comedy-thriller directed by Stanley Donen.

Diva (1981) In Jean-Jacques Beineix's stylish, off-beat thriller, a young opera fan's obsession with a diva (Wilhelmina Wiggins Fernandez) gets him mixed up with a bizarre bunch of underworld characters. An aria was filmed at the **Bouffes du Nord** theater, and there are motor-scooter chases that give viewers a good look at the streets of Paris.

Forget Paris (1995) Debra Winger plays an **Air France** employee in Paris who helps Billy Crystal find his lost luggage (his father's body) and fulfill his father's dream of being buried in Normandy. This offbeat comedy provides some memorable Paris streetscapes.

Frantic (1988) A Roman Polanski thriller features Harrison Ford as a North American doctor in Paris who becomes embroiled with Arab terrorists while hunting for his kidnapped wife. Lost luggage plays a key role in this one too.

French Can-Can (1955) This Jean Renoir film explores how the can-can was launched in Paris nightclubs and features great scenes of ramshackle Paris.

French Kiss (1995) A cutesy romantic comedy set in Paris and the South of France costars Meg Ryan as a North American hunting down her fiancé, who has run off with a young French woman, and Kevin Kline as the faux-French taxi driver who befriends her.

Funny Face (1957) Fred Astaire, Audrey Hepburn, and Kay Thompson star in the story of a fashion editor and photographer who discover a fashion model working in a bookshop. Great music, dancing, and art direction are all here.

Hôtel du Nord (1938) People with problems congregate at a small hotel on the **Canal St-Martin** in Paris; with Annabella, Louis Jouvet, Jean-Pierre Aumont, and Arletty.

Irma La Douce (1963) Shirley Maclaine and Jack Lemmon star in this saucy Billy Wilder film about a Paris policeman who falls for a prostitute and becomes her pimp. The street and cafe scenes offer classic images of Paris.

Last Tango in Paris (1972) Marlon Brando stars in this Bernardo Bertolucci film as a middle-age man who has a doomed love affair with a young Frenchwoman. The most memorable scenes take place in a Paris bathtub.

Les 400 Coups (The 400 Blows; 1959) In François Truffaut's autobiographical film, an alienated 12-year-old boy (Jean-Pierre Léaud) unloved by his selfish parents grows up wild in the city, gets thrown into a reformatory, and escapes at the end. The film gives a vivid impression of working-class Paris street life.

Les Amants (The Lovers; 1958) This Louis Malle film starring Jeanne Moreau and Alain Cuny tells the story of the secret life in Paris of a rich wife who has a passionate romance with a young man.

Les Amants du Pont-Neuf (The Lovers of the Pont-Neuf; 1991) An artist who fears she is going blind ends up on the **Pont-Neuf** with other down-and-out characters. This movie, directed by Léo Carax and starring Juliette Binoche, Denis Lavant, and Klaus-Michael Gruber, was one of the most expensive French films ever made, mainly because the City of Paris refused to let the film be shot on the Pont Neuf, and the producers had to build an elaborate set re-creating the bridge and its surroundings elsewhere.

Les Enfants du Paradis (1945) A street mime falls in love with an elusive young woman whose problems with other men keep them apart. Jean-Louis Barrault, Arletty, and Pierre Brasseur star in this epic melodrama set in the world of the mid–19th-century popular theater in Paris, considered by some to be the greatest French film of all time.

Paris Blues (1961) Two North American jazz musicians in Paris (Paul Newman and Sidney Poitier) fall in love with two tourists (Joanne Woodward and Diahann Carroll) in this Martin Ritt film. It has a great Duke Ellington score, fine black-and-white location shooting, and convincing performances all around.

Paris Underground (1945) Two women (Constance Bennett and Grace Fields) who are caught in Paris when the Nazis invade continue their Resistance activities.

Paris Vu Par. . . (Six in Paris; 1965) Six short stories, set in different parts of Paris, are told by six French New Wave directors.

Paris When It Sizzles (1963) A film writer and his secretary try out several script ideas together. William Holden and Audrey Hepburn star in the Hollywood remake of the 1952 French film *La Fête à Henriette.*

Phantom of the Opera (1925) This silent-film classic is the story of a disfigured man (Lon Chaney) who abducts the prima donna of the **Paris Opéra** (Mary Philbin) and takes her to his lair in the sewers below.

Playtime (1968) Barbara Dennek, Jacqueline Lecomte, and Henri Piccoli appear in this Jacques Tati romp in which Hulot and a group of North American tourists are bewildered by life in an airport, a business block, and a restaurant.

Prêt-à-Porter (Ready to Wear; 1995) Robert Altman's satirical look at the world of haute couture includes performances by Julia Roberts, Marcello Mastroianni, Sophia Loren, and Lauren Bacall. Paris, the fashion capital of the world, serves as the backdrop for this parody.

Round Midnight (1986) Real-life sax great Dexter Gordon turns in a brilliant performance in Bernard Tavernier's film about an alcoholic North American jazz musician in Paris who is befriended by a French fan (François Cluzet), with a fine studio recreation of jazz-crazy **St-Germain-des-Prés** in the 1950s and an Oscar-winning score by Herbie Hancock, who appears in the film.

Sabrina (1954) Audrey Hepburn plays a chauffeur's daughter who is wooed by Humphrey Bogart and William Holden. A scene in which Hepburn takes a cooking class at the **Cordon Bleu** inspired an actual course at the famous culinary institution.

Seventh Heaven (1927) In this silent film, a Paris sewer worker (Charles Farrell) shelters a street waif (Janet Gaynor), marries her, and then goes to war.

Subway (1985) Luc Besson directs Isabelle Adjani and Christophe Lambert in this stylish comedy/melodrama about an eccentric man on the run from thugs who takes refuge overnight in the platforms and tunnels of the Paris métro.

The Trial (1962) Kafka's nightmarish story of a man who is tried and convicted for an unspecified crime is directed by Orson Welles and features Welles, Jeanne Moreau, and Anthony Perkins. The old **Gare d'Orsay** (now the **Musée d'Orsay**) is the set for a huge office space with endless rows of desks.

100 Musée de Sculpture en Plein Air
This outdoor sculpture museum, built in 1980, was once the site of Henri IV's bathing beach. Here the king would pour water from a royal hat over the young Dauphin as the preamble to a swimming lesson. Today this long grassy lawn on the banks of the Seine is dotted with large modern sculptures in stone, wood, and steel, and there are benches for quiet contemplation of the river and a playground for children. But don't come here after dark; a less desirable brand of exhibitionist prowls then. ♦ Quai St-Bernard (between Pl Valhubert and Pont de Sully). No phone. Métros: Gare d'Austerlitz, Jussieu

INSTITUT DU MONDE ARABE

101 Institut du Monde Arabe (Arab Institute) Opened in 1987, this sociocultural institution was established to promote relations between France and the Arab world. It contains a library, exhibition space, and a top-floor restaurant that serves Moroccan specialties (see below). The architect, **Jean Nouvel**, who received the

Agha Kahn prize for his design, has given Islamic architectural elements a stunning space-age interpretation. Notice **Nouvel**'s treatment of the south facade: The wall is made up of thousands of cameralike shutters that open and close automatically according to the sun's brightness, thus regulating the amount of light let inside the building. ♦ Tu-Su. 1 Rue des Fossés-St-Bernard (at Quai St-Bernard). 01.40.51.38.38; www.imarabe.org. Métros: Jussieu, Cardinal Lemoine

Within L'Institut du Monde Arabe:

Le Ziryab ★★$$ The river view from this rooftop Moroccan restaurant is better than that of **La Tour d'Argent**—at a fraction of the price. Start a meal with one of the hot and cold hors d'oeuvres, such as marinated salmon or mini–chicken brochettes. Move on to *zaalouk d'aubergines* (eggplant pâté) or *kefta* (a mixture of minced beef and lamb with seven spices), and end the repast with an assortment of Oriental pastries and mint tea. Linger at a table on the terrace on a balmy summer evening. ♦ Tu-Su lunch and dinner. Reservations recommended. Ninth floor. 01.40.46.84.62

The life expectancy of French women is the highest in Europe: 82.1 years.

St-Germain

Hôtel des
Invalides

Place
Vauban

Place
Alphonse-
Deville

Tour
Montparnasse

N

km
mi   1/16   1/8   1/4
      1/8

Quai Anatole-France

Rue de Lille

Rue de l'Université

Rue de Constantine

Ave. du M.-Gallieni

Rue de Bourgogne

Rue de Grenelle

Rue de Varenne

Blvd. des Invalides

Rue de Soufferino

Rue de Bellechasse

Blvd. St-Germain

Rue de Poitiers

Rue de Verneuil

Rue de l'Université

Rue de St-Simon

Rue du Bac

Blvd. Raspail

Rue St-
Guillaume

Rue Barbet-de-Jouy

Rue Vaneau

Rue de Babylone

Rue du Bac

Rue Velpeau

Ave. de Breteuil

Ave. de Villars

Rue d'Estrées

Rue Monsieur

Blvd. des Invalides

Rue Oudinot

Rue de Sèvres

Rue d'Assas

Ave. Duquesne

Rue Eblé

Rue Masseran

Rue Duroc

Rue M.-de-la-
Sizeranne

Ave. de Saxe

Rue de Sèvres

Blvd. du Montparnasse

Rue Mayet

Rue St-Romain

Rue du Cherche-Midi

Rue St-Placide

Rue du Regard

Rue J.-Ferrandi

Rue Notre-Dame-
des-Champs

Rue Littré

Ave. du Maine

Rue de Rennes

Rue du Montparnasse

Blvd. Pasteur

Rue de Vaugirard

Rue Falguière

Rue Armand-
Moisant

Rue de l'Arrivée

Rue du Départ

1 2 3 4 5 6 7 8 9
10 11 12 13 14 15 16 17 18 19 20
21 22 23 24 25 26 27 28 29 30
39 40 41
73 74

St-Germain

The tree-lined **Boulevard St-Germain** originates near the tip of Ile St-Louis, then traverses the heart of literary Paris, and finally arrives back at the Seine at the **Pont de la Concorde** in the noble faubourg fashionable during the reign of Louis XV. This is the home of the **Académie Française**, the world's oldest cafe **(Le Procope)**, prestigious publishing houses, bookbinders, and a conclave of intellectuals' watering holes where Fitzgerald, Hemingway, and other North American scriveners wrote or drank in the Jazz Age (1920s and 1930s), and where Sartre, and Camus and company made existentialism a household name in the 1950s.

The St-Germain quarter is also the home of the inviting **Jardin du Luxembourg** (Luxembourg Gardens), the **Ecole des Beaux-Arts** (School of Fine Arts), and a plethora of art galleries. In this neighborhood, the painter Corot walked the quays; Manet lived on **Rue Bonaparte;** and Delacroix resided in the **Place de Furstemberg**. Ingres, Baudelaire, and Wagner stayed on **Quai Voltaire**, and Picasso painted *Guernica* on **Rue des Grands-Augustins**.

This St-Germain itinerary covers the boulevard's most interesting portion, in the vicinity of the church of **St-Germain-des-Prés**, site of the remains of the city's oldest abbey. The route leads down alleys where bookshops, poster stores, antiques dealers, and picture restorers do business side by side with chic dress shops and cafes frequented by students. In the 1990s, the high fashion industry invaded the old stomping ground of Sartre, de Beauvoir, and Camus. Some might bemoan the *quartier*'s drift from Sartre to the sartorial, but the new trend has reenergized an area that had been drifting into lethargy. And there are still plenty of places left that keep the myth of St-Germain alive.

Start at the **Musée d'Orsay**, a former Belle Epoque train station that is now devoted to art and culture from 1848 to World War I. En route to the Boulevard St-Germain, take **Rue du Bac** and stop at **Deyrolle**, an amusing taxidermy shop. On the boulevard is **Madeleine Gély**'s handmade-umbrella shop, an essential stop during those frequent April downpours. Consider having an early lunch and watching the world go by at one of the area's literary shrines: **Brasserie Lipp**, **Café de Flore**, or **Les Deux Magots**. When you can't eat another bite of **Brasserie Lipp**'s *choucroute* (sauerkraut) with boiled ham, pork, and sausages, visit the shaded Place de Furstemberg to look for the old studio of Delacroix, browse for antiques along **Rue Jacob**, or tour the African art galleries along **Rue de Seine**.

Also on this tour is the narrow **Cour du Commerce-St-André**, where the guillotine was invented and where the firebrand Marat had his printing press. You'll pass **Le Procope**, where Voltaire and Robespierre were among the regulars, and the **Rue de Buci**, the street market where Picasso bought his sausages. From the **Odéon**, where Sylvia Beach had her famous bookshop, nature lovers will want to detour through the **Jardin du Luxembourg**, one of Queen Marie de Médicis's legacies to the city. Those nostalgic for the Paris of the North American expatriates in the 1920s can proceed to neighboring **Montparnasse** and visit favorite haunts of writers and artists of that period that are still going strong, such as the **La Closerie des Lilas**, **Le Sélect**, and **La Coupole**.

At day's end, consider dining at a classic, Old World bistro such as **Allard**. Or catch an early Cary Grant film at the **Action Christine**, then dine in the splendor of **Jacques Cagna** around the corner on Rue des Grands-Augustins. After dinner, wander toward the river, stopping en route at **La Palette**, where you can have a beer at the bar, and afterward take a midnight stroll along the pedestrian bridge **Pont des Arts**, with its superb view of the Ile de la Cité, and ponder the magnificence that is Paris at night.

1 Hôtel D'Orsay $$ Forty-seven small, pleasant rooms with Oriental rugs, pastel walls, and floral wallpaper are available here at the former **Hôtel Solférino,** which was enlarged, renovated, and renamed in 1998. There's also a veranda where you can enjoy breakfast (but no restaurant). ◆ 93 Rue de Lille (between Rue de Solférino and Blvd St-Germain). 01.47.05.85.54; fax 01.45.55.51.16; espfranc@MicroNet.fr. Métros: Solférino, Assemblée Nationale

2 Bonpoint This pricey store offers exquisite couture for the little darlings in your life. Nearby on the same street are two sister stores—No. 65 for children's shoes and No. 86 for maternity gifts and junior fashions. ◆ M-Sa. 67 Rue de l'Université (at Rue de Solférino). 01.45.55.63.70. Métro: Solférino

3 Palais de la Légion d'Honneur Built by **Pierre Rousseau** for German prince Frédéric III de Salm-Kyrbourg in 1786, this palace is architecturally the most significant Louis XVI building in Paris. In 1804 Napoléon acquired it for the Légion d'Honneur. The *légion* was a society started by Napoléon to honor men, and later women, for outstanding service to France. Members may wear a woven bud of red wool stitched to their left lapel. The palace houses the **Musée de la Légion d'Honneur et des Ordres de Chevalerie,** which exhibits medals, insignia, and decorations related to the history of the *légion.* Included in the collection is Napoléon's Légion d'Honneur medal and his sword and breastplate. The California Palace of the Legion of Honor in San Francisco, which has an extensive collection of French art, is based on the palace here. ◆ Admission. Museum: Tu-Su 2-5PM. 2 Rue de Bellechasse (at Quai Anatole-France). 01.40.62.84.25. RER: Musée d'Orsay

4 Musée d'Orsay What was once an imposing turn-of-the-century train station, the **Gare d'Orsay,** is now a magnificent showcase for 19th-century art and culture. Opened in 1986, this museum houses the art that chronologically links the **Louvre** collections with those of the **Pompidou Center,** bridging the end of Romanticism and the origins of modern art. The museum transports visitors back to a time of grace and wit with the works of such geniuses as writer Henry James, actress Sarah Bernhardt, and artists Edouard Manet and James McNeill Whistler.

The collection (see floor plan at right) includes all the Impressionist paintings formerly in the **Jeu de Paume;** the post-Impressionist and Nabi works from the **Palais de Tokyo** (among them are 400 paintings by Odilon Redon); and

selected works that were formerly in the **Louvre,** including paintings and sculptures by artists who were born after 1820, such as Courbet and Millet, and various late paintings by Delacroix, Corot, Ingres, and the Barbizon landscape painters.

The Quai d'Orsay site was once occupied by the **Palais d'Orsay,** a government building that was devastated (as were the **Hôtel de Ville** and the **Tuileries Palace**) by the May 1871 fires set by the Commune at the end of France's tragic civil war period. The Orléans Rail Company bought the property and hired **Victor Laloux** (1850-1937), the architect who had rebuilt the **Hôtel de Ville,** to design a railway station and hotel. Construction lasted from September 1898 to July 1900 and was accomplished by a crew of 380 men working in round-the-clock shifts.

Upper Level

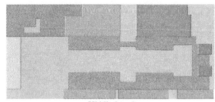

Middle Level

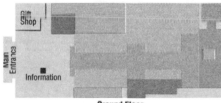

Ground Floor

Painting	Bookshop
Sculpture	Café des Hauteurs
Decorative Arts	Art Nouveau
Architecture	Restaurant
Temporary Exhibitions	

At one time, 200 trains a day used the **Gare d'Orsay,** but the growing electrification and lengthening of trains made its short platforms obsolete in the late 1930s. Over the years, the station took on other functions. Prisoners of war were garrisoned here after the Liberation; General de Gaulle announced his return to power at the **Gare d'Orsay** hotel on 19 May 1958; Orson Welles made a film version of the Franz Kafka book *The Trial* here in 1962; and in 1970, Bernardo Bertolucci used it as a setting for part of his film *The Conformist.*

As early as 1961, plans to raze the station and build a modern 870-room hotel complex were nearly realized; **Le Corbusier** even competed for the design job. But in 1971 the station was declared a historic landmark, and eight years later **ACT Architecture** (a group of three associated architects: **Pierre Colboc, Renaud Bardon,** and **Jean-Paul Philippo**) was selected to renovate the building for use as a museum. The famed Italian designer Gae Aulenti planned the interior.

The famous French Impressionist collection is displayed on the ground and upper levels of the museum. The term "Impressionism" was coined by a derisive critic after seeing Monet's painting *Impression: Sunrise.* The name stuck, and the movement effected as dramatic a change in the course of art history as the Renaissance had. Instead of choosing heroes, mythic deities, or saints for their subject matter, the Impressionists painted ordinary people in cafes, as well as trains chugging into Gare St-Lazare, with vivid color and undisguised brush strokes.

The museum collection also features paintings by more than 36 North American artists, including John Singer Sargent, William Merritt Chase, Robert Henri, Winslow Homer, and Henry Ossawa Tanner, many of whom worked and studied in Paris. And this is where you can visit that emblem of North American art, *Arrangement in Grey and Black: The Artist's Mother,* by Whistler. A restaurant, rooftop cafe, bookstore, and 380-seat auditorium round out the museum complex. ♦ Admission. Tu-W, F-Su; Th 10AM-9:45PM; closed Christmas and 1 May. 1 Rue de Bellechasse (at Quai Anatole-France). 01.40.49.48.14, recorded information 01.45.49.11.11. RER: Musée d'Orsay

Within the Musée d'Orsay:

Ground Level This floor features painting, sculpture, photography, and decorative arts dating from 1848 to 1870. The front of the gallery contains sculptures by Rude, Préault, and Pradier, and a great animal bronze by Barye. At the rear of the gallery stands *The Dance* by Carpeaux. Rooms at the end of the courtyard are dedicated to the **Paris Opéra** and its architect, **Charles Garnier.**

To the right of the central court are paintings by Romantics such as Delacroix and Ingres, as well as works by the eclectics and symbolists, including Puvis de Chavannes and Gustave Moreau, along with the pre-1870 work of Edgar Degas. To the left of the courtyard are works by Realists, including Daumier, Corot, Millet, and the Barbizon painters. They are neighbors to the masterpieces of Edouard Manet, such as *Olympia* and *Déjeuner sur L'Herbe,* and to the pre-1870 work of Monet, Bazille, and Renoir.

Upper Level To follow the chronological order of the artwork, ascend from the ground floor to the museum's upper level, where the light streaming through the glass roof shows off the post-1870 flowering of Impressionism. Here Manet, Degas, Monet, and Renoir are joined by Sisley, Pissarro, van Gogh, and Cézanne. Nearby, works by such post-Impressionists as Seurat, Signac, Cross, and Gauguin are shown with art from the Pont Aven and Nabi schools, including Denis, Bonnard, Vallotton, and Vuillard. Henri Rousseau's famous *Charmeuse de Serpents* and pieces by Toulouse-Lautrec are found here. There's also a special room devoted to graphic arts and photography from 1880 to 1914, including the works of early photographers Atget, Emerson, Steichen, and Stieglitz. On a landing between the upper and middle levels are works by Nadar, Legray, Baldus, Carroll, and Cameron.

Middle Level The terraces above the central court display the sculpture of Rodin, Maillol, and Bourdelle. The rooms along the Seine have figures created during the Third Republic, including works by symbolists Burne-Jones and Delville. Eight rooms are devoted to the era of Art Nouveau, with pieces by the Belgians Horta and van de Velde, by Gallé and Majorelle of the Nancy School, Guimard, and Thonet, the dean of bentwood furniture. On the Rue de Lille side are the 20th-century paintings of Klimt and Matisse, heralding the advent of modern art. Also on this level is an exhibition showing the evolution of the film industry.

Restaurant du Musée d'Orsay ★$$ Housed in the dining room of the old hotel on the museum's middle level, the restaurant is an ornately gilded period piece that has a ceiling covered with painted deities by Gabriel Ferrier, winner of the 1872 *Prix de Rome.* The decor may be the main attraction here, but the traditional French *menu du jour* is honest and inexpensive, and the 15-dish Nordic buffet is a real bargain at 96 francs. ♦ Tu-W, F-Su lunch and afternoon tea; Th dinner; closed Christmas and 1 May. 01.45.49.47.03

Café des Hauteurs ★$ Sharing space with Degas's pastels on the upper level, this airy cafe serves salads, snacks, light meals, and liquid refreshments. Service is cafeteria-style except during lunch and dinner hours. There's a grand view of the Seine, the **Tuileries,** and the **Louvre** from the balcony outside the cafe. ♦ Tu-W, F-Su; Th until 9:30PM; closed Christmas and 1 May. No phone

TAN - DINH

5 Tan Dinh ★★★$$$ The most elegant—and expensive—Vietnamese restaurant in Paris is conveniently located around the corner from the **Musée d'Orsay.** Delicate smoked-goose ravioli, light noodles with piquant shrimp, and lobster beignets with ginkgo are prepared by the affable Vifian brothers, who alternate nights in the kitchen. The exotic sorbets and remarkable Bordeaux are also memorable. ♦ M-Sa lunch and dinner; closed in August. Reservations recommended for dinner. 60 Rue de Verneuil (between Rues du Bac and de Poitiers). 01.45.44.04.84. Métro: Solférino

6 Ravi ★★$$$ Spicy and pricey, this aptly named Indian restaurant (*ravi* means "sun" in Hindi) outshines its competitors with Madras curries, kabobs, and outstanding tandoori prawns. Elephant sculptures stand guard outside, while the small dining room is charming and welcoming. ♦ M-Sa lunch and dinner. Reservations recommended. 50 Rue de Verneuil (between Rues du Bac and de Poitiers). 01.42.61.17.28. Métro: Solférino

7 Maxoff Restaurant ★$$ Such specialties as *tarama* (salmon roe spread), Baltic salad, beef stroganoff, Iranian caviar, *caviar d'aubergines* (eggplant caviar), Ukrainian borscht, strudel, and blintzes are served in a warm and convivial atmosphere. ♦ M-F lunch and dinner; Sa dinner; closed in August. Reservations recommended. 44 Rue de Verneuil (between Rues du Bac and de Poitiers). 01.42.60.60.43. Métro: Solférino

8 Rue du Bac The barracks that housed the swashbuckling heroes of *The Three Musketeers* by Alexandre Dumas were located on this street, which was built in 1564 and named after the *bac* (ferry) that used to transport Vaugirard quarry stone across the Seine to the construction site of the **Tuileries Palace.** ♦ Métros: Rue du Bac, Sèvres-Babylone

8 Lefèbvres & Fils Among those who have shopped at this century-old firm selling earthenware china and fanciful trompe l'oeil dishes were Victor Hugo, Marcel Proust, and Georges Feydeau. ♦ M-Sa; closed in August. 24 Rue du Bac (between Rues de l'Université and de Verneuil). 01.42.61.18.40. Métro: Rue du Bac

9 50 Rue de l'Université This is the former site of the **Hôtel de l'Intendance,** where Edna St. Vincent Millay wrote her Pulitzer Prize–winning poem, *The Ballad of the Harp-Weaver,* in 1921. The *hôtel* has since been replaced by an unattractive modern structure. ♦ Between Rues du Bac and de Poitiers. Métro: Rue du Bac

10 Galerie Maeght/Librarie Maeght The owner of this art gallery and art shop comes from a famous family of modern art dealers, and sells paintings, drawings, and original graphics, along with a huge selection of prints by modern artists from Matisse to Cucchi, deluxe art books, art exhibition posters, Miró T-shirts, and postcards. ♦ Tu-Sa. 42 Rue du Bac (between Blvd St-Germain and Rue de l'Université). Bookshop 01.45.48.45.15. Métro: Rue du Bac

10 Deyrolle This 150-year-old taxidermy shop has everything from mounted polar bears, ostriches, lions, and bewildered baby elephants to cobras, wild boars, and other citizens of Noah's Ark, all staring out of glass eyes. Deyrolle also acquires rare butterflies, tastefully stuffed cocker spaniels, and just about every crystal, geode, and mineral on earth. Kids could be left here to browse for hours. ♦ M-Sa. 46 Rue du Bac (between Blvd St-Germain and Rue de l'Université). 01.42.22.30.07. Métro: Rue du Bac

11 L'Oeillade ★★$$ An ever-changing, moderately priced three-course menu is offered by chef Jean-Louis Huclin, who makes all the sausages, terrines, and pasta himself. He also serves perfectly stewed pot-au-feu salad, cassoulet in a gleaming copper saucepan, succulent roast chicken, and *mousse au chocolat*. There are plenty of fine wines, and the ambience is warm and welcoming. ♦ M-F lunch and dinner; Sa dinner. 10 Rue de St-Simon (between Rue de Grenelle and Blvd St-Germain). 01.42.22.01.60. Métro: Rue du Bac

12 Hôtel Duc de St-Simon $$$ Two Swedish friends own this cozy antiques-furnished 34-room hotel on a hidden street just off the Boulevard St-Germain. It's popular among transatlantic diplomats, intellectuals, actors (including Lauren Bacall), writers (Nobel Prize–winner Toni Morrison, John Irving, P. D. James, and Nadine Gordimer stay here), film director Arthur Penn, and his photographer brother Irving. But despite the eminence of the company, the ambience remains very relaxed. Reservations for newcomers may be difficult to come by, but keep trying. Garden lovers should ask for room **No. 25,** which has a flower-bedecked terrace, if they don't mind a room that's a bit small. ◆ 14 Rue de St-Simon (between Rue de Grenelle and Blvd St-Germain). 01.44.39.20.20; fax 01.45.48.68.25. Métro: Rue du Bac

13 The General Store Homesick North Americans can comfort their taste buds with Paul Newman's spaghetti sauce, Hellman's mayonnaise, taco shells, Cheerios, maple syrup, peanut butter, and pecans, thanks to this grocery. Stuffed turkeys and homemade pumpkin pies are sold during Thanksgiving week, and French gourmands researching recipes for meat loaf or succotash will find such cookbooks as *La Cuisine Américaine*. ◆ M-Sa. 82 Rue de Grenelle (between Rues du Bac and de St-Simon). 01.45.48.63.16. Métro: Rue du Bac

14 Superlatif Popular with locals is this stationery shop that sells a wide variety of colored paper, designer pens, and assorted doodads. ◆ M-Sa. 86 Rue du Bac (between Rues de Varenne and de Grenelle). 01.45.48.84.25. Métro: Rue du Bac

OLIVIER DE SERCEY

15 Olivier de Sercey Ambassadors and government ministers from nearby offices frequent this tiny printing and engraving shop that makes dignified business cards. Wedding and party invitations are also a specialty. ◆ M-F; closed in August. 96 Rue du Bac (between Rues de Varenne and de Grenelle). 01.45.48.21.47. Métro: Rue du Bac

15 La Boîte à Musique This antiques shop specializes in 19th-century music boxes from France, England, and Switzerland. ◆ M 2-7PM; Tu-Sa; closed in August. 96 Rue du Bac (between Rues de Varenne and de Grenelle). 01.42.22.01.30. Métro: Rue du Bac

Restaurants/Clubs: Red
Shops/ 🌳 **Outdoors:** Green
Hotels: Blue
Sights/Culture: Black

16 La Cour de Varenne The back door of Etienne Lévy's antiques store opens onto a lovely courtyard where Madame de Staël's servants' quarters still stand. There are two floors of clocks, 17th- and 18th-century furniture, Japanese lacquer, mother-of-pearl–framed mirrors, and much more. ◆ Tu-Sa; closed in August.42 Rue de Varenne (between Rues du Bac and de Bellechasse). 01.45.44.65.50. Métro: Rue du Bac

17 110 Rue du Bac After the sale of *Arrangement in Grey and Black: The Artist's Mother* to the French government in 1893, James McNeill Whistler moved into a ground-floor apartment here and consorted with such artist-intelligentsia friends as Henry James, Edgar Degas, Edouard Manet, and Henri de Toulouse-Lautrec. It remains a residential building. ◆ Between Rues de Babylone and de Varenne. Métros: Rue du Bac, Sèvres-Babylone

18 La Pagode Sigh over your favorite François Truffaut and Jean Renoir classics in this authentic Chinese pagoda, the most unusual cinema in Paris. ◆ 57 *bis* Rue de Babylone (between Rues Vaneau and Monsieur). 08.36.68.75.07. Métro: St-François-Xavier

19 Le Bon Marché The granddaddy of all Paris department stores, which was founded in 1852, underwent *un lifting* (a major overhaul) during the 1990s, and is as up-to-date now as its big Right Bank competitors. Ready-to-wear collections include those of Corrine Saurrut, Ralph Lauren, Vivienne Westwood, and Comme des Garçons, and the store has its own line of menswear called Balthazar. Its **La Grande Epicerie** is especially famous, and is the largest of its kind in the city (9,075 square feet). Everything from fresh oysters to foie gras is sold here. ◆ Store: M-Sa. Epicerie: M-Sa 10AM-9PM. 22 Rue de Sèvres (at Rue du Bac). Store 01.44.39.80.00, épicerie 01.44.39.81.00. Métro: Sèvres-Babylone

20 Diners en Ville Tablecloths, candlesticks, china, earthenware, flatware—everything for the well-dressed table is available here. There's a wide selection of tinted wine and aperitif glasses from all over the world. ◆ M 2-7PM; Tu-Sa. 27 Rue de Varenne (at Rue du Bac). 01.42.22.78.33. Métro: Rue du Bac

21 Musée Maillol–Fondation Dina Vierny Located in an 18th-century mansion next to Bouchardon's splendid **Fontaine des Quatre**

Saisons, this museum is the result of the partnership of sculptor-painter Aristide Maillot and his model, Dina Vierny, whom he met when she was 15. Their collaboration lasted for 10 years until his death at 83 in 1944. Vierny's sublime form is seen in such works as *La Montagne, L'Air, La Rivière,* and Maillot's ultimate work *Harmonie.* She went on to become a successful Paris art dealer and worked for 30 years to create this foundation dedicated primarily to Maillot's work. The museum also includes pieces by such other 20th-century artists as Dufy, Matisse, Bonnard, Poliakoff, Kandinsky, Kabakov, and Duchamp. It mounts temporary exhibits on such artisans as Frida Kahlo as well. A pretty cafe in the vaulted basement serves light meals. ♦ Admission; free for children under age 18. M, W-Su 11AM-6PM. 59-61 Rue de Grenelle (between Blvd Raspail and Rue du Bac). 01.42.22.59.58. Métro: Rue du Bac

21 Fontaine des Quatre Saisons (Four Seasons Fountain) In the early 18th century, this, the wealthiest quarter in Paris, was almost totally without water. To remedy that problem, in 1739 sculptor Edme Bouchardon was commissioned to design this fountain to supply water to neighborhood residents. The Ionic-pillared fountain is adorned with a seated figure of Paris looking down on reclining personifications of the Seine and Marne Rivers. The sides are decorated with figures of the seasons and reliefs of cherubs. Voltaire protested the placement of this fountain in a narrow and confined street, arguing that "fountains must be elevated in public places and, like all beautiful monuments, be viewed on all sides." ♦ 57-59 Rue de Grenelle (between Blvd Raspail and Rue du Bac). Métro: Rue du Bac

22 Roland Barthélemy Fromager The Elysée Palace buys its cheese at this shop, which offers more than 50 kinds of fresh goat cheese, the finest vacherin (from October through February), and its special boulamour, a ball of enriched cow's cheese covered with Kirsch-soaked raisins. ♦ Tu-Sa. 51 Rue de Grenelle (between Blvd Raspail and Rue du Bac). 01.45.48.56.75. Métro: Rue du Bac

23 Pleats Please/Issey Miyake A fashion purist, Tokyo-based designer Miyake creates all his own fabrics and dresses his followers for maximum comfort and ease of motion. Miyake's main shop in Paris is in the Marais. ♦ M-Sa. 201 Blvd St-Germain (between Rue St-Guillaume and Blvd Raspail). 01.45.48.10.44. Métro: Rue du Bac. Also at: 3 Pl des Vosges (between Rues de Birague and des Francs-Bourgeois). 01.48.87.01.86. Métros: St-Paul, Bastille

24 Kenzo Star Japanese designer Kenzo splashes gorgeous colors over amusing, informal clothes and accessories. This is one of his eight shops in Paris. His flagship store is on Place des Victoires. ♦ M-Sa. 17 Blvd Raspail (at Rue de Grenelle). 01.45.49.33.75. Métro: Rue du Bac. Also at: 3 Pl des Victoires (between Rues Etienne-Marcel and Croix-des-Petits-Champs). 01.40.39.72.03. Métro: Bourse

HOTEL LUTETIA - PARIS

25 Hôtel Lutetia $$$$ The Left Bank's grandest of grand hotels, this 7-story, 250-room Art Nouveau gem opened in 1910 and its interior is a veritable museum of Art Deco style. The hotel was refurbished by fashion designer Sonia Rykiel in the 1980s and has been constantly refreshed since then. The guest rooms are large and luxurious, and many have views of the gilded dome of the **Invalides,** the **Eiffel Tower,** and beyond. Two dining spots grace the place: the highly rated gourmet restaurant **Paris,** which is elegantly decorated in Art Deco style, and the lively **Brasserie Lutetia.** ♦ 45 Blvd Raspail (at Rue de Sèvres). 01.49.54.46.46; fax 01.49.54.46.00; www.lutetia-paris.com. Métro: Sèvres-Babylone

26 Atelier Guillaume Martel Have a special 17th-century portrait or modern print you need framed? Martel, a graduate of the prestigious **Ecole du Louvre,** specializes in *dorure froide* (a cold-gilding technique) frames for both antique and contemporary prints. ♦ Tu-Sa; closed in August. 2 Rue du Regard (at Rue du Cherche-Midi). 01.45.49.02.07. Métros: Sèvres-Babylone, Rennes

27 Café Parisien ★★$ This modest cafe has garnered a large reputation. Its weekend brunches, hearty plats du jour, and *tarte tatin* (apple tart) draw a lively, often literary, throng. A branch, **Le Petit Café Parisien,** is at 35 Rue de Vaugirard (between Rues Jean-Bart and d'Assas, 01.45.49.47.15). ♦ M-F lunch and dinner; Sa-Su brunch and dinner. Reservations recommended. No credit cards accepted. 15 Rue d'Assas (between Rues de Vaugirard and de Rennes). 01.45.44.41.44. Métro: Rennes

Poilâne

28 Poilâne The most famous baker in France, if not the world, Lionel Poilâne continues a family tradition started by his Norman father,

Pierre, in 1933. His round sourdough country loaf, baked in wood-fired ovens, is served in some 400 Parisian restaurants and is flown daily to expensive gourmet shops in New York and Tokyo. If he's not too busy and you ask politely, Lionel may even take you down into the bakery's 12th-century cellars, where a baker in shorts and a T-shirt feeds lumps of dough to a wood-burning brick oven. ♦ M-Sa. 8 Rue du Cherche-Midi (between Pl Alphonse-Deville and Carrefour de la Croix-Rouge). 01.45.48.42.59. Métro: St-Sulpice

LE RÉCAMIER

29 Le Récamier ★★★$$$ Situated in a serene cul-de-sac in the well-trodden St-Germain shopping district, this elegant restaurant caters to the Paris publishing crowd and has one of the city's most peaceful outdoor terraces. Owner and certified wine expert Martin Cantegrit features dishes from his native Burgundy—fricassee of snails and wild mushrooms, *boeuf bourguignon sans pareil*, chateaubriand Récamier—as well as salmon *tartare* (raw chopped salmon, served with a sauce of herbs and spices), an excellent summer starter. Cantegrit's wine list, which he calls "my little Bible," merits the appellation. ♦ M-Sa lunch and dinner. 4 Rue Récamier (at Rue de Sèvres). 01.45.48.86.58. Métro: Sèvres-Babylone

30 Rue des Sts-Pères Known in the 13th century as the Chemins aux Vaches (Cow Path), this street became Rue de St-Pierre in the 16th century because of a nearby chapel dedicated to St. Peter. By 1652, people had worn the name down to Rue des Sts-Pères. ♦ Métros: Sèvres-Babylone, St-Sulpice, St-Germain-des-Prés

30 Au Sauvignon ★$ This old wine bar is predictably papered with maps of French wine regions. Still, in summer it's not such a bad thing to enjoy a plate of country-cured ham, some cantal cheese, and a Sancerre rosé while sitting at one of the sidewalk tables watching the world stroll by. ♦ M-Sa breakfast, lunch, and dinner until 10PM; closed in August. No credit cards accepted. 80

Rue des Sts-Pères (at Rue de Sèvres). 01.45.48.49.02. Métro: Sèvres-Babylone

31 Maude Frizon More than 1,500 styles of hand-crafted haute-couture footwear are carried here. ♦ M-Sa. 83 Rue des Sts-Pères (at Rue de Grenelle). 01.42.22.06.93. Métros: St-Sulpice, Sèvres-Babylone. Also at: 90 Rue du Faubourg-St-Honoré (at Pl Beauvau). 01.42.65.27.96. Métro: Miromesnil

31 Cassegrain There's nothing quite like a proper thank-you note or an engraved-in-gold place card. This stationer has been setting the standard since 1919. ♦ M-Sa. 81 Rue des Sts-Pères (between Rue de Grenelle and Blvd St-Germain). 01.42.22.04.76. Métros: St-Sulpice, Sèvres-Babylone

32 31 Rue du Dragon The **Académie Julian,** which was once here, admitted hundreds of aspiring North American painters who were hoping to study on the GI bill after World War II but were unable to meet the stricter entrance requirements of the **Ecole des Beaux-Arts.** The building now has both residential and commercial space. ♦ Between Carrefour de la Croix-Rouge and Rue Bernard-Palissy. Métro: St-Sulpice

32 Chez Claude Sainlouis ★$ Since opening in 1959, the unfailingly popular restaurant of ex-stuntman Claude Piau (Sainlouis was his *nom de cinéma*) has played it safe, serving an unchanging menu of traditional dishes. Steak, lamb chops, salad, and chocolate mousse are served in a casual setting. ♦ M-F lunch and dinner; Sa lunch; closed in August and one week at Christmas. Reservations recommended. 27 Rue du Dragon (between Carrefour de la Croix-Rouge and Rue Bernard-Palissy). 01.45.48.29.68. Métro: St-Sulpice

33 Yakijapo Mitsuko ★★$$ One of the best sushi bars in Paris also serves sashimi and yakitori at reasonable prices in a simple, elegant dining room. ♦ Daily lunch and dinner. 8 Rue du Sabot (between Rues du Four and Bernard-Palissy). 01.42.22.17.74. Métro: St-Sulpice

34 Via Palissy ★★$$ Climb to the tiny, crooked dining room of this Italian restaurant to sample risotto Milanese, gnocchi with gorgonzola, and homemade tiramisù. ♦ M-F lunch and dinner, Sa dinner; closed three weeks in August. Reservations recommended. 11 Rue Bernard-Palissy (at Rue du Sabot). 01.45.44.02.52. Métros: St-Sulpice, St-Germain-des-Prés

35 Baxter Old prints, etchings, and lithographs abound in this charming shop that specializes in European architectural and botanical illustrations from the 17th to 19th centuries. The friendly staff has both a knowledge of and affection for the wares. Framing services are available. ◆ M 1-7PM; Tu-Sa. 15 Rue du Dragon (at Rue Bernard-Palissy). 01.45.49.01.34. Métros: St-Sulpice, St-Germain-des-Prés

36 Korean Barbecue ★$$ The fare here includes marinated beef and vegetables that you grill over a gas stove at your table. The decor is clean, simple, and no-nonsense. ◆ Daily lunch and dinner. 1 Rue du Dragon (at Blvd St-Germain). 01.42.22.26.63. Métro: St-Germain-des-Prés

brasserie
LIPP

37 Brasserie Lipp ★★$$ A national landmark, where waiters still dress in black waistcoats and long white aprons, this famous Alsatian brasserie is always replete with editors (from Grasset, Gallimard, and Hachette) and politicians. De Gaulle and Pompidou used to lunch at these tables, and François Mitterand was also a regular. Ben Barka, a Moroccan militant, was arrested here. Today's familiar faces include Lionel Jospin, Yves Saint Laurent, and Sharon Stone. The ceilings are covered with buxom nudes; the walls are festooned with Art Nouveau ceramics and conveniently hung with mirrors so large you never need to crane your neck to watch the celebrities pass by.

The restaurant used to be run by the formidable Roger Cazes (whose father bought the establishment in 1920 from an Alsatian named Léopold Lipp), who didn't seem to care for Americans unless they were of the cultural stature of a William Styron. During the Cazes regime, an American's best ploy for getting seated was to arrive on a rainy February day just before 1AM—or shortly after a morning bomb scare. Anyone who was anyone sat on the main floor; upstairs was Siberia. After Cazes's death, the new management restored the second floor so diners there no longer feel banished. It is also possible to enjoy a Bavarian dark beer or cup of hot chocolate on the terrace; just don't tell anyone that's where you sat.

The food is solid, but hardly inspiring. Fresh oysters, smoked salmon, potato salad, and *choucroute* (sauerkraut) have long been the staples. But in the late 1980s (considered only yesterday here), four entrées—examples include roast pork, lamb, calf's liver, and monkfish—were added to the menu, with the selections changing twice a year. ◆ Daily 8:30AM-1AM. Reservations required. 151 Blvd St-Germain (between Rues de Rennes and du Dragon). 01.45.48.53.91. Métro: St-Germain-des-Prés

38 Sabbia Rosa Sexy teddies and other alluring lingerie can be purchased for or by the femme fatale. ◆ M-Sa; closed last half of August. 71-73 Rue des Sts-Pères (between Rue de Grenelle and Blvd St-Germain). 01.45.48.88.37. Métros: St-Sulpice, St-Germain-des-Prés

38 Y's Yohji Yamamoto Shop here for an outfit that's actually both fashionable and comfortable. This Japanese designer creates basic, high-style clothes for men and women. ◆ M-Sa. 69 Rue des Sts-Pères (between Rue de Grenelle and Blvd St-Germain). 01.45.48.22.56. Métros: St-Sulpice, St-Germain-des-Prés

38 Hôtel des Sts-Pères $$$ This tastefully renovated 39-room hotel was designed in 1658 by **Alphonse Daniel Gittard,** who founded the Academy of Architecture under Louis XIV and whose portrait hangs behind the reception desk. If dozing off while staring up at a 17th-century ceiling painting of the *Crowning of Jupiter* is your idea of luxury, ask for room **No. 100.** There's no restaurant, but the hotel has a pretty garden for breakfast in fair weather. ◆ 65 Rue des Sts-Pères (between Rue de Grenelle and Blvd St-Germain). 01.45.44.50.00; fax 01.45.44.90.83; espfranc@MicroNet.fr. Métros: St-Sulpice, St-Germain-des-Prés

39 La Maison de Verre (Glass House) Seeing the extraordinary glass house of **Pierre Chareau** and **Bernard Bijovet** is a must for any student of 20th-century design. You can get a glimpse of the exterior from the courtyard, but for a look at the inside of the early 1930s building—a tour de force in glass-block-and-steel construction—you must make a reservation. Send inquiries to: A.P. Vellay-Dalsace, 31 Rue St-Guillaume, 75006 Paris. ◆ Donation requested; send with reservations request. 31 Rue St-Guillaume (between Rue de Grenelle and Blvd St-Germain). Métros: Sèvres-Babylone, Rue du Bac

40 Madeleine Gély Since 1834 the finest umbrella shop in Paris has been selling and repairing handmade *parapluies*. The narrow

little boutique is crammed with umbrellas—large, small, new, and antique. And you needn't have a bad leg to buy one of Madeleine Gély's 400 new or antique canes. They include duck- and bulldog-headed canes, watch canes, whiskey-flask canes, and even a cane to measure the withers of a horse. There are also sturdy utilitarian models. ♦ Tu-Sa; closed in August. 218 Blvd St-Germain (between Rues St-Guillaume and du Bac). 01.42.22.63.35. Métro: Rue du Bac

41 Hôtel Montalembert $$$$ This chic Left Bank luxury hotel is popular with people from the worlds of publishing, fashion, and the fine arts. Designer Christian Liaigre's tasteful furnishings for the lobby and 56 rooms boast a wondrous attention to detail, from hand-crafted leather furniture to cast-bronze door handles. The modern guest rooms with customized furniture will suit guests who prefer contemporary style, while the Louis Philippe rooms with finely restored period furniture will please traditionalists. Everyone staying here should plan a few long, bubbly soaks in the opulent bathrooms, done in gray marble and chrome. ♦ 3 Rue de Montalembert (between Rues Sébastien-Bottin and du Bac). 01.45.49.68.68; fax 01.45.49.69.49; welcome@hotel-montalembert.fr; www.montalembert.com. Métro: Rue du Bac

Within the Hôtel Montalembert:

Restaurant Montalembert ★★$$
The congenial atmosphere and the creations of chef Fréderic Deswarte have made this intimate cafe a popular meeting place for Parisians. You can't go wrong with the lobster ravioli in vegetable court-bouillon, fillet of salmon in a Szechuan crust, sautéed lamb seasoned with licorice, or the dark and white chocolate cake with pear sherbet. ♦ M-Sa breakfast, lunch, and dinner; Su brunch and dinner. Reservations recommended. 01.45.49.68.68

42 Le Cabinet de Curiosité Lined with panels from an Empire-period pharmacy, this amusing shop displays stuffed penguins, brass hourglasses, ladies' shoes from the Louis XVI epoch, strange old primitive paintings, apothecary jars, an exquisite collection of Gothic keys and locks, and iron cork-crushers shaped like crocodiles. Owner Claudine Guerin is an expert in fine wrought iron. ♦ M-Sa; closed in August. 23 Rue de Beaune (between Rues de Verneuil and de Lille). 01.42.61.09.57. Métro: Rue du Bac

---

The ubiquitous green trash bins of Paris are called *poubelles* in honor of Eugène Poubelle, the Prefect of the Seine from 1883 to 1896. In 1884, he issued the order that all trash must be deposited in receptacles.

Le Bistrot de Paris

43 Le Bistrot de Paris ★★$$ This fashionable bistro has an innovative one-two punch: ravishing 1880s decor with Belle Epoque mosaics and a Provençal menu, with the specialties changing with the seasons. Lots of *gibier* (wild game) is featured during the hunting season. ♦ M-F lunch and dinner; Sa dinner. Reservations recommended. 33 Rue de Lille (between Rues de Beaune and du Bac). 01.42.61.16.83, 01.42.61.15.84. Métro: Rue du Bac

44 9 Rue de Beaune While living here at the **Hôtel Elysée** in July 1920, Ezra Pound convinced James Joyce to move from Trieste and bring his family to Paris, where Pound settled them in a small hotel nearby at 9 Rue de l'Université. Today this is a residential building. ♦ At Rue de Lille. Métro: Rue du Bac

44 7 Rue de Beaune In 1872 young Henry James, whose future novels *The American* and *The Ambassadors* would feature North American expatriates in Paris, came to this residential building to visit fellow Bostonian James Russell Lowell, and as a bonus found Ralph Waldo Emerson and his daughter Ellen in the sitting room. It was, as he wrote home, "a little Cambridge on the Seine." ♦ Between Rue de Lille and Quai Voltaire. Métro: Rue du Bac

45 Quai Voltaire This quay honors Voltaire, whose return in 1778 after a 30-year absence was greeted by a torchlight parade that wound from the **Comédie Française** (where his tragedy *Irène* had just opened) across the river to **27 Quai Voltaire,** where he died on 30 May 1778. The quay's history involves many artists: Jean-Dominique Ingres died on 14 January 1867 at **No. 11;** Delacroix and Corot, at different times, rented the top-floor studio at **No. 13;** in the hotel at **No. 19,** Baudelaire penned *Les Fleurs du Mal* in 1857; and Wagner composed *Die Meistersinger* here between 1861 and 1862. Today, it is a bazaar of first-rate antiques shops and galleries. Side by side are well-known dealers such as **Huguette Berès Bailly** (No. 25, 01.42.61.27.91) and **Jean Max Tassel** (No. 15, 01.42.61.02.01). ♦ Métro: Rue du Bac

HOTEL DU QUAI VOLTAIRE

45 Hôtel du Quai Voltaire $$ Charles-Pierre Baudelaire, Oscar Wilde, Richard Wagner, and Jean Sibelius each came to this hotel looking for a room with a view. Do the same: Ask for a front room (if you don't mind traffic noise) and wake up to a vista of the Seine and the **Tuileries.** There are 33 comfortable guest rooms. There's no restaurant, but the bar is open daily and serves a light lunch and evening snacks. ◆ 19 Quai Voltaire (between Rues des Sts-Pères and de Beaune). 01.42.61.50.91; fax 01.42.61.62.26; www.hotelduquaivoltaire.com. Métro: Rue du Bac

46 Sennelier The Left Bank's finest painters patronize this celebrated art-supply store. Even if you couldn't draw an apple to save your life, step inside and rub shoulders with the **Beaux-Arts** students shopping for linseed oil, blocks of brilliantly colored pastel chalks, and wooden palettes. ◆ M-Sa. 3 Quai Voltaire (between Rues des Sts-Pères and de Beaune). 01.42.60.72.15. Métros: Rue du Bac, St-Germain-des-Prés. Also at: 4 *bis* Rue de la Grande-Chaumière (between Rue Notre Dame-des-Champs and Blvd du Montparnasse). 01.46.33.72.39. Métro: Vavin

47 Hôtel de l'université $$$ This sedate hotel in a 17th-century town house has exposed stone walls and wooden beams, tapestries, antiques, and a small private courtyard. It offers 27 quaint, comfortably modernized rooms, but no restaurant. ◆ 22 Rue de l'Université (between Rues des Sts-Pères and de Beaune). 01.42.61.09.39; fax 01.42.60.40.84. Métro: Rue du Bac

48 Lenox $$$ The then 22-year-old T.S. Eliot spent a romantic summer here in 1910 on the old man's money, just before he took a job in a London bank and wrote "The Love Song of J. Alfred Prufrock." Restored with chic simplicity and a slightly New Wave bar, the 34-room hotel is a favorite of visiting fashion models. Ask for one of the top floor rooms—they have balconies and exposed beams. There's no restaurant, but the bar is open daily from 5PM to 2AM. ◆ 9 Rue de l'Université (at Rue du Pré-aux-Clercs). 01.42.96.10.95; fax 01.42.61.52.83. Métros: Rue du Bac, St-Germain-des-Prés

49 2-4 Rue de l'Université In 1776 Benjamin Franklin lived here at the former **Hôtel d'Entragues** while he was drumming up support for the American Revolution. It's still a residential building. ◆ At Rue des Sts-Pères. Métros: Rue du Bac, St-Germain-des-Prés

50 Debauve and Gallais This wood-paneled chocolate shop with a semicircular counter began as a pharmacy nearly 200 years ago, when medicated chocolate was a nostrum for flatulence, anemia, and other ills. Today, in addition to delicious nonmedicinal chocolate, the shop sells such delights as *croquamandes* (almonds roasted with caramelized sugar), hot chocolate mix, and real chocolate gift boxes. The old metal tea canisters date from 1804. ◆ M-Sa. 30 Rue des Sts-Pères (between Rues Perronet and de l'Université). 01.45.48.54.67. Métros: Rue du Bac, St-Germain-des-Prés

51 Coffee Saint-Germain ★★$$ Formerly the **Coffee Parisien,** this North American–style eatery was acquired in 1998 by *américainophile* Bruno Rivière, who continues to serve such culinary treats as pancakes with maple syrup, hash browns, bagels and cream cheese, eggs Benedict, and bacon cheeseburgers. Brunch is offered all day. ◆ Daily lunch, brunch, and dinner until 1AM. 5 Rue Perronet (between Rues des Sts-Pères and St-Guillaume). 01.40.49.08.08. Métros: Rue du Bac, St-Germain-des-Prés

52 Than ★★$ This tiny Asian canteen is a popular bargain in the pricey St-Germain quarter. The affable Mr. Than has been packing them in with his delicious and affordable Cantonese and Vietnamese specialties since 1968. He is especially proud of the lacquered duck and caramelized spare ribs. Regular diners include neighborhood editors, publishers, shop clerks, and medical students. ◆ M dinner; Tu-Sa lunch and dinner. 42 Rue des Sts-Pères (between Blvd St-Germain and Rue Perronet). 01.45.48.36.97. Métros: Rue du Bac, St-Germain-des-Prés

53 St-Vladimir le Grand Come on a Sunday morning and watch the rosy grandmothers wearing babushkas enter this Ukrainian church. ◆ 49-51 Rue des Sts-Pères (at Blvd St-Germain). Métros: Rue du Bac, St-Germain-des-Prés

54 Rue Jacob Named after the Old Testament patriarch, this street is chock-full of book and antiques shops selling everything from autographs and old manuscripts to theater props and scientific instruments. ◆ Métros: St-Germain-des-Prés, Mabillon

54 56 Rue Jacob The Treaty of Paris, by which England recognized the independence of the 13 American colonies, was signed in this building, formerly the **Hôtel d'York,** on 3 September 1783. Benjamin Franklin, John Jay, and John Adams endorsed the document on behalf of the US; David Hartley and Richard Oswald represented England. ◆ Between Rues Bonaparte and des Sts-Pères. Métro: St-Germain-des-Prés

55 Démons et Merveilles You'll find folk costumes from Romania, Hungary, Poland, Afghanistan, Tibet, and India; big silver bracelets from Morocco, Algeria, the Middle East; and heavy iron crucifixes from Ethiopia here. Faty, the Tunisian owner, left his law practice to start this shop. ♦ M-Sa. 45 Rue Jacob (between Rues St-Benoît and des Sts-Pères). 01.42.96.26.11. Métro: St-Germain-des-Prés

ALAIN BRIEUX

SCIENCES · TECHNIQUES · MÉDECINE

56 Alain Brieux This eclectic curio shop specializes in prints, Arabic astrolabes, and rare medical books that date back to the 16th century. Everything in the store is for sale except the crocodile hanging from the ceiling. This item was a traditional feature in old apothecaries and alchemists' labs. ♦ M-F; Sa 2-6PM; closed in August. 48 Rue Jacob (between Rues Bonaparte and des Sts-Pères). 01.42.60.21.98. Métro: St-Germain-des-Prés

57 Angleterre $$$ Among the notables who have stayed in this 18th-century hostelry are Washington Irving, Sherwood Anderson, and young Ernest Hemingway. It's now a picturesque 27-room hotel with a garden patio. The bar is open 24 hours for hotel guests only; there's no restaurant. ♦ 44 Rue Jacob (between Rues Bonaparte and des Sts-Pères). 01.42.60.34.72; fax 01.42.60.16.93. Métro: St-Germain-des-Prés

58 Le Petit St-Benoît ★★$ Offering indigent Left Bank intellectuals *blanquette de veau* (veal with béchamel sauce and mushrooms), shepherd's pie, and salted pork with lentils since 1901, this popular coach-house bistro has prices that are difficult to beat. The rest room features a celebrated blue-and-white-checkered washbowl. The restaurant publishes a quarterly newsletter, *Gazette du Petit Saint Benoît,* with articles and commentaries about St-Germain-des-Prés by area residents. ♦ M-F lunch and dinner. 4 St-Benoît (between Blvd St-Germain and Rue Jacob). 01.42.60.27.92. Métro: St-Germain-des-Prés

59 Le Muniche ★$$ Delicious fish soup, grilled sardines, fresh briny oysters, four kinds of sauerkraut, and an honest plate of liver and onions are some of the culinary choices at this crowded Alsatian bistro. In summer, reserve a table on the sidewalk.

♦ Daily lunch and dinner until 2AM. 7 Rue St-Benoît (between Rues Guillaume-Apollinaire and Jacob). 01.42.61.12.70. Métro: St-Germain-des-Prés

60 Le Bilboquet ★$$ On the former site of **Club St-Germain,** an old existentialist haunt, this upbeat dinner-jazz club serves grilled rack of lamb and sides of beef in a 1950s ambience. ♦ Daily dinner. Music: daily 10:30PM-2:45AM. 13 Rue St-Benoît (between Rues Guillaume-Apollinaire and Jacob). 01.45.48.81.84. Métro: St-Germain-des-Prés

61 Shu Uemura This Japanese cosmetics shop features compacts, lipstick, nail polish, creams, and brushes in every hue and shape imaginable. It's one of an international 6,000-shop chain started in 1986 by makeup artist Shu Uemura, who perfected the faces of Japan's most famous movie stars. ♦ M-Sa. 176 Blvd St-Germain (between Rues St-Benoît and des Sts-Pères). 01.45.48.02.55. Métro: St-Germain-des-Prés

Café de Flore

61 Café de Flore ★★$$ Jean-Paul Sartre wrote of hanging out in this great cafe during World War II: "Simone de Beauvoir and I more or less set up house in the **Flore.** We worked from 9AM till noon, when we went out to lunch. At 2PM we came back and talked with our friends till 4PM, when we got down to work again till 8PM. And after dinner, people came to see us by appointment. It may seem strange, all this, but the **Flore** was like home to us: even when the air-raid alarm went, we would merely feign leaving and then climb up to the first floor and go on working."

The drink to order here in winter is hot grog (rum, tea, and lemon slices); be sure to ask for extra lemon because they never bring enough. For early birds this is an excellent place to scrutinize *Le Monde* and have a breakfast of *oeufs sur le plat* (fried eggs), bacon, and croissants. Salads, sandwiches, and other typical cafe fare are served at lunch and dinner. The endearingly worn Art Deco interior—all red, mahogany, and mirrors—has changed little since the war. Many writers and journalists who live in the neighborhood still call this cafe their second home. Philosophy discussions are held monthly in English. ♦ Daily breakfast, lunch, and dinner until 1:30AM. 172 Blvd St-Germain (at Rue St-Benoît). 01.45.48.55.26. Métro: St-Germain-des-Prés

62 La Hune Wedged between **Café de Flore** and **Les Deux Magots** is one of the liveliest bookstores in Paris. It provides literary sustenance to the Parisian men and women of letters (and those trying to resemble them) who frequent the nearby shrines. Be warned, however: persistent rumors at press time labeled this bookstore an imminent victim of the *quartier*'s takeover by upscale pret-à-porter operations. ♦ M-Sa 10AM-midnight. 170 Blvd St-Germain (at Rue St-Benoît). 01.45.48.35.85. Métro: St-Germain-des-Prés

62 Les Deux Magots ★★$$ The best terrace in St-Germain-des-Prés is right here at this glamorous old cafe. From the tables fronting on the boulevard, patrons can indulge in the French national sport of people watching at its finest, while those on the more sedate Place St-Germain-des-Prés side can watch the sidewalk performers in the square in front of the church who are always amusing and occasionally brilliant. The cafe's name comes from the two statues of paunchy Chinese commercial agents—*magots*—that sit high on the center pillars inside.

The menu calls this place "The Rendezvous of the Intellectual Elite"—no empty boast. Like the **Café de Flore**, this place has long attracted poets, writers, and artists, including Paul Verlaine, Arthur Rimbaud, Stéphane Mallarmé, André Breton, Antonin Artaud, Jean Giraudoux, Oscar Wilde, and Picasso, who met Dora Marr here. Among the many North American regulars were Ernest Hemingway, *New Yorker* columnist Janet Flanner, Djuna Barnes, and Richard Wright. ♦ Daily breakfast, lunch, and dinner until 1:30AM. 6 Pl St-Germain-des-Prés (at Blvd St-Germain). 01.45.48.55.25. Métro: St-Germain-des-Prés

62 Arthus-Bertrand This establishment, started in 1803, casts reproductions of some of the **Louvre**'s treasures in sterling or in 18-karat gold. It also supplies 80 percent of the military medals and decorations used by African nations. For $6,000 to $20,000, it custom-designs the ceremonial swords worn by the "immortals" accepted into the **Académie Française.** The firm has a seriousness and a price list that will curb any idle browser. ♦ M-Sa. 6 Pl St-Germain-des-Prés (between Blvd St-Germain and Rue Guillaume-Apollinaire). 01.49.54.72.10. Métro: St-Germain-des-Prés

63 Embâcle This sculpture (whose name means "blockage") is not a ruptured water main but a practical joke of a fountain by Charles Daudelin. It was created in 1985. ♦ Pl du Québec. Métro: St-Germain-des-Prés

64 Annick Goutal Original perfumes, precious oils, lotions, and soaps are purveyed at this ivory- and gold-toned boutique. Goutal's beautifully packaged products celebrate nature with such women's and men's fragrances as Eau d'Hadrien, Eau du Ciel, Gardénia Passion, and Rose Absolute. The knowledgeable salespeople will cheerfully assist you in choosing the right scent. ♦ M-Sa. 12 Pl St-Sulpice (between Rues des Canettes and Bonaparte). 01.46.33.03.15. Métro: St-Sulpice

Hôtel de l'Abbaye

65 Hôtel de l'Abbaye $$$ Stone arches, antique furniture, and fresh-cut flowers enhance this exquisite 18th-century convent-turned-hotel. There are 40 peaceful rooms; ground-floor rooms **Nos. 2, 3,** and **4** open onto the trellised garden. There's no restaurant, but breakfast is served in the garden in fair weather, in the charming breakfast room when it's not. ♦ 10 Rue Cassette (at Rue de Mézières). 01.45.44.38.11; fax 01.45.40.07.06; hotel.abbaye@wanadoo.fr; www.hotel-abbaye.4in.com. Métro: St-Sulpice

66 58 Rue Madame The oldest brother of Gertrude Stein, Michael Stein, and his artist wife, Sarah, moved into a loft in this Protestant church building in 1903 and soon began buying canvases of the then-unknown Henri Matisse, who became a close friend. In a little more than a decade, Michael and Sarah, together with Gertrude and their brother Leo, had assembled one of the finest collections of Matisses, Renoirs, Cézannes, and Picassos in the world. ♦ Between Rues de Fleurus and de Vaugirard. Métros: St-Placide, Rennes

67 Perreyve $$ A quiet, modestly priced 30-room hotel, this place is just a minute's stroll from the **Luxembourg Gardens.** There's no restaurant. ♦ 63 Rue Madame (at Rue de Fleurus). 01.45.48.35.01; fax 01.42.84.03.30; www.paris-hotel.com/PERREYVE. Métros: St-Placide, Rennes

Hôtel de l'Avenir

68 Hôtel de l'Avenir $$ Conveniently located one block from the **Luxembourg Gardens,** this unassuming hotel has 35 neat, quiet, comfortable rooms at rates that are, as the French say, "très correct." There's no restaurant. ♦ 65 Rue Madame (at Rue de Fleurus). 01.45.48.84.54; fax 01.45.49.26.80. Métros: St-Placide, Rennes

69 Christian Constant ★★$ This tearoom-cum-chocolate-and-pastry shop serves 36 kinds of tea accompanied by 5 varieties of sugar, acacia honey, and fresh brioches, as well as luscious lemon meringue tarts. The pièce de résistance, however, is the pure bittersweet chocolate bar. ♦ Daily breakfast, lunch, and tea. 37 Rue d'Assas (at Rue de Fleurus). 01.45.48.45.51. Métros: St-Placide, Rennes

70 27 Rue de Fleurus The most famous of all North American expatriate addresses, this is where Gertrude Stein lived from 1903 to 1938, first with her brother Leo, then with her devoted companion, lover, and muse Alice B. Toklas. The walls of this large atelier were crammed with great Impressionist, Fauvist, and Cubist paintings. Gertrude and her family were among the first to buy works by Matisse and Picasso, who became regulars at her legendary Saturday night *salons*. An avant-garde writer and literary guru, she influenced many writers who visited her here, most notably the youthful Ernest Hemingway, in a friendship that eventually went sour. Stein gave her amusing account of their relationship in *The Autobiography of Alice B. Toklas*, but Hem got the vindictive last word in *A Moveable Feast*.

Stein's atelier is on the ground floor of the pavilion at the rear of the garden. It can be seen from the street through the glass doors of the main building, but the view from the inner court is better, if you can get someone to buzz you in. A wall plaque commemorates her residence here. ♦ Between Rue d'Assas and Blvd Raspail. Métros: St-Placide, Rennes

71 La Table de Fès ★★$$ Excellent North African couscous, chicken and lemon *tajine* (stew), and peppery *merguez* (lamb sausage) keep this friendly Moroccan restaurant crowded and hopping. The spicy change of pace from all those buttery French cream sauces is welcome. This spot is best late at night, when things are at their liveliest. ♦ M-Sa dinner; closed the last two weeks of August. Reservations required on Saturday. 5 Rue Ste-Beuve (between Blvd Raspail and Rue Notre-Dame-des-Champs). 01.45.48.07.22. Métros: Vavin, Notre-Dame des Champs

71 Le Sainte-Beuve $$$ Ideally situated equidistant from **La Coupole** and the **Luxembourg Gardens,** this handsome hotel was decorated by master designer David Hicks. It offers 22 refined and relaxing rooms in various shades of pastel. All are furnished in antiques, with air-conditioning, great bathrooms, and cable TV. There's no restaurant, but drinks are served at the little lobby bar, which, like the rooms, combines comfort with elegance. ♦ 9 Rue Ste-Beuve (between Blvd Raspail and Rue Notre-Dame-des-Champs). 01.45.48.20.07; fax 01.45.48.67.52. Métros: Vavin, Notre-Dame des Champs

72 26 Rue Vavin This luxury terraced apartment building was designed in 1925 by French architect **Henri Sauvage.** The splendid blue-and-white-tile complex, complete with ground-floor shops and indoor parking, was an early attempt at a self-contained building—what Le Corbusier would call *unité d'habitation*. ♦ Between Blvd Raspail and Rue Notre-Dame-des-Champs. Métros: Vavin, Notre-Dame des Champs

Within 26 Rue Vavin:

MARIE·PAPIER

Marie-Papier Attracting customers from Los Angeles to Tokyo, this famous French stationery store sells an elegant line of colored paper in single sheets or large albums. ♦ M-Sa. 01.43.26.46.44

Rouge et Noir Games galore! This handsome shop sells finely crafted miniature billiard tables, roulette wheels, hand-carved dominoes, Chinese checkers, Monopoly, and, yes, even Trivial Pursuit. Ask to see the reproductions of 15th- through 18th-century playing cards, as well as those with World War I, wine, and old costumes as themes— *les cartes à jouer* are kept in albums and are not on display. ♦ Tu-Sa. 01.43.26.05.77

73 La Coupole ★★$$ Along with **Brasserie Lipp** and **Brasserie Balzar,** this is a brasserie with a history. The landmark was the brainchild of René Lafond and his brother-in-law Ernest Fraux. While working at **Le Dôme,** Montparnasse's most popular cafe, in 1926, they took a 20-year lease on a wood and coal depot just down the street and transformed it into a huge dining room with red-velvet booths, jazz-age chandeliers, and its most original feature: 33 pillars and pilasters painted by Montparnasse artists. Painter Alexandre Auffray, whose studio was nearby, came up with the idea and recruited 31 artists from the *quartier* to do the painting. Lafond paid for the supplies and gave each artist a few good meals as an honorarium. Many had studied under Matisse, Léger, and Friesz, all of whose stylistic influences can be detected. In fact, the Cubist bathing beauty on the second pilaster to the left of the bar was long attributed to Léger, but turns out to have been done by his protégé Otto Gustav Carlsund. The most striking images were painted by Marie Vassillief: the elegant black man with a monocle and top hat, and the black rat dancing on the head of a flutist; they can be seen on the two center pilasters on the rear wall. Although these artists never achieved great renown, their paintings burst with the vibrant spirit of Montparnasse when the brasserie opened on the night of 20 December 1927 at the height of *Les Années Folles*.

Purchased for more than $10 million in 1988 and restored by brasserie czar Jean-Paul Bucher, the cavernous dining room has been classified as a historic monument (thus ensuring that its columns will be preserved). The restaurant seats 450 diners, and the tables are full every night. It's a watering hole for politicos, neighborhood merchants, aspiring actors, wandering poets, Scandinavian models, editors, and the suburban hordes that invade the Montparnasse movie theaters on Saturday nights. The restaurant, it is said, has the densest population of beautiful women in all of Paris on weeknights; it is most chic, however, to make an appearance Sunday night. But on any night the atmosphere will be festive. Expect to have a good time, but don't expect haute cuisine; the fare is simple and serviceable.

In the basement is an enormous ballroom where dancers literally kick off their shoes. There is salsa on Tuesday night, 1970s and 1980s music with a live band Friday and Saturday evenings, and tea dancing Saturday and Sunday afternoon. ◆ Restaurant: daily breakfast, lunch, and dinner until 2AM. Ballroom: W 8PM-4AM; F-Sa 9PM-4AM; tea dancing Sa-Su 3-7PM. No reservations taken after 9PM. 102 Blvd du Montparnasse (between Rues Delambre and du Montparnasse). 01.43.20.14.20. Métro: Vavin

74 Le Sélect ★★$ With its drab tan walls, kitsch ceiling molding, worn red banquettes, and beat-up wooden chairs and tables, this cafe, which opened in 1923, is the least altered of the hangouts favored by Kiki, Foujita, Ernest Hemingway, F. Scott Fitzgerald, Hart Crane, Henry Miller, and other writers

and artists in the heyday of Montparnasse. It remains a colorful spot where neighborhood regulars meet for coffee or a drink, or to partake of the fine selection of salads, omelettes, and sandwiches. The delicious *Croque "Sélect" pain Poilâne complet* (grilled ham, tomato, and egg sandwich on Poilâne sourdough bread) is a meal in itself. Grilled meat and bistro dishes are also served. ◆ M-F 8AM-2:30AM; Sa-Su 8:30AM-3:30AM. 99 Blvd du Montparnasse (at Rue Vavin). 01.45.48.38.24. Métro: Vavin

75 Dominique ★★$$ This restaurant/deli is as Russian as balalaikas. Grab a stool at the counter and snack on smoked salmon, pressed caviar, hot borscht, and blintzes with sour cream. Takeout is available. In the rear is an intimate restaurant for candlelight dining under a portrait of the Czar Nicholas II. ◆ M dinner; Tu-Sa lunch and dinner; closed one week in February and mid-July to mid-August. Reservations recommended. 19 Rue Bréa (between Blvd Raspail and Rue Notre-Dame-des-Champs). 01.43.27.08.80. Métro: Vavin

76 Académie de la Grande-Chaumière Any closet Cézannes, budding Bonnards, or rising Renoirs in your traveling party? At this modest art academy you can draw or paint your own masterpiece from live models and carry it home for less than the cost of those imitation Toulouse-Lautrec posters sold on Rue de Rivoli. ◆ Painting and drawing: M-Sa 9AM-noon. Sketching: M-Sa 3 6PM. Closed in August. 14 Rue de la Grande-Chaumière (between Rue Notre-Dame-des-Champs and Blvd du Montparnasse). 01.43.26.13.72. Métro: Vavin

77 Le Caméléon ★★$$ A bohemian bastion for famished painters in the 1960s, this eatery has become a thriving neighborhood bistro serving classic veal stew, hot sausage, smoked haddock, and a wide selection of salads. Those with a sweet tooth swoon for the white chocolate mousse and iced tea (with fresh mint) soufflé. Splurge on a delicious old Bourgueil wine with your meal. ◆ M-F lunch and dinner; Sa dinner; closed three weeks in August. Reservations recommended for dinner. 6 Rue de Chevreuse (between Blvd du Montparnasse and Rue Notre-Dame-des-Champs). 01.43.20.63.43. Métro: Vavin

78 La Closerie des Lilas ★★$$$ Since it opened in 1808, this legendary restaurant where lilacs once bloomed has attracted writers and artists, and the big names can be found engraved on the tables inside. Beaudelaire, Verlaine, and Jarry drank here in the 19th century, Fort held weekly poetry recitals in the years before World War I, and the Dadaists and Surrealists met here after the war. But the cafe is best known as one of Ernest Hemingway's favorite hangouts, where he wrote "true sentences" in notebooks, and talked life and literature with John Dos Passos, Archibald MacLeish, and F. Scott Fitzgerald. In *The Sun Also Rises,* part of which Hem wrote here, Lady Brett, Jake, and Bill Gorton stop in for a drink.

Today the place is frequented by young French film stars, people in publicity, communications, and fashion, and writers and artists with money. It's expensive and a bit pretentious, but fine for an after-dinner drink or a weekend lunch in the mottled light of its outdoor terrace in August when the rest of Paris shuts down. Try the steak *tartare, pigeon de Bresse rôti* (roasted pigeon from Bresse), *rumsteck flambé au cognac* (beefsteak flambéed with Cognac), or the best-selling *turbotin grillé* (grilled turbot). The piano kindles a certain warmth as well. ♦ Daily lunch and dinner until 1:30AM. Reservations required. 171 Blvd du Montparnasse (between Ave de l'Observatoire and Rue de Chevreuse). 01.40.51.34.50. RER: Port Royal

79 93 Boulevard St-Michel Sylvia Beach, founder of the famous Paris **Shakespeare and Company** bookstore (see page 81), holed up here in a top-floor kitchen after spending six months in a detention camp in Vittel. The first "liberator" she encountered was her old friend Ernest Hermingway, then a war correspondent, on 26 August 1944. They met in the street in front of her abandoned bookshop. As she later recalled, "We met with a crash; he picked me up and swung me around and kissed me while people on the street and in the windows cheered." ♦ Between Pl Louis-Marin and Rue Gay-Lussac. RER: Luxembourg

80 Le Petit Journal This old-time jazz *boîte* features French Dixieland and Swing groups and the occasional piano trio. Frequent performers include clarinetist Claude Luter, Sidney Bechet's longtime partner, and renowned pianist Claude Bolling. Clients can either pay a charge for the music and a drink, or enjoy the show over a prix-fixe dinner; prices for both options are quite reasonable. ♦ M-Sa until 2AM; closed in August. 71 Blvd St-Michel (between Pl Louis-Marin and Rue Gay-Lussac). 01.43.26.28.59. RER: Luxembourg. Also at: 13 Rue du Commandant-René-Mouchotte (between Pl de Catalogne and Ave du Maine). 01.43.21.56.70. Métros: Gaîté, Montparnasse-Bienvenüe

DALLOYAU

81 Dalloyau ★★$$ To sip a civilized cup of Chinese tea and indulge in a scoop of homemade ice cream or a delicate pastry while gazing over the **Luxembourg Gardens** from the terrace of this pastry shop and tea salon is to taste the luxury and leisure of an earlier, more gracious, era. ♦ Daily breakfast, lunch, and afternoon tea. 2 Pl Edmond-Rostand (at Blvd St-Michel). 01.43.29.31.10. RER: Luxembourg. Also at: 101 Rue du Faubourg-St-Honoré (between Rues du Colisée and La Boétie). 01.42.99.90.00. Métro: St-Philippe-du-Roule

82 Jardin du Luxembourg (Luxembourg Gardens) In the heart of the Left Bank, the 60-acre playground is graced with fountains, sculptures, ponds, flower beds, tennis courts, pony rides, a marionette theater, and outdoor band concerts. The *buvette,* a small open-air cafe (at the neat, modern public toilet in the basement, the cheerful attendant charges 2.5 francs per visit), is dappled with light filtered through the leaves of the surrounding trees, recalling the most pleasant moods of Impressionism. As a part of his draconian remodeling of Paris, Baron Haussmann had a plan to change this precious green expanse by turning part of it into roadways, but was thwarted when 12,000 Parisians signed a petition to save the park. A team of officious *gardiens* keeps the park under heavy surveillance, enforcing the following regulations: "The park is out of bounds to the drunk, beggars, and the indecently dressed; the playing of cards is restricted to the northwest corner of the gardens; the kicking of balls and sitting on the grass is prohibited entirely; and the park must be vacated precisely 30 minutes before sunset." These uniformed guards trill their whistles to chase lingerers from the gardens.

As for those ever-amusing North Americans in Paris: In 1900 Isadora Duncan was wont to dance here at 5AM, when the gardens opened, and Ernest Hemingway's destitute painter protagonist in *Islands in the Stream* captured and strangled pigeons for lunch. Don't miss the garden's many hidden delights: the small bronze replica of the Statue of Liberty; a series of statues of French queens and famous 19th-century women standing among the crocuses, daffodils, and azaleas; a beekeeping school run by André Lumaire, curator of the apiary, who gives practical classes from February to mid-September through the **Centrale d'Apiculture** (41 Rue Pernety, between Rues Raymond-Losserand and de l'Ouest, 01.45.42.29.08, Métro: Pernety); and the *pétanque* bowlers and chess players sequestered in their respective corners of the gardens. On the weekend, smartly dressed Latin Quarter grade-schoolers romp here and compete in the park's tricycle races and toy sailboat regattas held in the octagonal basin at the center of the park. ♦ Entrances at: Pl Paul-Claudel and Rue de Médicis. Métro: Odeon; Pl Edmond-Rostand and Blvd St-Michel. RER: Luxembourg; Pl André-Honnorat and Rue Auguste-Comte. RER: Luxembourg; Rue Guynemer (between Rues d'Assas and de Vaugirard). Métros: Notre-Dame des Champs, Rennes; Rue de Vaugirard (between Pl Paul-Claudel and Rue Guynemer). Métros: St-Sulpice, Rennes, Mabillon

Within the Jardin du Luxembourg:

Fontaine de Médicis (Medici Fountain)

At the end of a long, somewhat slimy pool filled with goldfish is one of the few Italianate stonework remnants of Marie de Médicis's day. White marble nude lovers, *Acis* and *Galatea,* are eyed from above by the bronze Cyclops *Polyphemus,* who waits to do the mythic Greek version of kicking sand in the face of the 98-pound weakling before making off with the girl. Notice that the water appears to flow uphill into the grotto. On the back side of the fountain is a delightful bas-relief of *Leda and the Swan* by Valois.

Luxembourg Gardens

MICHAEL STORRINGS

83 Palais du Luxembourg (Luxembourg Palace) The assassin Ravaillac could hardly have imagined that his murder of Henri IV in 1610 would result in the creation of this splendid palace and gardens. (Indeed, he didn't live long enough after committing his dastardly deed to imagine much of anything.) The widow of Henri IV, Queen Mother Marie de Médicis, grew tired of the **Louvre** and decided to build a palace that would recall her native Italy. She bought this vast property at the southern edge of the city from Duke François de Luxembourg and dispatched an architect to Florence to study her family residence, the Pitti Palace, before making plans for the new palace. Obediently, **Salomon de Brosse** designed this palace for her. Work began in 1615, but by the time the residence reached completion in 1631, Marie had been banished by her own son, Louis XIII, for turning against Cardinal Richelieu. She died penniless in Cologne 11 years later. During the Revolution, the palace served a short stint as a prison; it was here that British-born North American "Citizen Tom Paine" languished as an enemy Englishman for more than 10 months during the 1793 Reign of Terror and narrowly escaped execution.

Subsequently, the palace was remodeled to house the newly created French **Senate,** which met for the first time in 1804 and still resides here. Few of the trappings of Marie de Médicis's time remain; the 19th-century architect **Jean-François Chalgrin** (who also designed the **Arc de Triomphe**) made sure of that in his democratic remodeling. The 24 large canvases of the queen's life story created by Rubens were moved to the **Louvre** and the Uffizi Gallery in Florence. **Chalgrin** festooned the library with the paintings of Delacroix in homage to Virgil, Homer, and Dante. On the one day each month that the palace is open, visitors queue around the block. ♦ Admission. First Sunday of the month (call 01.44.61.20.89 or 01.44.61.21.69 before the 15th of the previous month to make a reservation for the guided tour). Rue de Vaugirard (between Pl Paul-Claudel and Rue Guynemer). Métro: Odéon

The city offers 72,778 registered hotel rooms.

In *A Moveable Feast,* Ernest Hemingway writes about walking in the Luxembourg Gardens to avoid food smells on the street when he was too poor to buy anything to eat. He also claims to have strangled pigeons and hidden them under the blanket in his son's stroller to take them home to cook.

Restaurants/Clubs: Red **Hotels:** Blue
Shops/ Outdoors: Green **Sights/Culture:** Black

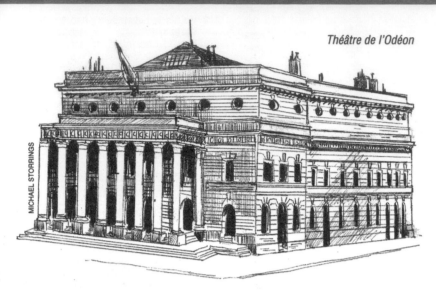

Théâtre de l'Odéon

MICHAEL STORRINGS

84 Théâtre de l'Odéon City architects **Marie-Josephe Peyre** and **Charles de Wailly** designed this rather clumsy building (pictured above) in 1782, intending it to look like an ancient temple. With 1,913 seats, it was the largest theater in Paris at the time. Beaumarchais's *Marriage of Figaro* premiered here on 27 April 1784 in an atmosphere of success and scandal; the author was jailed. After World War II, Jean-Louis Barrault and Madeleine Renaud revived interest in the theater with their productions of works by Beckett, Ionesco, Albee, and Claudel that became the talk of the town and, for a short period, made the theater the most popular in Paris. ♦ Box office: Daily 11AM-6:30PM. 1 Pl Paul-Claudel (at Rue Corneille). 01.44.41.36.36; www.theatre-odeon.fr. Métro: Odéon, RER: Luxembourg

LIBRAIRIE LE MONITEUR

85 Le Moniteur The best shop in Paris for books on architecture and landscape design also has a large selection of international design magazines and an array of unusual guidebooks and postcards. ♦ M-Sa. 7 Pl de l'Odéon (at Rue Racine). 01.44.41.15.75. Métro: Odéon

86 Rue Monsieur-le-Prince *Monsieur-le-Prince* is what every French king's brother was traditionally called. Since the early 19th century, this street has been a veritable North American alley, as evidenced by the events that took place at the following addresses. **No. 14:** A plaque on the building commemorates African-American novelist Richard Wright,

who lived in a third-floor apartment from 1948 to 1959, when Martin Luther King Jr. visited him there. **No. 22:** In 1892 James McNeill Whistler had a studio on the courtyard, where he completed a portrait of Count Robert de Montesquiou-Fezensac. (Years later, the count sold the painting for an exorbitant sum, thereby greatly offending Whistler. The portrait is now part of the Frick Collection in New York City.) **No. 49:** The poet Henry Wadsworth Longfellow lived here in June 1826. For $36 a week he received a room in the *pension de famille* of Madame Potet, French lessons with her daughters, and free laundry service. **No. 55:** Oliver Wendell Holmes lived here (now the site of the **Lycée St-Louis**) from 1833 to 1835 while he studied to be a doctor. To be on the safe side, the following year he obtained a second medical degree from Harvard. ♦ Métro: Odéon, RER: Luxembourg

86 Polidor ★★$ For well over a century, the home cooking served here has lured such struggling writers as Verlaine, Joyce, Valéry, and Hemingway out of their garrets for the earthy consolations of pumpkin soup, chicken in cream sauce, bacon and lentils, and rabbit in mustard sauce. Since its founding in 1845, little has changed; it's still a classic bistro with the traditional bistro decor, complete with lace curtains and tiny wooden drawers where the regulars store their linen napkins. Diners sit shoulder-to-shoulder at long tables, and the ambience is very convivial. The food is good, there are plenty of choices, and the prices have stayed within a garret-dweller's means. ♦ Daily lunch and dinner. No credit cards accepted. 41 Rue Monsieur-le-Prince (between Rues de Vaugirard and Racine). 01.43.26.95.34. Métro: Odéon

87 Bouillon Racine ★★$$ Built in 1906, this ornate Art Nouveau *bouillon,* a type of soup restaurant popular in Paris in the early 20th century, had great success in those days, but it eventually went downhill and was abandoned. The building was classified a historical monument, which meant that its interior could not be altered. A young Belgian chef, Olivier Simon, found it and fell in love with it in the early 1990s, and he and his partners spared no expense restoring it. When they opened in 1996, the mosaic floors, floral tile walls, serpentine chandeliers, and myriad other design elements were revealed once again in their full Belle Epoque efflorescence.

The cuisine is mainly Belgian, with beer used in many of the sauces. *Waterzooi* (Belgian pot-au-feu), is always on the menu, as is *carbonade de boeuf à la flamande* (Flemish-style *boeuf bourguignon*). But the menu changes frequently and offers such non-Belgian choices as ostrich steak or salmon sautéed with tandoori spices. And of course there's a vast array of Belgian beers, both bottled and on tap. The young staff is cheerful and efficient, the atmosphere lively. Reserve a table in the main dining room upstairs. The ground floor, where the bar is, can get a bit *too* lively. ♦ Daily lunch and dinner. Reservations recommended. 3 Rue Racine (between Blvd St-Michel and Rue Monsieur-le-Prince). 01.44.32.15.60. Métro: Cluny–La Sorbonne

88 Grand Hôtel des Balcons $$ This comfortable 55-room hotel, very reasonably priced for this area, is just down the street from the **Théâtre de l'Odéon.** There's no restaurant, but a buffet breakfast is served. ♦ 3 Rue Casimir-Delavigne (between Pl de l'Odéon and Rue Monsieur-le-Prince). 01.46.34.78.50; fax 01.46.34.06.27; www.balcons.com. Métro: Odéon

89 Chez Maître Paul ★★$$ The affable Debert family opened this quaint little restaurant in 1945. It looks like a country cottage hidden deep in the Franche-Comté region in the Jura Mountains in eastern France. The kitchen is famous for its variety of wine sauces and a winning way with chicken and veal. Specialties include free-range chicken in a sauce made with *vin jaune* (a wine similar to sherry), and calf's liver cooked with *vin de paille* (a Sauternes-like wine). ♦ Daily lunch and dinner. Reservations recommended. 12 Rue Monsieur-le-Prince (at Rue Casimir-Delavigne). 01.43.54.74.59. Métro: Odéon

90 San Francisco Book Company A few steps from Sylvia Beach's original **Shakespeare and Company** bookshop, Jim Carroll and Phil Wood carry on the worthy tradition of offering English-language books in a small, but remarkably well-stocked, store. They sell new and used books, hardcover and paperback, covering literature, music, art, film, philosophy, and the social sciences, and try to keep prices low to promote turnover. They also buy and swap books. ♦ M-Sa. 17 Rue Monsieur-le-Prince (between Rue Antoine-Dubois and Carrefour de l'Odéon). 01.43.29.15.70. Métro: Odéon

91 La Méditerranée ★★$$ Stunning interiors and good, fresh seafood continue to attract a stylish clientele at this glamorous old haunt of Marlene Dietrich, Orson Welles, Man Ray, Marc Chagall, and Jean Cocteau. Offerings range from fresh shellfish, marinated mussels, and grilled swordfish to more sophisticated dishes, including *chipirons* (little Basque squid) sautéed in herbs, *tartare* of fresh tuna, bouillabaisse, and fillet of bass roasted with dried tomatoes. ♦ Daily lunch and dinner. 2 Pl de l'Odéon (at Rue de l'Odéon). 01.43.26.02.30. Métro: Odéon

92 12 Rue de l'Odéon From 1921 to 1940 this was the famous bookstore **Shakespeare and Company,** run by Sylvia Beach, daughter of a Presbyterian minister from Princeton, New Jersey. Her shop was a Parisian hearth and home for such North American and British writers as Ezra Pound, Archibald MacLeish, Thornton Wilder, and F. Scott Fitzgerald, to whom Beach served as guardian angel. She was constantly lending books and money to Ernest Hemingway, who came to Paris in 1921 and, after the publication of *The Sun Also Rises* in 1926, became the city's most famous writer from across the Atlantic.

Beach was devoted to literature in general and to one writer in particular: James Joyce. If it hadn't been for this amazing woman, the most important literary event of the day—the publication, in full, of *Ulysses*—might never have happened. Beach became Joyce's secretary, editor, agent, and banker, and nearly bankrupted her bookstore in the process of publishing the book. A plaque on the building commemorates her achievement. The building now has residential and commercial space. ♦ Between Pl de l'Odéon and Carrefour de l'Odéon. Métro: Odéon

93 19 Rue de Tournon In May 1790 the American Revolutionary naval officer John Paul Jones, having served a year in the Russian navy, moved to Paris, where he was welcomed as a national hero for his epic 1779 capture of the *Serapis,* a British warship. When he told Ambassador Benjamin Franklin that he wanted to learn French, the wise old gentleman advised him to get "a walking dictionary." Jones died destitute in a second-floor flat in this building on 18 July 1792; he received a full-scale state funeral paid for by the French government. This is still a residential building. ♦ Between Rues de Vaugirard and St-Sulpice. Métro: Odéon

94 42-44 Rue de Vaugirard In a top-floor flat of this apartment building, William Faulkner set to work on his first novel, *The Mosquitoes,* in the summer of 1925. A plaque on the Rue Servandoni side of the building notes the future Nobel Prize laureate's sojourn in Paris. ♦ At Rue Servandoni. Métro: St-Sulpice, Mabillon

95 Au Bon St-Pourçain ★★$$ At this authentic old neighborhood bistro, Chef Franck Pasquet fuels his St-Germain regulars with escargots, *compote de lapereau* (young rabbit stew), cassoulet, beef with olives, and sole meunière, which they wash down with good, modestly priced St-Pourçain wine. ♦ M-Sa lunch and dinner. 10 *bis* Rue Servandoni (between Rues de Vaugirard and du Canivet). 01.43.54.93.63. Métros: St-Sulpice, Mabillon

96 Rue Férou This street has housed a number of artists over the years. Painter/photographer Man Ray occupied an atelier with a high ceiling at **No. 2** in 1951. Ernest Hemingway lived in the sphinx-protected *hôtel particulier* at **No. 6** in 1926, having left his wife, Hadley, for French *Vogue* staffer Pauline Pfeiffer.

Painter Henri Fantin-Latour had an apartment at **No. 13** in 1858, where he was sketched by his friend James McNeill Whistler (whose drawing was later purchased by the **Louvre**). ♦ Métro: St-Sulpice

97 Place St-Sulpice One of the most serene squares in Paris has a cafe, pink-flowering chestnut trees, and the marvelous stone **Fontaine des Quatre Points Cardinaux** (Fountain of the Four Cardinal Points) by Visconti. The fountain features four famous French clergymen oriented north, south, east, and west, with four regal lions snarling at their feet. Once flanked by shops peddling ivory crucifixes, rosary beads, and clerical garments, the square today is graced by two Yves Saint Laurent boutiques. It hosts antiques and book fairs in summer, and what many consider the finest of the Bastille Day balls. ♦ Métro: St-Sulpice

98 St-Sulpice Interrupted by insurrection, insolvency, and even bolts of lightning, the construction of this church required the services of architects, including the notable **Louis Le Vau** over a span of 134 years. Its dramatic Classical style was the inspiration of **Giovanni Servandoni,** a Florentine known for his theater and stage-set designs. The disparity of the two towers, an odd couple indeed, was the result of shifting architectural sands and patronly indecision. Named after St. Sulpicius, the sixth-century archbishop of Bourges, and dubbed the **Temple of Victory** during the Revolution, the church hosted a lavish banquet for 1,200 after Napoléon returned from his victories in Egypt. Inside the front door are two holy water stoups made from enormous shells given to François I by the Venetian Republic. The Chapelle des Anges (Chapel of Angels) was frescoed by an aging Eugène Delacroix. In a chapel at the rear of the church is the extraordinary *Virgin and Child* by Jean-Baptiste Pigalle. The organ, designed in 1776 by **Jean-François Chalgrin,** with 6,588 pipes, numbers among the largest in the world. In the floor, running along the north-south transept, is a bronze meridian line, a testament to France's 19th-century passion for science. Three times a year, on the equinoxes and the winter solstice, sunlight strikes the line so precisely that light runs along the metal strip, glances off an obelisk and globe at its top, and finally illuminates a cross. The inscription on the obelisk translates, more or less, as "Two Scientists with God's Help." ♦ Pl St-Sulpice (between Rues Palatine and St-Sulpice). 01.46.33.21.78. Métro: St-Sulpice

99 Marie Mercié The custom-made hats in Mercié's summer and winter collections here range from classic chapeaux to the amusing befeathered, beribboned fantasies that have earned her an international reputation. ♦ Tu-Sa. 23 Rue St-Sulpice (between Rues de

Tournon and Garancière). 01.43.26.45.83. Métros: Mabillon, Odéon

100 Le Petit Vatel ★★$ One of St-Germain's smallest and least expensive restaurants is filled with famished students and cost-conscious locals seated around its handful of tables. Owner Catherine Grandjacques and her garrulous chef Sixte, who is fluent in French, English, and Spanish, offer an amazing array of choices, given the minuscule size of the place. They include lime soup; homemade pâté; pot-au-feu; vegetarian plate; *pamboli* (mountain cheese and Spanish ham baked in an oven over toast with olive oil, a Catalan specialty); grilled, boiled, and baked sausages; lamb stew; moussaka; roast pork; chocolate cake; and *gratin de pommes* (baked apple casserole). ◆ M-Sa lunch and dinner; Su dinner. No credit cards accepted. 5 Rue Lobineau (between Rues de Seine and Mabillon). 01.43.54.28.49. Métros: Mabillon, Odéon

101 Marché St-Germain An old covered market has been converted into a bright, modern mall with **The Gap, The Body Shop,** several youth-oriented clothing boutiques, and **Coolin,** a convivial Irish pub (01.44.07.00.92). But the fishmongers, cheese and wine merchants, florists, and dairymaids are still to be found in the south side of the building, fronting on Rue Lobineau. Under the market building are a basketball court and a 25-meter (82.5-foot) public swimming pool, the **Piscine St-Germain** (01.43.29.08.15). ◆ Market: Tu-Sa; Su morning. Pool: Tu-Su hours vary. Rues Mabillon and Lobineau. Métro: Mabillon

102 Le Golfe de Naples ★★$ The best pizza in Paris is found at this little *ristorante* across the street from the **Marché St-Germain.** The pies come in 17 varieties, from the simple *Napoletana* to the appetite-sating *Amoureuse,* heaped with fresh shrimp, squid, mussels, and mushrooms. Italian appetizers, salads, pasta, meat, and fish dishes are also served at prices that are easy on the pocket. With its red tablecloths, big wood-burning oven, and happily chattering diners, the tone is decidedly upbeat. The late Marcello Mastroianni used to eat here every week during his frequent stays in Paris. There's a sidewalk terrace for alfresco dining in summer. A word of caution: the Neapolitan nonchalance of the waiters can be a problem for those in a hurry. ◆ Daily lunch and dinner. 5 Rue de Montfaucon (at Rue Clément). 01.43.26.98.11. Métro: Mabillon

103 Aux Charpentiers ★★$$ Formerly the lunch hall of an 18th-century carpenters guild, this reasonably priced bistro serves chef Pierre Bardeche's simple but well-prepared bacon and lentils, beef stew, sautéed veal, and other daily specials. ◆ Daily lunch and dinner. Reservations recommended. 10 Rue Mabillon (between Rues Guisarde and du Four). 01.43.26.30.05. Métro: Mabillon

103 Castel's This private club caters to dandies, back-biting gossips, "BCBGs" (for *bon chic, bon genre,* the French term for yuppies), and former cabinet ministers with socialites on their arms. Technically, no one crosses the threshold unaccompanied by a card-carrying member (some 2,500 privileged people), but if you're acceptably dressed (jacket and tie for men) and are willing to pay 2,200 francs (about $400 at press time) for a year's membership, you too might be permitted to join the elite. Drinks are correspondingly expensive, the decor is tacky, the food unremarkable, and the dance floor crowded—so what's all the fuss about? ◆ M-Sa dinner. Disco: M-Sa 11:30PM-dawn. 15 Rue Princesse (between Rues Guisarde and du Four). 01.40.51.52.80. Métro: Mabillon

104 Birdland The jazzy bar serves chili con carne and plays classic John Coltrane and Charlie Parker. ◆ M-Sa 7PM-dawn; Su 11PM-dawn. 20 Rue Princesse (at Rue Guisarde). 01.43.26.97.59. Métro: Mabillon

104 Chez Henri ★★$ This first-rate neighborhood bistro with a convivial ambience is known for its delicious *magret de canard* (duck fillet), green bean vinaigrette, *foie de veau* (veal liver), baked goat-cheese salad, au gratin potatoes, and homemade tarts. ◆ M-Sa lunch and dinner. Reservations recommended. No credit cards accepted. 16 Rue Princesse (between Rues Guisarde and du Four). 01.46.33.51.12. Métro: Mabillon

CyberParis

France moved into the Internet Age at an escargot's pace, and the country still lags way behind the US in all things computer-related. But Internauts traveling to Paris without computers will find several web cafes and other spots around town where they can get on-line for a modest fee. And for people seeking information about Paris, a vast quantity of material is available on the World Wide Web, in both English and French.

Where to Get On-line in Paris

Café Orbital (13 Rue du Médicis, between Pls Edmond-Rostand and Paul-Claudel, 01.43.25.76.77; info@orbital.com; www.orbital.fr; RER: Luxembourg) is a cozy Internet cafe by the **Luxembourg Gardens.**

Cyberport (Forum des Images, Nouveau Forum des Halles, 1 Rue Pierre-Lescot, at Rue Berger, 01.44.76.62.00; ebuazy@vdp.fr; www.forum.vdp.fr; RER: Châtelet–Les Halles, Métro: Les Halles) is Paris's most up-to-date multimedia center.

Galeries Lafayette (40 Blvd Haussmann, between Rues de la Chaussée-d'Antin and de Mogador, 01.42.82.36; welcome@galerieslafayette.com; www.galerieslafayette.com; Métro: Chaussée d'Antin) boasts the **Espace Internet,** a quiet room on the store's fifth floor that has several Internet setups.

Web Bar (32 Rue de Picardie, at Rue de Franche-Comté, 01.42.72.57.47; webbar@imaginet.fr; www.webbar.fr; Métro: République) is the coolest—both the people and decor—Internet cafe in town.

Useful Web Sites (in English)

Bonjour Paris's site (www.bparis.com) features well-written articles by experienced North American journalists in Paris, as well as a chat line.

Paris-Anglophone's guide (www.paris-anglo.com) is especially useful for people living in Paris and those planning to move here. It offers phone numbers and addresses of English-language contacts in Paris, a guide book oriented to the needs of English-speaking people who are planning a long stay in Paris, a cultural and practical guide for short-term visitors, and a chat room.

Paris Free Voice's (www.parisvoice.com) film, theater, and restaurant reviews, monthly cultural listings, journalistic pieces about the city, and want ads are featured here.

The **Paris Office de Tourisme**'s huge web site (www.paris-touristoffice.com) offers lots of valuable facts about the city. Also here is a list of hundreds of hyperlinked web sites for hotels, apartment-rental agencies, restaurants, monuments and museums, music, theater, cinema and sports venues, attractions for children, airlines and travel service companies, and several search engines (mostly in French, but easy to figure out).

Time Out's (www.timout.co.uk) reviews and listings are a helpful source of up-to-date information.

Useful Web Sites (in French)

Bibliothèque Nationale de France (National Library; www.bnf.fr).

Chateau of **Versailles** (www.chateauversailles.fr).

France Télécom (www.pageszoom.com/mescommercents.fr) has white and yellow pages for the whole country. Also here is an interesting search engine for streets that gives the name, address, and phone number of every business on the street; a click of the mouse on the name of an establishment brings up a photo of it.

Le Monde newspaper (www.lemonde.com).

Libération newspaper (www.liberation.com).

Museé du Louvre (www.louvre.fr).

Pariscope (www.pariscope.fr) features its weekly listings for movies, theater, opera, jazz, pop, and classical concerts and clubs.

Télérama magazine (www.telerama.com) offers its reviews and listings of movies, plays, operas, art exhibits, and TV shows.

Weather satellite photos and forecasts from the French national meteorological service (www.meteo.fr/temps).

Internet Access Numbers in France

AOL	08.36.06.13.10
CompuServe	08.36.06.13.19
MS Network	08.36.01.93.01

Village Voice

105 **Village Voice** In the intelligent tradition of those famous Left Bank bookstore/salons run by such women as Sylvia Beach and Adrienne Monnier, the English bookshop of Odile Hellier is a busy crossroads for *anglophone* writers, artists, and literati in Paris. Hellier has something for everyone: a fine selection of classical, contemporary, and small-press fiction, exceptional author readings, and the latest issues of *The New York Review of Books, The New Yorker,* and (naturally) *The Village Voice.* ◆ M 2-8PM; Tu-Sa. 6 Rue Princesse (between Rues Guisarde and du Four). 01.46.33.36.47. Métro: Mabillon

105 **Coffee Parisien** ★★$ Framed dollar bills on the wall, a 1950s Lucky Strike ad, the *New York Times* front page from the day President John F. Kennedy was assassinated in Dallas, and other Americana set the tone for

Franco–New Yorker Jonathan Goldstein's Big Apple–style luncheonette in the City of Light. Nachos, guacamole, and tortilla chips, chicken wings, spinach salad, pastrami sandwiches, cheeseburgers, hash browns, eggs Benedict, grilled tuna, vegetarian plate, cheesecake, Bud, Corona, Ben & Jerry's, it's all there, just like *chez vous*. ♦ Daily noon to midnight. 4 Rue Princesse (between Rues Guisarde and du Four). 01.43.54.18.18. Métro: Mabillon. Also at: 7 Rue Gustave-Courbet (between Rues de Longchamp and de la Pompe). 01.45.53.17.17. Métro: Rue de la Pompe

106 Chez Georges On an alley called Duckling Street, surrounded by a wealth of Italian restaurants, is this classic old French bar wallpapered with mug shots of the singers who once performed in the old cabaret downstairs. It's a nice place for a glass of Côtes-du-Rhône or Beaujolais before dining on cannelloni and pizza down the street. ♦ Tu-Sa noon-2AM. No credit cards accepted. 11 Rue des Canettes (between Rues Guisarde and du Four). 01.43.26.79.15. Métro: Mabillon

107 Rue des Ciseaux Named after a scissors craftsman who once resided here, this short street is home to three Japanese restaurants and a pizzeria. ♦ Métro: St-Germain-des-Prés

108 St-Germain-des-Prés For more than 15 centuries a church has stood on this corner, which in Roman times was a *pré* (open pasture). The first church, built in AD 452 by Merovingian king Childebert, was repeatedly destroyed by invading Normans and finally rebuilt to last in 1163. The Romanesque western gate tower is faintly reminiscent of the great abbeys on the outskirts of Paris. During the Middle Ages, this church, named after St. Germanus (AD 496-576), bishop of Paris, became a focal point for Easter fairs, with hundreds of stalls, performing theater troupes, live "statues," and dancing bears.

Inside the church is an altar dedicated to the victims of the September 1793 massacre, a shameful chapter of French history, when Paris was ruled by a bloodthirsty mob called the *sans-culottes* (because they wore linen trousers instead of aristocratic knee breeches). In 1793, after a mock trial on the weekend of 2-3 September, almost 200 prisoners sequestered in the church were led into the courtyard (at the corner of what is now Rue Bonaparte and Boulevard St-Germain), where they were stabbed and hacked to death by hired killers. Ministers of Louis XVI, his father confessor, and the Swiss Guards were slaughtered. The carnage was followed by an auction of the victims' personal effects. The skull of René Descartes, the 17th-century mathematician and philosopher, along with the body of John Casimir, a 17th-

century king of Poland who was abbot of St-Germain, are buried inside the church.

Today, however, the edifice is best known for its evening concerts of classical music. It also provides a cool place to meditate on muggy summer days. ♦ Guided tours: Tu, Th 1-5PM. Pl St-Germain-des-Prés (between Blvd St-Germain and Rue de l'Abbaye). 01.43.25.41.71, concerts 01.42.77.65.65. Métro: St-Germain-des-Prés

Next to St-Germain-des-Prés:

Hommage à Apollinaire In the small park to the left of the main portal is a bronze bust of a woman by Pablo Picasso, given to the city in 1958 in memory of his friend, the poet Guillaume Apollinaire (1880-1918), who lived and died at 202-04 Boulevard St-Germain. Of Polish origin (his last name was Kostrowitzki), Apollinaire wrote the famous *Alcools* in 1913 and was an early leader of the Paris avant-garde. Eventually renowned for his poetry, Apollinaire was best known in his time as the man who stole the *Mona Lisa*. The scandal began when Apollinaire's former personal secretary lifted two inconsequential Phoenician statues from the **Louvre** and sold them to Picasso. Coincidentally, the *Mona Lisa* disappeared shortly afterward. Apollinaire, trying to protect his secretary and Picasso from suspicion and incarceration, turned in the statues and was jailed for four days. The *Mona Lisa* eventually resumed her place in the **Louvre,** and Apollinaire was exonerated. He never, however, recovered his self-esteem. A short street nearby also honors Apollinaire.

109 St-Germain-des-Prés $$ In the heart of bustling St-Germain, this 30-room hotel is convenient though hardly tranquil. Breakfast is served in the garden room, but there's no restaurant. ♦ 36 Rue Bonaparte (between Pl St-Germain-des-Prés and Rue Jacob). 01.43.26.00.19; fax 01.40.46.83.63. Métro: St-Germain-des-Prés

110 Réunion des Musées Nationaux It's Tuesday. You forgot to buy a poster or catalog at the **Louvre** to take home, and now the museum is closed. Don't fret. This bookstore stocks all the catalogs and posters published by the national museums in France since 1966. ♦ M-Sa. 10 Rue de l'Abbaye (between Rues de Furstemberg and Bonaparte). 01.43.29.21.45. Métros: St-Germain-des-Prés, Mabillon

111 24 Rue Bonaparte In the spring of 1928, Henry Miller stayed here with his wife, June. The building now has both residential and commercial space. ♦ Between Rue Jacob and Quai Malaquais. Métro: St-Germain-des-Prés

---

Restaurants/Clubs: Red   **Hotels:** Blue

Shops/♦ **Outdoors:** Green   **Sights/Culture:** Black

112 Ecole des Beaux-Arts (School of Fine Arts) The city's fine arts school was established by Louis XIV and trained many of the architects and artists who have designed and decorated Paris over the centuries. It's worth a quick detour to view the lovely Renaissance archway, fountain, and sculpture, and the changing exhibitions of student work. Two well-known architects, **Richard Morris Hunt** and **Bernard Ralph Maybeck,** were among the first North Americans to be educated here, and each employed his own version of the Beaux Arts style in the US during the late 19th century. Ellsworth Kelly studied here after World War II. ♦ Daily. 14 Rue Bonaparte (between Rue Jacob and Quai Malaquais). 01.47.03.50.00. Métro: St-Germain-des-Prés

113 8 Rue Bonaparte The young Corsican conqueror once lived here, but this street wasn't named for him until 1852, when his nephew, Napoléon III, became emperor. ♦ Between Rue Jacob and Quai Malaquais. Métro: St-Germain-des-Prés

114 Restaurant des Beaux-Arts ★★$ Established in 1850, this bargain canteen is usually filled with art students. Go early to miss the lines but not the coq au vin, *boeuf bourguignon, confit de canard* (duck confit), and pot-au-feu. ♦ Daily lunch and dinner. 11 Rue Bonaparte (between Rue des Beaux-Arts and Quai Malaquais). 01.43.26.92.64. Métro: St-Germain-des-Prés

115 Franco Maria Ricci Editore This is the Paris shop of the celebrated Milan publisher, whose eclectic and elegant series of fine arts books and literature ranges in subject from decorative ceramics and iconography to deluxe Italian reeditions of Saki, Kafka, Borges, and Poe. ♦ Tu-Sa. 12 Rue des Beaux-Arts (between Rues de Seine and Bonaparte). 01.46.33.96.31. Métro: St-Germain-des-Prés

116 L'Hôtel $$$$ Formerly the **Hôtel d'Alsace,** this 27-room place is where Oscar Wilde stayed in 1899 after his release from Reading Gaol (the prison). He expired here the following year, sighing, "I am dying beyond my means." *Dorian Gray* fans can stay in the room where Wilde lived out his last days. Or, if you prefer, book the Art Deco bedroom of dance-hall belle Mistinguett. The hotel's seven-story light well is a triumph of Directoire architecture. Note: rooms with showers are far less expensive than those with baths. ♦ 13 Rue des Beaux-Arts (between Rues de Seine and Bonaparte). 01.44.41.99.00; fax 01.43.25.64.81; reservation@l-hotel.com; www.l-hotel.com. Métro: St-Germain-des-Prés

Within L'Hôtel:

Le Belier Bar Young art and antiques dealers bring their fancy North American friends here to experience the Parisian scene. ♦ Daily 2-11PM. 01.44.41.99.00

116 Galerie Claude Bernard One of the city's best, this internationally known gallery shows such modern heavyweights as Balthus, Giacometti, David Hockney, Louise Nevelson, and Jim Dine. ♦ Tu-Sa. No credit cards accepted. 7-9 Rue des Beaux-Arts (between Rues de Seine and Bonaparte). 01.43.26.97.07. Métro: St-Germain-des-Prés

117 5 Rue des Beaux-Arts Edouard Manet was born here in 1835. ♦ Between Rues de Seine and Bonaparte. Métro: St-Germain-des-Prés

118 Roger-Viollet The more-than eight million black-and-white and color photographs for sale at this press agency document the history of humankind from antiquity to the present. Stored here are glossies of the Temple of Ramses at Abou Simbel, the interior of a 14th-century baker's shop, Louis Armstrong, and the demolition of the Berlin Wall. Curious tourists are not admitted, but journalists, students, and other researchers are welcome. ♦ M-F. 6 Rue de Seine (between Rue des Beaux-Arts and Quai Malaquais). 01.55.42.89.00. Métro: St-Germain-des-Prés

119 24 Rue Visconti This was once the home of Racine. According to a historian's account, the brilliant 17th-century dramatist died here on 21 April 1699 of a combination of dysentery, erysipelas, rheumatism, a liver ailment, and, possibly, "the chagrin of no longer being in favor with the king." The building is still a private residence. ♦ Between Rues de Seine and Bonaparte. Métro: St-Germain-des-Prés

120 17 Rue Visconti Young Balzac set up his print shop at this address. A few years later, in 1836, Delacroix moved in. It was here that he painted his portraits of George Sand and Frédéric Chopin. It is now a private residential/commercial building. ♦ Between Rues de Seine and Bonaparte. Métro: St-Germain-des-Prés

120 Claude Boullé For a quarter of a century, Claude Boullé has been selling his landscapes represented in natural stones, cut and polished. Some of them are the mineral counterparts of Turner's seascapes on canvas. ♦ M-Sa. 28 Rue Jacob (between Rues de Seine and Bonaparte). 01.46.33.01.38. Métro: St-Germain-des-Prés

120 La Maison Rustique Green thumbs will enjoy browsing in this agricultural and horticultural bookstore. ♦ M-Sa. 26 Rue Jacob (between Rues de Seine and Bonaparte). 01.42.34.96.60. Métro: St-Germain-des-Prés

121 La Villa $$$ This 32-room hotel with a slick contemporary look is the place to stay on the Left Bank if rustic decor doesn't charm you. After 10:30PM Monday through Saturday you'll find an international assortment of beautiful people downstairs in the plush, modern **Club la Villa,** listening to live jazz and munching on caviar and foie gras. Filmmaker Spike Lee stays here. ♦ 29 Rue Jacob (between Rues de Furstemberg and Bonaparte). 01.43.26.60.00; fax 01.46.34.63.63. Métro: St-Germain-des-Prés

121 27 Rue Jacob The prestigious French publishing house Editions du Seuil has its offices in the building where Ingres, the master of French classical painting, lived more than 150 years ago. ♦ Between Rues de Furstemberg and Bonaparte. Métro: St-Germain-des-Prés

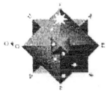

122 Librairie Maritime Outremer This bookstore specializes in maritime books. ♦ M-Sa. 17 Rue Jacob (between Rues de Furstemberg and Bonaparte). 01.46.33.47.48; 01.43.29.96.77. Métro: St-Germain-des-Prés

123 14 Rue Jacob German opera composer Richard Wagner lived here in 1841-42. The building now has both residential and commercial space. ♦ Between Rues de Seine and Bonaparte. Métro: St-Germain-des-Prés

124 7 Rue Jacob In 1656, at the age of 17, Racine lived here with his uncle. It's still a residential/commercial building. ♦ Between Rues de Furstemberg and Bonaparte. Métro: St-Germain-des-Prés

125 Yveline Tucked away in Place de Furstemberg is this charming antiques shop that is a fascinating place to browse. ♦ M-Sa; closed in August. 4 Rue de Furstemberg

(between Rues de l'Abbaye and Jacob). 01.43.26.56.91. Métros: St-Germain-des-Prés, Mabillon

125 Musée National E. Delacroix The old atelier of Eugène Delacroix, where he lived, worked, and, in 1863, died, is now a museum displaying his paintings, sketches, and letters. A quick tour will give you some idea of why Baudelaire described Delacroix as a "volcanic crater artistically concealed beneath bouquets of flowers." ♦ Admission. M, W-Su. 6 Rue de Furstemberg (between Rues de l'Abbaye and Jacob). 01.44.41.86.50. Métros: St-Germain-des-Prés, Mabillon

125 Place de Furstemberg Named after Egon de Furstemberg, a 17th-century abbot of **St-Germain-des-Prés,** this hidden treasure attracts French filmmakers, flamenco guitarists, and harpists who like to play in the courtyard because of its extraordinary acoustics. At the center of the square is a white-globed lamppost and four paulownia trees that Henry Miller described as having "the poetry of T.S. Eliot." In spring the trees burst into fragrant lavender bloom; Paris never smells as sweet anywhere else. ♦ Rue de Furstemberg (between Rues de l'Abbaye and Jacob). Métros: St-Germain-des-Prés, Mabillon

126 Manuel Canovas This showroom exhibits wallpaper and fabrics by the famed designer whose sumptuous works are often featured in *Vogue* and *Architectural Digest.* Within the shop is a small boutique offering home accessories including bed- and table linens. ♦ M-Sa. 7 Rue de Furstemberg (between Rues de l'Abbaye and Cardinale). 01.43.25.75.98. Métros: St-Germain-des-Prés, Mabillon

126 2 Rue Cardinale The Black Sun Press operated at this address under the aegis of Harry and Caresse Crosby, a couple of wild surrealists of the 1920s. They were the first to publish D.H. Lawrence's *Sun* and Hart Crane's *The Bridge.* Harry, who was a nephew of J.P. Morgan, died in a double suicide with his mistress at the Hôtel des Artistes in New York. ♦ Between Rues de l'Abbaye and de Furstemberg. Métros: St-Germain-des-Prés, Mabillon

127 Hôtel de Seine $$$ Once a family-run *pension,* this 30-room hotel has lost its bohemian charm of yore, but it's nonetheless a well-located and comfortable place that strives to please. Beat poet Lawrence Ferlinghetti, owner of City Lights Bookstore in San Francisco, used to stay here. There's no restaurant. ♦ 52 Rue de Seine (between Rues de Buci and Jacob). 01.46.34.22.80; fax 01.46.34.04.74. Métro: Mabillon

127 Cosi ★★$ This gourmet Italian sandwich and salad counter serves everything from salmon carpaccio to roasted red peppers—all on bread baked in wood-fired pizza ovens. Tuscan wines, opera by Verdi, and daily editions of *La Repubblica* lend to this place's Latin charm. Take your order to go, or if you prefer, eat here in the upstairs seating area. ♦ Daily lunch and dinner until midnight. 54 Rue de Seine (between Rues de Buci and Jacob). 01.46.33.35.36. Métro: Mabillon

128 Rue de Buci One of Paris's prettiest street markets is named after M. Buci, president of the Parliament of Paris during the Renaissance. On Tuesday through Saturday and Sunday mornings, the intersection of Rues de Buci and de Seine is thronged with operatic hawkers hustling endive, homemade fettuccine, freshly ground Colombian coffee, wild strawberries, fresh cherries, hot baguettes, and pink tulips.

From here, Rue de Seine shoots off toward the river, becoming a thoroughfare of art galleries. Bear that in mind when passing by in the early evening: a crowded gallery is most likely hosting a *vernissage* (literally a "varnishing," the French name for an exhibition opening). Put on your best French accent, join the party, and talk art while sipping a glass of Champagne. ♦ Market: Tu-Sa; Su morning. Métros: Mabillon, Odéon

On Rue de Buci:

Le Chai de l'Abbaye ★★$ Typical French fare is served here at one of the few good wine bars in Paris not crawling with yuppies. ♦ Daily breakfast, lunch, and dinner until 2AM. No. 26 (at Rue du Bourbon-le-Château). 01.43.26.68.26

128 2 Rue du Bourbon-le-Château Buzz yourself in and have a look at the circular-well courtyard in this 1824 apartment building. (**L'Hôtel** on Rue des Beaux-Arts is another example of this architectural device.) Try to imagine how items such as grand pianos are hoisted up to the fifth floor. ♦ At Rue de Buci. Métro: Mabillon

129 La Rhumerie Upper-crust imbibers, along with the rabble out for a good time, keep this place packed. The stiff punches made with 130 kinds of the tropical liquor make it worth fighting for a table. In addition to the usual daiquiris and planter's punch, try the *Père Serge,* which is named after a priest at **St-Germain-des-Prés** and is made with rum, lemon, and sugarcane syrup. The liquid refreshments are the real draw here, but meat and fish dishes are served at lunch and snacks such as *boudin* (sausage), *akra de morue* (fish fritters), and crab *farci* (stuffed and spiced crab) are available throughout the day and night. ♦ Daily 9AM-2AM. 166 Blvd St-Germain (between Rues de Buci and de l'Echaudé). 01.43.54.28.94. Métro: Mabillon

130 La Louisiane $$ If you want to stay right in the heart of Paris, this 80-room property is a

good choice. The hotel has hosted some famous French literati, including Jacques Prévert, Jean-Paul Sartre, and Simone de Beauvoir, who lived in one of the hotel's coveted oval rooms for years, and it was the favorite of North American jazz musicians during the heyday of the St-Germain jazz caves in the 1950s. The noise level can be high, so light sleepers should go elsewhere. There's no restaurant. ♦ 60 Rue de Seine (between Blvd St-Germain and Rue de Buci). 01.44.32.17.17; fax 01.46.34.23.87. Métro: Mabillon

131 Vagenende ★★$$ With the full effulgence of an 1885 Belle Epoque and Tiffany glass decor, this poor man's **Maxim's** has starred in films such as *Travels with My Aunt* and *Murder on the Orient Express.* Homemade foie gras, fresh shellfish, and pot-au-feu are good dishes to try. ♦ Daily lunch and dinner until 1AM. 142 Blvd St-Germain (between Rues Grégoire-de-Tours and de Seine). 01.43.26.68.18. Métros: Mabillon, Odéon

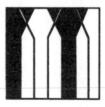

132 Galerie Documents Opened in 1954 by Michel Romand and now run by his daughter Mireille, this is the city's most distinguished antique poster shop, specializing in *affiches* from 1875 to 1930, particularly the works of Toulouse-Lautrec, Grasset, Mucha, and Steinlen. ♦ M 2:30-7PM; Tu-Sa. 53 Rue de Seine (between Rues de Buci and Jacques-Callot). 01.43.54.50.68. Métro: Mabillon

133 Galerie Arts des Amériques If pre-Columbian art from Central and South America is your passion, this gallery has treasures in store for you. ♦ M-Sa; closed in August. 42 Rue de Seine (between Rues Jacob and Visconti). 01.46.33.18.31. Métros: Mabillon, St-Germain-des-Prés

134 La Palette ★★$ This bohemian cafe is right out of a Jean Rhys novel. In fact, James Ivory filmed part of that down-and-out tale *Quartet* (with Alan Bates, Maggie Smith, and Isabelle Adjani) here in 1981. The artists' palettes that hang on the wall are more interesting than the paintings themselves, but don't miss the humorous 1920s tiled murals in the back room. House specialties include gruyère omelette, chef's salad, country ham served on Poilâne country bread, and a delicious *tarte tatin*. Bearded waiter Jean-François is grouchy but kindhearted and plays the part of a little Bonaparte; you must order quickly and without indecision or he'll ignore you until you've learned your lesson. One Aussie regular calls the crouch-style toilet an "authentic porcelain kangaroo trap." ◆ M-Sa breakfast and lunch until 2AM; closed in August. No credit cards accepted. 43 Rue de Seine (at Rue Jacques-Callot). 01.43.26.68.15. Métros: Mabillon, St-Germain-des-Prés

135 Librairie Fischbacher Along with a stunning collection of fine arts editions, this shop has books on history and primitive arts, critical studies, and biographies in French, English, German, and Italian. ◆ M-Sa. 33 Rue de Seine (between Rues Jacques-Callot and Mazarine). 01.43.26.84.87. Métros: Mabillon, St-Germain-des-Prés

135 Marie & Fils ★★$$ Although her *fils,* son Guillaume, has left, Marie carries on at her restaurant, serving the same mix of local artists, editors, and gallery owners for lunch and *la belle clientèle* at dinnertime (neighbor Catherine Deneuve among them). As one of the many ex-wives of record producer and inveterate playboy Eddie Barclay, Marie knows every glamorous face in town. Selections change seasonally except for two standbys: roast beef with mashed potatoes, and *foie de veau a la sauce aigre-douce* (veal liver in a sweet-and-sour sauce). The atmosphere is spirited. ◆ M dinner; Tu-Sa lunch and dinner. Reservations recommended. 34 Rue Mazarine (between Rues Jacques-Callot and de Seine). 01.43.26.69.49. Métros: Odéon, Mabillon

136 12 Rue Mazarine Here young Molière made his acting debut and later, with an inherited nest egg, opened a theater in an abandoned tennis court; this was the genesis of the **Comédie Française.** In 1673, after he died onstage, the theater company was orphaned and evicted. But the troupe started performing once again in another old tennis court at 14 Rue de l'Ancienne-Comédie after more than a decade of inactivity. ◆ Between Rues Jacques-Callot and de Seine. Métros: Odéon, Mabillon

137 Institut de France Situated across the Pont des Arts from the **Louvre,** this 17th-century masterpiece, designed by **Louis Le Vau** at the same time he was working on the **Louvre,** houses five academies, including the prestigious **Académie Française.** The academy began in 1635 as a salon of intellectuals who gathered informally to discuss French rhetoric and usage. Shortly thereafter, Cardinal Richelieu charged them with the protection and proliferation of the French language, hoping that Parisian French would eventually obliterate the less-refined regional dialects.

Academy membership is limited to 40 "immortals." At their induction ceremonies, the members wear silver-embroidered green robes and cocked admirals' bonnets and carry jeweled swords. The immortals don their robes for secret meetings, which are held every Thursday afternoon. Among their responsibilities are safeguarding the mother tongue and preparing new editions of the academy's dictionary, which first appeared in 1694.

Election to the academy is reserved for great writers, and even the list of runners-up comprises a pantheon of French literature: Descartes, Diderot, de Maupassant, Balzac, Flaubert, Verlaine, Stendhal, and Proust among them. Molière, the playwright/director/actor, was invited to join the academy on the condition that he give up acting. He refused the honor. No actor has ever been admitted to date. Emile Zola campaigned unsuccessfully for election 13 times; Nobel Prize–winners André Gide and Albert Camus never even tried. The late North American–born novelist Julian Green, who wrote his works in French, was elected in 1971. In 1981, history was made when Marguerite Yourcenar was inducted into the sacred ranks of the academy and became the first female immortal (the cloak she wore at the presentation was personally designed by Yves Saint Laurent).

The left wing of the institute (toward the mint building) is the site of the notorious **Tour Nesle,** from where, according to Dumas, Queen Margot (the first wife of Henri IV) would catapult that night's lover into the Seine. Among the exemplary statuary in the institute rotunda is a nude bust of Voltaire by Houdon. ◆ Open to cultural groups by appointment. 23 Quai de Conti (at Pl de l'Institut). 01.44.41.44.41. Métro: Pont Neuf

138 Pont des Arts Providing a pedestrian crossing between the **Institut de France** and the **Louvre,** this wooden-planked structure with latticed arches was the first iron bridge in Paris. Designed by an engineer named Dillon in 1804, the footbridge was originally landscaped with potted orange trees, rosebushes, and hothouses full of exotic tropical plants. Hordes of easel-toting artists from the nearby **Ecole des Beaux-Arts** come here to sketch and paint that familiar compact view spanning the Ile de la Cité, the rose-gray facade of Place Dauphine, and the dignified form of the Pont-Neuf, as well as the spires of **Notre-Dame** and **Sainte-Chapelle** in the distance. ◆ Métro: Pont Neuf

139 Galerie Larock-Granoff One of the city's most reputable modern art galleries sells works of the masters. ♦ M 2-6:30PM; Tu-Sa. 13 Quai de Conti (at Impasse de Conti). 01.43.54.41.92. Métro: Pont Neuf

139 Impasse de Conti On this street in 1792, a young Corsican named Napoléon Bonaparte rented an attic room in the **Hôtel de Guénégaud** (now part of the **Hôtel des Monnaies**) built by **François Mansart** in 1659. Twelve years later, he conquered Europe and crowned himself emperor of France. ♦ Métro: Pont Neuf

140 Hôtel des Monnaies/Musée des Monnaies (Mint/Money Museum) The austere Classical-style French mint is where the nation's centime and franc coins are designed and struck. In 1775, shortly after the original mint by **Jules Hardouin-Mansart** was demolished, the present edifice was built by **Jacques-Denis Antoine.** The museum traces the history of French coins back to Charlemagne's day and houses a collection of medals, currency, and commemorative coins. Hundreds of gold and silver medals are also for sale in the museum shop (2 Rue Guénégaud, 01.40.46.58.58). ♦ Admission. Museum: Tu-F 11AM-5:30PM; Sa-Su noon-5:30PM; Th 11AM-9PM. Tours of mint production area: W, F 2:15PM. Museum shop: M-Sa. 11 Quai de Conti (between Rue Guénégaud and Impasse de Conti). 01.40.46.55.33. Métro: Pont Neuf

141 Rue de Nevers Dating from the 13th century, this alley ends near a remnant of the King Philippe Auguste city wall (ca. 1200). It passes beneath an arch chiseled with an excerpt of the 17th-century poem *Le Paris Ridicule* by Claude Le Petit, which forecast the collapse of Henri IV's noble Pont-Neuf. The paper edition of this caustic verse was publicly burned in the Place de Grève (today's Place de l'Hôtel-de-Ville), along with its author. ♦ Métro: Pont Neuf

142 Galerie J.C. Riedel One of the most successful galleries in Paris, this springboard for European talent boasts the works of such promising and well-received artists as S.W. Hayter, François Audrum, Sanyu, and Garcia Tella. ♦ Sa 2-7PM. 12 Rue Guénégaud (between Rue Mazarine and Quai de Conti). 01.46.33.25.73. Métro: Odéon

142 Michel Cachoux Dig through the fossils, lapis, amethysts, and star-shaped calcites—there's something for everyone's hard-rock fantasy here. ♦ Tu-Sa; closed in August. 16 Rue Guénégaud (between Rue Mazarine and Quai de Conti). 01.43.54.52.15, 01.43.25.85.86. Métro: Odéon

---

Restaurants/Clubs: Red   **Hotels:** Blue
Shops/ 🌿 **Outdoors:** Green   **Sights/Culture:** Black

La Cafetière

143 La Cafetière ★★$$ This cozy restaurant features inventive Italian cuisine, varied with a few meat and fish daily specials prepared *à la française.* Among the Italian dishes are *bresaola girolles* (cured beef with hot mushrooms), lasagna with foie gras, and seafood risotto. For dessert, try the *cioccolata morbido,* a warm chocolate mousse. *Cafetière* means coffeepot, hence the collection that's scattered all about. ♦ Tu-Sa lunch and dinner; closed three weeks in August. Reservations recommended. 21 Rue Mazarine (between Rues Dauphine and Guénégaud). 01.46.33.76.90. Métro: Odéon

144 Alcazar ★★$$ British design and restaurant mogul Sir Terence Conran opened his new-fashioned version of the old-fashioned brasserie in November 1998. A former nightclub, the two-story, glass-domed space is now an ultramodern 250-place dining room, decorated in white, red, and gray, with a glassed-in kitchen where diners can watch their meals being prepared. Some traditional brasserie items are available—notably raw shellfish, which is impeccably fresh—but the menu is largely Mediterranean-inspired, with lots of fish, fresh vegetables, couscous, and goat cheese. With chef Gauillaume Lutard, formerly at **Taillevent,** assuring the quality of the cuisine, a bright, enthusiastic young team of servers, and a spectacular decor, everything is in place for an enjoyable dining experience. The only drawback is the high noise level. A large open bar on the mezzanine serves salads and other reasonably priced light fare and wine by the glass. A pianist and sax player entertain Thursday through Saturday from 8PM to closing. ♦ Daily lunch and dinner until 1AM. 62 Rue Mazarine (between Carrefour de Buci and Rue Jacques-Callot). 01.53.10.19.99. Métro: Odéon

145 Rue Dauphine The construction of the Pont-Neuf (see page 20) channeled traffic over to the Left Bank and led to this street's construction. When Henri IV's original request to put a highway through a monastery's vegetable gardens was denied, he snapped: "I will open the new road with cannonballs!" The gardens were sacrificed and the new road, named after the king's son, was built. Today the narrow road is lined with shops. ♦ Métros: Pont Neuf, Odéon

145 Le Monde en Marche Step into a magical world of wooden toys, puppets, and puzzles that are gaily colored and made by hand. ♦ M-Sa 10:30AM-7:30PM; closed in August. 34 Rue Dauphine (between Carrefour de Buci and Rue de Nesle). 01.43.29.09.49. Métro: Odéon

146 Hôtel le Régent $$$ Tastefully converted from a 1730 mansion, this comfortable 25-room hotel is nicely situated between the Seine and Rue de Buci, which boasts one of the prettiest outdoor markets in Paris. There's no restaurant. ♦ 61 Rue Dauphine (between Rues St-André-des-Arts and André-Mazet). 01.46.34.59.80; fax 01.40.51.05.07; hotel.leregent@wanadoo.fr. Métro: Odéon

147 Hôtel Left Bank St-Germain $$$ Best Western comes to France offering 31 rooms with flowered wallpaper, heavy furniture, white marble bathrooms, and such modern amenities as air-conditioning and cable television. The central location near the lively Carrefour de l'Odéon means that street-side rooms are subject to noise from the nearby all-night **Pub St-Germain-des-Prés;** light sleepers might want to ask for a *chambre* opening onto the pretty garden courtyard. The top floor penthouse suite has a splendid rooftop view of **Notre-Dame.** There's no restaurant. ♦ 9 Rue de l'Ancienne-Comédie (between Blvd St-Germain and Rue St-André-des-Arts). 01.43.54.01.70; fax 01.43.26.17.14; lbank@paris-hotels-charm.com. Métro: Odéon

148 Le Procope ★★$$ This colorful eatery bills itself as the world's oldest cafe. It was founded in 1686 by Sicilian Francesco Procopio dei Coltelli, the man credited with introducing coffee to France. The opening of the **Comédie Française** in a tennis court–turned-theater across the street in 1689 assured its success. Over the centuries, customers have included 17th-century writers La Fontaine, Rousseau, and Voltaire; 18th-century revolutionaries Benjamin Franklin, Thomas Jefferson, Robespierre, Danton, Bonaparte, and Marat; such ageless literati as Victor Hugo, Honoré de Balzac, Paul Verlaine, George Sand, and Mallarmé; and in the 1950s, when the tavern/cafe became a restaurant, Simone de Beauvoir and Jean-Paul Sartre.

The 18th-century decor is sumptuous, all red and gold, mirrors and crystal chandeliers, and there's furniture that belonged to Voltaire and Rousseau. The cuisine was long dismissed as bland and uninteresting, but the menu has improved markedly over the past few years. The fresh shellfish platters, grilled lobster, *coquilles St-Jacques,* and duck breast with orange are very good, and the prix-fixe menus are surprisingly reasonable. ♦ Daily lunch and dinner until 1AM. Piano bar: M-Sa 10PM-1AM. 13 Rue de l'Ancienne-Comédie (between Blvd St-Germain and Rue St-André-des-Arts). 01.40.46.79.00. Métro: Odéon

148 Pub St-Germain-des-Prés ★$$ Along with 26 brands of draft beer and 450 international varieties of bottled brew, this 600-seat pub offers such basic grub as mussels and beef cooked with—guess what?—beer. By the end of the evening, you may feel that you have been similarly stewed yourself. Open round-the-clock, it's a favorite of North American students abroad. ♦ Daily 24 hours. 17 Rue de l'Ancienne-Comédie (between Blvd St-Germain and Rue St-André-des-Arts). 01.43.29.38.70. Métro: Odéon

149 Hôtel de Fleurie $$$ This renovated 18th-century town house in the heart of St-Germain-des-Prés offers 29 quiet, air-conditioned rooms, including some in the attic with high ceilings and wood beams. Downstairs is a handsome stone-vaulted breakfast room, where the Marolleau family serves an excellent continental breakfast—slices of *quatre-quarts* (French pound cake), crisp baguettes, cheese, and freshly squeezed orange juice. There's no restaurant. ♦ 32-34 Rue Grégoire-de-Tours (between Rue des Quatre-Vents and Blvd St-Germain). 01.53.73.70.00; fax 01.53.73.70.20; bonjour@hotel-de-fleurie.tm.fr; www.hotel-de-fleurie.tm.fr. Métro: Odéon

149 Casa Bini ★★$$ Anna Bini and her family have prepared meals for Catherine Deneuve and Marcello Mastroianni at this casual, friendly Tuscan restaurant. Florentine appetizers include crostini with mozzarella and salmon, and swordfish carpaccio with herbs. There are new pasta, meat, and fish specials every day. Ask about Madame Bini's cultural and culinary tours to Italy. ♦ M-Sa lunch and dinner; Su dinner; closed one week in mid-August. Reservations recommended. 36 Rue Grégoire-de-Tours (between Rue des Quatre-Vents and Blvd St-Germain). 01.46.34.05.60. Métro: Odéon

150 Au Savoyard ★$$ This restaurant has been serving authentic French Alpine cuisine in the midst of Paris since 1932. The wooden chairs, wild-game trophies, paintings of mountain scenes, and peacock feathers provide an appropriately rustic setting for raclette, fondue, and smoked Savoie sausages. ♦ Daily lunch and dinner. Reservations recommended. 16 Rue des Quatre-Vents (between Carrefour de l'Odéon and Rue Grégoire-de-Tours). 01.43.26.20.30. Métro: Odéon

150 Christian Tortu Since opening in 1984, this has been one of the hottest florists in town, creating opulent and original designs with flowers and vegetables. Garden furniture is also sold. ♦ M-Sa. 6 Carrefour de l'Odéon (between Rue des Quatre-Vents and Blvd St-Germain). 01.43.26.02.56. Métro: Odéon

151 Carrefour de l'Odéon A crossroads of sorts is ruled over by a great pigeon-christened bronze of Georges-Jacques Danton. This Revolutionary leader's statements such as "We need audacity, more audacity, audacity forever. . . " cost him his head. Robespierre sent him to the guillotine in 1794. ♦ Métro: Odéon

152 Rue St-André-des-Arts This eclectic little street seems more like a pedestrian mall. ♦ Métros: Odéon, St-Michel

152 Le Mazet Once known as a hangout for seedy street musicians and pinball players, this cafe-bar-restaurant has cleaned up its act. The customers for its 125 cocktails, dozens of labels of beers, and traditional cafe fare are students from the many language and design schools in the area and the **University of Paris,** and a wide mix of locals who appreciate the relaxed ambience. ♦ Daily 10AM-2AM. 61 Rue St-André-des-Arts (between Rues de l'Eperon and de l'Ancienne-Comédie). 01.43.54.68.81. Métro: Odéon

152 Cour du Commerce-St-André Built in 1776, the city's first covered shopping mall was a hive of activity during the Revolution and inspired 17 other *passages* that sprang up on the Right Bank in the 19th century. Through the windows at **No. 4,** you can glimpse the remains of one of the towers in the city wall. At **No. 8** in 1789, Marat printed revolutionary exhortations in his inflammatory journal *L'Ami du Peuple.* Nearby, a German carpenter named Schmidt patiently perfected the guillotine (named after Dr. Guillotin, who recommended this apparatus for decapitation as a humane means of execution). Schmidt practiced on sheep, and the street ran red with the blood of the unfortunate beasts. It was also here that the artist Balthus had a studio and painted his famous picture *Le Passage du Commerce St-André* in 1954 (don't look for the shop with the golden key in the painting; it was abandoned long ago). **La Maison de la Catalogne** (01.40.46.85.28), Catalonia's attractive tourist office, art gallery, gift shop, and restaurant, occupies **Nos. 4, 6,** and **8.** ♦ 59-61 Rue St-André-des-Arts (between Rues de l'Eperon and de l'Ancienne-Comédie). Métro: Odéon

Within the Cour du Commerce-St-André:

Monsieur Baudrillart If you decide to have your Paris journal re-covered in leather, this bookbinding shop is the place to go. ♦ M-F. 01.46.33.19.88

A La Cour de Rohan ★★$ This English-style tearoom with apricot walls and paisley tablecloths offers fish or onion soup; melted goat cheese on toast; savory tarts; toothsome cakes, scones, and crumbles; exotic teas; and a 17th-century heirloom recipe for spicy marmalade. No smoking is allowed. ♦ M-W, Su lunch, afternoon tea, and dinner until 7:30PM; closed in August. 01.43.25.79.67

153 St-André-des-Arts $$ A friendly staff runs this modest, but comfortable 35-room hotel that was the 17th-century residence of the king's musketeers. The rooms are small, but they all have their original wood beams, and the bathrooms are perfectly modern. There's no restaurant. ♦ 66 Rue St-André-des-Arts (at Rue André-Mazet). 01.43.26.96.16; fax 01.43.29.73.34; hsaintand@minitel.net. Métro: Odéon

154 Jacques Cagna ★★★$$$$ In his elegant old inn, Cagna features traditional French cuisine with a nouvelle flourish. The prices are weighty, but the sauces are light, and the vegetables are treated with the gentleness they deserve. Specialties include escargots, Breton lobster salad, and foie gras; roasted turbot with crisply fried and puréed Granny Smith apples; roast Aveyron lamb; suckling pig casserole; Houdan farm hen; wild game in season; and a wild strawberry mille-feuille with light vanilla cream. The wine cellar stocks 60,000 bottles in 550 varieties. Most of the patrons are affluent older people. ♦ M, Sa dinner; Tu-F, Su lunch and dinner; closed in August, one week at Christmas, and holidays. Reservations required. 14 Rue des Grands-Augustins (at Rue Christine). 01.43.26.49.39. Métros: Odéon, St-Michel

154 Relais Christine $$$$ A 16th-century monastery was converted into this plush, well-run, fashionable hotel in 1980. It offers 51 rooms with either modern or antique furnishings as well as single or split-level apartments, some of which have luxurious marble bathrooms and access to a secluded courtyard. The basement breakfast room alone is worth the visit to this hotel (there's no restaurant). ♦ 3 Rue Christine (between Rues des Grands-Augustins and Dauphine). 01.40.51.60.80; fax 01.40.51.60.81; relaisch@club-internet.fr. Métros: Odéon, St-Michel

154 5 Rue Christine After being evicted from their famous atelier at 27 Rue de Fleurus, Gertrude Stein and Alice B. Toklas moved here in 1938. During the war, they fled to the countryside; in their absence, 5 Rue Christine was visited by the Gestapo, who attached a note to one of Stein's Picasso paintings reading "Jewish trash, good for burning." Stein died on 27 July 1946, and Toklas lived on here for another 18 years. The two women are buried side by side in **Père-Lachaise Cemetery.** ♦ Between Rues des Grands-Augustins and Dauphine. Métros: Odéon, St-Michel

155 La Rôtisserie d'en Face ★★★$$ Across the street from Jacques Cagna's famous namesake restaurant is his unpretentious bistro, where good, simple meals can be enjoyed in an agreeable setting. The menu features meats cooked on the rotisserie—chicken served with mashed potatoes, prime ribs of beef, and lamb with thyme. The *pastilla de pintade* (crispy pastry filled with guinea fowl, onion, eggplant, and mild spices) is a popular dish, and Cagna's mother has contributed family recipes, including *joues de cochon aux carottes et pommes de terre fondantes,* which translates inelegantly as pig cheeks with carrots and mashed potatoes. For dessert, the bistro's chocolate mousse rivals the best. ♦ M-F lunch and dinner; Sa dinner. Reservations recommended. 2 Rue Christine (at Rues des Grands-Augustins). 01.43.26.40.98. Métros: Odéon, St-Michel

155 Action Christine Two adjacent revival movie houses keep aficionados of Hitchcock and Lubitsch, as well as fans of Bogie and Bacall classics, happy. ♦ Daily. 4 Rue Christine and 10 Rue des Grands-Augustins. 01.43.29.11.30. Métros: Odéon, St-Michel

156 7 Rue des Grands-Augustins From 1936 to 1955, Pablo Picasso lived in this imposing house, where he painted *Guernica* in 1937. His friends Gerald and Sara Murphy, the quintessential North American expatriates in the 1920s, had an apartment in the pink building around the block on the Quai des Grands-Augustins. It was Picasso who got them work painting sets for Diaghilev and the Ballet Russe. They were also the models Fitzgerald used for Dick and Nicole Diver in *Tender Is the Night.* ♦ Between Rue de Savoie and Quai des Grands-Augustins. Métro: St-Michel

156 Quai des Grands-Augustins In 1313, one of the first *quais* (embankments) in Paris was constructed next to the monastery of St. Augustine. Hundreds of years later, Thomas Jefferson idled away many an afternoon here, browsing along this stretch of riverside, which is still known for its book- and print-sellers. ♦ Métro: St-Michel

156 Lapérouse ★★★$$$ This Old World quayside restaurant is housed in the former town mansion of the Comte de Bruillevert, Master of Waters and Forests under Louis XIV. In 1766 it was transformed by Lefèvre, the king's official wine merchant, into a public meeting place that was renowned for the quality of wines it served. In 1840 the establishment was named in honor of the French navigator Lapérouse, and thrived as a watering hole for such literary figures as Guy de Maupassant, Emile Zola, Alexandre Dumas, Victor Hugo, and Colette. Today chef Thierry Colas is attracting multitudes of gourmands to this elegant classic with such culinary sonnets as *brochette de langoustines, suprême de tourbot,* Bresse farm hen, and heavenly soufflés. ♦ M-F lunch and dinner; Sa dinner. Reservations required. 51 Quai des Grands-Augustins (between Rues Séguier and des Grands-Augustins). 01.43.26.68.04. Métro: St-Michel

157 Les Bookinistes ★★★$$ The enterprising Guy Savoy opened this attractive bistro on a quay by the Seine where book peddlers ply their trade. The contemporary decor by Daniel Humair and Léopold Gest features large mirrors with colorful hand-painted frames, cheerful red and yellow lampshades, and black modern chairs. In the kitchen, Savoy's protégé, William Ledeuil, has made a name for the restaurant with his imaginative combinations of raw and cooked products, and sweet and sour flavors. Roasted tuna with sautéed soy paste and black Chinese mushrooms, and roast young duckling with fig and turnip preserved in vinegar are a couple of examples. There's also a vegetarian menu. The service is alert and friendly, and the prices are very reasonable for the high quality and culinary inventiveness of the cuisine. ♦ M-F lunch and dinner; Sa, Su dinner. Reservations required. 53 Quai des Grands-Augustins (at Rue des Grands-Augustins). 01.43.25.45.94. Métro: St-Michel

158 46 Rue St-André-des-Arts e.e. cummings rented a single room in this building housing two bookshops. Today the structure has both residential and commercial space. ♦ Between Rues Séguier and des Grands-Augustins. Métros: Odéon, St-Michel

159 Rue de l'Ecole de Médecine During the Revolution, Jean-Paul Marat founded the biting journal *L'Ami du Peuple* and was forced to hide in the Paris sewers. The radical democrat was elected to the National Convention three years later with the support of Danton and Robespierre but soon learned that you can't please all of *le peuple* all of the time. On 13 July 1793 Marat was stabbed while taking a bath in his house on this street. His killer was Girondist Charlotte Corday, who had hidden a knife in her bodice. For a surprisingly ungory depiction of the assassination see David's painting in the **Louvre**'s **Salle des Etats.** ♦ Métros: Odéon, Cluny–La Sorbonne

160 Allard ★★$$ One of the old-time, honest bistros, this place has two zinc bars and a rotating selection of plats du jour as perennial as the clientele. The Allard family, who played host here to the Aga Khan, Brigitte Bardot, and Georges Pompidou, has sold the restaurant, but it still retains much of the old feeling. ♦ M-Sa lunch and dinner; closed the first three weeks of August. Reservations required. 41 Rue St-André-des-Arts (at Rue de l'Eperon). 01.43.26.48.23. Métros: Odéon, St-Michel

161 28 Rue St-André-des-Arts In *Satori in Paris*, Jack Kerouac described pleasant evenings spent here at what was then a bar called **La Gentilhommière** (ca. 1962) and is now a pizzeria. ♦ At Rue Gît-le-Coeur. Métro: St-Michel

162 Rue Gît-le-Coeur The name means "Where the heart lies," a French phrase that's a good deal more romantic than the street's preceding moniker: Gilles-le-Cook. **Nos. 1-9** were originally one mansion, built in the 16th century by François I for his love at the time, the Duchesse d'Etampes. ♦ Métro: St-Michel

On Rue Gît-le-Coeur:

Relais Hôtel de Vieux Paris $$$ In the 1950s this was a seedy crash pad known as "the Beat hotel," where Allan Ginsberg, Gregory Corso, Jack Kerouac, and William S. Burroughs holed up for long periods, and where Ginsberg helped Burroughs edit *Naked Lunch.* They'd be shocked if they could see it now: In 1991, the hotel underwent a total renovation, and its bohemian atmosphere gave way to distinctly more upscale charm, with 20 comfortable, tastefully decorated,

traditionally French rooms. The old days have not been forgotten, however: photos of the Beats taken here in the 1950s hang in the lobby. There is no restaurant. ♦ No. 9 (at Rue de l'Hirondelle). 01.44.32.15.90; fax 01.43.26.00.15; VieuxParis@soller.fr; www.sollers.fr/rhvp

163 Caveau de la Bolée A wooden door leads into a 13th-century dungeonlike cavern filled with late-night chess and checkers players. Dinner is served upstairs starting at 9PM and downstairs before the show, a cabaret act performed Monday through Saturday starting at 10:30PM. ♦ Daily dinner and late-night snacks. 25 Rue de l'Hirondelle (between Pl St-Michel and Rue Gît-le-Coeur). 01.43.54.62.20. Métro: St-Michel

164 L'Ecluse ★★$ A spectrum of 60 reds (18 of which can be ordered by the glass) are offered at this wine bar overlooking the Seine. Bordeaux is the specialty, a wine that goes wonderfully with the plates of smoked goose, carpaccio, and chavignol cheese served here. ♦ Daily lunch and dinner until 1AM. Reservations recommended. 15 Quai des Grands-Augustins (between Pl St-Michel and Rue Gît-le-Coeur). 01.46.33.58.74. Métro: St-Michel. Also at: 64 Rue François-1er (between Rues Lincoln and Quentin-Bauchart). 01.47.20.77.09. Métro: George V; 15 Pl de la Madeleine (between Blvd Malesherbes and Rue Chauveau-Lagarde). 01.42.65.34.69. Métro: Madeleine; 13 Rue de la Roquette (between Place de la Bastille and Rue Daval). 01.48.05.19.12. Métro: Bastille

165 Place St-Michel A relatively nonviolent crowd of students, bikers, and drug dealers gathers here on hot Saturday nights. The passable restaurants around the square cater to pizza and souvlaki eaters. ♦ Métro: St-Michel

On Place St-Michel:

165 Fontaine St-Michel (St. Michael Fountain) In 1860 Gabriel Davioud designed this 75-foot-high and 15-foot-wide spouting monster. The bronze of St. Michael fighting the dragon is by Duret.

166 Au St-Séverin ★$ The best people-watching perch in Place St-Michel has the famous Berthillon ice cream. The hot chocolate isn't bad either. ♦ Daily 7AM-2AM. 3 Pl St-Michel (at Rue de la Huchette). 01.43.54.19.36. Métro: St-Michel

167 Boulevard St-Michel This was one of the great boulevards of Baron Haussmann, scythed through the Left Bank from the edge of the Seine in a broad, tree-lined swath. The street was named in 1867 in memory of the ancient chapel of **St-Michel** that stood here once upon a time. ♦ Métros: St-Michel, Cluny–La Sorbonne

167 St-Michel Métro This is one of the Art Nouveau métro entrances designed by **Hector Guimard** in 1900. ♦ Pl St-André-des-Arts and Rue Danton

167 La Maison de la Lozère ★★$$ This crowded canteen with bare wooden tables is a trip straight to the Lozère region in France's heartland. Try one of the robust regional specialties such as *aligot d'Aubrac* (a heavenly concoction of mashed potatoes, garlic, and tomme cheese served only on Thursday), *maoucho* (grilled sausage stuffed with cabbage and other vegetables and ground pork), *assiette de cochonnailles* (a platter of cold sausage, ham, and pâté from the region), grilled Lozère lamb chops, bleu d'Auvergne cheese, and good *vin de pays* in carafes. ♦ Tu-Sa lunch and dinner; closed mid-July through mid-August and the last week of December. Reservations recommended. 4 Rue Hautefeuille (between Rue Serpente and Pl St-André-des-Arts). 01.43.54.26.64. Métro: St-Michel

168 Rue de la Harpe Named after Reginald the Harper, this medieval street, along with Rue de la Huchette, is one of the city's oldest. A youthful air emanates from the cheap restaurants jammed with students along this bustling byway. ♦ Métros: St-Michel, Cluny–La Sorbonne

169 Rue de la Huchette In medieval times this ancient thoroughfare was called Street of Roasters because it had a plethora of barbecue pits. Couscous and shish kebab joints continue the carnivorous tradition by roasting whole lambs and pigs in their front windows. You can always find cheap, sometimes risky, street food here. ♦ Métro: St-Michel

169 28 Rue de la Huchette Outside the **Hôtel Mt-Blanc** is one of the many wall plaques in Paris commemorating World War II Resistance fighters. It reads "Here fell Jean-Albert Bouillard, dead in the course of duty, killed by the Gestapo 17 May 1944 at 20 hours." ♦ Between Rue Xavier-Privas and Pl St-Michel. Métro: St-Michel

169 10 Rue de la Huchette For several months here in 1795, a young brigadier general languished in a sparsely decorated back room. Unemployed, unloved, and (he thought) dying of hunger, he saw no hope for the future. Soon thereafter, he dispersed a mob by firing grapeshot into its midst, and

from then on Napoléon Bonaparte was never ignored. ♦ Between Rue Xavier-Privas and Pl St-Michel. Métro: St-Michel

170 Théâtre de la Huchette Ever since Eugène Ionesco finished them in the mid-1950s, two of his plays, *The Bald Soprano* and *The Lesson,* have been running nonstop at this 85-seat theater. ♦ Box office: M-Sa. 23 Rue de la Huchette (between Rues Xavier-Privas and de la Harpe). 01.43.26.38.99. Métro: St-Michel

171 Rue du Chat-qui-Pêche The Street of the Fishing Cat, most likely named after a medieval fishmonger, is one of the narrowest and, arguably, grungiest alleys in Paris. ♦ Métro: St-Michel

50 ANS DE JAZZ

172 Caveau de la Huchette This is another crowded, dingy jazz cellar on a street that once rang with bebop. ♦ Cover; student discount available. M-Th, Su 9:30PM-2:30AM; F 9:30PM-3:30AM; Sa and holidays 9:30PM-4AM. 5 Rue de la Huchette (between Rues du Petit-Pont and Xavier-Privas). 01.43.26.65.05. Métro: St-Michel

173 St-Séverin This lesser-known edifice, which was constructed around 1220 on the burial site of a sixth-century hermit named Séverin, is the official church of the **University of Paris.** Recognized as the city's richest example of Flamboyant Gothic architecture, it was expanded between 1414 and 1520 with a bullet-shaped nave, a gaggle of gargoyles, and a five-aisled symphony of ribbed vaulting and stained glass. In 1673, the distinguished **Jules Hardouin-Mansart** tried his hand at enhancing the church, adding a small communion hall.

Don't miss the double ambulatory's slender medieval columns that shoot into vaulted arches, creating an effect that Joris-Karl Huysmans compared to being in a palm grove. The modern windows are by Jean Bazaine, the French abstract painter who created the mosaics for the **UNESCO** building and the **Cluny–La Sorbonne** métro station. Saint-Saëns and Fauré performed on the 18th-century Rococo organ in front of the west window; today the organ is frequently used for recitals. ♦ Rues des Prêtres-St-Séverin and St-Séverin. Métros: St-Michel, Cluny–La Sorbonne

174 Rue de la Parcheminerie In the Middle Ages this narrow street was crammed with scribes, copyists, and parchment peddlers. ♦ Métro: Cluny–La Sorbonne

Eiffel Tower/ Invalides

Ave. Kléber

Ave. Albert-de-Mun

Rue de Lübeck

Ave. du Prés.-Wilson

Ave. du Pres.-Wilson

Ave. Marceau

Ave. George-V

Rue Boccador

Rue Montaigne

Cours Albert-1er

Ave. d'Iéna

Rue de la Manutention

Pont de l'Alma

Place du Trocadéro-et-du-11-Novembre

105

Jardins du Trocadéro (Trocadéro Gardens)

Ave. des Nations-Unies

Passerelle Debilly

Place de la Résistance **87**

Quai d'Orsay

89

Rue Cognacq-Jay

Rue Malar

59

88

Ave. des Nations-Unies

Pont d'Iéna

Ave. de La Bourdonnais

Rue de l'Université

Cité de l'Alma

90

Rue de l'Université

Ave. Bosquet

86

67

68

66

Ave. du Prés.-Kennedy

Quai Branly

104

Ave. S.-de-Sacy

Ave. Franco-Russe

91

Rue de Monttessuy

93

Rue E.-Valentin

95

Ave. Rapp

Rue Sedillot

96

Rue Dupont-des-Loges

85

69

92

94

97

98 **99**

Rue du Gén.-Camou

100

Rue St-Dominique

80

79

Rue de l'Exposition

Ave. Gustave-Eiffel

Ave. Octave-Gréard

Ave. de Suffren

110

Ave. Charles Floquet

Rue du Maréchal-Harispe

Rue Augereau

82

81

83

78

77

101

Rue de Grenelle

84

109

Ave. Bouvard

Ave. Elisées-Reclus

Place Jacques-Rueff

Rue Marinoni

Ave. du Champ-de-Ma

106 Pont de Bir-Hakeim

107

Rue Jean-Rey

Rue de la Fédération

103 Parc du Champ-de-Mars

76

108 Blvd. de Grenelle

Rue St-Saëns

111

Ave. du Gén.-Détrie

Place Joffre

102

Rue Desaix

Blvd. du Docteur-Finlay

Rue de Presles

112

113

Rue Dupleix

Rue St-Charles

Rue Viala

Rue de Lourmel

Rue Dupleix

Rue de Pondichéry

Ave. de La Motte-Picquet

Ave. de Lowendal

Rue Rouelle

Rue Violet

Rue Frémicourt

Rue du Commerce

Place Cambronne

Blvd. Garibaldi

N

Ave. Emile-Zola

Rue de la Croix-Nivert

km
ml   1/16   1/8   1/4
1/8   1/4

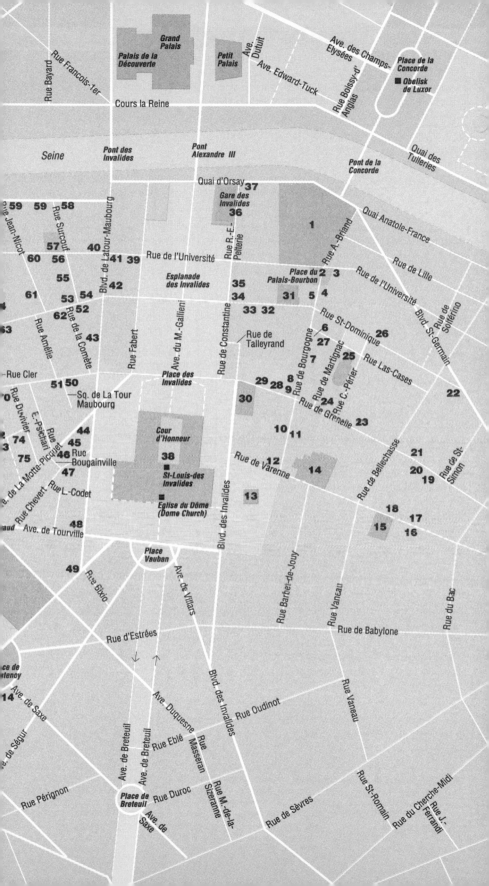

Eiffel Tower/Invalides

Overshadowed by the lacy mast of the **Tour Eiffel** (Eiffel Tower) and the sparkling gold dome of the **Hôtel des Invalides** (under which rest the remains of Napoléon Bonaparte), this district is one of pomp and grandeur. But nestled among the high-profile monuments are intimate streets lined with fancy food shops that cater to the residents of this upscale *quartier* (neighborhood), and some of the best restaurants in the city.

The following route encompasses two sectors bisected by the **Esplanade des Invalides**. The area to the east of **Les Invalides** is home to the **Assemblée Nationale**, situated in the elegant **Place du Palais-Bourbon,** and is scattered with stately 17th- and 18th-century mansions, including the **Hôtel de Biron**, where the famous sculptor Rodin lived and worked. The mansion is now the **Musée Rodin.**

The affluent neighborhood to the west of the esplanade is dominated by the symbol of Paris, the **Eiffel Tower,** which forms part of the grand axis from the **Ecole Militaire**, through the **Parc du Champ-de-Mars**, and across the river to the **Palais de Chaillot.** To learn some of the secrets of this neighborhood, meander in and out of the side streets off **Rue St-Dominique**, which are lined with exceptional restaurants, small antiques shops, Art Nouveau apartment houses, candy shops, and patisseries; this is also the site of the city's ritziest street market.

Keep in mind that much of this area shuts down in August, when the French take their annual vacation, and many of the restaurants here are closed for Saturday lunch and all day Sunday year-round.

To begin your explorations, set your watch by the clock over the courtyard facade of the **Assemblée Nationale** in the Place du Palais-Bourbon and grab a breakfast of coffee and croissants alongside publishers, *députés* (parliament members), and diplomats at the **Brasserie Bourbon.** If it's Saturday, you can start with a morning tour of the **Assemblée Nationale,** France's parliament building. Otherwise, head down the **Rue de Bourgogne**, taking detours onto Rue St-Dominique, **Rue de Grenelle**, and **Rue de Varenne** to view the neighborhood's 17th- and 18th-century mansions, including the **Hôtel de Noirmoutiers** and the **Hôtel Matignon.** You may only be able to catch a glimpse of these fancy former residences, however; many of them are now ministries and embassies sequestered behind stone portals and off-limits to the public. Upon reaching the **Hôtel de Biron**, spend the remainder of the morning in the **Musée Rodin;** be sure to take some time to stroll in the garden among some of the sculptor's best-known works.

This district's superb restaurants offer lunch possibilities to fit any pocketbook. Indulge in a meal at one of the neighborhood's elegant and pricey establishments such as **Arpège**, or cross the Esplanade des Invalides to **Paul Minchelli** or **Le Divellec.** Less expensive but also delicious alternatives are lunch at the classic family-run bistros **Thoumieux** and **La Poule au Pot;** **Bar au Sel** is a good place for fish. Those who want to save their three-star appetites (and budgets) for dinner could pick up a light bite at **Café Lunch.**

Spend the early afternoon touring the **Hôtel des Invalides**, a monumental 17th-century complex commissioned by Louis XIV to house the nation's veterans. This ensemble of buildings includes the magnificent Baroque **Eglise du Dôme** (Dome Church), which crowns the burial place of Napoléon Bonaparte, and the **Musée de l'Armée**, with its large collection of military paraphernalia.

Wander west along the Rue St-Dominique and notice its distinctly different character as compared to its sister leg to the east. With the distant **Eiffel**

Tower beckoning as your final destination, investigate the side streets such as **Rue Surcouf, Rue Malar,** and **Rue Augereau.** Visit the **Musée-Galerie de la Seita** (Tobacco Museum), which chronicles the history of the weed in Western Europe. Peruse the city's classiest street market along the **Rue Cler** and take in the beautiful displays of produce, baked goods, cheese, charcuterie, and flowers. If hunger sets in, stop for a coffee and *pain au chocolat* at **Jean Millet** or stroll a little farther for tea and scones at the lovely *salon de thé* **Les Deux Abeilles.**

As you reach the vicinity of the **Parc du Champ-de-Mars** stroll among some of the small side streets, which play peek-a-boo with the **Eiffel Tower,** noticing the elegant apartment houses along the way. Cross the Pont d'Iéna to reach the **Palais de Chaillot,** which houses three museums—the **Musée de la Marine,** the **Musée de l'Homme,** and the **Musée des Monuments Français.** From the building's terrace is a striking view of the **Eiffel Tower,** sweeping across the **Champ-de-Mars** to the **Ecole Militaire,** the military school that numbers Napoléon Bonaparte as its most famous cadet.

Dining spots abound in this neighborhood; you could end your day with dinner at **Vin sur Vin,** or really celebrate Paris with a table at **Le Jules Verne** within the weightless filigree of the **Eiffel Tower.** Linger after dinner over a good Cognac and ponder the glorious nighttime perspective of the City of Light.

1 Palais Bourbon/Assemblée Nationale The home of the French parliament was constructed in 1728 for the Duchess of Bourbon, one of Louis XIV's daughters. In 1807 **Bernard Poyet** designed the mansion's north facade for Napoléon in the Greek-Revival style, to mirror the **Madeleine** across the river; it now houses the **Assemblée Nationale** (the lower house of the French Parliament). Nearly 600 deputies convene in a chamber decorated in crimson and gold and adorned with a large Napoleonic eagle. Even the president of France is denied entrance into this exclusive club's assemblies. Ordinary people, however, can watch sessions from a public gallery, provided they have a pass signed by a deputy. If you tour the building, don't miss Delacroix's allegorical *History of Civilization* on the library ceiling. ♦ Free. Guided tours: Sa 10AM, 2PM, and 3PM; identification necessary; groups must call in advance. To arrange a group tour or to attend an assembly debate (October through June), call the administrative office of the Assemblée Nationale (01.40.63.64.08). 33 Quai d'Orsay (between Rues Aristide-Briand and Robert-Esnault-Pelterie). 01.40.63.60.00. Métro: Assemblée Nationale

2 Place du Palais-Bourbon This square boasts an elegant ensemble of Louis XVI buildings constructed in 1776. The *place* is dominated by the main entrance facade of the **Palais Bourbon** and a view of its inner courtyard. The facade and courtyard are the only surviving elements of the original mansion. ♦ Métro: Assemblée Nationale

3 Brasserie Bourbon ★★$$ The seasonally changing Alsatian and fish specialties served here are appreciated by the politicians from the **Assemblée Nationale** who lunch in the comfortable dining room and on the terrace. A winter meal could start with *moules marinières* (mussels steamed in white wine) or *foie gras,* followed by sirloin steak with *frites* (french fries) or *saucisson sec de montagne* (dry mountain sausage) and sauerkraut. In spring and summer diners might start with bouillabaisse or salmon and spinach salad, followed by *coquilles St-Jacques à la Provençale* (scallops in a sauce of olive oil, garlic, onions, tomatoes, and herbs) or a grilled fish plate. A good bottle of Gewürztraminer or Riesling will bring out the best in any of these dishes. ♦ M-Sa breakfast, lunch, tea, and dinner; Su breakfast, lunch, and tea. Reservations recommended. 1 Pl du Palais-Bourbon (at Rue de l'Université). 01.45.51.58.27. Métro: Assemblée Nationale

4 Marie-Pierre Boitard Silver napkin rings, a tiny silver escargot-shaped case, a silver baby rattle, and fine Hungarian china are displayed on tables draped with fancy brocades and embroidered fabrics and sold by

equally resplendent, but somewhat serious, saleswomen. ◆ M-Sa. 9-11 Pl du Palais-Bourbon (at Rue de Bourgogne). 01.47.05.13.30. Métro: Assemblée Nationale

4 Rue de Bourgogne Opened in 1719, this street, named for Louis Duc de Bourgogne (1682-1712), the son of Louis XIV, originally extended to the quay, but was modified in 1778 when the Place du Palais-Bourbon was created. ◆ Métros: Assemblée Nationale, Varenne

4 Hôtel Bourgogne et Montana $$$ This elegant hotel's name has nothing to do with the state of Montana; its previous owner hailed from Montana, Switzerland. The refined decoration of the 34 rooms is in keeping with the upscale neighborhood. The breakfast room (there's no restaurant) features handsome black leather upholstery and crisp white tablecloths. ◆ 3 Rue de Bourgogne (between Rue St-Dominique and Pl du Palais-Bourbon). 01.45.51.20.22; fax 01.45.56.11.98. Métro: Assemblée Nationale

4 Chez Marius ★★$$$ At lunch important-looking people speak in hushed tones over *soupe de poissons* (fish soup), *pavé de saumon poêlé à la niçoise* (salmon steak in a light tomato and garlic sauce), bouillabaisse, grilled lobster, or *poulet de Bresse rôti* (roasted Bresse chicken). In contrast to this seafood restaurant's subdued beige interior, the windows are covered with enough stickers to rival the rear window of a Winnebago; the various labels and logos represent the many guidebooks and organizations that have given the place their stamp of approval. ◆ M-F lunch and dinner; Sa dinner; closed in August. Reservations recommended. 5 Rue de Bourgogne (between Rue St-Dominique and Pl du Palais-Bourbon). 01.45.51.79.42. Métro: Assemblée Nationale

5 Galerie Naïla de Monbrison If you're looking for a gift or souvenir that's out of the ordinary, you'll find it in this small, narrow jewelry shop and art gallery designed by **Patrick Naggar** and **Dominique Lachevsky**. Such unassuming materials as glass, particleboard, oxidized bronze, and lead are

fashioned into well-crafted display cases that contrast with and complement the precious materials of the jewelry they contain. Mme. de Monbrison offers a superb collection of ethnographic jewelry, and drawers hold bounties of colorful hand-crafted trinkets from Asia, Africa, Siberia, Turkey, and North America. Contemporary art jewelry is also featured in the gallery's expositions. ◆ Tu-Sa; closed in August. 6 Rue de Bourgogne (between Rue St-Dominique and Pl du Palais-Bourbon). 01.47.05.11.15. Métro: Assemblée Nationale

6 Ombeline Maud Frizon sold the name of her famous line of haute-couture shoes; switched to her married name, Maud de Marco; and opened this shop. However, her stunning and creative footwear still has the same high quality and wild heel shapes that made her original line of shoes famous. ◆ M-Sa. 17 Rue de Bourgogne (between Rues de Grenelle and Las-Cases). 01.47.05.56.78. Métros: Assemblée Nationale, Varenne

7 Carole de Villarcy At this tiny boutique you can find top-quality women's haute couture (including clothing by Chanel, Guy Laroche, Yves Saint Laurent, and other designers) from seasons past at a fraction of the original prices. ◆ M 2-7PM; Tu-Sa; closed in August. 27 Rue de Bourgogne (between Rues de Grenelle and Las-Cases). 01.45.51.28.38. Métros: Assemblée Nationale, Varenne

Club des Poètes

8 Club des Poètes ★★$ *"La Poésie est vivante. Vive la Poésie!"* (Poetry is alive. Long live Poetry!) proclaims Jean-Pierre Rosnay, well-known French poet and owner of this dimly lit, cozy restaurant, where actors read works by poets from all over the world in the evenings. There are French poems from Villon to Boris Vian, and North American verses from Walt Whitman to Lawrence Ferlinghetti and Jack Kerouac, while diners savor *terrine de lapin* (rabbit pâté), *salade Drômoise* (with tomatoes, St. Marcellin cheese, and walnuts), *grillade St-Tropez* (beef with tomatoes and herbs), and *gâteau de Sarah* (chocolate cake from an old family recipe). Rosnay's wife and son are both poets, and together the family puts out a poetry journal three times a year, runs a radio station devoted to poetry, and started the Festival of Poetry in Paris. Visitors from the US will enjoy a warm welcome here; Rosnay, a resistance fighter during World War II, loves North Americans. ◆ M-Sa lunch and dinner; closed in August. Reservations recommended. 30 Rue de Bourgogne (between Rues de Grenelle and St-Dominique). 01.47.05.06.03. Métro: Varenne

9 Trenta Quattro ★★$$ Charming Francesca Ciardi serves delectable Italian fare in her cozy dining room. Ricotta and spinach ravioli, risotto with blueberries and cèpes, and veal in white wine or lemon marsala sauce are all worthy dishes. If you have any room left at the end of the meal, share the rich zabaglione and blueberries with your dinner companion. ♦ Tu-F lunch and dinner; Sa-Su dinner; closed Saturday in August. Reservations recommended. 34 Rue de Bourgogne (at Rue de Grenelle). 01.45.55.80.75. Métro: Varenne

10 Hôtel de Varenne $$ The entrance to this tranquil hotel is through a flower-filled courtyard with white iron garden furniture. Guests staying in the 24 fresh, pretty rooms can have breakfast alfresco in the spring and summer. There's no restaurant. ♦ 44 Rue de Bourgogne (between Rues de Varenne and de Grenelle). 01.45.51.45.55; fax 01.45.51.86.63. Métro: Varenne

11 Le Garde Manger ★★$$ In the back of this little wine and gourmet-food boutique you can take a table alongside *députés* from the **Assemblée Nationale** and staff members of the **Musée Rodin** to savor a lunch of foie gras or smoked salmon from the shop's shelves. Changing plats du jour might include *canard aux lentilles* (duck with lentils), *coquilles St-Jacques* (scallops), and sautéed veal, and such desserts as crème brûlée and *tarte aux pommes* (apple tart). Try one of the fine wines—perhaps the Cahors Château Quatre 1989 or the Côtes-de-Catillon Château Cap de Faugères 1990—with your repast. ♦ Restaurant: M-F lunch; Sa lunch and dinner. Shop: M-F 10AM-8PM. Closed in August. Reservations required. 51 Rue de Bourgogne (between Rues de Varenne and de Grenelle). 01.45.50.23.93. Métro: Varenne

12 Rue de Varenne The name of this street, like that of Rue de Grenelle, evolved over time from the word *garenne* (rabbit warren); Rue de Varenne was laid out in 1605 along a *garenne* belonging to the abbey of **St-Germain-des-Prés**. Today, the street is lined with ministries and foreign embassies housed in attractive old mansions. ♦ Métros: Varenne, Rue du Bac, Sèvres-Babylone

12 L'Arpège ★★★★$$$$ Daring but respectful of tradition, young chef Alain Passard executes a first-rate menu that includes *crème de truffe aux oeufs et parmesan* (scrambled eggs with parmesan cheese and truffle cream), sweet-and-sour Brittany lobster with rosemary, and *canard Louise Passard* (duck with orange and date purée and lemon conserve). Desserts include a heavenly lemon soufflé as well as *feuilletage au chocolat* (chocolate cake), and the wine list is one of the best in Paris. The skillful servers may add the final touches to dishes at your table. The mood of the small dining room is modern and subdued, with low lighting, wood paneling, sumptuous carpets, and classical-style nude figurines in crystal. ♦ M-F lunch and dinner; Su dinner. Reservations required. 84 Rue de Varenne (between Rue de Bourgogne and Blvd des Invalides). 01.45.51.47.33. Métro: Varenne

Musée Rodin

13 Musée Rodin The Hôtel de Biron, which houses this museum, is a Regency masterpiece of columns and pediments originally built in 1730 by **Jean Aubert** and **Jacques-Ange Gabriel** for a wealthy wig maker named Abraham Peyrenc. In 1753 it was bought by the Maréchal-Duc de Biron, who indulged quite a passion for gardening in the years before he went to the guillotine during the Reign of Terror; he spent 200,000 *livres* each year on tulips alone. During an unfortunate stint as a convent school, the *hôtel's* gold-and-white wood paneling was ripped out by the Mother Superior, who deemed it too Baroque and materialistic.

The Hôtel de Biron was subsequently subdivided into a cluster of artists' studios. In 1908, Auguste Rodin (1840-1917) moved in and stayed until his death. His neighbors in the *hôtel* included Rainer Maria Rilke, Jean Cocteau, Isadora Duncan, and Henri Matisse.

After viewing the ground-floor exhibits of Rodin works, bear left and gradually spiral upstairs. The works are displayed chronologically, beginning with Rodin's academic paintings and his sketches in both classic and modern modes. Notice that Rodin usually depicts only right hands; the one exception to this rule is *The Hand of the Devil*, which shows Satan's left hand crushing humanity.

The room containing Rodin's *Sculptor with his Muse* also displays several works by Camille Claudel, the talented sculptor who became Rodin's muse, model, and lover at the age of 17. Her portrait of Rodin, executed in 1888 at the peak of their affair, when he was nearly 50, reveals a rather cold man with small eyes.

Upstairs is a series of studies of Balzac created in the early 1890s. In one of them, a bronze, the writer stands stark naked and is 90 percent paunch. In the final version, which stands in the center of Boulevard Raspail between Boulevard du Montparnasse and Rue Vavin, Rodin draped Balzac in a concealing cloak.

The garden, the third largest of any of the *hôtels* in Paris (after those of the **Elysée Palace** and the **Hôtel Matignon**), provides the setting for some of Rodin's best-known works, *The Thinker, The Burghers of Calais, The Gates of Hell,* and, on an island in the center of the pool, the *Ugolin* group. On 30 January 1937, Helen Keller visited here and was permitted to touch the sculptures with her hands. Of *The Thinker,* she said: "In every limb I felt the throes of emerging mind." Keller said the sculpture of the *Burghers of Calais,* who surrendered their lives to the English to save their city, was "sadder to touch than a grave." ♦ Admission. Tu-Su. 77 Rue de Varenne (between Rue Barbet-de-Jouy and Blvd des Invalides). 01.44.18.61.10. Métro: Varenne

14 Hôtel de Villeroy This mansion was built in 1724 for actress Charlotte Desmarnes (1682-1753), who debuted at the age of 8 at the **Comédie-Française** and performed the roles of queens and maidservants there for more than 20 years. In the early 18th century the building served as the residence of the ambassador of Holland, then of the ambassador of England. In 1735 it was sold to the Duc de Villeroy. In 1886 a more modern building was erected behind the *hôtel,* dwarfing it. Today it houses the French Ministry of Agriculture. ♦ 78-80 Rue de Varenne (between Rues de Bellechase and de Bourgogne). Métro: Varenne

Child's Play

In addition to such obvious child-pleasers as the **Eiffel Tower,** Paris is filled with other attractions that will amuse and amaze young visitors. Here are 10 favorites:

1 Jardin du Luxembourg is the most marvelous garden in Paris, where children love to play and adults will recapture their childhood. There are special play areas for wee ones, with sandboxes and a lawn where, contrary to the usual Paris law, playing on the grass is allowed. Older children can enjoy the large playground crammed with numerous slides, swings, and monkey bars. Other delights include pony, donkey, and go-cart rides; a pond where you can rent toy boats to sail; and **Théâtre des Marionnettes** puppet shows.

2 The **Cité des Enfants** at **Parc de la Villette** has a grand array of stimulating interactive games and science displays for children ages 3 to 12.

3 Musée de la Poupée (Doll Museum) has a collection of more than 200 French porcelain dolls dating from 1860 to 1960. Stuffed animals and limited editions of porcelain dolls can be purchased in the museum's gift shop.

4 Musée Carnavalet, housed in a splendid 16th-century mansion, is the **Historical Museum of the City of Paris,** with exhibits on four centuries (1500-1900) of Parisian life. On the ground floor is an entire room full of old shop signs created to be understood by a population that was mostly illiterate—a bakery sign features a stalk of wheat, a butcher sign depicts a pig, and a locksmith sign is in the shape of a giant key. Also of interest to young museum-goers is the exhibit on the French Revolution, which includes a rope ladder used by a prisoner to escape from the **Bastille,** a model of the guillotine, and a pair of Revolutionary drums. Tours for children are offered on Wednesday, Saturday, and school holidays.

5 The Seine offers tired little feet (and big ones too) boat tours along the river in a *bateau mouche.* These excursions are especially dramatic on summer nights, when the buildings visible from the river are spectacularly, fantastically lit. Highlights include **Notre-Dame,** the **Conciergerie,** the **Louvre,** and the **Eiffel Tower.**

6 The Sewers of Paris afford children a place to explore underground Paris. The hourlong visit includes a film and a walk through the tunnels.

7 Disneyland Paris is a definite quick fix of North American "culture," where kids of all ages can spend a day with Mickey and Minnie. The theme park is similar to those in Florida and California with the requisite **Frontierland, Fantasyland, Adventureland, Discoveryland,** and **Main Street.**

8 The Zoological Park in the **Bois de Vincennes,** one of Europe's most beautiful zoos, is home to over 110 species of mammals and 115 types of birds. Visitors can help feed the animals their daily meals: pandas at 9:30AM and 5PM; pelicans at 2:15PM; penguins at 2:30PM; and seals and otters at 4:30PM. On the weekend a small train takes passengers on a tour of the zoo.

9 The Louvre is a daunting prospect to anyone, so when visiting the world's largest art museum with children, limit your itinerary to one museum department per day. A good place to start is the **Egyptian Antiquities Collection,** always a favorite of fledgling art connoisseurs. Highlights include: Akhout-Hetep's *mastaba* (funeral chapel); Middle Kingdom tomb objects, including model boats to help the deceased on their journey in the afterlife and blue-glazed terra-cotta hippopotami; and furniture, games, jewelry, and other objects illustrating daily life in the New Kingdom period.

10 The Museum of Natural History in the **Jardin des Plantes** possesses one of the world's richest mineral collections and some of the oldest fossilized insects on earth. The renovated **Grande Galerie** houses a superb display on the evolution of life. Highlights are a giant whale skeleton; an impressive grouping of stuffed African savanna animals, including giraffes, lions, and elephants; and an extinct and endangered species exhibit.

15 Hôtel Matignon Behind the immense porte cochere flanked by two pairs of Ionic columns is one of the most beautiful mansions in the city, built by **Jean Courtonne** in 1721. Inside are beautiful salons sumptuously decorated in period styles, the largest private garden in Paris, and a music pavilion. Former owners include Talleyrand, the diplomat who lived here from 1808 to 1811 and held infamous parties and receptions, and, later in the century, Mme. Adelaïde, the sister of Louis-Philippe. Since 1958 it has been the residence of the French prime minister. It's off-limits to the public. ♦ 57 Rue de Varenne (between Rues du Bac and Vaneau). Métros: Rue du Bac, Varenne

16 Hôtel de Boisgelin This mansion was constructed in 1732 by **Jean Sylvain Cartaud,** and has been the Italian Embassy since 1938. ♦ 47 Rue de Varenne (between Rues du Bac and Vaneau). Métros: Rue du Bac, Varenne

17 Hôtel de Gallifet This handsome 1739 mansion, with an Ionic peristyle facing the interior courtyard, is now the Italian Institute. The building was enlarged in 1938 with the annexation of **L'Hôtel de Boisgelin,** which stood behind it at 73 Rue de Grennelle. Many of the rooms have their original decoration, and the stairwell is ornamented with false windows framed by Ionic columns and lit by a cupola. The building is closed to the public. ♦ 50 Rue de Varenne (between Rues du Bac and de Bellechasse). Métros: Rue du Bac, Varenne

18 Hôtel de Gouffier de Thoix Built in 1719 for the Marquise de Gouffier de Thoix, this *hôtel particulier* was confiscated during the Revolution and later won in a lottery by a jeweler. The family of the original owners returned to Paris in the 19th century to reclaim it. Notice the magnificent doorway surmounted by a shell carving. It is now a government administration building. ♦ 56 Rue de Varenne (between Rues du Bac and de Bellechasse). Métros: Rue du Bac, Varenne

19 Hôtel d'Estrées Through the courtyard of this mansion, built by **Robert de Cotte** in 1713 for the Duchesse d'Estrées, is a triangular pediment supported by three stories of pilasters. In 1896, when the building served as the Russian Embassy, Czar Nicolas II and the czarina lived here. It is now a government administration building. ♦ 79 Rue de Grenelle (between Rues du Bac and de Bellechasse). Métro: Rue du Bac

20 Hôtel d'Avaray Constructed in 1728 by **Jean Baptiste Le Raux,** this *hôtel* stayed in the Avaray family for two centuries. In 1920 the government of Holland installed the Royal Netherlands Embassy. The garden facade has a triangular pediment with a tympanum framed by carved palm motifs. ♦ 85 Rue de Grenelle (between Rues du Bac and de Bellechasse). Métro: Rue du Bac

21 Temple de Pentémont This chapel was built by **Constant d'Ivry** in 1750 for the **Abbaye de Pentémont,** a convent where Joséphine de Beauharnais, future wife of Napoléon, lived for several years. The convent's main buildings (some are still visible at 37-39 Rue de Bellechase) housed an aristocratic school, famous for educating young ladies from the noble families of Paris. Thomas Jefferson's daughter was a student here when he was America's ambassador to France from 1785 to 1789. ♦ 104-06 Rue de Grenelle (between Rues de St-Simon and de Bellechasse). Métro: Rue du Bac

22 Rue St-Dominique Between 1355 and 1643 this street had nine different names; its present appellation comes from a monastery for Dominican novices that was once located here. The street originally stretched to Rue des Sts-Pères, but a large portion of it was amputated to make room for the opening of Boulevard St-Germain in 1866. Rue St-Dominique is more like two streets: The segment to the east of Esplanade des Invalides—often called St-Dominique–St-Germain—is characterized by fine *hôtels particuliers* that now hold government offices; the sector to the west of the esplanade—known as St-Dominique–Gros-Caillou—is largely a local shopping street that offers glimpses of the **Eiffel Tower** along its course. ♦ Métros: Solférino, Invalides, Latour Maubourg

22 1 Rue St-Dominique Known as the **Hôtel de Gournay** or the **Hôtel de Tingry,** this mansion was built in 1695 by **Germain Boffrand** for the Marquis de Gournay. In 1725 it belonged to Christian-Louis de Montmorency, Duc de Luxembourg, Prince de Tingry, and one of the first owners of the **Hôtel Matignon.** The private residence features a grand concave facade and an oval courtyard. ♦ At Blvd St-Germain. Métro: Solférino

22 3 Rue St-Dominique Dating from 1688, this mansion was at one time part of the **Dames de Bellechasse** convent. It was home to nobility in the 18th century, and a plaque commemorates chemist Jean-Baptiste Dumas, who was a resident in the 19th century. Between the ceiling of the second floor and the floor of the third was a *cachette,* used as a hiding place during *la Terreur.* It is now a government administration building. ♦ Between Blvd St-Germain and Rue de Bellechasse. Métro: Solférino

22 5 Rue St-Dominique Like its next-door neighbor, the **Hôtel de Tavannes** also was once the property of the **Dames de Bellechasse.** Sophie Soymonof, wife of the general Svetchine and known as the Russian Mme. de Sévigné, held a literary salon here from 1818 to 1857 that was frequented by many distinguished personalities. Illustrator Gustave Doré, who had his atelier nearby at 27 bis Rue de Bellechasse, lived here from 1832 until his death in 1883. The private mansion is one of the few in the city that's open to the public (albeit for a limited time and just the courtyard and staircase). It has an elegant arched doorway surmounted by a scallop and crowned by a triangular pediment. Inside there's a fine stairwell with a wrought-iron balustrade. ♦ Daily 9AM-noon, 2-4PM 20 Aug-30 Sept. Between Blvd St-Germain and Rue de Bellechasse. Métro: Solférino

23 Petit Hôtel de Villars This hôtel with elegant twin garlanded oval windows was constructed in 1712 by **Germain Boffrand** as an addition to the 1709 mansion he built next door, at **No. 116,** for the Duc de Villars. It is now the Lycée Paul Claudel, a private high school. ♦ 118 Rue de Grenelle (between Rues de Bellechasse and Casimir-Périer). Métros: Solférino, Varenne

24 Café Lunch ★$ Young arty-intellectual types serve Italian sandwiches and coffee drinks at this busy lunch counter that might be more at home in San Francisco's North Beach than among the mansions of this stately neighborhood. There's a selection of panini— try the Sicilian (with tomatoes, mozzarella, basil, and olive oil); various salads; quiche of the day; and such desserts as tarte au citron (lemon tart) and mousse au chocolat. The cappuccino is made with aromatic and rich Segafredo brand coffee beans. Order from the take-out window, or eat inside at the counter. ♦ M-Sa breakfast and lunch until 5:30PM. 130 Rue de Grenelle (at Rue de Martignac). 01.45.55.15.45. Métro: Varenne

25 Basilique Ste-Clothilde This Neo-Gothic church, designed in 1846 by **Christian Gau,** was the first of its kind to be built in Paris. It is the product of mid–19th-century enthusiasm for the Middle Ages, inspired by such writers as Victor Hugo. The church is notable for its prominent twin towers, visible from across the river. Composer César Franck was organist here from 1858 until his death in 1890, and a monument commemorating him stands in the pretty neighborhood park opposite the church. ♦ 23 bis Rue Las-Cases (between Rues Casimir-Périer and de Martignac). 01.44.18.62.60. Métro: Solférino

26 10-12 Rue St-Dominique The Ministry of Defense has occupied these buildings since 1804, but they were originally the **Couvent des Filles de St-Joseph,** a convent and home for orphan girls established in 1641. The orphans were taught a skill, such as embroidery, and at 20 were expected to find jobs, become nuns, or marry. In 1645 alone the convent housed 686 girls who worked in an embroidery workshop on the premises. The convent closed in 1790 and became

headquarters for the Ministry of War in 1793. ♦ Between Rues de Solférino and de Bourgogne. Métros: Solférino, Assemblée Nationale

26 14-16 Rue St-Dominique The **Hôtel de Brienne,** built in the early 18th century, was the home of Letizia Bonaparte, Napoléon's mother, from 1806 to 1817. Today it is occupied by the Ministry of Defense. ♦ Between Rues de Solférino and de Bourgogne. Métros: Solférino, Assemblée Nationale

27 Chapelle Jesus Enfant The catechism chapel of **Basilique Ste-Clothilde** (see left column) was built at the same time as its mother church. ♦ 29 Rue Las-Cases (between Rues de Martignac and de Bourgogne). 01.44.18.62.60. Métros: Solférino, Assemblée Nationale

28 Hôtel de Noirmoutiers Also known as the "Hôtel de Sens," this mansion was built in 1722 by **Jean Courtonne** on the lands of the Comte de Noirmoutiers. Mlle. de Sens, great-granddaughter of Louis the First of Bourbon, lived here in 1735 and had the interior decorated by Lassurance. The mansion was later the army headquarters, where Marshal Foch resided until his death in 1929. Today, **No. 140** houses the Ministry of Public Works and the headquarters of the Institut Géographique Nationale, and behind the impressive concave entryway of **No. 138** is the Ministry of the Sahara. ♦ 138-140 Rue de Grenelle (between Rues de Bourgogne and de Talleyrand). Métro: Varenne

29 Hôtel du Chanac de Pompadour Designed by architect **Pierre-Alexis Delamair** in 1704, this mansion has housed the Swiss Embassy since 1938. Inside is a subterranean swimming pool, surrounded by 20 Tuscan columns, with 5 niches for statues. Unfortunately, it is only open to the public once a year, on the third Saturday of September. ♦ 142 Rue de Grenelle (between Rues de Bourgogne and de Talleyrand). Métro: Varenne

30 Hôtel du Châtelet This mansion is a fine example of the Louis XV style, built in 1770 for the Duc du Châtelet, who was later beheaded in la Terreur. It was confiscated in 1796 to house a civil engineering school. In 1835 it became the Turkish Embassy, in 1843 the Austrian Embassy, and from 1849 to 1906 it was the Archbishop's Palace. Since then it has housed the Ministry of Employment. The courtyard facade is ornamented with four composite columns supporting an entablature and balustrade that extend along the whole facade. Several of the salons have their original Louis XV and XVI decoration, and the arched porte cochere is in the Tuscan style. ♦ 127 Rue de Grenelle (at Blvd des Invalides). Métro: Varenne

Hôtel des Invalides

31 28 Rue St-Dominique Pierre Lassurance, one of the builders of mansions in the Faubourg St-Germain area, constructed this *hôtel* in 1703. In 1764 it was owned by Maurice de Riquet, Comte de Caraman, who had a celebrated garden that Marie Antoinette visited in 1771 to get some ideas about how to transform her **Jardin de Trianon** at **Versailles.** In 1929 it became the headquarters for the Union Internationale de Chimie (International Union of Chemists). ♦ Between Rues de Bourgogne and de Constantine. Métros: Assemblée Nationale, Invalides

32 53 Rue St-Dominique Today home to the Ministry of Cultural Affairs, this mansion was built in 1770. Past renovations united its garden with that of **Nos. 43** and 55 Rue St-Dominique. ♦ Between Rues de Bourgogne and de Constantine. Métros: Assemblée Nationale, Invalides

33 57 Rue St-Dominique This grand mansion, visible through iron gates, is separated from the street by an unpaved courtyard and symmetrical fountains on either side of the entrance. Known as the **Hôtel de Monaco de Sagan,** it was built in 1784 by **Alexandre Théodore Brongniart** for the Princess of Monaco. Until 1825 it was the British Embassy. It was acquired in 1838 by Dutch banker William Hope, who distorted it by raising the first floor, moving the stair, and adding three dining rooms. Hope also enlarged the grounds, incorporating a little chapel dating from 1706 belonging to the Filles de Ste-Valère. Today the building houses the Polish Embassy. ♦ Between Rues de Bourgogne and de Constantine. Métros: Assemblée Nationale, Invalides

34 British Cultural Center The aim of the center, which is under the aegis of the British Council, is to promote cultural and scientific links between Great Britain and France by organizing exchange programs for French and British scientists, offering English-language classes, and operating a lending library of English-language books. The council promotes young artists and musicians, and

brings such British orchestras and theater companies as the **Royal Shakespeare Company** to France. ♦ Free. M-F. 11 Rue de Constantine (at Rue St-Dominique). Center 01.49.55.73.00, library 01.49.55.73.23. Métro: Invalides

35 Canadian Cultural Services This branch of the Canadian Embassy helps Canadian artists find contacts. It often hosts visual-arts shows and theater productions, and changing sculpture exhibits are displayed in the courtyard. ♦ M-F. 5 Rue de Constantine (between Rues St-Dominique and de l'Université). 01.47.05.89.68. Métro: Invalides

36 Rue Robert-Esnault-Pelterie Since 1965 this block has borne the name of the French astronomical engineer and pioneer of aviation (1881-1957), who lived at 23 Rue de Constantine. ♦ Métro: Invalides

On Rue Robert-Esnault-Pelterie:

Gare des Invalides At the **Air France** *aérogare* (air terminal), you can catch a bus to **Orly Airport,** change your ticket, or rent a car at the **Hertz, Avis,** or **Europcar** desks. Be forewarned: Even the French are confused by the drop-off procedure for rental cars, which involves parking in the lot underneath the Esplanade des Invalides and depositing the key in one of the hard-to-find boxes. ♦ No. 2 (at Quai d'Orsay). 01.43.23.94.93, 01.43.17.20.20

37 Ministère des Affaires Etrangères (Ministry of Foreign Affairs) The facade, roof, grand stair, and garden statuary of this structure, built by **Lacornée Lacornée** in 1845, are classified with the *Monuments Historiques.* ♦ 37 Quai d'Orsay (between Rues Aristide-Briand and Robert-Esnault-Pelterie). Métro: Invalides

38 Hôtel des Invalides Louis XIV ordered **Libéral Bruant** to erect this monumental group of buildings to house the king's old soldiers, many of them invalids who had been reduced to begging or seeking shelter in monasteries. When the *hôtel* (pictured above) was completed in 1676, 6,000 aging pensioners moved in. It is still used as a home for old soldiers, though only a dozen or so still live here. The year after its completion, the "Sun King" (Louis XIV's nickname, derived from his brilliance and his fondness for gold) commissioned a second church for the complex, which was built by **Jules Hardouin-Mansart.** Attached Siamese-twin–style to **Bruant**'s original church, **St-Louis-des-Invalides,** the **Eglise du Dôme** (Dome Church) is one of the most magnificent Baroque churches of the *Grand Siècle.* Its dome is decorated with garlands and crowned with a 351-foot-tall spire.

France's bravest soldiers and greatest warriors are entombed in the **Eglise du Dôme:** Turenne, Vauban, Duroc, Foch, and, of course, Napoléon. "I do not think that there is a more impressive sepulchre on earth than that tomb; it is grandly simple," wrote Theodore Roosevelt of Napoléon's resting place. "I am not easily awestruck, but it certainly gave me a solemn feeling to look at the plain, red stone bier which contained what had once been the mightiest conqueror the world ever saw."

Concealed by the outward simplicity of red porphyry, Napoléon's remains are contained in seven coffins, one inside the other, made of iron, mahogany, lead, ebony, oak, and marble. Napoléon was originally interred on the island of St. Helena, where he died in 1821. The British finally agreed to repatriate his remains in 1840, thus fulfilling the emperor's wish to be buried "on the banks of the Seine among the people of France whom I have loved so much." The tomb of Napoléon's son, the King of Rome, who died in Vienna at age 21, sounds a morbid footnote to history. In 1940 his remains were given to Paris in a grandiose gesture by a heady Hitler.

Bruant's church, **St-Louis-des-Invalides,** where the occupants of the *hôtel* worshiped, is separated by a glass barrier from the domed edifice. One of the church's most impressive features is the collection of captured banners hanging from the upper galleries. Among these tattered mementos of French military victories there is even the flag with the rising sun of Japan, a relic of World War II. In 1837 Berlioz's *Requiem* was performed here for the first time.

Visitors enter **St-Louis-des-Invalides** from the **Cour d'Honneur,** an impressive courtyard also designed by **Bruant.** This is where French army officer Alfred Dreyfus was publicly disgraced and where de Gaulle kissed Churchill. The statue of Napoléon by Seurre, which used to be on the top of a column in Place Vendôme, now stands in this courtyard. Among the other Napoleonic memorabilia exhibited here are the emperor's death mask, his dinner jacket, and the dog that was his

companion during his years on the island of Elba, stuffed for posterity. ◆ Admission. Daily. Pl Vauban. 01.44.42.37.72. Métro: St-François-Xavier

Within the Hôtel des Invalides:

Musée de l'Armée (Army Museum) At the north end of the **Invalides** complex, this museum houses one of the largest collections of military paraphernalia in the world. Swords, guns, armor, flags, and other articles are on display, along with innumerable models, maps, and images that trace the evolution of warfare from prehistoric times until World War II. Understandably, Napoleonic souvenirs are most conspicuous, but there are also intriguing exhibitions of medieval, Renaissance, and Asian militaria. ◆ Admission. Daily. Pl des Invalides (between Blvds des Invalides and de La-Tour-Maubourg). 01.44.42.37.72. Métros: Latour Maubourg, Varenne

39 Le Divellec ★★★$$$ The tasteful nautical decor of chef Jacques Le Divellec's restaurant emphasizes that the focus here is the sea. Le Divellec's book of seafood recipes, *Les Bons Plats de la Mer,* is none too discreetly displayed at the restaurant's entrance foyer. Some of his exceptional dishes include smoked bass, roasted, then flambéed with thyme; *homard à la presse avec son corail* (pressed lobster with lobster corral); baked turbot with lobster béarnaise sauce; and *cassolette de St-Jacques aux truffes* (scallop casserole with truffles). For dessert, top the meal off with an iced Cognac and coffee soufflé. ◆ M-Sa lunch and dinner. Reservations required. 107 Rue de l'Université (at Rue Fabert). 01.45.51.91.96. Métros: Invalides, Latour Maubourg

40 Petrossian Parisians have flocked here since 1924 for caviar, smoked salmon, and foie gras. Sit down at one of the three tables to sample some of the shop's wares and a glass of Champagne in an elegant atmosphere. ◆ Tu-Sa. 18 Blvd de Latour-Maubourg (at Rue de l'Université). 01.44.11.32.22. Métros: Invalides, Latour Maubourg

41 La Boule d'Or ★★$$ This invitingly calm restaurant, with its blond wood and beige-upholstered banquettes, offers such specialties as *foie gras de canard* (duck liver pâté); *filet de perche en barigoule* (perch in a stew of carrots, onions, artichokes, olive oil, chives, and cream); *pintade sauce diable* (roast guinea fowl with mustard and onion sauce); and warm lemon soufflé. ♦ M-F, Su lunch and dinner; Sa dinner. Reservations required. 13 Blvd de Latour-Maubourg (at Rue de l'Université). 01.47.05.50.18. Métros: Invalides, Latour Maubourg

42 La Mandarin de Latour-Maubourg ★$ One of many Chinese restaurants that dot the *quartier,* this informal place is always full. Its loyal local clientele appreciates the wide range of Mandarin dishes, including spring rolls, roasted spareribs, chicken with ginger and scallion sauce, crab and asparagus soup, and roast duck. ♦ Daily lunch and dinner. 23 Blvd de Latour-Maubourg (between Rues St-Dominique and de l'Université). 01.45.51.25.71. Métro: Latour Maubourg

43 Paul Minchelli ★★★$$$ The handsome wood facade and the nautical Art Deco interior of this *restaurant de poissons* (fish restaurant) provide a fine, if rather formal, setting for a meal of simple seafood dishes, fresh, subtle, and impeccably prepared. The chef knows that his high-quality fish and shellfish, with lobsters scooped right out of the tank, need little embellishment. Feast on fresh shrimp, *St-Pierre* (John Dory) with olive oil, and lobster with honey and pimiento. ♦ Tu-Sa lunch and dinner, closed in August. Reservations required. 54 Blvd de Latour-Maubourg (between Rues de Grenelle and St-Dominique). 01.47.05.89.86. Métro: Latour Maubourg

43 Le Bistrot du 7ème ★★$ The warmth that emanates from this neighborhood bistro may have less to do with the simple, traditional French food it serves than with Argentinean Mme. Beauvallet, who, with her husband, owns this cozy spot. Changing daily specials might include *bavette aux échalottes* (steak with shallots), *soupe de poissons* (fish soup), trout meunière, grilled pork sausage, crème brûlée, iced chocolate charlotte, and a fruit or chocolate tart. The restaurant's only nod to Mme. Beauvallet's Argentine roots is the inclusion of plump little bottles of San Felipe Tinto, an Argentine red wine, nestled among all the Bordeaux, Bourgognes, and Beaujolais. ♦ Daily lunch and dinner.

Reservations recommended. 56 Blvd de Latour-Maubourg (between Rues de Grenelle and St-Dominique). 01.45.51.93.08. Métro: Latour Maubourg

44 Café Max ★★$ One of the only beacons in this nighttime desert is this cozy French bistro that's particularly animated on Saturday nights. The place is agreeably dingy, with banquettes, mismatched chairs and tables, and such flea-market memorabilia as a stuffed swordfish and street signs on its red walls and wooden shoe lasts hanging from the ceiling. Jovial owner Max, who speaks very good English, presides over the dining room while his wife, Lili, rules in the kitchen. The food is simple and includes *cassoulet Landais* (a casserole of duck confit, garlic, sausage, beans, and ham); Lyons sausages; ham and potato salad; and *tarte tatin* (apple tart). For an aperitif, order a kir Max, the house cocktail made with sparkling white wine and Crème de Cassis. ♦ M dinner; Tu-Sa lunch and dinner; closed in August. Reservations recommended. 7 Ave de La Motte-Picquet (between Rue Bougainville and Blvd de Latour-Maubourg). 01.47.05.57.66. Métro: Latour Maubourg

45 Le Chambrelain M. Alexandre's hand-painted Limoges porcelain dishes are exquisitely decorated with fruits, flowers, and fish and come in handsome black gift boxes that accentuate the precious quality of this expensive tableware. Those on tighter budgets might consider buying dishes decorated by the traditional method known as *décalcomanie;* you can take home a set adorned with artichokes, rutabagas, pea pods, roses, and irises for about half the price of the hand-painted porcelains. Alexandre has been in the business since 1946 and had a big workshop that supplied **Bergdorf Goodman** and **Neiman Marcus** before he decided to scale down to this smaller boutique. The smell of turpentine permeating the shop emanates from the back-room atelier where he gives courses in hand-painting porcelain. ♦ M-F; closed in August. 11 Ave de La Motte-Picquet (between Rue Bougainville and Blvd de Latour-Maubourg). 01.45.55.03.45. Métro: Latour Maubourg

46 Au Liégeur Cork is the name of the game here: cork trivets, cork watches, cork jewelry, sheets of cork, corkscrews, and just plain old corks that come from the company's (what else?) cork factory. The shop carries a nice assortment of decanters, decorative corks, and the coveted *bouchon universal*, a cork specially designed to fit bottles of all sizes. ♦ Tu-Sa; closed in August. 17 Ave de La Motte-Picquet (between Rue Bougainville and Blvd de Latour-Maubourg). 01.47.05.53.10. Métros: Ecole Militaire, Latour Maubourg

46 Restaurant Le Champ de Mars ★★$$ At this comfortable restaurant you might start with Normandy oysters, then have a main course of *filet mignon de veau aux morilles fraîches* (veal filet mignon with fresh morels) or stuffed rabbit, followed by a dessert of nougat ice cream with *coulis de framboises* (raspberry sauce) and *profiteroles au chocolat.* ♦ Tu-Su lunch and dinner; closed mid-July to mid-August. Reservations recommended. 17 Ave de La Motte-Picquet (at Rue Bougainville). 01.47.05.57.99. Métros: Ecole Militaire, Latour Maubourg

47 Hôtel Muguet $$ Behind the pink-painted brick exterior of this well-maintained hotel are 45 calm and comfortable rooms with TV sets hung high on the wall, hospital style. Five of the rooms have a view of the **Eiffel Tower** and two look onto the **Hôtel des Invalides.** Breakfast is served, but there's no restaurant. ♦ 11 Rue Chevert (between Rue Louis-Codet and Blvd de Latour-Maubourg). 01.47.05.05.93; fax 01.45.50.25.37; muguet@wanadoo.fr; www.hotelmuguet.com. Métro: Latour Maubourg

48 Le Maupertu ★★$$ This intimate spot will convince you that dining in Paris can indeed be both grand and affordable. The decor is a blend of terra-cotta and marble and the menu is pleasing to the palate. The expertly prepared French specialties include *mille-feuille de torteau aux crevettes* (crab and shrimps in a flaky pastry) and *ravioli de champignons au coulis de cèpes* (ravioli stuffed with wild mushrooms with a sauce of cèpes). Such desserts as wafer-thin slices of chocolate and white chocolate mousse served with light egg custard are superb. There's also an excellent wine list. Reserve a table under the glass roof, with its lovely view of the gilded dome of the **Hôtel des Invalides;** it's especially splendid at night. ♦ M-F lunch and dinner; Sa dinner. Reservations recommended. 94 Blvd de Latour-Maubourg (between Ave de Tourville and Rue Louis-Codet). 01.45.51.37.96. Métro: Ecole Militaire

The oldest house in Paris is at 51 Rue de Montmorency (between Rues Beaubourg and St-Martin) in the third arrondissement. It was built by the alchemist Nicholas Flamel in 1407.

Restaurants/Clubs: Red **Hotels:** Blue
Shops/ ♥ Outdoors: Green **Sights/Culture:** Black

49 Auberge d'Chez Eux ★★$$$ In the shadow of the **Hôtel des Invalides,** Jean-Pierre Court and his father have specialized in a *cuisine familial* from France's southwest since 1963. The restaurant's enclosed terrace is draped with red-and-white-striped fabric and is a perfect spot for feasting on the homemade *foie gras d'oie* (goose liver pâté), which comes with a glass of Château Loubens Bordeaux Blanc; *cuisses de grenouilles Provençale* (frogs' legs sautéed in olive oil, garlic, and tomatoes); *magret de canard* (sliced fresh roasted duck breast) with honey vinegar; roast lamb chops; or *pavé de saumon d'Ecosse poêlé sauce béarnaise* (sautéed salmon steak with béarnaise sauce). Wines are reasonably priced; the Cahors Chateau Lagineste would be a good choice with any of the dishes. ♦ M-Sa lunch and dinner; closed three weeks in August. Reservations recommended. 2 Ave de Lowendal (at Blvd de Latour-Maubourg). 01.47.05.52.55. Métro: Ecole Militaire

50 Square de Latour-Maubourg Dating from 1897, this peaceful private drive is decorated with an ornamental pool that matches one in the Place François-1er across the river. ♦ Métro: Latour Maubourg

51 St-Jean This small Lutheran Evangelical church was built in the Neo-Gothic style in 1911; the interior is intimate and full of light, with a timber ceiling of boat hull construction. In 1990 the **American University** took out a 50-year lease on the land directly behind the church and constructed a new building to house its classrooms, computer lab, and faculty offices. The university's main building is located at 31 Avenue Bosquet. ♦ 147 Rue de Grenelle (between Sq de Latour-Maubourg and Cité du Général-Négrier). Métro: Latour Maubourg

52 Thoumieux ★★$$ For those seeking honest regional fare, here is an authentic bistro that has been in Jean Bassalert's family for more than 75 years. The comfortable dining room, with its sophisticated 1930s charm, glows with the warmth of a place well loved, and attentive but discreet waiters who deliver impeccable service. The menu includes many specialties from the La Corrèze region in southwest France, and changes daily according to what's fresh at the market.

Bassalert types each day's bill of fare on an old Remington typewriter and then mimeographs it, adding a wonderful, immediate quality to the experience. Experiment with a Correzien appetizer such as the earthy *soupe de châtaignes* (chestnut soup) or the *pâté de pomme de terre* (a pastry made with potatoes, pork, and garlic); then have a main course of *steak frites, confit de canard* (preserved duck breast), grilled beef with bordelaise sauce, or *gigot d'agneau rôti* (roast leg of lamb) with ratatouille. Your wine choice might be a lush Bordeaux, such as the Château David 1996, or a Nuits-St-Georges 1997 from Burgundy. For dessert the crème brûlée is warm and velvety, and the *gâteau Thoumieux crème anglaise* (chocolate cake with custard sauce) is as rich and delicious as it sounds. The banquet room is the site of a monthly wine class (normally for groups but there is often an extra space or two) during which six types of wine are served with six accompanying dishes. There's also a small hotel upstairs (see below). ♦ Daily lunch and dinner. Reservations recommended. 79 Rue St-Dominique (between Blvd de Latour-Maubourg and Rue de la Comète). 01.47.05.49.75. Métro: Latour Maubourg

At Thoumieux:

Hôtel Thoumieux $$ If you can land one of the 10 modern rooms here you will be surrounded by the amiable young staff of the restaurant downstairs. You could even indulge in dinner at **Thoumieux** every night! ♦ 01.47.05.49.75; fax 01.47.05.36.96

Hôtel Le Pavillon ★★

53 Hôtel le Pavillon $$ In 1889, when the Eiffel Tower was nearing completion and Paris buzzed in anticipation of the World's Fair, many former monastery and convent buildings became hotels to accommodate the flood of visitors to the city. This one, part of a convent built in 1585 by the Ursuline nuns, once sat in a large open field that extended all the way to the Seine. Today it is a humble 18-room hostelry that's inexpensive, well located, and quiet. An arched iron gate and a well-planted courtyard separate the building from the street. Regular guests return year after year. There's no restaurant. ♦ 54 Rue St-Dominique (between Rues Surcouf and Jean-Nicot). 01.45.51.42.87; fax 01.45.51.32.79. Métro: Latour Maubourg

53 Hôtel Saint Dominique $$ Another former-convent-turned-hotel, this one has 34 well-equipped *chambres,* a breakfast room in the vaulted basement (but no restaurant), and exposed beams in the lobby. The small courtyard has yellow-painted walls. ♦ 62 Rue St-Dominique (between Rues Surcouf and Jean-Nicot). 01.47.05,51,44; fax 01.47.05.81.28. Métro: Latour Maubourg

53 Boulangerie Gisquet The interior of this bakery is registered as a historic monument; notice the decorative faïence tiles and the painting on the trompe l'oeil ceiling that depicts a view of the sky from underneath an oval balustrade. Much more real are Mme. Gisquet's enticing country breads, fruit tarts, and macaroons. Don't leave without a *mille-feuilleaux* of pears with a caramelized topping, or a *Balkan* made with Chantilly cream, *fromage blanc* (sour cream), and raspberries. ♦ Tu-Su 7AM-8:30PM. 64 Rue St-Dominique (between Rues Surcouf and Jean-Nicot). 01.45.51.70.46. Métro: Latour Maubourg

54 Rue Surcouf In 1728 this street was called Rue de la Boucherie-des-Invalides because a slaughterhouse was located at its terminus on Rue St-Dominique. By 1867 the *boucherie* had disappeared and the street's name was changed to honor Corsair Robert Surcouf (1773-1827). ♦ Métros: Latour Maubourg, Invalides

54 Du Côté 7ème ★★$$ All meals at this simple but elegant eatery owned by M. and Mme. Brossard are prix-fixe. A classic French dinner might include an aperitif of kir; an appetizer such as crab flan or escargots with butter, parsley, garlic, and hazelnuts; *filet d'agneau rôti* (roasted lamb fillet) with garlic purée, or *confit de canard* roasted with spices; a bottle of red, white, or rosé wine (per two people); and either a selection of cheeses or a dessert such as *charlotte au chocolat* (molded chocolate cream) with *crème anglaise* (a light custard sauce) or one of the other featured goodies. ♦ Tu-Su lunch and dinner. Reservations recommended. 29 Rue Surcouf (between Rues St-Dominique and de l'Université). 01.47.05.81.65. Métro: Latour Maubourg

55 Le Bellecour ★★★$$ In his small, cozy dining room that recalls the bistros of days gone by, Chef Gérald Goutany offers classic and refined seasonal Lyonnaise specialties that have earned him a Michelin star. They include *truffière de St-Jacques rôties* (roasted scallops with truffles); wild duck and lentils in the hunting season; and medaillons de *lotte à la sauge avec jus balsamique* (angler fish with sage) and caramelized endive. TV journalists frequent the place and keep things lively. ♦ M-F lunch and dinner; Sa dinner; closed in August. Reservations required. 22 Rue Surcouf (between Rues St-Dominique and de l'Université). 01.45.51.46.93. Métros: Latour Maubourg, Invalides

55 Au Petit Tone ★★$$ Genet Boyar has been preparing *"use cuisine de femme"* for businesspeople, artists, and locals since 1979. In her dining room, with its compelling rundown charm, she serves *salade Bressane* (with chicken livers in raspberry vinaigrette), *rognons de veau* (veal kidneys) with Madeira sauce, *châteaubriand au poivre* (with pepper), and chocolate profiteroles. A plat du jour of fish changes depending on the day's catch; past specials have included *coquilles St-Jacques* and *turbot au beurre blanc* (in a butter sauce with vinegar and shallots) with fresh sorrel. ♦ Daily lunch and dinner. 20 Rue Surcouf (between Rues St-Dominique and de l'Université). 01.47.05.09.01. Métros: Latour Maubourg, Invalides

56 La Poule au Pot ★★$ "If God grants me a longer life, I will see to it that no peasant in my kingdom will lack the means to have a chicken in the pot *(une poule dans son pot)* every Sunday," promised King Henri IV. At this popular restaurant with prices a peasant could almost afford, you can enjoy comforting chicken stew every day *but* Sunday (when it's closed). *Poule* alone does not account for the always-full tables, however. Other tasty options include salad of warm foie gras with cèpes, *filet au poivre* (fillet of beef flambéed with Armagnac and served with béarnaise sauce), or *andouillette au chablis* (tripe sausage grilled in white wine). Dessert might be *croustillant poires au chocolat* (pear-filled pastry covered with chocolate). Come in anytime for a coffee or a *pression* (draft beer) and a warm welcome at the zinc bar. This restaurant belongs to the Dumond family, who own the equally friendly restaurant **Le Trumilou** on the Quai de l'Hôtel-de-Ville. ♦ M-F breakfast, lunch, and dinner; Sa dinner. 121 Rue de l'Université (at Rue Surcouf). 01.47.05.16.36. Métros: Latour Maubourg, Invalides

57 Musée-Galerie de la Seita (Tobacco Museum) This museum, housed in the administration building of a former tobacco factory, relates the history of tobacco since it was brought to Europe from the New World 500 years ago. The collection, which provides a fascinating insight into the uses and abuses of tobacco, covers smoking, snuff taking, tobacco chewing, and the medical uses of tobacco. Tobacco-related objects on display include Napoleon III's 19th-century cigar chest. ♦ Admission. Tu-Su. 12 Rue Surcouf (at Rue de l'Université). 01.45.56.60.17. Métros: Latour Maubourg, Invalides

Le Bar au Sel

58 Bar Au Sel ★★$$ There has always been a cafe or restaurant on the site that this intimate, friendly eatery has occupied since the beginning of the century. But carnivores beware: chef Jean-Jacques Philletas serves only seafood. Raw oysters, rockfish soups, and crab ravioli are some of the starters; main dishes include the eponymous *bar en croûte de sel* (salt-crusted sea bass), sole meunière, or pan-fried langoustines. ♦ Daily lunch and dinner. Reservations required. 49 Quai d'Orsay (at Rue Surcouf). 01.45.51.58.58. Métro: Invalides

59 53-65, 67-69, and 71-91 Quai d'Orsay From 1829 to 1909 this area was the site of a tobacco manufacturing center. A factory specializing in the fabrication of cigars with tobacco from Havana once stood at Nos. 53-65; in 1862 it employed more than 700 workers. ♦ Between Rue Surcouf and Pl de la Résistance. Métro: Invalides, RER: Pont de l'Alma

At 65 Quai d'Orsay:

American Church Built in 1931 by **Carrol Greenough** in the Gothic style, this interdenominational church serves the spiritual and social needs of the English-speaking community in Paris. Within the church complex are the bilingual **Montessori** and **Lenen Schools,** and a bulletin board renowned by apartment hunters for its listings of housing available in the city. The headquarters of the *Paris Free Voice*, a monthly English newspaper, is in the basement. ♦ 01.40.62.05.00

60 Rue Jean-Nicot This street is named after the 17th-century gentleman who introduced tobacco to France. ♦ RER: Pont de l'Alma

60 Conservatoire Municipal With its bold design of intersecting white forms and geometric cutouts, this structure is one of architect **Christian de Portzamparc**'s first well-known projects. After designing it in the 1980s, he went on to the **Café Beaubourg** and, more recently, the **Cité de Musique** at **Parc La Villette.** The building houses the seventh arrondissement's conservatory, where students are trained in music, dance, and dramatic arts. ♦ 135 Rue de l'Université (at Rue Jean-Nicot). Métro: Latour Maubourg

61 Poujauran One of the pioneers of the organic bread movement in France, Jean-Luc Poujauran made his name as a young *boulanger* (baker) in the early 1980s with his chewy *baguette biologique* made with organically grown, stone-ground wheat. He also makes a superb sourdough *pain de campagne,* flavored breads (e.g., apricot, fig), and a popular raisin-nut loaf. He is equally famous for his pastries. Poujauran's *galette des rois* is as light and flavorful as that traditional almond cake can get. ♦ Tu-Sa 8AM-8:30PM. 20 Rue Jean-Nicot (between Rues St-Dominique and de l'Université). 01.47.05.80.88. Métro: Latour Maubourg

62 81 Rue St-Dominique In the mid-18th century this building housed a cabaret called the **Canon-Royal.** It's now the site of several shops. ♦ Between Rues de la Comète and Amélie. Métro: Latour Maubourg

62 93 Rue St-Dominique All that's left of the clockmaker's workshop that was on this site in the early 19th century is its sign, which is composed of three bells, a lantern, shells, garlands of fruits and flowers, and, of course, a clock. It's classified with the *Monuments Historiques.* The building today is a mix of commercial and residential space. ♦ Between Rues de la Comète and Amélie. Métro: Latour Maubourg

63 Jean Millet Pastry chef Denis Ruffel makes dreamy honey madeleines and croissants, and his *pain au chocolat* has two sticks of chocolate instead of the typical one. Indulge in an afternoon snack of a St-Marc pastry (made with chocolate, Chantilly cream, and a caramelized cookie) and an espresso at one of the inviting tables. ♦ M-Sa; Su 8AM-1PM. 103 Rue St-Dominique (between Rues Amélie and Cler). 01.45.51.49.80. Métro: Latour Maubourg

Hôtel de la Tulipe

64 Hôtel de la Tulipe $$ This hotel's lively owner, actor Jean-Louis Fortuit, claims that the rooms in his charming hotel were once the cells of monks, and that the small rounded structure jutting out into the lush plant-filled courtyard was the chapel. Whatever the story, the atmosphere at this cottagelike hostelry is relaxed and friendly, and many of the guests are Fortuit's actor friends. Each of the 22 rooms is slightly different, and many have rustic wood beams and exposed stone walls; there's no restaurant. The name was inspired by a Belgian tulip seller who rented the entire hotel for four months during a *Salon d'Agriculture* in the 1950s. ♦ 33 Rue Malar (between Rues St-Dominique and de l'Université). 01.45.51.67.21; fax 01.47.53.96.37; www.hotelsinparis.com. Métro: Latour Maubourg

65 Chez L'Ami Jean ★$$ Here is a Basque restaurant full of sports memorabilia that is frequented by players of rugby and *pelota* (a Basque game similar to jai alai). Owner Jean, himself a former *pelotari* from Basque country, offers paunchy former ballplayers

and other patrons such dishes as *confit de canard des Landes,* pot-au-feu, paella Valenciana, fresh anchovies, foie gras, and Basque-style chicken, along with a selection of regional red wines. ♦ M-Sa lunch and dinner; closed in August. 27 Rue Malar (between Rues St-Dominique and de l'Université). 01.47.05.86.89. Métro: Latour Maubourg

66 L'Affriolé ★★★$$ In a serene Neo-Roman dining room with faux marble–painted architectural details, diners can feast on chef Alain Atibard's seasonal offerings that might include *côte de veau truffé* (veal ribs with truffles), *coquilles St-Jacques,* or *ravioli d'escargots au bouillon d'herbes* (ravioli stuffed with snails and herbs). The wine list is extensive—and expensive. ♦ M-F lunch and dinner; Sa dinner; closed first three weeks of August. 17 Rue Malar (between Rues St-Dominique and de l'Université). 01.44.18.31.33. Métro: Latour Maubourg, RER: Pont de l'Alma

67 Michel Chaudun Once chief *chocolatier* at **Maison du Chocolat,** Chaudun now turns out his own confections. Chocolate Eiffel Towers and Statues of Liberty, *colombes* (white and dark chocolate discs), a white-chocolate Tutankhamen, and several African totem sculptures in dark chocolate are on display. ♦ Tu-Sa; closed in August. 149 Rue de l'Université (at Rue Malar). 01.47.53.74.40. Métro: Latour Maubourg, RER: Pont de l'Alma

68 Beato ★★$$ This classy Italian restaurant with colors reminiscent of Siena is popular with good reason: its savory specialties include the Robespierre (cooked carpaccio perfumed with garlic and rosemary), *spaghetti Stromboli* (with olives, capers, and anchovies), *scampi alla griglia* (grilled shrimp), *scaloppine al limone* (veal scallopini with lemon), osso buco Milanese with saffron rice, and tiramisù with Amaretto. The prix-fixe lunch is a remarkable value. ♦ M-Sa lunch and dinner; closed three weeks in August. 8 Rue Malar (between Rues St-Dominique and de l'Université). 01.47.05.94.27. Métro: Latour Maubourg, RER: Pont de l'Alma

Though Paris is by far the most populous municipality in France, with 2.15 million people, it ranks only 113th in land surface, with 10,540 hectares (26,034 acres).

69 St-Pierre du Gros Caillou In 1652 the inhabitants of this neighborhood, then called Gros-Caillou, decided that their parish church of **St-Sulpice** was just too far away. It took 86 years to realize, but in 1738 the small chapel of **Notre-Dame-de-Bonne-Délivrance** was erected on this site. The present church, with its austere Doric facade and interior coffered vault, replaced the chapel in 1922. ♦ 92 Rue St-Dominique (at Rue Pierre-Villey). 01.45.55.22.38. Métro: Latour Maubourg

70 Rue Cler At Paris's most exclusive street market you'll see the best-dressed shoppers in town choosing from the colorful, bountiful displays of butchers, bakers, *fromagers* (cheese sellers), greengrocers, wine merchants, and florists that spill out onto the cobblestone street. This market, like most, is especially lively on Saturday morning. ♦ Tu-Sa morning. Between Ave de La Motte-Picquet and Rue de Grenelle. Métros: Ecole Militaire, Latour Maubourg

70 Le Repaire de Bacchus This small wine shop has a big selection of *grands vins français,* as well as many labels from small regional producers. The salespeople are expert wine counselors, able to offer advice on just the right wine to have with a particular dish or to help you select something for your wine cellar back home. You could try an inexpensive bottle of Le Vieille Ferme Côte du Ventoux 1996, with its distinct perfume of wood and raspberries, or splurge with a Château Senilhac 1995 Haut Medoc that envelops the mouth with its refined flavors. The shop also carries over 60 types of whiskey, including some rare bottles. ♦ Tu-Sa; Su morning. 29 Rue Cler (between Rues du Champ-de-Mars and de Grenelle). 01.45.56.99.99. Métros: Ecole Militaire, Latour Maubourg. Also at: 147 Rue St-Dominique (between Rue Augereau and Pl du Général-Gouraud). 01.45.51.77.21. Métro: Ecole Militaire

70 Fromagerie Cler Bleu de Bresse, creamy chèvre, and Morbier are just a few of the cheeses sold at this well-stocked shop that you could design a picnic around. ♦ Tu-Sa; Su 8AM-1PM. 31 Rue Cler (between Rues du Champ-de-Mars and de Grenelle). 01.47.05.48.95. Métros: Ecole Militaire, Latour Maubourg

DAVOLI
LA MAISON DU JAMBON

71 Davoli Also known as "La Maison du Jambon" (The House of Ham), this shop has Parma hams hanging from the ceiling and is literally stuffed with sausages and such take-

out dishes as lasagna, salads, and an assortment of tarts. It also sells marvelous *choucroute,* the Alsatian sauerkraut specialty. ♦ Tu, Th-Sa; W, Su 8AM-1PM; closed 15 July-15 August. 34 Rue Cler (between Rues du Champ-de-Mars and de Grenelle). 01.45.51.23.41. Métro: Ecole Militaire

72 Café du Marché ★★$ Escape the bustling Rue Cler street market by ducking into this cordial cafe for a quick coffee at the attractive copper bar, or stay for a lunch of *confit de canard* or farm chicken. You can also order a crepe at the little stand outside and eat it at a table inside. ♦ M-Sa 7AM-11PM; Su 7AM-4PM. 38 Rue Cler (at Rue du Champ-de-Mars). 01.47.05.51.27. Métro: Ecole Militaire

73 Hôtel Champ-de-Mars $ You'll wake up to the Rue Cler market when you stay at this charming 25-room *hôtel familial.* Adding to the appeal are the accommodating young owners, the friendly resident spaniel, Chipie, and the unbeatable prices. There's a downstairs breakfast room with high-backed tapestry-covered chairs, and rooms **No. 2** and **No. 4** have small terraces where guests can eat breakfast in the summer. There's no restaurant. ♦ 7 Rue du Champ-de-Mars (between Rue Cler and Ave Bosquet). 01.45.51.52.30; fax 01.45.51.64.36. Métro: Ecole Militaire

73 Ragut Charcuterie The mouthwatering take-out dishes displayed here make it difficult to leave empty-handed. Choices include trout with almonds, langoustine thermidor, paella, bouillabaisse, avocado stuffed with shrimp or crab, quiche Lorraine, Hungarian goulash, beef brochettes, spinach in cream, coq au vin, duck with peaches . . . the list goes on and on. ♦ M-Sa. 40 Rue Cler (at Rue du Champ-de-Mars). 01.45.51.29.35. Métro: Ecole Militaire

74 3 Rue du Champ-de-Mars Buzz yourself into the entrance foyer of this Art Nouveau apartment house to see how the leaf-and-lily design that appears on the facade's masonry and on the iron gates is repeated in the lovely tile mosaic on the floor. ♦ Between Rues Duvivier and Cler. Métro: Ecole Militaire

75 Le Lutin Gourmand This candy shop with the whimsical name (it means "gourmet imp") has something for everyone: glass cases full of colorful hard candies and mints; lollipops shaped like animals and hearts; tempting hazelnut treats called *feuilleté noisettes;* and pretty bottles of Port and Armagnac. All the candy is made right on the premises. ♦ Tu-Sa. 47 Rue Cler (between Ave de La Motte-Picquet and Rue du Champ-de-Mars). 01.45.55.29.74. Métro: Ecole Militaire

Over 91.2 percent of French people approve of premarital sex, the highest in Europe.

76 Hôtel Relais Bosquet
$$ The automatic sliding doors are the first tip-off that this 40-room establishment is strong on modern conveniences and limited in the charm department. However, you can count on a comfortable stay enhanced by **CNN**, hair dryers, and an iron and ironing board in your room. Some of the fifth- and sixth-floor rooms have a view of the tip of the **Eiffel Tower.** There's no restaurant. ♦ 19 Rue du Champ-de-Mars (between Rue Cler and Ave Bosquet). 01.47.05.25.45; fax 01.45.55.08.24; webmaster@relais-bosquet.com; www.relais-bosquet.com. Métro: Ecole Militaire

77 Rue de l'Exposition Formerly known as Passage de l'Alma, this quiet, narrow street received its current name at the time of the **1867 Exposition Universelle.** ♦ Métro: Ecole Militaire

77 Hôtel de l'Alma $$ A comfortable 32-room hotel on a calm street offers all the modern conveniences and makes no attempt at false charm. The lobby is pleasantly decorated with rattan furniture. Many North Americans stay here. ♦ 32 Rue de l'Exposition (between Rues de Grenelle and St-Dominique). 01.47.05.45.70; fax 01.45.51.84.47. Métro: Ecole Militaire

78 Auberge du Champ de Mars ★$ Michel Duclos wears the chef's hat while his wife, Madeleine, plays host in this softly lit, red-velvet–upholstered restaurant. The prix-fixe, three-course menu includes such appetizers as avocado and smoked salmon salad or *escargots à la Bourguignonne* (snails with butter, garlic, and parsley); a main course of *poulet Normandie* (chicken in a mushroom cream sauce) or turbot in hollandaise sauce; and a dessert of profiteroles with warm chocolate sauce or warm apple tart. ♦ M-F lunch and dinner; Sa dinner; closed two weeks in August. 18 Rue de l'Exposition (between Rues de Grenelle and St-Dominique). 01.45.51.78.08. Métro: Ecole Militaire

79 L'Auvergne Gourmande ★★$ Christiane Miquel has been serving her superb Auvergne-style home cooking in this charming former butcher's shop with tiled walls, utensils hanging from racks, and only four tables since 1980. Just a few starters, two entrées, and a couple of desserts are offered, but the choices change daily, and everything is fresh, robust, and savory. The salads (of ham, cheese, and egg, for example) are practically meals in themselves. A plat du jour might be duck thighs or sausages. The desserts are excellent, and like everything else

here, made that very day. If strawberry crumble is offered, be sure to ask for it while ordering your main meal, because quantities are limited (the best bet is to arrive early and order immediately). The chocolate fudge cake is delicious too. But then, so is everything here, which keeps Miquel's devoted clientele—mostly French people who work in the area—coming back again and again. ♦ M-F noon-5:30PM. 127 Rue St-Dominique (between Ave Bosquet and Rue de l'Exposition). 01.47.05.60.79. Métro: Ecole Militaire

79 La Fontaine de Mars ★★$$ Ever popular, Mme. Boudon's gem of a bistro is comfortable and cozy, with small dining rooms and a lively atmosphere. Locals keep coming back for the southwest-style cooking. Those looking for light fare might try the warm *pâté de cèpes*, poached fillet of turbot, sole meunière, and *pruneaux à l'Armagnac* (prunes in Armagnac), while diners with heartier appetites could opt for the *boudin aux pommes* (blood sausage with apples), duck cassoulet, or *côte de veau filet aux morilles* (veal fillet with morels), with a *truffé au chocolat for dessert*. A bottle of Madiran Château Bouscassé or Cahors Château Eugenie will aid in digestion. The outdoor dining terrace on the little square is delightful in warm weather. ♦ M-Sa lunch and dinner. Reservations recommended. 129 Rue St-Dominique (between Ave Bosquet and Rue de l'Exposition). 01.47.05.46.44. Métro: Ecole Militaire

79 Fontaine de Mars This freestanding fountain by **Henri Beauvarlet** was once situated in the center of a semicircle of poplars, replaced in 1859 with the present arcaded square. The fountain's bas-relief represents Hygeia, the goddess of health, giving a drink to Mars, the god of war. Between the pilasters are vases encircled by serpents, the symbol of Aesculapius, the god of medicine. ♦ Rues St-Dominique and de l'Exposition. Métro: Ecole Militaire

79 La Croque au Sel ★$ Two different prix-fixe menus are offered at this turn-of-the-century–style bistro. Winter salad with foie gras, pot-au-feu, grilled meats with herbs, *escalope de saumon* (thinly sliced salmon), *sauté de boeuf* (pan-fried beef), and grilled pork chops are among the specialties. The high ceilings, whirling fans, and palms give the restaurant a breezy, summery air, and the covered terrace makes a nice dining spot in the warm-weather months. ♦ M-F lunch and dinner; Sa dinner. 131 Rue St-Dominique (at Rue de l'Exposition). 01.47.05.23.53. Métro: Ecole Militaire

80 Duchesne Boulanger Pâtissier This pastry shop is most notable for its Louis XV–style interior of ornate wood paneling, mirrors, and mosaics, although the selection of pastries also makes it worth a stop. Enjoy a treat and a cup of coffee or tea at one of the four tables. ♦ M-Sa; closed one month in summer. 112 Rue St-Dominique (between Rues Dupont-des-Loges and Sedillot). 01.45.51.31.01. Métro: Ecole Militaire

81 Aryllis The master florist in the back room of this flower shop makes artful arrangements out of the long-stemmed roses, tulips, lilies, and ferns sumptuously displayed in urns and baskets. ♦ Tu-Sa; Su 8AM-1PM. 141 Rue St-Dominique (at Rue Augereau). 01.47.05.86.26. Métro: Ecole Militaire

81 Le Chariot du Roy At first glance one wonders whether the vibrant colors of the fruits and vegetables here are due to trickery with lighting: The strawberries, green beans, pencil-thin asparagus, mangoes, kiwis, kumquats, mini bananas, and other deluxe fruits and vegetables look too perfect to be real. There's also a cheese counter, a selection of nuts and dried fruits, and assorted delicacies such as quail eggs. ♦ Tu-Sa; Su 8AM-1PM; closed in August. 145 Rue St-Dominique (between Rue Augereau and Pl du Général-Gouraud). 01.47.05.07.08. Métro: Ecole Militaire

81 Dubernet Behind the wood-columned facade is a megaselection of tins and jars of foie gras, *confit d'oie* (goose confit), *boudin blanc truffé* (blood sausage with truffles), pâtés, pot-au-feu, and *gésiers de canard* (duck gizzards). On the last Friday and Saturday of each month the boutique sells its delicacies at a 25- to 30-percent discount. ♦ Tu-Sa; closed in August. 2 Rue Augereau (at Rue St-Dominique). 01.45.55.50.71. Métro: Ecole Militaire

82 Hôtel de Londres Eiffel $$ This calm, quiet, 30-room hotel just off Rue St-Dominique has some fifth- and sixth-floor rooms that look out on the top of the **Eiffel Tower;** these are also the smallest rooms on the premises (the double beds are a tight squeeze), but for many that's a small price to pay for a view of Paris's most famous edifice. Scrambled eggs, ham, or omelettes can be added to the continental breakfast (not included in the room rate) served in the breakfast room; there's no restaurant. ♦ 1 Rue Augereau (at Rue St-Dominique). 01.45.51.63.02; fax 01.47.05.28.96; reservation@londres-eiffel.com; www.londres-eiffel.com. Métro: Ecole Militaire

82 Chez Agnès ★★$$ In a homey salon with rows of tables in the front room and a discreet dog named Gipsy in the back, Agnès offers such fare from Les Landes as *salade au foie gras, pavé de thon au poivre* (tuna steak with black pepper), and *entrecôte sauce roquefort* (rib steak with roquefort sauce). Her menu also features unusual crepes: *la contre courante* has smoked salmon, butter, and lemon in it; the *feux de Bengale* has chicken, curry, mushrooms, and bananas; *l'Emeraude* is filled with mint and chocolate; and *le lemon incest* is stuffed with lots of lemon filling. ♦ M-Sa lunch and dinner; Su dinner; closed two weeks in August. 1 *bis* Rue Augereau (at Rue St-Dominique). 01.45.51.06.04. Métro: Ecole Militaire

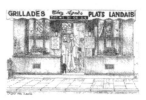

83 Café de Mars ★★$$ This relaxed, 1950s-looking cafe mixes French and North American flavors in its decor and cuisine—not surprising as its young owner, Thierry Steiner, is half-French, half–North American. Choose from traditional bistro fare or sample such New World treats as Buffalo wings, brownies, and cheesecake. A young artistic crowd frequents the place, and on weekends, students from the nearby **American University of Paris** come here to unwind. ♦ M-F lunch and dinner; Sa dinner; closed last two weeks of August. Reservations recommended. 11 Rue Augereau (between Rues de Grenelle and St-Dominique). 01.47.05.05.91. Métro: Ecole Militaire

84 The Real McCoy Longing for Pop Tarts, Lays potato chips, a peanut butter and jelly sandwich, or a sesame-seed bagel? You've come to the right place. This tiny grocery also has a sandwich counter. ◆ Daily. 194 Rue de Grenelle (between Rue Cler and Ave Bosquet). 01.45.56.98.82. Métro: Ecole Militaire

---

THE AMERICAN UNIVERSITY OF PARIS

---

85 The American University of Paris Established in 1962 as an independent arts and sciences institution, this university currently has 112 faculty members and over 800 students from 85 countries. Thirty-five percent of the students are from the United States, many on junior-year exchange programs from other schools. The largest department is International Business Administration, but the university is also strong in art history, comparative literature, European cultural studies, and international economics. This building houses some of the school's administrative offices, a student cafe, and some classrooms. The library, which is only open to university students, is located at 9 bis Rue de Montlessuy. Other school facilities are at 147 Rue de Grenelle. If you want to sit in on a class or enroll in a summer course, contact the director of admissions (admissions@aup.fr). ◆ 31 Ave Bosquet (between Rues St-Dominique and de l'Université). 01.40.62.07.20; fax 01.47.05.34.32. RER: Pont de l'Alma

86 Le 6 Bosquet ★★$$ Smooth service and a smart-looking modern dining room are just two of the draws of this sophisticated restaurant. Burgundy-born owner-chef Emmanuel Joinville creates such sensations as ravioli de foie gras de canard au bouillon d'épices douces (ravioli stuffed with foie gras served in a clear broth). Heartier appetites will enjoy parmentier tortue (crab with creamed potatoes), roast lamb with carrots in tarragon, and grilled prawns served with apple chutney and basmati rice. Savor the desserts—especially the chocolate fondant. There's a good selection of Burgundy wines. ◆ M-F lunch and dinner; Sa dinner; closed two weeks in August. Reservations required. 6 Ave Bosquet (at Cité de l'Alma). 01.45.56.97.26. RER: Pont de l'Alma

87 Place de la Résistance This intersection was named for the French forces who fought to free Paris from Nazi control from 1940 to 1944. ◆ RER: Pont de l'Alma

88 Rue Cognacq-Jay Opened in 1928, this street bisected the land owned by M. Cognacq and his wife, whose maiden name was Jay.

The two were philanthropists and founders of **La Samaritaine** department store. The area between Rue Malar and Avenue Bosquet was occupied in 1910 by an amusement park called **Magic City,** which disappeared in 1925. ◆ RER: Pont de l'Alma

89 Egouts (Sewers) The égouts of Paris are always a popular underground attraction. This 1,305-mile network of tunnels was constructed during the reign of Napoléon III and is considered one of Baron Haussmann's finest achievements. If laid end to end, the tunnels would reach from Paris to Istanbul. The sewers house freshwater pipes, telephone wires, traffic-light cables, and the city's pneumatic postal network, which was shut down in 1984. The hourlong sewer tour includes a film, photograph exhibition, and walk through the 18-foot-high by 14-foot-wide tunnels. Ever since a notorious bank heist in which the robbers made their getaway via the sewers, underground boat cruises have not been permitted. ◆ Admission. W-Sa. Quai d'Orsay and Pont de l'Alma. 01.47.05.10.29. RER: Pont de l'Alma

90 Les Deux Abeilles ★★★$ Here is a cozy tea salon that feels like a grandmother's cottage, with pink-flowered fabric on the walls, terra-cotta tiles, lace curtains, wooden sideboards, and homemade tarts cooling in the window. The food is substantial and good; menu items include gratiné d'aubergine (eggplant au gratin), omelettes with cèpes, tomato and thyme tarts, and salade de feuilleté au roquefort (salad with roquefort cheese). Desserts include Berthillon ice cream, a light, smooth tarte tatin served with homemade whipped cream; pear crumble; and raspberry tart soufflé. Teatime treats include scones with butter and confiture, warm cinnamon brioches, and chocolat à l'ancienne (old-fashioned hot chocolate) with cream. Everything is made daily by mother and daughter Anne and Valeria Arella, who opened the tearoom in 1985. They or the soft-spoken waitresses serve steamy hot tea in pink-flowered cups. ◆ M-Sa breakfast, lunch, and tea until 7PM. 189 Rue de l'Université (between Aves Rapp and Franco-Russe). 01.45.55.64.04. RER: Pont de l'Alma

91 Rue de Monttessuy This otherwise unremarkable street is impressive for its angular view of one of the **Eiffel Tower's** legs. The famous monument, usually depicted in its totality, becomes a revelation when seen at such close proximity and from such a refreshing perspective. ◆ RER: Pont de l'Alma

91 Au Bon Accueil ★★$$ For gourmet meals at reasonable prices, its location convenient to the **Eiffel Tower,** and the warm welcome its name promises, this place is hard to beat. Chef Jacques Lacipiere prepares a new menu daily, depending on what inspires him when he makes his rounds at the **Rungis** wholesale food market at 2AM. Since opening their doors in 1986, Jacques and his gracious wife, Catherine, who oversees the service in the pleasant coral and white dining room, have built a loyal following of residents of this affluent and famously *gourmand* arrondissement and staff members of the nearby **American University** and **American Library.** The prix-fixe menu is a real bargain: A typical meal might consist of a starter of *magret de canard* with truffle-flavored celery cream, a main course of crusty puff pastry with *brandade de cabillaud* (purée of fresh cod), and for dessert, a *moelleux chaud au chocolat* (a warm, soft-centered chocolate cake served with saffron-flavored black chocolate ice cream. The wine list matches the sophistication of the cuisine. ◆ M-F lunch and dinner. Reservations recommended. 14 Rue de Monttessuy (between Aves Rapp and de La Bourdonnais). 01.47.05.46.11. RER: Pont de l'Alma

92 American Library in Paris Founded in 1920, this is the largest English-language library in continental Europe, with more than 100,000 volumes. Anyone can become a member and partake of a collection that includes fiction, nonfiction, reference books, audio- and videocassettes, a CD-ROM and Internet reference center, more than 450 periodicals, and 8,000-plus children's books. There's a yearly fee for membership, but visitors can join for as little as a day. A free story hour is held every Wednesday afternoon in the children's room. Roughly once a month the library hosts "Evenings with an Author," a series of talks and readings by well-known English-language writers that is free and open to the public. Short-story writer Mavis Gallant, novelists William Wharton and Diane Johnson, biographer John Baxter, and New Yorker columnist Adam Gopnik are just some of the authors who have appeared in recent years. ◆ Tu-Sa; limited hours in August. 10 Rue du Général-Camou (between Aves Rapp

and de La Bourdonnais). 01.53.59.12.60; fax 01 45.50.25.83. RER: Pont de l'Alma

93 Pâtisserie de la Tour Eiffel ★$ Before attempting a trip to the summit of the **Eiffel Tower,** enjoy a novel view of the edifice's east leg from the terrace of this patisserie, which doubles as a tea salon. Fortify yourself for the ascent with a hot chocolate and a *tarte de framboise.* ◆ Tu-Su 6AM-8PM. 21 Ave de La Bourdonnais (at Rue de Monttessuy). 01.47.05.59.81. RER: Pont de l'Alma

93 Vin sur Vin ★★★$$$ Sunny yellow walls, flowers, and crisp white linen tablecloths on the nine comfortably spaced tables greet diners as they enter this small, but oh-so-elegant restaurant. The atmosphere is warm, yet discreet, like a private club. As its name indicates, the wine here is even more important than the food. Genial owner Patrice Vidal's list is magnificent, with more than 500 fine French vintages drawing from all the regions of the country; it includes some that are modestly priced. This is the kind of restaurant where regulars with a craving for a classic dish such as pot-au-feu with foie gras or veal liver *à la diable* (in a spicy sauce) can call and order it 24 hours in advance. Otherwise, the menu features a seasonally changing array of original dishes. Some past favorites include fresh scallop salad, duck with peaches, *turbot rôti à huile d'olive* (roasted turbot in olive oil), sardine cake with basil, crème brûlée, and a bitter-chocolate tart. ◆ Tu-F lunch and dinner; M, Sa dinner. Reservations required. 20 Rue de Monttessuy (between Aves Rapp and de La Bourdonnais). 01.47.05.14.20. RER: Pont de l'Alma

94 Le Sancerre ★★$ Jean-Louis Guillaume's atmospheric wine bar takes its name from the rich, dry, full-bodied Loire Valley wine that he features on his menu. Wine is the primary focus here; the menu offers very simple fare. Snuggle up in the warm, woody dining room and order a bottle with some *jambon fumé* (smoked ham) and an omelette. Those who have a problem with the dense cloud of cigarette smoke in the main room can find relief in the *non-fumeur* alcove in the rear. ◆ M-F breakfast, lunch, and dinner; Sa lunch; closed two weeks in August. 22 Ave Rapp (between Rues du Général-Camou and de

Monttessuy). 01.45.51.75.91. RER: Pont de l'Alma

95 Pharmacie Rapp Worth a peek even if you don't need *un adhésif* (Band-Aid) or *l'aspirine*, this corner pharmacy has an 1899 interior that's a pretty assemblage of delicately carved wood cupboards and reliefs of medicinal plants. Notice the original *pots à pharmacie* (blue glass jars) in the windows. ◆ M-Sa. 23 Ave Rapp (at Rue Edmond-Valentin). 01.47.05.41.25. RER: Pont de l'Alma

96 7 Rue Edmond-Valentin Irish writer James Joyce lived here from 1935 until 1939. It's still a residential building. ◆ Between Ave Bosquet and Rue Dupont-des-Loges. RER: Pont de l'Alma

97 Puyricard M. and Mme. Roelandts's shop features delectable chocolates from Aix-en-Provence. Heavenly coconut-praline, raspberry-marzipan, apricot-truffle, and mandarin-orange chocolates are some of the irresistible, award-winning cocoa fantasies available here. ◆ M 2-7PM; Tu-Sa 9:30AM-7:30PM. 27 Ave Rapp (between Sq Rapp and Rue Edmond-Valentin). 01.47.05.59.47. RER: Pont de l'Alma

97 29 Avenue Rapp Paris's prime example of Art Nouveau architecture won designer **Jules Lavirotte** first prize at the Concours des Façades de la Ville de Paris in 1901. A sense of humor can be seen in this apartment building's glazed terra-cotta decoration of animal and flower motifs intermingled with female figures, which was deliberately erotic and subversive for its day. ◆ Between Sq Rapp and Rue Edmond-Valentin. RER: Pont de l'Alma

98 Square Rapp This small private way was called Villa de Montlessuy before receiving its current name from the neighboring Avenue Rapp. Notice the trompe l'oeil perspective created by the dark green lattice on the building at the end of the street. ◆ RER: Pont de l'Alma

On Square Rapp:

No. 3 Another **Jules Lavirotte** construction, this 1899 apartment building features a wild conglomeration of balconies, railings, glazed brick and terra-cotta decoration, and a watchtower whose finial seems to be a hybrid of Tintin's rocket and the dome of **Sacré-Coeur**.

Société Théosophique de France This curious and ponderous brick building is the headquarters of the French Theosophical Society. The interior lobby, a cubic space surmounted by a dome, is somewhat reminiscent of the architecture of India, but unfortunately comes across as heavy and clunky rather than as uplifting and inspirational. The society sponsors some fine lectures (often on Sunday), and classes in religion and theosophy. ◆ Tu-Sa. No. 4. 01.47.05.26.30

At the Société Théosophique de France:

Librairie Adyar The society's bookstore stocks volumes about spirituality, psychology, parapsychology, and astrology, with some titles in English. You'll also find candleholders, crystal pyramids, tarot cards, incense, meditation tapes, and anything else you might need to start your journey toward enlightenment. ◆ Tu-Sa. 01.45.51.31.79

99 18 Rue Sedillot The vaguely Baroque overtones of this turn-of-the-century building by **Jules Lavirotte** are typical of the sinuous style employed by the Art Nouveau architect on several Paris apartment buildings. ◆ Between Rues St-Dominique and Edmond-Valentin. RER: Pont de l'Alma

100 Avenue de La Bourdonnais Opened in 1770, this avenue once had five entrance gates leading to the **Parc du Champ-de-Mars** along its route. The last survivor, the **Porte Rapp,** existed until 1920. Take time to explore this upscale residential neighborhood by strolling along the short, perpendicular streets (such as Avenue Silvestre-de-Sacy, Rue du Maréchal-Harispe, and Rue Marinoni) that lead from the Avenue de La Bourdonnais into the park. Here beautiful apartment buildings and gardens are set back from the street behind iron gates, and well-heeled ladies in fur coats walk their well-coiffed dogs. ◆ Métro: Ecole Militaire, RER: Pont de l'Alma

𝕶𝖓𝖎𝖆𝖟 𝕵𝖌𝖔𝖗

100 Kniaz Igor ◆ ¢¢ The atmosphere is all red velvet and balalaika music; beluga caviar, borscht with sour cream, chicken Kiev, *roulade de filet de boeuf* (rolled beef fillet), and vodka sorbet are featured menu items at this Russian restaurant. Faded photos of past dinner guest Roman Polanski are proudly displayed in the window. ◆ M-Sa dinner; closed last two weeks of July. Reservations recommended. 43 Ave de La Bourdonnais (between Pl du Général-Gouraud and Rue du Général-Camou). 01.45.51.91.71. RER: Pont de l'Alma

DECEMBRE *en mars*

101 Décembre en Mars British teddy bears, Bauhaus blocks, Annette Himstadt dolls, hobbyhorses, spinning tops, wooden trains, and rubber ducks are just a few of the colorful delights sold in this little toy store. ◆ Tu-Sa; closed in August. 65 Ave de La Bourdonnais (between Rue de Grenelle and Pl du Général-Gouraud). 01.45.51.15.45. Métro: Ecole Militaire

102 Ecole Militaire In an attempt to rival the **Hôtel des Invalides** of Louis XIV, Louis XV and his mistress, Mme. de Pompadour, hired **Jacques-Ange Gabriel,** the architect who created Place de la Concorde in the 1770s, to design a military school. Raising money for the project was a problem until Beaumarchais, who wrote *The Marriage of Figaro* and gave harp lessons to Louis XV's daughters, came up with the idea of paying for the building through a lottery and a tax on playing cards.

Standing at the foot of the **Champ-de-Mars,** the school, with its Corinthian columns, statues, dome, double colonnade, and elegant wrought-iron fence, is one of **Gabriel**'s masterpieces. The most famous graduate of the school, which is still in operation, was Napoléon Bonaparte. He spent a year here and left as a lieutenant when he was 16 with the comment on his report card, "Will go far if circumstances permit." ◆ By appointment

only. For information write to: Direction Générale, Ecole Militaire, 1 Pl Joffre, 75007 Paris. 1 Pl Joffre (at Ave de La Motte-Piquet). No phone. Métro: Ecole Militaire

103 Parc du Champ-de-Mars Named for the god of war, this large rectangular park stretching from the **Ecole Militaire** to the **Eiffel Tower** has long been a site of battles, both actual and preparatory. Here, in 52 BC, Roman legions defeated the Parisii; in 886 the Parisians beat back the invading Vikings; and, in the early 18th century, when this was the parade ground for the **Ecole Militaire,** Napoléon drilled with his fellow cadets.

Now the park, adorned with flowering trees, shrubs, and miniature cascades, is the site of pony rides, marionette theaters, organ-grinders, occasional parades for children, and Christmastime fairs and pageantry. You can do almost anything in the **Champ-de-Mars** except have a picnic on the lawns. French grass is sacred grass, and a bluecoat (guard) will appear and order you off before you've even had time to unwrap your salami and uncork the Bordeaux. ◆ Bounded by Allées Adrienne-Lecouvreur and Thomy-Thierry, and Pl Joffre and Ave Gustave-Eiffel. Métro: Ecole Militaire; RER: Pont de l'Alma, Champ de Mars–Tour Eiffel

104 Tour Eiffel (Eiffel Tower) In 1889, the world was drunk on science. The decade had produced one technological marvel after another: the automobile, the telephone, the electric light, and the **Eiffel Tower.** First dubbed a monstrosity, then considered the definitive symbol of Paris, the tower was built to commemorate the centennial of the storming of the **Bastille** and to stand as the centerpiece of the **1889 International Exhibition of Paris.** The now-classic design by **Gustave Eiffel** beat 700 other entries in the design competition. (Among the losers, for obvious reasons, were a giant guillotine and a mammoth lighthouse.) The tower was the tallest structure in the world until 1930, when the title was usurped by New York's Chrysler Building. **Eiffel,** who also engineered the iron bones of that city's Statue of Liberty (undergirding the **Frédéric Bartholdi** copper structure), was himself a diminutive man, only five feet tall.

Spanning 2.5 acres at its base, the tower is made of 18,000 metal parts held together with 2.5 million rivets and covered with 66 tons of brown paint. (The structure is repainted every 7 years and at last count received its 17th coat.) A thousand feet high, it weighs 7,000 tons and sways no more than 4.5 inches in strong winds. The weight is distributed so elegantly that it exerts no more pressure on the ground per centimeter than does a person seated in a four-legged chair. Three platforms are built into the tower—at 57 meters (187

Eiffel Tower

feet), 115 meters (377 feet), and 276 meters (906 feet)—and elevators and staircases serve each level. There are 1,652 steps to the top.

When the tower was first completed, much of Paris was unimpressed. Its stark, geometric structure offended the prevailing Beaux Arts sensibility. Prominent critics, including such luminaries as Paul Verlaine, Guy de Maupassant, the younger Dumas, and Emile Zola, denounced it as the "Tower of Babel" and a dishonor to Paris. Maupassant used to say he liked to have lunch at the tower because it was the only place in Paris where he didn't have to look at it.

In later years it was discovered that the tower could function as the world's largest antenna, and during World War I it became one of France's most vital weapons. Since then, it has served as a radio and meteorological post, and in 1985 was fitted with broadcasting equipment for France's fifth television channel.

Despite these eminently utilitarian applications, the **Eiffel Tower**'s primary effect is to excite the imagination. One man tried to fly from it and was killed when his wings failed him. In 1923 a bicycle-riding journalist careened down the steps to the ground from the top floor. A mountaineer scaled it in 1954, and in 1984 two Englishmen parachuted from it.

In 1989, a 9-year renovation program was completed in time for the tower's 100th birthday on the bicentennial of the French Revolution. About 1,500 tons of extraneous concrete (mostly in the form of concession areas) were removed from the first platform; 4 new electronic glass elevators and new visitors' facilities were installed; and the pavilion housing the tower's main restaurant, **Le Jules Verne** (see below), was remodeled. The most dramatic change of all, however, was a new 292,000-watt interior lighting system inaugurated on New Year's Eve 1986, replacing the old floodlights. The new lights illuminate the entire structure from within, creating a golden tracery against the sky at night. ♦ Admission varies for each of the three levels. Daily 9:30AM-11PM Jan-June, Sept-Dec; daily 9:30AM-midnight July-Aug. Ave Gustave-Eiffel (between Aves Octave-Gréard and Silvestre-de-Sacy). 01.44.11.23.23. RER: Champ de Mars–Tour Eiffel

Within the Tour Eiffel:

Le Jules Verne ★★★$$$ One of the most beautiful views of Paris, day or night, is from this perch in the second level of the **Eiffel Tower**. Sleek and seductive, the all-black decor is an elegant backdrop for the restaurant's chic clientele and the creative and refined cuisine of chef Alain Reix. *Entrecôte de veau de Corrèze au jus de laitue goût d'herbes*

(veal from Corrèze sautéed with herbs); *langoustines rôties et crabe, pommes croustillantes, et asperges* (roasted prawns with crabmeat, fried potatoes, and asparagus); and *tarte au chocolat Caraïbe et glace à la vanille de Tahiti* (a sweet and spicy chocolate tart with exotic vanilla ice cream) are just some of the reasons that reservations here are so difficult to obtain. Be sure to reserve far in advance and specify your view preference: a table on the Trocadéro side reveals a perspective all the way to **La Défense,** while the **Ecole Militaire** dining room looks out toward Montparnasse. ♦ Daily lunch and dinner. Reservations required. Second level (elevator at south pier). 01.45.55.61.44

Altitude 95 ★★$$ This silvery metallic restaurant wedged in among the 19th-century brown steel girders of the first level of the **Eiffel Tower** takes its design inspiration from a 19th-century vision of the future: There are shiny bolts on the tables, silver-riveted bucket seats on wheels, and altimeters reminding you of your elevation of 95 meters (312 feet) above sea level. Besides the great view, the restaurant offers honest cuisine at reasonable prices, especially with its prix-fixe menus featuring dishes from several regions in France that can be mixed and matched to create a meal. You might start with oysters from Brittany, then have a Franche Comté–inspired fillet of trout, followed by Provençal goat cheeses, and a dessert of crepes flambéed with Grand Marnier from the Ile-de-France. Parents will be pleased with the inexpensive children's menu. ♦ Daily lunch, tea, and dinner. Reservations recommended. First level (elevator at north pier). 01.45.55.20.04; 01.45.55.00.21

Over 180 million people have mounted the Eiffel Tower since it opened in 1889. Currently about 6 million visitors make the climb every year. At this rate, it's expected the 200 million mark will be topped by 2002.

The word "boulevard" was originally a military term for an embankment behind a rampart where cannons were placed. When the wall that stood along the current route of the Grands Boulevards was torn down in the late 18th century, the wide civilian roadway took its old martial name.

Paris in Print

Some of history's most compelling stories have taken place in the French capital. The following is a survey of three centuries of Paris-inspired literature.

The Age of Reason by Jean-Paul Sartre (Vintage Books, 1992) Set in 1938, this is the story of Mathieu, a professor of philosophy, who is motivated by an idealistic obsession to remain free, particularly when his mistress becomes pregnant.

The Ambassadors by Henry James (Oxford University Press, 1986) In this Henry James 1903 classic, Lambert Strether is sent to Paris by Mrs. Newsome, a wealthy widow whom he plans to marry, in order to persuade her son Chad to come home. Strether gradually realizes that life may hold more meaning for Chad in Paris than in Massachusetts.

The American by Henry James (Buccaneer Books, 1990) This 1877 novel describes how a rich, self-made American goes to Paris to enjoy his wealth and becomes engaged to a beautiful young French widow from a noble family.

An American in Paris by LeRoy Neiman (Harry N. Abrams, 1994) One of America's most celebrated artists illustrates his impressions of Paris.

Banners of Silk by Rosalind Laker (Doubleday, 1981) This historical romance portrays the rags-to-riches story of two couturiers, Charles Worth and Louise Vernet, in the world of 19th-century Paris fashion.

The Blessing by Nancy Mitford (Carroll & Graf, 1989) Grace, a beautiful but dull Englishwoman, marries a dashing French marquis and is swept into the complexities of Parisian society.

Camille by Alexandre Dumas *fils* (New American Library, 1984) Published in 1848, this novel depicts a beautiful courtesan in the fashionable world of 19th-century Paris who rejects a wealthy count for her penniless lover Armand Duval. They escape to the country, but at the request of his family she pretends she no longer loves him and goes back to her life in Paris. The story ends with a tragic reunion between the lovers.

The Cardinal and the Queen by Evelyn Anthony (Putnam Publishing Group, 1968) This novel is the story of the beautiful Anne of Austria, her humiliating marriage to Louis XIII, and her passionate love affair with Cardinal Richelieu, the king's minister. The **Louvre,** the **Palais du Luxembourg,** and other royal buildings of 17th-century Paris are the backdrops.

Cousin Pons by Honoré de Balzac (Viking Press, 1978) Part of the 1848 series, *Scenes of Parisian Life,* this book focuses on the friendship of two old musicians, Schmucke and Cousin Pons, and is set in the sordid mid–19th-century Parisian society of minor theaters, innkeepers, and impoverished artists and other bohemians.

Down and Out in Paris and London by George Orwell (Harvest 1961) First published in 1933, this account of the writer's sojourn among the lowlife of Paris in the late 1920s contains a hilarious exposé of the sanitary conditions in posh French restaurants, where he worked as a *plongeur* (dishwasher).

Gigi by Colette (French & European Publications, 1979) The 1952 story of a young girl brought up to be a high-class mistress, but who maneuvers a marriage proposal from a sophisticated man-about-town.

Giovanni's Room by James Baldwin (Laureleaf, 1985) In this groundbreaking gay novel, first published in 1956, most of the story takes place in Paris, where a young North American man is involved with both his fiancée and another man.

Good Morning, Midnight by Jean Rhys (W.W. Norton & Company, 1986) A middle-aged woman, lonely and adrift in Paris, seeks consolation in a relationship with a gigolo.

Héloïse and Abélard by George Moore (W.W. Norton & Company, 1974) This fictionalized version of the tragic 12th-century love affair between Héloïse, a beautiful and learned woman, and Pierre Abélard, the brilliant philosopher who served as her tutor, was first published in 1921.

The Hunchback of Notre Dame by Victor Hugo (Longmeadow Press, 1991) First published in 1830, this classic is set in Paris during 1482. With the harshness of medieval life and the grandeur of **Notre-Dame** as backdrops, the strange and fantastic romance between the hunchback Quasimodo and his Esmeralda unfolds.

I'll Always Have Paris: A Memoir by Art Buchwald (Putnam Publishing Group, 1996) The famed columnist recalls when he was a 22-year-old Paris-based writer for the *International Herald Tribune* during the 1940s and 1950s.

Imagining Paris: Exile, Writing, and American Identity by J. Gerald Kennedy (Yale University Press, 1993) An exploration of the imaginative process of five expatriate North American writers (Gertrude Stein, Ernest Hemingway, Henry Miller, F. Scott Fitzgerald, and Djuna Barnes) demonstrates how the experience of living in Paris shaped their careers and literary works.

Is Paris Burning? by Larry Collins (Simon & Schuster, 1965) A suspenseful and exciting retelling of the story of the liberation of Paris in 1944 and one German general's decision to save the city from being burned to the ground.

Le Divorce by Diane Johnson (Dutton, 1997) California film school dropout Isabel Walker (read Isabel Archer) comes to Paris to help her sister, who is going through a divorce from her French husband. This witty fin de *20ème* (20th) siècle satirical novel is based on the Jamesian theme of the cultural chasm between the innocent American and the wily, sophisticated French.

Le Rouge et le Noir *(The Red and the Black)* by Stendhal (French & European Publications, 1958) Published in 1830, this tale follows the fall of

Napoléon, as protagonist Julien's scandalous adventures take him to Paris.

Les Claudine by Colette (French & European Publications, 1969) Four semiautobiographical novels written from 1900 to 1903 follow Claudine through precocious girlhood, young womanhood in Paris, marriage, and an unusual love affair.

Les Enfants Terribles by Jean Cocteau (EMC Corp., 1977) In this historically and psychologically significant novel, two wild, poetic children withdraw to a small room in the midst of Paris after their mother's death.

Les Liaisons Dangereuses (Dangerous Liaisons) by Pierre Choderlos de Laclos (Knopf, 1991) Condemned in 1782 for being scandalous, this ruthless portrayal of sexual intrigue is a powerful moral analysis of the decadent society of mid–18th-century France.

Les Misérables by Victor Hugo (Penguin USA, 1982). A tale of the poor and the outcast in the early 19th century. First published in 1862, it recounts how an unjust system labels the noble Jean Valjean a criminal; other suffering victims of society are Fantine, her daughter Cosette, and Cosette's lover Marius.

Love in the Days of Rage by Lawrence Ferlinghetti (E.P. Dutton, 1988). Set against the turbulence and energy of the 1968 student riots in Paris, the love between a French banker and an expatriate North American woman grows as revolutionary ideas are debated in cafes.

The Mandarins by Simone de Beauvoir (W.W. Norton & Company, 1991) This 1954 book paints a portrait of the Existentialist clique and its adversaries, and re-creates the ambience of Paris after the German occupation.

Mrs. 'arris Goes to Paris by Paul Gallico (International Polygonics Ltd., 1989) A middle-aged London cleaning woman, determined to own a designer gown, invades Paris's **Christian Dior** salon in this 1958 classic tale.

A Moveable Feast by Ernest Hemingway (Scribner, 1996) Published posthumously in 1964, Papa's sketches of his years as a young writer in Paris (1921-26) are noted for their lovely descriptions of his **Left Bank** haunts, mean-spirited hatchet jobs on writers who befriended and helped him—Gertrude Stein and F. Scott Fitzgerald in particular—and self-pity about how the world somehow caused him to break up his idyllic first marriage.

Naked I Came by David Weiss (Wm. Morrow & Company, 1970) A fictionalized account of the life and work of sculptor Auguste Rodin portrays the controversies and love affairs that marked his life.

Nightwood by Djuna Barnes (New Directions, 1988) First published in 1936, this novel takes place in the 1920s in the world of Left Bank lesbian expatriates—of which Barnes was a prominent member. It recounts the tortured love affair of Nora and Robin and is set in a sinister ambience of nighttime Paris amid a bizarre cast of characters

estranged from all sense of identity. Barnes's dense, very brilliant prose denotes a civilization in decay.

The Notebooks of Malte Laurids Brigge by Rainer Maria Rilke (W.W. Norton & Company, 1992) A young Danish poet of noble birth moves to Paris and lives in poverty. This 1910 novel is written as if it were a series of diary entries, with observations of the poet's suffering and squalor and speculations on art and life.

Our Paris by Edmund White (Alfred A. Knopf, 1995) This sharply observed series of literary sketches traces the North American author's life with his French lover, Hubert Sorin, in **Châtelet** over the final two years of Sorin's losing battle with AIDS. Despite its underlying tragedy, the book is far from depressing, thanks to Sorin's courage and unflagging sense of humor and White's witty way with the people and places they encounter together. Sorin did the illustrations for the book.

Overhead in a Balloon: Twelve Stories of Paris by Mavis Gallant (W.W. Norton & Company, 1988) The 12 stories in this book are interconnected by characters who jump from one tale to another. Parisian life is well captured in pieces about a bourgeois debate over real estate law, roommates discussing domestic arrangements, and dissatisfied lovers.

Paris Noir by Tyler Stovall (Houghton Mifflin, 1996) A richly detailed account of the long, mutually stimulating cultural relationship between France and the many African-American writers, artists, and musicians who have lived and worked in the City of Light.

The Scarlet Pimpernel by Baroness Emmuska Orczy (Buccaneer Books, 1984) Sir Percy Blakeney, a foppish young Englishman, is found to be the daring Scarlet Pimpernel who rescues aristocrats from the guillotine during the French Revolution.

The Short Reign of Pippin IV by John Steinbeck (Penguin USA, 1994) In this satire on French politics published in 1957, the French run out of governments and decide to revive the monarchy. They choose Pippin, an amateur astronomer who is a descendant of Charlemagne.

The Sun Also Rises by Ernest Hemingway (Scribner, 1954) This classic tale of Jake Barnes, Lady Brett Ashley, and the "Lost Generation" of disillusioned World War I veterans in Paris was published in 1926 at the height of the post-war expatriate migration to **Montparnasse.** A literary sensation, it immediately established Hemingway as the dominant prose stylist in the English language.

Sylvia Beach and the Lost Generation by Noel Riley Fitch (Norton, 1985). This lively biography of the creator of the **Shakespeare and Company** bookshop, friend of Hemingway, Fitzgerald, Pound, Joyce, and numerous other expatriate writers, and the courageous publisher of Joyce's *Ulysses,* is the best single volume on the English-language literary explosion in Paris in the 1920s and 1930s.

105 Palais de Chaillot Perched on its hill across the Seine from the **Eiffel Tower,** this palace serves as the Right Bank termination of the monumental axis that sweeps up across the **Champ-de-Mars** from the **Ecole Militaire.** The white sandstone twin pavilions of the palace were built for the **1937 Exposition Universelle,** replacing the earlier **Palais du Trocadéro,** a massive barrel-shaped building erected for the 1878 exhibition. Although its stark forms and groups of heroic statuary uncomfortably recall the type of Fascist architecture that emerged during the period in Germany and Italy, the palace succeeds both as a monument and a cultural complex. Within its two curving wings (which cradle a series of descending gardens and pools) are three museums, a theater, library, and restaurant.

At press time the left wing of the palace was closed for a major renovation; it was scheduled to reopen in 2001 as the home of the **Cité de l'Architecture et du Patrimoine** (see below). The **Musée du Cinéma Henri Langlois,** and the screening room of the **Cinémathèque Français,** formerly located in the left wing, were expected to move to the fanciful building designed by **Frank Gehry** for the now-defunct **American Center** in the **Parc de Bercy** in eastern Paris; it was expected to open in 2001 as the **Maison du Cinéma.** In the right wing of the palace, the **Musée de la Marine,** the **Musée de l'Homme,** and the **Théâtre National de Chaillot** remain open (see below).

The palace's terrace offers a spectacular view of the **Eiffel Tower** directly across the river. ♦ Pl du Trocadéro-et-du-11-Novembre (between Aves Paul-Doumer and du Président-Wilson). Métro: Trocadéro

Within the Palais de Chaillot:

Musée de la Marine Founded in 1827 by order of Charles X and moved here in 1943, the museum displays magnificent scale models of ships; artifacts and mementos of naval heroes; and exhibits on the scientific and technical aspects of the history of navigation. ♦ Admission. M, W-Su. 01.53.65.69.69

Musée de l'Homme (Museum of Humankind) The museum traces human history through a series of anthropological, archaeological, and ethnological displays. ♦ Admission. M, W-Su. 01.44.05.72.72

Théâtre National de Chaillot Located beneath the **Palais Terrace,** this theater seats 1,200 people in the main **Salle Jean Villar** and features productions of mainstream European classics and musical reviews. The 400-seat **Salle Gémier** stages more experimental works. ♦ Box office: daily. 01.53.65.30.00

Cité de l'Architecture et du Patrimoine Scheduled to open at the beginning of 2001, this museum combines the collections of the **Musée des Monuments Français** (which occupied half of the left wing before it closed) and the **Institut Français d'Architecture.** This collaboration will present the full history of France's architectural heritage from the Middle Ages to the present.

Created in 1880, the older collection was the brainchild of **Eugène Emmanuel Viollet-le-Duc,** who restored **Notre-Dame,** as well as the medieval monastery in Mont St-Michel and the cathedral in Carcassonne, in the 19th century. Through drawings, models, and reproductions, visitors can trace the development of monumental sculpture, statuary, and mural painting on buildings from the early Romanesque period to the decoration of the great Gothic cathedrals, and thanks to the newly added collection, follow the story into the 20th century. ♦ Admission. M, W-Su. 01.44.05.39.10

106 Pont de Bir-Hakeim Along the top of this double-decker bridge runs one of the only aboveground métro lines in Paris, which provides a spectacular view of the **Eiffel Tower** as it is approached from the Seine. Board at the **Passy** station, just across the river, and travel toward **Nation.** The lower bridge is for pedestrians. It was constructed in 1903 to replace an inadequate pedestrian bridge, the Pont de Passy. In 1949 it was named for the 1942 Battle of Bir-Hakeim in the Libyan desert, when the Free French forces held off Rommel's armored divisions. ♦ Métros: Passy, Bir Hakeim

107 Allée des Cygnes A small narrow islet that divides the Seine provides a pleasant promenade from the Pont de Bir-Hakeim to the Pont de Grenelle with a view of **Radio France** (a modern building that housed the **French Broadcasting Service** until 1975) on the Right Bank and the **Front de Seine** (a modern urban-renewal project integrating high-rise apartment and office towers, public buildings, and a shopping center) on the Left Bank. On the upriver side of Pont Bir-Hakeim is a 1930s equestrian statue named *La France Renaissante* by Danish sculptor Wederkinch, and downriver on the Pont de Grenelle is a small replica of the **Statue of Liberty** donated by the North American community in Paris in 1885. ♦ Métros: Passy, Bir Hakeim

108 **8 Boulevard de Grenelle** A plaque records the roundup of thousands of Parisians, most of them Jews, in the *vélodrome* (cycling track) here on 16 July 1942 before their deportation to Nazi concentration camps. Of the approximately 150,000 adults and 20,000 children arrested by the Germans and the cooperating Paris police, only 3,000 adults and 6 children survived. The *vélodrome* was demolished in 1959. ♦ Between Rue St-Charles and Quai de Grenelle. Métro: Bir Hakeim

109 **Avenue de Suffren** Like Avenue de La Bourdonnais, this avenue opened in 1770 as a perimeter road around the **Parc du Champ-de-Mars.** It was named after Vice Admiral Bailli Pierre André de Suffren (1726-88), the justice administrator of St-Tropez and commander of the Ordre de Malte, who fought for the Americans during the Revolutionary War. ♦ Métros: La Motte Picquet–Grenelle, Ségur, Sèvres-Lecourbe; RER: Champ de Mars–Tour Eiffel

Hilton
Paris

109 **Paris Hilton** $$$$ Built in 1966, this sleek, International-style hotel has 11 stories of concrete and glass, and a vast, airy marble-floored lobby. It looks more like a corporate headquarters than a Parisian luxury hotel, but then, the hostelry makes no pretensions of Old World grandeur. Set in a quiet park overlooking the **Eiffel Tower** and the **Palais de Chaillot,** it offers 462 first-rate modern rooms and suites, along with several conference rooms and ballrooms. The 10th and 11th floors are the executive floors, with a private lounge and other extras. ♦ 18 Ave de Suffren (at Rue Jean-Rey). 01.44.38.56.00; fax 01.44.38.56.10; www.hilton.com. RER: Champ de Mars–Tour Eiffel

Within the Paris Hilton:

Pacific Eiffel ★★$$ Reckoning that Paris has all the French restaurants it needs, this eatery has placed its emphasis on a different culinary appeal: California cuisine, enlivened by touches of the Mediterranean and the Far East. Nebraska prime ribs, deli sandwiches, Caesar salad, pizza, ricotta and salmon ravioli, and grilled fish and meat from the rotisserie are featured, along with an attractive all-you-can-eat buffet at both lunch and dinner. The wines come from California, Australia, and South Africa, with a good selection from the main wine regions of France. The restaurant is a big, rambling double-decker with a cheerful red, blue, and yellow color scheme, and its sweeping white metal staircase with pipe banisters gives it the feel of a modern cruise ship. Although the restaurant is on the ground floor of the hotel, it has a separate entrance and identity. ♦ Daily breakfast, lunch, and dinner. 01.44.38.57.77, 01.44.38.56.00

Le Bar Suffren The staff at this comfy English-style bar with Robert Doisneau photos on the walls have invented some novel cocktails, including the *Aristobar* (vodka, Champagne, and wild strawberry liqueur) and the nonalcoholic *Soleil Rouge* (fresh grapefruit and orange juice, lemonade, and grenadine). Croissants and coffee are served in the morning, and snack service is offered all day. There is a terrace for alfresco sipping in good weather. ♦ Daily 10AM-2AM. 01.44.38.56.00

Le Toit de Paris ★★$$ "The rooftop of Paris," this grill on the hotel's top floor offers a superb view of the nearby **Eiffel Tower.** It is open to the public only on Sunday, for a Champagne brunch featuring main courses of lobster, prime rib, and salmon, and a large selection of salads and pastries. ♦ Su 11AM-3PM. 01.44.38.56.00

110 **Chez Ribe** ★★$$ The exquisite wood paneling dates from 1900, but the specialties on Jean-Antoine Père's prix-fixe menu are as fresh as can be. Start with *tartare* of smoked salmon or eggplant cake with tomato sauce, then try the cod with aïoli or duck with lavender honey. For dessert order the apples with warm caramel sauce. ♦ M-F lunch and dinner; Sa dinner; closed in August. Reservations recommended. 15 Ave de Suffren (at Ave Octave-Gréard). 01.45.66.53.79. RER: Champ de Mars–Tour Eiffel

111 **Le Backgammon** M. Borentain has been selling the shop's namesake games, along with chess sets, Chinese solitaire, and casino games, both old and new, since 1986. ♦ Tu-Sa 11AM-1PM, 3-7PM; closed in August. 62 Ave de Suffren (between Rues de Presles and Desaix). 01.45.67.59.18. Métro: La Motte Picquet–Grenelle

The guillotine was proposed by Dr. Joseph Guillotin in 1791 as an instantaneous and more humane method of execution. The beheading device was adopted for all capital crimes in France in 1792. Contrary to common lore, Dr. Guillotin was not killed by the machine that bears his name; he died in his bed in 1814 at age 76.

Restaurants/Clubs: Red **Hotels:** Blue
Shops/♥ **Outdoors:** Green **Sights/Culture:** Black

112 74 Avenue de Suffren During the **1900 Exposition Universelle,** this was the site of the **Grande Roue de Paris,** a 350-foot Ferris wheel (one-third the height of the **Eiffel Tower**). The wheel had 40 wooden cars divided into 5 series of 8 cars; it took 5 stops, boarding 8 cars at a time, to load the whole wheel. In what is perhaps a metaphor for the French mentality, each eight-car unit was composed of six second-class cars, one first-class car, and a restaurant. The Ferris wheel's axis was supported by two pylons set in concrete foundations; between them was a garden that was the site of a theater, restaurant, hotel, several souvenir stands, and a number of duels. Today the area is built up with a variety of structures, none as fanciful as the late lamented Ferris wheel. ♦ At Rue Dupleix. Métro: La Motte Picquet–Grenelle

Parlez-Vous Anglais?

If English is your first—or only—language, and you need a book fix in Paris, here are the English-language bookstores of choice:

Abbey Bookshop 29 Rue de la Parcheminerie (between Rues St-Jacques and de la Harpe). 01.46.33.16.24. Métro: Cluny–La Sorbonne

Albion 13 Rue Charles-V (between Rues Beautreillis and St-Paul). 01.42.72.50.71. Métro: Sully-Morland

Brentano's 37 Ave de l'Opéra (between Rues Danielle-Casanova and d'Antin). 01.42.61.52.50. Métros: Opéra, Pyramides

Galignani 224 Rue de Rivoli (between Rues d'Alger and de Castiglione). 01.42.60.76.07. Métro: Concorde

San Francisco Book Company 17 Rue Monsieur-le-Prince (between Rue Antoine-Dubois and Carrefour de l'Odéon). 01.43.29.15.70. Métro: Odéon

Shakespeare and Company 37 Rue de la Bûcherie (between Rues St-Julien-le-Pauvre and du Petit-Pont). 01.43.26.96.50. Métros: Maubert-Mutualité, St-Michel, Cité

Tea and Tattered Pages 24 Rue Mayet (between Rues du Cherche-Midi and de Sèvres). 01.40.65.94.35. Métros: Duroc, Falguière

Village Voice 6 Rue Princesse (between Rues Guisarde and du Four). 01.46.33.36.47. Métro: Mabillon

W.H. Smith and Son 248 Rue de Rivoli (at Rue Cambon). 01.44.77.88.99. Métro: Concorde

And if you need a library:

American Library in Paris 10 Rue du Général-Camou (between Aves Rapp and de La Bourdonnais). 01.53.59.12.60. RER: Pont de l'Alma

113 Foc Ly ★★★$$ You'll find no dragons or paper lanterns in this chic, contemporary Thai/Chinese restaurant with friendly young servers and a decor of blond wood and peach hues. Faithful clients, many of them patrons of the restaurant's former location of 20 years in the fashionable suburb of Neuilly, come for the *boeuf parfumé au soja noir* (beef in soy sauce), steamed sole *à la Cantonnaise,* Thai-style *brochettes de gambas* (shrimp kabobs), and sizzling meats cooked at your table on hot stones. ♦ Tu-Su lunch and dinner; closed mid-July through August. Reservations recommended. 71 Ave de Suffren (between Aves de La Motte-Picquet and du Général-Détrie). 01.47.83.27.12. Métros: La Motte Picquet–Grenelle, Ecole Militaire

114 UNESCO Secretariat This building was designed by architects from three member countries: **Bernard Zehrfuss** of France, **Luigi Nervi** of Italy, and **Marcel Breuer** of the US. When it was built in the late 1950s, the headquarters of the 158-member United Nations Educational, Scientific, and Cultural Organization was a hopeful symbol of a new era of international cooperation. The main building with its three crescent glass-and-concrete wings in the shape of a "Y" is a veritable time capsule of cutting-edge architecture of that period. Likewise, its art collection is a treasure trove of works by mid–20th-century masters: Henry Moore's *Reclining Figure;* a black metal Calder mobile; two ceramic walls executed by Artigas after designs by Miró; a sculpture by Giacometti; fresco by Tamayo; relief by Jean Arp; and a mural by Picasso, *The Victory of the Forces of Light and Peace over the Powers of Evil and Death.* An enchanting Japanese garden has a fountain designed by Noguchi. The gift shop in the lobby has a fine selection of handicrafts from around the world. Visitors must present their passports to pass through security. ♦ M-F. Group tours by appointment. 7 Pl de Fontenoy (between Aves de Saxe and de Lowendal). 01.45.68.10.00. Métros: Ségur, Cambronne, Ecole Militaire

France grants new mothers 16 weeks of paid maternity leave.

Eric Gaucheron
Manager, Familia Hotel

On a warm summer afternoon, have a sherbet or ice cream at **Berthillon** on **Ile St-Louis**. At this place, you are in the heart of Paris, and can choose between the **Right** and **Left Banks**. On the Left Bank, walk near the river and admire **Notre-Dame**. On the Right Bank, go to the **Place des Vosges**. Don't miss a boat ride, with or without dinner; it's another way of discovering Paris.

I prefer to use the bus system rather than the *métro*, it's a nicer way to see Paris. For example, take the *No. 63* and see **St-Germain-des-Près**, the **Musée d'Orsay, Les Invalides, Trocadero,** the **Eiffel Tower**. At the last stop discover the **Bois de Bologne** during the day. To see Paris from the top, you should go to the **Toupary** restaurant, on the top of **La Samaritaine**, which offers a great view while eating a pancake, or a lunch; at dinnertime you'll see the night lights of Paris. If you like open-air flea markets, go to the **Marché aux Puces de Vanves**.

Noël Riley Fitch
Author

After living part of each year in Paris since 1985, I still thrill to many of the same Parisian experiences, such as a visit to the **Louvre** during evening opening hours, spending early evening on the terrace of the **Les Deux Magots** cafe, and walking west along the **Seine** late during the white nights until I see the new filigree lights of the **Eiffel Tower**. I also suggest the following:

Have an afternoon ice cream at **Berthillon** on **Ile St-Louis** and then walk around the entire island.

Visit places of memory, homes of North American writers who once lived in the city, such as Hemingway's home around the corner from Place de la Contrescarpe or Edith Wharton's Rue de Varenne townhouse (both have large plaques).

Have lunch at **La Coupole**, that large restored brasserie for 1920s Left Bank artists; 1960s boomers may prefer a visit to Jim Morrison's grave at **Cimetière du Père-Lachaise**.

Visit **Place de Furstemberg**, one of the smallest and most beautiful squares (very near **Les Deux Magots**). Delacroix painted and died, forgotten, at No. 6.

Have oysters and Champagne (or Hemingway's favorite herring and potatoes in oil) for lunch in **Brasserie Lipp** and admire the mosaic tiles and Belle Epoque decor, then walk east to Rue du Four and right to Rue Princesse: check out the latest English-language publications at **Village Voice** bookshop (look for the blue front).

Visit the **Deportation Memorial** (during the daytime) at the tip of **Ile de la Cité** behind **Notre-Dame**.

Stand on the **Pont Alexandre III** at dusk and watch the tour boats float underneath you (on 14 July enjoy the fireworks from this or any other bridge closer to the **Eiffel Tower**).

Visit quiet and beautiful stops such as **Parc de Monceau** or **Place des Vosges**.

Enjoy dinner at one of my personal favorites: **Au Petit Marguéry**. Reservations recommended.

Have your pricey farewell lunch halfway up the **Eiffel Tower** at **Le Jules Verne** restaurant and enjoy looking at all the sites you have visited while in Paris.

Phil Wood
Co-Owner/Manager, San Francisco Book Co., Paris

The **Jardin du Luxembourg** any time of day, any time of year, in almost any weather. It's my favorite park in the world. I also like the **Jardin des Plantes** and often include both parks plus the banks of the **Seine** (**Rive Gauche** from **Notre-Dame** to **Pont d'Austerlitz**) and the market on **Rue Mouffetard** in the same walk.

For that matter any of the many street markets; e.g., on **Rue de Buci** and **Rue de Seine,** at **Place Maubert**. Going out of my way to walk through the **Marché St-Germain** on the way to work. Seeing the fresh food displayed in the morning is nourishment all by itself.

Walking along the **Seine** and watching the *péniches* (barges)—especially watching the ones waiting upstream of the **Ile St-Louis** for the light on the bridge **(Pont de Sully)** to change from red to green so they can continue downstream. Sometimes they wait a long time and during that time you might see a barge waiting for the gates to open so it can enter the **Canal St-Martin** on the **Rive Droite**.

The city at Christmastime with all the lights and decorations, and especially the music—opera, symphony, choral works, much of it performed in the churches.

Walking around **Montmartre,** where I live, on Sunday afternoon and watching the *boulistes,* i.e., the people playing *boules* (boccle). As you approach the place where they're playing you can hear the clatter of balls resulting from a shot all the way in the air, which has the aim of blasting the opponent's ball clear out of play. Trying to understand the game, see who's on which team, etc. I especially like to watch the group of six or eight people in **Place Suzanne-Buisson** who play with the large balls, and who are there every Sunday afternoon.

The reading room of the **Bibliothèque Ste-Geneviève** across from the **Panthéon**.

Hanging out and eating a late-afternoon lunch at the bar at **Joe Allen's** on the way home from the bookshop. It's about half-way on the *métro* (*No. 4* line) from the Left Bank to Montmartre, and the kitchen is always open.

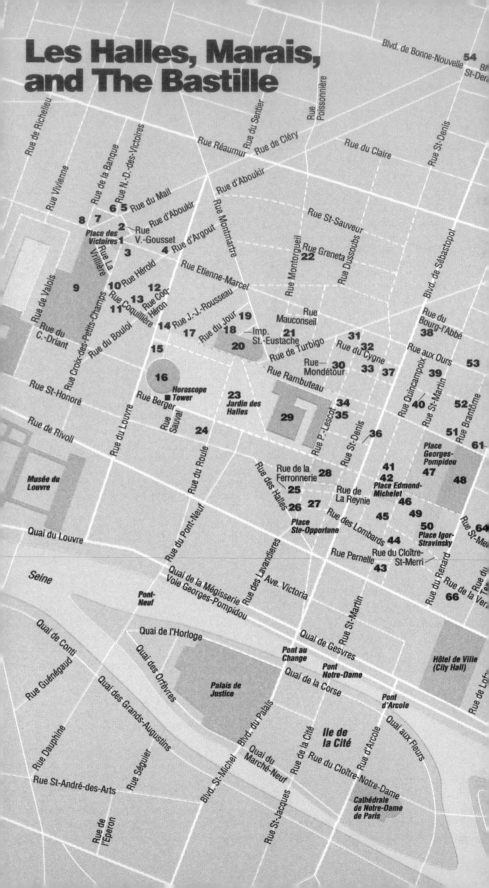

Les Halles, Marais, and The Bastille

This tour traverses 3 Parisian neighborhoods and 16 centuries of the city's history. It begins in the old Les Halles neighborhood, once the site of the great marketplace that Emile Zola called "the belly of Paris." Here you can wake up with the bustle of the marketplace and have a breakfast of coffee and croissants with local workers in one of the many cafes on the **Rue Montorgueil,** one of the surviving remnants of the old Les Halles food market. Thus fortified, head over to the fashionable **Place des Victoires** for some power shopping in the upscale boutiques (**Victoire,** for example). Then amble over to **St-Eustache,** to admire the towering parish church of Les Halles, second only to **Notre-Dame** in size and Gothic splendor.

Emerging from **St-Eustache,** you'll find yourself at the **Forum des Halles,** the huge modern, mostly underground mall that replaced "the belly" after it moved to the suburbs three decades ago. Here you can shop for practically anything *except* groceries in the almost-200 boutiques, catch the latest movie at one of the multiplex theaters, or swim a few laps in an Olympic-size pool. Back up on the street, stroll on to "the Beaubourg," as the **Centre Georges Pompidou** is popularly known. This huge and hugely controversial building (it looks like an oil refinery) is Paris's department store of modern culture, and home to the **Musée National d'Art Moderne.** At press time the structure was closed for a major renovation, but even seeing the building from the outside affords plenty of surprises. Indulge in a second cup of coffee on the terrace of chic **Café Beaubourg,** a choice perch from which to watch the myriad street performers in front of the center.

From the Beaubourg, move on to the city's most beautiful square, **Place des Vosges,** in a section of the Marais district that was once a snarl of medieval streets inhabited by rich viscounts and poor Jews. On the way, stop in at the **Musée d'Art et d'Histoire du Judaïsme,** a splendid museum of Jewish art and history that opened in December 1998. Browse the boutiques of **Rue des Francs-Bourgeois** or visit the **Musée Carnavalet** (the **Historical Museum of the City of Paris**) to peruse its collection of Revolution memorabilia and 18th-century shop signs, both of which are a big hit with children. Have lunch at one of the many tea salons (**Le Loir dans la Théière** is a good choice) or pick up a quick falafel or pastrami sandwich on **Rue des Rosiers,** the main artery of the old Jewish quarter, which is lined with storefront synagogues and kosher bakeries (remember, though, that much of the street closes on Saturday, the Jewish Sabbath). Your dessert will be the **Musée Picasso** in the **Hôtel Salé** on Rue de Thorigny. (If visiting the Marais during summer, inquire about the Festival du Marais, a series of opera, chamber music, and drama performances in the district's exquisite 17th-century mansions.)

The final stop on this tour is the reinvigorated **Place de la Bastille.** Here the **Opéra Bastille,** a huge silver whale of a building, looms over a neighborhood of artisans and woodworkers coexisting with trendy designer shops, art galleries, restaurants, cafes, and clubs, most of which have sprung up since the **Opéra Bastille** opened in 1990. Once the site of the prison whose storming marked the start of the bloody French Revolution, the Place de la Bastille is better known today for the dramas that take place onstage in the opera house. But there is plenty to do in the area, even if you don't have opera tickets. **Bofinger, Les Grandes Marches,** and **Thaï Elephant** are three popular dinner spots. Great dancing is afoot at the trendy **Casbah** and at Paris's most famous dance hall, **Le Balajo,** which opened in 1936 and is still kicking. Complete your Bastille rite of passage by sipping a glass of

Champagne at **Sanz-Sans** or a coco loco cocktail at the **Havanita Café.** More fashion-conscious night owls should check out the wee-hours scene at **Les Bains Douches** in Les Halles, a discotheque favored by movie stars, models, and other glitterati. If hunger strikes, two classic eateries, **Au Pied de Cochon** and **La Tour de Montlhery**, are open around-the-clock. Both places are full of characters with 3AM cravings for steak and Burgundy, oysters and Champagne, or the traditional Les Halles staple—a cheese-crusted bowl of onion soup.

Les Halles

The area known as Les Halles (the marketplace) takes its name from the great wholesale food market that began here in 1100. The colorful old market operated on this site until 1969 when it moved to Rungis near **Orly Airport,** leaving behind *le trou* (the hole). This was filled 10 years later by a huge underground shopping mall called the **Forum des Halles;** the attractive 12-acre **Jardin des Halles** surrounding it was created in the late 1980s. On the garden's northern perimeter are the church of **St-Eustache,** several old all-night restaurants serving onion soup and pig's feet, and a few bustling market streets where traditional food and kitchenware outlets have survived.

As recently as a few decades ago, this area was a rundown garment district and slum that stretched between **St-Merri** church and the old food market. The opening of the **Forum des Halles** and the nearby **Centre Georges Pompidou** in the late 1970s brought new commercial life into the area (as well as architectural controversy). Retired food merchants now share their turf with hordes of mall-bound youths, street performers, panhandlers, and tourists.

1 Place des Victoires Like those at the Place Vendôme, this circle of noble mansions was designed by **Jules Hardouin-Mansart** to celebrate a triumph of Louis XIV, in this case the Treaty of Nijmegen that marked his victory over Spain, Holland, Piedmont, and Germany. Originally at its center was a gilded bronze statue (1686) portraying the king being crowned by a goddess of victory, with four bound warriors at his feet representing the conquered nations. Destroyed during the Revolution, the statue was replaced in 1822 with the Astyanax Bosio equestrian version of Louis XIV that proudly rears here today. During the 19th century, the Place des Victoires fell into ruin and its buildings were converted into shops, but today it's the Right Bank's hub of high fashion. ♦ Métros: Bourse, Palais Royal–Musée du Louvre

2 Victoire Come here to find out what's new in the current fashion scene. This place takes pride in being the very first specialty store to discover new Paris design talent. ♦ M-Sa. 10-12 Pl des Victoires (at Rue Vide-Gousset). 01.42.61.09.02. Métros: Bourse, Palais Royal–Musée du Louvre

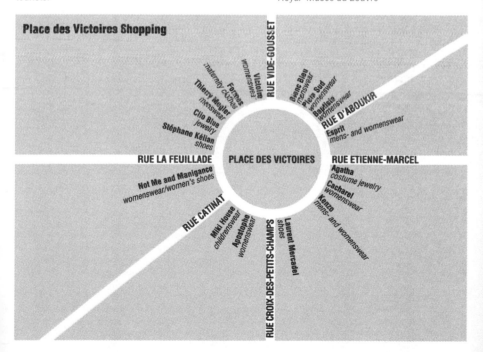

Place des Victoires Shopping

3 Kenzo For the young at heart: This appealing boutique, decorated with natural wood, has some of the most fanciful fashions and friendliest sales help in town. The menswear collection is downstairs, the womenswear upstairs. ♦ M-Sa. 3 Pl des Victoires (between Rues Etienne-Marcel and Croix-des-Petits-Champs). 01.40.39.72.00. Métros: Bourse, Palais Royal–Musée du Louvre

3 Cacharel Though company founder Jean Bosquet moved into politics long ago, the design flame remains bright with sensible sportswear and cotton paisley-print fabrics for men and women, some produced in collaboration with Liberty of London. Menswear is sold at 20 Rue Tronchet (between Pl de la Madeleine and Rue Vignon); the children's collection is at 34 Rue Tronchet (between Rue des Mathurins and Blvd Haussmann). ♦ M-Sa. 5 Pl des Victoires (between Rues Etienne-Marcel and Croix-des-Petits-Champs). 01.42.33.29.88. Métros: Bourse, Palais Royal–Musée du Louvre. Also at: 33 Rue Tronchet (between Rue des Mathurins and Blvd Haussmann). 01.47.42.12.61. Métro: Havre-Caumartin

4 Lina's ★★$ This airy sandwich bar with its ocher walls, blond-wood trim, and acres of windows is the perfect vantage point for spying on the chic fashion show that promenades in the vicinity of the Place des Victoires. Behind the counter, businesslike young men and women serve delicious roast beef, pastrami, and smoked-salmon sandwiches on crusty whole-grain *pain pavé* (country bread). ♦ Daily. 50 Rue Etienne-Marcel (at Rue d'Argout). 01.42.21.16.14. Métro: Sentier. Also at: Numerous locations throughout the city

Chez Georges

5 Chez Georges ★★$$ Handwritten menus, beveled mirrors, waitresses in black dresses, and an honest platter of beefsteak and fries are the hallmarks of this classic Parisian bistro. ♦ M-Sa lunch and dinner; closed three weeks in August. Reservations recommended. 1 Rue du Mail (at Pl des Petits-Pères). 01.42.60.07.11. Métro: Bourse

6 Basilique Notre-Dame-des-Victoires Using the plans of **Pierre Le Muet,** in 1740 architect **Jean Sylvain Cartaud** completed this rather undistinguished church, the name of which commemorates the Louis XIII trouncing of the Protestants in 1628 at La Rochelle. Inside the church are a 1702 bust of the composer Jean-Baptiste Lully, who lived down the street at 45 Rue des Petits-Champs, and an estimated 30,000 tablets blanketing the walls. ♦ Pl des Petits-Pères and Rue Notre-Dame-des-Victoires. 01.42.60.90.00. Métro: Bourse

7 Au Panetier Lebon Hundreds of crispy sourdough baguettes are baked daily in the wood-fired oven of Bernard Lebon. ♦ M-F. 10 Pl des Petits-Pères (between Rue des Petits-Pères and Passage des Petits-Pères). 01.42.60.90.23. Métro: Bourse

8 Legrand It's a joy to behold this renowned wine shop's bright red Belle Epoque facade, and its ceiling covered with corks. For three generations, the Legrand family has run this *épicerie* (grocery shop) stocked with an intelligent selection of wine, chocolate, tea, coffee, and jam. Francine Legrand, the daughter of the late Lucien, has a passion for younger, undiscovered (and less expensive) wines from France's smaller vineyards in Burgundy and Bordeaux. Ask her to recommend one—she loves to chat. ♦ Tu-Sa. 1 Rue de la Banque (at Rue des Petits-Pères). 01.42.60.07.12. Métro: Bourse

9 Banque de France The mansion, which became home to the Bank of France in 1812 by order of Napoléon, was originally built for the Comte de Toulouse, the son of Louis XIV and Mlle. de Montespan. Among its lavish treasures is a first-class work of art, *Fête à Saint Cloud,* which many art historians say is the best of Fragonard's landscape paintings. That huge (7-by-10-foot) canvas hangs in the private office of the governor of the bank, so unless you have specific business with the governor you'll have to content yourself with the smaller Fragonards down the street at the **Louvre.** The building is not open to the public. ♦ 39 Rue Croix-des-Petits-Champs (between Rues du Colonel-Driant and La Vrillière). Métro: Palais Royal–Musée du Louvre

10 La Coutellerie Suisse You can't miss this consummate cutlery shop with its giant red Swiss Army knife splayed in the window. ♦ M-F; closed in August. 44 Rue Coquillière (between Rues Hérold and Croix-des-Petits-Champs). 01.42.33.20.92. Métro: Palais Royal–Musée du Louvre

11 La Fermette du Sud-Ouest ★★$$ Jacky Mayer reigns supreme over this countrified restaurant, which is famous for homemade *boudin* (blood sausage) with onions and sautéed potatoes, cassoulet, magnificent entrecôtes, and hearty Cahors, Buzet, and Madiran wines. ♦ M-Sa lunch and dinner. Reservations recommended. 31 Rue Coquillière (between Rues du Bouloi and Croix-des-Petits-Champs). 01.42.36.73.55. Métro: Palais Royal–Musée du Louvre

12 Gérard Besson ★★$$$ One of the neighborhood's finest lunch menus (it's changed every three weeks) begins with owner/chef Besson's *foie gras de canard* (duck liver pâté), which may be followed by lobster with small vegetables. For dessert, try the *biscuit glacé à la framboise* (a cookie topped with raspberry ice cream). The detailed wine list is strong on Bordeaux. The service is attentive; the ambience, quiet and comfortable. ♦ M-F lunch and dinner; Sa dinner. Reservations recommended. 5 Rue Coq-Héron (between Rues Coquillière and du Louvre). 01.42.33.14.74. Métro: Les Halles

A LA Cloche DES halles

13 A La Cloche des Halles ★★$ This wine bar, named after the *cloche* (bronze bell) that for decades signaled the opening and closing of Les Halles market, offers not only superb Sancerres, Morgons, and Côtes-de-Brouillys, but scrumptious plates of baked country ham, assorted regional cheeses, quiche, and homemade fruit tarts. It's crowded with local merchants, journalists, and the folks in dark suits from the **Bourse** and **Banque de France** up the street. ♦ M-Sa breakfast, lunch and dinner; closed two weeks in August. No credit cards accepted. 28 Rue Coquillière (at Rue Coq-Héron). 01.42.36.93.89. Métros: Les Halles, Palais Royal–Musée du Louvre

14 Dehillerin Half warehouse, half hardware store, this family-run kitchen emporium has been supplying the great chefs of Europe with cooking vessels and utensils since 1820. It even furnishes the French Army with cast-iron frying pans, boxwood knives, spatulas, and the wire skimmers known as "spiders." Mail order is available to anywhere in the world.

The store also happens to be the city's leading specialist in re-tinning copper pots. Two of the staff speak English. ♦ M-Sa. 51 Rue Jean-Jacques-Rousseau and 18-20 Rue Coquillière. 01.42.36.53.13. Métro: Les Halles

15 Le Pavillon Baltard ★$ This warm and welcoming Alsatian brasserie serves *choucroute* (sauerkraut) with your choice of fish, pork, calf's head, or stuffed pig's tail. Nouvelle cuisine this ain't. Plan a long stroll after dinner. ♦ Daily lunch and dinner until 1AM. Reservations recommended. 9 Rue Coquillière (at Rue du Louvre). 01.42.36.22.00. Métro: Les Halles

16 La Bourse du Commerce (Commercial Exchange) One of the few buildings to escape the Les Halles demolition, this circular structure (built in 1887) is a graceful birthday cake of iron and glass. Not to be confused with the **Bourse des Valeurs** (the Roman temple to the north that houses the **Paris Stock Exchange**), here brokers in wheat, sugar, and other commodities do their trading. Beside the structure is a 101-foot Classical column, topped with what appears to be a giant iron birdcage. This curiosity, called the **Horoscope Tower,** was once attached to the **Hôtel de la Reine** of Catherine de Médicis and accommodated her stargazing astrologer, Ruggieri, during the late 16th century. ♦ Reception/information: M-F; open to the public by appointment only. 2 Rue de Viarmes (at Rue Sauval). 01.55.65.78.36. Métro: Louvre-Rivoli

17 Au Pied de Cochon ★$$ This nostalgic all-night eatery specializes in *fruits de mer* (mixed seafood) and pig's feet (hence the restaurant's name), and also serves an overrated onion soup gratinée. Local night owls gather here at 4AM, but otherwise it's a tourist spot. For a Parisian version of Sunday brunch, order oysters (a dozen varieties are available) and Champagne at the bar. Though open around the clock, service is as poky as the snails are delicious. If the ground floor is too boisterous, head upstairs to the more sedate dining rooms. ♦ Daily 24 hours. 6 Rue Coquillière (between Rues du Jour and Jean-Jacques-Rousseau). 01.40.13.77.00. Métro: Les Halles

agnès b.

18 agnès b. These cotton T-shirts, chic silk blouses, and skirts are comfortable and fashionable—black being the dominant tone. In her outlets along Rue du Jour, agnès b. outfits the 1990s generation. Her trademark cotton cardigans with mother-of-pearl snaps are de rigueur Parisian attire. Other shops on

Rue du Jour are at No. 2 (babies), No. 3 (men), No. 10 (teens), and No. 19 (household decoration). ♦ M-Sa. 6 Rue du Jour (between Rues Rambuteau and Montmartre). 01.42.33.04.13. Métro: Les Halles

19 Le Cochon à l'Oreille ★★$ Beautiful ceramic murals adorn this authentic turn-of-the-century working-class bar/cafe. Butchers, foie gras wholesalers, local merchants, and paunchy men of indefinite occupation wearing blue coveralls hang out here. They come for their coffee and Calvados before dawn or to share a *pastis* (an anisette drink) at the crowded zinc bar in the afternoon. ♦ M-Sa breakfast and lunch until 6PM. No credit cards accepted. 15 Rue Montmartre (between Impasse St-Eustache and Rue du Jour). 01.42.36.07.56. Métro: Les Halles

MICHAEL STORRINGS

20 St-Eustache This massive amalgam of Gothic flying buttresses, rose windows, and Flamboyant vaulting was built in the 16th and early 17th centuries to rival **Notre-Dame.** The incongruous Neoclassical main entrance was added in the mid-18th century. While its dimensions are enormous (346 feet long, with a 112-foot-high nave), the church is better known for its musical legacy than its architectural grandeur. Berlioz's *Te Deum* and Liszt's *Grand Mass* were first played here, and composer Jean-Philippe Rameau is buried in the church. At midnight Mass on Christmas Eve, the 8,000-pipe organ and talented church choir outshine even those of **Notre-Dame.** Notable treasures here are the Rubens painting *Pilgrims at Emmaus,* the Pigalle statue of the Virgin, and a colorful sculpted scene honoring the vegetable vendors forced out of Les Halles in 1969.

The church is dedicated to St. Eustache, a second-century Roman general who converted to Christianity when, like St. Hubert, he saw a vision of the cross poised between the antlers of a stag. (A sculpted stag's head and cross are beneath the gable in the church's Renaissance transept facade.) St. Eustache, as the story goes, was gruesomely martyred; he was roasted alive inside an immense bronze bull with his wife and children. This was once the parish church for the merchants of Les Halles and the nobility from the nearby **Louvre** and **Palais Royal.** It hosted the baptisms of Cardinal Richelieu, Jean-Baptiste Poquelin (Molière), and Mme. de Pompadour, as well as the funerals of fabulist Jean de La Fontaine, Colbert (prime minister of Louis XIV), Molière, and Revolutionary orator Mirabeau. During the Revolution the church was vandalized and renamed the "Temple of Agriculture," doubtless in honor of its proximity to Les Halles market. ♦ Fee for tour. Daily. 2 Impasse St-Eustache (just southwest of Rue Montmartre). 01.42.36.31.05. Métro: Les Halles

21 Rue Montorgueil Paris chefs have continued to shop on this colorful market street despite the demolition of the old Les Halles markets. The market starts at Rue de Turbigo at the rear of **St-Eustache** and runs several blocks north to Rue Réaumur. Rue Montorgueil and all its cross streets are paved in cobblestone and are closed to traffic. One of the finest and most beautiful old patisseries in Paris is at No. 51—**Stöhrer,** opened by a former pastry chef to Louis XV in 1730 (01.42.33.38.20). ♦ Market: Tu-Sa 6AM-1PM, 4PM-7PM; Su 6AM-1PM. Métros: Les Halles, Etienne Marcel, Sentier

On Rue Montorgueil:

L'Escargot Montorgueil ★★$$ One of the most authentic examples of 1830s decor in Paris, this restaurant has a black-and-gilt facade, enormous cut-glass mirrors, tulip chandeliers, and red banquettes. The old cooking allegory gracing the wall came from the dining room of actress Sarah Bernhardt. Champagne is served in carafes; escargots are served in mint, curry, roquefort, or *bourguignonne* (butter, garlic, and parsley) sauce; and the customers are of the **Maxim's, Lasserre, Grand Véfour,** and **La Tour d'Argent** variety, which is not surprising, as the place is run by Mme. Saladin-Terrail, the sister of Claude Terrail, who owns **La Tour d'Argent.** ♦ Daily lunch and dinner. Reservations recommended. No. 38 (at Rue Mauconseil). 01.42.36.83.51

22 La Reine de Sabah At this hair and beauty salon, body hair is removed using the old-fashioned method (presumably the same way as the 10th-century BC Queen of Sheba, after whom the shop is named, had it done). Instead of hot wax, the establishment uses cool liquid caramel, which takes the hair out at the roots and is consequently painless. Vivacious Israeli-born owner Vanessa Sitbon also performs tattoolike body staining in henna or black in patterns that fade in two weeks. Sitbon introduced the black stain to France and this is the only place in Paris that practices it. Hair treatments are also given. The salon has a distinctive North African/Middle Eastern flavor—most of the staff comes from that part of the world and Sitbon's line of hair and skin products are made from such exotica as musk and jasmine. ♦ M-Sa. 69 Rue Greneta (between Rues Dussoubs and Montorgeuil). 01.40.41.06.64. Métro: Etienne Marcel

23 Jardin des Halles The razing of Les Halles market left 36 acres of open space, of which the western 12 acres has been developed into an attractive tree-lined garden and children's playground in the shadow of **St-Eustache** church. Two escalators—one at Rue du Jour and the other to the south of the church—lead down to **Paul Chemetov's** spacious subterranean concourse that opened in 1986 (see "Forum des Halles" on page 134).

In the cobblestone plaza by **Porte St-Eustache,** be sure to note the colossal 70-ton stone head of a man with his chin in his hand. Sculpted by Henri de Miller, the statue is called *Ecoute,* presumably because it is listening to the church's beautiful organ music. ♦ Rue Rambuteau (between Rues Pierre-Lescot and du Jour). Métros: Les Halles, Châtelet

24 A La Tour de Montlhery ★★$$ The owner, Denise, who tends *la caisse* (the cash register), serves her loyal clientele of wine merchants, advertising executives, and visiting English novelists such stick-to-the-ribs specialties as stuffed cabbage, mutton with beans, and steak with shallots. This is a nice place to meet friends over a bottle of Brouilly. ♦ M-F 24 hours; closed mid-July through mid-August. Reservations recommended. 5 Rue des Prouvaires (between Rues St-Honoré and Berger). 01.42.36.21.82. Métro: Châtelet

25 Rue de la Ferronnerie Henri IV was murdered here in his carriage on 14 May 1610 as he passed along Ironmongers Row. His assassin, Ravaillac, was quartered by four horses in the Place de Grève, today called Place de l'Hôtel-de-Ville. ♦ Métro: Châtelet

On Rue de la Ferronnerie:

Papeterie Moderne If you've got enough patience to sort through this store's marvelous hodgepodge of old Parisian signs (for streets, butcher shops, bakeries, and the like), you can take home a fine souvenir. A copy of anything in the store may be ordered; allow 10 days for pickup. ♦ M-Sa; closed one week in August. No. 12. 01.42.36.21.72

Hôtel Ducs d'Anjou

26 Ducs d'Anjou $$ This pleasant 34-room hotel sits just off the charming Place Ste-Opportune. Rooms on the courtyard are somber but comfortable. There's no restaurant. ♦ 1 Rue Ste-Opportune (at Pl Ste-Opportune). 01.42.36.92.24; fax 01.42.36.16.63. Métro: Châtelet

27 Au Diable des Lombards ★$ Cheeseburgers, rabbit terrine, and homemade ice cream are among the menu items at this trendy bistro. ♦ Daily 9AM-1AM. 64 Rue des Lombards (between Rues St-Denic and Ste-Opportune). 01.42.33.81.84. Métro: Châtelet

MICHAEL STORRINGS

28 Fontaine des Innocents During the 16th century, Les Halles fishmongers and butchers drew their water from this fountain (pictured above), which was commissioned by Henri II and designed by Pierre Lescot in 1547. An important relic of early Renaissance Paris, it stands on the site of what was once the overcrowded, foul-smelling **Church of the Holy Innocents** cemetery. In 1786 the church was razed and some two million skeletons were transported from the cemetery to a quarry in the Denfert-Rochereau area (14th arrondissement), which was then most appropriately renamed the **Catacombs** (see page 246). Later, during World War II, the **Catacombs** were the macabre setting for the

133

headquarters of the French Resistance. Today, the area surrounding the fountain is the haunt of tattooed down-and-outers and indigent backpackers poring over out-of-print copies of *Europe on $20 a Day.* ♦ Sq des Innocents. Métro: Châtelet, RER: Châtelet–Les Halles

Forum des Halles

29 **Forum des Halles** **Victor Baltard**'s 12 marvelous 19th-century iron-and-glass food halls were torn down in the early 1970s after the 800-year-old wholesale market was moved to Rungis near **Orly Airport** in 1969. In its place, **Claude Vasconi** and **Georges Pencreach** designed a four-level shopping mall. The silvery greenhouselike pavilions that form an "L" at the intersection of Rues Rambuteau and Pierre-Lescot are just the proverbial tip of the iceberg. The three main levels are underground. This crater of consumerism is a labyrinth of 3.5 kilometers (2 miles) of walkways lined with more than 180 stores, dozens of snack bars and cafes, 12 restaurants, 32 cinemas, a recital hall, multimedia center, gymnasium, and Olympic-size pool.

Niveau 3, the third level down, is the **Forum**'s "Main Street." It extends from Rue Pierre-Lescot at the eastern end to **La Bourse du Commerce** at the west, a distance of five city blocks, and is very well lit by natural and artificial light. In the middle is an open-air plaza. On this level is the main branch of **FNAC** (01.40.41.40.00), an excellent book/CD/photo/audio and video equipment retailer, and a popular hangout where teenagers come to buy concert tickets, peruse the latest *bandes dessinées* (hardcover comic books), and listen to the most current CDs on headsets; roughly 100 boutiques for clothes, shoes, and accessories; 17 eating places; **Piscine Les Halles** (01.42.36.98.44), an Olympic-size swimming pool; and the 19 movie theaters of the **UGC Ciné Cité** (08.36.68.68.58) complex, the largest and most technically advanced in Paris.

Be forewarned: you won't be alone here. An estimated 36 million visitors a year pass through the mall. According to a survey conducted by **McDonald's,** 80,000 pedestrians walk past its doors alone every day. To maneuver your way through this labyrinth, pick up a copy of *Le Guide du Forum des Halles de Paris,* a well-designed booklet that has a map and directory of all the establishments, at **Point d'Information** (01.44.76.96.56) on **Niveau 3** at the foot of the escalators in front of the main entrance to

FNAC. To get there, take the escalator down from the **Porte Lescot** entrance.

Beneath the **Forum** is the **Châtelet–Les Halles** RER station. It is the world's largest underground train station, providing direct access to the métro, the **RER** (including lines to the **Roissy–Charles-de-Gaulle** and **Orly Airports**), and various underground parking lots. ♦ 1 Rue Pierre-Lescot (at Rue Berger). RER: Châtelet–Les Halles, Métro: Les Halles

30 **Pharamond** ★★$$ This bistro is a remnant of the old Les Halles days, with 19th-century colored tiles and mosaics, handsome woodwork, and lots of mirrors. Try the *tripes à la mode de Caen,* cooked in white wine and Calvados in classic Normandy fashion and served in old-fashioned charcoal-fired brass braziers. Nobody simmers it better. ♦ M dinner; Tu-Sa lunch and dinner. Reservations recommended. 24 Rue de la Grande-Truanderie (between Rues Pierre-Lescot and Mondétour). 01.42.33.06.72. Métros: Les Halles, Etienne Marcel

Duthilleul & Minart

31 **Duthilleul & Minart** For more than a century, this store has sold uniforms and work clothes, from waiters' aprons to chefs' toques, plus an array of uniquely French occupational garb. This is a great spot for gifts, such as the popular French watchmakers' smocks. Same-day service is also available. ♦ M-Sa. 14 Rue de Turbigo (at Rue Etienne-Marcel). 01.42.33.44.36. Métro: Etienne Marcel

32 **Joe Allen** ★$$ One of the most popular restaurants in Les Halles, this is a replica of its Manhattan namesake right down to the old photographs on the dark brick walls. The menu, which also mirrors its US counterpart, offers spareribs, chili con carne, black bean soup, and apple pie. ♦ Daily lunch and dinner until 1AM. 30 Rue Pierre-Lescot (between Rues du Cygne and Etienne-Marcel). 01.42.36.70.13. Métro: Etienne Marcel

33 **Chez Vong aux Halles** ★★$$ Refined Cantonese and Szechuan dishes may be found in the company of excellent French wines at this attractive Chinese bistro. Dim sum, beef in oyster sauce, and lacquered pigeon are good choices. Be sure to ask for the less expensive prix-fixe menu. ♦ M-Sa lunch and dinner. Reservations recommended. 10 Rue de la Grande-Truanderie (between Rues St-Denis and Pierre-Lescot). 01.40.39.99.89. Métros: Les Halles, Etienne Marcel

34 Au Père Tranquille ★$ French teenagers wearing penny loafers and fake US varsity-letter jackets crowd this late-night corner cafe. On a warm evening, order a kir on the terrace while you sit and watch the Les Halles parade pass by. Act III of e. e. cummings's play *Him* is set here. ♦ Daily breakfast, lunch, and dinner until 2AM. 16 Rue Pierre-Lescot (at Rue des Précheurs). 01.45.08.00.34. RER: Châtelet–Les Halles, Métro: Les Halles

35 Le Bon Pêcheur $ When the adolescents at **Au Père Tranquille** grow up, they graduate to this smoky cafe across the street. Decorated with orange neon lights, mirrored columns, a zinc bar, and maps of Brazil on the wall, it offers salsa music on the stereo, *caipirinha* (the fiery Brazilian drink) for the thirsty, and such fare as quiche Lorraine for the hungry. ♦ M-Th, Su breakfast, lunch, and dinner until 2AM; F-Sa breakfast, lunch, and dinner until 6AM. 12 Rue Pierre-Lescot (at Rue des Précheurs). 01.42.36.91.88. RER: Châtelet–Les Halles, Métro: Les Halles

36 Rue de la Cossonnerie Giovanni Boccaccio (1313-75), considered one of the founders of the Italian Renaissance, was born on this 13th-century street. He was the author of *Filocolo* and the *Decameron*. ♦ RER: Châtelet–Les Halles

37 Rue St-Denis Once the route by which France's kings entered Paris to be crowned and exited to be buried in the basilica at St-Denis, this street now unfurls a lurid panoply of Parisian sleaze: peep shows, prostitutes, and such fast-food joints as **Love Burger.** ♦ Métros: Châtelet, Les Halles, Etienne Marcel, Réaumur-Sébastopol, Strasbourg–St-Denis; RER: Châtelet–Les Halles

On Rue St-Denis:

St-Leu–St-Gilles This 14th-century church is of interest less for its unimposing exterior than for its unusual interior, with its mélange of sculptures, paintings, and architectural elements from many centuries. On a street epitomizing voyeurism, the glass doors of the church appropriately provide their own peep show of medieval architecture. ♦ No. 92 (between Rues de la Grande-Truanderie and du Cygne). 01.40.26.99.75

38 Les Bains Douches Architectural whiz kid **Philippe Starck** transformed these old public Turkish baths with their circa-1900 facade into one of the trendiest discos and restaurants in Les Halles. It's a favorite of Robert De Niro, Johnny Depp, and Madonna when they're in town. The doorman is very choosy about who gets in—you'll need "un look" to gain entrance. What would former baths patron Marcel Proust have to say? ♦ Restaurant: daily dinner (starting at 9PM). Disco: daily midnight-dawn. 7 Rue du Bourg-l'Abbé (between Rue St-Martin and Blvd de Sébastopol). 01.48.87.01.80. Métro: Etienne Marcel

39 Entrée des Artistes This whimsical bookstore/gallery specializes in marionettes, Venetian masks, posters, postcards, and books on cinema and theater. Ask the owner to crank up the mechanical performing circus, complete with lion tamer, acrobats, and hypnotist. ♦ M-Sa. 161 Rue St-Martin (between Passage Molière and Rue aux Ours). 01.48.87.78.58. Métros: Rambuteau, Etienne Marcel

40 Passage Molière Until recently a ramshackle spot with inexpensive tailor shops and one-room flats, this quaint 19th-century alleyway now houses art galleries and antiquarian bookshops. ♦ Métro: Rambuteau

On Passage Molière:

Galerie Lucette Herzog This gallery offers original prints and graphics by Alechinsky, Max Ernst, Bram Van Velde, Rassineux, Pandini, Tello, and others, along with some paintings and sculptures. ♦ W-F 2:30-6:30PM; Sa. No. 23. 01.48.87.39.94

41 Rue Quincampoix The Scottish financier John Law founded a bank on this narrow old street in 1719 after he became France's controller general, prompting a spurt of speculation in this part of the city. In more recent times, a rash of art galleries has sprung up here, drawn by the powerful magnet of the **Centre Georges Pompidou.** ♦ Métros: Etienne Marcel, Rambuteau, Châtelet; RER: Châtelet–Les Halles

On Rue Quincampoix:

No. 46 The cinema and theater of the **Centre Wallonie-Bruxelles,** a Belgian cultural center, are located in this complex. Don't miss the startling entryway sculpture of an army of nudes bursting through the seams in the wall. ♦ Between Rues Aubry-le-Boucher and Rambuteau

The first red light to control traffic was introduced in 1923 at the crossroads of Boulevards de Strasbourg and Saint-Denis. Green and orange lights were added later. There are now 11,650 traffic lights in Paris.

Restaurants/Clubs: Red   Hotels: Blue
Shops/♣ Outdoors: Green   Sights/Culture: Black

42 Galerie Alain Blondel This gallery features early–20th-century works, large canvases from the 1930s, trompe l'oeil, and surrealism. ♦ Tu-Sa. 4 Rue Aubry-le-Boucher (at Rue Quincampoix). 01.42.78.66.67. Métro: Rambuteau, RER: Châtelet–Les Halles

43 Benoit ★★★$$$ You need not take the train to Lyon to savor blood sausage with apples and roast potatoes, crab soup, or duckling with turnips. This charming 1912 bistro with yellow mock-antique walls and red plush dining banquettes is frequented by French businesspeople who definitely know their business when it comes to good eating. ♦ Daily lunch and dinner; closed in August. Reservations required; no credit cards accepted. 20 Rue St-Martin (at Rue Pernelle). 01.42.72.25.76. Métros: Châtelet, Hôtel de Ville

44 Rue de la Verrerie This narrow street, which takes its name from the 11th-century glassblowers guild, is where Jacquemin Gringoneur once lived. He invented playing cards to amuse King Charles VI ("The Beloved"), who ruled from 1380 to 1422. ♦ Métros: Hôtel de Ville, Châtelet

44 Hôtel St-Merri $$$ The former presbytery of the flamboyant Gothic **St-Merri** church next door, this hostelry has remained unswervingly faithful to its stylistic roots. For example, communion rails serve as banisters; stone, exposed beams, dark wood paneling, heavy wooden furniture, and wrought iron abound; and one guest room even has flying buttresses over the bed. All 11 rooms are very comfortable, and most are quite spacious. This place is the ideal honeymoon hotel for medieval scholars. There's no restaurant. ♦ 78 Rue de la Verrerie (at Rue St-Martin). 01.42.78.14.15; fax 01.40.29.06.82. Métros: Châtelet, Hôtel de Ville

45 Les Viennoiseries de St-Medard What a treat in this modish neighborhood to find an old-time bakery complete with a rosy-cheeked baker proudly displaying her fresh brioches, croissants, and tarts on the white marble counters. ♦ M, W-Su. 81 Rue St-Martin (between Rue des Lombards and Pl Edmond-Michelet). 01.42.72.84.24. Métros: Hôtel de Ville, Châtelet; RER: Châtelet–Les Halles

46 Café Beaubourg ★★$$ From the *terrasse* (terrace) of this chic, yet surprisingly relaxed cafe, you'll have a perfect vantage on the ever-amusing comings and goings around the **Pompidou Center**. Or if the weather's inclement, move into architect **Christian de Portzamparc**'s soaring interior. Inside or out, this place offers first-rate wines and practically anything else you can think of imbibing; brunch all day; a fine selection of sandwiches, salads, grilled fish and meat, snacks, desserts; and copies of *Le Monde* and *Libération*. ♦ M-F breakfast, lunch, and dinner until 1AM; Sa-Su breakfast, lunch, and dinner until 2AM. 100 Rue St-Martin (between Rue du Cloître-St-Merri and Pl Georges-Pompidou). 01.48.87.63.96. Métro: Rambuteau

47 Place Georges-Pompidou The large inclined plaza on the west side of the **Centre Georges Pompidou** is home to an impromptu circus of folk singers, hypnotists, quick sketch artists, kerosene garglers, sword swallowers, Hare Krishnas, rowdies, acrobats, jugglers, and (be forewarned) purse snatchers and panhandlers who prey on gawking tourists. ♦ Métro: Rambuteau

On Place Georges-Pompidou:

Atelier Brancusi Romanian-born Constantin Brancusi moved to Paris in 1904 and developed the pure, simple, and organic forms that made him one of Paris's greatest 20th-century sculptors. When he died in 1957, he willed his Left Bank atelier to France. The studio was eventually reconstructed here, with its original objects, and opened on the **Centre Georges Pompidou**'s 20th anniversary in 1997. It contains almost 104 sculptures, pedestals, sketches, and many of his photos. ♦ M, W-F noon-10PM; Sa-Su 10AM-10PM

48 Centre Georges Pompidou (Centre National d'Art et Culture Georges Pompidou) Critics took to calling the five-story jumble of glass and steel the "gasworks" and asked "Who forgot to take the scaffolding down?" Still, this surrealistic Tinkertoy temple of modern culture is the biggest attraction in Paris, outdrawing both the **Louvre** and the **Eiffel Tower**. A million people visited in 1977 during the first seven weeks it was open, an average of eight million a year since. More than half of all visitors are under age 35.

Created at the behest of then-president Georges Pompidou (1911-74) and designed by Italian **Renzo Piano** and Englishman **Richard Rogers** (whose proposal was selected from among a field of 681), the revolutionary (some say revolting) structure is home to one of the world's most important modern art museums **(Musée National d'Art Moderne/Centre de Création Industrielle);** Paris's largest public research library, with more than a half-million books **(Bibliothèque Publique d'Information);** an art workshop for children; a **Département du Développement Culturel** that puts on cinema and video arts programs in its screening rooms, and dance, performance art, and lectures in theater and public spaces; and a sixth-floor restaurant with a four-star view.

The center also mounts several major temporary exhibits yearly. **IRCAM** (the **Institut de Recherche et de Coordination Acoustique/Musique**), one of the world's most advanced computer music laboratories, is part of the complex, but is located in another building nearby (see below), as is the **Atelier Brancusi** (see page 136).

The high-tech design concept of the center celebrates the building's functional parts (heating ducts, ventilator shafts, stairways, and elevators) by brightly color-coding them: red for vertical circulation, green for water, blue for air, yellow for electricity, and white for structure. An escalator in a Plexiglas tube snakes up the front of the complex, offering one of the city's best panoramic vistas, the grand sweep from Montmartre to Montparnasse, from the top floor. Pompidou, who was a patron of modern art as well as a politician, is immortalized by Victor Vasarely in a hexagonal portrait that hangs on the ground floor.

Unfortunately, innovation and popularity carry a price. The center was built with the expectation that an estimated 5,000 people would visit daily. Instead, an average of

23,000 came each day. The wear and tear was enormous—tarnished steel, peeling paint, shredded carpets, and even floors that bowed. Critics blame not just the crowds, but the design. "To put the bones and intestines outside the skin," said one, "is to invite health problems."

The center was closed in October 1997 for a massive renovation to correct these problems. It was also decided to expand the exhibition spaces and areas for cultural activities and move the administrative offices to another building. **Renzo Piano** and **Jean-François Bodin** were hired to plan a complete redevelopment of the interior. The center was scheduled to reopen at press time.
♦ Admission. Call for hours. Pl Georges-Pompidou (between Pl Igor-Stravinsky and Rue St-Martin). 01.44.78.12.33. Métro: Rambuteau

Within the Centre Georges Pompidou:

Musée National d'Art Moderne/Centre de Création Industrielle (MNAM/CCI)
One of the world's largest collections of modern and contemporary painting, sculpture, graphic art, photographs, rare books, films, new media, architecture, and design is displayed here. The period covered begins with the Fauves in the first decade of the 20th century and goes up through the Cubist, Dadaist, Surrealist, Abstract Expressionist, Pop Art, Nouveaux Réalistes, Conceptual Art, and other major movements of the century, to the museum's latest acquisitions of works by contemporary artists. The permanent collection includes important works by Matisse, Bonnard, Duchamp, Picasso, Braque, Gris, Léger, Modigliani, Kandinsky, Delaunay, Klee, Mondrian, Chagall, Brancusi, Calder, Giacommetti, Dalí, Magritte, Miró, Balthus, De Staël, Klein, Pollock, De Kooning, Newman, Kelly, Warhol, Moore, Bacon, Jasper Johns, and many others.

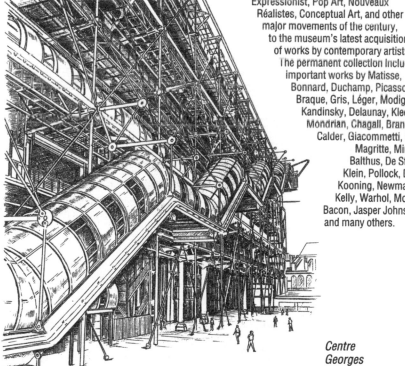

Centre Georges Pompidou

The fourth floor is devoted to the museum's contemporary collection (post-1960) of paintings; sculpture; graphics; photographs; film, video, and other media; architecture, and design. The fifth floor houses Modern Art (1900 through the 1950s) from the permanent collection. Most of the top floor (which it will share with the restaurant) is set aside for temporary exhibits.

Bibliothèque Publique d'Information (B.P.I.) Occupying the second and third floors of the center, this huge general research library with more than a half-million books on its open-stack shelves attracts 12,000 users per day. Most of the books are in French, but there are many in English on practically all subjects, including a substantial collection of literary works. The compilation is very strong in photography and art. The library carries 2,500 current periodicals, including 400 from the international press. It also has stereo set-ups for listening to its 10,000 CDs; VCRs to view its more than 2,400 documentaries; a modern language-study laboratory with interactive audio programs; 200 CD-ROM reference disks; and 400 computer terminals for consulting catalogs, CD-ROMs, the Minitel, and the Internet. Anyone can use the library, and everything is free, except for the photocopy machines.

49 IRCAM (Institut de Recherche et de Coordination Acoustique/Musique) One of the world's most advanced computer music centers is located in an innovative building with a brick panel facade designed by **Renzo Piano**. Toiling away in the institute's underground reaches, leading modern composer Pierre Boulez's studio of composers and electronic engineers is creating the music of the future. The building is usually not open to visitors, but you can enter the ground-floor level for information about concerts by **L'Ensemble InterContemporain** and the public lectures that frequently take place here. ♦ By appointment only. 1 Pl Igor-Stravinsky (between Rue du Cloître-St-Marri and Pl Georges-Pompidou). 01.44.78.12.33; fax 01.44.78.15.40. Métros: Rambuteau, Hôtel de Ville

50 Fontaine de Stravinsky The fantastic and frivolous ballet of squirting animals, serpents, and mermaids in this lively fountain created by Niki de Saint-Phalle and Jean Tinguely makes this a great spot for an urban picnic. Several inexpensive eating places line the eastern side of the square overlooking the fountain, including a branch of the imaginative **Dame Tartine** (2 Rue Brisemiche, 01.42.77.32.22). ♦ Pl Igor-Stravinsky. Métros: Rambuteau, Hôtel de Ville

ESPACE VIT'HALLES

51 Espace Vit'Halles This popular health club, started in 1983 by French Olympic wrestler Christophe Andanson and his wife, Claudy, is one of the hottest underground (in the literal sense) singles spots in the district. Among the more than 1,000 members are **Pompidou Center** staffers flocking to aerobics classes and young **Bourse** financiers pumping iron as a respite from lusting after gold. The clean and affordable facilities include a sauna, tanning rooms, and bodybuilding equipment. Memberships are available for one day, one week, and longer. ♦ Daily. 48 Rue Rambuteau (at Rue Brantôme). 01.42.77.21.71. Métro: Rambuteau

52 Defender of Time Inspired by the Rathaus clock in Munich, the one-ton Jacques Monestier kinetic sculpture (1975) in oxidized brass sends a sword-brandishing warrior to do battle with a bird, crab, and dragon (representing the three elements: air, water, and earth). As every hour strikes, one of the beasts attacks, and at noon, 6PM, and 10PM, the *Defender of Time* is forced to take on all the creatures at once, always emerging victorious. A bit kitschy (as is this whole mini–shopping mall, the **Quartier de l'Horloge**), but young children love it. ♦ Rues Brantôme and Bernard-de-Clairvaux. Métro: Rambuteau

53 Ambassade d'Auvergne ★★$$ Adorned with flickering oil lamps, a roaring fire, and cured hams dangling from heavy wood beams, this rustic restaurant serves hearty Massif Central cuisine. Specialties include *potée au choux* (stew), *aligot* (potatoes, cheese, and cream), roast suckling pig, lentil cassoulet, and blood sausage with chestnuts. ♦ Daily lunch and dinner. Reservations recommended. 22 Rue du Grenier-St-Lazare (between Rues Beaubourg and St-Martin). 01.42.72.31.22. Métro: Rambuteau

54 Porte St-Denis This imposing Roman-style triumphal arch celebrates Louis XIV's victorious battles in Flanders and the Rhineland. **François Blondel** modeled the 24-

meter-high (79 feet) structure after the Arch of Titus in Rome; Charles Le Brun's allegorical sculptured adornments were inspired by the reliefs on Trajan's Column. South of the arch, Rue St-Denis has long been a prime stomping ground of *les femmes de la nuit* (women of the night) who were so remarkably photographed by Brassaï in the 1930s. ♦ Blvd St-Denis and Rue du Faubourg-St-Denis. Métro: Strasbourg–St-Denis

55 Porte St-Martin In 1674 **Pierre Bullet** constructed this smaller arch—only 17 meters (56 feet) high—after plans made by **François Blondel** for **Porte St-Denis.** These two triumphal arches, astride the most important routes to the north, were erected by the Sun King to announce the grandeur of the French capital to visitors, right at the time he was tearing down the city's medieval walls, which he felt were no longer needed because of his military might. ♦ Blvd St-Denis and Rue du Faubourg-St-Martin. Métro: Strasbourg–St-Denis

56 Rue du Vertbois The remains of the walls of the **St-Martin-des-Champs** priory on this street date from 1270. An inflammatory letter from Victor Hugo is said to have saved the wall from demolition. ♦ Métros: Temple, Arts et Métiers, Réaumur-Sébastopol

57 Musée National des Techniques (National Technical Museum) This extraordinary collection of 80,000 machines traces the evolution of technology from the 16th century onward. In an odd juxtaposition of religion and science, part of the museum is in the remains of the **St-Martin-des-Champs** priory, one of the finest naves to survive the Middle Ages. The museum underwent a complete renovation and was scheduled to reopen at press time. The project was slowed because workers came across important archaeological artifacts in the museum's chapel, many of them dating from before the 10th century. ♦ Admission. Call for hours and information. 292 Rue St-Martin (between Rues Réaumur and du Vertbois). 01.40.27.23.71, 01.40.27.22.20, 01.40.27.23.31. Métro: Réaumur-Sébastopol

---

In a restaurant, *un menu* means a prix-fixe meal. The term for the list of dishes available is *la carte.*

Sainte Geneviève (ca. 423-500), the patron saint of Paris was said to have holy powers from birth. The story goes that Geneviève's mother lost her eyesight when she hit the young girl. The little saint restored her mother's sight by bathing her eyes with water from a well in the Paris suburb of Nanterre. The well is revered for its healing powers to this day.

58 St-Nicolas-des-Champs Construction on this church began in the 12th century, and it has acquired distinguished features throughout the ages: a Flamboyant Gothic facade, a Renaissance doorway, and many 17th-, 18th-, and 19th-century paintings. ♦ 254 Rue St-Martin (at Rue Cunin-Gridaine). 01.42.72.92.54. Métro: Réaumur-Sébastopol

404

59 404 ★★$$ The small open kitchen here puts bowls of exotic spices, plates of delicate pastries, and simple cooking techniques on display, all of which infuse this North African restaurant with an artistic ambience and heavenly aromas. Tasting one of the *tajines* (succulent stews of meat delicately blended with fruit, vegetables, and spices, and served in ceramic pots) is pure bliss. Choose a bottle of Moroccan wine to go with your meal, lean back on the plump pillows, and observe the hip-looking Parisians at the tables around you—friends, no doubt, of the popular comedian Smaïn, who owns the place. (The restaurant was named after the Peugeot 404, which, as car buffs will know, was a very cool car in the 1960s.) ♦ Daily lunch and dinner; closed the last two weeks of August. 69 Rue des Gravilliers (between Rues Beaubourg and St-Martin). 01.42.74.57.81. Métro: Arts et Métiers

60 Le Tango To dance here cheek-to-cheek among Brylcreem dandies and perfumed widows is to enter a time warp that leads back to 1906, when the tango first hit Paris. A harmonious mixture of gays, lesbians, and heteros dance to calypsos, salsas, beguines—any beat but hip-hop—all night long. This club is both authentic and inexpensive. ♦ Cover. W-Sa 11PM-dawn. 13 Rue au Maire (between Rues des Vertus and Beaubourg). 01.42.72.17.78. Métro: Arts et Métiers

61 Galerie Daniel Templon Daniel Templon helped launch conceptual art, language art, and a good deal of the "Support Surface" movement in France. His gallery is modeled after those in New York's SoHo. Among the many artists he now represents are Ross Bleckner, Eric Fischl, Malcolm Morley, Philip Pearlstein, David Salle, and Julian Schnabel. (To gain entrance to the gallery, which does not front on the street, ring the bell and walk to the rear of the passageway; it's on the left). ♦ M-Sa; closed in August. 30 Rue Beaubourg (between Rues Rambuteau and Michel-Le-Comte). 01.42.72.14.10. Métro: Rambuteau

61 Musée de la Poupée (Doll Museum)
This unusual museum is home to a private collection of over 200 porcelain-headed French dolls dating from 1860 to 1960, amassed by father and son Guido and Samy Odin. Each of the small museum's seven rooms is dedicated to an important phase of French dolldom or to themed temporary expositions often featuring dolls from other countries or dolls in regional costumes. The museum offers lectures on the history of dolls as well as doll-making classes, and the gift shop carries a nice collection of stuffed animals, limited-edition porcelain dolls, and doll-related accessories. ♦ Admission. Museum: Tu-Su. Lectures: Th 5:30PM by reservation. Doll-making courses: M-Tu by reservation. Impasse Berthaud (east of Rue Beaubourg). 01.42.72.55.90. Métro: Rambuteau

62 Café de la Cité ★$ No wider than a bowling lane, this cafe/luncheonette has become one of the most popular pit stops in the area. Decorated with wooden fans and prints of old Breton sailing vessels (the owner comes from Brittany), it offers tasty plats du jour. The management boasts that you can order, eat, and head out the door in less than 30 minutes. ♦ Daily lunch and dinner. Reservations required for dinner. 22 Rue Rambuteau (between Rues du Temple and Beaubourg). 01.48.04.30.74. Métro: Rambuteau

63 Musée d'Art et d'Histoire du Judaïsme (Museum of Jewish Art and History)
Located in the splendid 17th-century **Hôtel de St-Aignan,** this spacious modern museum, which opened in December 1998, traces the history, cultural heritage, and traditions of Jewish communities in the Middle East, North Africa, and Europe from the Middle Ages to the early 20th century through artistic expression.

The museum's collection combines the holdings of the former **Museum of Jewish Art** in Montmartre and the *Strauss-Rothschild* collection from the **Musée National du Moyen Age** at the **Hôtel de Cluny,** as well as adding many new acquisitions from France and abroad. Among the noteworthy pieces in the permanent collection are medieval Jewish scriptures, tabernacles, silver ceremonial articles, gravestones, and sculptures; ritual objects and garments from North Africa; many old prints on the rituals and iconography of Judaism; more than 3,000 original documents relating to the Dreyfus Affair; paintings and sculptures by Soutine, Chagall, Modigliani, Lipchitz, and other Jewish modern artists who worked in France in the early 20th century; photographs on the Jewish immigrant community that lived in the Marais in the years before World War II; and an installation by Christian Boltanski evoking the history of the people who resided in the **Hôtel de St-Aignan** on the eve of the war, some of whom were deported to the death camps.

The museum also mounts temporary art and photography exhibits—often on contemporary Jewish themes—and presents films and theatrical and musical performances in the 180-seat auditorium. A research library, workshop for children, tearoom, and book and gift shop are also open to the public. ♦ Admission. M-F 11AM-6PM; Su. 71 Rue du Temple (between Rues Rambuteau and Michel-Le-Comte). 01.53.01.86.53. Métro: Rambuteau

64 The Studio ★★$ In a 17th-century cobblestone courtyard it shares with several dance studios, this Tex-Mex canteen throws the hottest Fourth of July party in Paris. Margaritas, copious servings of Tex-Mex standards, and a simpatico atmosphere make for good times year-round. A traditional North American brunch is served on the weekend. ♦ M dinner; Tu-F lunch and dinner; Sa-Su brunch and dinner. 41 Rue du Temple (between Rues St-Merri and Simon-Le-Franc). 01.42.74.10.38. Métro: Rambuteau

65 Vieux Marais $$ Decorated with Chinese carpets and floral wallpaper, this 30-room hotel gives guests a warm welcome. There's a tearoom but no restaurant. ♦ 8 Rue du Plâtre (between Rues des Archives and du Temple). 01.42.78.47.22; fax 01.42.78.34.32. Métro: Rambuteau

66 Lescene-Dura Since 1875 this sprawling wine lover's warehouse has been offering all manner of enological paraphernalia, from corkscrews to Champagne buckets. ♦ Tu-Sa; closed in August. 63 Rue de la Verrerie (between Rues du Temple and du Renard). 01.42.72.08.74. Métro: Hôtel de Ville

Marais

This district in eastern Paris has been known as the *marais* (marsh) since Roman times. It was a vast, oozy swamp on the northern branch of the Seine until the 12th century, when the marsh was drained, making it habitable for humans. Like New York's fashionable SoHo district, the Marais is now a mélange of ruin and restoration, past and present. The historically rich neighborhood possesses at least one Roman road (along Rues François-Miron and St-Antoine), and numerous twisting, huddled medieval streets.

Among those streets are three (**Rues des Rosiers, des Ecouffes,** and **Ferdinand-Duval**) that are the backbone of the celebrated Jewish quarter, formed in the 13th century when King Philippe Auguste "invited" the Jewish merchants living in front of **Notre-Dame** to move outside his new city wall.

Seven French kings resided in the Marais, starting with Charles V (1337-80). Henri II (1519-59) was the last; he died during a freak jousting accident when the shattered lance of Montgomery, the captain of his Scots Guards, pierced the visor of his helmet. Henri's wife, Catherine de Médicis, tried to ease her grief by having their royal **Maison des Tournelles** in the Marais demolished.

A half-century after the accident, Henri IV chose to construct the **Place Royale** on the leveled crown land in the Marais. Its name was changed in 1800 to **Place des Vosges** to honor the Vosges in eastern France, which was the first provincial department to pay its taxes after the Revolution. "It's the blow of Montgomery's lance," Victor Hugo later wrote, "that created the Place des Vosges."

The Marais and Place Royale (des Vosges) figured prominently in Henri IV's building boom in the 17th century, which also included Pont-Neuf, Place Dauphine, and Ile St-Louis. In the Marais, the king employed the leading architects of the day: **Louis Le Vau, François Mansart,** and **Jules Hardouin-Mansart.**

During this era, Mademoiselle de Scudéry, Molière, Racine, Madame de Lafayette, and Madame de Sévigné were exchanging witty party conversation in the great salons of the Marais that Molière parodied in his play *Les Précieuses Ridicules.* Within a century the former swamp had become the heart of intellectual Paris. In 1630 Cardinal Richelieu, a Marais resident, founded the **Académie Française** here, and years later a seven-year-old Mozart played his first Paris concert in the Marais. This area became an island of urban civility and sophistication, far removed from the wild boars and party boors of **Versailles.**

After the Revolution the elegant town houses were abandoned or carved into small factories and rooming houses. Squatters took over, and the Marais fell into a shocking state of ruin. Over the centuries, 29 of the grand *hôtels particuliers* were destroyed; nearly 100 remained, dilapidated and on the verge of collapse. In 1964 André Malraux, Minister of Culture under Charles de Gaulle, came to the rescue and designated the Marais the first historic preservation district in Paris. Within its boundaries are 1,500 architecturally important structures, making the Marais the largest historic district in France.

Many of the old buildings have been given new life, as you'll see when you visit the **Archives Nationales, Musée Carnavalet** (the city's historical museum), the famous Place des Vosges, and the **Musée Picasso.** The Marais quarter, once a juxtaposition of splendor and squalor, is almost all splendor now.

67 Rue des Archives For generations, the lower section of this street bore the name Rue où Dieu fut Bouilli (street where God was boiled) after the legend of the moneylender who stabbed a communion wafer with his knife, then threw it into a steaming pot, where to his astonishment it began to bleed. ♦ Métros: Hôtel de Ville, Rambuteau, Arts et Métiers

On Rue des Archives:

Musée de la Chasse et de la Nature (Museum of the Hunt) Housed in a portion of the **Hôtel de Guénégaud** (1654) and designed by **François Mansart,** this museum presents three floors full of hunting paraphernalia and related items, including crossbows, muskets, game trophies, whole stuffed animals, and paintings of hunting dogs and animals by the likes of Rubens and Brueghel. Among the most lavish paeans to the slaughter are the paintings of Desportes, the court artist employed by Louis XIV to portray the royal hunts at **Versailles.** ♦ Admission. M, W-Su. No. 60 (at Rue des Quatre-Fils). 01.42.72.86.43

68 Hôtel de Rohan In 1705 the son of François de Rohan, prince-bishop of Strasbourg, commissioned **Pierre-Alexis Delamair** to build a mansion opposite the **Hôtel Soubise,** where his parents lived. In the courtyard to the right, above the entrance to the former stables, is one of the masterpieces of 18th-century French sculpture: Robert Le Lorrain's superb relief-sculpture *The Watering of the Horses of the Sun.* The building sometimes houses temporary exhibitions. ♦ 87 Rue Vieille-du-Temple (between Rues des Francs-

Bourgeois and des Quatre-Fils). Métros: Rambuteau, St-Sébastien–Froissart

69 Archives Nationales/Musée de l'Histoire de France The letters of Joan of Arc and Voltaire, the wills of Louis XIV and Napoléon I, a papyrus signed by Merovingian King Dagobert (622-38), the Edict of Nantes, the Declaration of the Rights of Man, and 6 billion other documents are stored on 175 miles of shelves in this admirable 18th-century mansion, the former **Hôtel Soubise.** Even if you have no interest in French history, the museum's fortified turrets, colonnaded courtyard (72 Corinthian columns in all), and the riot of Rococo in the **Oval Salon** make a visit worthwhile. Designed by **Pierre-Alexis Delamair** for François de Rohan, the prince of Soubise, the mansion has an ornate interior (1739) that was engineered by **Germain Boffrand,** a pupil of **François Mansart.** Boffrand hired the best artists of the day, among them François Boucher and Charles Natoire, to decorate the *hôtel.* The archives, housed in the **Hôtel Soubise** since 1808, expanded into the nearby **Hôtel de Rohan** in 1927. ◆ Admission. M-Sa. 60 Rue des Francs-Bourgeois (at Rue des Archives). 01.40.27.60.00. Métro: Rambuteau

70 Picard Surgelés Who said the French are all food snobs? The brave new world of French frozen food is displayed in this chilly, sterile mart (one of a chain of stores in Paris) that sells microwave ovens and anything you might want to defrost in them. Go inside and watch Parisians wheel their shopping carts around yellow, blue, and red freezers looking for tonight's TV dinner, and ask yourself what Julia Child would say. ◆ Daily. 48 Rue des Francs-Bourgeois (between Rues Vieille-du-Temple and des Archives). 01.42.72.17.83. Métro: Rambuteau

71 Crédit Municipal de Paris Paris's first municipal pawnshop is still a place for hocking ("putting it on the nail," as the French say). Auctions, especially for jewelry, are frequent and well attended; check the notices posted outside. ◆ M-Th; F 8:30AM-3:45PM. 55 Rue des Francs-Bourgeois (between Rues Vieille-du-Temple and des Archives). 01.44.61.64.00. Métro: Rambuteau

Paris Seen from Down Below

Strange as it may seem, some of the most memorable sights in the City of Light are to be found in the dark, deep in the ground where everything is so . . . *mystérieux:*

Archaeological Crypt of Notre-Dame Gallo-Roman and medieval ruins unearthed beneath the square in front of the cathedral have been imaginatively transformed into an archaeological museum. It includes sections of a late-Roman rampart, medieval cellars, and the foundations of the Enfants-Trouvés orphanage.

Canal St-Denis The barge cruise of **Paris Canal** (for more information, see "Tours" in the Orientation chapter) starts at the **Quai d'Orsay** on the Seine near the **Esplanade des Invalides,** enters the **Canal St-Martin** at the **Bastille** pleasure-boat port, and ends (or begins, if you prefer to take it in the opposite direction) at **Parc de La Villette.** The most mysterious part of the canal is where it goes underground for a mile between the **Bastille** and **Rue du Faubourg-du-Temple.** Shafts of light from the tunnel's intermittent skylights play on the water and create strange, haunting colors not seen anywhere else.

Catacombs In the late 18th century, millions of skeletons were removed from the ancient **Cemetery of the Innocents** at **Les Halles** and other Paris cemeteries. They were deposited here in the abandoned quarries of **Montrouge,** where the skulls and bones were piled in tidy but often gruesome arrangements. There's a one-hour tour.

Donjon of the Ancient Louvre No visitor to the **Louvre** should miss the massive stone foundation walls of the medieval fortress that the Louvre was before it became a Renaissance palace. They were unearthed in the 1980s during excavations for the Grand Louvre project and are now displayed, dramatically lit, in the underground level of the **Sully Wing,** along with thousands of ancient objects found during the digs.

Les Egouts de Paris The sewers of Paris is one of the city's biggest tourist attractions. A descent to the remarkable 1,305-mile network of vaulted canals laid out by 19th-century urban redevelopment czar Baron Haussmann will show you why. There's a one-hour tour.

71 Le Dôme du Marais ★$$ Covered by a large glass rotunda, sumptuously adorned with scarlet walls and bronze statues, this trading house-turned-restaurant features dinner concerts ranging from opera to gospel on Thursday nights. Owner-chef Pierre Lecoutre, formerly of the fine L'Atlantide restaurant in Nantes, took over this romantic spot at the end of 1998 and introduced some imaginative dishes. *Dorade royale au poivre de champignons* (red mullet cooked with mushroom pepper), *aiguillettes de canard laqué à l'orange et aux épices* (sliced duck fillet glazed with orange and served with cardamom turnips), and pheasant with endives, are a few examples. ♦ M, Sa dinner; Tu-F lunch and dinner; closed in August. Reservations recommended. 53 *bis* Rue des Francs-Bourgeois (between Rues Vieille-du-Temple and des Archives). 01.42.74.54.17. Métro: Rambuteau

72 Hôtel des Ambassadeurs de Hollande When this Baroque mansion (built in 1660) was named, there were no Dutch ambassadors to France, and none has ever lived here. (The building did, however, belong to the chaplain of the Dutch Embassy from 1720 to 1727). Subsequently the *hôtel* was rebuilt by Pierre Cottard; its most famous resident was Beaumarchais, author of *The Marriage of Figaro* and *The Barber of Seville*. The great wooden doors are embellished by what look like howling Medusas or perhaps a pair of baritones warming up. ♦ 47 Rue Vieille-du-Temple (between Rues Ste-Croix-de-la-Bretonnerie and des Blancs-Manteaux). Métro: St-Paul

73 Mariage Frères ★★★$$ The ritual of tea becomes an art at this handsome tea boutique and *salon de thé*. The shop sells 450 varieties of tea stored in smart black canisters lining the walls, along with teapots, sugars, spices, tea cakes, and jams. In the dining room, tea is served with a selection of scones, muffins, and pastries, as well as a superb brunch and lunch. ♦ Daily brunch, lunch, and afternoon tea. 30-32 Rue du Bourg-Tibourg (between Rues du Roi-de-Sicile and Ste-Croix-de-la-Bretonnerie). 01.42.72.28.11. Métro: Hôtel de Ville. Also at: 13 Rue des Grands-Augustins (at Rue de Savoie). 01.40.51.82.50. Métro: St-Michel

74 Hôtel Caron de Beaumarchais $$ Behind the brilliant blue facade of this superbly located hotel is a gem of a hostelry radiating 18th-century elegance and charm. Father and son hosts Etienne and Alain Bigeard are true gentlemen who receive guests with a natural warmth and enthusiasm. The interior is simply and tastefully decorated by Alain: The stone *cheminée* in the lobby boasts a crackling fire in the winter; the 19 guest rooms feature exposed beams, Louis XV–style fabrics, and hand-painted tile in the bathrooms; and the walls are hung with memorabilia from the comedies of playwright Pierre-Augustin Caron de Beaumarchais, the hotel's namesake, who, in 1778, wrote The *Marriage of Figaro* down the street at 47 Rue Vieille-du-Temple. Some rooms on the fifth and sixth floors have balconies looking out over the rooftops of the Marais. A continental breakfast with fresh croissants is served until noon, an unusual tradition that's appreciated by those guests who want to sleep in after taking advantage of the late-night spots in neighboring Les Halles and Bastille. There's no restaurant. ♦ 12 Rue Vieille-du-Temple (between Rues de Rivoli and du Roi-de-Sicile). 01.42.72.34.12; fax 01.42.72.34.63. Métro: St-Paul

75 Au Petit Fer à Cheval ★★$ Named after its 1903 marble-topped *fer à cheval* (horseshoe) bar, this neighborhood cafe offers lunchtime plats du jour in its back room, where one of the booths is an old wooden métro seat. ♦ Daily breakfast, lunch, and dinner until 2AM. 30 Rue Vieille-du-Temple (between Rues du Roi-de-Sicile and des Rosiers). 01.42.72.47.47. Métro: St-Paul

76 Le Colimaçon ★★$$ A pretty stone facade, built in 1732 by **Louis Le Tellier,** graces this popular restaurant. Inside, guests dine in a romantic setting of fresh floral arrangements, candlelight, and superb service. Such specialties as foie gras and *magret de canard landais aux fruits de saison* (duck's breast with seasonal fruit) are popular favorites. There's also a good wine list. ♦ M-Th dinner; F-Su lunch and dinner.

Reservations required. 44 Rue Vieille-du-Temple (between Rues des Rosiers and des Francs-Bourgeois). 01.48.87.12.01. Métro: St-Paul

77 Rue des Rosiers *Rosiers* means rosebushes and refers to the roses that bloomed nearby within the old medieval city wall, but the fragrances wafting along this narrow, crooked street today are anything but floral. Scents of hot pastrami, steaming borscht, chopped chicken livers, and fresh matzos emanate from the kosher butcher shops, delicatessens, and bakeries that line this street, the *Platzel* (little square) of the Jewish quarter since the Middle Ages. The adjoining Rue des Ecouffes takes its name from the Lombardian pawnbrokers who were derided as *écouffes,* French for kite, a rapacious bird. A terribly haunting reminder of the district's history was a plaque that used to hang outside an elementary school on the street. It read: "165 Jewish children from this school, deported to Germany during World War II, were exterminated in Nazi camps. Never forget." Down this street the Nazis and Vichy French marched and dragged away 75,000 Jews to concentration camps. ◆ Métro: St-Paul

77 Finkelsztajn A Jewish bakery has operated at this address since 1851, and today Sacha Finkelsztajn carries on the tradition, producing the richest cheesecake this side of Manhattan's Second Avenue. The affable baker offers newcomers a free taste of her Polish herring, chicken liver, and eggplant puree. ◆ W-Su; closed one week in winter and July to mid-August. 27 Rue des Rosiers (between Rues des Ecouffes and Vieille-du-Temple). 01.42.72.78.91. Métro: St-Paul

78 Rue des Francs-Bourgeois Originally called Rue des Poulies (Street of Spools) after a local community of weavers, this thoroughfare became known as the Street of the Free Citizens in the 14th century, when the local parish built an almshouse (on the site of 34-36 Rue des Francs-Bourgeois) for citizens so poor they were *francs* (free) of any obligation to the state tax jackals. Today affluent shoppers flock to the chic and unusual shops that line the street, especially on Sunday, when most shops in Paris are closed. ◆ Métros: Rambuteau, St-Paul, Chemin Vert

78 The Filofax Centre Here you'll find everything to gratify your Filofax fetish. The famous pocket-size, three-ring English notebooks come in myriad styles, from black leather to rubber, and with notepaper of every hue. Also in stock are sheaves of maps, calendars, and metric conversion charts to store in your portable file cabinet as well as a beautiful collection of handmade sterling silver pens. ◆ M-Sa. 32 Rue des Francs-Bourgeois (between Rues Elzévir and Vieille-du-Temple). 01.42.78.67.87. Métro: St-Paul

79 A l'Image du Grenier sur l'Eau Brothers Yves and Sylvain Di Maria have spent the last two decades assembling this remarkable collection of more than a million vintage postcards of locales from Avignon to Zaire, each one for sale. This shop, with its original tiled floors, also features French publicity photos from the 1950s and lithographs from the Art Nouveau period. ◆ M-Sa; Su 2-7PM. 45 Rue des Francs-Bourgeois (between Rues Pavée and Hospitalières-St-Gervais). 01.42.71.02.31. Métro: St-Paul

80 Galerie Yvon Lambert Works by On Kawara, Lewitt, Twombly, Schnabel, Nan Goldin, and Boltanski are showcased here. ◆ Tu-Sa. 108 Rue Vieille-du-Temple (between Rues des Coutures-St-Gervais and de Poitou). 01.42.71.09.33. Métro: St-Sébastien–Froissart

81 Musée Picasso In the first month after it opened on 23 September 1985, this museum received 80,000 visitors. "Give me a museum and I'll fill it up," said Pablo Picasso, considered one of the 20th century's most important and prolific painters. His wish was granted posthumously here in the **Hôtel Salé,** a 17th-century building that undoubtedly would have pleased the artist, who epitomized outlaw Modernism yet preferred old houses. Today the mansion enshrines the artist's collection of his own works, the largest assembly of Picassos in the world: 203 paintings, 158 sculptures, 16 collages, 29 relief paintings, 88 ceramics, 30 sketchbooks, more than 1,500 drawings, and numerous prints, including the *Vollard Suite,* his Neo-Classical etchings created in the 1920s. The museum also houses Picasso's personal art collection, including works by Matisse, Renoir, Cézanne, Braque, Balthus, and Le Douanier Rousseau.

In December 1912, at the age of 31, Picasso began to hoard his own work. He wrote his dealer, Daniel Henry Kahnweiler, that he would keep five paintings a year, as well as his self-portraits, family portraits, and most of his sculpture. For 70 years Picasso also made a habit of holding onto the works he painted during the week of his birthday, 25 October.

When Picasso died on 8 April 1973 with no will, France's tax collectors were quick to pounce on his estate. In lieu of $65 million in inheritance taxes, Picasso's heirs donated a quarter of his collection to the state. Dominique Bozo (former chief curator of the **Musée National d'Art Moderne** at the **Centre Georges Pompidou**) and a team of Picasso experts then carved up the artist's pie for France. Ironically, as late as 1945, there were only three Picassos in public collections in France, a handful far outnumbered by the many in the possession of the Museum of Modern Art in New York.

The **Hôtel Salé** has but a few of Picasso's masterpieces, *Still Life with Caned Chair*, *Two Women Running on Beach*, and the Neo-Classical *Pipes of Pan* among them. However, the works here are exhibited chronologically, and the collection affords an extraordinary odyssey through the artist's growth and psyche. Furthermore, revealing Picasso memorabilia are sprinkled throughout the museum: photos of Picasso at bullfights, posing on the beach with a fig leaf, hoisting a bull's skull at the beach of Golfe-Juan, playing with his children, and consorting with such friends as Jean Cocteau and Max Jacob. Also throughout the museum are portraits of the women in Picasso's life: Olga Kokhlova, the Russian dancer; Marie-Thérèse Walter, the 17-year-old earth mother; Dora Maar, the intellectual; Françoise Gilot, the painter; and his widow, Jacqueline.

You could spend the entire day wandering through the museum, but if it's 11:30AM and you've got a 1PM lunch date, it is best to concentrate on the second-floor collection, then stroll among the sculptures in the basement on your way out. Here are a few highlights: **Room 1** brings you face-to-face with one of Picasso's Blue Period masterpieces, the wintry 1901 *Self-Portrait at Age 20*, which shows the gaunt-looking artist clothed in an overcoat to ward off the drafts that undoubtedly plagued his bohemian existence. The influences of Toulouse-Lautrec and van Gogh are particularly evident in the Expressionist deathbed portrait of the poet Casagemas. **Rooms 2** and **3** contain sketches and drawings inspired by Cézanne's geometrical style and by the primitive sculpture from Africa and New Caledonia that so fascinated Picasso and ultimately led to the creation of *Les Demoiselles d'Avignon*. **Room 4**, especially *Still Life with Caned Chair*, reflects Picasso's years of Cubist inquiry (1909-17) with Georges Braque. The next several rooms feature his paper collages and three-dimensional paintings made of cigar-box wood, newspapers, and metal shards. **Room 5** contains the best of the 60 works in Picasso's personal art collection: masterpieces by Matisse, Braque, Rousseau,

and Cézanne. Of the latter, Picasso told the photographer Brassai in 1943: "He's my one and only master." The museum crescendos in **Room 6** with *La Lecture de la Lettre* and *The Pipes of Pan* from his classical period. A minuscule side room (**6B**) is devoted entirely to Picasso's theater and costume designs, created in collaboration with Cocteau, Massine, Stravinsky, and Diaghilev. Near the end of his life, Picasso's art became childlike and cartoonish. The last painting in the collection, dated 14 April 1972, is called *Young Painter*, a sketchy image of a smiling dauber. In his final years the artist confessed, "It has taken all my life to learn how to paint like a child again." Picasso's playfulness is perhaps most evident in his sculpture, which is fashioned from an amusing assortment of odds and ends. En route to the exit, descend into the museum's basement to find his sculpture collection, with originals of his celebrated monkey, goat, and skipping girl.

The **Hôtel Salé** was built from 1655 to 1659 by architect **Jean Bouillier** for Pierre Aubert de Fontenay, a man who got rich collecting taxes on salt for the king. With the fall of Nicolas Fouquet (1615-80), Louis XIV's greedy finance minister, Aubert lost his job, his house, and finally, in 1668, his life. Later the **Hôtel Salé** was leased to the embassy of the Venetian Republic and the naval minister of Louis XVI. After the Revolution, in 1793, it became a boys' school (Balzac studied here), a science laboratory, and, from 1887 to 1964, an exhibition hall for a bronze foundry. After Picasso's death, Minister of Culture Michel Guy secured a 99-year lease on the building from the City of Paris, and the government spent some 65 million francs on its restoration. **Roland Simounet**, winner of the 1977 Grand Prix for Architecture, was selected to design the museum. Simounet's plan preserved the architectural integrity of the building while doubling its interior space from 9,900 to 19,800 square feet. A design detail lost on most visitors: The museum's extraordinary benches, tables, and light fixtures were fashioned by the late Diego Giacometti, brother of artist Alberto.
◆ Admission. M, W-Su. 5 Rue de Thorigny (at Rue des Coutures-St-Gervais). 01.42.71.25.21. Métro: St-Sébastien–Froissart

---

"The French will only be united under the threat of danger. No one can simply bring together a country that has over 265 kinds of cheese."

Charles de Gaulle

Restaurants/Clubs: Red   **Hotels:** Blue
Shops/ 🍃 **Outdoors:** Green   **Sights/Culture:** Black

Within the Musée Picasso:

Museum Restaurant ★$ Salads, quiche, soups, grilled salmon, and fruit tarts are served in this small, attractive tea salon. ♦ M, W-Su breakfast, lunch, and afternoon tea. 01.42.71.25.21

82 Musée de la Serrure (Lock Museum)/Bricard Showrooms Roman door knockers, medieval chastity belts, and the key of the now-destroyed **Cimetière des Innocents** may be seen in the changing exhibits of this small, quirky museum, established by the time-honored locksmithing company Bricard and housed in the **Hôtel Libéral Bruant.** (Architect **Bruant** built this mansion as his residence, and it is considered his most important work after the **Hôtel des Invalides** and the **Salpêtrière** chapel.) The museum has been relegated to the building's vaulted cellar while handmade replicas of some of the museum pieces, such as the lock to Marie Antoinette's **Versailles** apartments, are sold in the **Bricard Showrooms.** Here you can also examine the rich detailing and historical styles of other Bricard products. ♦ Admission. Museum: Tu-Th 10AM-2PM, 4-5PM. Showroom: M-F 8:30AM-12:30PM, 1:30-5:30PM. 1 Rue de la Perle (at Pl de Thorigny). Museum 01.42.77.79.62, showroom 01.42.77.71.68. Métros: Chemin Vert, St-Sébastien–Froissart, St-Paul

83 Musée Cognacq-Jay This marvelously complete collection of 18th-century art was acquired by the husband-and-wife team of Louise Jay and Ernest Cognacq, who created **La Samaritaine** department stores and boasted of never having set foot in the **Louvre.** The collection was moved to the 5-story, 16th-century **Hôtel Donon,** and the works of Boucher, Tiepolo, Watteau, Fragonard, Greuze, La Tour, Rembrandt, Gainsborough, and Reynolds are as well displayed here as they were in their old home on Boulevard des Capucines. There's also a remarkable set of perfume cases and snuffboxes as well as Meissen porcelain statuettes. ♦ Admission. Tu-Su. 8 Rue Elzévir (between Rues des Francs-Bourgeois and du Parc-Royal). 01.40.27.07.21. Métro: St-Paul

84 Luthier Owner M. Brué buys, sells, makes, and restores violins, violas, bows, and old instruments at these quarters in the **Hôtel de Savourny.** ♦ W-Sa. 4 Rue Elzévir (between Rues des Francs-Bourgeois and du Parc-Royal). 01.42.77.68.42. Métro: St-Paul

85 Gallery Maison Mansart The ground floor of the house **François Mansart** built for himself (and inhabited until his death in 1666) now houses Alain Thiollier's stark, high-ceilinged gallery, which exhibits contemporary works by an international group of artists every month except August. On the second floor is a chapel (with an altar inscribed to "Humanism") built by a Brazilian follower of French positivist Auguste Comte. The chapel is not open to the public, but inquire about the occasional Baroque music concerts that are held here. ♦ Tu-Sa 3-7PM; closed in August. 5 Rue Payenne (between Rues des Francs-Bourgeois and du Parc-Royal). 01.48.87.41.03. Métro: St-Paul

86 Marais Plus Formerly a bookstore and tea salon, this jumble is now a *boutique en mouvement,* with an ever-changing stock of postcards, inflatable globes, dolls, stuffed animals, Christmas decorations, and handmade ceramic tea services. The tearoom serves delicious tarts, salads, and desserts, plus brunch on Sunday. ♦ Daily. 20 Rue des Francs-Bourgeois (at Rue Payenne). 01.48.87.01.40. Métro: St-Paul

87 Rue Pavée The construction of one of the city's first *pavée* (paved) streets was a pioneer achievement in the 14th century, when the city's muddy roads also served as open sewers and pigsties. ♦ Métro: St-Paul

87 Bibliothèque Historique de la Ville de Paris (Historical Library of the City of Paris) Designed in 1611 by **Baptiste du Cerceau,** the **Hôtel Lamoignon** (pictured on page 147) has housed the **Bibliothèque Historique de la Ville de Paris** since 1969 and is a mecca for French historians. The mansion was originally the property of Diane de France, the illegitimate daughter of Henri II. As the story goes, young Henri, while traveling in Italy, was in hot pursuit of the Duchess of Angoulême. When she refused to leave her house, he burned it down and had her kidnapped and taken to France. Out of their tumultuous union, Diane was born. At age 7, she was legally adopted by the king and given all the rights of nobility, among them this mansion, where she lived until her death at age 82.

Adorned with a colossal order of Italianate pilasters, this was the city's first private mansion. The low triangular pediment is embellished by a stag with antlers, a tribute to Diana, goddess of the hunt. On a rainy day, the library is one of the best places in Paris to read about Paris. Once in the courtyard, bear right, up the steps to the **Reading Room** door. If you manage to convince the guard you are a visiting scholar, he will give you a reader's card. Take a seat at one of the long wooden tables and gaze up at the gilded beams, one of which is ornamented with a painting of Diana and the hunt. The rest of the library is off-limits to the public. ♦ M-Sa; closed holidays and the first two weeks of August. 24 Rue Pavée (at Rue Malher). 01.44.59.29.40. Métro: St-Paul

88 Association Culturelle Israélite Agoudas Hakehilos The sinuous facade of the only synagogue (1913) designed by **Hector Guimard,** the Art Nouveau architect best known for his sculptural métro entrances, suggests an open book, perhaps the Torah. The building is closed to the public except during Saturday services. ♦ 10 Rue Pavée (between Rues du Roi-de-Sicile and des Rosiers). 01.48.87.21.54, 01.48.87.26.29. Métro: St-Paul

89 Le Loir dans la Théière ★★$ With its flea-market furniture, sprung-out sofas, wooden tables, and raffish air, this comfortable tea salon could be in Seattle or Berkeley. The name, "Dormouse in the Teapot," recalls *Alice's Adventures in Wonderland,* as does the mural of other characters from the Lewis Carroll fantasy. Yet the light, tasty salads and fine homemade cakes and tarts are very real. ♦ M-F lunch and afternoon tea; Sa-Su brunch and afternoon tea. No credit cards accepted. 3 Rue des Rosiers (between Rues Pavée and Ferdinand-Duval). 01.42.72.90.61. Métro: St-Paul

90 Jo Goldenberg ★★$$ The sweet aroma of spiced meat, the clatter of dishes, and, particularly on Sunday afternoon, the babble of strong, animated voices fill this Jewish delicatessen/restaurant. Try the *foie haché* (chopped liver), *poisson farci* (gefilte fish), Cracovian sausages, and strudel, washed down with a cold Pilsen. This famous spot was the site of a tragedy on 9 August 1982, when masked gunmen killed six customers. The PLO took credit, and the gunmen were never caught. ♦ Daily breakfast, lunch, and dinner; closed on Yom Kippur. Reservations recommended. 7 Rue des Rosiers (at Rue Ferdinand-Duval). 01.48.87.20.16, 01.48.87.70.39. Métro: St-Paul

91 L'As du Fallafel "The Falafel Ace" offers kosher North African, Israeli, and Middle Eastern specialties to go—hummus, falafel sandwiches, and shawarma. ♦ M-F, Su. 34 Rue des Rosiers (between Rues Pavée and des Hospitalières-St-Gervais). 01.48.87.63.60. Métro: St-Paul

92 La Tartine ★★$ This is the oldest wine bar in Paris, owned since 1940 by the family of M. Bouscarel, who selects the stock of more than 60 wines himself. He buys directly from Burgundy, Bordeaux, Rhône, and Loire Valley producers, keeping the prices down and the quality up. The cafe is always filled with a vibrant mix of ages and personalities, happily sipping wine and munching on *tartines,* simple sandwiches on *pain Poilâne* (sourdough bread) filled with pâté, cheese, ham, or sausage. ♦ M, Th-Su breakfast, lunch, and dinner; Tu-W lunch and dinner. No credit cards accepted. 24 Rue de Rivoli (between Rues Ferdinand-Duval and des Ecouffes). 01.42.72.76.85. Métro: St-Paul

Bibliothèque Historique de la Ville de Paris

MICHAEL STORRINGS

Hôtel et
Musée
Carnavalet

MICHAEL STORRINGS

93 Maison Suba A stone's throw from the Place des Vosges you will find a shop full of delicious red pepper conserves and oak-smoked Hungarian sausages. Don't pass up the Tokay wine, so loved by King George VI, the father of Queen Elizabeth II, that he ordered it in industrial quantities. ♦ Tu-Sa; closed in August. 11 Rue de Sévigné (between Rues de Rivoli and des Francs-Bourgeois). 01.48.87.46.06. Métro: St-Paul

94 Hôtel et Musée Carnavalet The laughing carnival mask sculpted in stone above the Rue des Francs-Bourgeois gate of this splendid mansion (illustrated above) is a misleading visual pun: This 16th-century building does not conceal a midway of clowns or a family of dancing bears. A truer clue to the building's contents is found in the ship (the symbol of Paris) on the gate. In 1880, the **Hôtel Carnavalet** was put into service as the **Musée Historique de la Ville de Paris** (Historical Museum of the City of Paris), and today it vividly displays four centuries (1500-1900) of Parisian life. The building's original 1540 design is attributed to **Pierre Lescot,** who was then the architect of the **Louvre.** The *hôtel* (mansion) was spruced up in 1655 by **François Mansart,** the architect for whom the mansard roof is named. The structure's name evolved from that of an early owner, the widow of the Breton Sire de Kernevency, whose surname Parisians constantly mispronounced and permanently corrupted to its present form.

The museum has something for everyone, even the most fidgety youngster. On the ground floor (see diagram at right) is an entire roomful of old metal shop signs and 18th-century billboards dating from an age of mass illiteracy. The baker advertised himself with a golden sheaf of wheat, the butcher with a suckling pig, and the locksmith with an ornate iron key. There is also a lively exhibit on the French Revolution; the royal family's itemized laundry bill; the young dauphin's penmanship book; the rope ladder used by a political prisoner to escape from the Bastille; a model of the guillotine; a pair of drums banged by the Revolutionaries; a *Who's Who* of the Revolution in portraits (from crazed Marat to stern Robespierre); and the penknife Napoléon Bonaparte used during the Egyptian campaign. The ground floor also houses temporary exhibits on topics related to Paris past and present.

On the second floor are exhibitions of fashionable furnishings from the reigns of the last Bourbon kings (Louis XIV, Louis XV, and Louis XVI), salon murals by Jean-Honoré Fragonard and François Boucher, and the apartments of Madame de Sévigné (1626-96). This "Grande Dame of the Marais" (who was born, baptized, and married in the district) lived at the **Hôtel Carnavalet** for the last 19 years of her life. Here she entertained the greatest thinkers of the day and, in her famous *Lettres,* inscribed her witty, incisive observations on the court of Louis XIV. Her association with the royals was not forgotten by well-read Revolutionary hotheads, who a century later exhumed her remains, beheaded the corpse, and triumphantly paraded through Paris with her skull. On your way out, catch Louis XIV, looking rather silly decked out as a Roman general with a wig (the Antoine Coysevox courtyard statue was brought here from the **Hôtel de Ville**). ♦ Admission. Tu-Su. 23 Rue de Sévigné (between Rues des Francs-Bourgeois and du Parc-Royal). 01.42.72.21.13. Métros: St-Paul, Chemin Vert

Ground Floor

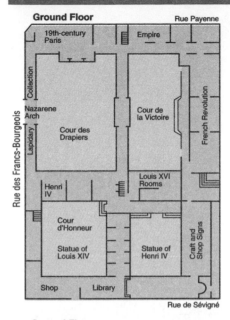

Rue Payenne

Rue des Francs-Bourgeois

- 19th-century Paris
- Empire
- Collection
- Nazarene Arch
- Lapidary
- Cour des Drapiers
- Cour de la Victoire
- French Revolution
- Henri IV
- Louis XVI Rooms
- Cour d'Honneur
- Craft and Shop Signs
- Statue of Louis XIV
- Statue of Henri IV
- Shop
- Library

Rue de Sévigné

Second Floor

- Paris Under Louis XVI
- Exhibitions
- Temporary
- 17th- and 18th-century Government of Paris
- Louis XIV and Regency Furniture
- Louis XV Rooms
- 18th-century Paris

95 Les Bourgeoises ★★$$ Dining here on the baked St. Marcellin cheese on toast, fresh ravioli stuffed with herbed cheese, lamb stew with coriander and ginger, or such Indian specialties as chicken tandoori is like dining in the living room of owner Martine Robin's grandmother. In fact, the oil paintings, chairs, and tables all come from Robin's grandparents' antiques shop. The homemade raspberry liqueur aging in a jar by the front window is, unfortunately, purely decorative. ◆ M-Sa dinner; Tu, Th-Sa lunch and dinner; Su afternoon tea. Reservations recommended. 12 Rue des Francs-Bourgeois (between Rues de Turenne and de Sévigné). 01.42.72.48.30. Métros: St-Paul, Chemin Vert

96 Jean-Pierre De Castro Such antique silver and silver-plated articles as Champagne buckets, candelabras, and sugar tongs are the specialties of this busy boutique. Forks and spoons are displayed by the basketful and sold by the kilogram. ◆ M 2PM-7PM; Tu-Su. 17 Rue des Francs-Bourgeois (between Rues de Turenne and de Sévigné). 01.42.72.04.00. Métros: St-Paul, Chemin Vert

97 L'Osteria ★★$$ Friendly service and deliciously prepared Italian fare are the reasons that so many Parisians make repeated stops here. Fresh pasta dishes are the most popular menu choices: Try *tagliolini* (wide noodles) with broccoli and Parma ham, *gnocchi di patate al gorgonzola,* or seafood spaghetti; the osso buco is also highly recommended. ◆ M-F lunch and dinner; closed in August. 10 Rue de Sévigné (between Rues St-Antoine and de Jarente). 01.42.71.37.08. Métro St-Paul

98 Auberge de Jarente ★★$ This warm, rustic restaurant serves such Basque specialties as *pipérade* (an omelet with tomatoes and peppers) and paella at modest prices. ◆ Tu-Sa lunch and dinner; closed two weeks in August and at Christmas. Reservations recommended. 7 Rue de Jarente (between Rues de Turenne and de Sévigné). 01.42.77.49.35. Métro: St-Paul

98 Bar de Jarente ★$ Whether you come for coffee and a croissant in the morning or an aperitif before hitting one of the neighboring restaurants, do as the locals do and let the energetic and feisty Mme. Renée take care of you. You will see why her hospitality is known throughout the *quartier* (area). ◆ M-Sa breakfast, lunch, and snacks; closed in August. 5 Rue de Jarente (between Rues de Turenne and de Sévigné). 01.48.87.60.93. Métro: St-Paul

98 Grand Hôtel Jeanne d'Arc $$ Its grandiose name will bring a smile when you see this little hotel in the heart of the Marais. *Mignon* would be more like it. Here everything is cozy and quaint, from the small antiques-furnished lobby and breakfast room to the 36 guest rooms: all neat, comfortable, and charming, but rather petite. But then this is an outstanding value for the price. Many North Americans like to stay here. The staff is helpful and well informed. There's no restaurant. ◆ 3 Rue de Jarente (between Rues de Turenne and de Sévigné). 01.48.87.62.11; fax 01.48.87.37.31; www.hoteljeannedarc.com. Métro: St-Paul

99 Place des Vosges The oldest and perhaps most beautiful square in Paris, this symmetrical ensemble of 36 matching pavilions with red and gold brick and stone facades, steep slate roofs, and dormer windows was designed in 1612 by **Clément Métezeau.** This marked the first time in Paris that an arcade was used to link houses, and balconies were employed for more than decorative purposes.

The original function of the square, commissioned by Henri IV, was to house a silk factory and its workers. The goal was to provide Marie de Médicis, his estranged queen, with lingerie cheaper than what could be imported from Genoa. Despite Henri's good intentions, his silk workers' housing project was gentrified before the last brick was laid. Into the apartments with 16-foot-high ceilings, red marble fireplaces, and parquet floors moved Richelieu, Corneille, Molière, and a covey of courtiers, cavaliers, ministers, and marquises.

It remained a high-class neighborhood until the summer of 1686, when Louis XIV moved to **Versailles** and the French aristocracy followed. In the early 18th century the Marais continued to decline and eventually became the city's industrial East End. Heavy machinery was bolted to the elegant floors of the great spaces, and magnificent salons were subdivided into minuscule apartments. The neighborhood was not pulled out of its nosedive until the early 1960s, when Minister of Culture André Malraux had the Place des Vosges and the Marais declared a historic district. Nowadays, the Place des Vosges is frequented by knitting grandmothers, toddlers digging in the dirt, and perhaps a group of North African immigrants enjoying an impromptu soccer game beside an equestrian statue of a smirking Louis XIII. **Numbers 18** and **23** have two of the best portals on the square. Also, don't miss the door knockers at **Nos. 4** and **17.** ♦ Between Rues de Birague and de Béarn. Métros: Bastille, St-Paul

100 Issey Miyake Something of an art gallery for clothes, this large boutique shows the latest looks from the Japanese master. Many of these pieces are made in limited editions, while his **Pleats Please** boutique (201 Blvd St-Germain, between Rue St-Guillaume and Blvd Raspail, 01.45.48.10.44) sells Miyake's regular clothing lines. Like the other newer structures on the square, this building is a masterpiece of trompe l'oeil. The facade is made of plaster on wood framing, and you have to get pretty close to see that the bricks are painted on. ♦ M-Sa; closed two weeks in August. 3 Pl des Vosges (between Rues de Birague and des Francs-Bourgeois). 01.48.87.01.86. Métros: St-Paul, Bastille

100 Hôtel de Coulanges The Marquise de Sévigné, whose correspondence with her daughter in Provence became one of the most famous series of letters in French literature, was born here on 6 February 1626. It's still a private residence. ♦ 1 Pl des Vosges (at Rue de Birague). Métros: St-Paul, Bastille

101 Coconnas ★$$ Boasting a Louis XIII dining room and a sidewalk terrace overlooking the mansions and garden of the Place des Vosges, this casual restaurant (run by Claude Terrail of **La Tour d'Argent**) has built its reputation on serving Good King Henri's *poule-au-pot* (commemorating Henri IV's famous political promise of a chicken in every pot) and *soufflé Grande Marnier*. North American tourists and expatriates predominate. ♦ Tu-Su lunch and dinner; closed mid-December to mid-January. Reservations recommended. 2 *bis* Pl des Vosges (between Rues de Birague and du Pas-de-la-Mule). 01.42.78.58.16. Métros: Bastille, St-Paul

101 Musée Victor Hugo This museum was the French writer's home from 1833 until 1848, when Napoléon III came to power and Hugo's voluntary exile in the Channel Islands began. The museum's eclectic assortment of Hugo mementos includes the cap he wore during the 1871 Siege of Paris, his bust sculpted by Rodin, and a model of an elephant sculpture that he proposed for Place de la Bastille. Haunting postage stamp–size pen-and-ink doodles of Rhine castles and ships at sea along with macabre sketches of witches, demons, and the hanging of John Brown show a nightmarish side to the author of *The Hunchback of Notre-Dame* (1831) and *Les Misérables* (1862).

The drawings are counterbalanced by the hodgepodge of Oriental furnishings Hugo designed for the Guernsey home of Juliette Drouet, his mistress for more than a half-century. Don't leave the museum without viewing the Place des Vosges from one of Hugo's upstairs windows and glancing at the Nadar photo of an old but ageless Hugo on his deathbed, 22 May 1885. ♦ Admission. Tu-Su. 6 Pl des Vosges (between Rues de Birague and du Pas-de-la-Mule). 01.42.72.10.16. Métros: Bastille, St-Paul

102 La Chope des Vosges ★$$ Architects working on restorations in the historic district hang out in this simple cafe/restaurant. Not found on any gourmet's restaurant roster, it does serve a sumptuous foie gras with a warm welcome. ♦ Daily lunch and dinner May through September; M, Sa lunch; Tu-F, Su lunch and dinner October through April. Reservations recommended. 22 Pl des

Vosges (between Rues de Birague and du Pas-de-la-Mule). 01.42.72.64.04. Métro: Chemin Vert

103 André Bissonnet Some years ago, a butcher named André Bissonnet laid down his meat cleaver, redecorated his *boucherie* (butcher's shop), and began buying antique musical instruments and restoring them in his cold-storage room. On any given day he might be working on a 1747 viola da gamba, a 17th-century harp, a porcelain trumpet, ancient hurdy-gurdies, or a black serpent, a bizarre 18th-century horn used to accompany chanting priests. Bissonnet claims to be an accomplished player of the Breton bombardon and upon request will proudly bleat out a few bars. ♦ M-Sa 2-7PM or by appointment; closed in August. 6 Rue du Pas-de-la-Mule (between Rue des Tournelles and Pl des Vosges). 01.48.87.20.15. Métro: Chemin Vert

104 Pavillon de la Reine $$$$ The most elegant hotel in the Marais, this 17th-century mansion, discreetly distanced from the *place* by its own garden courtyard, is quietly opulent, with antique tapestries, Persian carpets, a grand fireplace, marble floors, soft leather couches, and 55 luxurious rooms and suites. There's no restaurant. The property is operated in conjunction with the chic hotel **Relais Christine** across the Seine. ♦ 28 Pl des Vosges (at Rue de Béarn). 01.40.29.19.19; fax 01.40.29.19.20; pavillon@club-internet.fr. Métro: Chemin Vert

105 La Guirlande de Julie ★★$$ At his restaurant on the square, Claude Terrail,

owner of the celebrated **Tour d'Argent,** presents a small, seasonally inspired menu. Start with something light, such as baked breast of duck sautéed with spices, followed by the excellent pot-au-feu or fillet of salmon with an herb crust and vegetable tagiatelle, and a bottle of wine from the **Cave de la Tour d'Argent.** Conclude with the popular warm apple tart with cinnamon and ice cream. The weekday prix-fixe lunch menu is a bargain. At night, it's à la carte. In summer reserve a table outside beneath the brick arcade. ♦ W-Su lunch and dinner until 1AM. Reservations recommended. 25 Pl des Vosges (between Rues de Béarn and des Francs-Bourgeois). 01.48.87.94.07. Métro: Chemin Vert

105 21 Place des Vosges Cardinal Richelieu (1585-1642), the French prime minister under Louis XIII and the founder of the **Académie Française,** lived here. ♦ At Rue des Francs-Bourgeois. Métro: Chemin Vert

MA BOURGOGNE

106 Ma Bourgogne ★★$$ Owned by Aimé Cougoureux, this arcade-sheltered cafe is where the locals go for Sunday breakfast. Specialties include sausages from Auvergne, *foie gras des Landes andouillette* (foie gras from Landes with sausages), veal tripe, and spicy steak *tartare.* ♦ Daily breakfast, lunch, and dinner; closed in February and one week in March. No credit cards accepted. 19 Pl des Vosges (at Rue des Francs-Bourgeois). 01.42.78.44.64. Métro: Chemin Vert

107 L'Ambrosie ★★★★$$$$ One of the few Michelin three-star restaurants in Paris, this dining spot is owned by chef Bernard Pacaud, who trained under Claude Peyrot at **Le Vivarois.** Pacaud is a perfectionist and his brief bill of fare fulfills the promise of the restaurant's name—a menu fit for the gods. Some favorites have included John Dory braised with fennel, artichokes with foie gras, skate with sliced cabbage, *croustillant d'agneau* (rolled fillet of lamb stuffed with truffles), and the puff-pastry desserts. The dining room is discreetly romantic with subtle lighting, exquisite floral arrangements, and beautiful tapestries adorning the walls. ♦ Tu-Sa lunch and dinner; closed two weeks in February and three weeks in August. Reservations required (at least one month in advance). 9 Pl des Vosges (between Rues de Birague and des Francs-Bourgeois). 01.42.78.51.45. Métro: St-Paul

108 Hôtel de la Place des Vosges $$ Just down the street from the **Pavillon du Roi** entrance to the famous square sits this cozy, rather than regal, 16-room hotel. There's no restaurant. ♦ 12 Rue de Birague (between Rue St-Antoine and Pl des Vosges). 01.42.72.60.46; fax 01.42.72.02.64; globemar@easynet.fr; www.france-hotel-guide.com/h75004placedes vosges.htm. Métros: St-Paul, Bastille

109 L'Impasse ★★$$ One of the best-kept secrets in the Marais can be found tucked away in a narrow alley. In his delightful old neighborhood bistro—also known as "Chez Robert," the aproned *patron* Robert serves traditional bourgeois cuisine in a pleasant wood-beamed dining room. Baked goat cheese salads, terrines of rabbit and *girolle* mushrooms, fillet of duck in blueberry sauce, and rich chocolate profiteroles are offered here at bargain prices. The service is warm and attentive. ♦ M, Sa dinner; Tu-F lunch and dinner; closed two weeks in August. Reservations recommended. 4 Impasse Guéménée (just north of Rue St-Antoine). 01.42.72.08.45. Métro: Bastille

110 Hôtel de Sully The most richly decorated private mansion in Paris dates from the time of Louis XIII and was designed in 1630 by architect **Androuet du Cerceau** for the notorious gambler Petit Thouars, who is said to have lost his entire fortune in one night. Ten years later, the mansion was bought by the Duc de Sully, a minister to Henri IV. Today this is the site of the information office of the **Caisse Nationale des Monuments Historiques et des Sites** (Bureau of Historic Monuments and Sites), where you may rent any of 40 châteaux or historic mansions throughout France for private receptions, weddings, or conventions. It also houses the **Mission du Patrimoine Photographique** (Mission for the Photographic Patrimony), which mounts outstanding photo exhibits. Retrospectives of Dorothea Lange and W. Eugene Smith have been featured in recent years.

At the far end of the small, well-manicured rear garden, a gateway from the *orangerie* (orange grove) opens onto the Place des Vosges. ♦ Garden: Daily. Photo Gallery: open for exhibits only. 62 Rue St-Antoine (between Rues de Birague and de Turenne). 01.44.61.21.50. Photo exhibit information 01.42.74.47.75. Métro: St-Paul

111 The Hairy Lemon ★$ This comfortable Irish bar is the perfect drop-in spot for typical pub fare. There are generous burgers, hearty sandwiches, baked potatoes, and daily specials. ♦ M-F lunch and dinner; Sa-Su dinner. 4 Rue Caron (just north of Rue St-Antoine). 01.42.72.90.40. Métro: St-Paul

112 St-Paul–St-Louis Built for the Jesuits as part of their monastery in 1627, this Baroque church, with its classically ordered facade, superimposed columns, and dome, is

modeled on the Gesù Church in Rome. The spacious interior is well lit and ornate with decoration and sculptures. In the transept is the painting *Christ in the Garden,* by Delacroix. ♦ Rue St-Antoine (between Rues St-Paul and de Fourcy). 01.42.72.30.32. Métro: St-Paul

113 Maison Européenne de la Photographie Opened in 1996, this cultural institution is located in a classic 18th-century town house. Parisian architect **Yves Lion** has created a tasteful, contemporary interior that boasts a permanent collection of over 12,000 photographs and galleries for rotating exhibitions. Exploring the architectural diversity of the center is an adventure: the main promenade features rough stone walls; there's an elegant staircase; and vaults of the original house twist into the adjoining modern, spacious annex. Visitors are invited to participate in workshops, lectures, and conferences and to view films in the deluxe screening room. ♦ Admission. W-Su. Tours by appointment only. 5-7 Rue de Fourcy (between Rues de Jouy and François-Miron). 01.44.78.75.00. Métro: St-Paul

114 Village St-Paul This jumble of antiques shops crammed into a courtyard often becomes a lively outdoor market. It's one of the few places in Paris to shop on Sunday. ♦ M, Th-Su. Bounded by Rues St-Paul and des Jardins-St-Paul, and Rues de l'Ave-Maria and Charlemagne. Métros: St-Paul, Sully-Morland, Pont Marie

115 Thanksgiving ★★$$ Americans who long for familiar tastes can sate themselves at Judith Blysen's restaurant and shop. The store carries bottled barbecue sauce, packages of Cracker Jack and Pop-Tarts, while the restaurant features Louisiana Cajun and creole specialties. Here you can feast on Cajun popcorn shrimp, filé gumbo, and crawfish pie as appetizers; and jambalaya, crab cakes Louisiana, blackened swordfish, barbecued ribs, and red beans and rice for a main course. When Thanksgiving approaches, fresh turkey (cooked, if you call ahead), pumpkins, cranberries, and all the fixings are on hand. ◆ Restaurant: Tu-F lunch and dinner; Sa-Su brunch. Shop: Daily. Closed two weeks in August and one week in January. 20 Rue St-Paul (between Rues des Lions-St-Paul and Charles-V). Shop 01.42.77.68.29; restaurant 01 42 77 68 29. Métros: St-Paul, Sully-Morland

115 L'Enoteca ★★$$ The Italian food served here, beneath colorful glass lamps and wood beams, often varies in specifics but never in quality. Neighborhood residents come for *gigot d'agneau* (leg of lamb), or *soupe de coquillages* (shellfish soup). The wine bar is a pleasant place to pass the afternoon or late evening, with more than 300 Italian wines as well as Italian cheeses for nibbling. ◆ Restaurant: Daily lunch and dinner. Wine bar: Noon-1AM. Reservations recommended. 25 Rue Charles-V (at Rue St-Paul). 01.42.78.91.44. Métros: St-Paul, Sully-Morland

116 Albion Pick up a few paperback classics in English to read at cafes and on train rides. French people who are trying to learn English buy their books here. ◆ M-Sa; closed last three weeks in August. 13 Rue Charles-V (between Rues Beautreillis and St-Paul). 01.42.72.50.71. Métro: Sully-Morland

117 Hôtel St-Louis Marais $$ A rustic 16-room hotel is all that remains of the 18th-century **Hôtel des Célestins** that belonged to the **Celestine Monastery.** Around the corner on Rue Beautreillis is the original entrance to the convent, a stone portal with a weathered wooden door. Beware: The five-story hotel's landmark status prevents the owners from installing an elevator. The rooms are both charming and comfortable. There's no restaurant. ◆ 1 Rue Charles-V (at Rue du Petit-Musc). 01.48.87.87.04; fax 01.48.87.33.26; www.paris_hotel.tm.fr. Métro: Sully-Morland

118 Temple de Ste-Marie This circular temple was originally the chapel of the **Convent of the Visitation,** built by **François Mansart** in 1632, and is today a Protestant church. Nicolas Fouquet, the finance minister accused of embezzlement under Louis XIV, and Henri de Sévigné, the husband of Madame de Sévigné who was killed in a duel in 1651, are buried here. ◆ Rues St-Antoine and Castex. Métro: Bastille

119 Statue de Beaumarchais The 18th-century comedies of Pierre-Augustin Caron de Beaumarchais (1732-99), *The Barber of Seville* (1775) and *The Marriage of Figaro* (1784), were transformed by Rossini and Mozart respectively into operas whose factotum heroes were regarded as dangerously, even revolutionarily, independent. The radical sympathies of Beaumarchais were played out in real life, too: His office was secretly running guns to American revolutionaries. In keeping with the

dramatist's satiric tradition, residents of the Bastille neighborhood are constantly dressing up his statue in outrageous costumes. ◆ Rues St-Antoine and des Tournelles. Métro: Bastille

The Bastille

The area around the Bastille, rejuvenated by the building of a new opera house in 1990 and by scores of art galleries, today is often called the SoHo of Paris. But this neighborhood was not always on the cutting edge of fashion. Originally a convergence of roads leading to Paris, it became a center for jobs and industry in the 17th century when Louis XIV attracted artisans and craft guilds to the area by exempting them from taxes. A century later the working-class haven was to become the symbol of freedom, when, in July 1789, a crowd of citizens seized the **Bastille** and freed its prisoners, marking the start of the French Revolution.

In the 1930s, the district was filled with *bougnats,* Auvergnat dispensaries of wine and coal. Today the *quartier* has been discovered by painters and other bohemians, and the neighborhood has undergone a mind-boggling transformation. The once seedy **Rue de Lappe,** just off the **Place de la Bastille,** is now dubbed "the trendiest street in Paris." Quite a change from 1944, when Somerset Maugham wrote in *The Razor's Edge* that Rue de Lappe, "gave the impression of sordid lust." There are artisans' studios and ateliers and a handful of Auvergnat restaurants, side by side with oh-so-trendy bars and cafes, avant-garde art galleries, and more than one too many Tex-Mex restaurants. Upscale establishments like Jean Paul Gaultier's headquarters are causing rents to go up and forcing struggling artists and artisans to move elsewhere.

MICHAEL STORRINGS

120 Place de la Bastille On 14 July 1789, 633 people stormed the **Bastille** (the French counterpart to the Tower of London), captured its ammunition depot, released its prisoners (only 7, and none political), lynched its governor, and demolished the fortress, thus sparking the French Revolution. Every year on the 14th of July, these events are celebrated in Paris with parades and dancing in the streets.

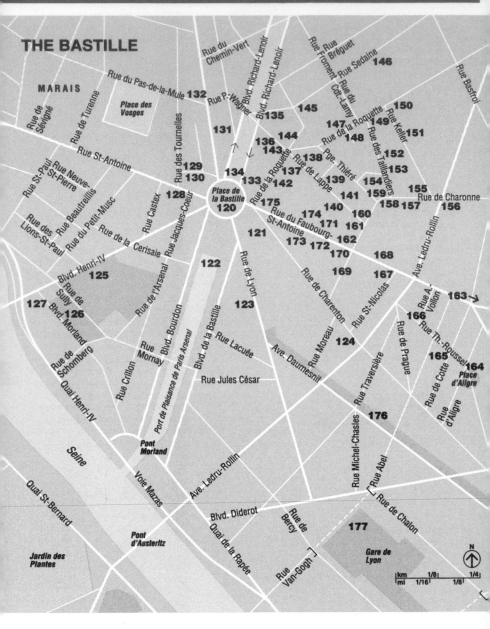

THE BASTILLE

MARAIS

Rue du Chemin-Vert
Rue du Pas-de-la-Mule **132**
Rue P.-Wagner
Blvd. Richard-Lenoir
Rue du Côt.-Lamy
Rue Froment
Rue Bréguet
Rue Sedaine **146**
Rue Bastroi

Place des Vosges
131
135
145
147
Rue de la Roquette
149 **150**
Rue Keller
151

Rue de Sévigné
Rue de Turenne
Rue des Tournelles
136 **144**
143 **138**
Rue de la Roquette
137 Rue de Lappe
148
Pge. Thiéré
152
Rue des Tallandiers
153

Rue St-Antoine
129
130
134
133 **142**
139
154
159
155
Rue de Charonne
156

Rue St-Paul
Rue Neuve-St-Pierre
128
Place de la Bastille
120
175
174 **140** **160**
141 **158** **157**

Rue Beautreillis
Rue du Petit-Musc
Rue Castex
Rue Jacques-Coeur
121
Rue du Faubourg-St-Antoine
173 **172**
171 **161**
170 **162**
168
Ave. Ledru-Rollin

Rue des Lions-St-Paul
Rue de la Cerisaie
122
Rue de Lyon
169 **167**
163→

Blvd. Henri-IV
125
Rue de l'Arsenal
Rue de Charenton
Rue St-Nicolas
Rue A.-Vollon
166
Rue Th.-Roussel
165
164
Place d'Aligre

Rue de Sully
Blvd. Moriand
127 Blvd. **126**
123
124
Rue de Prague
Rue de Cotte
Rue d'Aligre

Rue de Schomberg
Blvd. Bourdon
Rue de la Bastille
Rue Lacuée
Ave. Daumesnil
Rue Moreau
Rue Traversière

Quai Henri-IV
Rue Mornay
Port de Plaisance de Paris Arsenal
Rue Jules César
176

Seine
Pont Moriand
Voie Mazas
Ave. Ledru-Rollin
Rue Michel-Chasles
Rue Abel
Rue de Chalon

Quai St-Bernard
Pont d'Austerlitz
Blvd. Diderot
Rue de Bercy
Rue Van-Gogh
Quai de la Rapée
177
Gare de Lyon

Jardin des Plantes

N

| km | 1/8 | 1/4 |
| mi | 1/16 | 1/8 |

The eight-towered **Bastille** was built in 1370 by Provost Hugues Aubriot as a fortified palace for Charles V, and was later transformed by Cardinal Richelieu into a holding tank where political prisoners were detained without trial. During its baleful history, the prison held Voltaire, who was imprisoned for his biting verse, as well as the notorious Marquis de Sade and the mysterious "Man in the Iron Mask." Paving stones, laid where Rue St-Antoine intersects the square, mark the site of the original towers. The 170-foot **Colonne de Juillet** (July Column; pictured on page 153) in the center of the square commemorates the July 1830 Revolution, which overthrew the last of the Bourbon kings. The gilded figure perched on top is not an allegory of Liberty, as many suppose, but a winged Mercury. ♦ Métro: Bastille

121 Opéra Bastille In the early 1980s, the French government appointed **Carlos Ott,** a Canadian-Uruguayan architect, to design what was to be the largest opera house in the world on the Place de la Bastille. The gigantesque silver-surfaced structure came under heavy criticism as soon as it went up (the building was called the world's largest public toilet by some), but whatever its aesthetic merits, the edifice's presence sparked the renewal of the Bastille area, helping it to become the trendiest neighborhood in Paris. The facility, billed as the "people's opera house," entertains an estimated 700,000 ticket holders a year, and includes an amphitheater and a stage for smaller performances. Its opening was planned for the July 1989 bicentennial of the storming of the Bastille and the French Revolution, but dissension among administrators, including the axing (figuratively at least) of the director, and various technical problems delayed the opening of the amphitheater until March 1990, when a new production of Berlioz's *The Trojans* was premiered. Since then, all large-scale operas of the **Opéra National de Paris** have been presented here. (The **Opéra Garnier**—see page 218—is now reserved mainly for dance performances.) The 2,700-seat auditorium is blandly modern in style, but the seats are comfortable, the sight lines are clear, and the acoustics are excellent. After a series of acrimonious changes of musical directors, conductor James Conlon has succeeded in establishing order, and under his magical baton, the **Opéra National de Paris** is now one of the world's greatest opera companies.

Tours of the building are available for a small charge, but you must reserve in advance. ♦ Box office: M-Sa 11AM-6PM. 120 Rue de Lyon (at Pl de la Bastille). 08.36.69.78.68; fax 01.44.73.13.74. Métro: Bastille

121 Les Grandes Marches ★★$$ This large white brasserie next door to the **Opéra Bastille** began as a 17th century inn patronized by the artisans of the working-class Faubourg St-Antoine quarter. During the days preceding the Revolution it became a meeting place for patriots. Today tourists and famished post-opera diners gather here for the less urgent task of consuming *fruits de mer* (mixed seafood), fish dishes, and grilled meat. Begin your meal with oysters and langoustines from the *coquillage* (shellfish) bar, then proceed to the crusty-topped lobster and sea scallop casserole, or the chateaubriand with béarnaise sauce. For a grand finale, order the bitter-dark-chocolate cake with coffee sauce, or prunes soaked in red wine. The Belle Epoque–style dining rooms on the ground floor have elegant painted ceilings and enough mirrors to satisfy any narcissist. For a sweeping view over the Place de la Bastille, reserve (three days ahead) one of the tables by the front window in the wood-paneled upstairs *salon*. ♦ Daily lunch and dinner until 1AM. Reservations recommended for post-opera dinners. 6 Pl de la Bastille (between Rues de Lyon and de Charenton). 01.43.42.90.32. Métro: Bastille

121 FNAC Musique Bastille Your one-stop connection to the music scene carries a complete range of CDs and cassettes and a huge selection of videos and laser discs. Like all stores in the chain, this place is sleek and efficient. It features listening stations with headphones; a ticket outlet for musical, theatrical, and sports events; a photo gallery; and frequent music-related promotional events. ♦ M-Sa; W, F 10AM-10PM. 4 Pl de la Bastille (between Rues de Lyon and de Charenton). 01.43.42.04.04. Métro: Bastille. Also at: Forum des Halles, 1 Rue Pierre-Lescot (at Rue Berger). 01.40.41.40.00. RER: Châtelet–Les Halles, Métro: Les Halles

122 Canal St-Martin Dating from 1821, this industrial canal was dug to facilitate delivery of materials to the manufacturers in the Faubourg St-Antoine quarter. It flows under Boulevard Richard-Lenoir and Place de la Bastille and comes out at Port de Plaisance de Paris Arsenal, the pleasure-boat harbor immediately to the south of Place de la Bastille. Its northern end is at the Bassin de la Villette in the 19th arrondissement. Boat tours are offered from April through November by **Paris Canal** (01.42.40.96.97) and **Canauxrama** (01.42.39.15.00). The unusual cruises pass along the tree-lined canal, through more than a mile of tunnel and nine locks, and under two swinging bridges and eight footbridges, between the Port de Plaisance de Paris Arsenal and the **Parc de la Villette**. ♦ Métro: Bastille

123 Dame Tartine ★★$ Airy and no-frills, this eatery appeals to students and young people in search of a reasonably priced snack, light lunch, or dinner away from the bustle of Place de la Bastille. Duck stew with orange and fresh mint, and salmon with coconut milk and curry on slivers of zucchini are just a couple of the interesting combinations featured here. Every dish comes with a *tartine* (toasted bread), the restaurant's namesake. Portions are small, but inexpensive, so famished diners might want to order two courses. The bland vista of the **Opéra Bastille**'s bulky midsection across the street is the only drawback. ♦ Daily lunch and dinner. 59 Rue de Lyon (between Rue Lacuée and Pl de la Bastille). 01.44.68.96.95. Métro: Bastille. Also at: 2 Rue Brisemiche (at Rue du Cloître-St-Merri). 01.42.77.32.22. Métros: Rambuteau, Hôtel de Ville

124 China Club ★★$$ This Shanghai-chic place mixes cocktails for the gentry of the east side. The Chinese Deco atmosphere features a cozy drawing room with soft leather chairs, a 46-foot-long bar, and a restaurant where very good renditions of traditional Chinese dishes are served. The bourgeoisie from Paris's conservative west side like to come here, thinking they're living dangerously. ♦ Restaurant: Daily dinner. Bar: Daily 7PM-2AM; Happy Hour 7-9PM. 50 Rue de Charenton (between Ave Ledru-Rollin and Rue Moreau). 01.43.43.82.02. Métro: Ledru Rollin

125 Garde Républicaine This massive, rusticated stone complex houses the military barracks and horses' stables of the French National Guard. It was constructed in 1891 on the site of the garden of the former **Celestine Monastery** (founded in 1352), although all that remains today of the vast religious grounds is a stone portal on Rue Beautreillis. The compound is open to the public only two days a year (usually in June) but you may be lucky enough to catch the uniformed gendarmes parading on horseback through the streets of Paris on public holidays. Such processions are magnificent, although some of their pomp is diminished by the humorous and necessary presence of one of the city's bright green pooper-scoopers at the end of the parade. ♦ Open to visitors two days a year in June. 12-28 Blvd Henri-IV (between Rues de la Cerisaie and de Sully). 01.42.76.16.32. Métro: Sully-Morland

126 Bibliothèque de l'Arsenal Housed in the four stories of this long and slender sandstone building, constructed in 1594 as the mansion of the Grand Master of Artillery under Henri IV, is a library with an unparalleled collection of literature, illuminated manuscripts, French dramatic works, and books on literary history and the history of the theater. The archives encompass over a million printed volumes, 15,000 manuscripts, 100,000 engravings, and 300 musical works. The collection includes Louis IX's Book of Hours, Charles V's Bible, and many documents relating to the **Bastille**. To visit the fine 17th- and 18th-century salons, among them the **Salon de Musique** with its intricate Louis XV woodwork, you must make a reservation for a group tour through the **Caisse Nationale des Monuments Historiques** (Hôtel de Sully, 62 Rue St-Antoine, between Rues de Birague and de Turenne, 01.48.87.24.15). On the cornice of the south facade (along Boulevard Morland) is a row of eight life-size stone cannons, serving as a reminder of the original function of the building. ♦ Fee for tour. M-Sa; closed 1-15 September. 1 Rue de Sully (at Rue Mornay). 01.53.01.25.04. Métro: Sully-Morland

127 Pavillon de l'Arsenal This building's heavy stone facade hides a glass-and-steel structure constructed in 1879 for Laurent-Louis Borniche, an art lover and patron, as a place to display his almost 2,000 canvases. But Borniche didn't live to see his museum realized, and after his daughter sold the building it was used for various purposes, including workshops for **La Samaritaine** department store and archival storage for the City of Paris. Renovated in 1988 by **Bernard Reichen** and **Philippe Robert,** the building is now a fascinating museum that looks at the urban development of Paris. It also houses a center for documentation on current architectural projects, and a photographic library.

By presenting drawings and models of local urban design and architectural projects, the museum aims to enhance the public's understanding of the city's continual evolution. On permanent display is a model of Paris connected to a computer; at a visitor's request, a videodisc displays one of 30,000 images (of canals, monuments, green spaces, sectors under development, etc.) while a laser ray spots the corresponding locus on the model. There is also an exhibit on the successive phases of the city's construction, from the wall of Philippe Auguste to Haussmann's Paris to present-day developments. The changing exhibitions concentrate on contemporary urbanization. ♦ Free. Exhibitions: Tu-Su. Library: Tu-F 2-6PM. 21 Blvd Morland (between Rue de Schomberg and Blvd Henri-IV). 01.42.76.33.97. Métro: Sully-Morland

128 5 Rue St-Antoine This building marks the position of the **Bastille** courtyard where the angry mob gained access. A plaque at the site reads: *Ici était l'entrée de l'avant-cour de la Bastille par laquelle les assaillants pénétrèrent dans la forteresse le 14 juillet 1789* (Here was the entrance of the forecourt of the Bastille through which the assailants penetrated the fortress the 14th of July 1789). ♦ At Rue Jacques-Coeur. Métro: Bastille

129 Hotel Bastille Speria $$ One minute by foot from the Place de la Bastille and three minutes from the Place des Vosges, this bright, spotless, and tastefully decorated modern hotel should fill the bill for those who want to be in the heart of the action without going broke. All 42 rooms have good, firm beds, up-to-date bathrooms, cable TV, and a restful pale pink and gray color scheme, and there are plants everywhere. The hotel has no restaurant, but a buffet is served in the cheerful breakfast room. ♦ 1 Rue de la Bastille (at Rue des Tournelles). 01.42.72.04.01; fax 01.42.72.56.38; speria@micronet.fr. Métro: Bastille

---

Restaurants/Clubs: Red   **Hotels:** Blue
Shops/ ♣ Outdoors: Green   **Sights/Culture:** Black

129 Bofinger ★★$$ Dating from 1864, this is among Paris's oldest, busiest, and most spectacularly ornate brasseries. House legend holds that it was the first in the city to pour draft beer. Specialties are *fruits de mer* (mixed seafood), Alsatian *choucroute* (sauerkraut), Riesling and Gewürztraminer wines, and Belle Époque splendor. Reserve well in advance to secure a table *sous la coupole,* in the gorgeous glass-domed main dining room. ◆ Daily lunch and dinner until 1AM. Reservations recommended. 5-7 Rue de la Bastille (between Rues Jean-Beausire and des Tournelles). 01.42.72.87.82. Métro: Bastille

LE DÔME BASTILLE

130 Le Dôme Bastille ★★$$ This friendly seafood place features *friture d'éperlans* (fried smelts), salmon *tartare,* and *bar grillé à la Provençale* (grilled bass). With fish, the Mâcon Villages Domaine des deux Roches is an especially good choice from the wine list. The famous **Le Dôme** in Montparnasse (108 Blvd du Montparnasse, at Rue Delambre, 01.43.35.25.81, Métro: Vavin) is this bistro's *maison mère.* ◆ Daily lunch and dinner. 2 Rue de la Bastille (at Rue des Tournelles). 01.48.04.88.44. Métro: Bastille. Also at: 1 Rue Delambre (at Blvd Raspail). 01.43.35.32.00. Métro: Vavin

130 Le Bistrot de Bofinger ★$$ Spawned by **Bofinger** across the street in 1993, this *décontracté* (easygoing) 1940s-style bistro serves *pâté de tête* (headcheese), *salade d'endives* with cantal cheese and walnuts, steak *tartare,* very good grilled steaks, and in winter, a steamy pot-au-feu. There is also a special children's menu, a rarity in Paris. The mosaic floors and the 1945 wall mural depicting the Place de la Bastille were uncovered by workers during a renovation. ◆ Daily lunch and dinner. 6 Rue de la Bastille (between Pl de la Bastille and Rue des Tournelles). 01.42.72.05.23. Métro: Bastille

131 2-20 Blvd Beaumarchais Here once stood the luxurious mansion and gardens of Caron de Beaumarchais (1732-99), the 18th-century dramatist who wrote *The Marriage of Figaro* and who now resides in **Père-Lachaise Cemetery.** The garden was garnished with statues (including one of Voltaire), grottoes, a labyrinth, and an orchard. In 1818 his heirs sold the property to the city for less than a quarter of what Beaumarchais had invested, and it was demolished to facilitate the opening of Canal St-Martin. The buildings now have residential and commercial space. ◆ Between Pl de la Bastille and Rue Pasteur-Wagner. Métro: Bastille

132 Le Bar à Huitres ★★$$ Known for its fresh and reasonably priced seafood, this restaurant composes delicious platters of *coquillage* and serves fine entrées of grilled salmon and grilled lobster. The crisply decorated dining room is well run and casual. ◆ Daily lunch and dinner until 2AM. 33 Blvd Beaumarchais (at Rue du Pas-de-la-Mule). 01.48.87.98.92. Métros: Chemin Vert, Bastille. Also at: 33 Rue St-Jacques (between Blvd St-Germain and Rue Galande). 01.44.07.27.37. Métros: Maubert-Mutualité, Cluny–La Sorbonne; 112 Blvd du Montparnasse (at Blvd Raspail). 01.43.20.71.01. Métro: Vavin

133 Indiana Cafe ★$$ There are margaritas and tequila sunrises to go with the nachos, guacamole, bacon cheeseburgers, and barbecued ribs at this formula Tex-Mex restaurant and bar on the Place de la Bastille, animated until the wee hours of the morning. The sweeter side of the menu features brownies, hot fudge sundaes, and apple pie. ◆ Daily lunch and dinner. 14 Pl de la Bastille (at Blvd Richard-Lenoir). 01.44.75.79.80. Métro: Bastille. Also at: 130 Blvd St-Germain (between Rues de l'Eperon and de l'Ancienne-Comédie). 01.46.34.66.31. Métro: Odéon; 7 Blvd des Capucines (at Pl de l'Opéra). 01.42.68.02.22. Métro: Opéra

134 Boulevard Richard-Lenoir One of the city's most pleasant outdoor markets is situated in the center island of this wide boulevard, between Place de la Bastille and Rue St-Sabin. Fine produce and poultry are sold—some stalls feature organically grown fruits and vegetables, others offer roast chickens and ducks. In the fall several vendors deal in wild mushrooms. Sunday is the market's big day, when you'll find merchants earnestly hawking everything from antique furniture, cookware, and Savon (soap) de Marseille to chrysanthemums, pig's feet, and Babar the elephant beach towels, and singers and musicians entertain. ♦ Market: Th, Su mornings. Métros: Bastille, Bréguet Sabin

135 Le Sedaine Bastille Mme. and M. Rousseau's small corner bar peaks on Sunday between 10AM and 1PM when market workers escape their stalls for a quick *pastis* or rough Côte du Rhone. The floor is strewn with cigarette butts, sugar wrappers, and napkins. ♦ M-F; Su 6AM-8PM. 18 Blvd Richard-Lenoir (at Rue Sedaine). 01.47.00.90.40. Métros: Bastille, Bréguet Sabin

136 Cour Damoye Behind a rusted iron gate lies this deserted street, whose owner rents it out as a movie-filming location. Notice that almost all the shops along this little *allée*, such as the one with the sign reading "Boulanger," are only the false storefronts used in the last filming. ♦ Rue Daval (between Rue de la Roquette and Blvd Richard-Lenoir). Métro: Bastille

136 Relais du Massif Central ★★$ Softly smiling and amply built Mme. Caroline Coutinho makes sure that no one leaves her restaurant hungry. Auvergne-inspired specialties include frog's legs *Provençale*, grilled shrimp with Cognac-laced lobster sauce, *faux-filet* (beef sirloin) with roquefort cheese, *gratin de coquilles St-Jacques* (scallops au gratin), and sole meunière. Amidst the here-today-gone-tomorrow trendiness of the Bastille, this is the real thing—which is why neighborhood workers, residents, and tourists keep coming back. ♦ M-Sa lunch and dinner. 16 Rue Daval (between Rue de la Roquette and Blvd Richard-Lenoir). 01.47.00.46.55. Métro: Bastille

137 Rue de Lappe Once populated with natives of the Auvergne region of France and now the main artery of the trendy Bastille, this narrow cobbled street was named in 1652 for Girard de Lappe, who owned the gardens and marshland through which the street was pierced. On 23 December 1830, Louis Philippe passed down the Rue de Lappe during a royal visit to the Faubourg, filling the residents with such enthusiasm that the following year they named the street after him. In 1848, after the February Revolution in which "The Citizen King" was overthrown, the street reverted to its original name. Only a dreary little *passage* off Rue de Lappe is still named for the rejected hero. ♦ Métros: Bastille, Ledru Rollin

137 Chez Teil One of the few remaining Auvergnat establishments in the neighborhood, this shop sells products from the Auvergne region in central France. Take home a jar of *confit d'oie* (goose meat confit), some *saucisson sec* (dry sausages), a tasty nut cake, or a pair of *galoches* (the Auvergnat version of clogs). ♦ Tu-Sa. 6 Rue de Lappe (between Rues de Charonne and de la Roquette). 01.47.00.41.28. Métro: Bastille

137 66 Café ★$ The theme here is—you guessed it—Route 66 in the USA. The red vinyl seats, rough-hewn wood floor, and wagon wheel over the bar (which specializes in such drinks as whiskey sours, Long Island iced tea, and screwdrivers) all contribute to the all-American ambience. US-style grub includes fried chicken, T-bone steak, cheeseburgers, apple pie, and banana splits. The place is full of young North Americans and Yankee-loving French. ♦ Restaurant: daily 6PM-2AM. Happy Hour: daily 6-8:30PM. 8 Rue de Lappe (between Rues de Charonne and de la Roquette). 01.43.38.30.20. Métro: Bastille

138 La Pirada ★$ A gigantic bull's head keeps watch while Spanish-food enthusiasts drink sangria and consume tapas and paella. ♦ Daily lunch and dinner until 2AM. 7 Rue de Lappe (between Passage Louis-Philippe and Rue de la Roquette). 01.47.00.73.61. Métro: Bastille

138 Le Balajo Founded in 1936 by Jo France, the *bal à Jo* (Jo's ballroom) was Paris's most popular dance hall in the heyday of the *bal musette* (a dance or informal "ball" featuring a distinctive style of accordion music), frequented by Maurice Chavalier and Edith Piaf. After a long, steady decline following World War II, the place bounced back in the 1990s and is as *branché* (hot) as ever today. Announced by a giant neon sign, the dance hall is full of people straight out of a Fellini flick dancing to Latin, swing, or rock music on the small, cramped dance floor, or relaxing on sticky red vinyl seats. A deejay spins disks on the balcony where an orchestra once played, and on the opposite wall is a zany model of a fictitious city. Rock and swing are on tap on Wednesday night; Salsa on Thursday; a mixed bag on Friday and Saturday; Tango on

Sunday; and *bal musette* on Sunday afternoon. ♦ W 9PM-2AM; Th 10PM-5AM; F-Sa 11PM-5AM; Su 3-7PM and 9PM-1AM. 9 Rue de Lappe (between Passage Louis-Philippe and Rue de la Roquette). 01.47.00.07.87. Métro: Bastille

138 Havanita Café ★$ Buzzing with the warmth of the Caribbean, this Cuban restaurant has well-worn leather armchairs, colorful wall and ceiling murals, and palms galore. Join the **Balajo** crowd, which arrives late for dinner, and fill up on generous portions of sautéed langoustines with fried bananas, Cuban chicken salad, and exotic fruits, accompanied by mojitos, piña coladas, coco locos, and other Cuban cocktails. ♦ Daily dinner until 2AM. Happy Hour: Daily 5-8PM. 11 Rue de Lappe (between Passage Louis-Philippe and Rue de la Roquette). 01.43.55.96.42. Métro: Bastille

139 Hôtel les Sans-Culottes $ If you're lucky enough to land one of the 10 rooms in this charming old-fashioned inn, you're getting the best deal in the Bastille. Although small, the rooms are equipped with 20th-century comforts like showers and TV sets, and hotel guests get to have breakfast in the handsome 1900s-style **Bistrot les Sans-Culottes** downstairs (see below). ♦ 27 Rue de Lappe (between Rue de Charonne and Passage Louis-Philippe). 01.49.23.85.80; fax 01.48.05.08.56. Métro: Bastille

Within Hôtel les Sans-Culottes:

Bistrot les Sans-Culottes ★★$$
Entrepreneurial young owner Ahmed Arab opened this restaurant in 1991, but the zinc bar, elegantly curved stair, ornate ceilings, wall mirrors, and other fin de siècle–style details make it look as if it's been here for at least a century. The name *sans-culottes* (without knickers) was given to the French Revolutionaries, who wore the trousers of the working class rather than the knickers favored by the aristocracy. The menu, however, features both the traditional and the revolutionary: foie gras, grilled salmon with *pistou* (a creamy basil and garlic sauce) and saffron rice, veal kidneys with *pleurottes* (wild mushrooms), *crème brûlée pistaché*, and warm apple tart. The large outdoor terrace, the only one on the street, is the perfect vantage point from which to watch the wild parade along the Rue de Lappe. ♦ M breakfast for hotel guests only; Tu-Su breakfast, lunch, and dinner. 01.48.05.42.92

LILIANE & MICHEL DURAND-DESSERT

140 Galerie Liliane et Michel Durand-Dessert Located behind an art bookstore, this is one of the best-known galleries in Paris. Within its white lofty space is fine art in all mediums from noted artists including Joseph Beuys, Stanley Brouwn, Yan Pei-Ming, Yves Openheim, and Gerard Garouste. ♦ Tu-Sa. 28 Rue de Lappe (between Rues de Charonne and de la Roquette). 01.48.06.92.23. Métros: Bastille, Ledru Rollin

140 Galerie Zone & Phase A popular gallery for its use in *matière* (raw material, textures, and colors), as well as work by contemporary artists who make objects in the *esprit africain*. ♦ M by appointment; Tu-Sa. 30 Rue de Lappe (between Rues de Charonne and de la Roquette). 01.48.06.51.25. Métros: Bastille, Ledru Rollin

141 La Galoche d'Aurillac ★★$$ Mme. and M. Bonnet's *restaurant Auvergnat* is one of the last holdouts from the days when this neighborhood was heavily populated with craftsmen and others from the Auvergne region in central France. The eatery is named for the wooden or leather clogs traditionally worn by French workmen, and numerous examples of *galoches* are hung from the ceiling in neat rows. The menu features *salade du Cantal* (salad with cantal cheese), lentils *à l'Auvergnate* (cooked with bacon and goose fat), *confit de canard* (duck confit) with apples, and sausage from Auvergne. The regional cheeses such as cabécous, cantal, and bleu d'Auvergne are a good excuse for another bottle of Côtes d'Auvergne or Marcillac. ♦ Tu-Sa lunch and dinner. 41 Rue de Lappe (between Rue de Charonne and Passage Louis-Philippe). 01.47.00.77.15. Métros: Bastille, Ledru Rollin

141 Galerie Alain Gutharc This gallery specializes in exhibiting photographs, video, and sculpture with an emphasis on such young artists as Joël Bartoloméo and Claire Chevrier. ♦ Tu-F afternoon; Sa. 47 Rue de Lappe (between Rue de Charonne and Passage Louis-Philippe). 01.47.00.32.10. Métros: Bastille, Ledru Rollin

142 Sukiyaki ★$ It's all here: standard Japanese decor, a sushi bar, and a menu featuring sashimi, sushi, sukiyaki, and Japanese barbecue that you grill at your own table. ♦ M-Sa lunch and dinner; Su dinner. 12 Rue de la Roquette (between Pl de la Bastille and Rue de Lappe). 01.49.23.04.98. Métro: Bastille

143 Café Iguana ★★$ This two-story Tex-Mex bar has a woody interior and ceiling fans and serves omelettes, chili, grilled meat, carpaccio, sandwiches, and salads. However, drinking is the main purpose of most who come here, and the cocktail list offers blue lagoons, silver bananas, white Russians, 11 types of vodka, 16 kinds of whiskey, and the darkest draft Murphy's this side of Cork. There's a tiny *non-fumeur* (nonsmoking) room upstairs. ♦ Daily 9AM-4AM. 15 Rue de la Roquette (at Rue Daval). 01.40.21.39.99. Métro: Bastille

144 Hôtel Daval $ Didier Gonod's friendly hotel is nothing fancy—the 23 rooms are small and simply decorated—but who could ask for more than a clean, quiet, cheap room in the heart of the lively Bastille quarter? A friendly German shepherd named Malko is in residence. There's no restaurant. ♦ 21 Rue Daval (between Rue St-Sabin and Blvd Richard-Lenoir). 01.47.00.51.23; fax 01.40.21.80.26. Métro: Bastille

145 A la Petite Fabrique In this little chocolate factory, you can watch the artisans ply their luscious craft in the immaculate kitchen to the rear of the shop. At Easter the boutique is packed to the gills with the traditional chocolate fish, rabbits, and chickens stuffed with small candies, and with real eggshells filled with chocolate and praline. More than 40 kinds of chocolate bars are available year-round, including praline, hazelnut, and orange fondant. Buy a bag of *orangettes* (strips of candied orange peel in chocolate) with no guilt about the calories. Taped to the counter is a magazine article hailing the benefits of chocolate as a physical stimulant, an antidepressant, a source of minerals, and a cure for broken hearts. ♦ Tu-Sa. 12 Rue St-Sabin (between Rues de la Roquette and Sedaine). 01.48.05.82.02. Métros: Bastille, Bréguet Sabin

145 Papeterie Saint Sabin The two side-by-side boutiques of this elegant, modern stationery shop sell such classic French paper products as Canson Paper, colored paper from Nepal, and Oberthur agendas (which have been around more than 130 years longer than Filofax). There are also handmade sketchbooks, those wonderful Annonay notebooks and folders adorned with black blotches, and magnificent leather brief cases and carrying bags. ♦ Tu-Sa. 16 Rue St-Sabin (between Rues de la Roquette and Sedaine). 01.47.00.78.63. Métros: Bastille, Bréguet Sabin

145 Café de l'Industrie ★★$ Onion soup, carpaccio, roast beef with potatoes, and other simple, low-priced fare provide the sustenance, but the food here is strictly secondary. What fills the tables night after night at this quintessentially Bastille cafe is the ultra-easygoing, playful ambience. Spears, python skins, glamour shots of 1940s French movie starlets, and ridiculous oversized paintings grace the walls of this rambling, but curiously cozy place. The attractive and refreshingly unprofessional waitresses (models, no doubt) add to the charm, as does the good recorded jazz, making the young Parisian *intello-mode* crowd that congregates here feel right at home. The owner is self-confident enough to close down on Saturday, the most popular day to dine out. ♦ M-F, Su lunch, dinner, and late-night meals until 1AM. 16 Rue St-Sabin (between Rues de la Roquette and Sedaine). 01.47.00.13.53. Métros: Bastille, Bréguet Sabin

146 Lire Entre les Vignes ★★$ "Read Between the Vines" is the English translation of this wine bar's name, and not surprisingly, its superb list of vintages is the place's distinguishing feature. But the food is good here, too. The predominantly local clientele choose from items on the chalkboard, which change daily. Foie gras, beef carpaccio, cold cut platter, and *boudin noir* (pork blood sausage) with apples are some of the dishes you might find. Wash any of them down with a Saumur Château de Beauregard Rouge or a Chablis Domaine des Marronniers. The place is relaxed and airy, with a skylight over the main dining room, rough wooden floors, and old bottles, scales, and crockery. ♦ M-F lunch and dinner. 38 Rue Sedaine (between Rues Popincourt and du Commandant-Lamy). 01.43.55.69.49. Métros: Bréguet Sabin, Voltaire

147 Vue sur Toi Stylish men's and women's clothes to outfit the elegant Lycra crowd are featured at this small boutique. ♦ M-Sa. 41 Rue de la Roquette (between Rues du Commandant-Lamy and St-Sabin). 01.47.00.17.33. Métros: Bastille, Bréguet Sabin

147 Coyote Café ★$ This tiny restaurant offers the standard Mexican repertoire with a few Parisian twists, such as a quesadilla with smoked salmon. There's also a good selection of Mexican beers. ♦ Tu-Su lunch and dinner.

43 Rue de la Roquette (between Rues du Commandant-Lamy and St-Sabin). 01.47.00.70.85. Métros: Bastille, Bréguet Sabin

147 Thaï Elephant ★★★$$ The Tikki Room meets Thailand in this veritable jungle of exotic flora, with a little wooden bridge, a waterfall, and young waiters in silk robes gliding among the tables serving chef Oth Sombath's sweet and spicy specialties. Try the *tom yam khung* (spicy shrimp soup with lemon), *colvert Siamois* (duck with raisins, pineapple, basil, and coconut milk), *massaman d'agneau* (a southern Muslim lamb dish in a sweet sauce), or the chicken soufflé served in banana leaves. Other restaurants under the same ownership in London, Bangkok, Brussels, and Copenhagen go by the name Blue Elephant. ♦ M-F, Su lunch and dinner; Sa dinner. Reservations recommended. 43-45 Rue de la Roquette (between Rues du Commandant-Lamy and St-Sabin). 01.47.00.42.00. Métros: Bastille, Bréguet Sabin

148 Cité de la Roquette Pop into this small dead-end passage for a look at the charming brick ateliers of woodworkers and violin makers, through the gate to the left of the lumberyard. This is a favorite location spot for filmmakers. ♦ Métros: Bastille, Bréguet Sabin

149 Louis Philippe Fountain This stone fountain, decorated with delicately carved fruit, acanthus leaves, shells, and lions' heads was built in 1846 during the reign of Louis Philippe. The now-dry fountain is off-limits to the public, closed off by iron gates (which have been adopted by locals as a bike rack). Notice the ship, the symbol of Paris, carved in the center keystone. A similar fountain was erected on the Rue de Charenton but was demolished in 1906 for the opening of the Rue de Prague. ♦ 70 Rue de la Roquette (between Rues Keller and des Taillandiers). Métros: Bastille, Bréguet Sabin

150 Théâtre de la Bastille A red neon sign announces this theater, which, under the direction of the innovative Jean-Marie Hordé, features daring and inventive ventures in contemporary dance and theater. ♦ Box office: M-F by phone only; 30 minutes before performances. 76 Rue de la Roquette (between Rues Basfroi and Keller). 01.43.57.42.14. Métros: Bastille, Bréguet Sabin

151 Galerie Akié Aricchi Not limited by any particular style, Akié Aricchi shows the work of international painters and sculptors, both abstract and figurative. She is spontaneous and eclectic in her selection—if she likes the spirit of the artist's work, she shows it. Some of the artists she has taken to are Akiko Toriumi, Lechevallier, Tony Soulié, Helga Hommes, and Alan Simon. ♦ Tu-Sa 3-7PM. 26 Rue Keller (between Rues de Charonne and de la Roquette). 01.40.21.64.57. Métros: Bastille, Ledru Rollin

152 Les Taillandiers ★★$ The locals don't mind waiting for a table at this popular French bistro serving hearty fare at a reasonable price. Choose from such popular favorites as *petit salé* (salted pork with lentils) and *blanquette de veau* (veal in béchamel sauce with mushrooms and rice). ♦ M-Sa lunch. 22 Rue des Taillandiers (between Rues de Charonne and de la Roquette). 01.48.05.98.24. Métros: Bastille, Ledru Rollin

153 Galerie Jorge Alyskewycz For the last several years this gallery's Argentinian-Ukrainian curator has dedicated his space to installations and sculptures, with the occasional painting or photography exhibit. The sculptures of Roland Cognet, Michel Roginsky, and Alejandra Riera, and the conceptual installations of Arnold Schalks have been featured here. ♦ Tu-Sa 2:30-7PM. 14 Rue des Taillandiers (between Rues de Charonne and de la Roquette). 01.48.06.59.23. Métros: Bastille, Ledru Rollin

154 Galerie Jousse Seguin: Espace Gran Dia Behind this red-and-yellow–painted brick facade is a collection of original-edition architects' and designers' furniture, with a particular emphasis on pieces from the 1950s. There are many works by Jean Prouvé, Alexandre Noll, and Charlotte Perriand. ♦ M-Sa; if closed ask at main gallery (see page 162). 5 Rue des Taillandiers (between Rue de Charonne and Passage des Taillandiers). 01.47.00.32.35. Métros: Bastille, Ledru Rollin

---

More than half of French families own their own homes. One in eight owns a holiday home, often belonging to the extended family. Two-thirds of these are in the country and the other third by the sea or in the mountains.

From the time of Napoléon, the French national government—ever leery of the revolutionary potential of the Parisian masses—had always governed the capital. But in 1975, as part of a nationwide trend toward decentralization, Parliament adopted a new constitution for the city that gave Paris the power to administer itself. The code also established the position of Mayor of Paris, who was to be picked by the 109 municipal counselors who were elected by universal suffrage in the city's 20 arrondissements. The central government didn't trust Paris completely, however—it kept control of the police force. Jacques Chirac, the first mayor, served from 1977 to 1995, when he was elected president of France.

155 Centre Gai et Lesbien At the city's only gay and lesbian information center, interested folk can find information on the gay scene in Paris, including the inside scoop on restaurants, bars, and clubs. There is plenty of informational literature, a small gallery, a library of books and magazines (including *3 Keller,* the center's monthly magazine), and a small cafe in the corner. Numerous lesbian and gay groups hold meetings here. The friendly staff is happy to answer questions about health concerns or gay rights' issues either in person or on the phone. Free *préservatifs* (condoms) are there for the taking. ♦ M-Sa 2-8PM; Su 2-7PM. 3 Rue Keller (between Rues de Charonne and de la Roquette). 01.43.57.21.47; fax 01.43.57.27.93. Métro: Ledru Rollin

155 Le Souk ★★$$ To get to Marrakech in the wink of an eye, step past the colorful bins full of spices in front of this restaurant and into its cozy dining room, where amiable waiters in burnooses glide through the authentically Moorish decor lit by flicking mosque candles. The standard couscous and *tajine* with lamb, chicken, *mechoui* (oven-baked mutton), or *merguez* (spicy North African sausage) are excellent. But for some alternate takes on the tried and true recipes, try the *tajine* with duck, figs, and lemon, or with fish and fennel; or the couscous with chicken, raisins, spiced semolina, and cinnamon. The restaurant also serves complete vegetarian meals, and there's a small, but well-chosen, selection of French, Algerian, and Moroccan wines. Owner Lahlu Arab is the brother of Ahmed Arab, who owns the **Bistrot les Sans-Culottes** (see page 159). ♦ Tu-Su lunch and dinner. Reservations recommended. 1 Rue Keller (at Rue de Charonne). 01.49.29.05.08. Métro: Ledru Rollin

155 BPM Progressive music is sold at this techno house, one of many in the Bastille neighborhood. ♦ M-Sa. 1 Rue Keller (at Rue de Charonne). 01.40.21.02.88. Métro: Ledru Rollin

155 Pause Café ★★$ On a warm, sunny day, pause for a break and have a bottle of crisp white Montlouis Domaine Levasseur and a plate of assorted cheeses on the terrace of this popular local hangout. Or try the duck with orange, a roast beef sandwich, or warm goat cheese on *pain Poilâne.* If the weather isn't obliging, take a seat at the horseshoe-shaped bar or one of the tables in the airy dining room, which has tripled its size since the cafe was featured in the 1996 film, *Chacun Cherche son Chat,* a big hit in France. ♦ Tu-Sa lunch and dinner until midnight; Su lunch. 41 Rue de Charonne (at Rue Keller). 01.48.06.80.33. Métro: Ledru Rollin

156 Le Bistrot du Peintre ★★$ This corner cafe is an architectural jewel. It opened in 1907 as a bistro/billiard hall and retains the original Eiffel-era girders, carved wood panels, and peeling gold-leaf lettering. Have a *pastis* or some Berthillon ice cream on the terrace and luxuriate in the faded fin de siècle elegance. Traditional French bistro fare is also served. ♦ M-Sa breakfast, lunch, and dinner until 2AM; Su breakfast, lunch, and dinner. 116 Ave Ledru-Rollin (at Rue de Charonne). 01.47.00.34.39. Métro: Ledru Rollin

157 Galerie Jousse Seguin Since 1989, owners Patrick Jousse and Philippe Seguin have been showing a broad range of works by contemporary international artists. At opposite ends of the spectrum are Karin Kneffe's precise, realist watercolors of fruits and Thomas Grünfeld's disturbing installations of taxidermy misfits, featuring such fantastical creatures as a combination sheep/Saint Bernard, and a fox/pheasant/swan. Serge Comte, Stephen Hepworth, and Peter Hopkins also exhibited here. ♦ M-Sa. 34 Rue de Charonne (between Ave Ledru-Rollin and Rue du Faubourg-St-Antoine). 01.47.00.32.35. Métro: Ledru Rollin

158 La Chaiserie du Faubourg Hundreds of chairs waiting to be repaired or retrieved by their owners are stacked *pêle-mêle* from floor to ceiling, leaving only a small passage for Gérard Decourbe to squeeze through to his desk. It's a wonder Decourbe is able to find the particular chair he is looking for, but he has a special cataloguing system that makes even the **Louvre**'s look simple. If he's not too busy you may be able to talk him into a tour of the atelier in the **Passage l'Homme** where chairs are repaired and manufactured. There you'll meet paint-spattered crafter Gérard Brousset, who jokes with pride that he can make old chairs look new and new chairs that look old. ♦ M-Sa. 26 Rue de Charonne (between Ave Ledru-Rollin and Rue du Faubourg-St-Antoine). 01.43.57.67.51. Métros: Bastille, Ledru Rollin

158 Passage l'Homme Take a detour into this pleasant ivy-covered passage and peek through the windows of **Ateliers d'Art** (01.47.00.81.22), where artisans keep alive the traditional craft of binding books with leather and gold leaf. ♦ 26 Rue de Charonne (between Ave Ledru-Rollin and Rue du Faubourg-St-Antoine). Métros: Bastille, Ledru Rollin

159 Galerie Lavignes-Bastille In his large, light-bathed gallery, Jean-Pierre Lavignes displays contemporary and modern art works from all over the world that he sells *dépôt-vente* (on consignment). It's an eclectic variety of pieces, with everything from outrageous kitsch to real art (whatever that is). At the very least, it makes for an amusing foray, and with luck you may find something you like. M. Lavignes also represents the noted artists Jean-Claude Meynard and Calum Fraser. ◆ M-F 2-7PM; Sa 11AM-12:30PM, 2-7PM. 27 Rue de Charonne (between Rue des Taillandiers and Passage Thiéré). 01.47.00.88.18; fax 01.43.55.91.32. Métros: Bastille, Ledru Rollin

159 Charonne Café ★★$ East meets West at this cozy cafe owned by an Egyptian husband-and-wife team. Popular light-meal choices—such as Oriental cakes with mint tea, charcuterie, or a spicy homemade rice dish—will no doubt satisfy. ◆ M-Sa; Su brunch. 25 Rue de Charonne (at Passage Thiéré). 01.43.57.69.33. Métros: Bastille, Ledru Rollin

Les Portes

160 Les Portes ★$ Behind the rustic facade with its namesake doors, this restaurant's harried owner serves lunches of ricotta and tomato tarts; chicken, potato, and tarragon salad; salmon ravioli with peas and creamy fennel sauce; and such plats du jour as gingered salmon. At night the dining room becomes a well-populated bar. ◆ Restaurant: daily lunch. Bar: daily 5PM-2AM. 15 Rue de Charonne (at Rue de Lappe). 01.40.21.70.61. Métros: Bastille, Ledru Rollin

161 Chez Paul ★★$$ Although the customers look rather trendy, this eatery is unpretentious and old-fashioned, serving such authentic bistro fare as lamb with rosemary, and rabbit stuffed with goat cheese and mint. ◆ Daily lunch and dinner. Reservations recommended. 13 Rue de Charonne (at Rue de Lappe). 01.47.00.34.57. Métros: Bastille, Ledru Rollin

161 Axis This boutique's humorous collection of kooky objects includes an escargot plate with snail-shaped ceramic cups, Philippe Starck's daddy longlegs juice squeezer, leg-shaped nutcrackers, and a collection of cartoon character Géteon paraphernalia. ◆ Tu-Sa; closed in August. 13 Rue de Charonne (at Rue de Lappe). 01.48.06.79.10. Métros: Bastille, Ledru Rollin

162 L'Herbe Verte Behind the beautiful carved wood facade, once the entrance to a furrier's shop, young florist Marc Henri casually displays his colorful sunflowers, tulips, daisies, and roses in zinc buckets. Henri, who spent four years working with renowned florist Christian Tortu, designs arrangements for John Galliano. He works with the rhythms of the seasons, creating his splendid arrangements out of the fruits and flowers of the moment; in spring that might mean daisies and tulips, in winter, anemones and berries. He makes an exception for sunflowers, however, which he gets year-round from his native Auvers-sur-Oise, the village where Vincent van Gogh breathed his last and is buried with his brother, Theo. ◆ M-Sa. 5 Rue de Charonne (between Rues du Faubourg-St-Antoine and de Lappe). 01.48.06.50.69. Métros: Bastille, Ledru Rollin

162 Bar La Fontaine This busy spot at the junction of Rues de Charonne and du Faubourg-St-Antoine has been a watering hole for more than 100 years. Its location makes for great people watching, so take a sidewalk table, order a carafe of red wine, and observe the world as it strolls by. The bar is named after the 16th-century **Fontaine Trogneux** around the corner on the Rue du Faubourg-St-Antoine, where two bronze lion heads spout water rather unceremoniously from their mouths into the drains below. ◆ Daily. 1 Rue de Charonne (at Rue du Faubourg-St-Antoine). 01.47.00.58.36. Métros: Bastille, Ledru Rollin

163 Casbah Three bouncers at the door decide who will get into this nightclub, where everything from jeans to tuxedos is acceptable as long as you have an "un look." Those who pass muster can plunge into a magnificent Casablanca atmosphere created by rich colors, dim lighting, exotic cocktails, raï music, and incense. Don't even think of arriving before midnight. ♦ Bar: daily 9PM-dawn. Disco: W-Sa 11PM-dawn. 18-20 Rue de la Forge-Royale (between Rues du Faubourg-St-Antoine and Charles-Delescluze). 01.43.71.71.89. Métros: Ledru Rollin, Faidherbe-Chaligny

164 Place d'Aligre Market One of the most famous and cheapest in Paris, this outdoor market has a North African flavor (undoubtedly because the majority of the merchants are of North African origin). It's always lively and crowded, with shops, stalls, and a covered market offering fabric, white rum, spices, green bananas, and secondhand goods. ♦ Tu-Sa 8AM-1PM, 4-7PM; Su 8AM-1PM. Rue d'Aligre and Pl d'Aligre. Métro: Ledru Rollin

165 Le Baron Rouge ★★$ Close to the **Place d'Aligre Market,** this rough-and-ready wine bar is one of the most colorful and convivial in Paris. Workers from the market, neighborhood artists, and seriously dressed business types mingle in mellow camaraderie. Wine is sold by the glass or bottle (fine vintages from Bordeaux, Bourgogne, Alsace, and the Loire) at the always packed zinc bar, or on tap from the mountain of oak vats piled by the door for next to nothing. Platters of cheese and charcuterie are also available. Be forewarned: The toilet's out in the back courtyard, one of those "Turkish" models that's a hole in the floor. The bar is named for the famed World War I German flying ace, but nobody seems to know why. ♦ M-Th 10AM-2PM, 5-9:30PM; F, Sa 10AM-9:30PM; Su 10AM-3PM. 1 Rue Théophile-Roussel (at Rue de Cotte). 01.43.43.14.32. Métro: Ledru Rollin

LE SQUARE TROUSSEAU

166 Le Square Trousseau ★★$$ This classic Belle Epoque bistro draws lots of its regulars, including the ebullient Jean Paul Gaultier, from the fashion houses that have established themselves along Rue du Faubourg-St-Antoine. The ambience is easygoing; the cuisine honest and satisfying. The menu changes monthly, but examples of typical fare are braised leg of lamb; roast guinea fowl with green cabbage and country-style bacon; duck with prunes and white turnips; and roasted veal liver with melted lentils. The wines are first rate, but somewhat expensive. In good weather dine alfresco under the jaunty yellow awnings at a table on the peaceful square after which the restaurant is named. ♦ Daily lunch and dinner. 1 Rue Antoine-Vollon (at Rue Théophile-Roussel). 01.43.43.06.00. Métro: Ledru Rollin

167 Rue du Faubourg-St-Antoine The main artery of the old working-class Faubourg St-Antoine quarter, this street is latticed with courtyards and passages that have enticing names like Etoile d'Or, du Bel-Air, and St-Esprit. Here carpenters' and cabinetmakers' workshops are adjacent to furniture stores, fashion houses, and funky bars and restaurants. The intersection of Rue du Faubourg-St-Antoine and Avenue Ledru-Rollin was, until 1914, a crossroads where an outdoor furniture market was located; now it is home to such chain stores as **Monoprix** (the French version of K-mart), and **ED l'Epicier,** a no-frills grocery store. ♦ Métros: Bastille, Ledru Rollin, Faidherbe-Chaligny, Nation

167 80 Rue du Faubourg-St-Antoine In a niche above the door is a statue of St. Nicholas dating from 1895. Its presence recalls the 17th-century orphanage founded by *prêtre* (priest) Antoine Barberé that once stood on Rue St-Nicolas. With his outstretched hands, the saint seems to be pontificating, largely unnoticed, to the steady stream of traffic below. ♦ At Rue St-Nicolas. Métro: Ledru Rollin

At 80 Rue du Faubourg-St-Antoine:

Rémy

Rémy Here reproductions of antique furniture, chandeliers, curtains, rugs, and anything else you might need to furnish a somewhat stuffy apartment are sold by a somewhat stuffy staff of designer counselors. ♦ M-Sa. 01.43.43.65.58. Also at: 82 Rue du Faubourg-St-Antoine (at Rue St-Nicolas). 01.43.43.80.72. Métro: Ledru Rollin

168 Cour de l'Etoile d'Or This courtyard, part of which is inhabited by the workshops of the **Rémy** furniture shop down the street, is worth a detour. Just inside the entrance, look for the trompe l'oeil window display with abundant draperies, mirrors, chairs, vases, and decorative objects. Straight ahead you encounter another trompe l'oeil painting, this one of a woman standing at her ivy-covered balcony; through open doors you can glimpse the interior of her apartment. High up on the rear wall of the courtyard is the barely legible 1751 sundial set on a plaster wall. ♦ 75 Rue du Faubourg-St-Antoine (between Ave Ledru-Rollin and Rue de Charonne). Métro: Ledru Rollin

169 Passage du Chantier A sign at the entrance invites you to visit the artisans whose ateliers and showrooms line this passage. Look into the workshops of **Atelier Paul** (01.46.28.44.83.), where reproductions of furniture from many periods are created. ◆ Métros: Bastille, Ledru Rollin

170 Librairie L'Arbre à Lettres Strong on art and philosophy, this bookstore's great collection makes you want to improve your French in order to read all the volumes. The shop is beautifully designed by Thierry Claude, with well-organized stacks and great lighting. ◆ M 1-8PM; Tu-Sa; Su 2:30-7PM. 62 Rue du Faubourg-St-Antoine (between Passage du Chantier and Pl de la Bastille). 01.43.45.49.04. Métros: Bastille, Ledru Rollin

171 Sanz-Sans ★★$ This Bastille bar is named after its young owners, Messrs. Sanz and Sans. The exterior is rough and raw, with exposed brick and steel beams, and the interior features a framed video screen running a continuous closed-circuit film of the bar. The eclectic menu offers such dishes as salmon steak and steak tandoori, and pear tart for dessert. ◆ Daily breakfast, lunch, and dinner until 2AM. 49 Rue du Faubourg-St-Antoine (between Rue de Charonne and Pl de la Bastille). 01.44.75.78.78. Métros: Bastille, Ledru Rollin

172 La Distillerie ★★$$ The poem posted outside this creole restaurant promises to transport diners to the exotic world of the Antilles. Inside, the pink tablecloths, white ironwork chairs, and rum cocktails with names like *touloulou*, punch Soufrière, and *la vie en rose* will make you feel as if you've stepped into a Jean Rhys novel. Owner Elisabeth de Rozières offers such Caribbean inspired dishes as red snapper and shellfish terrine with langoustine sauce; spicy fish soup; mutton with Antillean curry sauce; shark with lime sauce; and exotic ice creams, including mango, banana, white rum, pineapple, and coconut. ◆ M-Th dinner until 2AM; F dinner until 5AM. 50 Rue du Faubourg-St-Antoine (between Passage du Chantier and Pl de la Bastille). 01.40.01.99.00. Métros: Bastille, Ledru Rollin

173 Jean Paul Gaultier The man who outfitted Madonna in ice-cream-cone bras has set up shop in the Faubourg, lending an aura of avant-garde establishment to the neighborhood's often trendy fashion design industry. The handsome black-and-white-striped building was derelict and full of squatters when Gaultier moved in. Now the interior has been revamped and features exposed steel beams, a galactic blue ceiling, mosaic floors embedded with video monitors showing the latest fashion shows, and model-thin salespeople peddling ready-to-wear for men and women, including the designer's trademark striped T-shirts. ◆ M-Sa. 30 Rue du Faubourg-St-Antoine (between Passage du Chantier and Pl de la Bastille). 01.44.68.85.00. Métro: Bastille. Also at: Galerie Vivienne (between Rues des Petits-Champs and Vivienne). 01.42.86.05.05. Métros: Bourse, Pyramides

ATELIER 33

174 Atelier 33 This discreet 17th-century building was an inn before the French Revolution, and today is one of the few remaining buildings on the street that witnessed the bloody events of 1789. It is notable for its architectural details, including mansard roofs, balcony, windows, ironwork, and the wood staircase visible through the double doors in the courtyard. Young fashion designer Henry Leparque has renovated this historic building—now the home of his boutique and ateliers—with respect and elegance, leaving the old stone walls as a backdrop for his simple, classic men's and women's clothing

The young *créateur* helped change the Faubourg from a street of furniture-making workshops to one of fashion houses, yet his fashions are anything but trendy. Leparque uses fine wools and cashmeres for his jackets and coats, which he sells to such established New York department stores as Saks Fifth Avenue and Bloomingdale's. Part of Leparque's success hinges on his interchangeable collections; because his ateliers are upstairs he is able to bring the mix-and-match concept to a new height. Clients can choose their own buttons, ask for another lining in a jacket, or order a pair of gloves and a hat to go with a coat, ending up with a customized ensemble that will be ready in a week. Friendly and excitable, Laparque can easily be persuaded to give you a tour of his upstairs ateliers, where his fashions are made. Note the chairs in the dressing rooms, which once graced the winter garden of the Côte d'Azur estate of the Gould family, the heirs of the 19th-century robber baron Jay Gould. ◆ Daily. 33 Rue du Faubourg-St-Antoine (between Rue de Charonne and Pl de la Bastille). 01.43.40.61.63. Métro: Bastille

174 Perrette Handmade clothes for *les petits* (children), some with lovely hand-embroidered details, are displayed on racks while women quietly continue stitching more garments. If you don't see exactly what you want for that special little girl or boy, keep in mind that they will do made-to-measure outfits. This is a nonprofit organization, and everything is made by seniors and workers with disabilities. ◆ Tu-Sa. 29 Rue du Faubourg-St-Antoine (between Rue de Charonne and Pl de la Bastille). 01.53.17.13.56. Métro: Bastille

175 Les Colonies du Paradis ★$ Unable to decide what it wants to be, this schizophrenic restaurant offers a bit of everything. Shrimp and spinach tandoori, coconut daiquiris, mango margaritas, carrot cake, mint tea, chocolate orange mousse, and dishes with such curious names as the Viking Specialty and the Inca Sandwich are served on glass-topped tables displaying compartments of dried pumpkin seeds, rose buds, black-eyed peas, and banana chips. ◆ M-Sa lunch and dinner until 1:30AM; Su brunch and dinner. 3 Rue du Faubourg-St-Antoine (between Rue de Charonne and Pl de la Bastille). 01.43.44.01.00. Métro: Bastille

175 Atelier Franck Bordas This gallery has put out its own editions of works on paper since 1978, when the curators established an adjacent atelier where artists can create prints on the premises. Such internationally known artists as Gilles Aillaud, Jean-Paul Chambas, Jan Voss, and Robert Wilson have all exhibited in the light and airy spaces, which are perfect for viewing the original prints, artists' books, and lithographed travel cards. ◆ Tu-Sa 2-7PM; closed in August. Cour Février, Passage du Cheval Blanc, 2 Rue de la Roquette (at Rue du Faubourg-St-Antoine). 01.47.00.31.61. Métro: Bastille

176 Viaduc des Arts President Mitterand's decision in the early 1980s to install the new home of the **Opéra de Paris** at the then-shabby Place de la Bastille set off a radical transformation of the long-neglected east side of Paris, a momentum that continues to this day. The most visually striking development since the completion of the **Opéra** is this former railway viaduct whose sixty stone arches have been imaginatively converted into magnificent studios for artisans.

Opened in 1994, this long row of vaulted ateliers begins near the rear of the **Opéra Bastille,** and continues seven blocks southeastward along tree-lined Avenue Daumesnil to Rue de Rambouillet. All the studios have glass walls on the street, and most have dazzling display windows. For the window shopping alone, it's worth the walk. But the real fun is going inside, where you can watch highly skilled toy makers, stone sculptors, furniture restorers, weavers, a glass-blower, flute and violin makers, embroidery workers, and other artisans ply their crafts. All have goods to sell, as do a number of high-class ceramics and home decoration boutiques.

Stop in at one of two large cafes in the vaults for a quick bite or drink—the chic **Viaduc Café** (41-43 Ave Daumesnil, at Rue Abel, 01.44.74.70.70) or the bustling, working-class **Au Père Tranquille** (73-75 Ave Daumesnil, at Blvd Diderot, 01.43.43.64.58). In good weather sit outside at either place on the sprawling sidewalk terraces under the trees.

Pick up the free brochure on the viaduct that the City of Paris, which subsidizes the artists, distributes. Available at all the studios and at the cafe, the brochure has an excellent map and directory of the occupants. ◆ 9-129 Ave Daumesnil (between Rues de Rambouillet and Moreau). Métros: Bastille, Ledru Rollin, Gare de Lyon

Atop the Viaduc des Arts:

Promenade Plantée The City of Paris has developed the path of the old railway line into a lovely promenade. Planted with flower beds, flowering bushes, and trees, it extends almost two miles, from the start of the **Viaduc** all the way to the Bois de Vincennes.

177 Le Train Bleu ★★★$$$ Suspended in time between here and there, this glorious Old World dining room in the monumental **Gare de Lyon** is a train station restaurant in the grand tradition. Named for the luxurious Belle Epoque express train that once took the elite down to the Riviera, this is a traveler's dream, striking wanderlust into the hearts of even the most sedentary. The restaurant, classified as a historic monument, is characterized by vaulted ceilings; extraordinarily intricate gold-leaf moldings, friezes, and carvings; and ceiling frescoes by different artists depicting destinations from the **Gare de Lyon.** Images of Mont Blanc, Marseille, Monaco, Evian, Nice, Montpellier, and Algeria are enough to give even those who come here for a meal (and aren't waiting for a train) the travel bug. The restaurant's guest book has been signed by the likes of such modern-day notables as

Jacques Chirac, François Mitterrand, and Serge Gainsbourg, and in the more distant past Sarah Bernhardt, Edmond Rostand, and Salvador Dalí nourished themselves here.

Upscale traditional French fare is featured. Appetizers include hot Lyonnaise sausage, *escargots*, and *duo de saumon et d'oeuf poché aux aubergines confites* (eggplant purée topped with poached egg and salmon); some of the classic main courses are sole meunière, grilled steak with béarnaise sauce, *canard à l'orange* (braised duck with oranges), and rabbit stew. The 1995 St-Emilion, Chapelle de la Trinité, or the 1997 Sancerre blanc, Domaine Montagu, would be fine choices from the restaurant's wine list, but Champagne might be more appropriate in this sumptuous space. The restaurant's comfortable lounge area overlooking the tracks is the perfect place for a drink while waiting for a train. ♦ Daily lunch and dinner. Reservations recommended. Gare de Lyon, 20 Blvd Diderot (at Rue de Chalon). 01.43.43.09.06. Métro: Gare de Lyon

Bests

Françoise Genty
Waiter/Former Editor and Writer, FAO-Rome and OECD-Paris

The "Concerts du Dimanche Matin" at the **Théâtre des Champs-Elysées** are a very special entertainment in Paris because of the excellent musicians' performances, the informal, intimate atmosphere, and because it is Sunday morning in Paris.

Walking in the narrow streets of the **Marais** gives you the impression that you are softly treading on HISTORY.

Most days of winter, strolling along the **Seine** makes you believe that the rainbow has turned gray—from the river glittering dark gray, to the whitish building walls with their gray zinc roofs, up to the pearl gray clouds of the Parisian sky.

It's a real pleasure to have a late morning breakfast with a long *tartine de beurre* (toasted bread with butter) and a rich warm *café crème*, standing at the bar with others as they take a pause after hours of work that they started in early morning.

Judith Wolfe
Artist

When I feel the need for big, open spaces, I head up to the **Parc de la Villette,** a very lively, popular park with lots to see and do: the **Cité des Sciences et de l'Industrie** (science museum); the concerts at the **Cité de la Musique,** including open-air ones in warmer weather; and excellent temporary exhibits at the **Maison de la Villette.**

For a long, interesting walk away from traffic, I enjoy following the Canal de l'Ourcq, which goes through the park, down to the Place de Stalingrad and then beyond where it becomes the **Canal St-Martin.**

An extra-special treat is the three-hour boat trip on the canal, starting at **Parc de la Villette** and ending at the **Musée d'Orsay.** Unforgettable views of Paris.

For more visual stimulation I do the rounds of some of the better art galleries in town. Not far from Canal St-Martin, and just beyond Place de la République, you'll find a still very authentic part of the historic **Marais** quarter. Starting on the corner of the lively market street Rue de Bretagne and Rue Charlot, I go down Rue Charlot. I carry on around to Rue Poitou and over to Rues Debelleyme, Vieille-du-Temple, and du Perche, all lined with interesting galleries. Pick up the free gallery guide in any one of these.

Mireille Johnston
Author

Living in Paris means getting used to small miracles.

Of course, some places are more blessed than others. For me and mine, instant happiness is:

Lingering along the Seine. There are lazy sea gulls gently carried by the river flow, eager joggers, wide stone benches, rows of trees, wide barges loaded with sand, potted flowers, canvas chairs, acrobatic cats. I snuggle on the stone stairs flowing from the flower market on the **Ile de la Cité** to the riverbank. I dream of all the travelers, Vikings, Romans, who sailed the river centuries ago, when Paris was young. And how it took 35 bridges to properly link the unkissing cousins: **Left Bank** and **Right Bank.**

Fresh from an inspiring show at the **Musée National d'Art Moderne de la Ville de Paris,** it's "market day" on the Avenue du Président-Wilson. At once a village festival and a family reunion rolled into one. Merchants and buyers exchange jokes, recipes, opinions over the extravagant offerings of flowers, pâtés, cheese, fish, a mind-boggling choice of breads, vegetables, barrels of nuts and flours. There always seems to be—for gourmands and experts and innocents passing by—the contagious same need to enjoy each other, to enjoy the moment. No strings attached.

Strolling in the **Luxembourg Gardens.** A quick visit to the beehives and the fruit trees, a lazy walk around the pond, a more attentive look at the program of the Guignol puppet theater, a nostalgic glance at the tiny donkeys and their even tinier riders, a long friendly pause in front of the statues of Baudelaire, Mendès France, and the local version of the Statue of Liberty.

Stopping at **Ladurée** pastry shop for grapefruit, lemon, and pistachio tiny macaroons and nibbling them on the **Invalides** lawn by my apartment with in-line skaters, soccer players, crawling infants, and bouncing dogs all around.

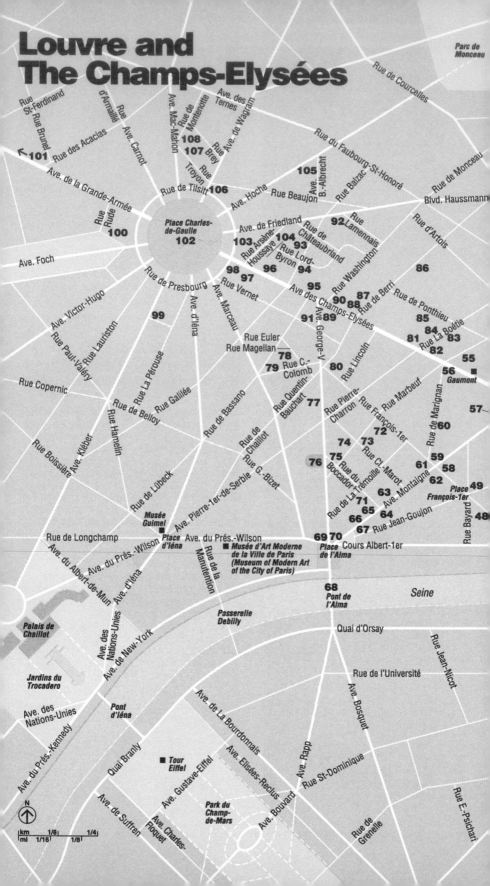

Louvre and
The Champs-Elysées

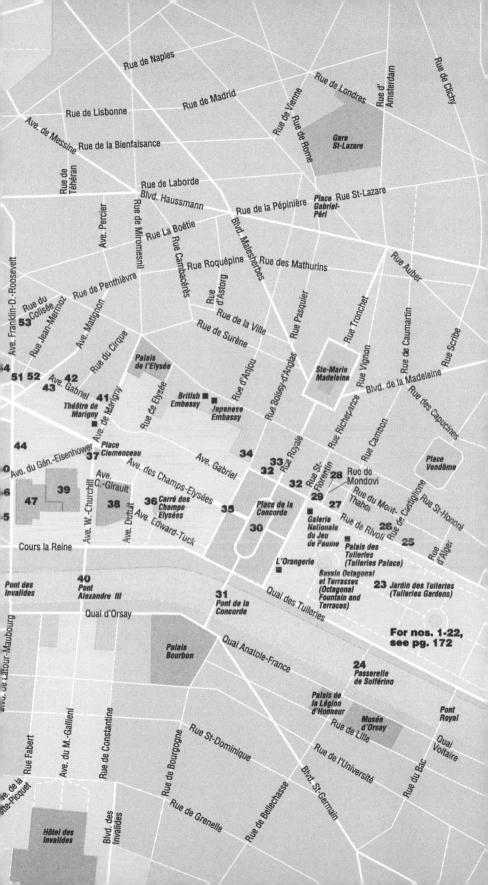

Rue de Naples
Rue de Madrid
Rue de Londres
Rue d' Amsterdam
Rue de Clichy
Rue de Lisbonne
Rue de Vienne
Rue de Rome
Ave. de Messine
Rue de la Bienfaisance
Gare St-Lazare
Rue de Téhéran
Rue de Laborde
Blvd. Haussmann
Rue de la Pépinière
Place Gabriel-Péri
Rue St-Lazare
Ave. Percier
Rue de Miromesnil
Rue La Boétie
Rue Cambacérès
Rue Roquépine
Blvd. Malesherbes
Rue des Mathurins
Rue Auber
Ave. Franklin-D.-Roosevelt
Rue du Colisée
Rue de Penthièvre
Rue d'Astorg
Rue de la Ville
Rue Pasquier
Rue Tronchet
Rue de Caumartin
Rue Scribe
Rue Jean-Mermoz
Ave. Matignon
Rue de Surène
Rue de la Madeleine
Ave. Percier
Rue du Cirque
Palais de l'Elysée
Rue d'Anjou
Rue de l'Anjou
Ste-Marie Madeleine
Rue Richepance
Rue Vignon
Blvd. de la Madeleine
Rue des Capucines
54
51 52
42
Ave. Gabriel
43
Ave. de Marigny
41
Rue Cr Elysée
British Embassy
Japanese Embassy
Rue Boissy-d'Anglas
Rue Cambon
Théâtre de Marigny
Place Vendôme
44
Avo. du Gén.-Eisenhower
37
Place Clemenceau
Ave. des Champs-Elysées
Ave. Gabriel
34
Rue Royale
Rue St-Florentin
28
Rue de Mondovi
Rue St-Honoré
Ave. C.-Girault
33
32
32
29
27
Rue du Mont-Thabot
Rue de Castiglione
39
38
36
Carré des Champs-Elysées
35
Place de la Concorde
30
Galerie Nationale du Jeu de Paume
Rue de Rivoli
26
25
Rue d'Alger
47
Ave. Dutuit
Ave. Edward-Tuck
L'Orangerie
Palais des Tuileries (Tuileries Palace)
Cours la Reine
40
Pont Alexandre III
31
Pont de la Concorde
Quai des Tuileries
Bassin Octagonal et Terrasses (Octagonal Fountain and Terraces)
23
Jardin des Tuileries (Tuileries Gardens)
Pont des Invalides
Quai d'Orsay
For nos. 1-22, see pg. 172
Palais Bourbon
Quai Anatole-France
24
Passerelle de Solférino
Rue Fabert
Ave. du M.-Galliéni
Rue de Constantine
Rue de Bourgogne
Rue St-Dominique
Palais de la Légion d'Honneur
Rue de Lille
Musée d'Orsay
Pont Royal
Quai Voltaire
Quai d'Orsay
Rue de l'Université
Rue du Bac
Rue de la Motte-Picquet
Blvd. des Invalides
Rue de Grenelle
Rue de Bellechasse
Blvd. St-Germain
Hôtel des Invalides
Ave. de Latour-Maubourg

Louvre and The Champs-Elysées

This superlative stroll includes the largest museum in the Western world (the **Louvre**), the world's most famous boulevard (the Champs-Elysées), the most ancient monument in Paris (the 3,300-year-old Egyptian **Obelisk of Luxor**), the best 360-degree view of Paris (from **La Samaritaine**'s rooftop cafe), some of the city's grandest hotels (the **Meurice, Crillon,** and **Plaza Athénée**), its oldest métro station (**Franklin D. Roosevelt**), its most elegant tea salon (**Angélina**), its best-stocked English paperback bookshop (**W.H. Smith and Son**), the world's most magnificent square (**Place de la Concorde**), the largest concert hall in Paris (**Théâtre du Châtelet**), the "hautest" of haute couture (the boutiques along **Avenue Montaigne**), the sexiest cabaret in Paris (the **Crazy Horse**), some of the city's best restaurants (**Les Ambassadeurs, Ledoyen, Laurent, Taillevent, Pierre Gagnaire, Guy Savoy**), and the world's biggest triumphal arch (**L'Arc de Triomphe**). That's a lot to absorb in one day, so get an early start, put on your most comfortable shoes, and *bon courage*—that's French for "keep a stiff upper lip."

Monday may be the best day to visit this area, for it's the only day the **Hôtel de Ville** (City Hall) is open, and the lines at the **Louvre Museum** slack off (on the first Sunday of the month, when admission to the **Louvre** is free, it's a mob scene). Monday is also discount night at the cinemas on the Champs-Elysées. Begin your tour with the **Hôtel de Ville**, then walk along the **Seine** past the pet and plant shops on **Quai de la Mégisserie** and stop for morning coffee and a spectacular panorama atop **La Samaritaine** department store. Next comes the **Louvre Museum** with all its wonders—take a two- to three-hour whirlwind tour of the history of art here that includes those three remarkable Mediterranean ladies: *Venus de Milo,* the *Winged Victory of Samothrace,* and the *Mona Lisa.* After the **Louvre** take a break at the nearby **Jardin des Tuileries** (Tuileries Gardens), then either splurge for lunch at **Ledoyen** or join the fashion models with fierce sweet cravings who order the *Mont Blanc* dessert at **Angélina**. En route to the **Place de la Concorde**, you might stop at **W.H. Smith and Son** for the latest *New Yorker* or an English-language novel to read on the plane home.

From the base of the **Obelisk of Luxor**, it is a mile to the **Arc de Triomphe.** If you need motivation to keep walking, consider the delights that lie ahead: the major art exhibition that can always be found under the huge glazed dome of the **Grand Palais**, the high fashion boutiques of the **Triangle d'Or** (bounded by the Champs-Elysées and Avenues Montaigne and George-V), and chef Philippe Legendre's *fruits de mer* (mixed seafood) with truffles at **Taillevent**. The eastern half of the Champs-Elysées is bordered by gardens (designed by André Le Nôtre, a gardener for Louis XIV, who also landscaped **Versailles**) that have not changed since novelist Marcel Proust played there as a child. On the right, you pass behind three fine structures: the **Japanese Embassy**, the **British Embassy**, and the **Palais de l'Elysée**. At **Rond-Point des Champs-Elysées**, a roundabout in the middle of the Champs-Elysées, shoppers should veer left to Avenue Montaigne, the high-fashion row, while art buffs and philatelists will want to go directly to the galleries on **Avenue Matignon** and to the stamp stalls on **Avenue Gabriel**.

The last stretch of the Champs-Elysées, which leads up to Napoléon's triumphal arch, is meant to be strolled in the evening, when Paris more than lives up to its nickname, the "City of Light." High rollers will want a cocktail on the terrace at **Fouquet's**, and dinner at **Taillevent, Chiberta**, or, perhaps, upstairs at **Lasserre**, where the ceiling rolls back for stargazing between courses. Those who are on a tighter budget might catch a first-run movie at the **Gaumont,** or a Beckett play at the **Théâtre du Rond-Point,** and then enjoy a late-night supper at the vivacious Art Deco brasserie **Le Boeuf sur le Toit.**

When the day's strolling is over, you may feel as if you've completed the Tour de France, the world's greatest bicycle race, which ends each July on the Champs-Elysées—also the finishing line for your one-day "Tour de Paris."

---

1 Place de l'Hôtel-de-Ville The present seat of the Paris city government, this square is where Etienne Marcel, one of the first mayors of Paris, established his city council in 1357. Marcel incited a mob to rise against the monarchy and storm the royal palace on Ile de la Cité. The next year he was killed— not by the king, but by his fellow Parisians. Centered in the granite on the square is the image of a boat, the city symbol, adopted from the 13th-century coat of arms of the Boatmen's Guild. ♦ Métro: Hôtel de Ville

2 Hôtel de Ville (City Hall) Another example of late 19th-century architectural eclecticism, this building (pictured below) is part Renaissance palace, part Belle Epoque fantasy. Its exterior is embellished with 146 statues, among them bronze effigies of the sentries who patrolled the perimeter of the city wall during the Middle Ages. Visitors on guided tours of the state rooms are shown the splendid staircase by Philibert Delorme, murals by Puvis de Chavannes, and a lesser-known Rodin sculpture, *La République.* ♦ Tours: M 10.30AM, departing from the Information desk at 29 Rue de Rivoli; call the previous Friday to confirm time. Pl de l'Hôtel-de-Ville (between Quai de l'Hôtel-de-Ville and Rue de Rivoli). 01.42.76.50.49. Métro: Hôtel de Ville

RESTAURANT

3 Le Trumilou ★$ The perfect way to enjoy this authentic Parisian bistro is at a window table overlooking the Seine and **Notre-Dame.** Jean-Claude Dumond and his family prepare home-cooked food at sensible prices. Favorites include *canard aux pruneaux* (duck with prunes), lamb with white beans, sole meunière, and the ever-popular *poulet Provençale* (chicken in tomato sauce with *herbes de Provence*). For dessert, try the *oeufs à la neige* (meringue floating in crème anglaise). ♦ Daily lunch and dinner. Reservations recommended. 84 Quai de l'Hôtel-de-Ville (between Rues du Pont-Louis-Philippe and de Brosse). 01.42.77.63.98. Métros: Pont Marie, Hôtel de Ville

Hôtel de Ville

MICHAEL STORRINGS

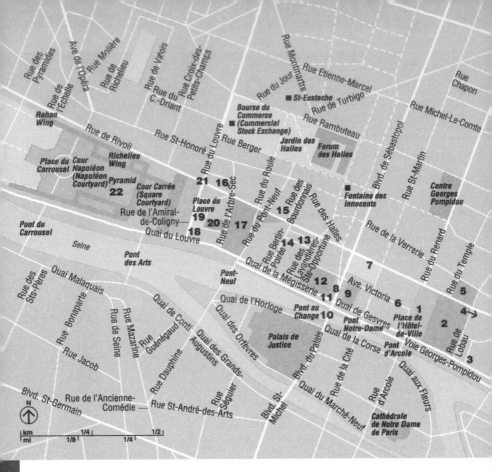

4 A l'Olivier Founded in 1860, this shop still sells every oil imaginable, including hazelnut oil for vinaigrettes, almond-honey–oil shampoo, and apricot-nut oil for massages. Tarragon mustard and dried figs are also available. The classic bottles would be worth buying empty, and the giant pottery casks for olive oil are not to be missed. ♦ Tu-Sa. 23 Rue de Rivoli (at Rue du Pont-Louis-Philippe). 01.48.04.86.59. Métro: Hôtel de Ville

5 Bazar de l'Hôtel-de-Ville (BHV) Situated directly across Rue de Rivoli from the **Hôtel-de-Ville,** this is one of Paris's largest department stores. Its five floors cover a

good-sized city block and are replete with everything this kind of store carries, including a maze of perfume and lingerie counters on the ground floor; clothes of all kinds for men, women, and children; toys; books; stationery; photo and video equipment; and a wide range of home furnishings, kitchenware, and appliances. But the store's most famous department is a huge hardware emporium in the basement, a do-it-yourselfer's paradise. Anyone trying to locate a hard-to-find part will be invariably directed here to **BHV** (pronounced "bay-aash-vay"). ♦ M-Tu, Th-Su; W 9:30AM-10PM. 52-64 Rue de Rivoli (between Rues des Archives and du Temple). 01.42.74.90.00. Métro: Hôtel de Ville

6 Avenue Victoria One of the shortest avenues in Paris doesn't commemorate any military victory, but rather the royal visit of the dowager Queen of England to Paris. ♦ Métros: Hôtel de Ville, Châtelet

7 Tour St-Jacques (St. Jacques Tower) This 1522 architectural anomaly was the Gothic belfry of **St-Jacques La Boucherie,** a church that was destroyed in 1802; the tower was spared to become a factory for manufacturing lead musket balls. The tower now doubles as a weather station, appropriately enough, for at the tower's base is a statue of Blaise Pascal (1623-62), one of France's first weather forecasters. In 1648, at the top of this tower, he used a barometer to calculate the weight of air. Cast your eyes up from outside the tower (it's closed to the public) and you'll see meteorological equipment lurking among the gargoyles. This place also has an important religious significance: It is the starting point for the pilgrimage to Santiago de Compostela in Spain. ♦ Sq de la Tour-St-Jacques. Métro: Châtelet

8 Place du Châtelet Named after a fortress and prison that once stood on this site, this square is the principal crossroads of Paris, a hub of east-west and north-south traffic. The **Châtelet Fountain** in the center, flanked by sphinxes, was designed in 1808 to celebrate the triumphant Egyptian campaign of Napoléon. Below the square, five métro lines intersect, making **Châtelet** the world's largest underground station. ♦ Métro: Châtelet

9 Théâtre de la Ville de Paris Formerly the **Sarah Bernhardt Theatre,** this mid–19th-century stage is now devoted to contemporary dance, jazz, and classical theater, but still preserves the dressing room of the "Divine Sarah." ♦ Box office: daily. 2 Pl du Châtelet (at Quai de Gesvres). 01.42.74.22.77. Métro: Châtelet

10 Pont au Change "Money-Changers' Bridge" was the ninth-century forerunner of an American Express office—a spot where travelers came to change foreign currency for French funds. Today this Second Empire bridge is flanked by identical state-owned theaters, both built by architect **Gabriel-Jean-Antoine Davioud** in 1862. ♦ Métro: Châtelet

11 Quai de la Mégisserie Once a malodorous *mégisserie* (sheepskin tannery), today this spot is rife with booksellers, pet shops, fish-tackle dealers, and plant stores where mice and goldfish are sold alongside dahlias and fertilizer. The cacophony of the parakeets, turkeys, and guinea fowls whose cages clutter the pavement vies pleasantly with that of the automobile traffic nearby. If you don't fancy house pets or have a green thumb, stroll here for the splendid views of **La Conciergerie,** the towers of **Notre-Dame,** and the spire of **Sainte-Chapelle.** ♦ Métro: Châtelet

12 Théâtre du Châtelet Built in 1862, this is the fourth-largest auditorium in Paris (after the **Opéra Bastille, Opéra Garnier,** and the **Palais des Congrès**) and the city's largest concert hall. Seating half as many people as the **Opéra Garnier,** the theater is primarily a venue for symphonies, operas, and ballets. On 21 May 1910, the New York Metropolitan Opera Company made its Paris debut here with *Aida.* Toscanini conducted, Caruso sang, and the audience, which included most of the French diplomatic corps, the Vanderbilts, and

Louis Cartier (who estimated that more than $3 million worth of jewelry was worn that evening), went wild. ♦ Box office: daily. Theater: closed in August. 1 Pl du Châtelet (at Quai de la Mégisserie). 01.40.28.28.28. Métro: Châtelet

13 Le Petit Opportun This little jazz club, which once featured such North American headliners as Clark Terry, Slide Hampton, and Pepper Adams, now presents French mainstream jazz groups and some Latino sounds. ♦ Cover. Shows: Tu-Sa 10:30PM-2:30AM. No credit cards accepted. 15 Rue des Lavandières-Ste-Opportune (between Rues Jean-Lantier and des Deux-Boules). 01.42.36.01.36. Métro: Châtelet

Grand Hôtel de Champagne
★★★

14 Grand Hôtel de Champagne $$$ Small, comfortable rooms (of which there are 40 and 3 suites) characterize this tastefully converted 16th-century stone mansion a short walk from the Place du Châtelet, the **Louvre, Sainte Chapelle, Notre-Dame,** and the Ile de la Cité. There's no restaurant. ♦ 17 Rue Jean-Lantier (between Rues des Lavandières-Ste-Opportune and Bertin-Poirée). 01.42.36.60.00; fax 01.45.08.43.33. Métro: Châtelet

15 Slow Club Dixieland jazz is alive and well at this former ballroom, now the oldest jazz club in the city. Enjoy live Dixieland, swing, boogie-woogie, R & B, and rock 'n' roll four nights a week in a refreshingly unpretentious, old-fashioned atmosphere. Wednesday is the only night that there's recorded music. ♦ Cover. Tu-Sa 10PM-3AM. No credit cards accepted. 130 Rue de Rivoli (between Rues des Bourdonnais and du Pont-Neuf). 01.42.33.84.30. Métro: Châtelet

16 Rue de l'Arbre-Sec This short street is long and rich in history. At **No. 52** is the **Hôtel de Trudon,** the former home of Louis XV's wine steward; nearby is the **Hôtel de François Barnon,** named after Louis XIV's barber; D'Artagnan of the Three Musketeers lived at **No. 4** (formerly the **Hôtel des Mousquetaires,** now **La Samaritaine** department store). The name *arbre-sec* (which literally means dry tree) suggests that a gibbet once stood in the street. ♦ Métro: Louvre-Rivoli, Pont Neuf

---

"Every man has two nations, and France is one of them."

Benjamin Franklin

16 Chez la Vieille ★★$$ True to its name, this bistro features fare that would make a French country grandmother proud. A typical meal that young chef Anne Desplanques prepares is *foie gras de canard* (duck liver pâté); followed by lamb shoulder with herbs from Provence, veal liver with shallots, or fish from the market; and for dessert, a grand selection from the *chariot* (cart). There's a well-chosen list of wines, mostly Bordeaux. The welcoming owner Marie-José Cervoni presides over the tiny five-table dining room. ◆ M-W, F lunch; Th lunch and dinner; closed in August. Reservations recommended for lunch; required for dinner. 1 Rue Bailleul (at Rue de l'Arbre-Sec). 01.42.60.15.78. Métro: Louvre-Rivoli

17 La Samaritaine One of the city's oldest department stores and possibly its most confusing, this emporium is named for an old Pont-Neuf water pump decorated with an image of the woman of Samaria offering Jesus a drink of water. Today the store sprawls through four grand old buildings offering everything from pop psychiatry books to kitchen sinks, all at bargain prices. Its best deal, however, is the rooftop panorama. On a pleasant summer day, walk into **Magasin II** (Store No. 2), designed by **F. Jourdan**, and ride the elevator to the ninth floor. Sip a *café* or *citron pressé* (lemonade) at the cafe, then mount the stairs and enjoy a 360-degree view of Paris. A ceramic legend locates points of interest. ◆ M-W, F-Sa; Th 9:30AM-10PM. 19 Rue de la Monnaie (between Pl de l'Ecole and Rue de Rivoli). 01.40.41.20.20. Métros: Pont Neuf, Châtelet, Louvre-Rivoli

Within La Samaritaine:

Toupary ★★$$ Suspended between the sky and the Seine, this apricot, turquoise, and electric blue restaurant designed by **Hilton McConnico** serves such specialties as cream of tomato soup with cardamom, *daurade* (sea bream) in fennel, a different fish dish every day, and lime crepes. Try to get a window table for a panoramic view of Paris. ◆ M-Sa lunch, tea, cocktails, and dinner until 1AM. Magasin II, Fifth floor. 01.40.41.29.29

18 Yvan sur Seine ★★$$ This riverside eatery with the look of an upscale pleasure barge is one of three restaurants owned by genial chef Yvan Zaplatilek, the darling of *Le Tout-Paris*. The banquettes buzz with the chatter of beautiful people at lunch and dinner. Show-biz types make their appearance late in the evening and keep the place open until the wee hours on Friday and Saturday. The fare is a mix of reinterpreted French and Italian dishes—ravioli of kidney, sea trout with anchovy butter, sea scallops *à la Provençale* (with oil, garlic, and tomatoes), and beef with Roquefort sauce and macaroni—along with specialties from Yvan's native Belgium, such as *waterzooï de volaille* (chicken stew). The prix-fixe menu, which includes wine, is reasonable, and the staff is efficient and charming. ◆ M-Th, Su lunch and dinner until 1AM; F lunch and dinner until 4AM; Sa dinner until 4AM. Reservations recommended. 26 Quai du Louvre (between Rues de l'Arbre-Sec and de l'Amiral-de-Coligny). 01.42.36.49.52. Métros: Louvre-Rivoli, Pont Neuf

18 Pâtisserie St-Germain-l'Auxerrois ★★$$ Embellished with crystal chandeliers, gilded pillars, and marble tables, this elegant pastry shop and tea salon—open since 1896—makes all its sweets and ice cream in a basement factory. Try the chocolate pastries (*la mousseline* and *le cador*). ◆ Tu-Su; closed two weeks in August and two weeks in September. No credit cards accepted. 2 Rue de l'Amiral-de-Coligny (at Quai du Louvre). 01.45.08.19.18. Métros: Louvre-Rivoli, Pont Neuf

19 Place du Louvre In 52 BC, Labienus, a lieutenant of Caesar, bivouacked with his troops between the present sites of the **Louvre** and **St-Germain-l'Auxerrois** before capturing the settlement of Lutetia. ◆ Métros: Louvre-Rivoli, Pont Neuf

MICHAEL STORRINGS

20 St-Germain-l'Auxerrois On St. Bartholomew's Day (24 August) in 1572, at the orders of Catherine de Médicis and Charles IX, the pealing bells of this church (illustrated above) signaled the beginning of a brutal religious massacre. Some 3,000 Huguenots, Protestant wedding guests of Henri de Navarre and Marguerite de Valois, were slain in their beds. The 38-bell carillon in the Neo-Gothic tower still rings every Wednesday afternoon, a grave reminder of the mass murder. The carillon is the only truly ancient one in Paris; all the others were melted down during the Revolution.

MICHAEL STORRINGS

Musée du Louvre

This gargoyle-laden edifice, designed in 1220 by **Jean Gaussel,** is named for St. Germain, the bishop of Auxerre (378-448), whose students included St. Patrick of Ireland, and Saint Geneviève of Paris. When Louis XIV and his court moved to **Versailles,** the artists' colony he had established there took over the **Louvre,** and **St-Germain-l'Auxerrois** became its parish church.

Among the luminaries buried here are architects **Louis Le Vau, Jacques-Ange Gabriel,** and **Jacques-Germain Soufflot;** the sculptor Antoine Coysevox; and painters Nöel Coypel, François Boucher, and Jean-Baptiste Chardin. Every Ash Wednesday a service is held to pray for artists throughout the world who will die in the coming year. Royalists flock here annually to a Mass said for Louis XVI on the anniversary of his 21 January 1793 execution. Notice the ornately canopied and sculpted oak bench on the right side of the aisle; painter Charles Le Brun designed this red-velvet pew for Louis XIV and his family in 1682. ◆ Daily; call for a schedule of Masses in English and organ and bell recitals. 2 Pl du Louvre (at Rue des Prêtres-St-Germain-l'Auxerrois). 01.42.60.13.96. Métros: Louvre-Rivoli, Pont Neuf

21 **Louvre-Rivoli Métro Station** The platform is a museum in itself, with softly illuminated copies of the sculptures found above it in the **Louvre.** This and the **Varenne** métro station (with replicas of Rodin sculptures) are two of the prettiest in Paris. ◆ Rues de l'Amiral-de-Coligny and de Rivoli

21 **Rue de Rivoli** On this arcaded street, an incongruous mix of luxury hotels and tacky souvenir shops lies demurely behind a graceful but rather monotonous First Empire colonnade designed by **Charles Percier** and **Pierre Fontaine** in 1811 at the behest of Napoléon. The street was named after the Italian town where the emperor thrashed the Austrians in 1797. Strict rules pertaining to the arcades forbade leasing shops to any

entrepreneur using ovens or metal tools, thus excluding such riffraff as bakers and butchers. ◆ Métros: Louvre-Rivoli, Châtelet, Hôtel de Ville, Palais Royal–Musée du Louvre, Tuileries, Concorde

22 **Musée du Louvre** This is the single largest building in Paris, the largest palace in Europe, the largest museum in the Western world, and probably the most dominating symbol of art and culture the world has ever known. "I never knew what a palace was until I had a glimpse of the Louvre," said 19th-century North American author Nathaniel Hawthorne. It has 224 halls, and its enormous **Grande Galerie** is longer than 3 football fields. It took 7 centuries to build, spanning the lives of 17 monarchs and countless architects.

The origin of the word *louvre,* though obscure, is believed to be either a derivation of the Old French word *louverie,* which meant wolf lodge, or a variation of an Old Flemish word meaning fortress. In 1190 King Philippe Auguste began surrounding Paris with a 30-foot-high city wall that included the fortified structure known as the **Louvre.** More than three centuries later, François I agreed to live in this fortress at the request of Parisian citizens who had ransomed him from captivity in Italy. In 1527 he tore down most of the old building, and by 1546 he had constructed the **Cour Carrée** (Square Courtyard).

In 1578 Catherine de Médicis built a new palace, the **Tuileries,** at the far end of the present **Louvre.** The two palaces were joined by Henri IV, who created a number of apartments in the long gallery for the use of court painters and their families in 1608. This same Henri was stabbed by an assassin here in 1610 (he was the only king to die within the **Louvre**'s walls). In the late 1660s, Colbert, a minister of finance to Louis XIV, hired the acclaimed Roman architect **Giovanni Bernini** to redesign the **Louvre.** But when Bernini suggested knocking the whole place down and starting from scratch, Colbert sent him

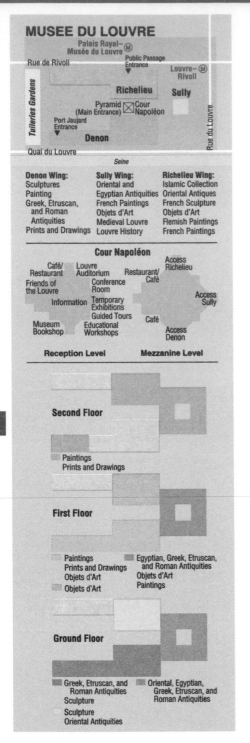

MUSEE DU LOUVRE

Denon Wing:
Sculptures
Painting
Greek, Etruscan,
  and Roman
  Antiquities
Prints and Drawings

Sully Wing:
Oriental and
  Egyptian Antiquities
French Paintings
Objets d'Art
Medieval Louvre
Louvre History

Richelieu Wing:
Islamic Collection
Oriental Antiques
French Sculpture
Objets d'Art
Flemish Paintings
French Paintings

Cour Napoléon

Café/
Restaurant
Friends of
the Louvre

Louvre
Auditorium
Conference
Room
Temporary
Exhibitions
Guided Tours
Educational
Workshops

Restaurant/
Café

Access
Richelieu

Access
Sully

Café

Access
Denon

Information

Museum
Bookshop

Reception Level   **Mezzanine Level**

Second Floor

Paintings
Prints and Drawings

First Floor

Paintings
Prints and Drawings
Objets d'Art
Objets d'Art

Egyptian, Greek, Etruscan,
  and Roman Antiquities
Objets d'Art
Paintings

Ground Floor

Greek, Etruscan, and
  Roman Antiquities
Sculpture
Sculpture
Oriental Antiquities

Oriental, Egyptian,
  Greek, Etruscan, and
  Roman Antiquities

Restaurants/Clubs: Red
Shops/ Outdoors: Green

Hotels: Blue
Sights/Culture: Black

packing. Louis XIV proceeded to reconstruct the **Cour Carrée** to his own tastes, consulting the architect **Louis Le Vau,** the painter Charles Le Brun, and Claude Perrault, a Parisian physician whose brother Charles was the author of *Puss in Boots.* After renovating the palace, Louis XIV established an artists' colony here; residents included painters such as Coustou, Boucher, and Coypel. Louis XIV left Paris for **Versailles** in 1678, and without royal occupants, the **Louvre** fell into disrepair. Overrun by freeloaders and squatters, it soon became a slum, and a shantytown of bars and brothels sprang up outside its walls.

After being dissuaded from tearing the structure down, Louis XVI magnanimously put some of the royal art collection on display in the **Louvre** shortly before he and Marie Antoinette were beheaded in 1793. Following his rise to power, Napoléon moved into the **Tuileries Palace** and built Rue de Rivoli for quick access to the **Louvre.** Napoléon also built the **Arc du Carrousel,** an arch celebrating some of his military victories (see page 178). During the Second Empire, Napoléon's nephew Napoléon III and Baron Georges-Eugene Haussmann, the radical urban planner, completed the **Louvre** (or so they thought) by building the **North Wing,** the **Flore** and **Marsan Pavilions,** and all the facades of the **Cour Napoléon.** The **Louvre's** art collection began with 12 paintings—including works by Titian, Raphael, and Leonardo da Vinci—that François I looted in Italy. (He not only took the *Mona Lisa* but also the man who had painted it, inviting Leonardo to his chateau at Amboise, where the artist remained until his death.) By the time of Louis XIV (who reigned from 1643 to 1715), the royal collection numbered more than 2,500 items. Until the Revolution, works in the **Louvre** were strictly for the pleasure of the kings and their courtiers. In 1793, after nearly burning the palace to the ground, the Revolutionaries opened the collection to the masses. Today the museum possesses more than 350,000 works of art, only 30,000 of which are on display at any given time. In a morning's hoofing, however, you can see many of the **Louvre's** greatest hits: the *Venus de Milo,* the *Winged Victory of Samothrace,* the *Mona Lisa,* the *Crown Jewels,* the David works, the *Eagle of Sugerius,* the *Law Code of Hammurabi,* the **Rubens Gallery,** Michelangelo's *Slaves,* the *Seated Scribe,* and other highlights of art history.

The collection is divided into seven categories (see floor plan at left): Greek, Etruscan, and Roman antiquities, Oriental antiquities, Egyptian antiquities, sculptures, objets d'art, paintings, and drawings. Although the Greek and Roman, Egyptian, and Oriental antiquities warrant at the very least a quick look, the museum's richest collection consists of paintings.

Some words of advice for touring the **Louvre:** 1. Don't even think about trying to see the museum's entire collection—or even half of it—in one day. Visit your favorite artworks the first time around, and come back for more another day. 2. In the summer or other high-season months, unless you buy tickets in advance (see below), count on a half-hour wait to purchase them. 3. Wear comfortable shoes. Check your coat as you enter, but in winter you might want to keep a pullover handy. 4. Guided tours in English are available; ask at the reception desk in the lobby. 5. When fatigue sets in, take a break in one of the museum's cafes. (If you prefer to lunch outside and come back, the tickets are valid all day, and reentry is allowed.) 6. Certain rooms are closed on a rotating basis; to find out in advance, phone or consult the Minitel or Internet site for the schedule of closings.

Museum tickets can be purchased in advance at any **FNAC** department store (including those in Belgium and the Netherlands); ordered by phone (01.49.87.54.54); by dialing 3615 Louvre on the Minitel in France; or by accessing the **Louvre**'s web site (www.louvre.fr). The buyer does not have to book for a specific date. The tickets are valid for any day. ◆ Admission, free first Sunday of the month. Museum: M 9AM-9:45PM (limited sections open in the evening); W 9AM-9:45PM (the full museum open in the evening); Th-Su. Bookstores and postcard shops: M, W-Su. Entrance at the Pyramid in the Cour Napoléon; the museum is bounded by Rues de l'Amiral-de-Coligny and de Rivoli, Ave du Général-Lemonnier, and Quais du Louvre and Qual des Tuileries. Recorded message 01.40.20.51.51, information desk 01.40.20.53.17. Métro. Palais Royal–Musée du Louvre

Within the Musée du Louvre complex:

Cour Napoléon (Napoléon Courtyard)
Under King Philippe Auguste, this was a patch of sparsely populated farmland. Over time, it sprouted a church, charity school, meat market, menagerie for wild animals, the castle kitchens, and a street for prostitutes frequented by soldiers from the castle garrison. Napoléon III leveled the houses and paved over the courtyard in the late 19th century.

On the Cour Napoléon:

Louvre Pyramid
Adding to the **Louvre** museum building seems to be an irresistible French pastime. The latest additions, officially opened in April 1989, were based on the designs of **I.M. Pei.** Now topping the courtyard is a 70.5-foot-tall glass pyramid, flanked by 3 smaller pyramids, a series of fountains, reflecting pools, and a lead replica of the Bernini statue of Louis XI. The largest

pyramid serves as the central entrance to the museum and as an enormous skylight above the **Hall Napoléon**—a 70,000-square-foot underground cavern.

The pyramid and its underground space contain an auditorium, an area for temporary exhibitions, and the remains of the 12th-century fortress that was unearthed prior to the pyramid's controversial construction, as well as ticket offices, conference rooms, laboratories, and museum shops. Stairs and escalators lead from under the pyramid to each side of the U-shaped **Louvre.** Traditionalists fear this latest addition has marred the museum's grandeur with a sort of Hyatt Regency glitz. Michel Guy, cultural minister under former French President Giscard d'Estaing, has said that **Pei**'s pyramids turn the **Louvre** into a "cultural drugstore that looks like an airport." However, the design has garnered fans, and, lest we forget, the **Eiffel Tower** was also first greeted with guffaws.

Excavations At the same time President François Mitterrand approved the **Pei** pyramid project, he also set aside close to $2 million for an immense archaeological excavation of the **Louvre**'s courtyard. This ambitious project brought 70 archaeologists to supervise the dig in the **Cour Napoléon** and the **Cour Carrée,** where the ancient dungeons of the King Philippe Auguste fortress were exposed. More than 11 million objects were retrieved, ranging from Chinese porcelain imported during the Ming Dynasty to coins from the first century AD and an eighth-century human skeleton. Visitors may descend from the pyramid to the 12th-century dungeons and view some of the objects uncovered in the dig.

Cour Carrée (Square Courtyard)
This elegant courtyard was built, in part, during the reign of François I, with additions commissioned by Louis XIII and Louis XIV.

Richelieu Wing Named after the famed 17th-century French cardinal and diplomat, this structure on the Rue de Rivoli side was long occupied by the Ministry of Finance. It opened in November 1993 as one of the main expansions under the Grand Louvre Project.

Within the Richelieu Wing:

Le Café Marly ★★$$ Restaurateurs Jean-Louis and Gilbert Costes's popular cafe serves everything from guacamole and *croque monsieurs* (toasted ham and cheese sandwiches) to grilled turbot and steak béarnaise, along with cheeses, pastries, and ice cream. A small but brilliant wine list features everything from a $20 Sauvignon Marionnet to a $250 Château Mouton-Rothschild Pauillac 1er Cru Classé 1987. The Venetian red walls, gold leaf, and velvet upholstered armchairs calls to mind a chic Italian disco. But if the weather is good, try for a table on the covered gallery overlooking the **Cour Napoléon** and **I.M. Pei**'s glass pyramid. It may take a while, especially at lunchtime, but it's well worth a wait for one of the best spots Paris has to offer for an alfresco lunch. ♦ Daily breakfast, lunch, tea, and dinner. 93 Rue de Rivoli (enter from the Cour Napoléon). 01.49.26.06.60

Le Grand Louvre ★★$$ Run by chef Yves Pinard, this elegant restaurant located under the **Louvre Pyramid** has a subdued wood-and-metal decor and features a range of well-prepared French specialties that should appeal to any taste bud: foie gras, crayfish on a spinach salad, poached fillet of sturgeon, salmon and mixed vegetables in a flaky pastry, a vegetarian dish, duck breast with orange, rack of lamb, rabbit stew, guinea fowl with chestnut puree, crème brûlée, and *Pyramide au chocolat,* a pyramid-shaped chocolate cake. ♦ M, W-Su lunch and dinner. 01.40.20.53.41

Carrousel du Louvre This underground shopping mall is skylit by a 150-ton inverted glass pyramid and features over 35 boutiques and businesses proffering everything from Lalique crystal to miniature Eiffel Tower souvenirs and château rentals to 1-hour film developing. **Restorama Universal** is a huge 700-seat international food hall on the mezzanine level with a dozen or so stalls that offer modestly priced fast food of nearly every description—Mexican, Lebanese, Asian, Spanish, Italian, American, vegetarian, and, of course, French. During the shopping center's construction, architects **I.M. Pei** and **Michel Macary** uncovered a 14th-century moat built by Charles V, which has been incorporated into the design and named the **Fossé Charles V.** During the fall and spring, the mall becomes a chic circus when more than 50 fashion designers parade their ready-to-wear collections through striped tents set up here. Check at the information stand for a schedule of events. ♦ Daily. Main entrance at 99 Rue de Rivoli (between Rue de l'Amiral-de-Coligny and Ave du Général-Lemonnier); also accessible from the Louvre Museum foyer. 01.43.16.47.47

Place du Carrousel This square was named to commemorate a *carrousel* (equestrian gala) held by King Louis XIV and his court in June 1662 to honor the birth of the king's first child. More than 15,000 spectators watched the king lead a thundering brigade of horsemen dressed as Romans, sporting golden helmets with red plumes, gold breastplates, and red stockings.

On Place du Carrousel:

MICHAEL STORRINGS

L'Arc du Carrousel This marble arch with pink pillars (see illustration above) was built in 1808 by Napoléon to celebrate Austerlitz and other military victories. It was then crowned with the famous bronze horses of San Marco, plundered from Venice during one of Napoléon's military campaigns (originally, the horses stood in the Temple of the Sun at Corinth). With the fall of Napoléon in 1815, Italy recovered the horses and copies were placed here. The arch can be used like a gun sight to line up the **Tuileries Fountains**, the Egyptian **Obelisk of Luxor** in the **Place de la Concorde** (a half-mile to the west), the Champs-Elysées, and the **Arc de Triomphe**, more than two miles away.

22 **Musée des Arts Décoratifs (Museum of Decorative Arts) and Musée de la Publicité (Poster and Advertising Museum)** With furnishings that date from the Middle Ages through the 20th century, the **Musée des Arts Décoratifs,** housed in the **Rohan Wing,** offers collections worthy of and complementary to its neighbor's displays of European art. Lovers of medieval religious art shouldn't miss the superb collection of painted, sculpted stone, and carved wood altarpieces from northern Italy, Catalonia, France, Germany, Flanders, and the Netherlands. Occupying nine rooms and a full floor, these pieces are housed in the museum's Middle Ages and Renaissance

department. Reopened in 1998 after a long renovation, this section also boasts a superb collection of Renaissance tapestries, furniture, glassware, ceramics, and enamelware, and a cozy wood-paneled Gothic bedroom and a grand Renaissance reception hall. The rest of the museum, with pieces covering the early 17th century to the early 20th century, was closed for restoration at press time; it was scheduled to reopen at the end of 2000.

In the same building is the **Musée de la Publicité,** also closed for renovation until the end of 2000. More than 40,000 posters from the 18th century to the present are housed here. Beautiful temporary exhibitions are also mounted on occasion. ♦ Admission. Tu, Th, F 11AM-6PM; W 11AM-9PM; Sa-Su. 107 Rue de Rivoli (at Ave du Général-Lemonnier). 01.44.55.57.50

22 Musée National de la Mode et du Textile (Fashion and Textile Museum)
Located in the **Rohan Wing,** this museum pays homage to the capital of fashion. Selections from its 20,000 outfits, 35,000 accessories, and 100,000 fabric samples are beautifully presented by theme in exhibitions that change every 6 months. The museum's sleek and chic collection consists of costumes dating back to the 17th century. Among the highlights of the collection are the 17th-century gloves worn by Anne of Austria, Brigitte Bardot's wedding dress (made by Jacques Esterel in 1958), a robe designed for Sarah Bernhardt, and the gown worn by the Empress Eugénie to please Napoléon III when he returned from a hard day of empire-building. There is also a library containing engravings, drawings, journals, photographs, and catalogs. The view of the **Tuileries Gardens** from the top floor is spectacular. ♦ Admission. Tu, Th, F 11AM-6PM; W 11AM-9PM; Sa-Su. 107 Rue de Rivoli (at Ave du Général-Lemonnier). 01.44.55.57.50

23 Jardin des Tuileries (Tuileries Gardens)
The elegant gardens *à la française* were designed in 1664 for Louis XIV by André Le Nôtre, the king's gardener, who was born in a cottage on the royal grounds. Le Nôtre also designed the gardens at **Versailles, Chantilly,** and the **Château Vaux-le-Vicomte.** It's hard to believe that this lovely and serene spot was the site of such violence during the Revolution (the **Palais des Tuileries,** then the home of the royal family, was attacked by an angry mob in 1792). Stroll through the manicured hedges and lawns near the 18 bronze nudes by Aristide Maillol. In 1998, 12 works by Rodin and such modern artists as Giacometti, Laurens, Max Ernst, Dubuffet, and Germaine Richier were permanently installed here for the pleasure of the 6 million people who visit the gardens every year. You'll see old women feeding the pigeons, vendors

lofting mechanical birds into the air in hope of attracting a sale, and kids racing sailboats on the fountain under the watchful eyes of their governesses. Four refreshment stands, a small merry-go-round, a swing set, and subdued pony rides for children are available.

From the upper terrace of the gardens is a splendid view of the Seine, the **Musée d'Orsay,** and the **Palais de la Légion d'Honneur,** which was begun by Napoléon to laud French accomplishment. Farther in the distance, you can glimpse the stern Neo-Classic **Palais Bourbon,** where the Chambre des Députés, France's congress, holds its sessions. This terrace has become known as a gathering spot for gay men. ♦ Bounded by Ave du Général-Lemonnier and Pl de la Concorde, and Quai des Tuileries and Rue de Rivoli. Métro: Tuileries, Concorde

Within the Jardin des Tuileries:

Palais des Tuileries (Tuileries Palace)
Designed in 1564 by **Philibert Delorme,** this palace stood until 1884. It connected the two corner pavilions of the **Louvre** (paralleling what is today Avenue du Général-Lemonnier) and took its name from the *tuile* (tile) factories that had previously stood on the site. Catherine de Médicis, for whom the palace was built, moved out after her astrologer, Ruggieri, told her she would die close to St-Germain. Since the **Tuileries** was in the parish of **St-Germain-l'Auxerrois,** Catherine built another palace near what is today the **Bourse du Commerce** (Commercial Stock Exchange), and there she died. As for Ruggieri's prediction: The priest who administered the last rites to Catherine de Médicis was named Julien de St-Germain.

Napoléon's second wife gave birth in the palace to a short-lived imperial heir, l'Aiglon, who was named the king of Rome. Subsequent royal residents included Charles X and Louis Philippe, who ruled from 1831 to 1848 and was popularly known as the "Grocers' King" for his custom of carving the Sunday roast himself. In 1871, during the Siege of Paris, the Communards set the palace afire. It burned for three days while the **Louvre Museum** staff worked frantically to save the collections. The palace was razed between 1882 and 1884; a single bay was preserved and stands unmarked in a remote corner of the **Tuileries Gardens** behind the **Jeu de Paume.**

Galerie Nationale du Jeu de Paume
The name of this museum, built in 1853 by Napoléon III, refers to the building's original function as an indoor court where royalty played the racket sport that was the precursor of tennis. The sport was created by medieval monks who started swatting wads of rags around the monastery courtyard with the palm

of their hands, *jeu de paume* meaning literally "the game of the palm." Rackets came later. In 1907, a group of painters called Impressionists commandeered the building and used it as a gallery. From 1947 until 1986, the **Louvre**'s collection of French Impressionist masterpieces was housed here, making this the most visited museum in the world relative to its size. The Impressionist collection was moved across the river to St-Germain's **Musée d'Orsay,** and since 1991 the renovated galleries here have hosted changing exhibitions by contemporary artists. On the terrace to the south of the museum is a monument to Charles Perrault, the 17th-century fabulist who convinced Colbert to make the **Tuileries** public. ♦ Call ahead for opening times; hours vary. 01.42.60.69.69

Bassin Octagonal et Terrasses (Octagonal Fountain and Terraces)
Between the **Jeu de Paume** and **L'Orangerie** (see below) is a series of 18th-century statues representing the Nile, the Tiber, the Loire and Loiret, the Marne, and the Seine Rivers, part of an overall garden design that also includes the adjoining **Octagonal Fountain,** terraces, slopes, and stairways. North of the fountain is a modest bust of André Le Nôtre, the landscape architect. The **Tuileries** is framed from the west by Coysevox's two winged horses, erected in 1719 at the western edge of the garden, along Place de la Concorde.

The first human ascent in a hydrogen balloon, on 1 December 1783, took place beside the **Octagonal Fountain.** Thousands packed the park to watch the historic flight of physician J.A.C. Charles and his mechanic Noel Robert. Among the spectators were Benjamin Franklin and French philosopher Denis Diderot, who conjectured that one day human beings might go to the moon. The hot-air balloon rose more than 2,000 feet and carried its passengers safely 25 miles to the north of Paris. Now, every New Year's Day, the celebrity-studded Paris-Dakar overland motor race across Europe and North Africa begins here.

Café Véry ★$ Located on the central alleyway a few steps east of the **Bassin Octagonal,** this cafe is the best place in the park to pause for liquid or solid refreshment—particularly in fair weather, if you're lucky enough to secure a table outdoors. The Dame Tartine group runs this cafe, and it features the same range of imaginative salads, sandwiches, and light dishes (smoked salmon on a bed of endives with fresh ginger sauce, and duck stew with orange and mint leaves) as at the other locations. ♦ Daily noon-11PM. 01.47.03.94.84. Also at: 2 Rue Brisemiche (at Rue Cloître-St-Merri). 01.42.77.32.22. Métros: Hôtel de Ville, Rambuteau; 59 Rue de Lyon (between Rue Lacuée and Pl de la Bastille). 01.44.68.96.95. Métro: Bastille

L'Orangerie This former citrus nursery is the permanent home of the *Walter-Guillaume Collection* of paintings, including 144 masterworks by such artists as Renoir, Monet, Cézanne, Henri Rousseau, Soutine, Picasso, Modigliani, Derain, and Matisse. The artists best represented are Pierre-Auguste Renoir (24 works) and André Derain (28 paintings). The Cézannes are exceptional, particularly *Apples and Biscuits,* whose audacious composition is held together by a drawer latch placed dead center in the picture. On the lower floor, mounted on curved panels, are Claude Monet's eight giant water lily murals, *Les Nymphéas.* ♦ Admission. M, W-Su. 01.42.97.48.16

24 **Passerelle de Solférino** Scheduled to open at press time, the city's newest bridge will provide pedestrian passage between the **Jardins des Tuileries** and the **Musée d'Orsay.** Constructed of a special type of steel used in naval architecture, the wood-planked *passerelle* (footbridge), designed by engineer **Marc Mimram,** will be the first to span the Seine with only one arch. The bridge will offer pedestrians direct access from either the upper or lower quays. ♦ Métros: Tuileries, Assemblée Nationale, Solférino

25 **Galignani** Established in 1802, the grande dame of Paris bookstores still sells plenty of books in French, but most of its works are now in English. The store is strong in literature, current affairs, politics, and history, and its international art book section is the most extensive in France.♦ M-Sa. 224 Rue de Rivoli (between Rues d'Alger and de Castiglione). 01.42.60.76.07. Métro: Concorde

ANGELINA

25 **Angélina** ★★★$$ The Rolls-Royce of Parisian tea salons, this place originally went by the name **Rumpelmayer's.** It was founded in 1903 on the former site of the king's stables. Amid marble pedestal tables, landscapes by Lorrant-Heilbronn, and gilt decor, the hardworking waitresses deliver justly celebrated pastries, sumptuous hot chocolate, and *Mont Blanc,* a weighty concoction of chestnut cream purée (a

favorite of the Aga Khan). The whipped cream is fresh and the ice water is served on silver trays. In spring and autumn, get a table near Rue de Rivoli, where you can watch top models and fashion designers returning from the ready-to-wear collection fashion shows. ◆ Daily breakfast, lunch, and afternoon tea. 226 Rue de Rivoli (between Rues d'Alger and de Castiglione). 01.42.60.82.00. Métro: Tuileries

25 Hôtel Meurice $$$$ Heads of state (vacationing and exiled), artists, writers, and other celebrities have long favored this refined 160-room property. Alphonse XIII of Spain stayed here for years, and Salvador Dalí made it his Paris home for three decades. During World War II, the hotel served as Nazi headquarters; it was here that Commandant General von Cholitz, after disobeying Hitler's orders to burn Paris, surrendered to the Allies in August 1944. Since the hotel opened in 1816, it has attracted many famous North American visitors, including Herman Melville, Henry James, Henry Wadsworth Longfellow, and Wilbur and Orville Wright, who stayed here in 1907 while trying to sell their airplane to the French. (The Wrights used the familiar argument that their invention was the weapon to end all wars. The French military didn't buy that, but the public was captivated by the biplane, which the Wrights had shipped all the way to Paris from Dayton, Ohio.)

The hostelry was extensively renovated in 1999—the number of rooms was reduced from 180 to 160 to make room for more suites (including a huge penthouse with a 360° view of Paris); a new subbasement was dug to house the heating and air-conditioning units; the electrical and plumbing systems were modernized; and a winter garden created. The styles of Louis XV and XVI still prevail throughout the property. Tea in the **Salon Pompadour** next to the charming bar is a discreet pleasure, especially in the late afternoon after the pianist settles at the keys. There's also an opulent restaurant, **Le Meurice,** which boasts one Michelin star. Note: There's no charge for children 14 and under when sharing a room with a parent or guardian; however, owners of dogs must pay for bunking their pets. ◆ 228 Rue de Rivoli (between Rues d'Alger and de Castiglione). 01.44.58.10.10; fax 01.44.58.10.78; reservations@meuricehotel.com; www.meuricehotel.com. Métro: Tuileries

HOTEL
INTER·CONTINENTAL
PARIS

26 Hôtel Inter-Continental Paris $$$$ Designed in 1878 by **Charles Garnier,** who built the **Opéra Garnier,** this 450-room establishment has 3 salons that are classified as historical landmarks. The fanciest receptions in town—including those celebrating the new haute couture collections of Yves Saint Laurent, Guy Laroche, and Jean Patou—take place in these ornate rooms. This hotel has always drawn a varied clientele: Victor Hugo and the Empress Eugénie were fans, as is Jerry Lewis. The rooms offer both turn-of-the-century elegance and modern conveniences. ◆ 3 Rue de Castiglione (between Rues de Rivoli and du Mont-Thabor). 01.44.77.11.11; fax 01.44.77.14.60; paris@interconti.com; www.interconti.com. Métros: Concorde, Tuileries

Within the Hôtel Inter-Continental Paris:

Rivoli 234

Brasserie 234 Rivoli ★★$$ The most upscale brasserie in Paris (*choucroute*—sauerkraut—isn't even on the menu), features two floors. At the upper level of this airy restaurant which overlooks the **Tuileries,** such à la carte dishes as pan-fried Dublin Bay prawns, turbot roasted on the bone, and roasted rack of lamb glazed with spices are offered. If the prices for these delicacies are beyond your budget, there's also a very affordable prix-fixe menu. On the lower level, a sumptuous buffet is served, again reasonably priced. The brasserie can be entered either from the hotel lobby or the street entrance at 234 Rue de Rivoli. ◆ Daily breakfast, lunch, and dinner. 01.44.77.10.40

Terrasse Fleurie ★★$$ This flowery terrace restaurant in the hotel's secluded central courtyard serves summery fare from May through September. It is a lovely spot for a buffet lunch or a romantic candlelight dinner. ◆ Daily lunch and dinner May-Sept. 01.44.77.10.44

Tuileries Bar Cozy and peaceful with soft lighting and red velvet walls, this bar serves sandwiches, snacks, and plats du jour. A piano player entertains Friday and Saturday from 10PM to closing. ◆ Daily breakfast, lunch, and dinner until 1AM. 01.44.77.10.47

27 W.H. Smith and Son This British book store on 2 levels has 70,000 titles available and is strong in current, recent, and classic fiction; history; travel books; and maps. It's also the best place in Paris to find English-language periodicals. The magazine section carries over 500 titles, and all major British, Irish, and North American international newspapers are delivered daily. ◆ M-Sa. 248 Rue de Rivoli (at Rue Cambon). 01.44.77.88.99. Métro: Concorde

28 Lescure ★★$$ Come to this unspoiled bistro during hunting season (autumn) to enjoy such dishes as *confit de canard* (duck confit), rabbit and sorrel, dandelion green salad, and wild game. ♦ M-F lunch and dinner; closed in August. Reservations recommended. 7 Rue de Mondovi (between Rues de Rivoli and du Mont-Thabor). 01.42.60.18.91. Métro: Concorde

29 Hôtel Talleyrand/American Consulate Designed by **Jacques-Ange Gabriel,** the architect for Louis XV, and **Jean-François Chalgrin** who designed the **Arc de Triomphe,** this *hôtel* was originally the residence of diplomat par excellence Charles-Maurice de Talleyrand-Périgord and subsequently housed Czar Alexander I, several French Rothschilds, and, during World War II, the German Navy, which kept prisoners of war in the cellars. Today this historic building houses the **American Consulate,** best known among travelers as the office where you replace lost or stolen passports. ♦ 2 Rue St-Florentin (at Rue de Rivoli). 01.40.20.01.99. Métro: Concorde

30 Place de la Concorde The largest square in Paris, covering 21 acres, was a swamp until royal architect **Jacques-Ange Gabriel** was asked by Louis XV to find a setting appropriate for an equestrian statue of the king himself. The statue stood on the square, originally named for Louis XV, less than 20 years; it was removed during the Revolution. On Sunday, 21 January 1793, the guillotine was set up on the square's west side (near the spot where the statue of Brest sculpted by Cortot stands today). Louis XVI was beheaded, and the 13-month Reign of Terror began. Among its thousands of victims were Marie Antoinette, Madame du Barry, Charlotte Corday, and Danton. On the evening of 28 July 1794, more than 1,300 townspeople gathered here to watch the execution of Robespierre. During the Revolution, no fewer than 1,343 victims were executed on the Place de la Révolution (as it was known then), and the square so reeked of gore that herds of oxen balked at crossing it. The *place* subsequently was given the name *concorde* (peace) as a way of laying to rest its violent past. ♦ Métro: Concorde

On Place de la Concorde:

Obelisk of Luxor This 3,300-year-old, 220-ton Egyptian obelisk is unquestionably the oldest monument in Paris. Originally erected around the 13th century BC in the Temple of Luxor, the 76-foot-tall monument was a gift to Louis Philippe from Mohammed Ali Pasha, who was viceroy of Egypt, in 1831. (He also gave Queen Victoria Cleopatra's Needle, a slightly shorter obelisk taken from Heliopolis.) The pink-granite Paris obelisk, which replaced the equestrian statue of Louis XV that was removed during the Revolution, traveled 600 miles by barge down the Nile to Alexandria, was towed through the Mediterranean and the Atlantic, was carted through Normandy, and finally was erected at Place de la Concorde in 1836, ending a political squabble over whose monument should adorn a square dedicated to neither a French king nor Napoléon's army. The designs on the pedestal are meant to illustrate the technological wizardry involved in the obelisk's journey from Egypt to Paris.

Visitors be forewarned: Pedestrians crossing the Place de la Concorde on foot are taking their lives in their hands. But go ahead; you only live once, and the obelisk is worth a close look. What's more, the island surrounding it provides an unobstructed view of the Champs-Elysées. Cross at the light!

Sculpture and Fountains Adorning Gabriel's original octagonal square are several groups of statuary, allegorical figures representing Bordeaux, Brest, Lille, Marseilles, Nantes, Rouen, and Strasbourg. Believe it or not, the tiny two-room pavilions underneath the statues were once rented out as dwellings. North and south of the obelisk stand two fountains, one representing maritime navigation and the other river navigation. The latter, ironically, is the farthest from the Seine. The fountains' sea nymphs and water gods are replicas of those found in fountains on St. Peter's Square in Rome.

31 Pont de la Concorde This five-arched bridge designed in 1791 by civil engineer Jean Rodolphe Perronet is constructed in part with stone souvenirs from the 1789 storming and demolition of the **Bastille,** allegedly so that people could forever trample the ruins of the old fortress. ♦ Métros: Assemblée Nationale, Concorde

32 North Facade of Place de la Concorde When royal architect **Jacques-Ange Gabriel** designed the Place de la Concorde, he made sure that buildings would face only its north side, and in 1757, work began on the two matching Neo-Classical north facades separated down the middle by Rue Royale. The facade's design was borrowed from the **Louvre** colonnades, which **Gabriel** himself had restored. The **Hôtel de la Marine,** part of the facade east of Rue Royale, was intended to be lodging for foreign ambassadors, but became first a royal-furniture storehouse and then, in 1792, the Admiralty (now known as the Ministry of the Navy). L'Automobile Club De France and the very elegant **Hôtel Crillon** (see below) now occupy the building on the opposite corner. On 6 February 1778, Louis XVI and American diplomats (including Benjamin Franklin) met at the **Crillon** to sign the Treaty of Friendship and Trade, which recognized the independence of the 13 American states. ♦ Between Rues St-Florentin and Boissy-d'Anglas. Métro: Concorde

32 Hôtel Crillon $$$$ The facade of this hotel, one of the swankiest properties in Paris, was designed in 1758 by **Jacques-Ange Gabriel** for the Count of Crillon. The family managed to hold onto the mansion right through the Revolution, in spite of the fact that the guillotine was set up practically on their doorstep. Today the 123-room, 40-suite institution is the last of the grand Parisian hotels to remain 100 percent French-owned. Should you decide that the kids don't need to go to college after all, rent one of the three royal suites (the **Red Suite,** the **White Suite,** or the **Blue Suite**) and enjoy some of the best possible views of the Place de la Concorde, the Seine, and the **Eiffel Tower.** Another option is the **Marie Antoinette Apartment,** where the queen is said to have taken her music lessons. Among the famous North American couples who have romanced here are Mary Pickford and Douglas Fairbanks, who stopped in during their 1920 honeymoon, and newspaper magnate William Randolph Hearst and his girlfriend, Marion Davies. The hotel's proximity to the American and British Embassies assures a clientele of diplomats, royalty, and wealthy foreigners. ♦ 10 Pl de la Concorde (between Rues Royale and Boissy-d'Anglas). 01.44.71.15.00; fax 01.44.71.15.02; crillon@crillon-paris.com; www.crillon-paris.com. Métro: Concorde

Within the Hôtel Crillon:

Ambassadeurs Restaurant ★★★$$$$ In this magnificent dining room, with marble walls, elaborate mirrors, 20-foot-high ceilings, and massive crystal chandeliers, innovative chef Dominique Bouchet concocts a cuisine that measures up to the setting. Medaillon of lobster with chives, small ravioli with duck foie gras, braised St-Pierre (John Dory), Brittany lobster, filet mignon of suckling pig, Vendée pigeon glazed with honey, and warm Grand Cru chocolate tart are among the specialties. The exemplary fare is complemented by outstanding views of the Place de la Concorde. ♦ Daily lunch and dinner. Reservations required. 01.44.71.16.16

> "What is the secret of the French attraction for most strangers? Why do foreign colonies flourish so easily in France? The secret is France's aloofness; they tolerate strangers and allow them to do as they please as long as they don't meddle in French national affairs or do anything to hurt their pride."
>
> Harlem Renaissance writer Claude McKay

Obélisque ★★$$ Serving delicious pasta and regional cheeses, this discreet eatery with wood-paneled walls offers meals suitable for lighter appetites and slimmer purses while remaining in step with the hotel's elegant atmosphere. ♦ Daily lunch and dinner; closed in August. Reservations recommended. 01.44.71.15.15

Bar du Crillon International journalists and visiting diplomats often stop here for a glass of Champagne before dinner. Its hot *feuilletés* (croissantlike pastries) are great snacks. ♦ Daily 11AM-2AM. 01.44.71.15.39

33 Maxim's ★★$$$$ Paris without **Maxim's?** *Pas possible.* Where would all those rich business executives lunch? And where would the bona fide blue bloods, glitzy jet-setters, and fashionably late diners find such a Belle Epoque setting? This venerable dining spot has given the royal treatment to Edward VIII of England and Leopold II of Belgium, as well as to such prominent North Americans as John Paul Getty, Jackie Onassis, and Elizabeth Taylor. Not everyone is admitted to this Pierre Cardin–owned landmark, which has been cloned in Beijing, Brussels, Mexico City, Moscow, Nagoya, New York, Rio de Janeiro, Shanghai, Singapore, and Tokyo. If you are lucky enough to be allowed to pass through the doors, however, expect unsurpassed Champagne and service, disappointing food, and a splendid and expensive Parisian evening. ♦ M-Sa lunch and dinner. Reservations required. 3 Rue Royale (between Pl de la Concorde and Rue du Faubourg-St-Honoré). 01.42.65.27.94. Métro: Concorde

34 American Embassy Designed in 1933 by the New York firm **Delano and Aldrich,** and flanked by two bald eagles in stone, the embassy and nearby consulate are staffed with about 500 people working for an alphabet soup of agencies including the IRS, CIA, and FBI, and the Departments of Defense, State, Agriculture, and Commerce. ♦ Rue Boissy-d'Anglas (between Pl de la Concorde and Rue du Faubourg-St-Honoré). 01.43.12.22.22. Métro: Concorde

35 Chevaux de Marly (Marly Horses) The two sculptures of rearing horses at the entrance to the Champs-Elysées are actually replicas. The originals by Nicolas and Guillaume Coustou, called *Africans Mastering the Numidian Horses,* were taken from the **Château de Marly** (the Louis XIV château that was destroyed in the Revolution) and placed here in 1795. Sixteen horses dragged the statues to Paris in five hours, a transportation feat considered so marvelous that the vehicle in which they were carried is exhibited in the **Conservatoire des Arts et Métiers.** In 1994, the original Coustou sculptures were moved to **La Cour Marly,** a glass-covered courtyard in the **Louvre.** ♦ Ave des Champs-Elysées and Pl de la Concorde. Métro: Concorde

35 Avenue des Champs-Elysées The neighborhood that is now the site of the world's most famous boulevard was forsaken marshland, unsafe after dark, until 1616, when Marie de Médicis, the wife of Henri IV, had a fashionable carriage-drive, the Cours-la-Reine (Queen's Way) built west of the **Tuileries** along the Seine. A half-century later, master landscaper André Le Nôtre planted double rows of chestnut trees to create another avenue to the northwest. Originally called the Grand Cours, this second avenue was later renamed the Avenue des Champs-Elysées (Elysian Fields). In 1724 the boulevard was extended to the top of the Butte de Chaillot. Fifty years later, architect **Jacques-Germain Soufflot** leveled it by 16 feet to ease the climb for carriage-towing horses.

Since its creation, the Champs-Elysées has always been the place to promenade. Processions marking the liberation of Paris (26 August 1944), the student-worker demonstrations (30 May 1968), the death of Charles de Gaulle (12 November 1970), and the French soccer team's victory in the **1998 World Cup,** all made their way down this street. If you fancy pomp and pageantry, show up here on Bastille Day (14 July), when the jets of the French Air Force streak overhead; Armistice Day (11 November), when the president lays a wreath on the **Tomb of the Unknown Soldier;** in late July when the grueling three-week Tour de France bicycle race ends here; and at Christmastime, when the avenue's trees twinkle with tiny white lights. The eastern half of the boulevard, from Place de la Concorde to Rond-Point des Champs-Elysées, is bordered by lush gardens of azaleas and mature chestnut trees. Within the gardens are theaters (the **Théâtre de Marigny** and **Théâtre du Rond-Point**) and exclusive restaurants with pretty garden terraces, such as **Ledoyen** and **Laurent.** The western half of the avenue leads from the Rond-Point des Champs-Elysées to the Place Charles-de-Gaulle, also known as Place d'Etoile, where the **Arc de Triomphe** bulks large at the top of the wide, tree-lined avenue. A major face-lift of this commercial section of the Champs-Elysées in the 1990s gave it new wide granite sidewalks, ended on-street parking, and toned down the garish decor of certain fast-food outlets that had tarnished the avenue's aristocratic image. Banks, airline offices, shops and shopping arcades, numerous cafes, restaurants, fast-food businesses, ice cream parlors, and several big cinemas line this lively stretch where strolling has become a delight once again, night or day. ♦ Métros: Concorde, Champs Elysées–Clemenceau, Franklin D. Roosevelt, George V, Charles de Gaulle–Etoile

Avenue des Champs-Elysées

36 Ledoyen ★★★$$$$ During the reign of Louis XVI (1774-92), this dining spot on the south side of the Champs-Elysées was a country inn and dairy bar serving fresh milk to travelers. Dinner here can still seem pleasantly bucolic; the view of the Champs-Elysées from the elegant upstairs dining room is superb. Young chef Christian Le Squer, who garnered two Michelin stars at his previous restaurant, **Le Grand Opéra** at **Le Grand Hôtel Inter-Continental** (see page 217), continues on his imaginative way here with his exquisitely prepared and served offerings. For starters, choose from whole roasted foie gras of Landes duckling sliced at your table, giant langoustines rolled in fine noodles, or simple and elegant grilled *coquilles St-Jacques* (scallops). Main courses include sole sautéed in sage butter with a *rémoulade* of cucumber and fresh ginger, and turbot topped with finely chopped truffles on a bed of mashed potatoes. The desserts are stupendous, and the restaurant has one of the finest wine lists in Paris. ◆ M-F lunch and dinner. Reservations required; jacket and tie required. Carré des Champs-Elysées (just north of Ave Edward-Tuck). 01.53.05.10.00. Métro: Champs Elysées–Clemenceau

Within Ledoyen:

Cercle Ledoyen ★★$$ Downstairs from the glamorous gourmet restaurant and sharing the same bucolic view and chef is its relaxed, lively junior version featuring exquisite, but relatively simple fare. The cuisine here is French bourgeois, with an à la carte menu that changes daily, offering at least a half-dozen choices each of starters, fish, meat, and poultry dishes, and desserts. The wine list is excellent and honestly priced. Regular patrons become members of "Le Cercle," a sort of dining club, and benefit from a special prix-fixe menu. The restaurant is very popular with businesspeople at lunch, and at dinnertime French couples come for an elegant, yet affordable, night on the town. ◆ M-Sa lunch and dinner. 01.47.42.76.02

37 Statue de Clemenceau Georges Clemenceau (1841-1929) was the outspoken French politician who formed a coalition government in 1917 and galvanized French morale in the final phases of World War I. Sculptor François Cogne has captured Clemenceau's trademarks in bronze: the walrus mustache, high leather boots, walking stick, and wool scarf flapping in the wind. ◆ Pl Clemenceau and Ave des Champs-Elysées. Métro: Champs Elysées–Clemenceau

38 Petit Palais This little turn-of-the-century palace houses the fine arts museum of the City of Paris, with a collection specializing in such 19th-century French painters as Delacroix, Courbet, Monet, Cézanne, and Bonnard. The architect, **Charles Girault**, crowned the building with a graceful cupola and decorated its two wings with Ionic columns and Rococo embellishments. ◆ Admission. Tu-Su. Ave Winston-Churchill (between Cours la Reine and Ave Charles-Girault). 01.42.65.12.73. Métro: Champs Elysées–Clemenceau

39 Grand Palais Along with the Pont Alexandre III and the **Petit Palais,** this exuberant stone, steel, and glass structure is an example of Art Nouveau architecture at its most excessive. The **Grand Palais** and **Petit Palais** were built for the **1900 Exposition Universelle,** the first world's fair in Paris. Famous for its domed and vaulted glass roof and superb staircase, the **Grand Palais** was the work of three architects: **Henri Deglane** designed the principal facade; **Albert Thomas,** the rear facade; and **Louis-Albert Louvet,** the rest. With 54,000 square feet of floor space (equivalent to nearly 14 basketball courts), this structure is used for book fairs, car shows, and blockbuster art exhibitions. ◆ Admission. Open only for special exhibitions and events; call for schedule or check *Pariscope* or *L'Officiel des Spectacles.* Ave Winston-Churchill (between Cours la Reine and Pl Clemenceau). 01.44.13.17.17. Métro: Champs Elysées–Clemenceau

40 Pont Alexandre III Between the **Invalides** and the **Grand Palais** is an elegant Belle Epoque bridge embodying the architectural giddiness that celebrated the French spirit of ingenuity and optimism at the turn of the century. The bridge is encrusted with every Greco-Roman frippery in the book: human-size cupids; lavish garlands; huge golden statues of Pegasus and Renown; prides of lions; and a plethora of trumpets, tridents, shells, and shields. Built to commemorate the 1892 French-Russian alliance, the bridge bears the Russian and French coats of arms side by side and teams a sculptural allegory of the Seine with one of the Neva. ◆ Métros: Champs Elysées–Clemenceau, Invalides

41 1 Avenue de Marigny In 1954, when novelist John Steinbeck and his family moved into this house, he described it in a letter to Richard Rodgers and Oscar Hammerstein: "It is next to the Rothschilds and across the street from the president of France. How's that for an address for a Salinas kid?" It's still a private residence. ◆ At Ave Gabriel. Métro: Champs Elysées–Clemenceau

---

The Rond-Point des Champs-Elysées, the large roundabout halfway down the Champs-Elysées, is circled by 70,000 vehicles on a working day.

Restaurants/Clubs: Red	**Hotels:** Blue
Shops/🎋 Outdoors: Green	**Sights/Culture:** Black

42 Résidence Maxim's $$$$ Near the intersection of the Champs-Elysées and the Place de la Concorde, Pierre Cardin has created a 43-room confection, most of it Art Nouveau, that accommodates visiting executives, sheiks, and the rich and famous for anywhere from $400 to $3,000 per night, depending on whether you prefer, say, the Sarah Bernhardt bed or the Toulouse-Lautrec painting in your room. There's also a classic Belle Epoque bar and restaurant. ♦ 42 Ave Gabriel (between Rue du Cirque and Ave Matignon). 01.45.61.96.33; fax 01.42.89.06.07. Métros: Champs Elysées–Clemenceau, Franklin D. Roosevelt

RESTAURANT LAURENT

43 Restaurant Laurent ★★★$$$$ Just down the street from the official residence of the French president, the parking lot of this restaurant is always crowded with chauffeured limousines bearing diplomatic license plates. The drawing cards here are the lovely garden terrace, impeccable service, and nouvelle cuisine bourgeoise, which includes salmon carpaccio with caviar, rack of lamb, langoustines in pastry crust, roast lobster, and warm raspberry soufflé. The chef is Philippe Braun, a disciple of Joël Robuchon, and the aptly named Philippe Bourguignon oversees the wine list. In addition to the terrace, there are tables in a covered garden pavilion and in dining rooms on two floors in a 19th-century building. The interior decor is plush, with high ceilings, Impressionist paintings, and a nostalgic Belle Epoque theme. ♦ M-F lunch and dinner; Sa dinner. Reservations required. 41 Ave Gabriel (between Aves de Marigny and Matignon). 01.42.25.00.39. Métros: Champs Elysées–Clemenceau, Franklin D. Roosevelt

THEATRE
DU ROND-POINT

44 Théâtre du Rond-Point The company of Marcel Marechal took up residence in this newly renovated theater just off the Champs-Elysées in the fall of 1995. Contemporary French theater, including the works of Camus and Claudel, is featured. ♦ Call for box office hours. 2 bis Ave Franklin-D.-Roosevelt (between Ave du Général-Eisenhower and Rond-Point des Champs-Elysées). 01.44.95.98.00. Métros: Champs Elysées–Clemenceau, Franklin D. Roosevelt

Within the Théâtre du Rond-Point:

Théâtre du Rond-Point Restaurant ★$$ On the theater's lower level, this restaurant serves reasonably priced traditional French and international dishes. Try such items as smoked salmon with shallot cream, gazpacho, grilled sea bass on a bed of fennel, and roast rack of lamb with garlic. In the summer, dine on the delightful terrace overlooking the gardens along the Champs-Elysées. ♦ Daily lunch, afternoon tea, and dinner. Reservations recommended. 01.44.95.98.44

45 France Amérique If you want to give a party and insist on nothing less than a Second Empire town house for your setting, consider this place, which rents its three Louis XVI rooms (200 square meters/660 square feet) for festivities lasting just until midnight. Have **Angélina** (see page 180) take care of the catering for the perfect lavish bash. ♦ 9 Ave Franklin-D.-Roosevelt (between Rues François-1er and Jean-Goujon). 01.43.59.51.00. Métros: Franklin D. Roosevelt, Champs Elysées–Clemenceau

46 Lasserre ★★★$$$$ In the same luxurious league (and price range) as **Tour d'Argent** and **Grand Véfour**, this restaurant is famous for its caviar, 1930s ocean-liner decor, and service bordering on perfection (owner René Lasserre got his start in the restaurant business washing dishes at the age of 13, and all that experience shows). Located in a small town house, the main dining room is reached by a velvet-lined elevator. In warm weather, the ceiling, painted by Touchagues, rolls away, providing patrons with a view of the stars and a little cool air. Masterpieces from a rather traditional repertoire include: Belon oysters, canard (duck) à l'orange, sea bass with sorrel, and soufflé Grand Marnier. The restaurant's wine cellar has 140,000 bottles. ♦ M dinner; Tu-Sa lunch and dinner; closed in August. Reservations required; jackets required. 17 Ave Franklin-D.-Roosevelt (between Rues François-1er and Jean-Goujon). 01.43.59.53.43. Métros: Franklin D. Roosevelt, Champs Elysées–Clemenceau

47 Palais de la Découverte The western part of the **Grand Palais** houses a sprawling science museum offering holography exhibitions, Jacques Cousteau festivals, daily demonstrations on everything from ants to astronomy, and 9,000 stars twinkling on the ceiling of its celebrated planetarium. Kids love the Madagascar agates and, of course, the metal replicas of dinosaurs. ♦ Admission. Tu-Su. Ave Franklin-D.-Roosevelt (between Cours la Reine and Ave du Général-

Eisenhower). 01.40.74.80.00. Métros: Franklin D. Roosevelt, Champs Elysées–Clemenceau

48 7 Rue François-1er During World War II, this building, formerly the **Hôtel du Palais,** was the headquarters of the American Red Cross. It was here that North American poet e.e. cummings, a volunteer ambulance driver, spent a glorious May in 1917 detached from his unit. This act of independence resulted, through a tragicomic series of events, in his spending six months in a French prison, an experience that provided cummings with ample material for his autobiographical prose work, *The Enormous Room,* published in 1922. The building is now privately owned. ♦ Between Cours Albert-1er and Pl François-1er. Métro: Franklin D. Roosevelt

49 San Régis $$$$ This sophisticated and discreet 44-room hotel has hosted Raquel Welch and Lauren Bacall. It's decorated with fine antiques and paintings and sits close (but not too close) to the **Champs-Elysées.** There's a restaurant and a bar. ♦ 12 Rue Jean-Goujon (between Ave Franklin-D.-Roosevelt and Pl François-1er). 01.44.95.16.16; fax 01.45.61.05.48; message@hotel-sanregis.fr; www.hotel-sanregis.fr. Métro: Franklin D. Roosevelt

50 25 Avenue Franklin-D.-Roosevelt From 1862 until the end of the Civil War, John Slidell, the Confederate commissioner to France, spent his time in a vain attempt to gain diplomatic recognition and financial support for the Southern cause. After the Confederacy's defeat, Slidell chose to remain in this house in Paris. It's still a private home. ♦ Between Rue Jean-Goujon and Rond-Point des Champs-Elysées. Métros: Franklin D. Roosevelt, Champs Elysées–Clemenceau

51 Yvan ★★$$$ In his handsome restaurant *gastronomique,* chef Yvan Zaplatilek presents dishes largely influenced by his Belgian roots: potatoes with caviar, *waterzooï de faisan* (pheasant stew), poached salmon, rabbit with lemon confit, and *gateau au chocolat* (chocolate cake). The pastel-and-ivory dining room is filled with fresh flowers and softly lit with chandeliers and candlelight. ♦ M-F lunch and dinner; Sa dinner. Reservations required. 1 *bis* Rue Jean-Mermoz (between Rond-Point des Champs-Elysées and Rue de Ponthieu). 01.43.59.18.40. Métro: Franklin D. Roosevelt

51 Le Petit Yvan ★★$$ Chef Yvan Zaplatilek's little bistro is cheery, with brightly colored mismatched plates, red paper napkins, a hodgepodge collection of art on the walls, and a polite young staff. It's a tight squeeze, but the beautiful people here don't seem to mind rubbing elbows with each other. The inexpensive prix-fixe menu offers such dishes as langoustine bisque, roast chicken with mushrooms, steak *tartare, baba au rhum,*

and poached pears. ♦ M-F lunch and dinner; Sa dinner. Reservations recommended. 1 *bis* Rue Jean-Mermoz (between Rond-Point des Champs-Elysées and Rue de Ponthieu). 01.42.89.49.65. Métro: Franklin D. Roosevelt

52 Avenue Matignon This is "gallery alley" for Right Bank art and antiques. Take note of the stamp-collectors' market along this street and the connecting Avenue Gabriel, which is held Thursday, Saturday, Sunday, and holidays. ♦ Métros: Franklin D. Roosevelt, Miromesnil

On Avenue Matignon:

Le Berkeley ★$$ A classic oysters-and-Champagne, steak-and-fries restaurant, it features the red decor of a first-class dining car. ♦ Daily breakfast, lunch, and dinner until 2AM. Reservations recommended. No. 7 (at Rue de Ponthieu). 01.42.25.47.79, 01.42.25.72.25

BŒUF SUR LE TOIT

53 Le Boeuf sur le Toit ★★$$ With its high mirrored walls, period chandeliers, and velvet banquettes, this 1930s Art Deco gem is the most glamorous of Jean-Paul Bucher's vintage brasseries in Paris (the others are **Flo, Julien, Terminus Nord, Vaudeville, La Coupole,** and **Le Balzar**). Named after a 1919 musical by Jean Cocteau and Darius Milhaud, "Le Boeuf" had the hottest jazz, the prettiest women, and the best gossip in Paris at its earlier location during *Les Années Folles* of the 1920s. Cocteau, Picasso, the Dadaists, the Surrealists, everyone who was anyone in the arts came to see and be seen. The memorabilia collection by the front door recalls those days. There's no jazz band now, just the tinkling of a cocktail piano, but the aura of glamour remains strong. Fashion models, actors, and other high livers still pack the place, especially after the theaters let out. This is one of the most stimulating spots in Paris for a late night snack or supper. Fresh shellfish, grilled fish, *tajine de lotte aux olives et gingembre* (a spicy Moroccan stew of monkfish with olives and ginger), and well-prepared brasserie fare are served. ♦ Daily lunch and dinner until 2AM. Reservations recommended. 34 Rue du Colisée (between Rue du Faubourg-St-Honoré and Ave Franklin-D.-Roosevelt). 01.53.93.65.55. Métros: St-Phillipe-du-Roule, Franklin D. Roosevelt

53 Escrouzailles ★★$$ This friendly and refreshingly simple restaurant serves mouthwatering specialties from France's gastronomic heartland, the Massif Central. Appetizers include pumpkin soup, duck foie gras, and sautéed goose gizzards with lima beans. For the main course, try the remarkable *croustillant Quercynois en croûte de pomme de terre* (two crispy potato wafers filled with preserved duck breast, foie gras, and potato gratin), roast salmon, or honeyed roast lamb. Wild game is served in season. A bottle of Château Montus 1995 Madiran red goes beautifully with everything. Be sure to save room for either one of the homemade fruit sherbets or the *tout chocolat noir* (a square of dark mousselike chocolate). To increase the allure, the yellow walls are hung with original paintings by local artists that are for sale. The very reasonably priced food keeps the place filled with businesspeople at lunch, and Parisian regulars and foreign visitors at dinner. ♦ Daily lunch and dinner. Reservations recommended. 36 Rue du Colisée (between Rue du Faubourg-St-Honoré and Ave Franklin-D.-Roosevelt). 01.45.62.94.00. Métros: St-Philippe-du-Roule, Franklin D. Roosevelt. Also at: 83 Ave de Ségur (between Blvd Garibaldi and Ave de Suffren). 01.40.65.99.10. Métro: Ségur

54 Jadis et Gourmande A chocolate-lover's sweetest dream, this candy store sells chocolate letters of the alphabet to compose messages, **Arcs de Triomphe,** chocolate Bordeaux bottles filled with coffee beans, and dozens of other original ideas for gifts. ♦ M-Sa. 49 *bis* Ave Franklin-D.-Roosevelt (between Rond-Point des Champs-Elysées and Rue de Ponthieu). 01.42.25.06.04. Métro: Franklin D. Roosevelt

55 Hôtel Colisée $$ Quilted bedspreads and bamboo furniture embellish the 44 rooms of this comfortable, well-located member of the Best Western hotel group. There's no restaurant. ♦ 6 Rue du Colisée (between Rue de Ponthieu and Ave des Champs-Elysées). 01.56.88.26.26; fax 01.56.88.26.00; www.bestwestern.com. Métro: Franklin D. Roosevelt

56 Franklin D. Roosevelt Métro Station This is the oldest métro station in Paris. The *métro* (short for *métropolitain*), was born on 4 October 1898, when men with picks and shovels began digging a labyrinth beneath the city as directed by engineer Fulgence Bienvenue. ♦ Rue de Marignan and Ave des Champs-Elysées

57 Avenue Montaigne This street is to haute couture what the **Louvre** is to art. The swank avenue is lined with high-fashion temples

(**Christian Dior, Nina Ricci, Jean-Louis Scherrer, Valentino, Louis Vuitton, Ungaro,** and **Laroche**). You will also find the **Canadian Embassy,** the luxurious **Plaza Athénée** hotel, and two smart theaters (the **Comédie des Champs-Elysées** and the **Théâtre des Champs-Elysées**). ♦ Métros: Franklin D. Roosevelt, Alma-Marceau

57 Artcurial An essential stop for art lovers, this prestigious gallery and bookstore sells modern and contemporary prints, sculptures, original art objects and jewelry, and art books in the glamorous new space it settled into in 1998. ♦ Tu-Sa; closed three weeks in August. 61 Ave Montaigne (between Rond-Point des Champs-Elysées and Rue François-1er). 01.42.99.16.16. Métro: Franklin D. Roosevelt

CHANEL

58 Chanel The dashing Chanel collections are displayed here to their best advantage: in a setting of crisp white walls, gleaming mirrors, and spacious dressing rooms. ♦ M-Sa. 42 Ave Montaigne (between Rues Bayard and François-1er). 01.47.23.74.12. Métros: Alma-Marceau, Franklin D. Roosevelt

59 L'Avenue ★★$$ In this chic brasserie/restaurant, located on one of the most sumptuous avenues in the world, chef Jean Philippe Liotté prepares appropriate temptations: classic Caesar salad, *gazpacho de tomates du soleil* (with sun-dried tomatoes), marinated scallops and salmon with lemon sauce, risotto with snails, prawns with ginger, and *noisette* (tenderloin) of lamb. ♦ Daily breakfast, lunch, afternoon tea, and dinner. Reservations recommended. 41 Ave Montaigne (at Rue François-1er).01.40.70.14.91. Métros: Franklin D. Roosevelt, Alma-Marceau

60 Spoon Food & Wine ★★$$ Back from a global trot, six-Michelin-star chef Alain Ducasse offers his take on "world food"—which comes mainly from Asia, the Americas, and Italy—in this bright, modern, and resolutely un-French bistro. Even the menu is un-French—the dishes are described first in English, then translated (in smaller print) into *français.* Diners can mix and match their dishes from all over the globe: pork or shrimp ravioli, seviche, Thai squid in curry sauce, a BLT or pastrami sandwich, pan-seared tuna with satay sauce, or barbecue spare ribs. And for dessert, what else but Ben & Jerry's ice cream? The wine list is equally eclectic. Half the 120 selections come from the US, the rest mainly from Chile, South Africa, and Australia, with only 10 percent hailing from France. It's an interesting culinary experiment. Only time will tell if the public is ready for so much globe trotting. ◆ M-F lunch and dinner; Sa lunch. Reservations recommended. 14 Rue de Marignan (between Rue François-1er and Ave des Champs-Elysées). 01.40.76.34.44. Métro: Franklin D. Roosevelt

61 Nina Ricci Perhaps the most beautiful lingerie in the world is sold here, along with a stylish array of dresses, scarves, scents, and jewelry. **The Ricci Club,** an elegant menswear shop, is next door at 19 Rue François-1er, and around the corner at 17 Rue François-1er this haute couture designer's fashions from the year before are sold at a discount. ◆ M-Sa. 39 Ave Montaigne (at Rue François-1er). All three stores 01.49.52.56.00. Métros: Alma-Marceau, Franklin D. Roosevelt

62 Christian Dior In 1949 Dior signed the first designer licensing contract (for stockings). Today, women can dress in his wares from head to toe. Roam through this ultrachic gray-and-white complex, which sells dresses, furs, jewelry, makeup, accessories, and gifts, to select your ensemble. ◆ M-Sa. 30 Ave Montaigne (between Rue François-1er and Pl de la Reine-Astrid). 01.40.73.54.00. Métros: Franklin D. Roosevelt, Alma-Marceau

62 26 Avenue Montaigne In 1857, when he was 14, Henry James moved into this apartment building with his family. ◆ Between Rue François-1er and Pl de la Reine-Astrid. Métros: Franklin D. Roosevelt, Alma-Marceau

◪
PLAZA ATHÉNÉE PARIS

63 Plaza Athénée $$$$ Elegant and charming, this 205-room property has long enjoyed a reputation as the most fashionable palace hotel in Paris, largely because its **Relais Plaza** restaurant (see below) remains the favored lunchtime hangout of Paris couturiers. In fact, when the great designer Pierre Balmain died, the management retired his table. Also on the premises are the one-Michelin-star **Régence** restaurant and a classic Parisian cocktail bar (see below). The Louis XV– and XVI–style decor features a profusion of flowers—the hotel staff boasts that the monthly florist's bill is higher than the electric bill. In 1918 West Point graduate Captain George Patton stayed here while learning to fence at the French Military Academy in Saumur. While in residence, Patton discussed combat with then 28-year-old Charles de Gaulle. Today the hotel's select out-of-town clientele includes Rockefellers, rich Brazilians, and the like. ◆ 25 Ave Montaigne (between Rues Clément-Marot and du Boccador). 01.53.67.66.65; fax 01.53.67.66.66. Métro: Alma-Marceau

Within the Plaza Athénée:

Relais Plaza ★$$ For a late-night, after-theater meal, try the fillets of sole or braised beef in aspic, accompanied by a good house wine. *Tout Paris* lunches here, particularly during the fashion shows. ◆ Daily lunch and dinner. Reservations recommended. 01.47.23.78.33

Bar Anglais After a performance at the **Théâtre des Champs-Elysées,** the concert crowd may come here and mix with the South American night owls staying at the hotel. There's piano music after 11PM. ◆ Daily 11AM-1AM. 01.47.23.78.33

Régence-Plaza ★★★$$$ The most expensive of the hotel's restaurants is peopled, as a rule, by the rich and famous who dine in an opulent setting. Young chef Eric Briffard creates such elegant dishes as *St-Pierre au curry et aux aubergines fondants* (John Dory with curry and melted eggplant) and roast peach with fresh almond and lavender. Patrick Jeanne, the restaurant's manager, has mastered the art of mingling the stars and the not-yet-famous so that everyone can get a look at everyone else. In summer dine on the ivy-decked terrace. ◆ Daily lunch and dinner. Reservations recommended. 01.53.67.65.00

64 Bar des Théâtres ★★$$ This noisy bar/restaurant is patronized by theater critics before, bored ticket holders during, and worn-out actors after performances. The fare is simple: steak, Welsh rarebit, osso buco, and the like. It's a favorite lunch spot of film director Roman Polanski. ◆ Daily lunch and dinner until 2AM. 6 Ave Montaigne (between Rue François-1er and Pl de la Reine-Astrid). 01.47.23.34.63. Métro: Alma-Marceau

65 Valentino The Milan designer's Paris boutique, all beige marble and glass, shows his sophisticated men's and women's fashions as well as the casual, less expensive clothes sold under his younger label, Miss Valentino. ◆ M-Sa. 17-19 Ave Montaigne (at Rue du Boccador). 01.47.23.64.61. Métro: Alma-Marceau

66 Théâtre des Champs-Elysées Here, on 29 May 1913, the **Ballet Russe** of Sergei Diaghilev first performed to the music of the Stravinsky piece *Le Sacré du Printemps.* Riots followed the performance, which was

shocking in its originality and modernity. Diaghilev, Stravinsky, Nijinsky, and Cocteau fled the mobs for the **Bois de Boulogne** and drove around while Diaghilev wept.

Inaugurated in 1913, the theater was one of the first buildings of reinforced concrete in Paris; it was designed by **Auguste Perret,** who was later hired to reconstruct the entire port city of Le Havre after World War II. Today it is the city's most celebrated classical music venue; it also hosts opera and dance performances.

North American footnotes: On 2 October 1925 *La Revue Nègre* opened here; John Dos Passos painted the show's stage set, Sidney Bechet played clarinet, and Josephine Baker danced to "Yes, Sir, That's My Baby." In May 1927 a Charles Lindbergh autograph sold for $1,500 at an auction held at the theater (the name of his plane, *The Spirit of St. Louis,* pleased the French, who associated it not with Missouri, but with the saintliest of their line of kings). And on 16 April 1928, the Gershwins attended the opening of a performance of *La Rhapsodie en Bleu* by the **Ballet Russe.** ♦ Box office: M-Sa. No performances 1 July through the first week of September and holidays. 15 Ave Montaigne (between Rue du Boccador and Pl de l'Alma). 01.49.52.50.00. Métro: Alma-Marceau

Atop the Théâtre des Champs-Elysées:

Maison Blanche ★★★$$$ René Duran's trendy restaurant attracts a business and haute couture clientele. The space is decorated in simple monochromes, and the culinary magic of José Martinez is as pleasing to the eye as to the palate: special taste treats include *beignets d'huitres aux neuf saveurs* (oyster fritters with nine flavors), *le pigeon rôti à la cannelle* (cinnamon roast pigeon), and heavenly desserts. ♦ Daily lunch and dinner. 01.47.23.55.99

67 2 Avenue Montaigne Back when this was the **Hôtel Elysée-Bellevue,** Sinclair Lewis passed the winter of 1924 here writing *Arrowsmith.* It is now a private residential building. ♦ At Pl de la Reine-Astrid. Métro: Alma-Marceau

68 Pont de l'Alma Built in 1855 to honor the first French victory in the Crimean War (1854), this bridge is decorated with a statue of a Zouave soldier that acts as a watermark; during the flood of 1910, the Seine reached his chin. The *bateaux mouches* and dinner cruises embark on their tours of the Seine from the quay below Place de l'Alma. A full-scale replica of the Statue of Liberty's torch on Place de l'Alma by the Right Bank end of the bridge was erected by the *International Herald Tribune* in 1987 to commemorate the newspaper's 100th anniversary. It has since become an ad hoc memorial to Princess Diana

and Dodi Al Fayed, who died in the underpass beneath this spot in 1997. For a year after the tragedy, mourners heaped the monument with flowers and plastered it with poems and placards in their honor. At press time, people continued to bring notes and flowers here and to cover the walls near the torch with weird graffiti. ♦ Métro: Alma-Marceau

69 Chez Francis ★★$$ Formerly a *relais de poste* (stable for the post office's horses), this bistro boasts a three-star view of the **Eiffel Tower** and the largest outdoor terrace in Paris. A show-biz crowd assembles here for fresh seafood platters, tuna or beef carpaccio, *moules marinières* (mussels steamed in white wine and shallots), grilled sole, and *confit de canard* with sautéed apples. ♦ Daily lunch and dinner. Reservations recommended. 7 Pl de l'Alma (at Ave George-V). 01.47.20.86.83. Métro: Alma-Marceau

70 Avenue George-V Along this grand avenue named after the English king, you will find the **American Cathedral;** the salons of **Givenchy** and **Balenciaga;** the Chinese and Mexican embassies; a swank hotel (the **Four Seasons Hotel George V**); and the **Crazy Horse,** with its sophisticated girlie shows. ♦ Métros: Alma-Marceau, George V

70 Marius et Janette ★★★$$$ For a taste of some of the finest Provençal cuisine available in Paris, reserve a table at this gracious seafood restaurant, which is set on a large yacht. Chef Laurent Odiot serves classic bouillabaisse, lobster salad, sea bass flambé, and a selection of other seafood dishes. A favorite of celebrities (Sylvester Stallone, Michelle Pfeiffer, and Robert De Niro have all dined here), this place has an appropriately nautical feel, with lots of wood and photos of fishermen on the walls. Note: bouillabaisse lovers must call two days in advance to order the dish. ♦ Daily lunch and dinner. Reservations recommended. 4 Ave George-V (between Pl de l'Alma and Rue de La Trémoille). 01.47.23.41.88. Métro: Alma-Marceau

70 Le Bistrot de Marius ★★$$ Pagnol's Marius may have run away to sea, but the chef here seems to have just returned. The bill of fare at this warm, Provençal-style spot revolves around the freshest of raw shellfish, rockfish soup, sea scallops, and for carnivores, roast lamb fillets with sautéed potatoes. ♦ Daily lunch and dinner. 6 Ave George-V (between Pl de l'Alma and Rue de

La Trémoille). 01.40.70.11.76. Métro: Alma-Marceau

70 Crazy Horse Saloon The originality of *l'art du nu* (the art of the nude) in Paris's sexiest floor show lies in the play of light patterns projected onto the nearly nude bodies of the 18 women dancers—"living pictures," as the spectacle's creator, Alain Bernardin, called them. Updated every year, the show has attracted millions of spectators since the club opened in 1951. The women come from all over Europe, but they must be of uniform height—between 5 feet, 4 inches and 5 feet, 5 inches tall—so that their salient features line up neatly on stage. The performers adopt fanciful stage names—Loulou Looping, Tita de Cucufa, Sleepy Nightmare, and Pussy Duty-Free were just some of the more appealing appellations at press time. The show also features brilliant puppet and magic acts. The club has an arrangement with neighboring **Chez Francis** (see above) where spectators can dine either before or after the show. ♦ Cover. Shows: M-F, Su 8:30PM, 11PM; Sa 7:30PM, 9:45PM, 11:50PM. Reservations recommended. 12 Ave George-V (between Pl de l'Alma and Rue de La Trémoille). 01.47.23.46.46. Métro: Alma-Marceau

71 Hôtel de la Trémoille $$$$ This impressive-yet-relaxed 107-room hotel is a bit of *Vieux France* in the heart of the high-fashion district. The rooms are furnished with antiques and feature sumptuous bathrooms. After an afternoon of shopping at **Christian Dior** and **Nina Ricci**, dine here or at one of the restaurants in the nearby **Plaza Athénée** and charge your meal to your room. ♦ 14 Rue de La Trémoille (at Rue du Boccador). 01.47.23.34.20; fax 01.40.70.01.08. Métro: Alma-Marceau

Within the Hôtel de la Trémoille:

Le Louis d'Or ★★$$$ A fire burns in the *cheminée* (fireplace) of this elegant but cozy dining room. With an emphasis on traditional cuisine, a fine meal here might consist of a starter of potato cakes with truffles and Port or scallop salad with lime, a main course of sole meunière, or roast lamb with fresh thyme, and a dessert of crème brûlée or *tarte tatin* (apple tart). ♦ M-F breakfast, lunch, and dinner; Sa-Su breakfast and lunch. Reservations required. 01.47.23.34.20

72 Claridge-Bellman $$$ Decorated with antiques, paintings, 17th-century tapestries, and Chinese vases, this posh 42-room hotel is home to the Italian couturiers during the seasonal fashion shows. The quietly elegant dining room is open to the public. Reserve well in advance. ♦ 37 Rue François-1er (at Rue Marbeuf). 01.47.23.54.42; fax 01.47.28.08.84. Métro: Franklin D. Roosevelt

73 Chez André ★★$$ Unchanged since 1938, this bistro bustles at lunchtime with the dressed-for-success crowd from the Champs-Elysées and matronly waitresses loping through with hot plates. Recommended dishes include poached haddock, short ribs, roast leg of lamb with mashed potatoes, sponge cake with rum sauce, and the affordable house Muscadet and red Graves. ♦ Daily lunch and dinner until 1AM. Reservations recommended. 12 Rue Marbeuf (at Rue Clément-Marot). 01.47.20.59.57. Métro: Franklin D. Roosevelt

RISTORANTE

74 Ristorante Romano ★★$$ Highlights of this simple, casual, and warm Italian eatery include its smiling owner Romano and a seasonally changing menu that might include *insalata caprese* (mozzarella, tomato, and basil), *spaghetti alle vongole* (with clams), ravioli in a morel sauce, scampi, and saltimbocca with mozzarella. ♦ Daily lunch and dinner. Reservations recommended. 11 Rue Marbeuf (between Rues du Boccador and Clément-Marot). 01.47.20.85.98. Métros: Franklin D. Roosevelt, Alma-Marceau

La Table des Gourmets

75 La Fermette Marbeuf 1900 ★★★$$ In 1978, when Jean Laurent purchased what had been a self-service restaurant since 1950, he had no idea of the treasure that lay behind the plastic and Formica. Renovations began, and as workers were tearing down the partition walls they discovered the tile, stained glass, and cast-iron pillars of a spectacular Art Nouveau room that had been hidden for 30 years. The room, it turns out, had been created in 1898 by two young, unknown designers named Hutre and Wielharski. Although the real star here is the decor, the cuisine runs a close second. Among the delectations are crab meat with avocado, green beans, and mayonnaise; grilled young turbot with béarnaise sauce; saddle of rabbit stuffed with fennel; prime ribs of beef; peach soup with apricots and Beaumes de Venise liqueur; and mint-flavored dark and white chocolate cake. A fine selection of eaux-de-vie, Cognacs, and liqueurs await the end of your meal. ♦ Daily lunch and dinner. Reservations required. 5 Rue Marbeuf (at Rue du Boccador). 01.53.23.08.00. Métros: Franklin D. Roosevelt, Alma-Marceau

75 24 Rue du Boccador In the late 1940s this apartment building was rife with such movie stars as Brigitte Bardot, Ivy League CIA agents posing as novelists, and legitimate North American writers, including Theodore H. White, Art Buchwald, and Irwin Shaw. This is where White, after working for six years as *Time* magazine's Beijing bureau chief, wrote his Pulitzer Prize–winning World War II novel, *The Mountain Road.* In a fifth-floor studio, Buchwald wrote his "Paris After Dark" column for the *Herald Tribune,* and Shaw, in much grander digs, completed his best-selling novel *The Young Lions,* which was published in 1948. ♦ Between Rue Marbeuf and Ave George-V. Métros: Franklin D. Roosevelt, Alma-Marceau

76 American Cathedral This spired Gothic Revival church was designed by **George Edmund Street,** the architect of London's New Law Courts, and consecrated in 1886. It has 42 Pre-Raphaelite stained glass windows and a fine 15th-century triptych by the Roussillon Master, probably Gaubert Gaucelm. In addition to its Anglican-Episcopalian services in English held on Monday through Friday and Sunday, the church presents numerous choral concerts and organ recitals. ♦ 23 Ave George-V (between Pl de l'Alma and Ave Pierre-1er-de-Serbie). 01.53.23.84.00. Métro: Alma-Marceau

77 Four Seasons Hotel George V Paris $$$$ Opened in 1928, this was one of the most glamorous and expensive hotels in Paris, and attracted a long parade of celebrities and extremely wealthy people. In 1996, one of the latter, Prince Al Waleed of Saudi Arabia, bought the hotel, and commissioned a long, drastic program to refurbish the property while maintaining its Old World charm. The hotel was scheduled to reopen at press time, under Four Seasons management. There are 245 elegant guest rooms (including 61 suites)—each with a marble bathroom and 30 with a private balcony, a restaurant, bar, lounge, health club, pool, and spa. ♦ 31 Ave George-V (between Ave Pierre-1er-de-Serbie and Rue Quentin-

Bauchart). 01.53.53.28.00; fax 01.53.53.28.10; www.fourseasons.com. Métro: George V

77 37 Avenue George-V On their honeymoon in 1905, Franklin and Eleanor Roosevelt visited Franklin's aunt, Deborah Delano, who had an apartment at this address. She used to take the newlyweds driving; in fact it was in the **Bois de Boulogne** that FDR learned to drive. ♦ Between Ave Pierre-1er-de-Serbie and Rue Quentin-Bauchart. Métro: George V

Hôtel François 1er

78 Hôtel François I $$$$ This luxurious 40-room hostelry off the Champs-Elysées is a favorite of business travelers. The spacious lobby, bar, and restaurant feature tasteful Art Deco decor. All rooms afford luxurious bath amenities, mini-bar, and room service. ♦ 7 Rue Magellan (between Rues Christophe-Colomb and de Bassano). 01.47.23.44.04; fax 01.47.23.93.43. Métro: George V

79 16 Rue Christophe-Colomb In 1898 Henry Adams, grandson of John Quincy Adams and professor of history at Harvard University, stayed in several rooms in this apartment building while reading medieval manuscripts for his book on art and culture, *Mont-Saint-Michel and Chartres.* ♦ Between Rue Magellan and Ave Marceau. Métro: George V

80 L'Ecluse ★★$$ The second in a chain of six classy wine bars, this place offers vintage Bordeaux and light meals of smoked salmon, carpaccio, and goat cheese. ♦ Daily lunch and dinner until 1AM. 64 Rue François-1er (between Rues Lincoln and Quentin-Bauchart). 01.47.20.77.09. Métro: George V. Also at: Numerous locations throughout the city

81 Guerlain Institut de Beauté Make an appointment at least a week in advance if you wish to visit this Regency-paneled beauty salon and undergo the royal treatment from the perfumed ladies in pink. ♦ M-Sa. 68 Ave des Champs-Elysées (between Rues La Boétie and de Berri). 01.45.62.11.21. Métros: Franklin D. Roosevelt, George V

82 Virgin Megastore This majestic music and multimedia shop looks like a Cecil B. De Mille movie set, complete with a monumental marble staircase. Its various levels are replete with a mind-bending selection of records, CDs, tapes, and videos (in English and French), as well as books on music and stereo equipment. There's also a lively cafe on the mezzanine. ♦ M-Sa 10AM-midnight; Su noon-midnight. 52-60 Ave des Champs-Elysées (at Rue La Boétie). Recorded message 01.49.53.50.00, 01.49.53.52.45. Métro: Franklin D. Roosevelt

83 Institut Géographique National
The French counterpart of the National
Geographic Society in Washington, DC,
is a cartographer's heaven, selling maps
of the entire universe (at least that which
is recognized by the French) and more.
You may purchase wall-size maps of the
Paris métro, navigation charts of the Seine,
infrared satellite photos of France, 1618 city
maps of Paris, and four-by-four-foot color
aerial photographs of different sectors of
downtown Paris so detailed you can make
out pedestrians on the Champs-Elysées.
♦ M-Sa. 107 Rue La Boétie (between Rue
de Ponthieu and Ave des Champs-Elysées).
01.43.98.80.00. Métro: Franklin D. Roosevelt

84 Chesterfield Café This large Tex-Mex
cafe puts on free concerts by an all–North
American lineup of rising rock and R&B
artists, and big names on the comeback
trail. Alanis Morissette, the Spin Doctors,
Widespread Panic, Jeff Healey, and Ian Moore
have performed here. Live gospel is played
Sunday from noon to 4PM. ♦ Daily 11AM-
5AM. Live music: Tu-Sa midnight-2AM.
Happy Hour: M-F 4-8PM. 124 Rue La Boétie
(between Rue de Ponthieu and Ave des
Champs-Elysées). 01.42.25.18.06. Métro:
Franklin D. Roosevelt

85 Régine's Régine, the celebrated
queen of Paris nightlife, puts in only
rare appearances at her enticing, dimly lit
private club off the Champs-Elysées, but the
Ritz/Tour d'Argent/Maxim's crowd keeps
coming back anyway. ♦ Cover. Daily 11PM-
dawn. 49 Rue de Ponthieu (between Rues La
Boétie and de Berri). 01.43.59.21.13. Métro:
Franklin D. Roosevelt

86 Gymnase Club The largest health club
in Paris offers five floors of aerobics studios,
body-building equipment, saunas, Jacuzzis,
a solarium, and juice bar. ♦ M-Sa. 26 Rue
de Berri (between Rues de Ponthieu and
d'Artois). 01.43.59.04.58. Métro: George V

87 Lancaster $$$$ Set in a renovated,
handsome 19th-century town house, this
50-room and 10-suite first-class hotel has
an atmosphere more like a luxurious private
home than a grand hostelry. The guest rooms
are furnished with antiques, and each has
individual charm. There's also a fitness center
and sauna, a relaxed and refined cafe/bar, and
a charming courtyard garden. Helen Keller
stayed here in 1937, John Steinbeck in 1954,
and Robert Capa made the hotel his home in

the late 1940s. A continuing parade of
North American luminaries has sojourned
here since. ♦ 7 Rue de Berri (between Ave
des Champs-Elysées and Rue d'Artois).
01.40.76.40.76; fax 01.40.76.40.00;
pippaona@hotel-lancaster.fr; www.hotel-
lancaster.fr. Métro: George V

87 The Chicago Pizza Pie Factory ★★$
Midwesterners pining for a taste of home
should descend to the cavernous brick
basement, bright with red-and-white
checkered tablecloths and reverberating with
Chuck Berry, where they can order a deep-
dish pizza with such traditional toppings as
pepperoni and mushrooms. ♦ Daily 11:30AM-
1AM. Happy Hour: M-F 4-7PM. 5 Rue de Berri
(between Ave des Champs-Elysées and Rue
d'Artois). 01.45.62.50.23. Métro: George V

88 1 Rue de Berri On 17 October 1785,
42-year-old Thomas Jefferson succeeded
Benjamin Franklin as minister to France
and moved into this mansion, the **Hôtel
de Langeac,** designed by architect **Jean-
François Chalgrin.** Jefferson resided here
for the next four years. It's now divided into
shops and offices. ♦ At Ave des Champs-
Elysées. Métro: George V

89 Le Queen As the name suggests, the
crowd at this ultra-*in* (pronounced "ultra-
een") disco is predominantly made up
of gay men. Straight men and women are
welcome Wednesday nights, however, if
they're young enough and chic enough to
get by the doorman. The other nights are gay,
with drag queens galore. Top DJs from Paris
and London provide the music. It's jammed
every night, and the dance floor is pure
delirium. ♦ Cover charge M, F-Sa. M-Sa
midnight-dawn. 102 Ave des Champs-Elysées
(between Rues de Berri and Washington).
01.53.89.08.90. Métro: George V

Fouquet's

90 Fouquet's ★★$$$ This famous cafe has
been a watering hole for show-biz celebrities,
the glamour set, and big names in literature
and the arts since it opened in 1899. James
Joyce dined here almost every night once
he got in the chips (there's a dining room
upstairs named after him), and every March
the French film industry presents the Césars,
its version of Hollywood's Oscars, in the
sumptuous banquet room. The restaurant
serves traditional French fare, including some
specialties that have been on the menu for
the past 50 years: *maquereaux* (mackerel) in
white wine, *merlan au colbert* (fried whiting),
and *hachis parmentier* (mashed potatoes
mixed with beef and spices). The big outdoor
terrace with its trademark red awning

straddles the southeastern corner of Avenue George-V and the Champs-Elysées and is a popular spot for lunch or a drink. Some of the best people watching in Paris is found here. Sit on the George-V side to rub shoulders with celebrities. ♦ Daily breakfast, lunch, and dinner until 1AM. Reservations recommended. 99 Ave des Champs-Elysées (at Ave George-V). 01.47.23.70.60. Métro: George V

91 Barfly ★★$$
Food is secondary here—getting a chance to gawk at the international assemblage of the rich and famous is more to the point.

However, there is a perfectly acceptable eclectic menu of Japanese sushi or traditional French fare including puff pastry desserts. As reservations can be hard to come by, dropping in for a drink at the bar is the quicker way to check out the scene. ♦ Daily lunch and dinner until 1AM. Reservations recommended. 49-51 Ave George-V (at Rue Vernet). 01.53.67.84.60. Métro: George V

92 Taillevent ★★★★$$$$ This is as close as a restaurant comes to perfection. Jean-Claude Vrinat, the owner and idea man, and chef Philippe Legendre have made this establishment one of the best dining spots in Paris. Set in a town house with high ceilings, oak-paneled walls, and Louis XV furniture, the place has the feel of a grand bourgeois private club. Its namesake is Guillaume Tirel (a.k.a. Taillevent), the 14th-century royal cook who wrote the first treatise on French cooking, and it offers such innovative signature dishes as *fruits de mer* (mixed seafood) with truffles and pistachios, langoustines with fresh pasta, Barbary duck, veal kidneys, and almond ice cream. The wine list draws on a cellar of 130,000 bottles ranging from such collector's items as a Lafite-Rothschild 1806 to a less risky and far less expensive Château Haut Brion. This is the perfect choice for a top-of-the-line business lunch or that once-in-a-lifetime dining experience. ♦ M-F lunch and dinner; closed one week in February and in August. Reservations required well in advance. 15 Rue Lamennais (between Rue Washington and Ave de Friedland). 01.44.95.15.01. Métros: Charles de Gaulle-Etoile, George V

93 Hôtel de Vigny $$$$ Sumptuous wood paneling, a lobby resembling a private London club, and 37 bright and airy rooms that are royally furnished with antiques, puffy down comforters, and private Jacuzzis are just some of the features of this hostelry. There's an attractive bar where sandwiches and salads are served, but no restaurant. ♦ 9-11 Rue Balzac (at Rue Lord-Byron). 01.42.99.80.80; fax 01.42.99.80.40; De.Vigny@wanadoo.fr. Métros: George V, Charles de Gaulle–Etoile

94 Pierre Gagnaire ★★★★$$$$ This dining spot has garnered rave reviews from the moment it opened. One of the most skilled practitioners of blending exotic ingredients, chef Gagnaire prepares such dishes as poached salmon with chutney, duck foie gras wrapped in bacon, roasted duck topped with lime and served with bitter melons, veal with tomato marmalade and tiny squid, and herbed sea bass with fresh vegetables. His use of sweet and sour is legendary. Desserts are just as captivating—the dried grapefruit *dacquoise* (filled meringues) is a hit. Here the decor is minimalist, almost self-effacing, as if to highlight the creativity of the cuisine, which has elevated this restaurant to the apotheosis of Michelin three-stardom. ♦ M-F dinner; closed mid-July to mid-August. Reservations recommended. 6 Rue Balzac (between Ave des Champs-Elysées and Rue Lord-Byron). 01.44.35.18.25. Métros: George V, Charles de Gaulle–Etoile

95 Lido The largest cabaret in Paris, this lavish extravaganza outglitters Las Vegas with its $15-million revue starring the famous **Bluebell Girls,** whose dance numbers are choreographed by computer and who wear $4 million worth of high-tech costumes incorporating fiber optics, fake fur, leather, and the obligatory feathers and sequins. Dazzling special effects include aerial and aquatic ballets, a motorized flying dragon, water sprays, and a skating rink that rises out of the floor. Throw in a few jugglers, acrobats, and bare-breasted dancers decorously lowered from the ceiling and you have your basic night at the **Lido.** It's always packed with Japanese tourists, car salesmen, and sailors on leave. Famed chef Paul Bocuse is the food consultant for the international menu. ♦ Cover. Shows: Daily 10PM and midnight; doors open at 8PM for dinner and dancing before the show. Reservations recommended. 116 *bis* Ave des Champs-Elysées (between Rues Washington and Balzac). 01.40.76.56.10. Métro: George V

96 La Boutique Flora Danica ★★$
The pleasures of Danish dining—pickled herring, eel, marinated salmon, shrimp salad, roast beef with onions, Ceres beer on tap, and the flakiest pastries around—abound in this cheerful luncheonette with blond-wood tables fronting on the Champs-Elysées. ♦ Daily lunch and dinner; takeout available in the evening. 142 Ave des Champs-Elysées (between Rues Balzac and Arsène-Houssaye). 01.44.13.86.26. Métros: George V, Charles de Gaulle–Etoile

96 Flora Danica ★★$$ More refined Nordic cuisine is served at this sister restaurant that's located in a somewhat secluded setting to the rear of **La Boutique Flora Danica**. Here salmon is featured in many incarnations (poached with dill, smoked, marinated, or grilled) and served with draft Danish beer or French wine. This place is famous for its flaky pastries. In summer, meals are served in an umbrella-shaded courtyard; the rest of the year in the Danish Modern dining room. ♦ Daily lunch and dinner. 142 Ave des Champs-Elysées (between Rues Balzac and Arsène-Houssaye). 01.44.13.86.26. Métros: George V, Charles de Gaulle–Etoile

96 Copenhague ★★★$$$ Upstairs from **Flora Danica** and **La Boutique Flora Danica**, this restaurant serves more sophisticated, and more expensive, Danish cuisine in an elegant modern dining room. Reindeer terrine, marinated herring, and pre-salted *duck à la danoise* are among chef Denis Schneider's specialties. ♦ M-F lunch and dinner; Sa dinner; closed in August and the first week of January. 142 Ave des Champs-Elysées (between Rues Balzac and Arsène-Houssaye). 01.44.13.86.26. Métros: George V, Charles de Gaulle–Etoile

OFFICE DE TOURISME DE PARIS

97 Office de Tourisme de Paris Home of the city's official tourist bureau, this office provides visitors with free maps and brochures, sight-seeing information, and same-day hotel reservations for those stuck without a room for the night. ♦ Daily 9AM-8PM. 127 Ave des Champs-Elysées (between Rues Galilée and de Presbourg). 08.36.68.31.12; fax 01.49.53.53.00; www.paris-touristoffice.com. Métros: Charles de Gaulle–Etoile, George V

98 133 Avenue des Champs-Elysées After World War II, General Dwight D. Eisenhower, supreme commander of the Allied Forces in Europe, had his headquarters here in what was the old **Hôtel Astoria**. He asked for a room with a view of the **Arc de Triomphe**, his favorite structure in Paris. The hotel was destroyed in a fire in 1972; the present building houses offices and a drugstore. ♦ At Rue de Presbourg. Métro: Charles de Gaulle–Etoile

Within 133 Avenue des Champs-Elysées:

Drugstore des Champs-Elysées In addition to aspirin and Band-Aids, this drugstore sells gourmet groceries, quick brasserie meals, wristwatches, banana splits, and Cuban cigars. ♦ Daily 9AM-2AM. 01.44.43.79.00, 01.47.20.39.24

99 Raphael $$$$ This luxurious 87-room lodging place with Louis XVI and Louis XV decor attracts Italian and North American movie stars. There's a sumptuously decorated restaurant. ♦ 17 Ave Kléber (at Ave des Portugais). 01.44.28.00.28; fax 01.45.01.21.50; management@raphael.hotel.com; www.raphael.hotel.com. Métro: Kléber

100 Le Duplex ★★$$ The beautiful people who frequent this restaurant and nightclub come to see and be seen. If you don't want to stand outside under bright lights hoping you're cool enough to be allowed into the nightclub, make dinner reservations. You'll enjoy typical bistro food along with a stupendous view of the **Arc de Triomphe**, and afterwards you can go directly downstairs to the club, which boasts the best sound system in Paris. ♦ Restaurant: Tu-Sa dinner. Nightclub: daily 11PM-4AM. Reservations recommended. 8 Ave Foch (between Rues de Presbourg and Rude). 01.45.00.45.00. Métro: Charles de Gaulle–Etoile

101 Le Méridien Etoile $$$$ Conveniently located across from the **Palais des Congrès**, this 1,025-room hotel is perfect for the business traveler. The hotel's **Le Club Président** is a 112-room hotel-within-the-hotel on two adjoining floors, designed to resemble a private British club; it offers quick check-in/-out service, meeting rooms, traditional business services, voice mail, and individual fax and phone lines on request. There are three restaurants: the **Café Harlequin** (01.40.68.30.85), for Mediterranean and traditional French cuisine; **Le Yamoto** (01.40.68.30.41), a Japanese restaurant and sushi bar; and **Le Clos Longchamp** (01.40.68.30.40) for breakfast to the general public, and private lunches, dinners, and cocktail parties. There are two bars, a **Häagen-Dazs** ice-cream shop, and a jazz club. A Sunday jazz brunch is held in the lobby. ♦ 81 Blvd Gouvion-St-Cyr (between Pl de la Porte-Maillot and Rue Belidor). 01.40.68.34.34; fax 01.40.68.31.31; www.forte-hotels.com. Métro: Porte Maillot

Within Le Méridien Etoile:

Lionel Hampton Jazz Club Known throughout Paris for its high-quality music, this hospitable club attracts well-known international jazz and blues players and bands. Performers here have included B.B. King, Oscar Peterson, the Count Basie

Orchestra, and Fats Domino. ♦ Cover. M-Sa 10PM-2AM. Reservations recommended. 01.40.68.30.42

102 Place Charles-de-Gaulle Once called Place d'Etoile (Square of the Star), this square was created by Baron Haussmann in 1854 when he added 7 avenues to the existing 5 to form a 12-pointed star. Although the area is a snarl of traffic, it was always the place where the rich and famous, such as Aristotle Onassis, Maria Callas, Claude Debussy, the Shah of Iran, and Prince Rainier of Monaco, lived. One of the avenues that begins here, Avenue Foch, is the widest (390 feet) in Paris; it leads to the **Bois de Boulogne.** ♦ Métro: Charles de Gaulle–Etoile

On Place Charles-de-Gaulle:

L'Arc de Triomphe If Emperor Napoléon hadn't changed his mind in the nick of time, Parisians would be staring not at this magnificent arch (pictured above), but at a 160-foot-high elephant squirting water from its trunk. The decision was so close that a model of the elephant was made and stood for a while at the Place de la Bastille. In the end, Napoléon chose the more tasteful triumphal arch to honor his army's victory at the Battle of Austerlitz. (The sun sets exactly along this axis on 2 December, the anniversary of that victory.) This triumphal arch is 164 feet high and 148 feet wide.

Construction of the arch began in 1806, and the walls had scarcely risen above the ground by the time Napoléon divorced the childless Empress Josephine and wed Princess Marie Louise of Austria in 1810. The bridal procession passed through a fake arch of canvas, hastily constructed for the occasion by the architect **Jean-François Chalgrin.** The arch was not completed until 1836, well after Napoléon's downfall; only four years later, a chariot bearing his body would pass beneath the arch on its way to the **Invalides.** On 14 July 1919, victorious French soldiers marched through the structure. The following month, pilot Sergeant Godefroy flew a plane with a wingspan of 29 feet through the 48-foot-wide arch. On 11 November 1920 the

body of the Unknown Soldier was laid in state here to commemorate the dead soldiers of World War I. The eternal flame at the tomb (first kindled in 1923) is lit each evening at 6:30PM. On 26 August 1944, after the Germans had been routed from the capital, General Charles de Gaulle led a jubilant crowd to the arch, then walked down the Champs-Elysées to **Notre-Dame,** where the *Te Deum* Mass was celebrated in thanksgiving. On state occasions, an enormous French flag hangs inside the arch.

It would be suicide to cross the Place Charles-de-Gaulle on foot (cars have a hard enough time); pedestrians can take an underground passage. An elevator or 284 steps will take you (during daylight hours only) to the platform at the top, which affords a magnificent panorama of Paris.

On the Arc de Triomphe:

Departure of the Volunteers
Known as *La Marseillaise,* this sculpture by François Rude is the arch's most inspired and noteworthy stonework. (It is on the right with your back to the Champs-Elysées.) In 1916, on the day the Battle of Verdun started, the sword brandished by the figure representing the Republic broke and fell off. The disarmed sculpture was immediately hidden to conceal the accident from the superstitious, who might have seen it as a bad omen.

103 Chiberta ★★★$$$ The most chic nouvelle cuisine restaurant in Paris is made even more hip by its Art Deco decor. Chef Eric Coisel offers such seasonal specialties as wild mushroom fricassee in winter, truffle-and-parsley ravioli in autumn, and salmon with fresh artichokes and asparagus come spring. For dessert try the poached pear on crumbled biscuits in spiced syrup. The house Bordeaux is more than passable and the service good-natured and impeccable. This dining spot caters to a business clientele at noontime and an upscale international crowd in the evening. ♦ M-F lunch and dinner; closed in August. Reservations recommended. 3 Rue Arsène-Houssaye (between Aves des Champs-Elysées and de Friedland). 01.53.53.42.00. Métro: Charles de Gaulle–Etoile

104 Androuët ★★$$ Cheese lovers will be delighted with this combination *fromagerie* and cheese-oriented restaurant where they can order a *dégustation fromage,* six plates of cheese progressing from mellow to strong, accompanied by bread, salads, and wine—all in all, a remarkable culinary experience. Other specialties include *croquettes de camembert,* whole lobster in roquefort sauce, and lamb cutlets with Saint Marcellin. The shop at the restaurant's entrance offers a selection of 120 different cheeses. ♦ Restaurant: Tu-Sa lunch and dinner. Shop: M-Sa 10:30AM-8:30PM. Reservations recommended. 6 Rue Arsène-Houssaye (between Ave des Champs-Elysées and Rue Lord-Byron). 01.42.89.95.00. Métro: Charles de Gaulle–Etoile

105 Royal Monceau $$$$ This luxurious hotel has a decidedly theatrical air, with a vast marble-floor, mirrored lobby bedecked with huge arrangements of flowers, and 220 rooms and suites that are correspondingly grand. Not surprisingly, it has hosted such celebrities as Arnold Schwarzenegger, Sylvester Stallone, Tina Turner, Sting, and Madonna, who shot a video here. The saunas, steam rooms, herbal massages, and "spa cuisine" dining at the sumptuous **Thermes Health Spa** are open to hotel guests. There are also two exceptionally fine restaurants. ♦ 37 Ave Hoche (between Ave Berthie-Albrecht and Rue Beaujon). 01.42.99.88.00; fax 01.42.99.89.90; royalmonceau@jetmultimedia.fr.; www.royalmonceau.com. Métros: Ternes, Charles de Gaulle–Etoile

Within the Royal Monceau:

Le Jardin ★★★$$$ Set in the hotel's garden, this pretty glass dining pavilion is the best address in Paris for Mediterranean-Provençal cuisine (Michelin awarded it one star). Trained by Jacques Maximin and Alain Ducasse in their Côte d'Azur palaces, chef Bruno Cirino has proved himself an imaginative creator in his own right in this savory and certifiably healthy olive oil–based style of cooking. For a starter, try a generous portion of cèpes sautéed with tiny breaded wild nuts, or succulent roasted *écrevisses* (little freshwater crayfish) on a bed of truffle-laced spaghetti. Main courses of note include a casserole of langoustine tails and fresh peppers served with grilled langoustine heads stuffed with a peppery green roe; line-caught Mediterranean bass with seasonal garniture; and rack of lamb with pine nuts and summer savory. For dessert try the astounding dark chocolate ravioli with licorice ice cream. To accompany this feast, ask sommelier Stéphane Lochon to choose from his remarkable selection of southern French wines. The waiters are warm and relaxed, but very attentive, and the restaurant's flowery garden setting makes it a bright, cheerful place for lunch, and quiet and romantic for a candlelight dinner. ♦ M-F lunch and dinner. 01.42.99.98.70

Le Carpaccio ★★★$$ This airy Italian restaurant with sunny yellow Venetian decor and Murano glass chandeliers features the cuisine of Milanese-born chef Umberto Zanassi. His specialties include carpaccio with white truffles; risotto with scampi; grilled fish of the day; sautéed bass with artichokes and asparagus; grilled lamb cutlets; and a grand array of antipasti, pastas, and Italian desserts. Bruno Malara, the sommelier here since 1983, was chosen Sommelier of the Year for 1999 by Le Pudlo de Paris Gourmand for his astute selection of Italian wines. Jeanne Moreau, Catherine Deneuve, Ornella Mutti, Jean-Paul Belmondo, and other celebrities in love with Italian cooking can often be found dining here. ♦ Daily lunch and dinner; closed in August. Reservations recommended. 01.42.99.98.90

106 14 Rue de Tilsitt In April, 1925, novelist F. Scott Fitzgerald, his wife Zelda, and their young daughter Scotty moved into an apartment at this address. *The Great Gatsby* had just come out to excellent reviews, but sales were disappointing. Fitzgerald's drinking, always a problem, went from bad to worse. He would stumble into the Paris bureau of the *Chicago Tribune* and make a scene, and his pals William L. Shirer and James Thurber had to drag him back to Rue de Tilsitt in a taxi. This is still an apartment building. ♦ At Ave de Wagram. Métro: Charles de Gaulle–Etoile

107 Guy Savoy ★★★ $$$$ This large, handsome dining room simply decorated with Japanese-style flower arrangements perfectly complements the remarkable cuisine of Chef Savoy, a shining star in the Parisian culinary firmament. Try the artichoke soup with parmesan and truffles or *the bar en écaille grillé aux epices douces* (sea bass grilled in sweet spices). Everything looks as good as it tastes—and vice versa. ♦ M-F lunch and dinner; Sa dinner. Reservations recommended. 18 Rue Troyon (between Aves de Wagram and Mac-Mahon). 01.43.80.40.61. Métro: Charles de Gaulle–Etoile

108 L'Etoile Verte ★★ $$ Coq au vin, sautéed veal, and chateaubriand béarnaise are just some of the basic, well-prepared fare served at this little neighborhood eatery. With its pleasant decor of light wood-paneled walls, white tablecloths, and red banquettes, jolly waitresses, and good food at remarkably reasonable prices for this high-rent part of town, it's little wonder this restaurant is packed at lunchtime every day. ♦ Daily lunch and dinner. 13 Rue Brey (between Ave de Wagram and Rue de Montenotte). 01.43.80.69.34. Métros: Charles de Gaulle–Etoile, Ternes

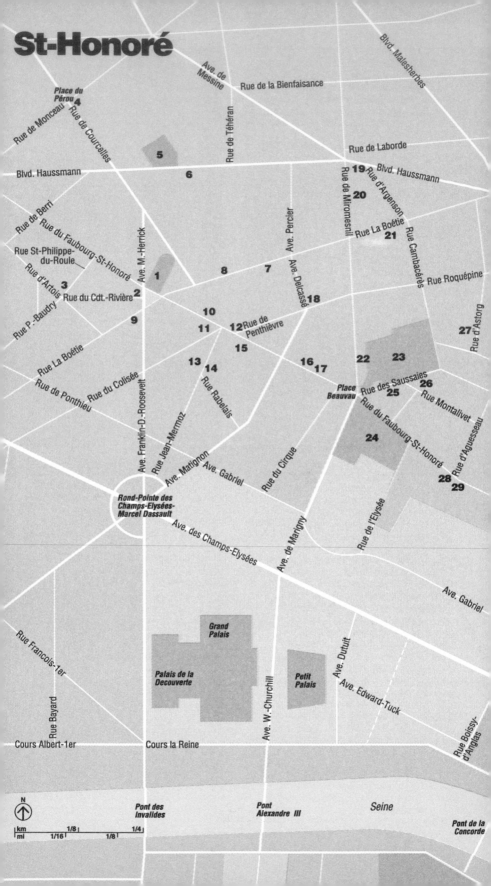

Rue de Vienne

Rue de Rome

Rue du Rocher

Rue de Londres

Rue de Clichy

Gare St-Lazare

Rue d'Amsterdam

Place d'Estienne-d'Orves

For nos. 96–150, see pg. 219

Rue St-Lazare

Place Gabriel-Péri

Rue de la Pépinière

Rue du Havre

Rue de Rome

Rue de Mogador

Rue de la Chausée-d'Antin

Square Louis-XVI
52

Rue de Provence
93

94

Rue des Mathurins

Rue Auber

Rue Gluck

Blvd. Malesherbes

Rue de Castellane

54

59

Rue Pasquier

Rue de l'Arcade

Rue Vignon

92
Place Charles-Garnier

95

Rue Halévy

Rue de la Ville-l'Évêque

Rue Chauveau-Lagarde

53

57 58

Rue Tronchet

Place de l'Opéra
91

Rue de Surène

51

50

49

47 48

55 56

56

Rue de Sèze

Rue de Caumartin

Rue Scribe

90

Ave. de l'Opéra

Rue d'Anjou

35 46

Kiosque Théâtre

La Madeleine (Eglise Ste-Marie Madeleine)

87

89
88

Rue Daunou

Blvd. des Capucines

85

45

Blvd. de la Madeleine
70

Rue des Capucines

Rue Volney
86

Rue de la Paix

84

31
30

32

Cité Berryer
43

44 Place de la Madeleine

60

Rue Richepance

69

83

Rue Danielle-Casanova

Rue La Grand

33 36

Rue Duphot

66

37

41 42
40

65

68

67

72

71
Place Vendôme 82

34

61

38 39

62

63

Place Maurice-Barrès
64

Rue St-Honoré

73

74

81

80

Rue Royale

Rue St-Florentin

Rue Cambon

Rue du Mont-Thabor

75 77
76

79

78

Rue de Castiglione

Rue d'Alger

Rue St-Roch

Rue des Pyramides

Place de la Concorde

Galerie Nationale du Jeu de Paume

Rue de Rivoli

Obelisk of Luxor

L'Orangerie

Jardin des Tuileries (Tuileries Gardens)

Quai des Tuileries

St-Honoré

Forget Fifth Avenue and Rodeo Drive. The **Faubourg St-Honoré,** named after the patron saint of pastry chefs, takes the cake as the world's most glamorous shopping district. *La plus haute* of international haute couture is here: Christian Dior, Yves Saint Laurent, Lanvin, Gucci, Hermès, Pierre Cardin, Guy Laroche, Ungaro, Courrèges, and Jean Paul Gaultier, not to mention countless purveyors of such extravagances as diamonds, crystal, silver, mink, caviar, truffles, and Champagne.

This district includes other dazzling sights as well. Among them are a small, remarkable art collection at the **Musée Jacquemart-André;** many architectural jewels, including **St-Roch** (the city's finest Baroque church) and the splendid **Palais Royal** and its gardens; the city's two most important old theaters, the **Opéra Garnier** and the **Comédie Française;** and several grand hotels, such as **Hôtel Le Bristol, Le Grand Hôtel,** and the **Hôtel Ritz,** whose name is synonymous with luxury. **Rue du Faubourg-St-Honoré** is made for that favorite Parisian pastime, tasteful loitering.

Plan on visiting St-Honoré on a weekday from Tuesday through Friday, since many shops and exhibits are closed on Monday, and the streets are crowded on weekends. Start with an early-bird pastry and coffee at one of the Right Bank's finest bakeries, **Boulangerie St-Philippe,** and continue down Rue du Faubourg-St-Honoré to the street's most fashionable stretch, which lies between the presidential **Palais de l'Elysée** and **Rue Royale.** Those getting a late jump on the day might consider visiting **Ma Bourgogne,** a popular neighborhood wine bar, where an elite crowd stands with a mid-morning glass of Beaune. While lovers of the Italian Renaissance keep their date with Donatello, Botticelli, and Titian at the **Musée Jacquemart-André,** serious shoppers will head down **Embassy Row** (where the US, British, and Japanese ambassadors hang their hats) and make a mandatory stop at **Hermès,** the world-famous leather and accessories shop.

As you pass onto Rue Royale, which starts at the **Place de la Concorde** and ends at the **Place de la Madeleine,** you will gaze upon the finest in antiques, tapestries, jewelry, and silver. By midday you will have reached Place de la Madeleine. Survey the plaza and whet your appetite with truffles at **La Maison de la Truffe,** chocolates at **Marquise de Sévigné,** and cheese at **La Ferme St-Hubert.** When you're finished with those delicacies, why not spend your life's savings on the four-star nouvelle cuisine at **Lucas Carton** or on a feast of caviar and Champagne at **Caviar Kaspia?** If you're down to your last few francs, you'll have to settle for a modest, though tasty, repast at **Ladurée** or **L'Ecluse.** Those feeling brash and regal by turns could knock back a shot of one of the 156 whiskeys sold at **Harry's New York Bar** and weave into **Charvet** to buy a cravat, as Edward VII was in the habit of doing not so long ago.

While your companion is changing money at **American Express,** line up for tickets inside the **Opéra Garnier** (also known as the **Opéra de Paris**), **Charles Garnier's** architectural birthday cake. If you're an antiques hound, **Le Louvre des Antiquaires,** with 240 dealers under one roof, will keep you occupied for hours. Otherwise, watch (as everyone from Louis XIV to Colette has) the sun set on the gardens of the **Palais Royal.**

Dinnertime already? Why not go for broke at the almost 200-year-old grande dame of gastronomy, **Le Grand Véfour,** or the century-old **Restaurant Drouant?** An evening in the neighborhood might consist of polishing your French at the **Comédie Française,** catching a classical ballet or modern dance performance at the **Opéra Garnier,** taking in a movie on **Boulevard**

Haussmann, or people watching from the terrace of **Café de la Paix.** If you still have energy to spare, you can return to where you began the day's outing and spend the night dancing till dawn at **Keur Samba.** Glittering St-Honoré offers glamour and grandeur around the clock.

---

1 St-Philippe-du-Roule Before this church was completed in 1784, its parishioners prayed in the chapel of a local leprosy asylum. Designed by **Jean-François Chalgrin** (better known for his **Arc de Triomphe**), it has three aisles divided by two rows of fluted Ionic columns, a floor plan resembling that of the early Christian basilicas. ♦ 154 Rue du Faubourg-St-Honoré (at Ave Myron-Herrick). 01.43.59.24.56. Métro: St-Philippe-du-Roule

2 Boulangerie St-Philippe ★★$ This bakery's luncheonette (beside the crowded bread counter) features *foie de veau à la vapeur* (steamed veal liver), delicious house terrines, grilled meats, and wine by the glass. Order one of the éclairs, a slice of lime tart, or *tarte tatin* (apple tart) for dessert and find out why the bakery is always crowded. ♦ M-F, Su 7AM-8PM. 73 Ave Franklin-D.-Roosevelt (at Rue du Commandant-Rivière). 01.43.59.78.76. Métro: St-Philippe-du-Roule

3 Hôtel Bradford-Elysées $$$ A surprising oasis of calm and friendliness, this Best Western member is wedged between the harried Champs-Elysées and Rue du Faubourg-St-Honoré. The 50 rooms are spic-and-span and big enough to dance in. There's no restaurant. ♦ 10 Rue St-Philippe-du-Roule (between Rues d'Artois and du Faubourg-St-Honoré). 01.45.63.20.20; fax 01.45.63.20.07; astotel@astotel.com; www.bestwestern.com. Métro: St-Philippe-du-Roule

4 C.T. Loo and Co. Located in a fantastic three-story pagoda equipped with a Chinese elevator, Michael Du Bosc's Asian art gallery deals in Orientalia. Get a close look at the lacquered hardwood furniture from the Ming Dynasty and the 13th-century Nepalese sculptures. ♦ M-Sa; closed in August. 48 Rue de Courcelles (at Pl du Pérou). 01.45.62.53.15, 01.42.25.17.23. Métros: St-Philippe-du-Roule, Courcelles

5 Musée Jacquemart-André Originally this late-19th-century Neo-Classical building—a magnificent mansion with a large reception room, winter garden, monumental staircase, and elegant private apartments—was the private residence of banker Edouard André and his artist wife, Nélie Jacquemart. The couple poured considerable amounts of money into their exquisite art collection, which now belongs to the **Institut de France.** The collection features Italian Renaissance and French 18th-century art, including works by Donatello, Botticelli, Uccello *(Saint George Slaying the Dragon)*, Tintoretto, Titian,

Bernini, Watteau, Fragonard, and Madame Vigée-Lebrun. It also has paintings by Rembrandt, Hals, Murillo, Van Dyck, and Reynolds, and six frescoes by Tiepolo, the only ones in France. Four of these grandiose scenes painted in 1750 illustrate the arrival of French King Henry III in Venice to visit the Doge in 1574. The frescoes were restored in 1998, with the work done in front of museum visitors. The Beauvais tapestries are also noteworthy.

Stop in the museum's cafe for a light lunch (including superb salads), tea, or dessert. This lovely setting has tapestries on the walls and a ceiling painted by Tiepolo. You can go to the cafe without paying the museum's entrance fee. ♦ Admission, including an audio guide. Museum: daily; group tours available. Cafe: daily 11:30AM-5:30PM. 158 Blvd Haussmann (between Rues de Téhéran and de Courcelles). 01.45.62.39.94, 01.42.89.04.91. Métros: Miromesnil, St-Philippe-du-Roule

6 Ma Bourgogne ★★$$ This reputable wine bar is known for such hot daily lunch specials as *oeufs en Meurette* (eggs cooked in red wine with bacon) and steak with béarnaise sauce. Bourgogne and Beaujolais wines are featured. ♦ M-F breakfast, lunch, and dinner; closed in July. Reservations recommended for lunch. 133 Blvd Haussmann (between Ave Percier and Rue de Courcelles). 01.45.63.50.61. Métros: Miromesnil, St-Philippe-du-Roule

7 Salle Gaveau Classical and chamber music performances are held in this concert hall. On 26 May 1926, six young North American composers, most of them studying in Paris with famed music professor Nadia Boulanger, presented new works in a concert here. George Antheil, Theodore Chanler, Aaron Copland, Herbert Ewell, Walter Piston, and Virgil Thomson gave French music lovers their first exposure to the new vigor and self-confidence in classical composition from across the Atlantic. ♦ Admission. Box office: daily; closed in August. 45 Rue La Boétie (between Ave Delcassé and Rue du Faubourg-St-Honoré). 01.49.53.05.07. Métro: Miromesnil

8 Galerie Lambert Rouland Engravings, lithographs, paintings, and sculptures are featured at this contemporary art gallery. ♦ M-F 10AM-12:30PM, 2-7PM; Sa 11AM-12:30PM, 2-6PM. 62 Rue La Boétie (between Ave Percier and Rue de Courcelles). 01.45.63.51.52. Métros: Miromesnil, St-Philippe-du-Roule

9 Keur Samba This nightclub uncorks around 2AM when actors, models, musicians, and diplomats of every stripe and color stop by here. This black-upholstered, jumping, after-hours playpen is located near **Régine's** (see page 193). ♦ Cover. Daily midnight-7AM. 79 Rue La Boétie (between Ave Franklin-D.-Roosevelt and Rue de Ponthieu). 01.43.59.03.10. Métro: St-Philippe-du-Roule

10 Cailleux This shop is full of works of art, primarily by 18th-century artists, including drawings and paintings by Watteau, Boucher, and Fragonard. ♦ M-F; closed in August. 136 Rue du Faubourg-St-Honoré (between Rues de Penthièvre and La Boétie). 01.43.59.25.24. Métro: St-Philippe-du-Roule

11 Dalloyau Sample the *buisson* (chocolate cake with raspberry), *gâteau mogador* (a confection of chocolate cake and chocolate mousse with a racing stripe of raspberry jam), or the best-selling *Opéra,* with layer upon layer of multitextured chocolate at this dessert shop that's been perfecting its chocolate since 1802. The Sunday morning lines attest to the best croissants in town. ♦ Daily. 101 Rue du Faubourg-St-Honoré (between Rues du Colisée and La Boétie). 01.42.99.00.00. Métro: St-Philippe-du-Roule. Also at: 2 Pl Edmond-Rostand (at Blvd St-Michel). 01.43.29.31.10. Métro: Cluny–La Sorbonne

12 H. Picard et Fils Founded in 1860, this exquisite bookstore deals in such bound treasures as Diderot's 35-volume, 18th-century encyclopedia, and Alexis de Tocqueville's *Democracy in America.* ♦ M-Sa; closed in August. 126 Rue du Faubourg-St-Honoré (at Rue de Penthièvre). 01.43.59.28.11. Métro: St-Philippe-du-Roule

13 Chez Germain ★$ The models, fashion designers, and art dealers who work in the neighborhood flock to this inexpensive bistro for a quick lunch. Sample the *pastilla de pintade* (baked, glazed guinea fowl), *jarret du porc aux raisins du Puy* (ham hock with grapes), or brochette of lamb. ♦ M-F lunch. Reservations recommended. 19 Rue Jean-Mermoz (between Rues de Ponthieu and du Faubourg-St-Honoré). 01.43.59.29.24. Métro: St-Philippe-du-Roule

14 Le Merisier ★★$$ In keeping with this restaurant's name, which means "the wild cherry tree," owners Jean-Paul and Françoise Boyrie have paneled the dining room in cherry wood. The warm and handsome room is often filled with people from the nearby embassies, who come here for breakfast and lunch. Good choices are the *terrine à l'ancienne et sa confiture d'oignons* (duck pâté with Armagnac and onion preserves), the steak *tartare,* and the *pavé de rumsteck aux morilles* (steak with morels). For dessert, the *larme au chocolat griottines* (a tear-shaped chocolate shell filled with chocolate mousse and Kirsch-soaked cherries) is much acclaimed. The ambience is exceptionally relaxed and friendly. There's guitar music in the evening. ♦ M-F breakfast, lunch, and dinner. Reservations recommended. 28 Rue Jean-Mermoz (at Rue Rabelais). 01.42.25.36.06. Métro: St-Philippe-du-Roule

15 Galerie Berheim-Jeune Impressionist to contemporary works, including those by such masters as Renoir, Bonnard, and Dufy, are exhibited in this art gallery. Around 1840 William Thackeray took a small pied-à-terre in the same building. ♦ Tu-Sa. 83 Rue du Faubourg-St-Honoré (between Ave Matignon and Rue Jean-Mermoz) 01.42.66.60.31. Métros: Miromesnil, St-Philippe-du-Roule

16 Hôtel Le Bristol $$$$ One of the last and perhaps the most prestigious of Paris's grand hotels, this glamorous establishment caters to the diplomats and dignitaries who conduct business down the street at the **Palais de l'Elysée.** All 185 rooms and 4 suites feature luxurious silk fabrics, antiques, Persian carpets, crystal chandeliers, and marble bathrooms, placing the hotel in a class by itself. Ulysses S. Grant was a guest here in 1877, and Sinclair Lewis stayed here in 1925, the year he won the Pulitzer Prize (which he declined to accept) for his novel *Arrowsmith.* More recently, this has been Robert De Niro's home away from home while working on movies in France. Many rooms overlook the lovely private garden. A modern fitness center, sauna, and pool are on the top floor. ♦ 112 Rue du Faubourg-St-Honoré (between Pl Beauvau and Ave Matignon). 01.53.43.43.00; fax 01.53.43.43.01; resa@hotel-bristol.com; www.hotel-bristol.com. Métro: Miromesnil

Within Hôtel Le Bristol:

Le Bristol ★★★$$$$ This formal dining room of the hotel, which has been awarded a Michelin star, brings forth images of elegance with its Regency-style and wood-paneled decor. Chef Michel del Burgo presides over the kitchen, adding the flavors of his southern

French background to create some of the best cuisine in Paris. Try the *risotto d'epeautre du plateau de Sault* (wild wheat risotto mixed with chicken wings stuffed with herbs and braised mushrooms), *noix de Saint-Jacques dorées à la poêle* (pan-fried sea scallops served with squid cooked with lemon juice, capers, and dried tomatoes), or pigeon cooked on a brochette. There's a grand selection of desserts, including melted chocolate on crunchy nougat with burnt coffee ice cream, to round out an exceptional meal. ♦ Daily lunch and dinner. Reservations recommended. 01.53.43.43.40

Bar du Bristol This comfy lounge opening out onto the lobby serves breakfast and light lunch, and refreshments any time of the day. ♦ M-F 8:30AM-2AM; Sa-Su 10:30AM-2AM.

17 Le Sphinx Together with its sister shop, **L'Aigle Impériale** (around the corner at 3 Rue de Miromesnil, 01.42.65.27.33), this place has one of the city's largest collections of antique weapons and Napoleonic memorabilia. Here you'll find portraits of the emperor, a bottle of 1811 Cognac he never got around to drinking, and one of Napoléon's trademark hats enshrined in a glass case. The proprietor, Pierre de Souzy, will part with the latter item for a mere $100,000. ♦ M-Sa. 104 Rue du Faubourg-St-Honoré (between Pl Beauvau and Ave Matignon). 01.42.65.90.96. Métro: Miromesnil

18 Trompe-l'Oeil On the corner of Rue de Penthièvre and Avenue Delcassé, a man gazes from his balcony at a bronze nude as two doves flutter away, casting shadows on the walls. Painted by artist Rieti in 1985, this trompe l'oeil enlivens an otherwise unremarkable intersection. ♦ Rue de Penthièvre and Ave Delcassé. Métro: Miromesnil

19 René-Gérard Saint-Ouen Instead of clay, this sculptor uses bread dough to create shapes—elephants, chickens, half-moons, bicycles, even the **Eiffel Tower**—for any whim or occasion. If you can't bring yourself to eat these yeasty works of art, brush on some varnish and hang them in the kitchen. ♦ M-Sa. 111 Blvd Haussmann (at Rue d'Argenson). 01.42.65.06.25. Métro: Miromesnil

20 Le Marcande ★★$$$ Chef Joël Verron prepares such dishes as pigeon with wild mushrooms, langoustines with Chinese cabbage and balsamic vinegar, lentil and foie gras terrine, and a delicious *chausson aux pruneaux et à l'armagnac* (plum turnover with Armagnac). Ask for a table in the breezy dining room with a view of the charming courtyard where alfresco eating is de rigueur in the summer. ♦ M-F lunch and dinner; closed two weeks in mid-August. Reservations recommended. 52 Rue de Miromesnil (between Rue La Boétie and Blvd Haussmann). 01.42.65.19.14. Métro: Miromesnil

21 19 Rue La Boétie Thirteen-year-old Henry James developed an addiction to the croissants sold across the street when he lived here from 1856 to 1857. It's still a residential building. ♦ Between Rues Cambacérès and de Miromesnil. Métro: Miromesnil

22 8 Rue de Miromesnil In May 1961, pop artist Robert Rauschenberg's first solo show was held here and received rave reviews. The building now houses several shops. ♦ Between Pl Beauvau and Rue de Penthièvre. Métro: Miromesnil

At 8 Rue de Miromesnil:

Arts et Marine A veritable armada of hand-crafted model wooden sailing vessels floats before your eyes. Among the replicas are the *Navire Négrier* (an 1870s slave ship). Also for sale are old brass compasses, ivory-clad binoculars, and frigates in bottles. There's sufficient nauticalia to salt up any landlubber. ♦ M-F; Sa 2-6PM; closed in August. 01.42.65.27.85

23 Hôtel de Beauvau Le Camus de Mezières designed this mansion for Prince Charles de Beauvau, but the Revolution transferred its ownership to the state. The Ministry of the Interior has resided behind its ornate iron gates since 1861. ♦ 96 Rue du Faubourg-St-Honoré (at Pl Beauvau). Métro: Miromesnil

In 1858, a would-be assassin known as Orsini the Carbonaro threw a homemade bomb at a carriage carrying Napoléon III to an opera house. Though the emperor was unharmed, 156 bystanders were killed or injured. With this in mind, architect Charles Garnier added a special entrance to his design for another opera house on Rue Auber; it allowed Napoléon III's coach to be driven directly to the level of the dress circle via a double ramp into the royal box. Rumor has it that this thoughtful touch helped Garnier's design win out over those of 171 other competing architects.

Restaurants/Clubs: Red		**Hotels:** Blue
Shops/♥ Outdoors: Green		**Sights/Culture:** Black

24 Palais de l'Elysée The most famous address on Rue du Faubourg-St-Honoré, if not in all of France, is the French version of the White House. Built in 1718 according to a design by **Armand-Claude Mollet**, the palace was purchased in 1753 by Mme. de Pompadour, Louis XV's rich and spoiled mistress, who hired the architect **Jean Lassurance** to expand the building and extend the gardens to the Champs-Elysées. Expropriated during the Revolution to serve as a government printing office (for the *Bulletin des Lois*) and dance hall, it later was known as the **Hameau Chantilly** and became a hideaway for the Empress Joséphine after she was divorced by Napoléon. On 22 June 1815 Napoléon signed his second abdication here. The mansion was subsequently the site of a restaurant and fairgrounds run by an ice-cream maker named Velloni. Still later, the Duke of Wellington and Czar Alexander I stayed here. The palace has been the official residence of the French president since 1873. The public is not admitted, but you can glimpse the dignified facade through the gateway. ♦ 55 Rue du Faubourg-St-Honoré (between Rue de l'Elysée and Ave de Marigny). Métro: Miromesnil

25 Muriel A remnant of Old Paris, this is one of the few remaining Parisian boutiques that sells only gloves. ♦ M-Sa Jan-July, Sept-Dec; M-F Aug. 4 Rue des Saussaies (between Rue Montalivet and Pl Beauvau). 01.42.65.95.34. Métro: Miromesnil

26 Au Vieux Saussaies This shop trades in 18th- and 19th-century silver—from sugar bowls to samovars and Champagne ice buckets, specializing in gifts for weddings and christenings. Here you'll find top-name *orfèvrerie* (silverware) at lower prices than you'll see at some of the other dealers. ♦ Tu-Sa. 14 Rue des Saussaies (between Rues Montalivet and de Surène). 01.42.65.32.71. Métro: Miromesnil

Madame de Pompadour, Louis XV's mistress, once gave a party at the Hôtel d'Evreux, now the Palais de l'Elysée (the French presidential palace), with a rustic theme inspired by Watteau's paintings of shepherds. For authenticity, she had a flock of sheep in pink ribbons brought into the building. When the lead ram spotted what he thought was a rival in the mirrored grand gallery, he charged it and shattered the mirror. The flock ran amok and trashed the whole palace.

ASTOR

WESTIN DEMEURE HOTELS · PARIS

27 L'Astor Westin Demeure $$$$ The 135 rooms and suites, as well as the public areas of this renovated hostelry, have been completely transformed by **Frédéric Méchiche**, who incorporated oak paneling, primitive trompe l'oeil paintings, and bold black-and-beige designs throughout. Rooms reflect a Regency-style elegance with modern conveniences including marble bathrooms, TV sets, CD stereos, and fax machines. Top-floor rooms afford unbeatable views of the city from their private terraces. ♦ 11 Rue d'Astorg (between Rues de la Ville-l'Evêque and Roquépine). 01.53.05.05.05; fax 01.53.05.05.30; hotelastor@aol.com. Métro: St-Augustin

Within L'Astor Westin Demeure:

Le Restaurant de l'Astor ★★★$$$ Though you'll be captivated by the comings and goings of fashionable Parisians, the cuisine is worthy of your attention too. A glass ceiling and soft yellow trompe l'oeil columns add an elegant touch to this oval-shaped dining room where the menu of chef Eric Le Cerf (a protégé of the legendary Joël Robuchon) is the star. Order such specialties as *tart friand de truffes aux oignons et lard fumée* (truffle, onion, and smoked bacon tart), roasted squab wrapped in linden leaves, and chestnut and truffle lobster. Desserts are tempting: Try the exceptional *crème caramélisée à la cassonade* (crème caramel with brown sugar). The wine list is limited but good. ♦ M-F lunch and dinner. Reservations recommended. 01.53.05.05.20

28 American Ambassador's Residence In the 19th century the **Hôtel de Pontalba** was owned by financier and art collector Baron Edmond de Rothschild. (When the baron died in 1934 at the age of 89, he left 3,000 drawings and 43,000 postage stamps to the **Louvre**.) Subsequently, the US government had the good taste to rent the *hôtel particulier* from Baron Maurice de Rothschild to serve as the residence of the US ambassador. The 40-room, 13-bathroom building is not open to the public, but if you are invited for dinner with the ambassador, you'll see the original Oudry wood paneling and paintings by John Singer Sargent, Cézanne, and van Gogh. In one of the upstairs guest rooms is the bed where Charles Lindbergh slept after completing the first nonstop solo flight across the Atlantic on 21 May 1927. ♦ 41 Rue du Faubourg-St-Honoré (between Rues Boissy-d'Anglas and de l'Elysée). Métros: Concorde, Madeleine

Rue du Faubourg-St-Honoré Shopping

Christian Lacroix
clothing
RUE DU CIRQUE

A Fragonard
womenswear
Galerie Nichido
Pierre Cardin
menswear
AVENUE DE MARIGNY

RUE DE MIROMESNIL
Perrin
antiques
Armorial
engravers/leather goods

RUE DES SAUSSAIES
Galerie de la Présidence
19th and 20th century art
Maud Frizon
women's shoes
Lilane Romi
womenswear
Louis Féraud
womenswear
Popoff *gallery*
Floriane
childrenswear
Marina
children'swear
Lecoanét Hemant
women's shoes and clothing
Maxim's *clothing*

RUE DE DURAS
Sotheby's
womenswear
J.J. Garella *womenswear*
Chopard *jewelry*
Sonia Rykiel *womenswear*
Artan *jewelry*
Van Laack *menswear*
Roberto Cavaili
womenswear
Etro *accessories*
Pomellato *jewelry*
Gianni Versace
womenswear

RUE D'AGUESSEAU
Mont Blanc
writing supplies
Gaimattiolo
womenswear
Electre
womenswear
Fratelli Rossetti
men's and women's shoes
Chloé *womenswear*
Map continues on right

RUE DU FAUBOURG-ST-HONORE

RUE DE L'ELYSEE
Ungaro
womenswear
Mondi
womenswear
Alimia
womenswear
Jean Lupu
antiques
Apostrophe
womenswear

Hervé Leger
womenswear
Lacôme
cosmetics
Valentino
womenswear
Oscar de la Renta
womenswear

Holland & Holland
sportswear
Rena Lange
womenswear

Cartier
jewelry

RUE BOISSY-D'ANGLAS
Lanvin
Café Bleu/menswear
Sergio Rossi
women's shoes and accessories
Carita
salon
La Bagagerie
leather goods
Façonnable
menswear
Jean de Bonnot
rare books
Oliver Lapidus
womenswear
Jaeger
womenswear
Nicolas Villani
mens- and womenswear

Cour aux Antiquaires
antiques
Franck Namani
womenswear
JP TOD'S *shoes*
Salvatore Ferragamo
leather goods
Leonard
womenswear

RUE D'ANJOU
Maxandre
womenswear
Hôtel de Castiglione
Yves Saint Laurent
womenswear
Jacques Fath
womenswear
Aramis *menswear*
Jun Ashida
womenswear
Yves Saint Laurent
beauty products
Guy Laroche
womenswear
Givenchy
womenswear
Hermès
leather goods/scarves

RUE DU FAUBOURG-ST-HONORE

Lanvin
women's boutique
La Perla
lingerie
André Chékière
menswear
Lolita Lempicka
womenswear/ wedding gowns
Iceberg *womenswear*
Lott *menswear*
Joan & David
men's and women's shoes
Christina Richard
jewelry
Les Copains
womenswear
Gucci
mens- and womenswear

29 British Embassy The lovely **Hôtel de Charost**, built by **Antoine Mazin** in 1723, was bought by Napoléon's sister, Pauline, who, after a tumultuous series of love affairs and marriages, became the Princess Borghese. In 1815, after Waterloo, the princess sold her **Palais Borghese** to George III of England, who turned it into his nation's embassy. Upstairs is Pauline's bed with gilded curtains descending from the talons of a Napoleonic eagle. The building is not open to the public. ♦ 39 Rue du Faubourg-St-Honoré (between Rues Boissy-d'Anglas and de l'Elysée). Métros: Concorde, Madeleine

30 33 Rue du Faubourg-St-Honoré Built by the architect **Grandhomme** in 1714, this house was the home of Duc Decres, who was minister of the French Navy until 1820, when a bomb hidden beneath his bed dealt him a mortal wound. For seven subsequent years, it housed the Russian Embassy, until it was sold to Nathaniel Rothschild. In 1918, the house was born anew as Cercle de l'Union Interalliée, a swank international club for business people. It is not open to the public. ♦ Between Rues Boissy-d'Anglas and de l'Elysée. Métros: Concorde, Madeleine

30 Japanese Embassy In 1718 **Pierre Lassurance** built this *hôtel* for Louis Blouin, confidant and premier *valet de chambre* of Louis XIV. Napoléon's sister and brother lived here, as did the king of Bavaria. It's now the Japanese ambassador's turn. ♦ 31 Rue du Faubourg-St-Honoré (between Rues Boissy-d'Anglas and de l'Elysée). Métros: Concorde, Madeleine

31 Georges Bernard Antiquités This intriguing shop specializes in Far Eastern artifacts: Chinese and Japanese ceramics, paintings, and bronzes, and sacred art from Southeast Asia. ♦ M-Sa; closed two weeks in August. 1 Rue d'Anjou (at Rue du Faubourg-St-Honoré). 01.42.65.23.83. Métros: Concorde, Madeleine

32 Castiglione $$$$ The high prices in this 117-room hotel are in keeping with its choice location amid the splendorous boutiques. Unfortunately, a modern face-lift has left it a hostelry in search of character. There's an unremarkable restaurant on the premises. ♦ 38-40 Rue du Faubourg-St-Honoré (between Rues Boissy-d'Anglas and d'Anjou). 01.44.94.25.25; fax 01.42.65.12.27. Métros: Concorde, Madeleine

HERMÈS
PARIS

33 Hermès Started in 1837 as a saddle store by Thierry Hermès, *artisan d'élite,* this is perhaps the most celebrated leather-goods emporium in the world. Having outlasted the age of the horse and carriage, Hermès now furnishes the leather fittings for Lear jets. Its bags are considered necessities, not accessories, while its gloves are unsurpassed in craftsmanship. The signature scarves are huge and come in more than 200 styles, the most popular of which is the Brides de Gala; more than a half-million of these silken trifles are sold every year. ♦ M-Sa. 24 Rue du Faubourg-St-Honoré (at Rue Boissy-d'Anglas). 01.40.17.47.17. Métros: Concorde, Madeleine

Within Hermès:

Musée Hermès On the top floor of the store is a private museum displaying old saddles, ornamented trunks, and even Napoléon's stirrups. ♦ For admission, write in advance to Mme. de Bazelaire (Hermès, 24 Rue de Faubourg-St-Honoré, Paris 75008) or call 01.40.17.48.36

33 John Lobb The Paris branch of the reputable London shoe- and boot maker is located on the ground floor rear of **Hermès**. To join the ranks of satisfied **Lobb** alumni, which have included Lyndon Johnson, the Shah of Iran, Gary Cooper, and the Duke of Edinburgh, stop in to be measured heel to toe. Using the measurements, one of **Lobb**'s cobblers will fashion two wooden lasts (one for each foot) on which to model your shoes. In the nearby studio, the skins are cut and stitched, and in one month (first-time customers must wait a year), this labor will have produced a noble pair of handmade shoes sure to last at least a decade—and for a mere $3,000 per pair. The shop also has an entrance at 21 Rue Boissy-d'Anglas. ♦ M-Sa. 01.42.65.24.45

34 buddha-bar ★★ $$ A two-story-high gilded Buddha presides over this spectacular bar and restaurant conveniently situated halfway

between **Hermès** and the **Hôtel Crillon** (see page 183). Chic shoppers, models, and celebrities, including Naomi Campbell and Prince Albert of Monaco, frequent the place. Not surprisingly, the cooking is Asian—spring rolls, tempura, sashimi, Korean braised beef, and Pacific Rim fare—but the music blasted out by the DJs is unlikely to move this crowd very far on the path to Nirvana. There's a balcony for people who just want a drink and a gander at the *beau monde* doing its thing in the cavernous main room below. ♦ Restaurant: daily lunch and dinner. Bar: daily 6PM-2AM. 8 Rue Boissy d'Anglas (between Pl de la Concorde and Rue du Faubourg-St-Honoré). 01.53.05.90.00. Métro: Concorde

35 28 Rue Boissy-d'Anglas Le Boeuf sur le Toit, the famous avant-garde nightclub, was once located here. Its 10 January 1922 inaugural party was thrown by Jean Cocteau and attended by Constantin Brancusi, Pablo Picasso, and Max Beerbohm, among others. Leading the club's orchestra that night was Vance Lowry, an African-American saxophonist who was partially responsible for introducing the French to jazz and the music of George Gershwin. ♦ Between Cité Berryer and Blvd Malesherbes. Métro: Madeleine

36 Lanvin Shop here for women's scarves, perfumes, haute couture, and prêt-à-porter. ♦ M-Sa. 22 Rue du Faubourg-St-Honoré (at Rue Boissy-d'Anglas). 01.44.71.31.73. Métros: Concorde, Madeleine

37 15 Rue du Faubourg-St-Honoré In 1804, Claude Rouget de l'Isle, composer of the *Marseillaise,* lived here, and after him, Felix, hairdresser to Empress Eugénie. The building now has both commercial and residential space. ♦ At Rue Boissy-d'Anglas. Métros: Concorde, Madeleine

At 15 Rue du Faubourg-St-Honoré:

Lanvin This is the place for fine men's fashion and accessories, including classic silk ties. ♦ M-Sa. 01.44.71.31.33

Within Lanvin:

Café Bleu ★★$ The cafe in the basement of the **Lanvin** boutique is a good place to fuel up with a light lunch or tea before continuing along the Faubourg St-Honoré for more power shopping. The menu is the brainchild of hot, young chef Marcel Baudis and presents salads, foie gras, fresh vegetable ravioli, club sandwiches, and several filling meat and fish dishes. They showcase *Les Vins des Stars* (Wines of the Stars)—wines produced by actors Gérard Départdieu and Pierre Richard, director Francis Coppola (a big budget item), and other big names. ♦ M-Sa lunch and tea. 01.44.71.32.32

37 Carita This lavishly decorated hair salon (whose clients have included Catherine Deneuve, Paloma Picasso, and French rocker Johnny Hallyday) has a relaxed, down-to-earth staff that sets hairstyle trends. There are separate entrances for men and women. The salon is also noted for its skin-care treatments. ♦ Tu-Sa. 11 Rue du Faubourg-St-Honoré (between Rues Royale and Boissy-d'Anglas). 01.44.94.11.11. Métros: Concorde, Madeleine

38 Christofle Want to make your little one's first lost baby tooth even more precious? How about encasing it in silver? Nothing is impossible for this shop, which has provided silver-plating services for more than a century. There's also a fine selection of silverware and antique gold, as well as the stunning yellow and blue tableware Claude Monet designed for his house at Giverny. Peek into the museum at the same address. ♦ M-Sa. 9 Rue Royale (between Pl de la Concorde and Rue du Faubourg-St-Honoré). 01.49.33.43.00. Métro: Concorde

LACHAVME

39 Lachaume The city's oldest and most exquisite florist has catered to haute couturiers and other well-heeled clientele (who can afford long-stemmed red roses in December) since 1845. For an instantaneous cure of the midwinter blues, gaze into the shop window at the gorgeous bunches of tulips and orchids. ♦ M-Sa; closed in August.

10 Rue Royale (between Pl de la Concorde and Rue St-Honoré). 01.42.60.59.74, 01.42.60.57.26. Métro: Concorde

40 Ladurée ★★★$ This turn-of-the-century *salon de thé* par excellence is posh and ultra-Parisian but not snobbish. The heavenly taste of the croissants is ample reason for having breakfast here. Habitués recommend *financiers* (almond cakes), chocolate macaroons, *babas au rhum,* and *royals* (almond biscuits iced with chocolate or mocha frosting). Don't miss the painting of the rosy-cheeked cherub-turned-pastry chef on the downstairs ceiling. ♦ Daily breakfast, lunch, and afternoon tea. 16 Rue Royale (at Rue St-Honoré). 01.42.60.21.79. Métros: Madeleine, Concorde

GUCCI

41 Gucci A four-floor marble palazzo is filled with the trademark Gucci red and green. ♦ M-Sa. 21 Rue Royale (between Rue du Faubourg-St-Honoré and Cité Berryer). 01.42.96.83.27. Métro: Madeleine

42 La Maison du Valais ★★$$ An Alpine-style chalet, this restaurant serves *à volonté* (all you can eat) raclette, delectable fondue, assortments of thinly sliced charcuterie, and cool Fendant wine. The cheerful waiters and Swiss food are heartening in winter when you fancy a ski weekend in the mountains but haven't time to escape the gray skies of Paris. ♦ M-Sa lunch and dinner. Reservations recommended, especially in winter. 20 Rue Royale (between Rue St-Honoré and Pl de la Madeleine). 01.42.60.23.75, 01.42.60.22.72. Métro: Madeleine

43 Cité Berryer The alley, formerly an open-air market, has been classified as a historic monument. It is now a classy shopping arcade called **Le Village Royale** and is lined with fashion boutiques and galleries. ♦ Métro: Madeleine

"I needed Paris. It was a feast, a grand carnival of imagery, and immediately everything good there seemed to offer sublimation to those inner desires that had for so long been hampered by racism back in America. For the first time in my life I was relaxing from tension and pressure. My thoughts, continually rampaging against racial conditions, were suddenly becoming as peaceful as snowflakes. Slowly a curtain was dropping between me and those soiled years."

Gordon Parks, *Voices in the Mirror,* 1990

Place de la Madeleine Shopping

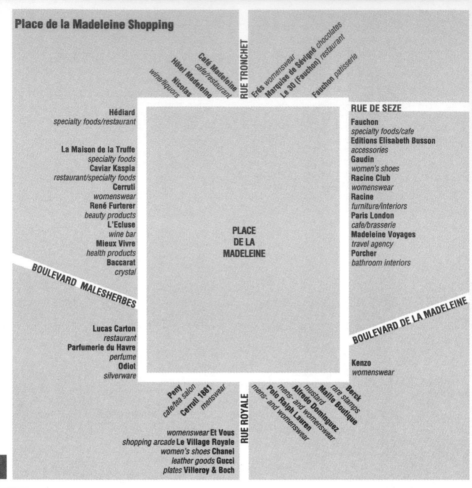

Café Madeleine
cafe/restaurant
Hôtel Madeleine
Nicolas
wine/liquors

RUE TRONCHET

Erès *womenswear*
Marquise de Sévigné *chocolates*
Le 30 (Fauchon) *restaurant*
Fauchon *patisserie*

Hédiard
specialty foods/restaurant

La Maison de la Truffe
specialty foods
Caviar Kaspia
restaurant/specialty foods
Cerruti
womenswear
René Furterer
beauty products
L'Ecluse
wine bar
Mieux Vivre
health products
Baccarat
crystal

PLACE
DE LA
MADELEINE

RUE DE SEZE
Fauchon
specialty foods/cafe
Editions Elisabeth Busson
accessories
Gaudin
women's shoes
Racine Club
womenswear
Racine
furniture/interiors
Paris London
cafe/brasserie
Madeleine Voyages
travel agency
Porcher
bathroom interiors

BOULEVARD MALESHERBES

Lucas Carton
restaurant
Parfumerie du Havre
perfume
Odiot
silverware

BOULEVARD DE LA MADELEINE

Kenzo
womenswear

Peny
cafe/tea salon
Cerruti 1881 *menswear*

womenswear **Et Vous**
shopping arcade **Le Village Royale**
women's shoes **Chanel**
leather goods **Gucci**
plates **Villeroy & Boch**

RUE ROYALE

Alfredo Dominguez *mens- and womenswear*
Polo Ralph Lauren *mens- and womenswear*
Maille Boutique *mustard*
Berck *rare stamps*

44 Place de la Madeleine Around the edges of this square, the heart of upscale noshing in Paris, are specialty shops to spoil the spoiled (see the shopping map above). Amid the fumes of buses and a more-or-less perpetual rush hour, a lively flower market (open Tuesday through Saturday and Sunday morning) blossoms just east of the **Madeleine** church. Here, at her funeral in 1975, entertainer Josephine Baker, having already received the Légion d'Honneur and the Médaille de la Résistance, became the first North American woman to be honored with a 21-gun salute. ♦ Métro: Madeleine

On Place de la Madeleine:

Public Lavatory Even if nature isn't calling, look for a sign that reads: "Hommes et Dames W.C." It will lead you underground to an elegant 1905 facility with Art Nouveau wood paneling, stained glass, and tile built by Etablissements Porcher, now one of the largest plumbing suppliers in France. ♦ At Rue Royale

MICHAEL STORRINGS

La Madeleine (Eglise Ste-Marie Madeleine) The 28 monumental steps of this church rise to meet 52 immense Corinthian columns, defining an edifice (pictured above) that dominates the hub of the financial district. However, the building has always been an architectural orphan. Begun as a church in 1764 under the reign of Louis XV and modeled after a Greek temple, the structure, at various times in its turbulent past, has been slated to become a bank, parliament building, theater, stock exchange, banquet hall, and yet another temple to glorify Napoléon's army (as if the **Arc de Triomphe**

and the **Invalides** were not enough). In 1837 the windowless edifice, designed by **Pierre Vignon** and **Jean-Jacques Huvé,** was selected to be the capital's first railway station but was consecrated as a church dedicated to St. Mary Magdalene five years later.

Not a single cross adorns the pediments of this church, and its rose marble and gilt interior is surprisingly sensual. The imposing bronze door portraying the Ten Commandments is by Philippe Joseph Henri Lemaire, and his gigantic *Last Judgment* on the south pediment is the largest work of its kind in the world (and it contains one of the chubbiest Christs in Europe). On the north side of the church, the inscription beneath a headless statue of St. Luke reads, "On 30 May 1918, a German shell struck the church of the Madeleine and decapitated this statue." The splendid organ was played by composer Camille Saint-Saëns, and the *Funeral March* of Chopin resounded here as the composer himself was laid to rest. The grandest funeral ever accorded a North American in Paris was that of Josephine Baker, held here on 15 April 1975. ♦ 01.44.51.69.00

Kiosque-Théâtre This kiosk sells half-price tickets to theater, dance, music hall, concert, cafe theater, and, occasionally, opera performances on the day of the event. During the first 2 years of operation it sold 140,600 tickets. ♦ Daily. No phone

45 Peny ★$ The coconut cake, *croque monsieur* (grilled ham and cheese sandwich), and yellow table umbrellas at this old-fashioned *salon de thé* are summertime favorites with North Americans. ♦ Daily breakfast, lunch, afternoon tea, and dinner. 3 Pl de la Madeleine (between Rue Royale and Blvd Malesherbes). 01.42.65.06.75. Métro: Madeleine

46 Lucas Carton ★★★★$$$$ The nouvelle cuisine of superstar chef Alain Senderens is better (and more expensive) than ever. In fact, this is one of the Parisian capitals of nouvelle cuisine, made even more memorable by the gorgeous Majorelle Belle Epoque maple and sycamore woodwork in the dining room. Try the delicious foie gras in steamed cabbage, *canard Apicus* (duck roasted with honey and spices), Breton lobster with vanilla, ravioli filled with clams, bittersweet chocolate soufflé, and licorice ice cream with peppermint meringue. ♦ M dinner; Tu-F lunch and dinner; Sa dinner; closed three weeks in August and two weeks at Christmas. Reservations required. 9 Pl de la Madeleine (at Blvd Malesherbes). 01.42.65.22.90. Métro: Madeleine

47 Au Verger de la Madeleine Since 1936 this has remained one of Paris's finest family-operated *épiceries* (grocery shops). Jean-Pierre Legras, who features wines dating from 1789, will help you find an old Sauternes bottled in the year you were born, got married, or made your first trip to Paris. ♦ M-Sa. 4 Blvd Malesherbes (between Pl de la Madeleine and Rue de l'Arcade). 01.42.65.51.99. Métro: Madeleine

48 L'Ecluse ★★$$ One of a chain of six wine bars selling marvelous old Bordeaux by the glass, this spot is lively, fashionable, affordable, and ideal for people watching. ♦ Daily lunch and dinner until 1AM. 15 Pl de la Madeleine (between Blvd Malesherbes and Rue Chauveau-Lagarde). 01.42.65.34.69. Métro: Madeleine. Also at: Numerous locations throughout the city

49 Caviar Kaspia ★★★$$$ Besides purveying the finest in Russian and Iranian caviars, the chic little upstairs restaurant adorned in czarist turquoise and overlooking Place de la Madeleine offers vodka, aquavit, and blintzes languidly draped with smoked salmon. The shop downstairs sells all the makings for a Russian dinner. ♦ Restaurant: M-Sa lunch and dinner until 1AM. Store: M-Sa 9AM-midnight. 17 Pl de la Madeleine (between Blvd Malesherbes and Rue Chauveau-Lagarde). 01.42.65.33.52. Métro: Madeleine

50 La Maison de la Truffe ★★$$$ Brooklyn delicatessens never looked like this fancy place, which specializes in black gold (fresh truffles, in season from November through February), and foie gras, caviar, smoked salmon, or any other delicacy your gourmand's heart could desire. Savor the tasty treasures at one of the 15 tables here or purchase them at the shop to enjoy on a picnic. ♦ Restaurant: M-Sa lunch and dinner until 8:30 PM. Shop: M-Sa 9AM-8PM. 19 Pl de la Madeleine (between Blvd Malesherbes and Rue Chauveau-Lagarde). 01.42.65.53.22. Métro: Madeleine

50 Hédiard This *épicerie* was founded in 1854 by Ferdinand Hédiard, who was the first to import the exotic pineapple into France. Marcel Proust once lingered here, surveying Hédiard's extraordinary selection of Asian and

African delicacies: spices, oils, vinegars, 30 blends of tea, freshly roasted coffee beans, baskets of rare jams and jellies, and old rums. A late–20th-century renovation turned the charming Old-World food shop into a modern souk. There are specialty food counters on two levels around a glass-roofed market that is a worthy rival of the more famous **Fauchon** across the square. In fact, the best selection of Bordeaux wines in Paris may well be here. ◆ M-Sa 9:30AM-9PM. 21 Pl de la Madeleine (between Blvd Malesherbes and Rue Chauveau-Lagarde). Shop 01.43.12.88.88, take-out delivery service 01.42.65.06.16. Métro: Madeleine. Also at: 126 Rue du Bac (between Rues de Sèvres and de Babylone). 01.45.44.01.98. Métro: Sèvres-Babylone

Atop Hédiard:

Hédiard ★★$$ Overlooking Place Madeleine, this bright, pleasant restaurant serves such tasty Provençal dishes as crusty-skinned *rouget* (red mullet) with trumpet mushrooms sautéed in olive oil and peppers stuffed with codfish paste. The dining spot buzzes with the excitement of upscale shoppers at lunch, and is more subdued in the evening. ◆ M-Sa lunch and dinner. 01.43.12.88.99

51 Hôtel Beau Manoir $$$ Serious shoppers will appreciate this hotel's central location—down the street from the Faubourg St-Honoré and next to the gourmet food boutiques in the Place de la Madeleine. Cozily refurbished with gold and red damask walls, exposed beams, marble bathrooms, and walnut cabinetry, the 32-room hostelry is part of the French Best Western Association. There's no restaurant. Next door is its less expensive sister, the **Hôtel Lido** (4 Passage de la Madeleine, 01.42.66.27.37; fax 01.42.66.61.23; lido@paris-hotels-charm.com; www.paris-hotels-charm.com). ◆ 6 Rue de l'Arcade (between Blvd Malesherbes and Rue Chauveau-Lagarde). 01.42.66.03.07; fax 01.42.68.03.00; bm@paris-hotels-charm.com; www.paris-hotels-charm.com. Métro: Madeleine

52 Chapelle Expiatoire (Expiatory Chapel) This memorial chapel, commissioned by Louis XVIII and designed by **Pierre Fontaine**, has become a shrine for French royalists. It was erected in 1815 on the grounds of the cemetery where, among the thousands of other victims of the Revolution, Marie Antoinette, Louis XVI, and Charlotte Corday are buried. In the chapel's right apse is a statue of Louis XVI being ushered into heaven by an angel resembling Henry Essex Edgeworth, the friend who escorted the king to the guillotine. Downstairs, an altar marks the spot where Louis XVI's body was buried. ◆ W; open to groups Th by appointment. 29 Rue Pasquier (at Sq Louis-XVI). 01.42.65.35.80. Métro: St-Augustin

53 New Hôtel Roblin $$ English travelers who cross the channel for a weekend of dance at the **Opéra Garnier** and luxurious take-out food from the Place de la Madeleine find refuge in this comfortable 77-room hotel. Its restaurant serves traditional French fare. ◆ 6 Rue Chauveau-Lagarde (between Pl de la Madeleine and Rue de l'Arcade). 01.44.71.20.80; fax 01.42.65.19.49; parisroblin@new-hotel.com; www.new-hotel.com. Métro: Madeleine

54 Hôtel Opal $$ For the frugal traveler, here's a property with cheerful yellow decor in the lobby, a friendly young team at the front desk, and 36 small, but neat and pleasant guest rooms with modern bathrooms. Located behind the **Madeleine** church, it's a handy place to stay if you love going to the ballet and shopping in the nearby stores. There is no restaurant, but breakfast is included in the rate. ◆ 19 Rue Tronchet (at Rue de Castellane). 01.42.65.77.97; fax 01.49.24.06.58; hotel_opal@club-internet.fr; www.hotels.fr/opal. Métros: Havre-Caumartin, Madeleine

55 Marquise de Sévigné The ambience in this combination tea salon/chocolate shop is as sublime as the rich hot chocolate it serves. Customers who order a coffee, tea, or hot chocolate at the little bar are entitled to all the chocolates they want to eat on the spot. There are no tables. ◆ Daily. 32 Pl de la Madeleine (between Rues de Sèze and Tronchet). 01.42.65.19.47. Métro: Madeleine

FAUCHON

56 Fauchon At Paris's most famous food emporium, window shopping is an aesthetic experience at all its three stores which span the northeast corner of the Place de la Madeleine. **No. 26** sells *traiteur* (prepared) dishes that look too beautiful to eat—every exotic fruit on earth is artfully arranged; along with gift baskets of pâtés, foie gras, truffles, jams, and rare honeys. The store's spacious, elegant *salon de thé* is the place to sample some of these products. **No. 28** is the patisserie, virtually impossible to walk past without popping in for one of its amazing treats (the pear and crunchy caramel tart with almond-caramel cream, for example). Finally, at **No. 30,** is a restaurant—**Le 30 (Fauchon)**; and an *épicerie* stocked with more than 17,000 items, including 119 kinds of jam, 44 flavors of mustard, and 93 varieties of tea. A newly opened magnificent wine cave in the basement boasts 12,000 beautifully displayed bottles of wines and spirits, a friendly team of sommeliers, and a large crescent-shape bar where wines by the glass are offered. The quality is stratospherically high, and so, for the most part, are the prices—although not for everything. There's a bottle of wine that sells for as little as 22 francs.♦ M-Sa. 26, 28, and 30 Pl de la Madeleine (at Rue de Sèze). 01.47.42.60.11. Métro: Madeleine

Within Fauchon:

Le 30 (Fauchon) ★★$$ Fauchon's casual restaurant upstairs features a view of the illuminated **La Madeleine.** Chef Bruno Deligne's menu includes such delicacies as hot oysters and leeks with truffle sauce, and, for lighter summer fare, melon and Sauternes soup. Catering is also available. ♦ M-Sa lunch and dinner. 01.47.42.60.11

57 La Ferme St-Hubert ★★$$ Cheese is the focus at this rustic restaurant, and Chef Henry Voy serves the best *croque monsieur* in Paris. Other specialties include fondue, raclette, and *tartiflette au reblochon* (melted reblochon cheese on a gratin of potatoes with bacon). Also on the premises is a shop selling 140 different varieties of cheese; this cheese-lover's heaven is especially known for its excellent roquefort and beaufort. ♦ M-Sa lunch and dinner. 21 Rue Vignon (between Rues de Sèze and Tronchet). 01.47.42.79.20. Métro: Madeleine

58 La Maison du Miel Run by the Gallands family since 1908, this shop is devoted entirely to honey and products containing honey, such as soap and oil. There are sample tastings and you can choose from a selection of various honeys in miniature jars. Don't pass up the *bruyère* (heather) honey. ♦ M-Sa. 24 Rue Vignon (between Rues de Sèze and Tronchet). 01.47.42.26.70. Métro: Madeleine

59 Le Roi du Pot-au-Feu ★★$$ For some warm consolation on a frigid evening, visit this offbeat little bistro with its red-checkered tablecloths and tableside jukeboxes. The specialty is its namesake: pot-au-feu, a marrow-rich beef broth served with the meat and vegetables that gave up their substance to the stew. ♦ M-Sa lunch and dinner. 34 Rue Vignon (between Rues de Sèze and Tronchet). 01.47.42.37.10. Métro: Havre-Caumartin

60 Edouard Berck Now run by the founder's daughter, Elysabeth, this shop buys and sells stamps from all over the world; offers estimates; and sells magnifying glasses, albums, catalogs and other tools of the hobby. It's the city's most renowned stamp dealer. ♦ M-Sa. 6 Pl de la Madeleine (between Blvd de la Madeleine and Rue Royale). 01.42.60.34.26; fax 01.42.60.68.11. Métro: Madeleine

60 Boutique Maille This is the ideal place to stock up on mustard to suit all tastes—Champagne or Cognac, for example. The shop also sells fresh mustard, flavored vinegars, pickles, and beautifully decorated ceramic jars in which to store your favorite condiment. ♦ M-Sa. 6 Pl de la Madeleine (between Blvd de la Madeleine and Rue Royale). 01.40.15.06.00. Métro: Madeleine

60 4 Place de la Madeleine Alas, this is no longer the home of Durand's, the famous music publisher, where, in 1831, Liszt first met Chopin. The building now has both commercial and residential space. ♦ Between Blvd de la Madeleine and Rue Royale. Métro: Madeleine

61 Rue St-Honoré This ranks as one of the oldest and most historic thoroughfares in Paris. In 1622 Molière was born on this street at the corner of Rue Sauval, near Les Halles. On 6 October 1793, a tumbril traveled down Rue St-Honoré, carrying a woman whose prison-shorn hair was hidden under a frumpy bonnet. Nearby, Jacques-Louis David sketched her as she passed, bequeathing to history a poignant image of Marie Antoinette, her hands tied behind her back, en route to the guillotine. ♦ Métros: Concorde, Madeleine, Tuileries, Pyramides, Palais Royal–Musée du Louvre, Louvre-Rivoli, Châtelet

61 Au Nain Bleu The Paris equivalent of FAO Schwarz sells toys luxurious enough to spoil any child. ♦ M-Sa. 406-10 Rue St-Honoré (at Rue Richepance). 01.42.60.39.01. Métros: Madeleine, Concorde

62 Toraya ★★$$ In Japanese, *toraya* means "tiger"; for Parisians, it denotes this elegant black-and-gray Japanese tea salon and pastry shop. Savor *abekawa mochi* (chunks of rice paste sugared and dusted with grilled soy powder), *kuzukiri* (noodles made from jellied arrowroot), and energizing pots of *sencha* (green tea). ♦ M-Sa lunch and afternoon tea. 10 Rue St-Florentin (between Rues de Rivoli and St-Honoré). 01.42.60.13.00. Métro: Concorde

---

Tennis went professional in 1687 when the top competitors in Paris started getting paid for playing matches.

63 Notre-Dame-de-l'Assomption This church, built in 1676, was originally part of a convent where destitute widows and abandoned wives were given shelter; it has served as a Polish parish since 1850. The massive cupola on top has been dubbed *le sot dôme* (the silly dome). ♦ 263 *bis* Rue St-Honoré (at Pl Maurice-Barrès). 01.42.60.07.69. Métro: Concorde

64 Cadolle Hermine Cadolle, the lady who is credited with inventing the brassiere in 1900, was the great-great-grandmother of the shop's current proprietor, Poupie Cadolle. All manner of deluxe lingerie, French beachwear, and perfume is sold here. The company also makes items to order. ♦ M-Sa. 14 Rue Cambon (between Rues du Mont-Thabor and St-Honoré). 01.42.60.94.22. Métro: Concorde

65 Goumard ★★★$$$ Scallop carpaccio with oysters, jumbo crab salad, grilled or poached Brittany lobster, sea bass with pan-roasted vegetables, and roast St-Pierre (John Dory) with baby vegetables, fig crisp and *dôme au chocolat* (shiny dome of chocolate mousse) are some of the specialties served at this restaurant. The dining room boasts original 19th-century architectural elements, complemented by beautiful Lalique light fixtures and sculptures. ♦ M-Sa lunch and dinner. Reservations recommended. 9 Rue Duphot (between Rues St-Honoré and Richepance). 01.42.60.36.07. Métro: Madeleine

66 L'Estaminet Gaya ★★$$ Settle on one of the comfortable banquettes in this fine seafood bistro and order the fresh shellfish, *tartare* of red tuna with ginger, tuna grilled with spicy olive oil, or bouillabaisse. Meat dishes are also available. ♦ M-Sa lunch and dinner. Reservations recommended. 17 Rue Duphot (between Rues St-Honoré and Richepance). 01.42.60.43.03. Métro: Madeleine. Also at: 44 Rue du Bac (between Blvd St-Germain and Rue de l'Université). 01.45.44.73.73. Métro: Rue du Bac

67 Hôtel Burgundy $$$ The last pages of *Look Homeward, Angel* sprang from the fertile imagination of Thomas Wolfe while he was here in 1928. Today it is a clean, comfortable, warmly decorated hotel with 90 guest rooms, a spacious lobby, and an attractive restaurant, **Le Charles Baudelaire,** that serves traditional French fare. ♦ 8 Rue Duphot (between Rue St-Honoré and Blvd de la Madeleine). 01.42.60.34.12; fax 01.47.03.95.20; hotel.burgundy@iname.com; www.perso.wanadoo.fr/hotel.burgundy. Métro: Madeleine

68 29 Rue Cambon Upon his return to Paris in November 1875, young *New York Tribune* correspondent Henry James took up residence on the third floor of what is now Chanel headquarters. This is where he wrote *The Americans,* his first novel set in Paris. ♦ Between Rue St-Honoré and Blvd de la Madeleine. Métros: Concorde, Madeleine

69 Demeure Castille $$$$ The **Opera Wing** of this elegant hotel features 87 Venetian-style rooms, with marble, colorful damasks, and a faux patina on the walls. The 20 traditionally French guest rooms in the more intimate **Rivoli Wing** were decorated by designer Jacques Grange. Some of the accommodations have views of the Chanel ateliers, where Coco Chanel created her first haute couture designs. The hotel has sumptuous public rooms, an outstanding restaurant, and a delightful courtyard with a trompe l'oeil mural and an impressive 18th-century fountain. ♦ 33-37 Rue Cambon (between Rue St-Honoré and Blvd de la Madeleine). 01.44.58.44.58; fax 01.44.58.44.00; castille_hotel@compuserve.com.fr. Métro: Madeleine

Within Demeure Castille:

Il Cortile ★★★$$ Young chef Nicolas Vernier, yet another Alain Ducasse protégé, has made a great name for himself and this restaurant with the sunny Northern Italian cuisine he offers here. Some of his impeccably prepared specialties include a vast array of antipasti—sardines stuffed *à la venetienne, pissaladière* (little Provençal onion and anchovy pizzas), grilled aubergines, and deep-fried zucchini flowers, just to name a few—several varieties of risotto, roasted fresh cod with ratatouille in a seafood sauce, sage-flavored veal piccata with Swiss chard, and spit-roasted pigeon with herb sauce served with polenta. For dessert, tiramisù, saffron-roasted pear with honey ice cream, or any of a dozen other Italian goodies are temptations that anyone will be glad to have given in to. A chic crowd from nearby fashion houses lunches either in the airy, Venetian-inspired dining room, decorated with pale blue, white, and yellow mosaics, or alfresco in the courtyard in fair weather. ♦ M-Sa lunch and dinner. 01.44.58.45.67

CHARLES JOURDAN

70 Charles Jourdan In 1957, the celebrated M. Jourdan became the first cobbler to use glue instead of nails to hold his shoes together; the result was the first truly delicate feminine footwear. The most up-to-the-minute styles are still featured at this fashionable shoe boutique. ♦ M-Sa. 5 Blvd de la Madeleine (between Rues Cambon and Duphot). 01.42.61.15.89. Métro: Madeleine

71 Place Vendôme Like the Place de la Concorde, Place des Victoires, and other magnificent squares, this was conceived as a setting for a royal equestrian statue. The subject was Louis XIV, and the sculptor was François Girardon. In 1685, to make way for his monument, Louis bought and demolished the Duke of Vendôme's town house and the nearby Capucines convent. **Jules Hardouin-Mansart** designed gracefully formal mauve limestone facades with Corinthian pilasters and sculpted masks that were added to the square's periphery in 1715. The Sun King, a budding real estate shark, encouraged speculators to buy the lots behind the facades, then hire their own architects to fill in the blanks. During the Revolution the heads of nine victims of the guillotine were displayed here on spikes, and for a while the Place Vendôme was known as the Place des Piques (Pike Square).

On 19 June 1792 the Revolutionaries lit a huge bonfire here that incinerated bundles of genealogical documents concerning the French nobility's title deeds. Needless to say, the king's gilt statue didn't survive the mob's wrath, either; it was felled in August of the same year. Today the 440-by-420-foot octagon is characterized by an aloof opulence. It is the home of the **Hôtel Ritz** and it boasts the world's greatest concentration of banks, perfumeries, and jewelers, including **Boucheron, Van Cleef & Arpels, Cartier, Chaumet, Schiaparelli,** and **Guerlain** (see shopping map at right). ♦ Métros: Opéra, Tuileries, Concorde, Madeleine

On Place Vendôme:

Vendôme Column In place of the toppled statue of Louis XIV, Napoléon raised a 144-foot-high monument modeled on Trajan's column in Rome. Made to commemorate Napoléon's military victories in Germany, the stone colonnade is faced with 378 spiraling sheets of bronze supplied by 1,200 cannons captured from the Austrian and Russian armies defeated at the Battle of Austerlitz in 1805. The column was originally topped with a statue of Napoléon dressed as Julius Caesar, but that was replaced by one of Henri IV in

1814. After Napoléon's defeat at Waterloo, the Bourbons commandeered the monument and mounted their symbol, the fleur-de-lis, at the top. Along came Louis Philippe, and the fleur-de-lis was replaced with a small statue of Napoléon. But on the afternoon of 1 May 1871, the column was toppled, crashing down along Rue de la Paix and breaking into 30 pieces. This act of destruction was masterminded by the painter Gustave Courbet for aesthetic and political reasons. When the Third Republic took power, it ordered Courbet to restore the monument at his own expense. The column was thrust up again (this time topped with a replica of the original statue), and Courbet was plunged into bankruptcy.

Place Vendôme Shopping

RUE DES CAPUCINES

RUE DANIELLE-CASANOVA

Emporio Armani *mens- and womenswear*

Alexandre Reza *jewelry*
Pierre Dubail *jewelry*
Hôtel Ritz
Cartier *jewelry*

Hôtel Vendôme

PLACE VENDOME

Charvet *mens- and womenswear*
Comptoir sud Pacific *accessories*
Boucheron *jewelry*
Van Cleef & Arpels *jewelry/watches*
Mauboicsin *jewelry*
Chanel *jewelry*
Piaget *watches*
Robergé *jewelry*
Chaumet *jewelry*
Patek Philippe *watches*
Mikimoto *jewelry*
Repossi *jewelry*
Giorgio Armani *mens- and womenswear*
Gianmaria Buccellati *fine silver/jewelry*
Galerie Alexander Butman
Lhullier *florist*
Guerlain *perfume/accessories*

RUE ST-HONORE

chocolates **Godiva**
bar/restaurant **Le Lotti**
accessories **Ilonka**
jewelry **Michaela Frey**
Galerie d'Art Castiglione
Weedly
childrenswear/T-shirts

costume jewelry **Anémone**
menswear **Namani**
optician **Meyrowitz**
jewelry **H. Stern**

RUE DE CASTIGLIONE

Annick Goutal *oils/perfume*
Rhodes & Brousse *menswear*
Agry *engraving*
Carré des Feuillants *restaurant*
Clio *jewelry*
Kenneth Jay Lane *jewelry*
Dallas *womenswear*
Claude Litz *furs*
Aquascutum *mens- and womenswear*
Luce Brett *antiques*
Payot *beauty products/salon*

RUE DU MONT-THABOR

Hotel Inter-Continental
purses/jewelry **Casty**

Cristal Vendôme *crystal*

Les Arcades *books*
Parfumeria Catherine *perfume*
Swann Pharmacy
Jacqueline Perès *womenswear*
Sulka *menswear*

RUE DE RIVOLI

72 Hôtel Ritz $$$$ If any hotel deserves to be called "legendary," it is this hostelry opened by César Ritz in 1898. Millionaires, Arab princes, divas, and cinema stars have favored this ritzy establishment, whose name has became a synonym for luxurious glamour. F. Scott Fitzgerald wrote a story called "The Diamond as Big as the Ritz," set big scenes in his fiction in the hotel, and downed more drinks than were good for him in the **Ritz Bar.** Marcel Proust used to arrive sporting lavender gloves and a variety of clothes that never seemed to fit him. Coco Chanel liked it so much she took up residence here. There are 440 employees (a third of whom have been here more than a quarter-century) catering to the occupants of the hotel's 187 opulent rooms and suites. Sixty of these stalwarts are available for duty as private servants if your vacation just isn't a vacation without Jeeves. The prices are astronomical but, by all accounts, justified. The suites on the second floor overlooking the Place Vendôme are actually registered with the Bureau of Fine Arts. Mohammed Al Fayed bought the hotel in 1979 for $30 million and spent 10 times that amount restoring and expanding it. The hotel's legend took a turn for the tragic in 1997, however, when Princess Diana and Dodi al Fayed left from here to their fatal flight from the paparazzi. ♦ 15 Pl Vendôme (between Rues St-Honoré and des Capucines). 01.43.16.30.30; fax 01.43.16.36.68; resa@ritzparis.com. Métros: Opéra, Tuileries, Concorde, Madeleine

Within the Hôtel Ritz:

Ritz Espadon ★★★★$$$$ The culinary reputation of this lovely restaurant was made from the very start by the presence of that great turn-of-the-century chef, Auguste Escoffier. He first met César Ritz when Ritz was manager of the Grand Hotel in Monte Carlo. Escoffier's celebrated recipe for foie gras in Port is still used. Under chef Guy Legay, in charge since 1980, this restaurant has maintained its standing as one of Paris's temples of *haute cuisine.* Latter-day creations include fillet of St-Pierre studded with olives and served with a saffron sauce, and lobster medaillons in a tarragon sauce. The crystal and silver and china are magnificent, and the army of waiters and dining room assistants is almost oppressively attentive. As is to be expected, the wine list is nonpareil and the prices are unsurpassed. In summer dine outside on the delightful garden patio. ♦ Daily lunch and dinner. Reservations recommended. 01.43.16.30.80

Hemingway Bar Just off Rue Cambon is this famous little bar, which Hemingway "liberated" at the end of World War II (he was the first to arrive for a drink after the liberation of Paris). Here the legendary barman Georges served drinks to President Teddy Roosevelt, just back from an African safari. Other big-time tipplers who have imbibed here include the Prince of Wales, Greta Garbo, Noel Coward, Douglas Fairbanks, Winston Churchill, J.P. Morgan, Andrew Carnegie, F. Scott Fitzgerald, and Marlene Dietrich. It's still an English-style pub, right down to its tweedy, rubicund patrons. ♦ Daily 6:30PM-1AM. 01.43.16.33.65

Vendôme Lesser known than the hotel's other watering hole, this bar has a terrace for drinks or tea in the summer. ♦ Daily 11AM-1AM. 01.43.16.33.63

Ritz Health Club Where else can you work out alongside the likes of Tom Cruise, Gregory Peck, Madonna, Woody Allen, and any number of top models, politicians, and members of the crème de la crème of Parisian society? Staying at the **Ritz** makes you an official member, and there are flexible membership programs for others as well. Facilities include a fully equipped gymnasium, squash courts, saunas, Jacuzzis, Turkish baths, spa treatments, and the largest private pool in Paris. ♦ Daily. 01.43.16.30.60.

72 11-13 Place Vendôme This is the **Ministry of Justice** where, in 1848, the official measure for the meter was set in the facade. ♦ Between Rues St-Honoré and des Capucines. Métros: Opéra, Tuileries, Concorde, Madeleine

Cartier

73 Cartier Since 1847 this jewelry store has offered the best and the brightest in French *bijoux,* with commensurately dazzling price tags. The 14-percent tourist discount on gold, however, almost brings the pretty baubles within reach. ♦ M-Sa. 7 Pl Vendôme (between Rues St-Honoré and des Capucines). 01.44.55.32.50. Métros: Tuileries, Concorde

74 3-5 Place Vendôme This was formerly the **Hôtel Bristol.** From 1890 to 1910, whenever financier and art collector John Pierpont Morgan came to Paris, he would stay in the same corner suite in the old hotel, which was run by one of his father's butlers. The Sultan of Brunei now owns it. ♦ Between Rues St-Honoré and des Capucines. Métros: Tuileries, Concorde

hôtel costes

75 Hôtel Costes $$$$ In 1996 enterprising Jean-Louis Costes took over the faded old **Hôtel France et Choiseul,** transformed it into Paris's most glamorous small hotel, and made its restaurant the most sought-after canteen for fashion masters and victims. Star designer Jacques Garcia deserves the credit for the opulent Second Empire decor that magically combines grandeur and coziness, both in the public areas and the luxurious guest rooms. All 85 rooms are individually decorated with remarkable combinations of fabrics, fully furnished in antiques, and equipped with the most up-to-date modern conveniences, including satellite TV, a CD player, fax machine, and mini-bar. ♦ 239 Rue St-Honoré (between Rues de Castiglione and Cambon). 01.42.44.50.00; fax 01.42.44.50.01; www.hotelcostes.com. Métros: Concorde, Tuileries

Within Hôtel Costes:

Costes ★★$$$ This ultra-"in" spot for the haute couture crowd boasts more pretty faces and show-biz names than any other restaurant in Paris. The menu is Mediterranean/international: penne with tomato and basil, tomato and goat cheese tart, melon with Parma ham, shrimp tempura, chicken with balsamic-dressed arugula, grilled fish or meat, or a simple club sandwich or omelette. The food is far less important than the scenery, but it's perfectly fine all the same. Eat under the white parasols in the Italianate courtyard when the weather is fine or in the plush Second Empire dining room when it's not. ♦ Daily 7AM-1AM. 01.42.44.50.25.

75 Godiva The world-renowned chocolatier takes its name from the 11th-century English noblewoman who sacrificed her modesty and rode naked through the streets of Coventry to plead with her husband, the earl, to reduce taxes on the townsfolk. If these exquisite bonbons had been available then, they might have made a better bribe. ♦ M-Sa. 237 Rue St-Honoré (at Rue de Castiglione). 01.42.60.44.64. Métros: Concorde, Tuileries

HOTEL ⊕ LOTTI

76 Hôtel Lotti $$$$ This 130-room luxury hotel is favored by British and Italian bluebloods who are drawn to the large, tastefully decorated rooms, period furniture, and impeccable service. There's a restaurant on the premises. ♦ 7 Rue de Castiglione (between Rues du Mont-Thabor and St-Honoré). 01.42.60.37.34; fax 01.40.15.93.56; hotel.lotti@wanadoo.fr. Métros: Concorde, Tuileries

77 Carré des Feuillants ★★★$$$$ Alain Dutournier runs the show at this 19th-century–style restaurant near Place Vendôme. His specialty is inventive southwestern French cuisine that includes parsley-crusted scallops with endive, fried eels with herb-and-sweet-garlic salad, wild hare with truffles, and braised veal with cèpes. For dessert try the *russe pistache* (shortbread biscuits with pistachio mousse and raspberry puree). ♦ M-F lunch and dinner; Sa dinner; closed in August. Reservations required. 14 Rue de Castiglione (at Rue St-Honoré). 01.42.86.82.82. Métros: Concorde, Tuileries

78 4 Rue du Mont-Thabor In the summer of 1820, still enjoying the afterglow of the triumphant reception of *Rip Van Winkle* and *The Legend of Sleepy Hollow,* 39-year-old Washington Irving moved into an apartment here. Mitigating his pleasure was Irving's powerful fear of growing old, the same problem that obsessed ol' Rip. The building is now the unremarkable **Hôtel Mont-Thabor.** ♦ Between Rues d'Alger and de Castiglione. Métro: Tuileries

79 Royal Saint-Honoré $$$$ Just one block from the **Tuileries Gardens,** this hotel has an elegant lobby, 72 quiet rooms with marble bathrooms, and a refined air. There's a handsome bar and breakfast room with original Louis XVI woodwork that serves light snacks, but no restaurant. ♦ 221 Rue St-Honoré (at Rue d'Alger). 01.42.60.32.79; fax 01.42.60.47.44; rsh@hroy.com; www.hroy.com/st-honore. Métro: Tuileries

80 Giorgio Armani This ultramodern designer boutique is set in the former **Hôtel du Rhin,** which became the temporary residence of Napoléon III during his 1848 presidential campaign. ♦ M-Sa. 6 Pl Vendôme (between Rues St-Honoré and Danielle-Casanova). 01.42.61.55.09. Métros: Tuileries, Concorde

81 12 Place Vendôme In 1849 Frédéric Chopin, Polish composer and pianist, died here at the age of 39. It's now an office building. ♦ Between Rues St-Honoré and Danielle-Casanova. Métros: Opéra, Tuileries, Concorde, Madeleine

82 16 Place Vendôme Here Franz Anton Mesmer (1734-1815), the Austrian charlatan physician who invented mesmerism (later called hypnosis), conducted "animal magnetism" seminars wrapped in robes decorated with astrological signs. Later, in the 1930s, Obelisk Press had its office at this address. Headed by Englishman Jack Kahane, Obelisk published works that no one else would, such as Henry Miller's *Tropic of Cancer,* which appeared in 1934. It's still an office building. ♦ Between Rues St-Honoré and Danielle-Casanova. Métros: Opéra, Tuileries, Concorde, Madeleine

83 Charvet Edward VII bought his neckties and cravats here. ♦ M-Sa; closed Monday in August. 28 Pl Vendôme (at Rue Danielle-Casanova). 01.42.60.30.70. Métros: Opéra, Madeleine

84 Ermenegildo Zegna The understated high fashions for men at this sophisticated shop are made with the richest of fabrics and have an appeal that's beyond snobbery. For more than a century the Zegna family has been known for making the world's finest wools, providing the best European designers with their raw materials. ♦ M-Sa. 10 Rue de la Paix (between Rues Danielle-Casanova and Daunou). 01.42.61.67.61. Métro: Opéra

85 Hôtel Westminster $$$$ Fully renovated in 1997 by talented designer-architect **Pierre-Yves Rochon,** this venerable hotel is one of Paris's loveliest and most comfortable luxury establishments. It is also one of the most prestigious, just as it was when the Duke of Westminster was a regular guest here in the 1840s. The duke liked it so much, in fact, that he authorized the hotel to use his coat of arms. Henry James and his family stayed here in 1856, when the future novelist was 12. The "carriage trade" continues to favor the hotel, but so do such film and theater personalities as Monica Vitti, Ute Lemper, and Michelangelo Antonioni. The hotel's executive floor and business center also make it attractive to business travelers. The 102 guest rooms, which include 18 superb suites, are each personalized with antique furniture, lovely pastel fabrics and wallpapers, and modern marble bathrooms. The lobby exudes the atmosphere of a refined British club, and Chief Concierge Patrice Delamare's staff is a model of affable efficiency. The hotel boasts a fine restaurant, colorful bar, and a great location midway between Place Vendôme and the Opéra. ♦ 13 Rue de la Paix (between Rues des Capucines and Daunou). 01.42.61.57.46; fax 01.42.60.30.66; www.hepta.fr/westminster. Métro: Opéra

Within the Hôtel Westminster:

Le Céladon ★★★$$$ This delightful restaurant makes diners feel right at home, especially if they happen to live in a Regency-era mansion. Each of the three small interconnected dining rooms has warm yellow walls hung with old paintings, crystal chandeliers, and a handful of well-spaced tables. There is much celadon on display, the graceful Chinese porcelain from which the restaurant takes its name. Young chef Emmanuel Hodencq has quickly made a name for himself (and garnered a Michelin star) with his refined array of risottos, roasted prawns, turbot casserole with celeriac and truffles, pigeon breast and foie gras baked in a cabbage leaf, and other imaginative specialties. The selection of wines is outstanding, as is the service. The prix-fixe lunch and dinner menus are surprisingly affordable. ♦ M-F lunch and dinner; closed in August. Entrance at 15 Rue Daunou. 01.42.61.77.42

Bar Les Chenets Frequented by a neighborhood business clientele, this cozy bar specializes in Champagne-based cocktails, which sounds misleadingly innocent. The bar also serves light lunches and a very British tea in the afternoon; and there is cocktail piano from 6:30 to 9PM. ♦ Daily 8:30AM-midnight. 01.42.61.57.46

85 Alfred Dunhill The Paris branch of a famous English company, this mahogany-paneled shop sells all manner of smoking paraphernalia. Dunhill pipes made from the best French brier, with ebony mouthpieces, are among the world's finest (and most costly). And where else will you find a thuja-wood cigar box? ♦ M-Sa. 15 Rue de la Paix (between Rues des Capucines and Daunou). 01.42.61.57.58. Métro: Opéra

86 Kitty O'Shea's The most Irish of pubs in Paris serves Guinness on tap. Businesspeople headquartered around the **Opéra** congregate here. ♦ M-Sa noon-2AM; Su noon-1:30AM. 10 Rue des Capucines (at Rue Volney). 01.40.15.00.30. Métros: Madeleine, Opéra

L'OLYMPIA

87 L'Olympia Edith Piaf sang her heart out on this stage. Years later so did a group of Brits named the Beatles, who had just launched their first world tour. Playing here is still an obligatory engagement for top pop singers. ♦ 28 Blvd des Capucines (between Rues Scribe and de Caumartin). 01.47.42.25.49. Métros: Madeleine, Opéra

Fragonard

88 Musée Fragonard Get a sense of what the perfume industry is all about at this museum devoted entirely to fragrance and its history. Priceless perfume-related objets d'art are also on display. There's also a shop that sells perfumes. ♦ Admission. M-Sa. 39 Blvd des Capucines (between Rues Daunou and des Capucines). 01.42.60.37.14. Métro: Opéra

89 14 Boulevard des Capucines On 28 December 1895 the brothers Auguste and Louis Lumière, inventors of the cinematograph, projected their first public movie here in what was called the **Salon Indien.** This is now an office building. ♦ At Rue Scribe. Métro: Opéra

89 Hôtel Scribe $$$$ This deluxe hotel is a full-blown Second Empire confection, from the harmonious 6-story Haussmann facade to the stately Napoléon III decor in the lobby to the 217 plush, spacious rooms. The Allied forces' press corps set up headquarters here in 1944. It was the only hotel in Paris that had hot water during the bitterly cold winter of 1944-45, and journalists who couldn't get rooms here would come to take a bath. Correspondent John Dos Passos, one of the lucky people to secure a room, wrote about the then-little-known General de Gaulle's performance at a press conference: "He has two voices, the Sorbonne voice and the *père de famille Henri Quatre, bonne soupe* kind of voice. There's more to him than we had been led to believe." ♦ 1 Rue Scribe (between Blvd des Capucines and Pl Charles-Garnier). 01.44.71.24.24; fax 01.42.65.39.97; www.sofitel.com. Métro: Opéra

Within the Scribe:

Les Muses ★★★$$$ In keeping with the hotel's style, its dining room is elegant in both decor and cuisine. Chef Philippe Pleuën and his team at this Michelin-one-star restaurant offer such imaginative and consistently well-prepared dishes as warm foie gras of Vendée duck with creamed and smoked potatoes; crusty scallops with risotto and boletus mushrooms; fillet of smoked lamb with its kidney served with a fricassee of green cabbage and bacon; and for dessert, roasted figs with honey and fresh goat cottage cheese, or the pastry chef's selection. The prix-fixe menu, available both at lunch and dinner, is an exceptional value. ♦ M-F lunch and dinner; closed in August. Reservations recommended. 01.44.71.24.26

Le Bar Business executives habitually gather around the elegant mahogany bar here, sipping the cocktail of the day. A pianist entertains Tuesday through Friday from 6:30PM to 9PM. A continental breakfast is served in the morning. ♦ Daily 8AM-2AM. 01.44.71.24.24

90 Le Grand Hôtel Inter-Continental $$$$ Designed in 1861 by **Alfred Armand** and inaugurated by Empress Eugénie the following year, this 514-room property occupying a full city block in the heart of the Opéra Quartier remains one of Europe's grandest luxury hotels. Major renovations directed by **Pierre-Yves Rochon**in the early 1990s streamlined some of its Belle Epoque grandeur; the hotel also now offers such first-class perks as a gymnasium, sauna, tanning rooms, and massage. The rooms and suites are spacious, tastefully modernized, and thoroughly comfortable. Its proximity to the **Opéra Garnier** makes it a favorite of visiting prima ballerinas. Business travelers appreciate the hotel's modern, 20-room **Centre de Conference Opéra**, and Parisian haute couture houses often use **Le Grand Salon Opéra**—the huge, spectacularly ornate circular ballroom—for fashion shows. ♦ 2 Rue Scribe (at Blvd des Capucines). 01.40.07.32.32; fax 01.42.66.12.51; legrand@interconti.com; www.interconti.com. Métro: Opéra

Within the Grand Hôtel Inter-Continental:

La Verrière ★★$$ Light-filled and spacious, with a glass roof and numerous plants and trees, this airy eatery serves a breakfast buffet Monday through Friday, and brunch on Sunday. Specialties at lunch and dinner include turbot grilled with sage, lobster fricassee, lamb curry, and duck wings with roasted pears and sesame seeds. For dessert, try the wild strawberry and rhubarb pastry or the island fruit with coconut milk. ♦ M-F breakfast, lunch, and dinner; Su brunch; closed in August. 01.40.07.32.32

Bar du Grand Hôtel Tucked under the arches of the hotel is this multilevel **Opéra**-goers' watering hole. ♦ Daily 11AM-1AM. Entrance at 12 Blvd des Capucines. 01.40.07.31.37

Café de la Paix ★★$$ Looking like a scene painted by Renoir—brightly clothed patrons, green-and-white-striped umbrellas, dappled light—this lovely old cafe is classified as a historic landmark. Guy de Maupassant, Emile Zola, Sir Arthur Conan Doyle, André Gide, and Oscar Wilde frequented its large terrace on the Place de l'Opéra. Salvador Dalí enjoyed it, as did Harry Truman, Maurice Chevalier, Josephine Baker, Maria Callas, Marlene Deitrich, and General Charles de Gaulle, who ordered a take-out cold plate here on 25 August 1944—the first in liberated Paris. Tradition holds that if you sit on the terrace long enough, you will see someone you know walk by. House specialties include steak *tartare* and sole meunière; the cafe is also famous for its fresh shellfish from September through June. ♦ Daily lunch and dinner until 1AM. Entrance at 3 Pl de l'Opéra. 01.40.07.30.20

Le Restaurant Opéra ★★★$$$$ This glamorous dining spot recalls the 19th-century heyday of the **Opéra Garnier**, thanks to its **Charles Garnier**-inspired architectural elements, including ethereal ceiling frescoes and old gold columns and moldings. Champagne-colored table linen, Sèvres porcelain plates, and fine crystal add to the elegant ambience. A perfect match for this visual splendor is young chef François Rodolphe's splendid cuisine. His creamy pumpkin soup with truffles served with chicken livers and croutons, and roasted king prawns from Brittany have elicited raves. For diners who've always been reluctant to try frogs' legs, this is the place to give them a whirl. The succulent little *cuisses de grenouille* are as tender as perfectly cooked poultry, delicately flavored with garlic and hazelnuts, and served with mashed leeks and wild mushrooms. For a main course, the pan-fried fillets of *rouget* (red mullet), Brittany lobster, wild duck from Sologne, and leg of Pyrénées lamb are all excellent choices. The cheese cart is remarkable (the goat cheeses from Rocmadour and Chambertin are positively uplifting), and for dessert, the lemon praline puff pastry with homemade hazelnut ice cream makes a bright topper to any meal. The wine list is extensive and magnificent. Meals are quite costly à la carte, but relatively reasonable prix-fixe menus are available. Bankers and businesspeople are the main clientele at lunch, and in the evening hotel guests, tourists, and opera- and theater-goers take their place. The service is personable, discreet, and efficient—upscale French professionalism at its best. ♦ M-F lunch and dinner; closed in August. Reservations recommended. Entrance at 3 Pl de l'Opéra. 01.40.07.30.10

91 **Place de l'Opéra** Six wide thoroughfares lined with bank headquarters, theaters, luxury boutiques, and **Le Grand Hôtel Inter-Continental** are the spokes emanating from this hub in front of the **Opéra Garnier**. It was the keystone of Baron Haussmann's massive redevelopment of the center of Paris under Napoléon III. Back when the **Opéra** was where one scaled the social heights, the haut monde and demimonde frequented the nearby **Café de la Paix, Café de Paris,** and **Café Riche.** ♦ Métro: Opéra

92 **American Express** If you did leave home without it, go no farther. Here you'll find traveler's checks, a foreign exchange bank, tours and travel services, and the famous American Express mail pickup counter. ♦ M-F; Sa for currency exchange only. 11 Rue Scribe (at Rue Auber). 01.47.77.74.75. Métro: Opéra

93 **Boulevard Haussmann** This drab expanse fronted with mammoth department stores becomes festive in December, when it's strung with Christmas lights. In 1784, two months after his arrival in Paris as American ambassador to France, Thomas Jefferson signed a nine-year lease on a new town house located on what is now the north side of Boulevard Haussmann. The Virginian filled it with furniture, then set about acquiring a collection of paintings, books, and engravings that would eventually adorn his beloved Monticello. History records that during his sojourn in Paris, Jefferson kept a black servant, James Hemings, whom he apprenticed to a local caterer, Combeaux, perhaps so he could take home some French culinary art along with his other acquisitions.

He also started a liaison here with his deceased wife's half-sister, his young mulatto slave Sally Hemings. ♦ Métros: Richelieu-Drouot, Chausée d'Antin–La Fayette, Havre-Caumartin, St-Augustin, Miromesnil

93 **Au Printemps** In the late 19th century Paris introduced the world to *grands magasins* (department stores) such as **Le Bon Marché** and **La Samaritaine,** and the city's shopping giants have been drawing crowds ever since. Today, two outclass the rest: **Au Printemps,** which opened in 1864, and **Galeries Lafayette** (see below), which opened in 1894, right next to each other along the Boulevard Haussmann. These are great places to get a peek at the latest in Parisian fashion as well as some indication of what it costs. Rest your feet and have a cup of tea or a slice of tart in the sixth-floor tea salon beneath the Belle Epoque blue stained-glass rotunda. If possible, shop on weekday mornings, as the afternoon and all day Saturday can resemble a stampede at the Chicago stockyard. ♦ M-W, F-Sa; Th 9:35AM-10PM. 64 Blvd Haussmann (between Rues de Caumartin and du Havre). 01.42.82.50.00. Métro: Havre-Caumartin

94 **Galeries Lafayette** With its magnificent glass-and-steel dome, this 10-story department store is classified as a historic monument. More than 10,000 customers visit its fashion department every day. An added attraction is **Galeries Lafayette Gourmet:** At sit-down counters throughout the food department, shoppers can sample each section's specialty, such as grilled meats near the butcher, salads in the produce area, etc. On the top floor there's incomparable browsing and a marvelous vista of the Right Bank's rooftops. ♦ M-W, F-Sa; Th 9:30AM-9PM. 40 Blvd Haussmann (between Rues de la Chaussée-d'Antin and de Mogador). 01.42.82.34.56; 01.42.82.36.40 in English. Métro: Chaussée d'Antin–La Fayette

95 **Opéra Garnier (Paris Opera)** An opera house fit for an emperor, the pièce de résistance of Baron Haussmann's revamped Paris, and a last hurrah of Second Empire opulence, this grandiose culture palace was once the world's largest theater, with an area of nearly 3 acres and a stage vast enough to accommodate 450 performers. Designer **Charles Garnier,** a 35-year-old previously unknown architect, was selected from among a field of 171 other competitors (including the empress's favorite architect, **Eugène-Emmanuel Viollet-le-Duc).** Garnier gave the facade an unusual, ornate look with friezes, winged horses, golden garlands, and busts of famous composers. He crowned his architectural extravaganza with a copper-

green cupola topped by Millet's *Apollo* thrusting a lyre above his head. A golden bust of the architect stands on the Rue Scribe side of the theater. **Garnier**'s orgiastic mishmash of styles (from Classical to Baroque) and materials (every possible hue of marble, from green to red to blue) was less than the hit he hoped it would be. The empress, wife of Napoléon III, is said to have barked in disgust, "What is this style supposed to be? It is neither Greek nor Roman nor Louis XIV nor Louis XV!" **Garnier** diplomatically replied: "It is Napoléon III, Your Majesty." Second Empire advocates of family values were in an uproar over the sensual Carrier-Belleuse lamp-bearing statues and the famous sculpted group *La Danse* by Carpeaux.

Inside, however, the effect is eminently upright, even majestic. Though Renoir loathed it, you will find a night at the opera house well worth your while, although it's mainly classical ballet and modern dance, rather than opera, that is performed here now; all grand operas take place at the **Opéra Bastille**. The gold ornaments, allegories in marble, Chagall ceilings, and the parade of Parisian society are all good for a gape. Horror fans will be interested to know that the underground grotto where Leroux's Phantom of the Opera lurked lies beneath the **Opéra**'s cellars, an artificial lake that provides water for the city's fire brigade. The **Opéra Museum** in the **West Pavilion** displays opera and ballet memorabilia (such as the crown Pavlova wore when dancing in *Swan Lake* and the ballet slippers and tarot cards of Nijinsky). ♦ Admission. Box office: M-Sa. Museum: M-Sa. Pl de l'Opéra (between Rues Halévy and Auber). Reservations 08.36.69.78.68, opera house 01.44.73.13.00, museum 01.47.42.07.02. Métro: Opéra

Within the Opéra Garnier:

Grand Foyer and Staircase Of this apotheosis of splendor Henry James wrote: "If the world were ever reduced to the domain of a single gorgeous potentate, the foyer would do very well for his throne room." The Baroque white Carrara marble **Grand Staircase,** with its Algerian onyx balustrade, is 32 feet wide at its center. At the first landing, it divides and sweeps upward in two flights of steps to the second-floor gallery. The **Grand Foyer,** 175 feet long and decorated with mirrors and allegorical paintings, is encrusted with gilt ornamentation, and its ceiling glows with Venetian mosaics and colored marble from the island of Murano. The annual **Ecole Polytechnique Ball** and presidential galas take place here.

95 Auditorium The theater is famous for its six-ton chandelier and five tiers of loges dressed in red velvet and gold. The ceiling is adorned with Marc Chagall's 1964 masterpiece depicting Parisian scenes and images from operas ranging from *Giselle* to *The Magic Flute;* the work is as colorful as the rest of **Garnier**'s palace, yet oddly out of place. Backstage is the **Foyer de la Danse** so often painted by Edgar Degas.

96 8 Boulevard des Capucines It was at this address in 1880, the year of his death, that 61-year-old Jacques Offenbach composed his masterpiece *The Tales of Hoffmann*. It's now an office building. ♦ Between Rue de la Chaussée-d'Antin and Pl de l'Opéra. Métro: Opéra

LE GRAND CAFE
CAPUCINES

97 Le Grand Café Capucines ★★$$ This is one of the rare Parisian bistros to stay open 24 hours a day, and has a lavish Belle Epoque decor to boot. It serves fresh shellfish platters; and grilled, poached, or sautéed fish and grilled meat. Opened in 1895, this haunt of Oscar Wilde is now a lively hangout for journalists, the after-show crowd (in addition to the **Opéra Garnier,** there are several big theaters within a few blocks), graveyard-shift laborers, and anyone else out walking the streets in the wee hours. ♦ Daily 24 hours. 4 Blvd des Capucines (between Rue de la Chaussée-d'Antin and Pl de l'Opéra). 01.43.12.19.00. Métro: Opéra

98 6 Rue Daunou Dr. Oliver Wendell Holmes (father of the famous jurist) knew this as the **Hotel d'Orient** and stayed here when he made a brief trip to Paris in 1886 to meet Louis Pasteur, who had just developed the vaccine for rabies. It's now the nondescript **Hôtel Daunou.** ♦ Between Rues Louis-Le-Grand and de la Paix. Métro: Opéra

99 Harry's New York Bar Opened in 1911, "Sank-Roo-Doe-Noo" (the US pronunciation of the bar's address) really came into its own two years later, when it was purchased by a bartender named Harry MacElhone. Here F. Scott Fitzgerald stared blearily at successive scotches and watched the plot lines of his stories take form; George Gershwin dreamed up his great fantasy *An American in Paris;* Ernest Hemingway dodged swinging fists; Gloria Swanson glowed; Noel Coward quipped; and Jean-Paul Sartre, despite himself, discovered both bourbon and hot dogs. The night before each US presidential election, the regulars around the bar are polled as to their guesses of the outcome; the legendary poll has an uncanny track record for predicting the winner. There is a piano bar downstairs with music from 10PM to 2AM. ♦ Daily 10:45AM-4AM. 5 Rue Daunou (between Rues Louis-Le-Grand and de la Paix). 01.42.61.71.14. Métro: Opéra

100 Brentano's For the greatest hits in English literature, try this, one of the best and oldest English-language bookstores in Paris. ♦ M-Sa. 37 Ave de l'Opéra (between Rues Danielle-Casanova and d'Antin). 01.42.61.52.50. Métros: Opéra, Pyramides

101 Yakitori ★$ Try the morsels of cheese-stuffed pork, teriyaki chicken, and marinated shrimp skewered and grilled *à la Japonaise*. This restaurant is perpetually crowded, but it's worth the effort to grab a seat at the counter and watch the chefs perform. ♦ M-Sa lunch and dinner. 34 Pl du Marché-St-Honoré (between Rues du Marché-St-Honoré and Gomboust). 01.42.96.10.18. Métro: Pyramides

102 Flo Prestige For those who enjoy picnicking and can afford not to bother with preparing the meal, this take-out gourmet deli offers a delectable selection of cheeses, charcuterie, salmon, salads, daily specials, desserts, and pastries of a quality that merits a limo for the tailgate picnic. For a setting, the nearby **Tuileries** gardens should do just fine. Or if you prefer, they will deliver to your hotel. ♦ Daily until 11PM. 42 Pl du Marché-St-Honoré (at Rue du Marché-St-Honoré). 01.42.61.45.46. Métro: Pyramides. Also at: Numerous locations throughout the city

103 Tuileries $$$ Down a quiet side street, this small hotel was the mansion of Queen Marie Antoinette's principal lady-in-waiting in the 18th century. It retains much of its period charm, despite 20th-century modifications— private bathrooms, color TVs, direct-dial phones, mini bars, and air-conditioning— that have made its 26 rooms eminently comfortable. There's no restaurant. ♦ 10 Rue St-Hyacinthe (between Rues de La Sourdière and du Marché-St-Honoré). 01.42.61.04.17; fax 01.49.27.91.56; members@aol.com/htuileri/. Métros: Pyramides, Tuileries

104 Delices St. Roch ★$ For a tasty lunch on the run, try this modest little eatery that serves quiches and a few family-style daily specials. The quiches are filled with imaginative combinations of ingredients, including chicken and carrot with mustard, fennel, and mushroom, and *oseille* (sorrel) and chavignol cheese. For plats du jour, there are such choices as *blanquette de veau* (veal with béchamel sauce and mushrooms), stuffed tomato, and roast turkey stuffed with olives. For dessert try the green rhubarb pie or the coconut cream. A horde of well-heeled St-Honoré office workers and the occasional Birkenstock-shod Californian keep this place busy at lunchtime. ♦ M-F lunch until 4PM. 21 Rue St-Roch (between Rues St-Honoré and Gomboust). 01.42.97.59.40. Métro: Pyramides

105 Dave ★★$$ A hideout for such celebrities as George Michael and Yves Saint Laurent, this excellent Sino-Vietnamese restaurant is named after its starstruck maître d', who keeps a Polaroid collection of his most famous customers. The small dining room is decorated with deep red carpets and Chinese lamps, lending it an intimate ambience. Recommended dishes include the sweet and spicy spareribs, Vietnamese rolls served with mint, and shrimp sautéed in a spicy black bean sauce. ♦ M-F lunch and dinner; Sa-Su dinner. 39 Rue St-Roch (between Rues St-Honoré and Gomboust). 01.42.61.49.48. Métro: Pyramides

106 St-Roch The bullet holes in this church's facade recall one of the most significant military debuts in French history. This is the site of a fierce Revolutionary skirmish that occurred on the steps of the church on 5 October 1795, when a Royalist mob was scattered by a then-little-known 27-year-old general named Napoléon Bonaparte. Ten days later Napoléon was appointed commander-in-chief of the home forces. An architectural mix-and-match, the structure is the city's finest Baroque church and is best known today for its splendid 1752 Rococo organ and weekly evening concerts. Built to handle the overflow from **St-Germain-l'Auxerrois**, it was originally designed by **Jacques Lemercier**, and no less a personage than Louis XIV laid its cornerstone in 1653. But it took another century to complete.

Jules Hardouin-Mansart was responsible for the oval **Lady Chapel**, and sculptor René Charpentier decorated the edifice in carved imagery. The church is dedicated to an Italian holy man who ministered to plague victims in the 14th century. Inside are memorials to the playwright Corneille, the philosopher Diderot, and Louis XIV's beloved gardener, André Le Nôtre, whose bust by Antoine Coysevox is to the left of the chancel. ♦ 296 Rue St-Honoré (at Rue St-Roch). 01.42.44.13.20. Métros: Pyramides, Tuileries

107 St-James et Albany $$$ Portions of this elegant hotel date back to the reign of Louis XIV, which is appropriate, since for years its clientele was strictly old European aristocracy. It now offers 208 rooms, suites, duplexes, and home-away-from-home studios equipped with kitchenettes. The nicest accommodations are nestled in the attic beneath low-beamed ceilings. The hotel incorporates parts of the old **Noailles Mansion**, where General Lafayette married one of the Noailles daughters in 1774, and where Queen Marie Antoinette paid a visit in 1779. It is built around a garden and interior courtyard, away from the traffic noise of Rue de Rivoli. ♦ 202 Rue de Rivoli (between Rues St-Roch and du 29-Juillet). 01.44.58.43.21; fax

01.44.58.43.11; stjames_albany@compuserve.com. Métro: Tuileries

Within St-James et Albany:

Les Noailles ★$$ Love will blossom when you stroll through the **Tuileries** with that special someone and then dine tête-à-tête in the courtyard of this elegant dining spot. Recommended dishes include *pavé de cabillaud mi-fumé* (lightly smoked cod) and *magret de canard au miel* (preserved duck breast in honey). ◆ Daily lunch and dinner. 01.44.58.43.40, 01.44.58.43.21

Bar St-James ★★$$ This library-turned-bar is one of the coziest spots in town for a quiet drink or a light lunch. The luncheon special, which changes daily, is dependable and inexpensive. ◆ Bar: 5PM-1AM. Restaurant: daily lunch. 01.44.58.43.21

108 Comfort Hotel Louvre Montana $$ Clean, modern, and conveniently located near the **Tuileries** and **St-Roch** (which has marvelous evening concerts), this 25-room hotel is an isle of economy in an archipelago of extravagance. There's no restaurant. ◆ 12 Rue St-Roch (between Rues de Rivoli and St-Honoré). 01.42.60.35.10; fax 01.42.61.12.28; commercial@hotels.emeraude.com. Métro: Tuileries

109 Statue de Jeanne d'Arc This gilded equestrian statue by 19th-century sculptor Frémiet honors Joan of Arc (1412-31), the French national hero and Roman Catholic saint. Born during the Hundred Years' War (1337-1453), this charismatic peasant girl claimed she heard the voices of saints urging her to save France from the English. She was able to convince the Dauphin Charles VII to provide her with troops that, under her generalship, took back Orléans and routed the English forces in the Loire. In 1429, during an unsuccessful attempt to liberate Paris from the occupying English army, Joan stationed a cannon on Butte St-Roch (leveled some three centuries ago as landfill for the Champ-de-Mars) to attack the St-Honoré Gate (which is now 163 Rue St-Honoré). A year later Joan of Arc was captured by Burgundians and turned over to the English, and the following year she was convicted of witchcraft and heresy by a tribunal of French clerics who supported the English, then burned at the stake in Rouen. She was canonized in 1920, and today France honors her with a national holiday. ◆ Pl des Pyramides. Métro: Tuileries

110 Hôtel Regina $$$$ Offering a splendid view of the **Tuileries Gardens,** this quiet 121-room hotel is furnished with antiques, crystal chandeliers, and a Louis XV-style elevator cage that has been retired from service and put on display in the lobby. The Belle Epoque–style restaurant serves standard French fare. ◆ 2 Pl des Pyramides (at Rue de Rivoli). 01.42.60.31.10; fax 01.40.15.95.16; helene@regina-hotel.com; www.regina-hotel.com. Métro: Tuileries

111 Le Canard Enchaîné France's famous leftist satirical weekly, celebrated for its irreverent cartoons and editorials, is based here. The paper specializes in covering scandals and is usually first to the scene of the crime. ◆ 173 Rue St-Honoré (between Rues de l'Echelle and des Pyramides). 01.42.60.31.36. Métros: Tuileries, Pyramides, Palais Royal–Musée du Louvre

112 Gargantua ★★$$ King Kong could leave here with a full tummy—the portions are so grand, the food (lamb curry, salmon and spinach tarts, foie gras) so delicious, the prices so reasonable. There's a lunch counter in the rear, but this is mainly a take-out place. Pastries, charcuterie, wines, and salads are packed to go. The croissants and *pain au chocolat* are renowned. ◆ Daily breakfast, lunch, and dinner. 284 Rue St-Honoré (between Rues de l'Echelle and des Pyramides). 01.42.60.52.54. Métros: Tuileries, Pyramides, Palais Royal–Musée du Louvre

112 Auberge des Trois Bonheurs ★★$$ Despite the oh-so-French name, classic, elegant Chinese cuisine is what you'll find here. The chef is from Hong Kong and specializes in steamed trout, Peking duck, and jumbo shrimp *à la Cantonaise*. The pretty dining room has Chinese paintings on the walls and fresh flowers on the tables. ◆ Daily lunch and dinner. Reservations recommended. 280 Rue St-Honoré (between Rues de l'Echelle and des Pyramides). 01.42.60.43.24. Métros: Tuileries, Pyramides, Palais Royal–Musée du Louvre

113 Place André-Malraux In 1874, this square, formerly called Place du Théâtre-Français, was graced by a duo of elegant but simple Davioud fountains decorated with bronze nymphs by Carrier-Belleuse and Math Moreau. ◆ Métro: Palais Royal–Musée du Louvre

114 163 Rue St-Honoré Here once stood the old **St-Honoré Gate,** where Joan of Arc was wounded in the thigh by an English archer in 1429. She was hit while measuring the depth of the moat with her lance in preparation for an assault on the city. ◆ Between Rues de Rohan and de l'Echelle. Métro: Palais Royal–Musée du Louvre

115 Hôtel du Louvre $$$ This modern 200-room hotel—fully renovated in 1998—is situated beside the **Palais Royal, Tuileries,** and **Comédie Française,** and within walking distance of the **Opéra** and the **Louvre.** It offers contemporary comforts, traditional Second Empire–style decor, and a brasserie. Request the **Pissarro Suite,** from which the artist

painted the Place du Théâtre-Français.
♦ Pl André-Malraux and Rue de Rohan.
01.44.58.38.38; fax 01.44.58.38.00;
www.hoteldulouvre.com. Métro: Palais
Royal–Musée du Louvre

115 A la Civette For more than two centuries this store has been in the forefront of tobacconists—it was the first shop in Paris to import the fine Montecristo cigar from Cuba. Shelves are cluttered with chewing tobacco, pipes, cigarillos, and stogies to delight the wheeziest connoisseur. ♦ M-Sa. 157 Rue St-Honoré (between Pl du Palais-Royal and Rue de Rohan). 01.42.96.04.99. Métro: Palais Royal–Musée du Louvre

115 Delamain The window of this wonderful old bookshop displays museum-worthy items, from 18th-century hand-bound volumes on King Clovis to modern editions of Samuel Beckett. ♦ M-Sa 10AM-10:30PM. 155 Rue St-Honoré (between Pl du Palais-Royal and Rue de Rohan). 01.42.61.48.78. Métro: Palais Royal–Musée du Louvre

116 Le Louvre des Antiquaires An association of more than 240 antique shops encompasses 3 floors here. You'll find Art Deco prints, period perfume bottles, miniature 16th century manuscripts, rare Japanese woodcuts, fin de siècle dolls and children's clothes, African tribal masks, and Thai Buddhas. In fact, one can find any old thing here except a bargain. Be advised that many of these dealers have their main antique shops (generally larger and less expensive) on the Left Bank, so take a card and pay them a visit when you're on the other side of the river. Also, before making a purchase, be sure you understand the complicated regulations concerning the removal of antiques from the country.

This building was formerly the **Grand Hôtel du Louvre,** where Mark Twain stayed in 1867. It was here that Twain met the tour guide Ferguson who figures in *The Innocents Abroad* (1869). ♦ Tu-Su; closed Sunday in July and August. 2 Pl du Palais-Royal (at Rue de Rivoli). 01.42.97.27.00. Métro: Palais Royal–Musée du Louvre

117 Maison Micro This Greek bazaar offers produce from Hellas: vats of olives and hot peppers, burlap sacks of whole grains and flour, crates of dried fruits, and barrels of *tarama*. Step inside and take a whiff of the Aegean. ♦ M 2-7PM; Tu-Sa 10AM-12:30PM, 1:30PM-7PM. 142-44 Rue St-Honoré (between Rues du Louvre and Jean-Jacques-Rousseau). 01.42.60.53.02. Métro: Louvre-Rivoli

117 Chez Nous ★$$ The city's best jock bar and restaurant is run by Gilbert Ghiraldi, an ex-rugby player. If you manage to outmaneuver the French national rugby team

that huddles here, grab a table and order one of the Basque specialties. ♦ Daily lunch and dinner. 150 Rue St-Honoré (between Rues du Louvre and Jean-Jacques-Rousseau). 01.42.61.76.28. Métro: Louvre-Rivoli

118 Christian Louboutin The specialty of this women's shoe designer is shoes with hand-sculpted heels. The heels covered in gold leaf give you a dazzling walk. ♦ M-Sa. 19 Rue Jean-Jacques-Rousseau (at Galerie Véro-Dodat). 01.42.36.05.31. Métro: Louvre-Rivoli

119 Galerie Véro-Dodat Named after two pork butchers who were here from the start, this covered passageway was the city's first public thoroughfare to be illuminated by gas lighting. ♦ Métros: Louvre-Rivoli, Palais Royal–Musée du Louvre

On Galerie Véro-Dodat:

Robert Capia This antiques shop specializes in dolls, and old photographs and old phonograph records, including original recordings of Sarah Bernhardt and Enrico Caruso. The store is a favorite of Catherine Deneuve. ♦ M-Sa. Nos. 24-26. 01.42.36.25.94

Restaurant Véro-Dodat ★★$$ Tasty nouvelle cuisine is served in this charming little restaurant In Paris's prettiest *galerie*, with a prix-fixe menu that offers a great range of tempting choices at prices that are more than reasonable. Duck pâté with mushrooms and cream sauce; white leeks with balsamic sauce and goat cheese; sea bass poached with saffron sauce; roast lamb with garlic sauce; and apples, walnuts and cream in a pastry shell with Grand Marnier are a few of the items featured. ♦ M lunch; Tu-Sa lunch and dinner; closed in August. Reservations recommended. No. 19. 01.45.08.92.06

120 L'Epi d'Or ★★$$ This humble 1950s Les Halles standby serves honest fillets of herring with warm potatoes, ham hock and lentils, *entrecôte bordelaise* (beef rib steak with Bordeaux-style brown sauce), *magret de canard de Landes aux cerises aiguës et airelles* (duck breast from Landes with sour cherries and cranberries), and unsophisticated Rhônes and Bordeaux. ♦ M-F lunch and dinner; Sa dinner; closed in August. Reservations recommended. 25 Rue Jean-Jacques-Rousseau (between Galerie Véro-Dodat and Pl des 2-Ecus). 01.42.36.38.12. Métro: Louvre-Rivoli

121 Palais Royal This six-acre enclave of flowering serenity is surrounded by, yet separate from, the urban bustle. Commissioned by Cardinal Richelieu and designed by his architect **Jacques Lemercier** in 1642, the mansion was christened **Palais Royal** when Anne of Austria temporarily lived here with her son, young Louis XIV. In 1780 the property fell into the hands of the shrewd

Philippe, Duke of Orléans, who embarked on a lucrative and fancy bit of real estate speculation. He hired the architect **Victor Louis** (who built the nearby **Théâtre Français**) to design a square like Venice's Piazza San Marco, but containing a garden (700 feet by 300 feet) to be faced on 3 sides with elegant apartments incorporating arcades that had space for 180 shops, which the duke then sold for immense profit. (He also named the bordering streets after his three sons: Valois, Beaujolais, and Montpensier.)

Strolling through the lime-tree groves here became the fashion for French aristocrats as well as for visitors from across the Atlantic, including Thomas Jefferson and Washington Irving. The garden's elegance soon frayed, however, when the profligate Philippe became chronically broke and began renting the galleries to magicians, wax museums, circuses, and brothels. Under his dissolute management, the palace and gardens attracted the Parisian rabble, questionable dandies, and women of easy virtue; it became a raffish, depraved enclave. (As late as 1804, historians listed the presence of 11 loan sharks, 18 gambling houses, and 17 billiard halls in the palace arcades.) Marat referred to the gardens as the "nucleus of the Revolution." It was here that Charlotte Corday bought the dagger she used to kill Marat. It was also here on 13 July 1789 that Camille Desmoulins incited his fellow Parisians to take up arms. Like the **Tuileries Palace,** the **Palais Royal** was ransacked during the revolt of 1848; a giant bonfire was kindled in the courtyard with gilt chairs, paintings, and canopies thrown from the windows by the mob. Among the furniture destroyed was the throne on which Louis Philippe first sat as king of France.

By the 20th century the luxurious apartments overlooking the gardens housed a number of famous residents. Poet and dramatist Jean Cocteau lived here, as did writer Colette. She resided at 9 Rue de Beaujolais and was often seen writing at her window overlooking the courtyard. Colette died as stylishly as she'd lived: suddenly and painlessly after drinking a glass of Champagne.

Today the buildings of the **Palais Royal** house private residences and offices that are closed to the public. However, visitors may stroll through the gardens and browse among the antiques, old books, jewelry, lead soldiers, medals, and rare stamps in the arcade's curiosity shops. The garden is embellished by the fountain where the infant Louis XIV once sailed his toy boats, and by two quite modern fountains resembling giant ball bearings. The larger court of the palace has been the focus of an aesthetic debate reminiscent of the one surrounding the **Louvre** transformation. Minister of Culture Jack Lang initiated a project (conceived by sculptor Daniel Buren) that involved the planting of 252 black-and-white striped columns, deep pools, and airport lights in the courtyard floor. In the winter of 1986 residents of the palace who objected to the scheme won a court order to halt construction on the site temporarily. The project, however, was completed the following summer. ♦ Bounded by Rues de Valois and de Montpensier, and Pl du Palais-Royal and Rue de Beaujolais. Métros: Palais Royal–Musée du Louvre, Pyramides, Bourse

Within the Palais Royal:

Le Grand Véfour ★★★★$$$$
A favorite haunt since the 1760s, this glamorous restaurant is named after Jean Véfour, chef to Philippe, the Duke of Orléans (who voted to send his relative Louis XVI to the guillotine and later wound up there himself). Seductively and appropriately timeworn, the gilt and wood-paneled Louis XVI–Directoire interior with the famous red velvet banquettes is classified as a historic monument. Here Napoléon courted Joséphine, Victor Hugo romanticized, and Colette and Jean Cocteau, who lived nearby, enjoyed regular repasts. The menu offers exquisite cuisine *gastronomique* by chef Guy Martin; favorites include foie gras ravioli with truffle cream, noisettes of lamb with fennel sauce, wild duck with quince, *parmentier de queue de boeuf* (oxtail with puréed potatoes), and *galette aux endives* (endive cake). Don't miss the rare cheeses and the Burgundy wines. ♦ M-F lunch and dinner; closed in August. Reservations required. 17 Rue de Beaujolais (between Rues de Valois and de Montpensier). 01.42.96.56.27

122 Comédie Française In 1673, while performing in his own *Le Malade Imaginaire,* the 51-year-old dramatist Molière collapsed onstage and died as the curtain came down. (Legend has it that there were several doctors in the audience who were so enraged by the play's criticism of medicine that they would not treat its dying author.) Seven years later Louis XIV founded the **Comédie Française** with the remaining members of the playwright's troupe. Today it is France's most prestigious theatrical group, residing since the end of the 18th century in this rather small Doric-style theater designed by **Victor Louis.** The company has survived the Bourbon monarchy, the Revolution, two empires, and four republics, and still plays to packed houses. After Molière, the theater's most celebrated thespian was the spirited tragic actress Sarah Bernhardt (the "Divine Sarah," born Rosine Bernard in Paris), who played roles ranging from Cleopatra to Hamlet, thereby reviving Shakespeare in

France. Bernhardt was a dynamic character who was fond of saying, even in old age, "Rest? With all eternity before me?"

Today the **Comédie Française** is the bastion of French theater. It aims to keep classical theater alive while also staging works by the best modern playwrights, both French and foreign. A foyer-bar opens onto a gallery displaying busts of famous playwrights. The upstairs foyer is graced with a notable stone statue of Voltaire by Houdon and the leather armchair into which Molière collapsed during his last act on stage.

Additional theatrical performances may be seen at the **Comédie Française Studio Théâtre** at the **Carrousel du Louvre** (99 Rue de Rivoli, between Rue de l'Amiral-de-Coligny and Ave du Général-Lemonnier, 01.44.58.98.58). Reservations are not accepted at this venue; tickets are sold one hour before each performance. ♦ Individual tours: third Su of each month at 10:15AM starting at the administration entrance on the Place Colette. Group tours: second and fourth Su of each month (must be reserved three to four months in advance). Box office: daily; a special window around the side of the building opens 45 minutes before the curtain to sell reduced-price tickets for the night's performance. 2 Rue de Richelieu (at Pl André-Malraux). 01.44.58.15.15. Métro: Palais Royal–Musée du Louvre

123 Manufacture Nationale de Sèvres (Sèvres Porcelain Factory) This showroom is an outlet for the famous and venerable (ca. 1738) Sèvres porcelain factory. An exhibition of designs ranges from Louis XVI dinner plates to contemporary pieces by Louise Bourgeois. All items sold here are tax-free. ♦ M-F. 4 Pl André-Malraux (between Rue de Richelieu and Ave de l'Opéra). 01.47.03.40.20. Métro: Palais Royal–Musée du Louvre

124 Pierre au Palais Royal ★★★$$$ In the shadow of the **Comédie Française,** this restaurant, entered through a deluxe flower shop, offers a warm immersion in the mood of France's Massif Central region. Try veal kidneys, roast rabbit with mustard sauce, *gratin dauphinois* (potatoes au gratin), or the refined pike with chives. ♦ M-Sa lunch and dinner. Reservations recommended. 10 Rue de Richelieu (between Pl André-Malraux and Rue des Petits-Champs). 01.42.96.09.17. Métros: Palais Royal–Musée du Louvre, Pyramides

124 Montpensier $$ Once the residence of a baroness who was a favorite of Louis XV, this hotel lacks the style that such a history suggests. The 43 plain rooms are of varying dimensions, and the room rates vary accordingly. There's no restaurant. ♦ 12 Rue de Richelieu (between Pl André-Malraux and Rue des Petits-Champs). 01.42.96.28.50; fax 01.42.86.02.70. Métros: Palais Royal–Musée du Louvre, Pyramides

124 Dynasty ★★$ Reasonably priced, this Chinese restaurant with pink tablecloths features a menu that's enlivened by several incendiary Thai specialties. ♦ M-Sa lunch and dinner. 12 Rue de Richelieu (between Pl André-Malraux and Rue des Petits-Champs). 01.42.86.06.58. Métros: Palais Royal–Musée du Louvre, Pyramides

125 L'Incroyable Restaurant ★$ What's incredible about Claude and William Breyer's eight-table restaurant hidden on a narrow cobbled passage are the generous portions and bargain prices. Traditional French dishes—*cuisses de canard confit sucrée d'oignons* (duck thighs with sugared onions), sautéed potatoes, and *clafouti* (apple, cherry, and black currant baked custard)—are served. ♦ M, Sa lunch; Tu-F, Su dinner. No credit cards accepted. 26 Rue de Richelieu (between Pl André-Malraux and Rue des Petits-Champs). 01.42.96.24.64. Métros: Palais Royal–Musée du Louvre, Pyramides

125 La Boutique du Bridgeur The only store in Paris catering strictly to bridge players, this boutique sells bridge tables, score pads, playing cards, and instruction manuals. If you write in advance, its affiliated bridge club might help find you a partner. ♦ M-Sa. 28 Rue de Richelieu (between Pl André-Malraux and Rue des Petits-Champs). 01.42.96.25.50. Métros: Palais Royal–Musée du Louvre, Pyramides

126 Les Boucholeurs ★★$$ *Boucholeurs* are the farmers who cultivate the small, finer tasting variety of mussels featured in many of the dishes served here. These particular mussels come from a *parc à huitres* (oyster farm) near La Rochelle on the west coast, while the bankers and stockbrokers who eat them come from the nearby **Bourse.** Try the superb *mouclade Rochelaise* (small mussels in a creamy saffron and Cognac sauce) with a bottle of Fiefs Vendéen de Pissotte. Other specialties include *moules sauce au gingembre* (mussels in a ginger sauce), *moules au curry,* and haddock *poché.* Intimate and tasteful, the small blue dining room has subtle nautical details. ♦ M-F lunch and dinner; Sa dinner; closed the first two weeks of May (or whenever the mussel season has run its course), and two weeks in mid-August. Reservations recommended. 34 Rue de Richelieu (between Pl André-Malraux and Rue des Petits-Champs). 01.42.96.06.86. Métro: Pyramides

---

Restaurants/Clubs: Red	**Hotels:** Blue
Shops/♥ Outdoors: Green	**Sights/Culture:** Black

126 Matsuri Sushi ★$$ Customers hunker around a circular bar to snag plates of raw salmon and tuna sailing by on a conveyor belt. To tally the check, waiters simply count the dishes in front of each diner. At lunch, every fifth item is free. So is home delivery throughout the day within Paris city limits. ♦ M-F lunch and dinner; Sa dinner; closed in August. 36 Rue de Richelieu (between Pl André-Malraux and Rue des Petits-Champs). Reservations 01.42.61.05.73, delivery 01.40.26.12.13. Métro: Pyramides

127 Fontaine Molière The fountain, designed by **Ludovico Visconti,** was dedicated in 1773, the centennial of the playwright's death. Seurre's statue of Molière, pen in hand, is seated atop, flanked on either side by marble statues by Pradier representing light and serious comedy. ♦ Rues Molière and de Richelieu. Métro: Pyramides

128 Le Poquelin ★★$$ Original nouvelle cuisine is served here; menu items include steamed fish with mushrooms, salmon *unilatérale* (cooked on one side), spicy chicken, and roast game. Top off your meal with a hot apple tart. The formal dining room has red theater curtains and a big portrait of Molière (né Jean-Baptiste Poquelin). Actors from the nearby **Comédie Française** dine here. ♦ M-F lunch and dinner; Sa dinner; closed first three weeks of August. Reservations recommended. 17 Rue Molière (between Ave de l'Opéra and Rue Thérèse). 01.42.96.22.19. Métro: Pyramides

129 Chez Pauline ★★$$$ When tradition works this well, why change? This relaxed restaurant serves such French classics as *boeuf bourguignon, poularde de Bresse* (chicken from Bresse), creamed wild mushrooms with chives, warm foie gras salad, fricassee of sole and crayfish, game in season, and a variety of plats du jour, such as stuffed cabbage, cassoulet with preserved goose, bacon with lentils, and calf's liver. ♦ M-F lunch and dinner, Sa dinner Jan-May, Sept-Dec; M-F lunch and dinner June-Aug. Reservations recommended. 5 Rue Villedo (between Rues de Richelieu and Ste-Anne). 01.42.96.20.70. Métro: Pyramides

130 Juveniles ★★$$ This lively *bistrot à vin* just down the street from the **Bibliothèque Nationale de France** is the brainchild of wine-lovers Mark Williamson (of **Willi's Wine Bar,** see below) and his partner, Tim Johnston. It's a comfortable spot for noshing on tapas, grilled quail, chicken wings, and salads, or on more substantial fare, including grilled tuna steak, sautéed lamb chops with ratatouille, and lamb curry, and afterwards enjoying a slice of the dense, flourless chocolate cake. Wash it all down with a reasonably priced Rioja or one of the many other excellent wines from Spain, Italy, France, and Australia. ♦ M-

Sa lunch and dinner. 47 Rue de Richelieu (between Rues Villedo and des Petits-Champs). 01.42.97.46.49. Métro: Pyramides

131 Macéo ★★★$$ It may be named after funk sax man Maceo Parker, but there's nothing funky about Mark Williamson's latest food and wine venture, two steps down the street from his wine bar. Williamson kept the Rococo ceilings, large mirrors, and zinc bar left by the previous occupant, the staid old **Mercure Galant** restaurant, but made it into an elegantly modern dining space with blonde wood paneling and burgundy walls, and curtainless windows to let in the light.

Complementing the decor is Jean-Paul Deyries's bright, sophisticated cuisine, with a menu that changes daily, following the seasons. Pumpkin soup with oysters, carpaccio of salmon with pesto, *sandre* (a perchlike fresh water fish) in a casserole with clams and shallots, Lozère lamb roasted with rosemary and sea salt, and preserved chestnut tart with a bitter cocoa sauce, or warm almond tart with chopped mangoes, are but a few of the young chef's imaginative offerings. The restaurant also offers vegetarian gastronomic menus daily. The wine list is large, eclectic, and absolutely splendid, with great and intriguing wines from all over the world, but especially strong on southern France. This is the perfect place to sample the marvelous wines of Bandol or Palette, or a Châteauneuf-du-Pape from the illustrious Château de Beaucastel. ♦ M-Sa lunch and dinner. Reservations recommended. 15 Rue des Petits-Champs (between Rues Vivienne and de Richelieu). 01.42.97.53.85. Métros: Bourse, Pyramides

131 Willi's Wine Bar ★★$$ The city's most elegant wine bar bustles nonstop with journalists, lawyers, fashion designers, and the public relations crowd who come to partake of 300 French wines and such changing daily specials as grilled fillet of sea bass, guinea fowl with olives, peppers, and sage, sautéed lamb with thyme, veal chops in sherry with grilled polenta, and other inventive bistro fare. The place is run by the affable Brit Mark Williamson, who knows his Côtes du Rhônes. ♦ M-Sa lunch and dinner. Reservations recommended. 13 Rue des Petits-Champs (between Rues Vivienne and de Richelieu). 01.42.61.05.09. Métros: Bourse, Pyramides

131 Herboristerie du Palais-Royal Herbs, oils, and lotions for needs both medicinal and pleasurable are crammed floor to ceiling in this small shop. Every potion is designed to stimulate the senses. Michel Pierre, who has coauthored a book on salutary plants, can select just the herb to remedy your ailment. Passiflore from South America promotes relaxation, eleuterocoque from Siberia increases energy, and harpagophytum from Namibia helps ease arthritis and rheumatism. ♦ M-Sa. 11 Rue des Petits-Champs (between Rues Vivienne and de Richelieu). 01.42.97.54.68. Métros: Bourse, Pyramides

132 Galerie Colbert Like the adjoining **Galerie Vivienne** (see below), this arcade, opened in 1826, has enjoyed a stylish renaissance. The **Bibliothèque Nationale de France,** which owns the passage, spent millions to restore the walkways, glass-roofed rotunda, faux marble pillars, and 19th-century bronze fixtures. The *galerie* has two public exhibition halls featuring prints and photos, and a small theater that hosts lunch and evening concerts. ♦ Free. Daily. 01.47.03.85.71. Métros: Bourse, Pyramides

133 Galerie Vivienne From its mosaic floors to the arching glass canopy, this gussied-up *galerie,* established in 1823, is a most fashionable arcade. Boutiques here sell everything from high-tech jewelry and rare books to children's masks and the best brownies in Paris. ♦ Daily. Métros: Bourse, Pyramides

Within Galerie Vivienne:

Si Tu Veux Babar, the universally loved French elephant, comes in plush, plastic, or posters at this old-fashioned toy store. There are also enough paper hats and masks available here to outfit any party of six-year-olds. ♦ M-Sa. No. 68. 01.42.60.59.97. Also at: 10 Rue Vavin (between Rues d'Assas and Notre-Dame-des-Champs). 01.55.42.14.14. Métro: Notre-Dame des Champs

Jean Paul Gaultier Here's the designer boutique of the man who brought miniskirts to men and ice-cream-cone bras to women. Check out the video screens—in the floor! ♦ M-Sa. 01.42.86.05.05

Legrand Filles et Fils From the back of this Rue de la Banque *épicerie,* Francine Legrand sells French wines by the bottle, the cubit, or the case, and an astonishing array of corkscrews and other devices for opening bottles. This is the most prestigious wine shop in Paris, and one of the few important ones to remain in family hands. ♦ Tu-Sa.No. 12. 01.42.60.07.12

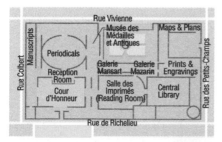

A Priori Thé ★★$ US expatriate Margaret Gilbert-Hancock owns this charming tearoom and luncheon spot, whose wicker chairs and tables decorated with silk flowers from Emilio Robba's shop next door spill into the **Galerie Vivienne.** A creative selection of quiches and salads is served, followed by divine apple crumble and brownies for dessert. Francine Legrand, whose shop (see above) is in the same arcade, chooses the wine list. ♦ M-Sa breakfast, lunch and afternoon tea; Su brunch and afternoon tea. Nos. 35-37. 01.42.97.48.75

MICHAEL STORRINGS

134 Bibliothèque Nationale de France, Site Richelieu (National Library of France, Richelieu) In 1537 a copyright act was passed to ensure that a copy of every book published in France would be housed in a royal library. Although most of this amalgamation of 4.5 centuries of book and document assembly has been moved to another site of the library, this building continues to house manuscripts, engravings, photographic material, maps and plans, coins and medals, and performing arts and music materials in a building whose architectural design is as impressive as its collection.

The library came to occupy its present site in the 17th century, when Cardinal Mazarin merged two of his mansions, the **Hôtel Tubeuf** and the **Hôtel Chivry.** The collection initially included 500 pictures and art objects owned by the cardinal himself. When Colbert, finance minister to Louis XIV, moved the library to his own mansion on Rue Vivienne in 1666, the collection numbered 200,000 volumes. In 1720, the library was combined again with the original Mazarin collection.

The library received its most dramatic space in 1854, when the architect **Henri Labrouste** was commissioned to design a reading room within the old courtyard of the **Palais Mazarin.** The result is the magnificent top-lit

Salle des Imprimés (illustrated on page 227), which consists of 9 square vaulted bays supported by 16 cast-iron columns and a network of perforated semicircular iron arches. The room reveals a further development of ideas **Labrouste** first explored in the design of his **Bibliothèque Ste-Geneviève,** a landmark building that was the first monumental public edifice to freely employ iron as both a structural and a decorative element. The reading room (admittance is for members and/or scholars only, although proof that you're an architect often works) features beautifully attenuated columns, gleaming lenslike skylights in the ceiling, and graceful curves of iron latticework. In the **Salon d'Honneur** (State Room) on the ground floor is an Houdon statue of Voltaire; the writer's heart is ensconced in the pedestal.

The library's vast book collection was transferred to the **Bibliothèque Nationale de France, Site François Mitterand/Tolbiac** (see page 246) when it opened in 1998. What remains here is reserved for researchers and scholars; none are open to the public except for one weekend every year in October, although tours are given to the public one day a month. Groups may arrange for private tours by calling ahead.

There are several public galleries and exhibition spaces in the library. The **Musée des Médailles et Antiques** features a collection of vases, precious stones, jewelry, furniture, and other antique objets d'art. The **Galeries Mazarin** and **Mansart** and the **Photo Galerie Colbert** mount temporary exhibitions. ◆ Free. Tour: first Tu of the month 2:30PM. Galeries Mazarin and Mansart: open for special exhibitions only. Musée des Médailles et Antiques: M-Sa 1-5PM; Su noon-6PM. Galerie Colbert: M-Sa noon-6:30PM. 58 Rue de Richelieu (between Rues des Petits-Champs and Colbert). 01.47.03.81.26. Métros: Bourse, Pyramides

135 Brûlerie San José The Cahen family, owners of this tiny stand-up coffee bar, roast their own beans and serve the best cappuccino in town. At midday, neighborhood workers seeking a caffeine fix swarm here. ◆ M-F 7AM-7PM. 30 Rue des Petits-Champs (between Rues Chabanais and Ste-Anne). 01.42.96.69.09. Métro: Pyramides

136 Issé ★★★$$$ One of the city's best (and most expensive) sushi bars also serves impeccable sashimi, grilled salmon, steaming miso soup, red caviar, delectably light tempura, and *chirashi* (raw fish on a bed of rice and served in a large bowl), the house specialty. ◆ M, Sa dinner; Tu-F lunch and dinner. Reservations recommended. 56 Rue Ste-Anne (at Rue Rameau). 01.42.96.67.76. Métros: Pyramides, Bourse, Quatre Septembre

137 Restaurant Drouant ★★★$$$$ At the end of each November since 1914, 10 novelists have met here to award the Prix Goncourt, France's prestigious prize for the year's best fiction. (The prize isn't much money, but fame and fortune in the form of lucrative publishing contracts follow.) The wood-paneled **Salon Goncourt** with its round table for 10 and the magnificent staircase designed by **Emile Rhulmann,** "the Pope of Art Deco," in 1930 are the highlights of this century-old restaurant's decor. The specialties are turbot roasted in clay, Bresse chicken with onion and lemon chutney, and a chocolate and pistachio fondant. The dining room is popular with the elegant crowd from the **Opéra.** If you forget to make reservations, consider having a meal in the cafe. ◆ Daily lunch and dinner. Reservations required. 18 Rue Gaillon (at Pl Gaillon). 01.42.65.15.16. Métros: Quatre Septembre, Opéra

138 La Tour de Jade ★★$ This Vietnamese and Chinese eatery was founded by a former minister to Indochina's Emperor Bao-Dai. Sautéed mussels and curry, sautéed lamb with ginger, whole pomtret fish with hot sauce, and duck with lotus seeds, and grilled prawns Vietnam style are the menu highlights. The dining room has the typical Chinese-restaurant decor—dim lighting, simple furniture, and kitschy decorative items. ◆ M-Sa lunch and dinner; Su dinner. 20 Rue de la Michodière (between Rue de Hanovre and Blvd des Italiens). 01.47.42.07.56. Métro: Quatre Septembre

139 5 Rue des Italiens The prestigious Parisian daily newspaper *Le Monde* is headquartered here. ◆ Between Blvd des Italiens and Rue Taitbout. Métros: Quatre Septembre, Richelieu-Drouot

140 Au Petit Riche ★★$$ A favorite of journalists, this lively 1880 restaurant, all mahogany, mirrors, and polished brass, offers fresh *fruits de mer* (mixed seafood), tasty Lyonnais sausage, roast lamb, duck served with figs, hot apple tarts, and carafes of Bourgueil. It's a popular spot for after the theater. ◆ M-Sa lunch and dinner until 1:30AM. Reservations recommended. 25 Rue Le Peletier (at Blvd Haussmann). 01.47.70.68.68. Métro: Richelieu-Drouot

141 Hôtel Drouot The closest thing to a Sotheby's in Paris, this establishment specializes in estate sales and auctions of everything from Cartier jewels, Louis XIV furniture, and African sculpture to baskets of kitchenware and collections of rare illustrated manuscripts. On the top floor, the most valuable objets d'art are overseen by renowned auctioneers Ader Picard. Auctions take place in the afternoon starting at 2PM, but arrive early to scan the merchandise—a great experience in itself. ◆ M-Sa; occasionally on Sunday. 9

Rue Drouot (at Rue Rossini). 01.48.00.20.20. Métro: Richelieu-Drouot

142 Chopin $$ Amid shops selling old books, toys, and clothes in the glass-covered **Passage Jouffroy** (which is classified as a historic monument), this charming hotel with salmon-colored wallpaper and green carpets offers 36 small rooms at correspondingly small rates. Some rooms have skylights. There's no restaurant. ◆ 46 Passage Jouffroy (between Blvd Montmartre and Rue de la Grange-Batelière). 01.47.70.58.10; fax 01.42.47.00.70. Métro: Grands Boulevards

143 Chartier ★$ This cavernous turn-of-the-century soup kitchen with pinwheel fans and surly waiters offers better theater than cuisine, but it's worth a visit nevertheless. Basic, inexpensive French food—egg salad, pâté, roast chicken—is served with rough red wine. The place is always mobbed with tourists, so get here early. ◆ Daily lunch and dinner until 9:30PM. 7 Rue du Faubourg-Montmartre (between Blvd Montmartre and Rue de la Grange-Batelière). 01.47.70.86.29. Métro: Grands Boulevards. Also at: 103 Rue de Richelieu (between Rue St-Marc and Blvd des Italiens). 01.42.96.68.23. Métro: Richelieu-Drouot

144 Musée Grevin The city's largest wax museum is populated with distinguished paraffin personalities, including Charles de Gaulle, Catherine Deneuve, Woody Allen, Yehudi Menuhin, Bill Clinton, Tony Blair, and Leonardo di Caprio. Children love it. ◆ Admission. Daily 1-7PM. 10 Blvd Montmartre (between Rue du Faubourg-Montmartre and Passage Jouffroy). 01.47.70.85.05. Métro: Grands Boulevards

145 49 Rue Vivienne On this site stood the **Salle Musard,** a concert hall where Tom Thumb, headliner for P.T. Barnum's show, performed in 1844. An office building stands here now. ◆ Between Rue St-Marc and Blvd Montmartre. Métros: Bourse, Richelieu-Drouot, Grands Boulevards

146 Aux Lyonnais ★★$$ Long patronized by **Bourse des Valeurs** traders in the neighborhood, this bistro's reputation is founded on classic, unadventurous cuisine. ◆ M-F lunch and dinner; Sa dinner. Reservations recommended. 32 Rue St-Marc (between Rues de Richelieu and Favart). 01.42.96.65.04. Métro: Richelieu-Drouot

147 Passage des Panoramas Nineteenth-century US inventor Robert Fulton painted and displayed 18 panoramas in 2 large cylindrical towers off Boulevard Montmartre. The French flocked to see the sagas, and, with his profits, Fulton bankrolled his steamboat and submarine schemes. ◆ Between Rue St-Marc and Blvd Montmarte. Métros: Bourse, Grands Boulevards

148 Clementine ★★$$ In this homey bistro named after the owner's daughter, chef Franck Langrenne prepares savory, unpretentious fare, with a handwritten menu that changes daily. Starters of homemade foie gras or mackerel croquettes and main dishes of rabbit in lemon mustard sauce, lamb chops with garlic, and roast chicken with chèvre are some of the possible choices. As for dessert, the luscious dark chocolate fondant is always available. The service is unusually relaxed and friendly. ◆ M-F lunch and dinner. Reservations recommended. 5 Rue St-Marc (between Rues Montmartre and Vivienne). 01.40.41.05.65. Métros: Bourse, Grands Boulevards

149 Le Vaudeville ★★$$ This vintage 1925 brasserie was rescued from decline and obscurity by brasserie king Jean-Paul Bucher and is now packed at lunchtime by execs from the **Bourse des Valeurs,** and at night by theater patrons. Specialties include *andouillette* (tripes*),* foie gras, grilled lobster, shellfish (year-round), homemade *saumon rillette* (salmon spread), and a chilled house Riesling. Dining on the sidewalk is pleasant in summer. ◆ Daily lunch and dinner until 2AM. Reservations recommended. 29 Rue Vivienne (between Rues du Quatre-Septembre and de la Bourse). 01.40.20.04.62. Métro: Bourse

150 Bourse des Valeurs (Stock Exchange) Napoléon commissioned this "Temple of Money" in 1808, and architect **Alexandre Théodore Brongniart** was inspired to adorn it with 64 massive Corinthian columns. The building's design is epic, befitting the frenzied battles that once took place on its trading floor. But in 1987, the *corbeille* (the basket), as the trading area is called, was closed, and all stock trades are now done through a decentralized computer network. Nevertheless, visitors are welcome to tour the building and see the old trading floor. There are guided tours in French and English, an audiovisual program that shows how a stock market works, and a small museum of stock market memorabilia. ◆ Free. M-F 1:15-5PM. Rue Notre-Dame-des-Victoires and Pl de la Bourse. 01.40.41.62.20. Métro: Bourse

151 Hollywood Savoy ★★$$ This stockbrokers' luncheon canteen becomes a nightclub when the **Bourse des Valeurs** goes to sleep. Waiters and waitresses join the band and the featured singer belts out creditable renditions of "Stormy Monday" and other Yankee classics. As for the cuisine, the foie gras, grilled fish and meat, and other simply prepared classics are fine. ◆ M-Sa lunch and dinner until 1AM. Reservations recommended. 44 Rue Notre-Dame-des-Victoires (between Rues Réaumur and Montmartre). 01.42.36.16.73. Métro: Bourse

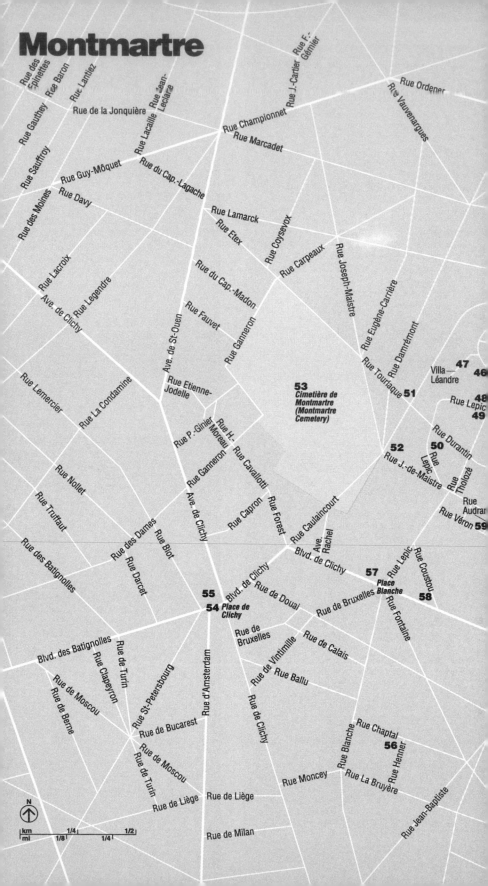

Montmartre

Rue des Spinettes
Rue Baron
Rue Lantiez
Rue Gauthey
Rue de la Jonquière
Rue Jean-Leclaire
Rue Lacalle
Rue J.-Cartier
Rue F.-Gémier
Rue Ordener
Rue Vauvenargues
Rue Sauffroy
Rue Guy-Môquet
Rue du Cap.-Lagache
Rue Championnet
Rue Marcadet
Rue des Moines
Rue Davy
Rue Lamarck
Rue Etex
Rue Lacroix
Rue Coysevox
Rue Legendre
Rue du Cap.-Madon
Rue Carpeaux
Ave. de Clichy
Rue Fauvet
Rue Joseph-Maistre
Rue Eugène-Carrière
Ave. de St-Ouen
Rue Gannéron
Rue Damrémont
Rue Lemercier
Rue La Condamine
Rue Etienne-Jodelle
Rue Tourlaque

Villa—Léandre

47
46

53
Cimetière de
Montmartre
(Montmartre
Cemetery)

48
Rue Lepic
49

Rue P.-Ginier
Rue H.-Moreau
Rue Cavallotti
52
Rue J.-de-Maistre

Rue Durantin

50
Rue Lepic

51

Rue Gannéron

Rue Nollet
Ave. de Clichy
Rue Tholozé

Rue Truffaut
Rue Capron
Rue Forest
Rue Audran
Rue Véron
59

Rue des Batignolles
Rue des Dames
Rue Biot
Rue Caulaincourt
Ave. Rachel

Rue Darcet
Blvd. de Clichy

55
Blvd. de Clichy
Rue de Douai
Blvd. de Clichy
Rue Lepic
Rue Coustou

57
Place
Blanche
58

54 Place de
Clichy
Rue de Bruxelles
Rue Fontaine

Blvd. des Batignolles
Rue de Turin
Rue de Bruxelles
Rue de Vintimille
Rue de Calais

Rue de Moscou
Rue Clapeyron
Rue St-Petersbourg
Rue de Vintimille
Rue Ballu

Rue de Berne
Rue d'Amsterdam
Rue de Clichy

Rue de Bucarest
Rue Chaptal
56
Rue Henner

Rue de Moscou
Rue Blanche
Rue La Bruyère

Rue de Turin
Rue Moncey

Rue de Liège
Rue de Liège
Rue Jean-Baptiste

N

km
mi
1/4
1/2
1/8
1/4

Rue de Milan

Montmartre

Crowned with that alabaster wedding-cake church known as **Sacré-Coeur,** Montmartre is the balcony of Paris—half dream, half nightmare. It is a tangle of contradictions: meandering country roads, seedy strip joints, early Christian sites, tourist clichés, sublime vistas, and hidden passages. The **Butte** (which is what Parisians call this sandstone height) is geographically the highest point in town (427 feet) and the traditional home of poets, singers, painters, and bohemians of all kinds.

The best day to visit Montmartre is on Tuesday, when many museums in other parts of Paris are closed, or any day when you feel like fleeing the center of the city for a few hours. Emerging from **Hector Guimard's** Art Nouveau **Abbesses** métro station, start your tour with café au lait and brioches in one of the cafes along **Rue des Abbesses**, which is crowded with butchers, bakers, and fishmongers from the **Rue Lepic** market. Then begin the ascent to **Place du Tertre**, a 14th-century square that in summer harbors a lively crowd of street artists, outdoor restaurant waiters, and tourists. The best bets for lunch are crepes at **Le Tire Bouchon** or fish at **La Crémaillère 1900** on Place du Tertre. After the obligatory pilgrimage to **Sacré-Coeur**, wind down Rue Lepic past the **Moulin de la Galette** until you see the red neon signs of the Butte's other storied temple, the **Moulin Rouge.** Come back later in the evening for the can-can show or for the cabaret at the legendary **Au Lapin Agile.** Métro service ends at 12:45AM, but you'll find a taxi just down the hill on **Rue Caulaincourt**, which is filled with revelers during the wine-festival parade held in October.

The name Montmartre has two possible origins: the "Mount of Mercury," for the Roman temple to Mercury that once stood on the Butte, or the "Mount of Martyrs," commemorating St. Denis, the first bishop of Paris, who, along with the priest Rusticus and the deacon Eleutherius, was tortured and decapitated here by the Romans in AD 250. According to the legend, St. Denis picked up his severed head and carried it from Montmartre to another hill several kilometers to the north. A thousand years later, the **Basilique de St-Denis** was built on that hill. Streets in Montmartre were named for the priest and deacon, who did not join St. Denis in the headless trek.

A lesser-known local martyr is mill owner Pierre-Charles Debray, who during the Franco-Prussian War was crucified on the blades of his **Moulin de la Galette**, a windmill with a garden tavern and dance hall that a half-century later would symbolize "Gay Paree" in a painting by Renoir. Such artists as Renoir, Van Gogh, Dufy, and Utrillo; poets Apollinaire, Max Jacob, and Jacques Prévert; and novelist Boris Vian, songwriter Aristide Bruant, and illustrator André Gill all worked in Montmartre. In the late 19th century, Toulouse-Lautrec sketched the can-can dancers at the **Moulin Rouge**, and in the early 1900s, Pablo Picasso, Georges Braque, and Juan Gris, working out of an abandoned piano factory nearby, gave birth to Cubism. Cabarets such as **Au Lapin Agile** further encouraged *la vie de bohème,* and the life was much romanticized by North Americans in Paris. Writer John Dos Passos, for instance, rhapsodized in 1918 that he wanted his heart "to be preserved in a pitcher of *vin de Beaujolais* in the restaurant in Place du Tertre on the summit of Montmartre."

After World War I, Paris's artistic center moved to another of the city's seven hills, Montparnasse, on the Left Bank. Its nightlife, however, remained in Montmartre and grew in notoriety. Though the neighborhood is the site of what is reputedly the oldest church sanctuary in Paris (**St-Pierre**) and was dominated in the 12th century by an abbey run by women, today the area is best known for women (and men disguised as women) plying an older, less pious profession. Painters may once have looked for portrait models among the seamstresses and dancers in **Place Pigalle**, but seamier live sex shows, porn theaters, and peep shops took over at the end of World War II. Nevertheless, the area is generally safe, even at night.

The Butte is packed on the weekend, especially the first Saturday and the first or second Sunday of October, the dates of the local annual wine-harvest festival and the vintage-car rally, respectively. You can avoid the masses by visiting on a weekday, or just come on the weekend and join in the joie de vivre of the crowd. For those who wish to avoid the steep climb to the top, *Le Montmartrain,* a small train, departs Place Pigalle for **Sacré-Coeur** daily every half-hour (for more information, see page 236).

1 Abbesses Métro Station Named after *les abbesses*, the nuns who ran the abbey here in the Middle Ages, this métro station is the deepest in Paris—300 feet below ground level. The reason for the great depth lies in Montmartre's old gypsum mines. Gypsum, a soft stone, was burned to make the internationally famous plaster of paris used to mold, among other things, busts of George Washington and Thomas Jefferson in the US capitol. Over the years, the growing network of quarry tunnels beneath Montmartre turned the hill, geologically speaking, to Swiss cheese. In the 1840s the mines were closed, but not before 27 houses and several Parisians had disappeared into the void. The city of Paris is still filling Montmartre's cavities with high-pressure concrete. The métro platform was built at bedrock, precisely 285 steps below Place des Abbesses. Take the elevator and save your breath for the Montmartre summit.

The turn-of-the-century exterior of the station, with its green, vinelike, wrought-iron arches and amber lights, is one of the most picturesque in Paris and typifies the early Art Nouveau designs of architect **Hector Guimard.** At first, nationalistic Parisians criticized **Guimard's** choice of German green and suggested that he paint his métro stations *bleu, blanc, et rouge* (blue, white, and red, like the French flag). His concession to chauvinism was a ship shield (the symbol of the city of Paris) in the middle of the roof, but he stubbornly held his ground on garden green. This is one of only two **Guimard** stations that still have their original glass roofs (the other is **Porte Dauphine** near the **Bois de Boulogne**). However, the **Abbesses** métro entrance is not original to the Butte. For decades it stood in front of the **Hôtel de Ville** (City Hall), but when Mayor Jacques Chirac gussied up the plaza in 1977, he moved **Guimard's** masterpiece to Montmartre. New York's Museum of Modern Art has an old *Métropolitain* sign and early **Guimard** arches similar to these. ♦ Pl des Abbesses and Rue des Abbesses

2 Hôtel Régyn's Montmartre $$ This 22-room hotel is in the heart of Montmartre, but otherwise it's nothing fancy. There's no restaurant. ♦ 18 Pl des Abbesses (at Rue des Abbesses). 01.42.54.45.21; fax 01.42.23.76.69; hotelreg@club-internet; www.paris.com. Métro: Abbesses

3 St-Jean-de-Montmartre Soon after its construction, this church, a Moorish grab bag of architectural tricks trimmed with what looks like turquoise Art Nouveau jewelry, was given the nickname "St-Jean-des-Briques" due to its redbrick facade. Looking amazingly contemporary for a nonagenarian, the 1904 church was the first in Paris built with reinforced concrete. ♦ 19-21 Rue des Abbesses (between Rues Houdon and Germain-Pilon). 01.46.06.43.96. Métro: Abbesses

4 L'Abat-Jour Patrick Rossignol and Chantal Juan want people of all ages, professions, and lifestyles to feel comfortable in their cozy hair salon. No photographs of pouty models with trendy hairdos are displayed. The stylists will cut, shape, color, or perm your hair to suit you, using many products with natural ingredients. The salon's name means "the lamp shade," which refers not to any coiffure but to the business formerly located at this address, a lamp shade manufacturer. ♦ Tu-Sa. 19 Rue Yvonne-Le-Tac (between Rue des Martyrs and Pl des Abbesses). 01.42.64.39.32. Métro: Abbesses

5 Martyrium Just off the Street of Martyrs, where St. Denis was thought to have been decapitated, is the **Chapelle des Martyres.** In the crypt of an earlier medieval sanctuary on this site, Spaniards Ignatius Loyola and Francis Xavier founded the Jesuit order of priests on 15 August 1534. ♦ M-W, F-Su. 11 Rue Yvonne-Le-Tac (between Rues des Trois-Frères and des Martyrs). No phone. Métro: Abbesses

6 Gaspard de la Butte Annie Baron and Catherine Malaure sell their original line of

colorfully patterned children's clothes in this darling little shop. You can catch a glimpse of the fabric samples and sewing machines in the backroom workshop. ◆ Daily. 10 *bis* Rue Yvonne-Le-Tac (between Rues des Trois-Frères and des Martyrs). 01.42.55.99.40. Métro: Abbesses

La Boutique des Anges

7 La Boutique des Anges Wing your way into this shop where owners Brigitte and Patricia sell everything from heavenly inspired CDs, jewelry, and lamps to books and paper goods—all with an angelic twist. One popular item is the personal guardian angel pin (selected to correspond with your birth date) designed by local artisans. ◆ Daily. 2 *bis* Rue Yvonne-Le-Tac (between Rues des Trois-Frères and des Martyrs). 01.42.57.74.38. Métro: Abbesses

8 Le Progrès ★$ Patronized by Parisians rather than tourists, this neighborhood cafe and bar is economical and authentic. The simple food isn't gourmet, but it is tasty, and decent wines are poured by the pitcher. There's a daily prix-fixe lunch—examples include roast beef and potatoes or *rognons provençaux* (kidneys with tomatoes, olive oil, and garlic). Charcuterie and cheese are served all day. ◆ M-Sa lunch and snacks until 2AM. 1 Rue Yvonne-Le-Tac (at Rue des Trois-Frères). 01.42.51.33.33. Métro: Abbesses

9 Claude & Nicole ★★$ This cozy neighborhood bistro has a faithful clientele of young Montmartre residents who come for the herring fillet, *jambon persil* (ham in parsley aspic), and *blanquette de veau* (veal with béchamel sauce and mushrooms), or one of the other rotating plats du jour. ◆ Tu-Sa lunch and dinner; Su lunch. 13 Rue des Trois-Frères (between Rues Yvonne-le-Tac and de la Vieuville). 01.46.06.12.48. Métro: Abbesses

10 Wanouchka ★$$ Eastern European immigrants swarm to this very small restaurant for classic Polish cuisine (pirogi, blintzes, Baltic herring, and borscht) prepared by chef Roman Rybicki. Forget the wine list and order the plum-and-lemon vodka—when in Warsaw, do as the Poles do. The dining room is formal, with traditional Polish decoration. ◆ M-Tu, Th-Sa dinner; Su lunch. Reservations recommended. 28 Rue la Vieuville (between Rues des Martyrs and des Trois-Frères). 01.42.57.36.15. Métro: Abbesses

Restaurants/Clubs: Red   Hotels: Blue
Shops/◆ Outdoors: Green   Sights/Culture: Black

11 Bonjour l'Artiste Sold here are juggling balls, batons, magic rings, trick cards, clown noses, and any other paraphernalia you might need in order to run away with the circus. ◆ M-Sa. 35 Rue des Trois-Frères (between Rues de la Vieuville and Ravignan). 01.42.51.44.53. Métro: Abbesses

12 Fontaine de Quatre-Grâces (Four Graces Fountain) Layered in green paint, this drinking fountain and 99 other identical ones around Paris were given to the city in the 1840s by Richard Wallace, an Englishman who collected 18th-century French art and frequently lamented that it was impossible in his beloved Paris to enjoy a glass of water in a cafe without paying for it. The metal drinking cup originally attached to it disappeared in the 1950s when the city adopted sanitation standards. ◆ Pl Emile-Goudeau. Métro: Abbesses

13 13 Place Emile-Goudeau On this site stood the famous old piano factory that art historians call the "Villa Médici of Modern Art." By the turn of the century this place had attracted poets Apollinaire and Max Jacob, and modern painters Picasso, Braque, Gris, and Modigliani. Picasso worked here for eight years, painting such works as *Les Demoiselles d'Avignon* (which is now in the collection of New York's Museum of Modern Art and is often cited as the first example of Cubism). This ramshackle building, which had but one water spigot to serve the 40 artists housed here, was sarcastically dubbed *Bateau Lavoir* after the laundry barges that used to travel along the Seine. The original structure burned in 1970, but the city of Paris built a concrete replica and now rents studios (and provides plenty of water) to the far more prosperous, though not necessarily more talented, artists of today. ◆ At Rue Ravignan. Métro: Abbesses

13 Tim Hôtel $$ Had this 60-room hotel been here in the 1920s, you might have asked neighbors Pablo Picasso or Georges Braque over for coffee and croissants. Today this member of a French budget hotel chain offers modern amenities (superior to those at most places in the same price range) but has the sterile atmosphere typical of chain hostelries. The charming location, however, makes up for the bland character. The upper-floor rooms on the south side have a spectacular view of the center of Paris. There's no restaurant. ◆ 11 Rue Ravignan (at Pl Emile-Goudeau). 01.42.55.74.79; fax 01.42.55.71.01; www.timhotel.fr. Métro: Abbesses

14 Rue de la Mire Getting lost in the twisting streets of Montmartre can be done with the greatest of ease, except on this short pedestrian street. An 18th-century *mire* (trail marker) points due north. ◆ Métro: Abbesses

15 Auberge de la Bonne Franquette ★$$
This former van Gogh studio is now an intentionally rustic restaurant/cabaret serving escargots, *confit de canard* (duck confit), and *pâté en croûte* (pâté in a pastry crust) to Japanese, Dutch, and German bus tours. Guitarist Jacques Lescure and accordion player Jacques Vassart lead the equivalent of a nightly French hootenanny and hawk their cassettes and records at intermission. ♦ Daily lunch and dinner. Reservations recommended. 18 Rue St-Rustique (between Rues du Mont-Cenis and des Saules). 01.42.52.02.42. Métro: Abbesses

16 Au Clair de la Lune ★★$$ In his cheerful restaurant with murals of **Le Moulin de la Galette** and the streets of Montmartre, talented chef Alain Kerfant presents such seasonal specialties as pheasant terrine with foie gras, fish soup with rouille, salmon steak simmered in Champagne, and wild hare casserole. Finish the meal with vanilla crème brûlée or chocolate profiteroles. The excellent wine list includes a 1993 Château Abbaye de Brandey Côtes de Castillon and 1992 Château du Terte Margaux Bordeaux. ♦ M dinner; Tu-Sa lunch and dinner. 9 Rue Poulbot (south of Rue Norvins). 01.42.58.97.03. Métro: Abbesses

17 Le Tire Bouchon Cabaret ★★$ If you're in the mood for a little "Maple Leaf Rag" to accompany an apricot crepe or some *cidre bouché* (bottled cider), go no farther: this *crêperie* has a jazz pianist upstairs playing the works of Fats Waller and Scott Joplin. The decor is reminiscent of an early-1960s Amsterdam jazz dive, with a vintage Coke dispenser, graffiti-scarred beams, and walls papered with posters and photos of stringy-haired musicians. ♦ Daily afternoon snacks, dinner, and late-night snacks until 2AM. No credit cards accepted. 9 Rue Norvins (between Pl du Tertre and Rue Poulbot). 01.42.55.12.35. Métro: Abbesses

18 Place du Tertre Part village carnival, part operetta set, this 14th-century square (*tertre* means hillock or mound) is the hub of Montmartre, where busloads of tourists descend to pay homage to the Unknown Artist's awful landscapes and pathetic paintings of melancholy wide-eyed children. In summer (when the square sprouts parasoled restaurant tables), white-aproned waiters and hustling artists jealously guard their territories; the daily border wars make for great theater. During the Middle Ages the abbey had a scaffold here to hang anyone who disobeyed its rules, including any vineyard owner on the Butte who refused to donate a quarter of the wine he pressed to the ladies of the cloth, *les abbesses*. The tradition of exhibiting paintings in Place du Tertre dates from the 19th century, but unfortunately the quality of art has deteriorated over the years. Located in front of **St-Pierre-de-Montmartre**, the square is hard to miss, though you may wish you had. ♦ Métro: Abbesses

19 La Mère Catherine ★$$ Founded in 1793 and, as house legend has it, commandeered in 1814 by the Russians who conquered the Montmartre villagers, this is still the oldest brasserie on Place du Tertre, and the waiters swagger as if to show it. You'll find escargots, rack of lamb, and *tournedos Mère Catherine* (beef fillets cooked in Port and foie gras sauce) on the menu. The dining room is adorned with Belle Epoque reproduction mirrors and red-velvet benches, and piano and violin music from the 1920s accompanies your meal. There's also outdoor dining on the terrace. ♦ Daily 9AM-1AM. 6 Pl du Tertre. 01.46.06.32.69, 01.42.58.78.21. Métro: Abbesses

19 La Bohème du Tertre ★$$ No-frills traditional French cuisine—*boeuf bourguignon,* au gratin potatoes, apple tarts—is served here. ♦ Daily 8AM-8PM; closed in January. 2 Pl du Tertre. 01.46.06.51.69. Métro: Abbesses

LA CRÉMAILLÈRE 1900

20 La Crémaillère 1900 ★★$$ This brasserie, with an arbored garden, fin-de-siècle decor, and Edith Piaf's greatest hits played nightly on the piano, has a healthy neighborhood following. Seafood (fresh oysters, mussels, and sole stuffed with shrimp mousse) is the strong suit. ♦ Daily lunch and dinner. 15 Pl du Tertre. 01.46.06.58.59. Métro: Abbesses

21 Au Clairon des Chasseurs $ In this bustling artists' cafe, where all the patrons seem to have sketchbooks under their arms and charcoal pencils behind their ears, painters gather by the window to case prospective clients in the square. Here you get the standard international spread: everything from pizza and *croque monsieur* (grilled ham and cheese sandwich) to club salads, omelettes, *boeuf bourguignon,* and *spaghetti bolognese* (with a meat sauce). Nevertheless, this cafe scores big points as a refuge. Ironically, the only way to escape the nagging street artists of Place du Tertre is by entering their midst; they come to this cafe strictly to take a break and won't pester you here. A jazz band plays Django Reinhardt–style music starting at 9PM. ♦ Daily 7AM-3AM. 3 Pl du Tertre. 01.42.62.40.08. Métro: Abbesses

22 St-Pierre-de-Montmartre An important example of early Gothic architecture, this modest, 3-aisled church was begun 16 years before **Notre-Dame** and claims to be the oldest sanctuary in Paris (two other structures, **St-Germain-des-Prés** and **St-Julien-le-Pauvre**, make similar claims). What appears to be a tiny provincial church is all that remains of the original abbey, which was founded in 1134 by King Louis VI (the Fat) and his wife, Queen Adélaïde, who is buried here. The church was dedicated and consecrated by Pope Eugene III in 1147. Both Dante and St. Ignatius Loyola worshiped here.

Architecturally, the church is a composite. The vaulted choir definitely dates from the 12th century (notice the walls buckling beneath the weight of more than 800 years), but archaeologists remain divided over whether the 4 capitaled columns incorporated in the church came from a Roman temple to Mercury or a Merovingian church (AD 500-751) on the site. The original church windows were shattered at the end of World War II by a bomb intended for a nearby bridge. New windows added in 1953 closely resemble in style the original Gothic stained glass; the three bronze west doors and the cemetery door depicting the Resurrection are by a contemporary Italian sculptor. Each Good Friday, the archbishop of Paris carries a crucifix up this "Mount of Martyrs" to **St-Pierre** as part of a stations-of-the-cross service.

The church's tiny cemetery is the smallest in Paris, with only 85 occupants, among whom are the sculptor Pigalle, the navigator Bougainville (after whom the purple flowering creeper is named), and Montmartre's first mayor, Felix Desportes. The Debray family, the original owners of the **Moulin de la Galette,** is also buried here; the family grave is easy to find—look for the miniature windmill on top. It's open only on All Saints' Day (1 November). ♦ 2 Rue du Mont-Cenis (at Rue St-Eleuthère). 01.46.06.57.63. Métro: Abbesses

MICHAEL STORRINGS

23 Basilique Sacré-Coeur Diocesan architect **Paul Abadie**'s Roman Byzantine marble tribute, universally panned by his peers, has nevertheless become enshrined in the Tourists' Top Ten. For most people, the highlight of the church (pictured at left) is not its design, but the view from its steps—or even better, from the dome (access through the north aisle) at dusk or dawn. The church was built as atonement for the massacre of some 58,000 citizens during the Franco-Prussian War, and within its mosaic-encrusted interior you can see priests praying for forgiveness for those war crimes 24 hours a day, a tradition that has been carried on since the church was consecrated more than a half-century ago. Begun in 1876, **Sacré-Coeur** took decades to complete; for the first 15 years of construction, pylons were sunk below grade to stabilize the foundation over the old quarry mines. The towering campanile was added in 1904 by **Lucien Magne;** one of the world's heaviest bells, the 19-ton **Savoyarde,** hangs in the belfry.

From the north side of the dome you can see in the distance the green roof of the basilica built on the site where St. Denis finally put down his head. A trip to the **Basilique de St-Denis** is worthwhile (one métro ticket will get you there), if only to see the extraordinary collection of tombs where France buried its kings until the time of the Revolution. (For more information, see page 252.) ♦ Admission to dome. Pl du Parvis-du-Sacré-Coeur. 01.42.51.17.02. Métros: Abbesses, Anvers

24 Funicular The shortest, steepest métro line in Paris runs every few minutes between Place Suzanne-Valadon and the base of **Sacré-Coeur.** While fitness freaks take the stairs, the rest ride up in comfort and enjoy the view, all for the price of a normal métro ticket. ♦ Top station: Rues du Cardinal-Dubois and Foyatier; bottom station: Pl Suzanne-Valadon and Rue Foyatier. Métro: Anvers

24 Rue Foyatier The most photographed steps in Montmartre, all 266 of them, run from Rue Azais down to Place Suzanne-Valadon (named after Maurice Utrillo's mother, a talented painter in her own right). All hell breaks loose here at 4:30PM each day when an elementary school lets out and scores of screaming children with miniature leather briefcases on their backs dart across the square in search of their mothers and fathers—the local butchers, bakers, and souvenir makers—who have come to walk them home. ♦ Métro: Anvers

25 Le Gastelier ★$ The tea salon at the foot of **Sacré-Coeur** is a perfect luncheon stop before making the final ascent up the white stairs. Try a Milanese tart (spinach, tomato, and cheese) and a dish of fresh mandarin-orange sorbet. Better yet, indulge in a few scoops of nougat ice cream or a plate of macaroons, and then waddle over to the **Funicular** and ride up. ♦ Tu-Su breakfast, lunch, and afternoon tea until 8PM. 1 *bis* Rue Tardieu (at Pl St-Pierre). 01.46.06.22.06. Métro: Anvers

26 Marché St-Pierre Paris's most celebrated discount fabric warehouse is the hub of the city's garment district. Pandemonium reigns over acres of tweed, bolts of polyester, and bins of last year's argyle socks in this five-story bazaar. Everyone comes here: students searching for cheap curtains, Punjabi women rummaging for sari silk, and New Wave couturiers stalking ersatz panther pelts. The costumes of the surly sales clerks range from three-piece suits to studded leather jackets and turquoise tights. The method in this madness? Take it from the top: fifth floor, linens and sheets; fourth floor, lace curtains and duvet covers; third floor, silks, velours, and *incroyables* (exotic odds and ends); second floor, wools and polyesters; ground floor, a bit of everything. ♦ M 1:30-6:30PM; Tu-Sa. 2 Rue Charles-Nodier (at Rue Livingstone). 01.46.06.92.25. Métro: Anvers

27 L'Eté en Pente Douce ★★$ This cafe and *salon de thé*, whose name means "summer on a soft slope," is hidden on a little square at the base of **Sacré-Coeur**'s sloping grassy park. Its outdoor terrace is a peaceful haven in this lively neighborhood. Such daily specialties as rabbit in mustard sauce are served along with the typical salad niçoise and the not-so-typical *filet mignon Sylvestre aux champignons* (wild boar steak with mushrooms). ♦ Daily lunch, afternoon tea, and dinner. 23 Rue Muller (at Rue Paul-Albert). 01.42.64.02.67. Métros: Château Rouge, Anvers

28 L'Ermitage Hôtel $$ Those who crave an elegant yet soothing atmosphere will delight in this small hotel, housed in a three-story 1860 residence. The warm and smiling owner, Maggie Canipel, makes each guest feel right at home. The 12 breezy rooms, each lovingly decorated by Maggie, contrast with the more somber corridors. **Rooms 11** and **12** open onto a bewitching terraced garden full of chirping birds, while other rooms have splendid views of the city. Breakfast, served in each guest's room, is included in the reasonable price. There's no restaurant. ♦ No credit cards accepted. 24 Rue Lamarck (between Rues du Chevalier-de-la-Barre and Becquerel). 01.42.64.79.22; fax 01.42.64.10.33. Métros: Château Rouge, Lamarck-Caulaincourt

29 Aux Négociants ★★$$ A favorite with locals is this simple bistro where the menu changes daily. The amiable owners, Jean and Rosa Navier, who opened the bistro in 1981, serve such hearty French fare as *blanquette de veau* (veal with béchamel sauce and mushrooms), steak *tartare* with *pommes de terre sautées* (raw, chopped steak and sautéed potatoes), *andouillettes frites* (fried sausage of chitterlings with fries), and *pâté creusois* (potato pie). Wines featured are from the Loire Valley. ♦ M-F lunch and dinner. 25 Rue Lambert (between Rues Labat and Custine). 01.46.06.15.11. Métros: Château Rouge, Lamarck-Caulaincourt

30 24 Rue du Mont-Cenis Composer Hector Berlioz lived with his English wife in a house on this site from 1834 to 1837. The present building was built in 1925. ♦ Between Rues Becquerel and Lamarck. Métro: Lamarck-Caulaincourt

31 Au Poulbot Gourmet ★★$$ Innovative Jean-Paul Langevin runs a simple, cozy restaurant decorated with early Montmartre photos and original Poulbot illustrations. His specialties are *foie gras de canard* (duck liver pâté), large curried escargots stuffed with tomatoes, and a two-chocolate charlotte with pistachio sauce. ♦ M-Sa lunch and dinner; Su lunch. 39 Rue Lamarck (between Rues du Mont-Cenis and des Saules). 01.46.06.86.00. Métro: Lamarck-Caulaincourt

32 A. Beauvilliers ★★★$$$ Its name is borrowed from Antoine Beauvilliers—*officier de bouche* (literally, officer of the mouth) to the gluttonous Count of Provence (the future Louis XVIII) and founder of the first restaurant in Paris in 1790—but this restaurant has a style all its own. Edouard Carlier has created one of the most elegant *salons à manger* (dining rooms) in Paris; what was once an old bakery is now three intimate Louis Philippe–style dining rooms. One room is full of bridal bouquets, the second features 18th- and 19th-century engravings of the Montmartre windmills, and the third is a portrait gallery of Beauvilliers's contemporaries painted by Louis-Léopold Boilly and the like. All three are adorned with a profusion of bouquets that seem even more numerous when reflected in the wall mirrors and lacquered ceilings. The decor is like that of a 19th-century bourgeois boudoir.

The menu changes weekly; memorable specialties have included *cul d'artichaut frais au torteau* (fresh artichoke heart filled with crabmeat), *timbale de macaroni au ris de veau au foie gras et aux morilles* (molded sweetbread macaroni with foie gras and morel mushrooms), spiced squab, and lemon pie in white rum for dessert. The wine is expensive. Be careful, or your bill will climb like Rue Lepic. ♦ M dinner; Tu-Sa lunch and dinner. Reservations required for dinner. 52 Rue Lamarck (between Rues du Mont-Cenis and Caulaincourt). 01.42.54.54.42. Métro: Lamarck-Caulaincourt

33 Musée de Montmartre Located just behind 12 Rue Cortot (whose roll call of former tenants includes Renoir, Utrillo, and Dufy), this pleasant little museum is housed in a delightful 17th-century town house called **Le Manoir de Rose de Rosimond.** The house, which is surrounded by two charming gardens, was the country residence of Rosimond, a 17th-century actor who appeared frequently in the plays of Molière and who, like Molière, died while performing *Le Malade Imaginaire.*

The museum's eclectic collection includes caricatures by Daumier and André Gill, posters and drawings by Toulouse-Lautrec, stunning Clignancourt porcelain, and the piano on which Gustave Charpentier wrote his opera *Louise* in 1900.

Though it seems outlandish in Paris to visit a museum in order to look at a bistro, an original 19th-century bistro complete with a scalloped zinc bar is on display here. The exhibition relates the apocryphal story that the term "bistro" originated on the Butte, where impatient Russian soldiers used to shout at Montmartre's waiters: "*Bistraou, bistraou!*" (Russian for "Get a move on"). On Wednesday evenings, the Art et Humour Montmartrois meets in the museum for poetry readings and art exhibitions; lectures on local culture sponsored by the Société du Vieux Montmartre are held Saturday evenings. ♦ Admission. Tu-Su. 12 Rue Cortot (between Rues du Mont-Cenis and des Saules). 01.46.06.61.11. Métro: Lamarck-Caulaincourt

34 Vignes de Montmartre (Montmartre Vineyards) This is one of the last two remaining vineyards in Paris. Each year's harvest yields enough grapes for about 500 bottles of red Clos Montmartre wine. The labels are designed by Montmartre artists, and half-bottles are sold each year in the basement of the 18th arrondissement's **Mairie** (Town Hall; see page 240). The wine is nothing special, but the harvest fete, on the first or second Saturday of October, is not to be missed. Crowds line Rue Lamarck for a celebration that feels like a combination of an academic procession, the Rose Bowl Parade, and Halloween. Participants might include baton twirlers, Auvergnat farmers in wooden clogs, and the mayor's wife, who traditionally picks the first grape. The vineyards are not open to the public, but note the plaque in front on Rue St-Vincent dedicated to Poulbot, the popular cartoonist who prevented the vineyards from being sold to high-rise developers in the 1930s. ♦ Rues des Saules and St-Vincent. Métro: Lamarck-Caulaincourt

35 La Maison Rose ★$ Utrillo once painted a picture of this pink restaurant, and pink it has stayed—even the cutlery is rose-tinted. In the summer the tables spill onto Rue de l'Abreuvoir, and if the view doesn't make you dizzy, order foie gras with a bottle of Champagne to ensure that your head spins. Such standard French fare as escargots and smoked salmon is served, but it's not that well prepared. ♦ Daily lunch and dinner. 2 Rue de l'Abreuvoir (at Rue des Saules). 01.42.57.66.75. Métro: Lamarck-Caulaincourt

36 Au Lapin Agile The original **Cabaret des Assassins** was rechristened in 1880 when André Gill painted a rabbit with a red bow tie bounding from a copper kettle on the sign outside. The *lapin à Gill* (rabbit by Gill) became the *lapin agile* (nimble rabbit), and this famous cabaret turned into a stomping ground for intellectuals and artists who came for poetry readings and folk songs. (In 1985 the French government issued a five-franc stamp depicting Utrillo's oil painting of the cabaret.) A century later you can still grab a wooden stool, order a kir, and sing along to those same old songs, as updated by pianist Roger Lesouad. Don't miss the 19th-century whimsy in front: a concrete fence made to look like knotty pine. No food is served. ♦ Tu-Su 9:15PM-2AM. No credit cards accepted. 22 Rue des Saules (at Rue St-Vincent). 01.46.06.85.87. Métro: Lamarck-Caulaincourt

37 Cimetière St-Vincent (St. Vincent Cemetery) Composer Arthur Honegger and painters Théophile-Alexandre Steinlen and Maurice Utrillo are buried in Paris's most intellectual cemetery. Enjoy the ivy-covered walls, a tranquil view of **Sacré-Coeur,** and (if you need to get off your feet) south-facing benches that catch the afternoon sun. The old caretaker is generally helpful but becomes cantankerous between noon and 2PM, when he is emphatically out to lunch. ♦ Daily. Rues St-Vincent and des Saules. Métro: Lamarck-Caulaincourt

Corridors of Nostalgia

First introduced at the end of the 18th century, glass-covered pedestrian arcades called *passages* quickly became the rage in Paris. By the mid-19th century, as many as 140 of these ancestors of our modern shopping malls had snaked their way through the center of the city, filling every shopping, eating, and entertainment wish and need of the bourgeoisie, all in a setting protected from bad weather and the messy horse traffic on the main streets.

Today only 30 of these old *passages* have survived. The best of them carefully cultivate their old-fashioned charm, with lacquered wood storefronts, ceramic tile floors, ornate iron skylight supports, and many unusual shops. Strolling through these *passages* (or *galeries,* as the fancier ones are known) creates a pleasantly artificial sensation, almost like being on the movie set of an Emile Zola novel (in fact, important scenes in his 1879 novel, *Nana,* take place in the **Passage des Panoramas**).

The following are some of the more colorful *passages:*

Galerie Colbert (Métros: Bourse, Pyramides) adjoins and is connected to the **Galerie Vivienne**. The elegant 1826 arcade houses a **Bibliothèque Nationale** bookshop, theater museum, and **Le Grand Colbert,** a splendid Belle Epoque cafe.

Galerie Véro-Dodat (Métros: Louvre-Rivoli, Palais Royal–Musée du Louvre) is a few steps east of the **Palais Royal.** The blocklong *passage* with a black-and-white tile floor was created by two butchers-turned-land speculators in 1826. Beautifully restored, the front of the shops here are of highly polished dark brown wood, and their windows trimmed in brass. Among the residents are a delightful antique doll shop **(Robert Capia)**, a *luthier* (stringed instrument maker), antiques dealers, a fine bookshop, and **Le Véro-Dodat,** a decent restaurant with period decor. (*Note:* unlike the other *passages* listed, the shops here are closed on Monday).

Galerie Vivienne (Métros: Bourse, Pyramides) opened in 1823. This cozy and vivacious *galerie* near **Place des Victoires** is home to the prestigious **Lucien Legrand** wine shop; the charming **A Priori** tearoom; sellers of antiques, antiquarian books, hats and umbrellas, women's clothes, fine fabrics, artificial flowers, toys, original prints; and a large **Jean Paul Gaultier** boutique.

Passage Jouffroy (Métro: Grands Boulevards) is the liveliest and most colorful of all. The long 1845 arcade features the **Librairie de Passage**'s lengthy line of stalls heaped with art books and old novels; the **Musée Grevin** wax museum; shops for cinema books and posters, Oriental carpets and curios, antique walking sticks, semi-precious stones, old-fashioned doll houses and furnishings; and **Le Chopin,** a cute little hotel.

Passage des Panoramas (Métros: Bourse, Grands Boulevards) is Paris's oldest *passage.* Opened in 1800, it takes its name from a series of huge panoramic paintings of the burning of Moscow, the battle of the Port of Toulon, and other dramatic scenes that were shown in two cylindrical viewing spaces flanking the Boulevard Montmartre end of the *passage.* This popular attraction of the early 19th century was created by Robert Fulton, the North American artist and steamship inventor. The **Stern** engraving shop at **No. 40** still has its 1840 facade and ornate interior woodwork. Other attractions include shops selling women's clothes, toys, and trompe l'oeil fruit; a tearoom; a quaint old bar; the *entrée des artistes* (stage door) of the **Théâtre des Variétés** described by Zola in *Nana;* and no less than six stamp dealers.

Passage Verdeau (Métros: Grands Boulevards, Le Peletier) was built in 1847. This passage is particularly rich in used and antiquarian bookshops and galleries specializing in old prints and photographs.

Galerie Vivienne

38 Le Château des Seigneurs de Clignancourt Along with **St-Pierre-de-Montmartre**, this is one of the oldest relics of this district's past. The original manor house was home to the famous porcelain manufacturer (founded in 1767) that provided Louis XVIII with plates and saucers. Regrettably, the early 16th-century house was demolished in 1861 and all that remains is its renovated turret, which now decorates the corner of a modern restaurant. ◆ Rues du Mont-Cenis and Marcadet. Métro: Jules Joffrin

39 Mairie du 18e Arrondissement (City Hall of the 18th Arrondissement) When artist Maurice Utrillo died in 1955, he left two of his paintings to the local *mairie* (town hall)—not in payment of estate taxes as Picasso did, but simply as a gift. The paintings are displayed here; ask the *secrétariat général* on the second floor. Half-bottles of wine from the **Montmartre Vineyards** are for sale in the basement. ◆ M-F. 1 Pl Jules-Joffrin (at Rue Ordener). 01.42.52.42.00. Métro: Jules Joffrin

40 René Raveau (Pâtisserie de Montmartre) It's tough choosing between the heavenly cherry tarts and the divine *Rose-Maries* (brioches filled with almond cream) at this pastry shop. ◆ M-Sa. 81 Rue du Mont-Cenis (between Rues Ordener and Versigny). 01.46.06.39.28. Métro: Jules Joffrin

41 Rue du Poteau Along this street (where Utrillo was born in 1883) lies a charming and lively neighborhood market. From behind a fog of simmering *choucroute* (sauerkraut), ruddy-faced women chant *"Chaud, chaud, Mesdames! Le boudin noir"* ("Hot, hot, ladies! Blood sausage"). Nearby, their husbands peddle pheasants and Normandy cheeses. Follow your nose to the left, up Rue Duhesme, and pass gingerly through the crowd of determined wicker-basket-toting householders who shop with the finesse and subtlety of football players. The market operates daily. ◆ Between Rues Ordener and Duhesme. Métro: Jules Joffrin

On Rue du Poteau:

Fromagerie de Montmartre Mme. Delbey offers 250-300 cheeses from all over the world, including nearly 50 varieties of goat cheese. She also makes her own pasta and ravioli and sells the famous sourdough *pain Poilâne*. ◆ Tu-Sa. No. 9. 01.46.06.26.03

42 Hôtel Damrémont $ This clean, often noisy, 35-room hotel is a good 20-minute hike from **Sacré-Coeur**, but the rates border on the philanthropic. There's no restaurant. ◆ 110 Rue Damrémont (between Rues Ordener and Championnet). 01.42.64.25.75; fax 01.46.06.74.64. Métro: Lamarck-Caulaincourt

Le Maquis

43 Le Maquis ★★$$ Located at the base of Avenue Junot, this lovely little bistro features such dishes as fish soup, escargots, skate with lemon, and saffron haddock with poached egg, and inexpensive light prix-fixe lunches. ◆ M-Sa lunch and dinner. 69 Rue Caulaincourt (between Rues Lamarck and Tourlaque). 01.42.59.76.07. Métro: Lamarck-Caulaincourt

44 Square Suzanne-Buisson This unexpected little square (named after a World War II Resistance fighter) was once the backyard of the adjoining **Château des Brouillards** (Castle of Fog), an 18th-century mansion turned dance hall. According to religious lore, St. Denis paused here to rinse his severed head. Today a statue of the forlorn-looking bishop surveys neighborhood elders playing an afternoon game of *pétanque,* a Lyonnais sand bowling game similar to boccie. The bowling alley has stone benches for spectators, and there's no better way to learn about the old Montmartre than to eavesdrop on the conversations of these tweed-capped codgers. Admission is free (as is the gossip), and the games pick up steam around mid-afternoon. ◆ Métro: Lamarck-Caulaincourt

45 Ciné Théâtre 13 In 1983 French filmmaker Claude Lelouch built this elegant 130-person private screening room beside his Montmartre town house. Directors and their stars still come here to screen their rushes, and it is also used for live stage productions open to the general public. For a reasonable $150 an hour ($300 after 7PM), you can rent this exclusive movie theater and show home movies if you like. No popcorn is permitted, but the theater can arrange catering. Call ahead for hours and for screening and catering reservations. ◆ 1 Ave Junot (at Rue Girardon). 01.42.54.15.12. Métro: Lamarck-Caulaincourt

46 Hameau des Artistes Behind the gate marked *Interdit* (No Trespassing) are footpaths leading to opulent artists' studios in structures ranging from a gray cement castle to a Tuscan villa. The gate to the "Artists' Hamlet" is open during the day; be adventurous but discreet. ◆ 11 Ave Junot (between Rue Girardon and Villa Léandre). Métro: Lamarck-Caulaincourt

46 13 Avenue Junot This is the former residence (1879-1946) of Francisque Poulbot, the Montmartre illustrator who drew chubby little children with cowlicks. Four of his cartoon characters frolic across the tile frieze of the house. In homage to the artist, Montmartre residents still call their children *petits poulbots;* at the corner of Rue Norvins and Impasse du Tertre, near **Place du Tertre**, you will find a sign that reads: *Ralentissez. Faites attention aux petits poulbots.* (Drive slowly. Watch out for the little poulbots.) This local folk hero is also credited with saving **Montmartre Vineyards** and with founding the Fraternal Association of Wooden Billiard Players (wooden billiards is a faddish Montmartre bar game in which winning is considered immoral—the winner always pays for the drinks). The house is still a private residence. ♦ Between Rue Girardon and Villa Léandre. Métro: Lamarck-Caulaincourt

46 Maison Tristan Tzara In the 1920s Viennese architect **Adolf Loos,** a pioneer of the Modern movement, was the only designer whose work reflected Dadaism. It is not surprising, then, that his "architecture without qualities" should have appealed to the Romanian Dadaist poet Tristan Tzara, who brought Loos to Paris with a commission to build this house. Set into a rising embankment, the five-story building has a rigorously symmetrical facade that is punctured by a huge double-height square terrace. The arrangement is a superb example of the Loos predilection for tensely juxtaposed, unadorned cubic forms. The interior is just as eccentrically organized. The patchwork of intersecting split-level spaces, typical of Loos's *raumplan* (room plan), provided Tzara with the sort of ironic, theatrical, and vaguely aggressive setting that befitted a Dadaist artist. This is still a private residence. ♦ 15 Ave Junot (between Rue Girardon and Villa Léandre). Métro: Lamarck-Caulaincourt

47 Villa Léandre Down this unexpected country lane leading off Avenue Junot is a hidden village where the eccentric little houses mirror the idiosyncrasies of the people who have inhabited them (a ballerina, two successful painters, and a few genuine hermits). It's worth a quick detour. ♦ Métro: Lamarck-Caulaincourt

48 Rue Lepic Montmartre's meandering old quarry road is the site of an antique-car rally held on the first or second Sunday in October (for information call 01.42.52.42.00). ♦ Métros: Lamarck-Caulaincourt, Blanche, Abbesses

48 Moulin de la Galette Painted by Renoir and many others, this windmill (and its former dance hall) is the best known of the scores of mills that once crowned Montmartre. In the 19th century, the hoi polloi of Paris journeyed here on Sunday afternoons with their sweethearts to dance, drink wine, and eat *galettes* (cakes made with flour from the mills). This windmill has a grisly history as

well. During the Franco-Prussian War, Montmartre was overrun by 20,000 Prussian soldiers, some of whom crucified the heroic mill owner, Pierre-Charles Debray, on the sails of his *moulin.* It's not open to the public. ♦ 79 Rue Lepic (between Rues Girardon and Tourlaque). Métro: Lamarck-Caulaincourt

49 La Petite Galette ★$ Right across the street from **Moulin de la Galette,** this bistro provides an inexpensive post-theater stop for a steak and *tarte tatin* (apple tart). Other specialties are foie gras, escargots, and "the Colonel" (lemon sherbet and vodka). ♦ Daily dinner until 2AM. 86 *bis* Rue Lepic (at Rue Tholozé). 01.42.52.99.72. Métro: Lamarck-Caulaincourt

50 54 Rue Lepic Vincent van Gogh and his brother Theo lived in this apartment building. ♦ Between Rues des Abbesses and Durantin. Métro: Blanche

51 21 Rue Caulaincourt Innovative graphic artist Toulouse-Lautrec spent his most productive years (1886-97) at a studio in this building, just a stroll away from his favorite nocturnal haunts. ♦ 21 Rue Caulaincourt (at Rue Tourlaque). Métro: Blanche

52 Terrass Hôtel $$$ Built in 1912, this is the only luxury hotel in Montmartre. It has marble floors and a magnificent fireplace in the lobby, a stellar panorama that takes in the **Opéra, Arc de Triomphe,** and **Eiffel Tower,** and 101 sumptuous rooms. Ask to stay on the cemetery side, which in local parlance means a room with a view, unobstructed because you're overlooking the low-rise **Montmartre Cemetery.** ♦ 12-14 Rue Joseph-de-Maistre (at Rue Caulaincourt). 01.46.06.72.85; fax 01.42.52.29.11; terrass@FranceNet.fr; www.hotels.fr/terrass. Métro: Blanche

"Everything I saw—the chestnut trees scattering their leaves along the walks, the wide bridges clustered with bookstalls at either end of the medieval town of Ile le la Cité over which Notre-Dame raised its ponderous, Gothic stones—evoked that strange pang which even first-time visitors to Paris recognize, with some astonishment, as *nostalgia.* A buried memory seems to stab at your consciousness in Paris, and you follow in the steps of an elusive phantom *déjà vu,* but never quite catch up. So deeply embedded in the world's dream of freedom, youth, art, and pleasure has this city become, that the feeling that the stranger in Paris has is feeling of *return.* Perhaps one misses friends so keenly there because all of one's senses are pitched to such a keen note of receptivity, and one vibrates with an awareness that one longs to share."

John Clellon Holmes, *Displaced Person,* 1987

Within the Terrass Hôtel:

La Terrasse ★★$$ From May through September the hotel moves its restaurant to the seventh floor terrace where you can dine under big white umbrellas and enjoy one of the finest views in Paris. Specialties include prawn salad, *rascasse à la tapenade* (scorpion fish with Provençal olive and anchovy paste), beef grilled with sea salt, and other grilled meat and fish. The rest of the year, the dining room can be found in its courtly winter quarters on the ground floor. ◆ Daily lunch and dinner. Reservations required for a terrace table with a view. 01.44.92.34.00

53 Cimetière de Montmartre (Montmartre Cemetery) A veritable academy of writers, composers, and painters, this is the final resting place of Zola, Stendhal, Dumas, Offenbach, Degas, Fragonard, and Greuze, whose eloquent headstone lauds him for having depicted "virtue, friendship, beauty, and innocence, thereby breathing soul into his paintings." Another striking memorial is François Rude's bronze of a reclining Cavaignac. Composer Hector Berlioz lies between his first wife, an English actress, and his second wife, an opera singer. ◆ Daily. 20 Ave Rachel (north of Blvd de Clichy). 01.43.87.64.24. Métros: Blanche, Place de Clichy

54 Place de Clichy Stop by the *Académie de Billard Clichy-Montmartre* (84 Rue de Clichy, 01.48.78.32.85), a billiards hall set in a converted 1900 stable, and then wander down Rue d'Amsterdam, past carpet shops, used-furniture stores, and homeopathic pharmacies. ◆ Métro: Place de Clichy

55 Charlot, Le Roi des Coquillages ★★ $$$ If you happen to be in Montmartre during an "R" month (the months spelled with the letter R—September through April—denote prime shellfish season), stop at this Art Deco–style bistro for a no-nonsense lunch of crabs, shrimps, oysters, and the like. Menu choices include bouillabaisse, *moules à la marinière* (mussels cooked in onions with white wine), and grilled shrimp coated with sea salt. Fine wines are served, including Muscadet and Chardonnay. ◆ Daily lunch and dinner until 1AM. 12 Pl de Clichy (between Ave de Clichy and Rue Biot). 01.53.20.48.00. Métro: Place de Clichy

56 L'Annexe ★$$ This lively bistro wallpapered with can-can scenes is only a quick stroll from the glitter of Pigalle. Try the *suprême de pintade* (breast of guinea fowl) cooked in cider, grilled beef with béarnaise sauce, or if you have the stomach for it, *androuillette grillé* (grilled tripe sausage). ◆ M-F lunch and dinner; closed in August. 15 Rue Chaptal (at Rue Henner). 01.48.74.65.52. Métro: Blanche

57 Moulin Rouge Founded in 1889 (the year the **Eiffel Tower** was built) and still kicking after all these years, this legendary temple of the risqué proffers all the bare-breasted women, ostrich plumes, rhinestones, and multicolored lights the stage can support. The show recalls the days of the famous can-can dancers: Jane Avril, Yvette Guilbert, Valentin le Désosse, and La Goulue, who were limned by Toulouse-Lautrec. The 60 indefatigable Doriss Girls carry on the tradition. Dinner is rather expensive and nothing to write home about, so you might want to skip it and take in the show from the bar. ◆ Cover. Dinner: daily. Show: daily 7PM, 9PM, and 11PM. Reservations recommended for dinner and show. 82 Blvd de Clichy (between Rue Lepic and Ave Rachel). 01.53.09.82.82; www.moulinroue.com. Métro: Blanche

57 Cité Véron Don't let its shabby entrance on the boulevard deter you, because this cul de sac to the left of the **Moulin Rouge** is quite intriguing. Surviving family members of French writers Jacques Prévert and Boris Vian make their homes here, and you will find the highbrow **Théâtre Ouvert** (No. 4 *bis*, 01.42.55.74.40), which features the works of contemporary French playwrights; the **Boris Vian Foundation** (No. 6 *bis*, 01.46.06.73.56), which is housed in an old hunting lodge and offers exhibitions, dance, and theater classes; and an amazing warehouse-cum-boutique for used clothing, old costumes and stage props called **Ophir** (No. 8, 01.42.64.58.40), whose doorbell you must ring to get in. Some of the best stuff collected by the owners Jacqueline and André Marcovici is not for sale (19th-century wooden carousel figures and **Moulin Rouge** stage props, for instance), but there's plenty more here to satisfy the most jaded of rummage sale shoppers. **Ophir** is open Monday through Friday from 9AM to 1PM; afternoons and weekends by appointment only. ◆ 92 Blvd de Clichy (between Rue Lepic and Ave Rachel). Métro: Blanche

58 Musée de l'Erotisme A touch of class amid the sleazy sex shops and strip joints of

Pigalle, this attractive, modern museum of erotic art was created by three passionate collectors in 1997. More than 2,000 works are on display—sculptures, paintings, photographs, fetishes, and furnishings from Africa, Asia, Oceania, Europe, and the Americas. The two upper floors of the five-story building are devoted to temporary exhibits of works by present-day artists. ◆ Admission. Daily 10AM-2AM. 72 Blvd de Clichy (between Rues Coustou and Lepic). 01.42.58.28.73. Métro: Blanche

59 Le Restaurant ★★$$ Modern, minimalist decor complements owner-chef Yves Peladeau's imaginative array of original and traditional dishes: mussels sautéed in olive oil, lemon, and pepper; Basque-style fish casserole; grilled free range chicken stuffed with preserved lemon, vegetables, and saffron; and an exquisite crème brûlée. A chic crowd dines here. ◆ Tu-F lunch and dinner; Sa dinner; closed the second half of August. Reservations recommended. 32 Rue Véron (at Rue Audran). 01.42.23.06.22. Métro: Abbesses

60 Bruno Would you like a goldfish on your ankle? Perhaps a mermaid on your chest? Bruno, one of the more popular body artists in Paris and an officer of the artisanal Order of Artistic Merit, practices safe tattooing, using only fresh needles and disposable ink cartridges. Even if you're not ready to commit to a permanent bodily souvenir of your trip, it's fun to look in the window and imagine. ◆ M-Tu, Th-Sa. 4 Rue Germain-Pilon (between Blvd de Clichy and Rue Véron). 01.42.64.35.59. Métro: Pigalle

61 Place Pigalle Nineteenth-century sculptor Jean-Baptiste Pigalle's celebrated rendering of the Virgin Mary is displayed in **St-Sulpice Church,** but his name became synonymous with porn theaters, sex shops, and prostitutes by being associated with this square. Known as **Pig Alley** to World War II GIs who came stalking the professional wildlife, Place Pigalle has lost many of its hookers to Rue St-Denis and **Bois de Boulogne;** these days transvestites predominate.

Le Montmartrain (06.08.26.38.38) is a small white tourist train that takes visitors on a circuit of the Butte de Montmartre with a stop at **Sacré-Coeur.** It departs from the Place Pigalle *métro* entrance on the center island of Boulevard de Clichy daily every half-hour from 10AM to 7 or 8PM (depending on the weather) from Easter through October; daily every 30 minutes from 10:30AM to 5PM the rest of the year. ◆ Métro: Pigalle

62 Caravelle $$ This hotel has 31 comfortable, but minimally decorated rooms. Ask for one in back and avoid the traffic noise. There's no restaurant. ◆ 68 Rue des Martyrs (between Ave Trudaine and Blvd de Rochechouart). 01.48.78.43.31; fax 01.40.23.98.72. Métro: Pigalle

63 Carlton's $$$ Surprise, surprise—there's a comfortable, well-appointed modern hotel offering 103 peaceful rooms amid the strip joints and kung fu cinemas of Pigalle. Have a drink on the rooftop terrace, which offers a spectacular 360° panorama of Paris, with **Sacré-Coeur** right up on the hill. There's no restaurant. ◆ 55 Blvd de Rochechouart (at Rue Lallier). 01.42.81.91.00; fax 01.42.81.97.04; carltons@club-internet.fr. Métro: Pigalle

64 L'Oriental ★★$ Moroccan specialties are served at this intimate restaurant where decor is accented with touches of marble and mirrors. Thoughtful preparation is the keyword here: Choose from among such dishes as *pastilla au poulet* (puff pastry filled with chicken, almonds, and mint), *tchakchouka* (a zesty mixture of scrambled eggs, onions, peppers, and spices), or prawn and saffron *tajine* (stew). ◆ M-Sa lunch and dinner; closed in August. Reservations required. 76 Rue des Martyrs (between Blvd de Rochechouart and Rue d'Orsel). 01.42.64.39.80. Métro: Pigalle

65 Résidence Charles-Dullin $$ These 76 kitchen-equipped apartments, located on a tranquil square, are rented by the night or week. ◆ 10 Pl Charles-Dullin (at Rue des Trois-Frères). 01.42.57.14.55; fax 01.42.54.48.87; www.pierre-vacances.fr. Métro: Anvers

66 Théâtre de l'Atelier When this charming theater was first built in 1822 on this cobblestoned square (named in 1957 after actor Charles Dullin), it was known for the Stefan Zweig adaptation of Ben Jonson's *Volpone* and for *L'Opéra Bouffe,* which critics called the best stage performances outside Paris (Montmartre was not yet part of the city proper). Today, under the direction of Pierre Franck, the theater is truly Parisian, and there isn't a bad red-velvet seat in the house. ◆ Box office: M-Sa 11AM-7PM. 1 Pl Charles-Dullin (at Rue d'Orsel). 01.46.06.49.24. Métro: Anvers

Additional Highlights

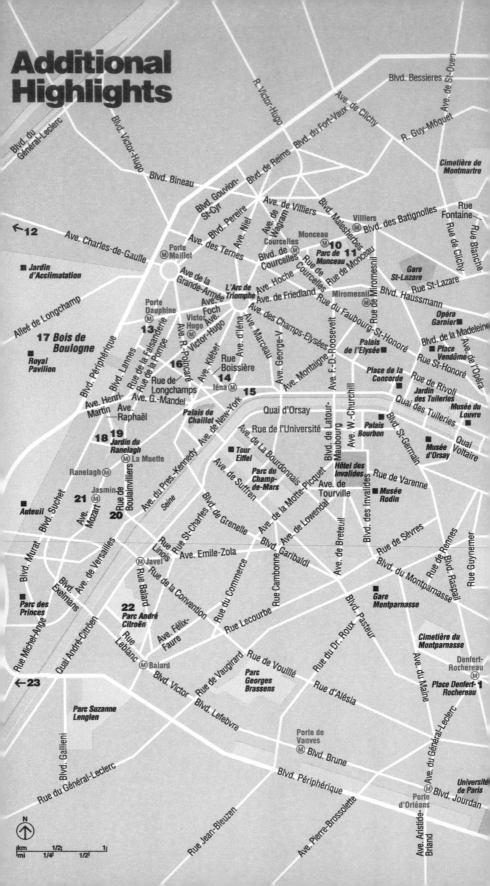

←12

Blvd. du Général-Leclerc

Blvd. Victor-Hugo

Blvd. Bineau

R. Victor-Hugo

Blvd. de Reims

Blvd. du Fort-Vaux

Ave. de Clichy

Blvd. Bessieres

Ave. de St-Ouen

R. Guy-Môquet

Cimetière de Montmartre

Rue Fontaine

Blvd. Gouvion-St-Cyr

Blvd. Pereire

Ave. Niel

Ave. de Wagram

Ave. de Villiers

Blvd. Malesherbes

Villiers

Blvd. des Batignolles

Rue de Clichy

Rue Blanche

Ave. Charles-de-Gaulle

Porte Maillot

Ave. des Ternes

Blvd. de Courcelles

Courcelles

Monceau

Parc de Monceau

10 11

Ave. de Friedland

Rue de Courcelles

Rue de Monceau

Gare St-Lazare

Rue St-Lazare

Blvd. Haussmann

Jardin d'Acclimatation

Ave. de la Grande-Armée

L'Arc de Triomphe

Ave. Hoche

Miromesnil

Rue du Faubourg-St-Honoré

Opéra Garnier

Blvd. de la Madeleine

17 Bois de Boulogne

Royal Pavilion

Porte Dauphine

Victor Hugo

Ave. R-Poincaré

Ave. Victor-Hugo

Ave. Kléber

Ave. d'Iéna

Ave. des Champs-Elysées

Ave. Marceau

Ave. George-V

Ave. Montaigne

Rue de Miromesnil

Palais de l'Elysée

Rue du Faubourg-St-Honoré

Place Vendôme

Rue St-Honoré

Ave. de l'Opéra

13

Blvd. Périphérique

Blvd. Lannes

Rue de la Faisanderie

Rue de la Pompe

Rue de Longchamps

16

Rue Boissière

14

Iéna

15

Ave. F.-D.-Roosevelt

Place de la Concorde

Rue de Rivoli

Jardin des Tuileries

Musée du Louvre

Ave. Henri-Martin

Ave. G.-Mandel

Ave. Raphaël

Palais de Chaillot

Ave. de New-York

Quai d'Orsay

Quai des Tuileries

Quai Voltaire

Musée d'Orsay

18 19

Jardin du Ranelagh

La Muette

Ranelagh

Ave. de La Bourdonnais

Rue de l'Université

Blvd. de Latour-Maubourg

Ave. W.-Churchill

Palais Bourbon

Blvd. St-Germain

Musée d'Orsay

Ave. du Prés.-Kennedy

Ave. de New-York

Seine

Tour Eiffel

Ave. de Suffren

Parc du Champ-de-Mars

Ave. de La Motte-Picquet

Hôtel des Invalides

Ave. de Tourville

Rue de Varenne

Musée Rodin

Jasmin

Rue de Boulainvilliers

21

Ave. Mozart

20

Rue St-Charles

Blvd. de Grenelle

Ave. de la Motte-Picquet

Ave. de Lowendal

Blvd. des Invalides

Rue de Sèvres

Auteuil

Blvd. Suchet

Rue de Rennes

Blvd. Raspail

Rue Guynemer

Parc des Princes

Blvd. Exelmans

Ave. de Versailles

Javel

Linois

Rue de la Convention

Ave. Emile-Zola

Rue du Commerce

Blvd. Garibaldi

Rue Cambronne

Ave. de Breteuil

Rue du Dr.-Roux

Blvd. du Montparnasse

Rue Michel-Ange

Quai André-Citroën

Rue Balard

22

Parc André Citroën

Ave. Félix-Faure

Rue Leblanc

Balard

Blvd. Victor

Rue de Vaugirard

Rue Lecourbe

Parc Georges Brassens

Rue de Vouillé

Rue d'Alésia

Gare Montparnasse

Blvd. Pasteur

Cimetière du Montparnasse

Ave. du Maine

Denfert-Rochereau

Place Denfert-Rochereau 1

←23

Parc Suzanne Lenglen

Blvd. Gallieni

Rue du Général-Leclerc

Rue Jean-Bleuzen

Blvd. Lefebvre

Porte de Vanves

Blvd. Brune

Blvd. Périphérique

Ave. Pierre-Brossolette

Ave. Aristide-Briand

Porte d'Orléans

Ave. du Général-Leclerc

Blvd. Jourdan

Université de Paris

N

km   1/2   1
mi   1/4   1/2

Additional Highlights

There are some wonderful spots in Paris that are not in the areas covered elsewhere in this book. This chapter features Paris's other highlights, which include something for everyone: eerie catacombs; pleasant parks, including the well-known **Monceau** and **Bois de Boulogne**; the famous **Cimetière du Père-Lachaise**, the burial place of generations of writers, musicians, and artists, from Chopin to Jim Morrison; and a variety of interesting museums, including the high-tech **La Villette** science museum, several fine art collections, and museums devoted to the lives and works of such notables as singer Edith Piaf and architect **Le Corbusier.**

1 Catacombs The catacombs began as a network of quarries that extended for miles beneath Paris. In 1785, several million skeletons were transported to these quarries from the overcrowded Innocents Cemetery near Les Halles. Here the skulls, femurs, and tibias of 30 generations of Parisians were stacked in a neat but rather macabre fashion. Carved near the entrance is an ominous medieval sign: "Stop. Beyond Here Is the Empire of Death." Apparently the warning deterred the occupying Nazis, because they never discovered that the secret headquarters of the French Resistance was literally under their feet. The dark reaches of the catacombs then housed radios capable of reaching London, as well as a telephone switching system handling Resistance communications for hundreds of miles around.

Today visitors can explore the catacombs and view the skeletal inhabitants as part of an hourlong tour. Bring along a flashlight and a sweater, be prepared for a lot of steps, and be sure to stay close to the group. In 1793 a Parisian took a wrong turn from his own wine cellar, got lost in the catacomb tunnels, and was not discovered until nine years later, by which time he was mummified. ♦ Admission. Tu-F 2-4PM; Sa-Su 9-11AM, 2-4PM. 1 Pl Denfert-Rochereau (at Blvd St-Jacques). 01.43.22.47.63. Métro: Denfert Rochereau

2 Parc Montsouris Prior to the 19th century, this park was an abandoned granite quarry stubbled with windmills. At the turn of the century the 50-acre swath of green was a refuge for the artists and literati of nearby Montparnasse; Hemingway often came here. Today, joggers run the park's one-mile perimeter, matrons feed the swans, and brass bands play marches in the band shell. ♦ 20 Rue Gazan (between Blvd Jourdan and Ave Reille). RER: Cité Universitaire

Within Parc Montsouris:

Le Pavillon de Montsouris ★★$$ The outdoor terrace of this Belle Epoque glass-and-iron restaurant has accommodated a great many famous customers, including Trotsky and Sartre. Not to be missed are the *purée de guacamole* and *soupe de fruits rouge.* ♦ Daily lunch and dinner. 01.45.88.38.52

3 Bibliothèque Nationale de France, Site François Mitterand/Tolbiac (National Library of France, François Mitterand/Tolbiac) The **Bibliothèque Nationale**'s vast collection of 11 million books was moved from its former home on Rue de Richelieu (see page 227) to this ultramodern building that includes four seven-story glass towers. The controversial spires, designed by architect **Dominique Perrault,** are L-shaped—like open books—and are connected to each other by an immense public esplanade the size of the garden at the **Palais Royal.** The reading rooms are located in two long sections of the building that parallel the river. The **Haut-de-Jardin** (Upper Garden) chambers have 1,600 seats, 180,000 volumes on open shelves, 2,500 periodicals, 10,000 reels of microfilm, 340,000 microfiches, 100,000 digitized images, and a huge audiovisual collection. The public can also order books (a day in advance) from the stacks that are delivered to the reading rooms via a 7-kilometer (4-mile) rail system. A research area on the **Rez-de-Jardin** (Garden Level) is open only to scholars by special arrangement. The complex was inaugurated in December 1996 and fully opened in October 1998.

Unlike the other parts of the **Bibliothèque Nationale,** which are free, this one charges a modest daily or yearly fee. ♦ Fee. Tu-Sa 10AM-8PM; Su noon-7PM; closed two weeks between the first and third Monday in September and national holidays. 11 Quai François-Mauriac (between Rues de Tolbiac and Raymond-Aron). 01.53.79.59.59. Métro: Bibliothèque François Mitterand

4 Bois de Vincennes Only slightly smaller than the **Bois de Boulogne,** this large park on the eastern edge of Paris is the city's second main recreation area. Like the **Bois de Boulogne,** this was a former royal hunting ground; it was given to the city by Napoléon III in 1860. The major attraction here is the **Château de Vincennes,** a stern medieval fortress that has served variously as a royal residence, prison, porcelain factory, and arsenal. King Henry V of England died here in 1422. The *bois* (woods) that extends to the south of the château contains the 80-acre **Parc Floral de Paris; Daumesnil Lake,** where rowboats and bicycles are available for rent; the **Kagyu Dzong Buddhist Center,** which boasts the largest sculpture of Buddha in Europe; the **Hippodrome de Vincennes** (01.49.77.17.17), a trotters' racecourse; and the **Zoological Park.** The zoo, with 550 mammals, including the giant pandas Yen-Yen and Lili, and more than 700 birds, provides a welcome contrast to the **Menagerie** at the **Jardin des Plantes—** here the animals live in surroundings similar to their natural habitats. In the zoo's center is a 230-foot-high artificial mountain, home to wild mountain sheep, goats, and ibex. A frisky colony of gibbons lives at the foot of the mountain. ♦ Admission for château. Daily. Château 01.48.08.31.20, zoological park 01.44.75.20.10. Métros: Porte Dorée, Porte de Charenton, Liberté, Charenton-Ecoles, Château de Vincennes; RER: Vincennes

5 Cimetière du Père-Lachaise (Père-Lachaise Cemetery) Named after Louis XIV's confessor, Father La Chaise, and designed by **Alexandre Théodore Brongniart,** this is the largest and most elite cemetery in Paris. The remains of France's most famous lovers, Abélard and Héloïse, keep company with Molière, Balzac, and the painters Corot, Daumier, David, Pissarro, Modigliani, and Seurat. Also buried here are the 19th-century photographer Nadar; the city-shaping Baron Haussmann; Jane Avril and Yvette Guilbert, two can-can dancers who modeled for Toulouse-Lautrec; Fulgence Bienvenue, who built the Paris métro; and Ferdinand de Lesseps, who designed the Suez Canal.

In remembrance of things past, a single red rose may grace the black marble slab marking Marcel Proust's grave, and singer Edith Piaf's unremarkable resting place is always surrounded with flowers. Music lovers might also search out the graves of Callas, Bizet, or Poulenc. Chopin's body is buried here (his heart is interred in Warsaw), as are the remains of Eugène Delacroix, Prosper Mérimée, and Alfred de Musset, who, like Chopin, loved George Sand, the great woman luminary of 19th-century French literature. Literati, as well as gays and lesbians, flock to Oscar Wilde's tomb, a stylish sphinx sculpted by Sir Jacob Epstein in 1909, and leftists make the pilgrimage to the grave of Laura Marx, daughter of Karl. Sarah Bernhardt lies here, as

does Jim Morrison, the Doors' lead singer who died in Paris in 1971. Lovers Gertrude Stein and Alice B. Toklas are together in death as they were in life. One side of their gravestone memorializes Gertrude, the other, Alice.

A monument to deported World War II Resistance fighters in the cemetery's southeast corner is right near the **Federalists' Wall** where the last 147 survivors of the Paris Commune insurgency were shot by government forces on 28 May 1871. They were buried on this spot in a common grave that has been a place of pilgrimage for leftwing sympathizers ever since.

This lush 108-acre sanctuary in eastern Paris is a museum of French history, but it's as much a park as a cemetery. Parisians by the hundreds come here to picnic, harvest escargots off the tombs, or neck on the benches. Chopin's tomb is used for posting love letters, and legend holds that women who kiss or rub the statue of Victor Noir, a French journalist (1848-70) killed by Pierre Bonaparte, will marry within a year. If you're lucky you may encounter Vincent de Langlade, who has spent his life studying this most famous of graveyards; he is the author of a dozen books on the necropolis. If you can't find him, pick up the detailed map available for sale at the cemetery's entrance and set out on your own celebrity search ♦ Daily. Blvd de Ménilmontant (between Blvd de Charonne and Rue du Repos and Pl Auguste-Métivier). 01.43.70.70.33. Métro: Père Lachaise

6 Musée Edith Piaf In a tiny museum filling two rooms of a private apartment near her grave in the **Père-Lachaise Cemetery,** the renowned French chanteuse lives on through the adoration of her fans, who come to look at her dressing gown, shoes, birth certificate, autographed letters, photographs, and portraits of her lovers. Recordings of the "little sparrow" play softly in the background and the museum's devoted curator is always present to recount the final days of the great entertainer's life. ♦ M-Th 1-6PM by appointment only. 5 Rue Crespin-du-Gast (just south of Rue Oberkampf). 01.43.55.52.72. Métro: Ménilmontant

7 Parc des Buttes-Chaumont If you're tired of the crowds in the **Luxembourg Gardens** and need a break from the deadly symmetry of the **Tuileries,** do as the French do. Buy some ripe brie, a baguette, and a hearty Bordeaux, and head for this urban wilderness in the northern end of Paris.

The unusual park was built in 1867 by Baron Haussmann, who also laid out the sewers and the city's grand boulevards for Napoléon III. Before Haussmann, **Buttes-Chaumont** was a city dump. In what must be the most inspired use of landfill in history, a then-new material—concrete—was used to form natural-looking cliffs, ravines, rivers, and an artificial lake. There's even a grotto and waterfall that have been restored. **Buttes-Chaumont**'s lake island is capped with a Classical colonnaded temple and commands one of the city's most striking views of Montmartre and **Sacré-Coeur**. Visitors not inclined to mountaineering may prefer sipping a *citron pressé* (lemonade) on the terrace of the **Pavillon du Lac,** which serves tea and light lunches and is located on the park's west side. ♦ Daily. Bounded by Rues de Crimée and Manin, and Rue Botzaris and Ave Simon-Bolivar. Métro: Buttes Chaumont, Botzaris

8 **Parc de la Villette** The old slaughterhouse district, a 75-acre site in northeastern Paris, was transformed in the mid-1980s into a huge complex of buildings and parks devoted to science and technology. A series of bright-red "follies"—whimsical structures designed by architect **Bernard Tschumi**—are laid out in a grid pattern throughout the park. They serve a variety of functions, including a cafe, weathervane, children's play area, and belvedere. ♦ Ave Jean-Juares and Pl de la Fontaine-aux-Lions. 01.40.03.75.03. Métros: Porte de Pantin, Porte de la Villette

Within Parc de la Villette:

Cité des Sciences et de l'Industrie La Villette's centerpiece is an 880-footlong, $600-million research and exhibition building designed by French architect **Adrien Fainsilber.** The gray granite, glass, and dark steel structure was built around the shell of an enormous 19th-century slaughterhouse, whose lack of central pillars created 1.5 million square feet of usable space. Exhibits are organized around such general themes as the earth and space, matter and physics, language and communication, and life on earth; many are multilingual and interactive. The most popular attraction is **La Géode,** a polished-steel sphere, 117 feet in diameter, where films are projected on a huge 180º screen. **La Mediathèque** houses 1,000 videodiscs, 150,000 books, and a large conference center. ♦ Admission. Tu-Su. 30 Ave Corentin-Cariou (at Blvd McDonald). 08.36.68.29.30, 01.40.05.12.12

Cité de la Musique Opened in 1995, this complex is **Parc de la Villette**'s newest attraction. Architect **Christian de Portzamparc**'s monumental ensemble of buildings is arranged along a glass-roofed interior street and includes two concert halls, an opera house, and a museum. The schedule of high-quality programs includes dance performances, operas, and concerts of classical and contemporary music from around the world. The **Conservatoire National de Musique et de Danse** (National Conservatory of Music and Dance), where students often give free recitals, is based here, as is the **Ensemble InterContemporain,** a research and educational institution devoted to late–20th-

century music. The 5-story **Musée de la Musique** displays a collection of over 4,500 music-related items, including 16th-century Venetian lutes; the 19th-century instruments of Adolphe Sax, inventor of the saxophone; 5 Stradivarius violins; and Frank Zappa's modular E-Mu synthesizer. ♦ Admission. Box office: W-Su noon-6PM. Museum: Tu-Su. 01.44.84.45.45, 01.44.84.44.84

9 **Rue de Paradis** This shabby little street is the domain of the finest French and European tableware outlets. Nearly 50 shops selling porcelain, silver, earthenware, crystal, and glass are crowded along its three blocks. All the most elegant brands of tableware may be found here at prices that are 30 to 50 percent lower than in the US. ♦ Métros: Château d'Eau, Poissonnière

On Rue de Paradis:

Musée Baccarat A glittering collection of Baccarat crystal is displayed here. Some of the pieces were used by heads of state, including the Queen of Siam and King Louis Philippe. Also on view are the Baccarat glasses commissioned for Henry Ford II's yacht and Franklin Roosevelt's White House. The most dazzling pieces are the 2 1-ton 79-light candelabras ordered by Czar Nicholas II for his St. Petersburg palace. Baccarat crystal is sold here as well. ♦ Free; fee for group tours. M-Sa. No. 30 *bis* (between Rues du Faubourg-St-Denis and d'Hauteville). 01.47.70.64.30

10 **Parc de Monceau** This small and quirky park dates from 1778, when Philippe-Egalité, the Duke of Orléans, commissioned the painter Carmontel to design a private garden on the Monceau Plain, then outside the city limits. Carmontel created a whimsical landscape full of architectural follies: a pyramid, a pagoda, a Roman temple, windmills, and artfully placed ruins. The park changed hands a few times after the Revolution, and by 1862 it had been revamped by Alphand, an engineer under Baron Haussmann. Alphand gave the landscape the picturesque, English garden–inspired elements still evident today. Of particular interest are the **Naumachie,** an oval basin with a colonnade said to have come from the unfinished mausoleum of Henri II at St-Denis, and the round **Barrière Monceau,** one of the many *barrières* (tollhouses) built along the old city wall (now destroyed) in 1784 by **Claude-Nicholas Ledoux.** Although Ledoux's commission called for 55 such tollhouses, historians are unsure how many were actually built; only 4 still stand. ♦ Entrances at: Blvd de Courcelles (between Blvd Malesherbes and Ave de Vigny). Métro: Monceau; Ave Velasquez (west of Blvd Malesherbes). Métro: Villiers; Ave Ruysdaël (north of Pl de Rio-de-Janeiro). Métro: Miromesnil; Ave Van-Dyck (northeast of Rue de Courcelles). Métro: Courcelles

11 Musée Cernuschi A fine collection of Chinese art is housed in the former mansion of wealthy financier Henri Cernuschi. This small but exceptional museum is near the east gate of the **Parc de Monceau.** ◆ Admission. Tu-Su. 7 Ave Velasquez (west of Blvd Malesherbes). 01.45.63.50.75. Métro: Villiers

11 Musée Nissim de Camondo Around the corner from the **Musée Cernuschi,** this museum exhibits the furniture and decorative art (including several **Gobelins** tapestries) of the Count de Camondo, who once owned this house. ◆ Admission. W-Su. 63 Rue de Monceau (between Blvd Malesherbes and Pl de Rio-de-Janeiro). 01.53.89.06.40. Métro: Villiers

12 Grande Arche de La Défense The axis that starts with the **Carrousel Arch** in front of the **Louvre** and runs westward through the **Tuileries Gardens** to the **Obelisk of Luxor,** then down the Champs-Elysées to the **Arc de Triomphe,** has been extended westward with this 300,000-ton white Carrara marble monument in the La Défense district. Designed by **Johan Otto von Spreckelsen,** who won an international competition for the commission, the arch is actually a hollow cube built on 12 pillars set 99 feet into the ground.

The building houses the Ministry of Planning and Development, the Foundation for the Rights of Man, headquarters for several cultural foundations, and private offices. Inaugurated in July 1989 as part of the 200th anniversary of the French Revolution, the building brings monumental dazzle to the sterile high-rise jungle that has become Paris's business district ◆ 1 Parvis de la Défense (just west of Pl de la Défense). Métro: Grande Arche de la Défense

13 Musée de la Contrefaçon (Forgeries Museum) It is not unusual to see the great ladies of Parisian society stopping by this one-room museum in the elegant 16th arrondissement to compare a new handbag or a Cartier watch to the near-perfect forgeries on display. The museum is a veritable capitalist's cabinet of curiosities, where *authentique* products are exhibited surrounded by bogus imitations from Japan, Korea, Italy, Morocco, Taiwan, and elsewhere. Note the ingenious copies of Louis Vuitton luggage, which wear counterfeit tags guaranteeing they are genuine Vuitton. A short visit here is enough to cast doubt forever on that little shop near the hotel selling Dior key chains, Omega watches, bottles of Benedictine, flacons of Chanel No. 5, and magnums of Cordon Rouge Champagne at bargain-basement prices. ◆ Admission. M-Th 2-5PM; F 9AM-noon. 16 Rue de la Faisanderie (between Rue de Longchamp and Ave Foch). 01.45.01.51.11. Métro: Porte Dauphine

14 Musée Guimet The finest collection of Asian art in Paris is on view here. Founded by industrialist Emile Guimet in 1879 to house his private collection of Oriental antiquities, the museum later became the **Département des Arts Asiatiques des Musées Nationaux** (National Museum of Asian Art). As such, it exhibits most of the **Louvre**'s Far East collection and has steadily expanded its holdings to include more than 50,000 works from China, Japan, India, Indochina, Afghanistan, and Tibet. At press time the museum was scheduled to reopen after renovations took place. ◆ Admission. M, W-Su. 6 Pl d'Iéna (at Ave d'Iéna). 01.45.05.00.98. Métro: Iéna

15 Musée d'Art Moderne de la Ville de Paris (Museum of Modern Art of the City of Paris) The City of Paris's rich modern art collection is housed in the **Palais de Tokyo,** a large Art Deco pavilion built for the **1937 Exposition Universelle.** The exhibits have a distinctly Parisian flavor—they are mainly paintings, drawings, graphics, sculptures, and photographs by 20th-century artists who have lived and worked here. Fauvism (Matisse, Derain, Vlaminck), Cubism (Braque, Gris, Picasso, Léger), Surrealism (De Chirico, Picabia, Brauner), the so-called School of Paris, Abstraction, Nouveau Realisme, and conceptual art are all well-represented.

Recent acquisitions include works by Simon Hantaï, Magdalena Abakanaowicz, Tony Stoll, and Louise Bourgeois, and photographs by Marc Riboud and Willy Ronis. Of the approximately 200 works the museum has on permanent display, the most spectacular are the monumental paintings by Matisse (two panels of *La Danse*), Sonia and Robert Delaunay, and Raoul Dufy (including his amazing 6,095-square-foot *La Fée Electricité,* the world's largest painting). The museum also puts on first-rate temporary exhibitions—retrospectives on Calder, Giacametti, Chagall, and Mark Rothko are just some of the latest. ◆ Admission. Tu-Su. 11 Ave du Président-Wilson (between Pls de l'Alma and d'Iéna). 01.53.67.40.00. Métro: Iéna

16 Alain Ducasse ★★★★$$$$ Joël Robuchon may have retired from the restaurant scene, but his legacy continues under the guidance of famed chef-owner Alain Ducasse. The magnificent 18th-century *hôtel particulier*—one of the few Paris restaurants to be awarded three Michelin stars—features a mosaic fountain and trompe l'oeil tapestries in the three wood-paneled dining rooms. Ducasse's own renditions—freshwater crayfish with wild mushrooms, langoustine wrapped with strips of squid and served with crunchy vegetables in ginger—are outstanding. Diners with heartier appetites can feast on pig's head on a bed of salad and truffles with caramelized potatoes and bacon. All this, plus an impressive collection of wines, make this quite a dining experience. ♦ M-F lunch and dinner. Reservations recommended at least two months in advance. 59 Ave Raymond-Poincaré (between Rue de Longchamp and Pl Victor-Hugo). 01.47.27.12.27. Métro: Victor Hugo

16 Le Parc $$$$ Located in the well-to-do 16th arrondissement, across the river from the **Eiffel Tower,** this aristocratic hotel is as noble and cozy as an English manor. The 120 sumptuous rooms and suites were decorated by leading British designer Nina Campbell, and the furniture was commissioned from Viscount Linley, the nephew of Her Majesty the Queen. The public areas, including the cozy lobby bar, are decorated in the style of an English gentlemen's club. The **Relais du Parc** restaurant is on the premises (see below). ♦ 55-57 Ave Raymond-Poincaré (between Rue de Longchamp and Pl Victor-Hugo). 01.44.05.66.66; fax 01.44.05.66.00. Métro: Victor Hugo

Within Le Parc:

Relais du Parc ★★★$$$ Don't despair if you can't get a reservation at **Alain Ducasse** next door—the master's touch is clearly felt at this restaurant, where, having taken over the Robuchon empire, he is consulting chef. The menu tends toward the southwest of France with such dishes as peppers stuffed with cod, tomatoes stuffed with crispy vegetables, and melon soup and John Dory with fennel. The dining room is English colonial–style and in summer you can dine beneath chestnut trees in the verdant garden courtyard. ♦ Daily breakfast, lunch, and dinner. Reservations required. 01.44.05.66.10

17 Bois de Boulogne Stretching along the western flank of Paris and occupying more than 2,200 acres, this is the city's ultimate playground. The Merovingians hunted wild boar and wolves in the *bois* in the 6th century, it was enclosed by Henri II in 1556, and in the 17th century **Jean-Baptiste Colbert** transformed the land into royal hunting grounds. After Napoléon III gave the forest to the city of Paris, Baron Haussmann remodeled the landscape; using London's Hyde Park as his guide he built many of the lakes, restaurants, racetracks, and paths that are here today. Haussmann designed the park so it would be entered from Avenue Foch, which he also designed, and which leads grandly down to the Porte Dauphine. Once in the park, you can choose from a seemingly infinite variety of activities and attractions. The most notable include the **Bagatelle** (01.40.67.97.00), a magical 50-acre park with an 18th-century villa built by the then future king, Charles X, a rose garden with 8,000 bushes of 700 varieties, and a

grand iris garden; the **Jardin d'Acclimatation** (01.40.67.90.80), an amusement park and miniature zoo; the **Auteuil** steeplechase racecourse (01.40.71.47.47) and the **Longchamp** flats track (01.44.30.75.00); the **Shakespeare Garden** (01.42.71.44.06), where the bard's works and classic French plays are performed in an open-air theater in summer; **Les Serres d'Auteuil** (01.40.71.74.00), a magnificent 19th-century greenhouse complex where concerts are given in May and June; and **Le Pré Catelan**, another flower and tree garden that shelters a luxurious cafe/restaurant of the same name (see below). There are numerous sports facilities, including the **Roland Garros Stadium** (01.47.43.48.00.), where the French Open tennis tournament is held. Bicycles can be rented opposite the main entrance to the **Jardin d'Acclimatation** (at the Carrefour des Sablons) and near the **Royal Pavilion** (at the Carrefour du Bout-des-Lacs) daily May through September and on Saturday and Sunday the rest of the year. ♦ Métros: Porte Dauphine, Porte Maillot, Porte d'Auteuil

Within the Bois de Boulogne:

Le Pré Catelan ★★★$$$ Elegant and romantic, this beautiful Belle Epoque, two–Michelin-star restaurant in the middle of the park features terrace dining in the summer. Chef Frédéric Anton, a Joël Robuchon protégé, is one of the young stars of the Parisian culinary scene. Some of his specialties include cauliflower and Greek-style marinated artichokes with fresh coriander, creamy mushroom risotto, grilled turbot with spinach purée, free-range guinea hen cooked on a spit, and *bergamot* (caramel) orange ice cream. ♦ Tu-Sa lunch and dinner; Su lunch. Route de la Grande-Cascade and Allée de la Reine-Marguerite. 01.44.14.41.14

18 Musée Marmottan The 16th arrondissement in Paris, which stretches from the **Arc de Triomphe** down between the **Bois de Boulogne** and the Seine, is a haven for the Proustian bourgeoisie. Out-of-town shoppers know this quarter as a place to buy old table linens, fine chocolates, and designer silk dresses, and others know it as the location of Omar Sharif's private gambling club. The best-kept secret of the select 16th, however, is the 19th-century Passy town house that contains this museum, which features more than a hundred original paintings, pastels, and drawings by Monet. This treasure trove of the artist's work from Giverny is relatively deserted, except when busloads of Japanese tourists descend.

After you take a good look at the 300 illuminated medieval manuscripts on the ground floor, skip the 2 floors devoted to the cold First Empire furniture and Flemish tapestries, and head straight for the basement.

Here amidst the joyous splashes and swirls of poppies, tulips, irises, and apple blossoms you'll experience the essential spirit of Monet's Giverny work. The exhibition culminates in a circular gallery with the artist's notebooks and palette in the center and 16 of his water-lily canvases on the walls. Stand in the middle of the room and pivot around to behold Monet's magical pond as it changed with the sun's daily round. (In summer you can visit the actual pond and gardens at Monet's Normandy home in Giverny. For more information, see "Day Trips" on page 256.) ♦ Admission. Tu-Su. 2 Rue Louis-Boilly (at Ave Raphaël). Recorded message 01.42.24.07.02, 01.44.96.50.33. Métro: La Muette

19 Jardin du Ranelagh Directly across Avenue Raphaël from the **Musée Marmottan** are these sumptuous English-style gardens, home to one of the last hand-cranked merry-go-rounds in Europe. The carousel is powered by a middle-aged woman with forearms rivaling those of Arnold Schwarzenegger. Children in ruffled dresses or seersucker suits hold on for dear life with one hand while wielding rod sticks in the other, trying to hook the elusive brass ring. ♦ Aves Raphaël and Prudhon. Métro: La Muette

20 Castel Béranger French architect **Hector Guimard** established his reputation in 1898 as the country's premier Art Nouveau designer with this seven-story apartment building, which sits along a quiet residential street in the 16th arrondissement. Guimard's quasi-organic Expressionism is seen here in its full glory, particularly in the curvilinear floral details of his ironwork, faience, and carved-wood elements, which prefigure the architect's more purely sculptural métro entrances of 1900. The private building contains 36 apartments, no two alike. ♦ 14-16 Rue La Fontaine (between Rue de Boulainvilliers and Ave Mozart). Métro: Ranelagh, RER: Ave du President Kennedy–Maison de Radio-France

21 Foundation Le Corbusier Charles-Edouard Jeanneret, better known as **Le Corbusier** (1887-1965), was the Swiss architect who helped revolutionize today's urban environment with his passion for cubist forms. Within Paris and its suburbs stand 15 of his modular buildings, including the apartment house in which he lived in 1933 (24 Rue Nungesser-et-Coli, south of Blvd d'Auteuil); a **Salvation Army** headquarters (12 Rue Cantagrel, between Rues du Chevaleret and de Tolbiac) built in 1933 of glass, brick, and exposed concrete; and the famous **Swiss Dormitory** and **Brazilian Pavilion** (constructed in 1932 and 1959, respectively) at Cité Universitaire (19-21 Blvd Jourdan, at Ave David-Weill). The headquarters and research library of the **Foundation Le**

Corbusier are housed in **Villa Jeanneret;** the adjoining **Villa La Roche,** also designed by the architect in 1923, contains a sparse collection of Le Corbusier's own painting, sculpture, and furniture design and is open to the public. ♦ Admission. M-F; closed in August. 8-10 Sq du Docteur-Blanche (southeast of Rue du Docteur-Blanche). 01.42.88.41.53. Métro: Jasmin

22 Parc André Citroën When the offices of automobile manufacturer André Citroën moved outside the city in the 1980s, an expanse of land the size of 50 football fields was left free in the quiet 15th arrondissement. The city transformed half this area into public grounds, now the only park in Paris where sitting on the grass is not forbidden. Landscape designers Alan Provost and Gilles Clément have made water a dominant feature here: Shallow pools border the park, and waterfalls tumble from small stone structures. The park's north side has six small gardens, each with a different theme and dominant color. The red garden, for example, contains cherry and apple trees. ♦ 25 Rue Leblanc (between Rue St-Charles and Quai André-Citroën). 01.45.57.13.35. Métros: Balard, Javel

23 Jardins Albert Kahn Turn-of-the-century banker and idealist Albert Kahn envisioned a society in which there would be a crossbreeding of cultures; these enchanting gardens, in which 360 species of plants from around the world thrive in one place, are the horticultural embodiment of his sociological ideas. Here you'll find an English garden, French flower beds, a rose garden, and a meticulous Japanese garden with a wooden teahouse (where Japanese tea ceremonies are conducted two days a month in September and April; call for days and times). This Eden has been a sanctuary of meditation for such notables as Colette, Einstein, Ferdinand Foch, Edouard Herriot, and Arthur Honegger. When your stomach's needs transcend those of your spirit, go to the **Palmarium,** a glass-and-iron rotunda where sandwiches and pastries are served.

Kahn also had an interest in photography that was furthered by his friendship with cinematography inventor Louis Lumière. Between 1910 and 1920, Kahn sent documentary photographers all over the world to compose his *Archives de la Planète.* More than 72,000 photographs and in excess of a half-million feet of film are housed in the **Musée Albert Kahn,** on the grounds of the gardens. ♦ Admission. Tu-Su. Reservations required for tea ceremonies; call the museum. 14 Rue du Port (between Rue des Abondances and Quai du 4-Septembre), Boulogne-Billancourt. Museum 01.46.04.52.80. Métro: Boulogne–Pont de St-Cloud

Day Trips

1 Basilique de St-Denis Around AD 250, St. Denis, the first Christian evangelist to come to Paris, was beheaded by the Romans. Legend has it that he picked up his head and carried it from Montmartre several kilometers north until, finally, he fell and was buried by a peasant woman. Whatever the facts, the grave of St. Denis became a place of pilgrimage. By the 12th century, pilgrims were so numerous that many were actually trampled to death in the stampede to the saint's shrine. Abbot Suger (1081-1151) decreed that a new church, large and full of light, be constructed on the site. The result was the first Gothic edifice in the world and one of the lesser-known treasures of Paris. The basilica became the starting place for the Crusades and the burial place of three dynasties of French royalty. Most macabre are the tombs of Marie de Médicis and Henri IV, who are depicted twice in marble. On the tops of their tombs are sculptures of the two in their finest Renaissance collars and jewels; below, their skeletons are shown being eaten away by worms. Badly neglected after the Revolution, the structure has been restored and is now a repository of exquisite funerary sculpture. The soaring nave glows with a rainbow of light from the stained-glass windows, illuminated most brightly on winter mornings. ◆ Admission to tombs. Rues de Strasbourg and de la Légion-d'Honneur, St-Denis. 01.48.09.83.54. Métro: Basilique de St-Denis

2 Château de Chantilly In 1671, Louis de Bourbon entertained King Louis XIV in his newly completed gardens at this château in the town of Chantilly. On that occasion, Vatel, the most famous chef in France, failed to deliver the fish course on time and, rather than live with the shame, promptly took his own life. Such is the tradition of excellence here.

Rising like a mirage from a moat in the midst of a dense beech forest 48 kilometers (30 miles) north of Paris, the château, which now houses the **Musée Condé,** is an artful conglomeration of the best of 16th-, 18th-, and 19th-century French architecture. During the Revolution the original château, built in the early 15th century, was razed, stone by stone, by vengeful mobs. The Duc d'Aumale, who was responsible for the subsequent reconstruction in 1844, showed his fine eclectic taste in other areas as well: His art

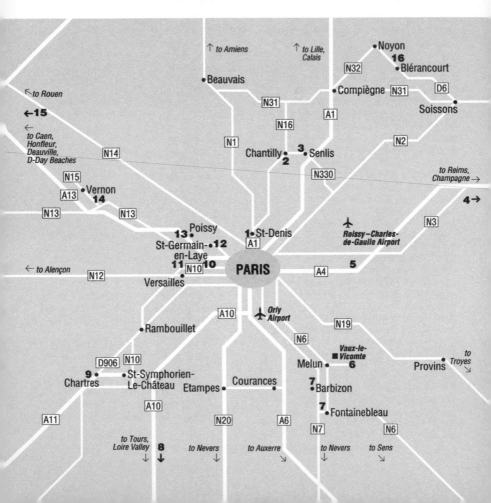

collection of medieval miniatures and French, Flemish, and Italian paintings is now on display in the **Musée Condé.** Each June the famous Prix de Diane horse race is run at a track on the edge of the palace grounds, and the **Grandes Ecuries,** Chantilly's extensive stables, are in use today as part of the **Musée Vivant du Cheval** (Living Museum of the Horse). The dressage exhibitions are great entertainment for children. ◆ Admission. M, W-Su. Trains leave from the Gare du Nord station. Paris Vision and Cityrama (see "Orientation" chapter) offer seasonal half-day trips on Sunday. Rte de l'Aigle (east of Rte N16), Chantilly. Musée Condé 03.44.57.08.00, Musée Vivant du Cheval 03.44.57.40.40

3 Senlis This entire town is classified as a historical monument. It is girdled by 23-foot-high, 13-foot-thick Roman walls that are punctuated by watchtowers and pierced by massive gates. The town's cathedral is older than **Notre-Dame-de-Paris** or **Chartres** and lofts a lacy spire considered the most beautiful in France. After visiting the cathedral, tour the ruins of the royal castle, the 28 towers of the Gallo-Roman wall, and the thousand-seat Roman amphitheater just outside of town. The streets of Senlis, such as the Rue du Châtel and Rue de la Treille, are winding, stone-paved canyonways dark with history. The best bet for exploring them is to follow the small arrows that indicate a walking route through town. ◆ Trains leave from the Gare du Nord station. 40 km (30 miles) north of Paris

4 Champagne The Champagne region is a realm of flowing hills dotted with vineyards, medieval stone towns, and châteaux. Its capital Reims was the coronation site of French kings, beginning with Clovis in 496. The cathedral here is stunning and definitely worth a stop. Epernay, the region's second city, is the home of Moët et Chandon, the giant among an estimated 145 Champagne producers in the region. Most of the largest producers offer tours, which usually culminate in some free sampling and (be forewarned) a persuasive sales pitch once your resistance is down. Five minutes north of Epernay is one of Champagne's best restaurants—the **Royal Champagne** in Champillon (Rte N2051, 03.26.52.87.11). **Boyer** in Reims (64 Blvd Henry-Vasnier, at Ave du Général-Giraud, 03.26.82.80.80) is one of France's most outstanding dining spots. For information contact Reims's **Office de Tourisme** (2 Rue Guillaume-de-Machault, 03.26.77.45.25). ◆ Trains to Reims leave from the Gare de l'Est

5 Disneyland Paris After a disappointing start, things have turned around for this all-American institution in Paris. In 1992 the 4,806-acre resort and amusement park opened in Marne-la-Vallée only 32 kilometers (20 miles) east of central Paris, offering a **Magic Kingdom** theme park similar to those in California, Florida, and Japan, as well as 6 hotels, 29 restaurants, a campground, golf course, and office, retail, and residential space. Originally called **Euro Disneyland,** the $2.5-billion property lost $1.1 billion in its first year, but announced its first quarterly profit in the summer of 1995 and has steadily increased since then. The park now draws more than 12 million visitors a year. In addition to adopting a new name, the amusement park has introduced 11 new attractions in recent years in an effort to boost attendance; among them is **Space Mountain,** a Jules Verne–inspired roller coaster that reaches the speed of 47 miles per hour—20 percent faster than any other Disney ride. Like its counterparts, the amusement park is divided into five major "lands": **Adventureland, Discoveryland, Fantasyland, Frontierland,** and **Main Street, USA.** And, like the US parks, there tend to be lines at the ticket windows and for the rides inside. ◆ Admission. Hours vary according to day and season; call ahead. Rte A4 (just east of Rte D231). 01.60.30.60.30. RER: Marne-la-Vallée/Chessy

6 Vaux-le-Vicomte When Nicolas Fouquet, superintendent of finances for Louis XIV, threw a housewarming party in July 1661 to celebrate the completion of this château, he spared no expense. Molière's troupe was there to perform; the guests ate from solid-gold plates; and horses, jewels, and swords were the party favors. But this excess was not generous enough. Because he neglected to offer the château itself to the seethingly jealous king, Fouquet was thrown in prison on trumped-up charges. Louis then commandeered the architects and artisans who had built the château and put them to work on what was to be the royal palace at **Versailles.** Today, Fouquet's château—58 km (36 miles) from Paris—is the largest private property in France. It's generally uncrowded and beautifully restored, and the gardens, which cover more than 125 acres, are simply stunning. Candlelight concerts of Baroque music are given on Thursday and Saturday evenings from May to mid-October. ◆ Admission. Daily April through 11 November; hours are irregular the rest of the year; for information call 01.64.14.41.90. Rte D215 (just east of Rte N36). RER: Melun

7 Château de Fontainebleau and Barbizon Newly returned from ignominious imprisonment in Spain, French King François I (who reigned from 1515 to 1547) was determined to recoup his dignity by creating a new court that would dazzle the world. He chose an old hunting lodge in the forest of Fontainebleau as its site and commanded the services of scores of Italian artists and craftsmen, who, the artist Vasari wrote, turned it into a "new Rome."

Keep in mind that the château is the size of an entire town; to tour it even casually requires at least a couple of hours. And that doesn't count a tour of the **Fontainebleau Forest,** a magnificent 96-square-mile expanse of towering trees and dramatic promontories where you can ride, climb rocks, or simply walk. At one edge of the forest is the hamlet of Barbizon, once the hub of the pre-Impressionist movement of painting. Rousseau, Millet, Daubigny, and Corot painted here, and many of their houses and studios have been lovingly restored and opened to the public. ◆ Admission. M, W-Su. Paris Vision and Cityrama (see "Orientation" chapter) offer day-trip tours. Trains run from the Gare de Lyon station to the Fontainebleau station, where there is a bus to the palace. 66 km (41 miles) southeast of Paris. 01.60.71.50.70

8 **Loire Valley** The Loire Valley would be a perfect destination for a day trip were it not for the profusion of magnificent châteaux: Two weeks spent in the valley would only begin to do it justice. Throughout the centuries French nobles have chosen to build their country houses along this calm river with lush banks. Visit as many châteaux as you can—**Chambord, Chenonceaux, Cheverny, Chinon, Loches,** and **Villandry** are particularly beautiful. But take your time, each château warrants at least a morning of contemplation. Save your afternoons for wine-tasting. For information about this region, contact **Comités Régionaux de Tourisme, Pays de Loire Hôtel de Région** (2 Rue de la Loire, 44200 Nantes, 02.40.48.24.20) or **Centre-Val de Loire** (9 Rue St-Pierre-Lentin, 45041 Orléans Cedex, 02.38.70.30.30). ◆ Take the train to Blois or Tours and from there catch a bus to Chambord or Cheverny (two buses M, W, and F). Paris Vision and Cityrama (see "Orientation" chapter) offer day tours to Cheverny, Chenonceaux, and Chaumont

9 **Chartres** The cathedral at Chartres must be among the most spiritual places in the world. Though the town has changed dramatically since the building of the cathedral, you can still see the signature spire cutting into the sky above the wheat fields, a sight that for medieval pilgrims meant they had reached one of five primary holy places to be visited on the path to heaven. Carved in the cathedral's celebrated portals and glowing in its stained-glass windows, Bible stories unfold with an overwhelming panoply of symbols and images. This imagery is brilliantly interpreted by Malcolm Miller—an English scholar who has devoted decades to research and writing on the cathedral—during his morning and afternoon tours. Before or after the tour, spend some time alone sitting in a pew and absorb the majesty of the cathedral. The 12th- and 13th-century stained-glass windows (the finest in France) are so brilliant that in medieval times peasants believed they were made of ground-up gems. Modern science disproves this notion, but no one has explained how medieval glassmakers at Chartres created such beauty.

After touring the cathedral, stroll around the old town and along the banks of the Eure River. Or explore the area on two wheels—there are bicycles for rent at Place Pierre-Semard. If you are interested in 20th-century folk art, visit **Picassiette's House** (20 Rue du Repos, 02.37.34.10.78), an extraordinary complex of rooms, chapels, and gardens constructed entirely from broken glass by a cemetery worker; it is open from Easter to All Saints Day; there's an admission charge. **Picassiette's House** is a 30-minute walk or a 5-minute taxi ride from the cathedral and is only open a few hours a week; inquire about the schedule at the tourist office in the Place de la Cathédrale (02.37.21.50.00) before you set out. Stay overnight at **Château d'Esclimont** (02.37.31.15.15), a gorgeous 16th-century castle just 15 kilometers (9 miles) from Chartres in St-Symphorien-Le-Château. ◆ Trains leave from the Gare Montparnasse station; Paris Vision and Cityrama (see "Orientation" chapter) offer half-day trips. 94 km (58 miles) southwest of Paris

Chartres Cathedral

10 Parc de St-Cloud For true escapists, this 1,100-acre park, lying just outside of Paris and landscaped by André Le Nôtre, is a little dream come true: a province of leafy woods that is a world apart from the urban bustle and a delight for children. For just a few francs, you can rent a tandem bicycle and take a romantic ride by the park's 17th-century fountains. ♦ Rte N185, St-Cloud. Métro: Boulogne–Pont de St-Cloud

11 Château de Versailles What can you say about the palace that has everything? On a royal whim, Louis XIV transformed a small hunting lodge bordering a marsh into the most lavish statement of monarchic privilege that has ever existed. Owing to just such excesses, the monarchy has long since fallen, but **Versailles** has not. Since 1978 the French government has spent over $19 million on the restoration of this palace, concentrating on 50 rooms in the more private family apartments. The **Hall of Mirrors**, designed by **Jules Hardouin-Mansart**, may well be the most dazzling room ever built, and it offers a grand view of the gardens. Unfortunately, all that splendor can be numbing: One grand hall begins to resemble the next soon. To get the most from a visit, read up on the palace's history beforehand and reserve plenty of time for loitering. Indeed, some visitors prefer to spend the entire day just wandering in the 250 acres of gardens.

Designed by the incomparable André Le Nôtre, the gardens are too big to be crowded and too varied to bore. The air smells of damp earth and the place is as quiet as Eden, but the precise geometry and balance of the designs betray the fact that nature, along with everything else, was forced to bow before the Sun King. The famous fountains, **Grandes Eaux,** splash Sunday at 3:30PM on from May through September. The **Neptune Basin** floodlight-and-fireworks show is held four times a year; find out when—it's worth the trip. There are rowboats for rent on the Grand Canal and bicycles for rent on the Allée St-Antoine by the start of the Grand Canal. If you are traveling with small children, don't miss the **Hameau** (the Hamlet), a cute little mock farm village on a duck pond built for Marie Antoinette so that she and her ladies-in-waiting could play at being peasant girls; there is a delightful zoo with farm animals. ♦ Admission to château. Château: Tu-Su. Gardens: daily. Paris Vision and Cityrama (see "Orientation" chapter) offer various tours. Trains leave from the Gare Montparnasse station. There is also a bus *(No. 171)* from the Pont de Sèvres métro station. Pl d'Armes (between Aves de Sceaux and de St-Cloud), Versailles. 01.30.84.76.18. RER: Versailles–Rive Gauche

12 Château de St-Germain-en-Laye For Louis XIV, this fortress in the town of St-Germain-en-Laye meant security. Born and bred in St-Germain, he later took refuge here during the popular uprising in 1648-53 known as the *Fronde.* Built in 1122 around a château that guarded the western flank of Paris, **St-Germain-en-Laye** contains an earlier version of Paris's **Sainte-Chapelle** (though it has long been without its glass), also designed by architect **Pierre de Montreuil.** Today the château also houses the **Musée des Antiquités Nationales.** The château's gardens were designed by the industrious André Le Nôtre before he was whisked away to landscape **Versailles.** In one corner of the gardens is the Pavillon Henri IV (21 Rue Thiers, east of Pl du Général-de-Gaulle, 01.39.10.15.15), where Louis XIV was born and Alexandre Dumas wrote *The Three Musketeers.* Since 1830 this building has also been a restaurant/hotel and a good place to lunch overlooking the Seine. ♦ Admission. M, W-Su. There is a bus *(No. 158)* from the Grande Arche de la Défense métro station. Pl du Général-de-Gaulle and Rue Thiers, St-Germain-en-Laye. 01.39.10.13.00. RER: St-Germain-en-Laye

13 Villa Savoye More than 70 years after its conception, this structure continues to be a striking evocation of modernist architectural purity. The last of several houses built in and around Paris in the 1920s by **Le Corbusier,** this "machine for living" synthesized many of the radical ideas the great Swiss architect espoused in his book *Vers une Architecture.* **Le Corbusier** wished to build a new type of bourgeois suburban villa, one that would reflect the precise, controlled rationalism made possible by modern technology. The result is an independent domestic mechanism separated from the landscape, which, in this case, it barely even touches. The villa is essentially an I-shaped series of rooms laid into a square tray that is elevated on slender *pilotis* (columns). As you travel on a continuous internal ramp into the building, you experience various light-filled spaces that eventually dissolve into the open air of the rooftop solarium. The strip windows, glass walls, flat roofs, cubic forms, and grid of columns were revolutionary at the time but now are familiar components of the International style that **Le Corbusier** helped establish. For more information on **Le Corbusier,** see **Foundation Le Corbusier** on page 251 ♦ Admission. M, W-Su. 82 Chemin de Villiers, Poissy. 01.39.65.01.06. RER: Poissy

There are 240 *bouquinistes* plying their bookselling trade from outdoor stalls, mainly along the banks of the Seine.

14 Giverny Anyone who's seen the beloved Claude Monet water-lily paintings knows what this place looks like. Monet's Normandy house and gardens have been well tended and restored, looking much as they did when the Impressionist painter lived here from 1883 to 1926. After the **Académie des Beaux-Arts** moved Monet's paintings to the **Musée Marmottan** (see page 250) in Paris in 1966, **Giverny** was neglected. Grass grew in the studio and a staircase caved in. But a renovation that was begun in 1977 and funded in part by Lila Acheson Wallace has awakened its former charms. Unfortunately, this is no secret, so on the weekend and in warm weather tourists swarm over the four-acre property.

Spring, when the early flowers are blooming and before the foreign tide hits France, is the best time to visit this horticultural/artistic shrine 50 kilometers (31 miles) northwest of Paris. Autumn, when you'll be able to see all the colors of the great painter's palette but with fewer distractions, is another good time. Two unexpected pleasures to be found here: Monet's collection of Japanese prints on display in the house, and the reproductions of the blue-and-yellow plates and cups designed by Monet on sale in the gift shop. ♦ Admission. Tu-Su; closed November through March. Cityrama and Paris Vision offer seasonal tours. Trains leave from the Gare St-Lazare station in the direction of Rouen. Get off at Vernon, which is about three miles from Giverny, and take a bus or taxi. Drivers should exit the Normandy autoroute A13 at Bonnières. Rte D5, Giverny. 02.32.51.28.21

15 Honfleur and Deauville Normandy, with its rugged coast, is the country of camembert, Calvados, apple orchards, and brick-and-beam-crossed plaster houses topped by steep shingled gables. Honfleur is one of the coast's most solidly Norman and picturesque harbors; Samuel de Champlain departed from here in 1608 to found Québec. Don't miss the Saturday morning market bustling around the old wooden Ste-Catherine church. The old port section of Honfleur has many seafood eateries, and just outside of town lies **La Ferme St-Siméon** (Rte Adolphe-Marais, 02.31.89.23.61), one of Normandy's finest restaurants.

Farther west along the coast is Deauville, the summer playground of Europe's social elite. Known for its casinos, private mansions, racetracks, and a film festival each fall, Deauville has a broad boardwalk and sandy stretch of beach that is a mere two-hour train ride from the center of Paris. ♦ Trains leave frequently from the Gare St-Lazare station. Drivers should exit the Normandy autoroute A13 at Beuzeville

MUSÉE DU DÉBARQUEMENT ARROMANCHES

15 D-Day Beaches Before arriving at the D-Day beaches, you pass Dives-sur-Mer, the site from which William the Conqueror embarked in 1066 to vanquish England. It was an important moment in history, but further from memory than the events of 6 June 1944. To the west, in Bénouville, is the Pegasus Bridge, the first spot taken by the Allies in Normandy. Farther on, the D-Day beaches begin, each with its own museum, its own monuments, and its own stories to tell. Most poignant is the US cemetery at Omaha Beach, 13 kilometers (8 miles) short of Pointe du Hoc, where 9,000 of the 23,000 North Americans killed in the invasion are buried. Even if you have come to experience modern history and the sorrows of the victors, it is worth visiting Bayeux to see the magnificent 231-footlong Bayeux Tapestry (1076) depicting William's conquests and the Norman invasion of England—a good meditation on the constancy of war. The tapestry is located in the **Centre Guillaume le Conquérant** (13 *bis* Rue de Nesmond, between Rues Larcher and Bienvenu, 02.31.51.25.50), which is open daily. The **Bayeaux Office de Tourisme** is at Pont St. Jean (02.31.51.28.28). Two important museums devoted to the Normandy campaign are the **Musée de la Bataille de Normandie** in Bayeux (02.31.92.93.41) and the **Musée du Débarquement Arromanches** in Arromanches (02.31.22.34.31).

16 Musée National de la Coopération Franco-Américaine Created by Anne Morgan, J.P.'s youngest daughter, who led a major civilian war relief and postwar recovery operation in this area during and after World War I, the museum was built in the ruins of a 17th-century château 106 kilometers (66 miles) northeast of Paris by **Salomon de Brosse,** architect of the **Luxembourg Palace** in Paris. In 1989 it was renovated for France's bicentennial by Frenchman **Yves Lion** and Canadian **Alan Levitt.** Exhibits include hundreds of historic war photographs, war memorabilia, and a collection of graceful late–19th- and 20th-century paintings, drawings, and sculptures on loan from the **Musée d'Orsay.** Represented here are Whistler, Calder, and Childe Hassam, as well as French artists who worked in the US. The handsome gardens were designed by Mark Rudkin. ♦ Admission for museum. Museum: M, W-Su. Gardens: daily. Château de Blérancourt, Blérancourt. 03.23.39.69.86

History

300 BC A tribe called the Parisii lives in a small settlement known as **Lutetia** on what is the modern-day **Ile de la Cité**. These early hunters and fishermen are well organized; they circulate their own gold coins.

52 BC After a fierce resistance effort during which most of their settlement is destroyed, the Parisii are conquered by the Romans. Lutetia is rebuilt and spreads out to the left bank of the **Seine**. Roman prefects rule from a compound on the site of the **Palais de la Cité**, the place from which future French kings will govern.

AD 100 Trade and fishing are the main commercial activities of Lutetia. Boatmen play a central role in government and in the thriving economy of the young town. A coat of arms bearing the likeness of a boat and representing the Boatmen's Guild becomes the official symbol of Lutetia. A similar coat of arms remains the official seal of modern Paris.

250 St. Denis (or Dionysius) leads a Christian mission to the city and establishes a community near the Seine. Twenty years later, Denis, the first bishop of what will become Paris, is killed at **Montmartre** (Martyr's Mount, or Mount of Mercury).

276 Lutetia continues to grow beyond the confines of the original settlement on Ile de la Cité, but the outlying parts of the city are vulnerable to attack by barbarians. A raid destroys the Left Bank settlements and forces the villagers to retreat to the island, where they build a fortified wall.

300 Lutetia becomes known as Paris.

450 Attila the Hun and his armies rampage through Europe and come close to taking Paris but are turned back at Orléans. The prayers of a 27-year-old nun named Geneviève are credited with halting the Huns' advance on Paris. She later becomes the female patron saint of Paris.

452 King Childebert builds a church in an open pasture on the outskirts of Paris. In later centuries, the church is repeatedly destroyed by invaders and rebuilt. The final building, erected in 1163, is named **St-Germain-des-Prés** after St Germanus, an early bishop of the city.

476 An invading tribe of Franks, under the leadership of King Clovis, captures Paris from the Gauls, marking the end of Roman rule over Paris and the founding of France. Clovis and the Franks convert to Christianity.

508 King Clovis makes Paris the capital of his kingdom of Franks, settling in the **Palais de la Cité**. Thus begins the Merovingian dynasty, which will rule until the eighth century.

751 The first of the Carolingian kings assumes the French throne. The dynasty is named for Charlemagne, who went on to rule the entire Western World as head of the Holy Roman Empire. Charlemagne subsequently makes Aix-la-Chapelle (Aachen) his foremost city, and Paris declines.

885 Paris in the Middle Ages is under constant attack by roaming tribes, most notably the Normans. After decades of invasions and sieges, the Normans are defeated by Count Eudes, who is later crowned King of France.

987 Hugh Capet, a Parisian nobleman, becomes King of France and moves the throne back to Paris.

1050 King Henri I, grandson of Hugh Capet, appoints a representative called the *prévôt de Paris* (provost of Paris) to function as mayor of the city and maintain order.

1100 A marketplace in **Les Halles** appears for the first time. A permanent market is built about 80 years later and survives in the same location until 1969.

1135 The **Basilique de St-Denis** is built on the outskirts of Paris in the new Gothic style.

1163 Pope Alexander III lays the foundation stone for the cathedral of **Notre-Dame**, based on a design sketched out by Bishop Maurice de Sully. Work takes two centuries to complete.

1171 An ancient, loosely organized association of river merchants and fishermen is formally chartered as a guild by King Louis VII. The guild receives monopoly rights to river trade, and its coat of arms is adopted by Paris as the city's official seal. The guild becomes immensely powerful.

1180 King Philip II begins an extensive building program in Paris. A 30-foot-high city wall is built and, within it, the **Louvre** fortress is constructed.

1190 King Philip II leaves Paris to lead a crusade. In his absence, he leaves the Boatmen's Guild, not the provost, in charge of Paris.

1215 The **University of Paris** is founded.

1220 The crown cedes to the Boatmen's Guild all tariff-collection rights, another sign of the growing power of the guilds. Paris is now clearly divided into three separate entities. The government is located on the Ile de la Cité, the **Rive Gauche** (Left Bank) is dominated by university and academic life, and the **Rive Droite** (Right Bank) is home to most commercial activity.

1239 King Louis IX purchases sacred relics—including the crown of thorns and pieces of the cross—from the Emperor of Constantinople and later builds the Gothic **Sainte-Chapelle** (Holy Chapel) to house them.

1253 The **Sorbonne** is founded. The world-famous university begins as lodgings for a handful of theology students. It expands quickly, and by the late 13th century is headquarters for the **University of Paris** and has more than 15,000 students. (Except for a period shortly after the Revolution, it has remained open continuously to the present.)

1260 Louis IX appoints the Boatmen's Guild to administer the affairs of the city. The power of the guild is beginning to threaten that of the king.

1300 The earliest surviving house in Paris is built.

1337 As France sinks into the drawn-out campaigns of the Hundred Years' War, building and expansion in Paris come to a virtual standstill.

1348 The plague, also called the Black Death, rages throughout Europe. Paris is hit particularly hard; thousands die.

1357 Etienne Marcel, leader of the Boatmen's Guild and an early mayor of Paris, leads a revolt against the young King Charles V. The king moves the royal residence to the **Marais** district. Marcel establishes a city council at the **Place de l'Hôtel-de-Ville,** site of the present seat of Paris city government. Marcel later allies himself with the British and is subsequently killed by a mob.

1364 Restored to power after the death of Marcel, King Charles V builds a new city wall around Paris.

1370 Wary of an uprising and threats against his rule by the powerful guilds, Charles V has his provost build a fortified palace called the **Bastille.** The eight-towered palace is later converted into a prison and becomes a symbol of corruption and abuse of power.

1413 Construction begins on **Pont Notre-Dame.**

1420 English armies under Henry V capture France. John Plantagenet, Duke of Bedford, is appointed regent of France. France is under British rule.

1429 Joan of Arc leads an attack on Paris in an effort to win back and liberate the city. She is wounded in the unsuccessful siege.

1431 King Henry VI of England dispenses with the regency and has himself crowned King of France in **Notre-Dame** cathedral.

1437 Charles VII leads a counterattack against the British and succeeds in recapturing Paris.

1453 With the Hundred Years War finally over, Paris can begin rebuilding after years of neglect. Recovery is slow but steady.

1510 The **Hôtel de Cluny,** originally built in 1330 but largely destroyed during the invasions, wars, and revolutions that followed, is rebuilt. (It now houses the **Musée de Cluny.**)

1527 King François I tears down most of the original structures of the **Louvre.**

1529 The prestigious **Collège de France** is founded by King François I.

1534 Ignatius Loyola and some of his followers take the vows that lead to the founding of the religious order called the Society of Jesus, whose members are known as Jesuits.

1537 A law is passed to ensure that at least one copy of every book published in France is kept in a royal library. The **Bibliothèque Nationale de France** (National Library of France) is founded.

1546 François I reestablishes Paris as the seat of royalty and commissions the building of a new Italian Renaissance palace on the grounds of the **Louvre.**

1559 Henri II dies of wounds received in a jousting tournament. His widow, Catherine de Médicis, has the **Maison des Tournelles** in the Marais demolished and commissions a new palace at the **Tuileries.**

1564 The **Palais des Tuileries** is completed. Designed by **Philibert Delorme,** it connects the two corner pavilions of the **Louvre** and takes its name from the *tuile* (tile) factories that had previously stood on the site. (It is razed in 1882-84.)

1572 Charles IX orders the assassination of 3,000 Huguenots on St. Bartholomew's Day.

1578 Work starts on the **Pont-Neuf.**

1594 Henri IV converts to Catholicism, settles in Paris, and continues building and expanding the **Louvre** and **Tuileries** palaces.

1605 Henri IV commissions a new palace in the Marais district.

1610 While waiting to move into his new palace, Henri IV is killed, becoming the only king to die within the **Louvre.**

1612 Under Louis XIII the Marais district becomes fashionable with the aristocracy.

1616 Marie de Médicis, Henri IV's widow, orders the construction of an avenue called the **Cours la Reine** (Queen's Way).

1627 The development of **Ile St-Louis** begins.

1631 The **Palais du Luxembourg** is built for Marie de Médicis; she never actually occupies the structure.

1632 Cardinal Richelieu commissions the **Palais Cardinal** (now the **Palais Royal**).

1635 The **Institut de France,** home of the prestigious **Académie Française,** is founded.

1666 Landscaper André Le Nôtre creates a wide, tree-lined avenue dubbed the **Grand Cours.** It is later renamed the **Avenue des Champs-Elysées.**

1672 Louis XIV transfers the court to **Versailles.** Most of the aristocracy follows.

1676 The **Hôtel des Invalides** is founded by Louis XIV to shelter several thousand veterans, most destitute.

1685 The **Place Vendôme** is built as a setting for a monument to Louis XIV. During the Revolution the monument is destroyed and the heads of victims of the guillotine are displayed on spikes, giving it the temporary name **Place des Piques** (Pike Square).

1718 The **Palais de l'Elysée** is built. Since 1873, it has been the official residence of the French president.

1728 The **Palais Bourbon** is constructed by the Duchess of Bourbon, one of Louis XIV's daughters. Today it houses the Assemblée Nationale, the lower house of the French Parliament.

1744 Louis XV vows to build a temple dedicated to Saint Geneviève if he recovers from an illness. He does recover and builds the **Panthéon,** which later becomes a necropolis for France's distinguished atheists, among them Voltaire, Rousseau, and Hugo.

1755 Louis XV commissions a large square beside the Seine as the site for an equestrian statue of himself. The resulting 21-acre **Place de la Concorde** is the largest square in Paris.

1786 The remains of the dead from the **Cimetière des Innocents** are moved to the **Catacombs.**

1789 A mob storms the **Bastille** prison on 14 July, captures the ammunition depot, releases the half-dozen prisoners kept there, kills the warden, and destroys the fortress. The French Revolution has begun.

1792 The **Comédie Française,** France's most prestigious theater troupe, moves into a new theater at the **Palais Royal.**

1793 A bloodthirsty mob takes over Paris and conducts a massacre of former government officials. Louis XVI is guillotined in the Place de la Concorde. During the next 13 months the Reign of Terror kills thousands, most executed at the guillotine.

1804 Napoléon crowns himself emperor in a ceremony at **Notre-Dame.**

1806 On Napoléon's orders, work commences on the **Arc de Triomphe.** The structure is not completed until 1836, well after Napoléon's downfall.

1841 The church of **Ste-Marie Madeleine,** better known as **La Madeleine,** is consecrated.

1848 The revolutionary fervor spreading throughout Europe is especially strong in Paris. The monarchy is overthrown once and for all.

1850 Baron Haussmann begins a series of public works projects and restorations that over the next two decades completely transform Paris.

1860 The city of Paris expands its boundaries by annexing outlying villages, including Montmartre.

1870 The Franco-Prussian war brings an end to a period of growth and prosperity. The population starves during the siege of Paris and the Paris Commune is suppressed. The **Palais des Tuileries** and the **Hôtel de Ville** are virtually destroyed.

1875 The **Opéra Garnier,** also known as the **Paris Opéra,** opens. Designed by **Charles Garnier,** the opulent Second Empire structure is for a time the largest theater in the world.

1876 Work commences on the **Basilique du Sacré-Coeur** in Montmartre. Construction will take decades.

1889 Amidst considerable controversy and opposition, the **Tour Eiffel** (Eiffel Tower), designed by **Gustave Eiffel,** is built for the Exposition Universelle (International Exhibition). It later becomes the most widely recognized symbol of Paris.

1900 The first underground railway line in Paris (the métro) opens. The **Grand Palais, Petit Palais,** and **Pont Alexandre III** are built for the Exposition Universelle. The city enjoys a period of commercial and artistic growth known as the Belle Epoque.

1914 During World War I, Paris is saved from a German invasion by the Battle of the Marne.

1920 **Montparnasse** replaces Montmartre as the center of artistic life in the city.

1937 The **Palais de Chaillot** is built for another Exposition Universelle. The structure houses four museums, two theaters, a library, and a restaurant.

1940 In the early days of World War II, the city is bombed. But France falls quickly and occupation rather than destruction follows.

1944 Paris is liberated by the Allies. General Charles de Gaulle leads a victory parade down the Champs-Elysées.

1950 Existentialism is in full bloom and its major proponents, Jean-Paul Sartre and Albert Camus, are the intellectual stars of Europe. Paris is once again a center of intellectual fervor.

1962 The **Mémorial de la Déportation** (Deportation Memorial) opens, commemorating the thousands of French, mostly Jews, who died during the Holocaust.

1968 Student demonstrations in the **Latin Quarter** and violent labor disputes throughout the city threaten to topple the government.

1977 Much like the **Eiffel Tower** of the last century, the **Centre Georges Pompidou** opens to a critical outcry. It quickly becomes the most popular tourist destination in Paris.

1985 The **Musée Picasso** opens and becomes an immediate hit.

1986 The **Musée d'Orsay,** a showcase for 19th-century art and culture, is unveiled.

1988 The renovation of the Les Halles district is completed.

1989 As the bicentennial of the fall of the **Bastille** is celebrated, a new addition to the **Louvre** is greeted with tremendous criticism. Designed by American architect **I.M. Pei,** the project includes a 70.5-foot glass pyramid. Again, the critics are silenced by enormous crowds of visitors.

1992 The inaugural performance is held at the new **Opéra Bastille.** The huge new opera house revitalizes the Bastille area.

1995 Socialist President François Mitterrand's 14-year term comes to an end. Conservative leader Jacques Chirac, former mayor of Paris, is elected president of the republic.

1996 President Jacques Chirac declares the banning of nuclear tests in the South Pacific.

Writer Marguerite Duras dies at age 81. Author of more than 70 books, she is most famous for *The Lover.*

1997 After dissolution of the Assemblée Nationale by President Jacques Chirac, the Socialist Party obtains the majority vote, and Lionel Jospin is named prime minister.

Europeride 97, a gay and lesbian rights landmark event, takes place in Paris.

Diana, Princess of Wales, is killed in a car accident.

1998 The French national football (soccer) team wins the **World Cup** at the Stade de France in the northern suburbs.

High school students stage massive nationwide demonstrations to protest overcrowding and poor funding of schools.

1999 Along with 10 other members of the European Community, France adopts the Euro as its official currency.

Index

A

Abadie, Paul 236
Abbesses Métro Station 233
Abbots' Chapel 50
A. Beauvilliers ★★★$$$ 237
Académie de la Grande-Chaumière 77
Accommodations 11
ACT Architecture 66
Action Christine 93
Additional Highlights 244 (chapter and map)
Addresses 11
Aerial views of Paris 29
agnès b. 131
Airlines, Orly Airport 7
Airlines, Roissy–Charles-de-Gaulle Airport 6
Airport minibus 7, 8
Airports 6
Airport services, Orly Airport 7
Airport services, Roissy–Charles-de-Gaulle Airport 6
A la Bonne Source 57
A la Civette 223
A La Cloche des Halles ★★$ 131
A La Cour de Rohan ★★$ 92
Alain Brieux 74
Alain Carion 31
Alain Ducasse ★★★★$$$$ 249
A la Petite Fabrique 160
A La Tour de Montlhery ★★$$ 133
Albion 153
Album 46
Alcazar ★★$$ 90
Alfred Dunhill 216
A l'Image du Grenier sur l'Eau 144
A l'Imagerie 46
Allard ★★$$ 94
Allée des Cygnes 122
A l'Olivier 172
Altitude 95 ★★$$ 119
Ambassade d'Auvergne ★★$$ 138
Ambassadeurs Restaurant ★★★$$$$ 183
American Ambassador's Residence 204
American Cathedral 192
American Church 110
American Consulate/Hôtel Talleyrand 182
American Embassy 183
American Express 218
American Library in Paris 116

The American University of Paris 115
André Bissonnet 151
Androuët ★★$$ 196
Angélina ★★★$$ 180
Angleterre $$$ 74
Annick Goutal 75
Antoine, Jacques-Denis 90
A Priori Thé ★★$ 227
Arab Institute (Institut du Monde Arabe) 61
Archaeological Crypt (Crypte Archéologique) 26
Archives Nationales/Musée de l'Histoire de France 142
Arènes de Lutèce (Roman Arena) 58
Armand, Alfred 217
Army Museum (Musée de l'Armée) 106
Artcurial 188
Arthus-Bertrand 75
Arts et Marine 203
Aryllis 114
Assemblée Nationale/Palais Bourbon 99
Association Culturelle Israélite Agoudas Hakehilos 147
Atelier Brancusi 136
Atelier Franck Bordas 166
Atelier Guillaume Martel 69
Atelier 33 165
Auberge d'Chez Eux ★★$$$ 108
Auberge de Jarente ★★$ 149
Auberge de la Bonne Franquette ★$$ 235
Auberge des Trois Bonheurs ★★$$ 222
Auberge du Champ de Mars ★$ 113
Aubert, Jean 101
Au Bon Accueil ★★$$ 116
Au Bon St-Pourçain ★★$$ 82
Au Clair de la Lune ★★$$ 235
Au Clairon des Chasseurs $ 235
Au Diable des Lombards ★$ 133
Auditorium (Opéra Garnier) 219
Au Gourmet de l'Isle ★★$$ 33
Au Lapin Agile 238
Au Liégeur 107
Au Lys d'Argent ★$ 31
Au Nain Bleu 211
Au Pactole ★★$$ 43
Au Panetier Lebon 130
Au Père Tranquille ★$ 135

Au Petit Fer à Cheval ★★$ 143
Au Petit Marguery ★★$$ 57
Au Petit Riche ★★$$ 228
Au Petit Tone ★★$$ 109
Au Pied de Cochon ★$$ 131
Au Poulbot Gourmet ★★$$ 237
Au Printemps 218
Au Rendez-Vous des Camionneurs ★$$ 23
Au St-Séverin ★$ 94
Au Sauvignon ★$ 70
Au Savoyard ★$$ 91
Au Verger de la Madeleine 209
Au Vieux Campeur 50
Au Vieux Saussaies 204
Aux Anysetiers du Roy ★$$ 31
Aux Charpentiers ★★$$ 83
Aux Lyonnais ★★$$ 229
Aux Négociants ★★$$ 237
Avenue de La Bourdonnais 117
1 Avenue de Marigny 185
Avenue des Champs-Elysées 184
133 Avenue des Champs-Elysées 195
Avenue de Suffren 123
74 Avenue de Suffren 124
25 Avenue Franklin-D.-Roosevelt 187
Avenue George-V 190
37 Avenue George-V 192
13 Avenue Junot 240
Avenue Matignon 187
Avenue Montaigne 188
2 Avenue Montaigne 190
26 Avenue Montaigne 189
29 Avenue Rapp 117
Avenue Victoria 172
Axis 163

B

Babble, Money, and César Towers (Tours de Bonbec, d'Argent, et de César) 23
Baltard, Victor 134
Banque de France 130
Bar Anglais 189
Bar Au Sel ★★$$ 110
Bar de Jarente ★$ 149
Bar des Théâtres ★★$$ 189
Bardon, Renaud 66
Bar du Bristol 203
Bar du Crillon 183
Bar du Grand Hôtel 217
Barfly ★★$$ 194
Bar La Fontaine 163
Bar Les Chenets 216
Bar St-James ★★$$ 222
Basilique de St-Denis 252

Basilique Notre-Dame-des-Victoires 130
Basilique Sacré-Coeur 236
Basilique Ste-Clothilde 104
Bassin Octagonal et Terrasses (Octagonal Fountain and Terraces) 180
The Bastille 126 (chapter and map), 153, 154 (map)
Baxter 70
Bazar de l'Hôtel-de-Ville (BHV) 172
Beato ★★$$ 111
Beauvais College Chapel/Eglise Roumaine (Romanian Church) 50
Beauvarlet, Henri 113
Benoit ★★★$$$ 136
Bernini, Giovanni 175
Berthillon 33
Bibliothèque de l'Arsenal 156
Bibliothèque Historique de la Ville de Paris (Historical Library of the City of Paris) 146
Bibliothèque Nationale de France, Site François Mitterand/Tolbiac (National Library of France, François Mitterand/Tolbiac) 246
Bibliothèque Nationale de France, Site Richelieu (National Library of France, Richelieu) 227
Bibliothèque Publique d'Information (B.P.I.) 138
Bibliothèque Ste-Geneviève 53
Bicycles 9
Bijovet, Bernard 71
Birdland 83
Bistrot les Sans-Culottes ★★$$ 159
Blondel, François 138, 139
Boats 9
Bodin, Jean-Francois 137
Boffrand, Germain 103, 104, 142
Bofinger ★★$$ 157
Bois de Boulogne 250
Bois de Vincennes 247
Bonjour l'Artiste 234
Bonpoint 65
Books about Paris 120
Bookstores, English 124
Bouillier, Jean 145
Bouillon Racine ★★$$ 81
Boulangerie Beauvallet Julien 42
Boulangerie Gisquet 109
Boulangerie Rioux 33

Boulangerie St-Philippe ★★$ 201
2–20 Blvd Beaumarchais 157
8 Boulevard de Grenelle 123
8 Boulevard des Capucines 219
14 Boulevard des Capucines 216
Boulevard Haussmann 218
Boulevard Richard-Lenoir 157
Boulevard St-Michel 95
93 Boulevard St-Michel 78
Bourse des Valeurs (Stock Exchange) 229
Boutique Maille 211
B.P.I. (Bibliothèque Publique d'Information) 138
BPM 162
Brasserie Balzar ★★$$ 53
Brasserie Bourbon ★★$$ 99
Brasserie des Deux Palais ★$ 25
Brasserie 234 Rivoli ★★$$ 181
Brasserie Lipp ★★$$ 71
Brentano's 221
Dreuer, Marcel 124
Bricard Showrooms/Musée de la Serrure (Lock Museum) 146
British Cultural Center 105
British Embassy 205
Brongniart, Alexandre Théodore 105, 229, 247
Bruant, Libéral 105, 146
Brûlerie San José 228
Bruno 243
buddha-bar ★★$$ 206
The Building Baron 22
Bullet, Pierre 139
Buses 7, 8, 9

C
Cacharel 130
Cadolle 212
Café Beaubourg ★★$$ 136
Café Bleu ★★$ 207
Café de Cluny ★$ 49
Café de Flore ★★$$ 74
Café de la Cité ★★$$ 140
Café de la Paix ★★$$ 217
Café de l'Industrie ★★$ 160
Café de Mars ★★$$ 114
Café des Hauteurs ★$ 66
Café du Marché ★★$ 112
Café Iguana ★★$ 160
Café Lunch ★$ 104
Café Max ★★$ 107
Café Parisien ★★$ 69
Cafes 12
Café Véry ★$ 180

Cailleux 202
Campagne et Provence ★★★$$ 42
Canadian Cultural Services 105
Canal St-Martin 155
Caravelle $$ 243
Carita 207
Carlton's $$$ 243
Carole de Villarcy 100
Carré des Feuillants ★★★$$$$ 215
Carrefour de l'Odéon 92
Carrousel du Louvre 178
Cars, rental 7, 8
Cartaud, Jean Sylvain 103, 130
Cartier 214
Casa Bini ★★$$ 91
Casbah 163
Cassegrain 70
Castel Béranger 251
Castel's 83
Castiglione $$$$ 206
Catacombs 246
Cathédrale de Notre-Dame de Paris (Cathedral of Our Lady of Paris) 27
Caveau de la Bolée 94
Caveau de la Huchette 95
Caviar Kaspia ★★★$$$ 209
Centre de Création Industrielle/Musée National d'Art Moderne (CCI/MNAM) 137
Centre Gai et Lesbien 162
Centre Georges Pompidou (Centre National d'Art et Culture Georges Pompidou) 136
Centre Guillaume le Conquérant 257
Centre National d'Art et Culture Georges Pompidou (Centre Georges Pompidou) 136
Cercle Ledoyen ★★$$ 185
Chalgrin, Jean-François 79, 82, 182, 193, 196, 201
Champagne 253
The Champs-Elysées 168 (chapter and map)
Chanel 188
Chapelle Expiatoire (Expiatory Chapel) 210
Chapelle Jesus Enfant 104
Charles Jourdan 213
Charlot, Le Roi des Coquillages ★★$$$ 242
Charonne Café ★★$ 163
Charreau, Pierre 71
Chartier ★$ 229
Chartres 254
Charvet 216
Château de Chantilly 252

Château de Fontainebleau and Barbizon 253
Château d'Esclimont 254
Château de St-Germain-en-Laye 255
Château de Versailles 255
Château de Vincennes 247
Chaussures Georges 57
Chemetov, Paul 133
Chesterfield Café 193
Chevaux de Marly (Marly Horses) 183
Chez Agnès ★★$$ 114
Chez André ★★$$ 191
Chez Claude Sainlouis ★$ 70
Chez Francis ★★$$ 190
Chez Georges (Les Halles) ★★$$ 130
Chez Georges (St-Germain) 85
Chez Germain ★$ 202
Chez Henri ★★$ 83
Chez L'Ami Jean ★$$ 111
Chez la Vioille ★★$$ 174
Chez Maître Paul ★★$$ 81
Chez Marius ★★$$ 100
Chez Nous ★$$ 223
Chez Paul ★★$$ 163
Chez Pauline ★★$$$ 226
Chez Pento ★★$$ 53
Chez René ★$$ 42
Chez Ribe ★★$$ 123
Chez Teil 158
Chez Toutoune ★★$$ 42
Chez Vong aux Halles ★★$$ 134
Chiberta ★★★$$$ 196
The Chicago Pizza Pie Factory ★★$ 193
Chieng-Mai ★★$$ 45
Child's Play 102
China Club ★★$$ 156
Chopin $$ 229
Christian Constant ★★$ 76
Christian Dior 189
Christian Louboutin 223
Christian Tortu 91
Christofle 207
Cimetière de Montmartre (Montmartre Cemetery) 242
Cimetière du Père-Lachaise (Père-Lachaise Cemetery) 247
Cimetière St-Vincent (St. Vincent Cemetery) 238
Ciné Théâtre 13 240
Cité Berryer 207
Cité de la Musique 248
Cité de l'Architecture et du Patrimoine 122
Cité de la Roquette 161
Cité des Sciences et de l'Industrie 248

Cité Métro Station 26
Cité Véron 242
City Hall (Hôtel de Ville) 171
City Hall of the 18th Arrondissement (Mairie du 18e Arrondissement) 240
The City of Light on the Big Screen 60
Claridge-Bellman $$$ 191
Claude Boullé 86
Claude & Nicole ★★$ 234
Clementine ★★$$ 229
Climate 12
Clock Tower (Tour de l'Horloge) 24
Club des Poètes ★★$ 100
Club Jean de Beauvais 50
Club Quartier Latin 42
Coconnas ★$$ 150
Coffee Parisien ★★$ 84
Coffee Saint-Germain ★★$$ 73
Colbert $$$ 45
Colbert, Jean-Baptiste 250
Colboc, Pierre 66
Collège de France 52
Comédie Française 224
Comfort Hotel Louvre Montana $$ 222
Commercial Exchange (La Bourse de Commerce) 131
Conservatoire Municipal 110
Conservatoire National de Musique et de Danse 248
Consulates 12
Copenhague ★★★$$$ 195
Corridors of Nostalgia 239
Cosi ★★$ 87
Costes ★★$$$ 215
Cour Carrée (Square Courtyard) 177
Cour Damoye 158
Cour de l'Etoile d'Or 164
Cour du Commerce-St-André 92
Cour Napoléon (Napoléon Courtyard) 177
Courtonne, Jean 103, 104
Coyote Café ★$ 160
Crazy Horse Saloon 191
Crédit Municipal de Paris 142
Crocojazz 51
Crypte Archéologique (Archaeological Crypt) 26
C.T. Loo and Co. 201
CyberParis 84

D
Da Capo 50
Dalloyau (St-Germain) ★★$$ 78
Dalloyau (St-Honoré) 202
Dame Tartine ★★$ 155

Dave ★★$$ 221
Davioud, Gabriel-Jean-Antoine 173
Davoli 112
Day Trips 252 (chapter and map)
D-Day Beaches 257
Deauville 256
Debauve and Gallais 73
de Brosse, Salomon 79, 257
Décembre en Mars 117
de Chelles, Jean 27
de Cotte, Robert 103
Defender of Time 138
Deglane, Henri 185
Dehillerin 131
Delamain 223
Delamair, Pierre-Alexis 104, 141, 142
Delano and Aldrich 183
Delices St. Roch ★$ 221
Delorme, Philibert 179, 258
Demeure Castille $$$$ 212
de Mezières, Le Camus 203
Démons et Merveilles 73
de Montreuil, Pierre 24, 27, 255
Département des Arts Asiatiques des Musées Nationaux (National Museum of Asian Art) 249
Departure of the Volunteers 196
Deportation Memorial (Mémorial de la Déportation) 30
de Portzamparc, Christian 110, 136, 248
de Wailly, Charles 80
Deyrolle 67
Diners en Ville 68
Diptyque 43
Disneyland Paris 253
d'Ivry, Constant 103
Doll Museum (Musée de la Poupée) 140
Dominique ★★$$ 77
Drinking 12
Driving 7, 8, 9
Drugstore des Champs-Elysées 195
Dubernet 114
du Cerceau, Androuet 20, 152
du Cerceau, Baptiste 146
Duchesne Boulanger Pâtissier 114
Du Côté 7ème ★★$$ 109
Ducs d'Anjou $$ 133
Duthilleul & Minart 134
Dynasty ★★$ 225

E

Ecole des Beaux-Arts (School of Fine Arts) 86

Ecole Militaire 118
Ecole Polytechnique 51
Edouard Berck 211
Eglise du Dôme 106
Eglise Roumaine (Romanian Church)/Beauvais College Chapel 50
Eglise Ste-Marie Madeleine (La Madeleine) 208
Egouts (Sewers) 115
Eiffel, Gustave 43, 118, 259
Eiffel Tower/Invalides 96 (chapter and map)
Eiffel Tower (Tour Eiffel) 118
Embâcle 75
Embassies 12
Emergencies 16
English bookstores 124
Entertainment 12
Entrée des Artistes 135
Ermenegildo Zegna 216
Escrouzailles ★★$$ 187
Esmeralda $$ 47
Espace Vit'Halles 138
Excavations 177
Expiatory Chapel (Chapelle Expiatoire) 210

F

Facchetti & Co. Charcuterie Fine 57
Fainsilber, Adrien 248
Familia Hôtel $$ 43
Fashion and Textile Museum (Musée National de la Mode et du Textile) 179
Fauchon 210
A Festival of Food in Paris's Outdoor Markets 44
Fêtes et Foires (Festivals and Fairs) 16
The Filofax Centre 144
Finkelsztajn 144
Fitch, Noël Riley 125 (bests)
Flood Marker 34
Flo Prestige 221
Flora Danica ★★$$ 194
FNAC Musique Bastille 155
Foc Ly ★★★$$ 124
Fondation Dina Vierny, Musée Maillol 68
Fontainebleau Forest 254
Fontaine de Mars 113
Fontaine de Médicis (Medici Fountain) 79
Fontaine de Quatre-Grâces (Four Graces Fountain) 234
Fontaine des Innocents 133
Fontaine des Quatre Saisons (Four Seasons Fountain) 69
Fontaine de Stravinsky 138
Fontaine du Pot-de-Fer 57

Fontaine Molière 226
Fontaine, Pierre 175, 210
Fontaine St-Michel (St. Michael Fountain) 94
Food markets 44
Forgeries Museum (Musée de la Contrefaçon) 249
Forum des Halles 134
Foundation Le Corbusier 251
Fouquet's ★★$$$ 193
Four Graces Fountain (Fontaine de Quatre-Grâces) 234
Four Seasons Fountain (Fontaine des Quatre Saisons) 69
Four Seasons Hotel George V Paris $$$$ 192
France Amérique 186
Franco Maria Ricci Editore 86
Franklin D. Roosevelt Métro Station 188
Fromagerie Cler 112
Fromagerie de Montmartre 240
Funicular 236

G

Gabriel, Jacques-Ange 101, 118, 175, 182, 183
Galerie Akié Aricchi 161
Galerie Alain Blondel 136
Galerie Alain Gutharc 159
Galerie Arts des Amériques 88
Galerie Berheim-Jeune 202
Galerie Claude Bernard 86
Galerie Colbert 227
Galerie Daniel Templon 139
Galerie Documents 88
Galerie J.C. Riedel 90
Galerie Jorge Alyskewycz 161
Galerie Jousse Seguin 162
Galerie Jousse Seguin: Espace Gran Dia 161
Galerie Lambert Rouland 202
Galerie Larock-Granoff 90
Galerie Lavignes-Bastille 163
Galerie Liliane et Michel Durand-Dessert 159
Galerie Lucette Herzog 135
Galerie Maeght/Librairie Maeght 67
Galerie Naïla de Monbrison 100
Galerie Nationale du Jeu de Paume 179
Galeries Lafayette 218
Galerie Urubamba 45
Galerie Véro-Dodat 223

Galerie Vivienne 227
Galerie Yvon Lambert 144
Galerie Zone & Phase 159
Galignani 180
Gallery Maison Mansart 146
Garde Républicaine 156
Gare des Invalides 105
Gargantua ★★$$ 222
Garnier, Charles 66, 181, 200, 217, 218, 259
Gaspard de la Butte 233
Gaucheron, Eric 125 (bests)
Gau, Christian 104
Gaussel, Jean 175
Gehry, Frank 122
The General Store 68
Genty, Françoise 167 (bests)
Georges Bernard Antiquités 206
Gérard Besson ★★$$$ 131
Getting around Paris 8
Getting to Paris 6
Giorgio Armani 215
Girault, Charles 185
Gittard, Alphonse Daniel 71
Giverny 256
Glass House (La Maison de Verre) 71
Gobelins Tapestry Factory (Manufacture des Gobelins) 58
Godiva 215
Goldsmiths Quay (Quai des Orfèvres) 23
Goumard ★★★$$$ 212
Grande Arche de La Défense 249
Grand Foyer and Staircase (Opéra Garnier) 219
Grandhomme 205
Grand Hôtel de Champagne $$$ 173
Grand Hôtel des Balcons $$ 81
Grand Hôtel Jeanne d'Arc $$ 149
Grand Palais 185
Greenough, Carrol 110
Ground Level 66
Gucci 207
Guerlain Institut de Beauté 192
Guimard, Hector 26, 95, 147, 233, 251
Guy Savoy ★★★$$$$ 197
Gymnase Club 193

H

The Hairy Lemon ★$ 152
Hameau des Artistes 240
Hardouin-Mansart, Jules 90, 95, 106, 129, 141, 213, 221, 255
Harry's New York Bar 219

Haussman, George Eugène, Baron 22
Havanita Café ★$ 159
Health care 12
Hédiard ★★$$ 210
Hédiard 209
Hemingway Bar 214
Herboristerie du Palais-Royal 226
Hermant, André 26
Hermès 206
H.G. Thomas 43
Historical Library of the City of Paris (Bibliothèque Historique de la Ville de Paris) 146
Historical Museum of the City of Paris (Musée Historique de la Ville de Paris) 148
History 257
Holidays 12
Hollywood Savoy ★★$$ 229
Hommage à Apollinaire 85
Honfleur and Deauville 256
Hotel Bastille Speria $$ 156
Hôtel Beau Manoir $$$ 210
Hôtel Bourgogne et Montana $$$ 100
Hôtel Bradford-Elysées $$$ 201
Hôtel Burgundy $$$ 212
Hôtel Caron de Beaumarchais $$ 143
Hôtel Champ-de-Mars $ 112
Hôtel Chenizot 32
Hôtel Colisée $$ 188
Hôtel Costes $$$$ 215
Hôtel Crillon $$$$ 183
Hôtel Damrémont $ 240
Hôtel Daval $ 160
Hôtel d'Avaray 103
Hôtel de Beauvau 203
Hôtel de Boisgelin 103
Hôtel de Cluny, Musée de Cluny (Musée National du Moyen-Age), and Palais des Thermes 49
Hôtel de Coulanges 150
Hôtel de Fleurie $$$ 91
Hôtel de Gallifet 103
Hôtel de Gouffier de Thoix 103
Hôtel de l'Abbaye $$$ 75
Hôtel de l'Alma $$ 113
Hôtel de la Place des Vosges $$ 151
Hôtel de la Trémoille $$$$ 191
Hôtel de la Tulipe $$ 111
Hôtel de Lauzun 35
Hôtel de l'Avenir $$ 75
Hôtel de Londres Eiffel $$ 114

Hôtel de l'université $$$ 73
Hôtel de Lutèce $$$ 31
Hôtel de Noirmoutiers 104
Hôtel de Rohan 141
Hôtel des Ambassadeurs de Hollande 143
Hôtel des Deux-Iles $$$ 32
Hôtel de Seine $$$ 87
Hôtel des Grandes Ecoles $$ 56
Hôtel des Grands Hommes $$$ 54
Hôtel des Invalides 105
Hôtel des Monnaies/Musée des Monnaies (Mint/Money Museum) 90
Hôtel des Sts-Pères $$$ 71
Hôtel d'Estrées 103
Hôtel de Sully 152
Hôtel de Varenne $$ 101
Hôtel de Vigny $$$$ 194
Hôtel de Ville (City Hall) 171
Hôtel de Villeroy 102
Hôtel-Dieu Hospital 27
Hôtel D'Orsay $$ 65
Hôtel Drouot 228
Hôtel Duc de St-Simon $$$ 67
Hôtel du Chanac de Pompadour 104
Hôtel du Châtelet 104
Hôtel du Collège de France $$ 50
Hôtel du Jeu de Paume $$$ 33
Hôtel du Louvre $$$ 222
Hôtel du Quai Voltaire $$ 72
Hôtel et Musée Carnavalet 148
Hôtel François I $$$$ 192
Hôtel Henri IV $ 21
Hôtel Inter-Continental Paris $$$$ 181
Hôtel Jardin des Plantes $$ 59
Hôtel Lambert 35
Hôtel Le Bristol $$$$ 202
Hôtel Left Bank St-Germain $$$ 91
Hôtel le Pavillon $$ 109
Hôtel le Régent $$$ 91
Hôtel les Sans-Culottes $ 159
Hôtel Lotti $$$$ 215
Hôtel Lutetia $$$$ 69
Hôtel Matignon 103
Hôtel Meurice $$$$ 181
Hôtel Montalembert $$$$ 72
Hôtel Muguet $$ 108
Hôtel Opal $$ 210
Hôtel Regina $$$$ 222
Hôtel Régyn's Montmartre $$ 233
Hôtel Relais Bosquet $$ 113

Hôtel Ritz $$$$ 214
Hôtel Saint Dominique $$ 109
Hôtel St-Louis $$ 31
Hôtel St-Louis Marais $$ 153
Hôtel St-Merri $$$ 136
Hôtel Scribe $$$$ 217
Hotels, rating 6
Hôtel Talleyrand/American Consulate 182
Hôtel Thoumieux $$ 109
Hôtel Westminster $$$$ 216
Hours 13
H. Picard et Fils 202
Hunt, Richard Morris 86
Huvé, Jean-Jacques 209

I

Il Cortile ★★★$$ 212
Ile de la Cité 18 (chapter and map)
Ile St-Louis 18 (chapter and map), 30
Impasse de Conti 90
Indiana Cafe ★$$ 157
Information, essential 11
Institut de France 89
Institut du Monde Arabe (Arab Institute) 61
Institut Géographique National 193
Internet 84
Invalides 96 (chapter and map)
IRCAM (Institut de Recherche et de Coordination Acoustique/Musique) 138
Isami ★★$$ 33
The Islands: Ile de la Cité and Ile St-Louis 18 (chapter and map)
Issé ★★★$$$ 228
Issey Miyake 150
Issey Miyake/Pleats Please 69

J

Jacques Cagna ★★★$$$$ 92
Jadis et Gourmande 188
Japanese Embassy 205
Jardin des Halles 133
Jardin des Plantes 59
Jardin des Tuileries (Tuileries Gardens) 179
Jardin du Luxembourg (Luxembourg Gardens) 78
Jardin du Ranelagh 251
Jardins Albert Kahn 251
Jean Millet 111
Jean Paul Gaultier (Les Halles, Marais, and The Bastille) 165

Jean Paul Gaultier (St-Honoré) 227
Jean-Pierre De Castro 149
Jean-Pierre Stella 45
Joe Allen ★$$ 134
Jo Goldenberg ★★$$ 147
John Lobb 206
Johnston, Mireille 167 (bests)
Jourdan, F. 174
Juveniles ★★$$ 226

K

Kenzo (Les Halles) 130
Kenzo (St-Germain) 69
Keur Samba 202
Kiosque-Théâtre 209
Kitty O'Shea's 216
Kniaz Igor ★$$ 117
Korean Barbecue ★$$ 71

L

L'Abat-Jour 233
La Bohème du Tertre ★$$ 235
La Boîte à Musique 68
La Boule d'Or ★★$$ 107
La Bourse du Commerce (Commercial Exchange) 131
La Boutique des Anges 234
La Boutique du Bridgeur 225
La Boutique Flora Danica ★★$ 194
La Brasserie de l'Isle Saint-Louis ★★$$ 31
La Bûcherie ★★★$$$ 48
La Cafelière ★★$$ 90
La Castaflore ★★★$$ 32
La Chaiserie du Faubourg 162
La Charlotte de l'Isle ★★$ 34
Lachaume 207
La Chaumière en l'Ile ★$$ 31
Lachevsky, Dominique 100
La Chope ★$ 56
La Chope des Vosges ★$$ 150
La Closerie des Lilas ★★$$$ 77
La Conciergerie 23
Lacornée, Lacornée 105
La Coupole ★★$$ 76
La Cour de Varenne 68
La Coutellerie Suisse 131
La Crémaillère 1900 ★★$$ 235
La Croque au Sel ★$ 113
La Distillerie ★★$$ 165
Ladurée ★★★$ 207

La Ferme St-Hubert ★★$$ 211
La Fermette du Sud-Ouest ★★$$ 131
La Fermette Marbeuf 1900 ★★★$$ 191
L'Affriolé ★★★$$ 111
La Fontaine de Mars ★★$$ 113
La Fourmi Ailée ★★$ 46
La Galoche d'Aurillac ★★$$ 159
La Guirlande de Julie ★★$$ 151
La Hune 75
La Louisiane $$ 88
Laloux, Victor 65
La Madeleine (Eglise Ste-Marie Madeleine) 208
La Maison de la Lozère ★★$$ 95
La Maison de la Truffe ★★$$$ 209
La Maison de Verre (Glass House) 71
La Maison du Miel 211
La Maison du Valais ★★$$ 207
La Maison Lafitte 31
La Maison Rose ★$ 238
La Maison Rustique 87
La Mandarin de Latour-Maubourg ★$ 107
La Marée Verte ★★★$$ 42
L'Ambrosie ★★★★$$$$ 151
La Méditerranée ★★$$ 81
La Mère Catherine ★★$ 235
La Mosquée de Paris 59
Lancaster $$$$ 193
La Nef Parisienne 51
Language 40
L'Annexe ★$$ 242
Lanvin 206, 207
La Pagode 68
La Palette ★★$ 88
Lapérouse ★★★$$$ 93
La Petite Galette ★$ 241
La Pirada ★$ 158
La Poule au Pot ★★$ 110
L'Arc de Triomphe 196
L'Arc du Carrousel 178
La Reine de Sabah 132
La Rhumerie 88
La Rose de France ★★$$ 21
La Rôtisserie d'en Face ★★★$$ 93
La Rôtisserie du Beaujolais ★★$$ 39
L'Arpège ★★★★$$$$ 101
La Samaritaine 174
L'As du Fallafel 147
Lasserre ★★★$$$$ 186
Lassurance, Jean 204

Lassurance, Pierre 105, 205
L'Astor Westin Demeure $$$$ 204
La Table de Fès ★★$$ 76
La Tartine ★★$ 147
La Terrasse ★★$$ 242
The Latin Quarter 36 (chapter and map)
L'Atlas ★★$$ 39
La Tour d'Argent ★★★★$$$$ 39
La Tour de Jade ★★$ 228
La Truffière ★★$$ 56
La Tuile à Loup 58
L'Auberge de la Reine Blanche ★$$ 34
Laundry 13
L'Auvergne Gourmande ★★$ 113
L'Avenue ★★$$ 188
La Verrière ★★$$ 217
La Villa $$$ 87
Lavirotte, Jules 117
Law Courts (Palais de Justice) 24
Le Backgammon 123
Le Balajo 158
Le Bar 217
Le Bar à Huitres (Les Halles, Marais, and The Bastille) ★★$$ 157
Le Bar à Huitres (The Latin Quarter) ★★$$ 48
Le Bar du Caveau ★$ 22
Le Baron Rouge ★★$ 164
Le Bar Suffren 123
Le Belier Bar 86
Le Bellecour ★★★$$ 109
Le Berkeley $$ 187
Le Bilboquet ★$$ 74
Le Bistrot de Bofinger ★$$ 157
Le Bistrot de Marius ★★$$ 190
Le Bistrot de Paris ★★$$ 72
Le Bistrot du Peintre ★★$ 162
Le Bistrot du 7ème ★★$ 107
Le Boeuf sur le Toit ★★$$ 187
Le Bon Marché 68
Le Bon Pêcheur $ 135
Le Bristol ★★★$$$$ 202
Le Cabinet de Curiosité 72
Le Café Marly ★★$$ 177
Le Caméléon ★★$$ 77
Le Canard Enchaîné 222
Le Carpaccio ★★★$$ 197
Le Caveau du Palais ★★$$ 21
Le Céladon ★★★$$$ 216
Le Chai de l'Abbaye ★★$ 88
Le Chambrelain 107

Le Chariot du Roy 114
Le Château des Seigneurs de Clignancourt 240
L'Ecluse (Louvre and The Champs Elysées) ★★$$ 192
L'Ecluse (St-Honoré) ★★$$ 209
L'Ecluse (St-Germain) ★★$ 94
Le Cochon à l'Oreille ★★$ 132
Le Colimaçon ★★$$ 143
Le Corbusier 66, 246, 251, 255
Le Coupe-Chou ★$$ 52
Le Divellec ★★★$$$ 106
Le Dôme Bastille ★★$$ 157
Le Dôme du Marais ★$$ 143
Ledoux, Claude-Nicholas 248
Ledoyen ★★★$$$ 185
Le Duplex ★★$$ 195
Lefèbvres & Fils 67
Le Flore en l'Ile ★★$ 31
Le Garde Manger ★★$$ 101
Le Gastelier ★$ 236
Le Golfe de Naples ★★$ 83
Legrand 130
Le Grand Café Capucines ★★$$ 219
Legrand Filles et Fils 227
Le Grand Hôtel Inter-Continental $$$$ 217
Le Grand Louvre ★★$$ 178
Le Grand Véfour ★★★★$$$$ 224
Le Jardin ★★★$$$ 197
Le Jules Verne ★★★$$$ 119
Le Loir dans la Théière ★★$ 147
Le Louis d'Or ★★$$$ 191
Le Louvre des Antiquaires 223
Le Lutin Gourmand 112
Le Maquis ★★$$ 240
Le Marcande ★★$$$ 203
Le Maupertu ★★$$ 108
Le Mazet 92
Le Ménagerie 59
Lemercier, Jacques 52, 221, 223
Le Méridien Etoile $$$$ 195
Le Merisier ★★$$ 202
Le Monde des Chimères ★★$$ 31
Le Monde en Marche 90
Le Moniteur 80
Le Mouffetard ★★$ 57
Le Muet, Pierre 130
Le Muniche ★$$ 74
L'Enoteca ★★$$ 153

Lenox $$$ 73
Le Paradis Latin 43
Le Parc $$$$ 250
Le Pavillon Baltard ★$ 131
Le Pavillon de Montsouris ★★$$ 246
Le Petit Journal 78
Le Petit Opportun 173
Le Petit St-Benoît ★★$ 74
Le Petit Vatel ★★$ 83
Le Petit Yvan ★★$$ 187
L'Epicerie 32
L'Epi d'Or ★★$$ 223
Le Poquelin ★★$$ 226
Le Pré Catelan ★★★$$$ 250
Le Procope ★★$$ 91
Le Progrès ★$ 234
Le Queen 193
Le Raccard ★★$$ 51
Le Rallye ★$ 39
Le Raux, Jean Baptiste 103
Le Récamier ★★★$$$ 70
Le Repaire de Bacchus 112
Le Restaurant ★★$$$ 243
Le Restaurant de la Mosquée ★$ 59
Le Restaurant de l'Astor ★★★$$$ 204
Le Restaurant Opéra ★★★$$$$ 217
L'Ermitage Hôtel $$ 237
Le Roi du Pot-au-Feu ★★$$ 211
Le Sainte-Beuve $$$ 76
Le Sancerre ★★$ 116
Les Bains Douches 135
Les Bookinistes ★★★$$ 93
Les Boucholeurs ★★$$ 225
Les Bouchons de François Clerc ★★★$$ 46
Les Bourgeoises ★★$$ 149
L'Escargot Montorgueil ★★$$ 132
Lescene-Dura 140
Les Colonies du Paradis ★$ 166
Les Comptoirs de la Tour d'Argent 38
Lescot, Pierre 148
Lescure ★★$$ 182
Les Deux Abeilles ★★★$ 115
Les Deux Magots ★★$$ 75
Les Deux Tisserins 43
Le Sedaine Bastille 158
Le Sélect ★★$ 77
Les Fontaines ★$$ 54
Les Fous de l'Ile ★★$ 33
Les Grandes Marches ★★$$ 155
Les Halles 129
Les Halles, Marais, and The Bastille 126 (chapter and map)

Le 6 Bosquet ★★$$ 115
Les Muses ★★★$$$ 217
Les Noailles ★$$ 222
Le Souk ★★$$ 162
Le Sphinx 203
Les Portes ★$ 163
Le Square Trousseau ★★$$ 164
Les Taillandiers ★★$ 161
L'Estaminet Gaya ★★$$ 212
Les Trois Maillets 47
Les Viennoiseries de St-Medard 136
Le Tango 139
L'Eté en Pente Douce ★★$ 237
Le Tellier, Louis 143
Le Tire Bouchon Cabaret ★★$ 235
L'Etoile Verte ★★$$ 197
Le Toit de Paris ★★$$ 123
Le Train Bleu ★★★$$$ 166
Le 30 (Fauchon) ★★$$ 211
Le Trumilou ★$ 171
Le Vaudeville ★★$$ 229
Le Vau, Louis 34, 35, 82, 89, 141, 175, 176
Le Vieux Bistro ★★$$ 30
Levitt, Alan 257
Le Ziryab ★★$$ 61
L'Herbe Verte 163
L'Hôtel $$$$ 86
Librairie Adyar 117
Librairie Fischbacher 89
Librairie Gourmande 46
Librairie L'Arbre à Lettres 165
Librairie Maritime Outremer 87
Librairie Présence Africaine 51
Librairie Ulysse 34
Librairie Maeght/Galerie Maeght 67
Lido 194
Limousines 7, 8
L'Impasse ★★$$ 152
Lina's ★★$ 130
L'Incroyable Restaurant ★$ 225
Lionel Hampton Jazz Club 195
Lion, Yves 152, 257
Lire Entre les Vignes ★★$ 160
Living Museum of the Horse (Musée Vivant du Cheval) 253
Lock Museum (Musée de la Serrure)/Bricard Showrooms 146
L'Oeillade ★★$$ 67
Loire Valley 254
L'Olympia 216

Loos, Adolf 241
L'Orangerie (Ile St-Louis) ★★$$$ 34
L'Orangerie (Louvre and The Champs Elysées) 180
L'Oriental ★★$ 243
L'Osteria ★★$$ 149
Louis Philippe Fountain 161
Louis, Victor 224
Louvet, Louis-Albert 185
Louvre and The Champs-Elysées 168 (chapter and map), 172 (map)
Louvre Pyramid 177
Louvre-Rivoli Métro Station 175
Lucas Carton ★★★★$$$$ 209
Luthier 146
Luxembourg Gardens (Jardin du Luxembourg) 78
Luxembourg Palace (Palais du Luxembourg) 79
Lycée Henri IV 54
Lycée Louis Le Grand 53

M

Ma Bourgogne (Les Halles, Marais, and The Bastille) ★★$$ 151
Ma Bourgogne (St-Honoré) ★★$$ 201
Macary, Michel 178
Macéo ★★★$$ 226
Madeleine Gély 71
Magne, Lucien 236
Mairie du 18e Arrondissement (City Hall of the 18th Arrondissement) 240
Maison Blanche ★★★$$$ 190
Maison Européenne de la Photographie 152
Maison Micro 223
Maison Suba 148
Maison Tristan Tzara 241
Mansart, François 90, 141, 142, 146, 148, 153
Manuel Canovas 87
Manufacture des Gobelins (Gobelins Tapestry Factory) 58
Manufacture Nationale de Sèvres (Sèvres Porcelain Factory) 225
Map key 6
Marais 126 (chapter and map), 141
Marais Plus 146
Marché St-Germain 83
Marché St-Pierre 237
Mariage Frères ★★★$$ 143

Marie & Fils ★★$$ 89
Marie Mercié 82
Marie-Papier 76
Marie-Pierre Boitard 99
Marius et Janette ★★★$$$ 190
Marly Horses (Chevaux de Marly) 183
Marquise de Sévigné 210
Martyrium 233
Matsuri Sushi ★$$ 226
Maude Frizon 70
Maxim's ★★$$$$ 183
Maxoff Restaurant ★$$ 67
Maybeck, Bernard Ralph 86
Mazin, Antoine 205
McConnico, Hilton 174
Méchiche, Frédéric 204
Medical care 12
Medici Fountain (Fontaine de Médicis) 79
Mémorial de la Déportation (Deportation Memorial) 30
Métezeau, Clément 150
Metric Conversions 14
Métro See inside front cover (map), 9
Michel Cachoux 90
Michel Chaudun 111
Middle Level 66
Mimram, Marc 180
Ministère des Affaires Etrangères (Ministry of Foreign Affairs) 105
Mint/Money Museum (Hôtel des Monnaies/Musée des Monnaies) 90
Mirama ★★$ 48
MNAM/CCI (Musée National d'Art Moderne/Centre de Création Industrielle) 137
Mobilier National (National Storehouse) 58
Moissonnier ★★★$$ 43
Mollet, Armand-Claude 204
Money 13
Money Museum/Mint (Musée des Monnaies/Hôtel des Monnaies) 90
Monsieur Baudrillart 92
Montagne Ste-Geneviève 51
Montmartre 230 (chapter and map)
Montmartre Cemetery (Cimetière de Montmartre) 242
Montmartre Vineyards (Vignes de Montmartre) 238
Montpensier $$ 225
Moulin de la Galette 241
Moulin Rouge 242
Movies 60
Muriel 204

Musée Adam Mickiewicz 32
Musée Baccarat 248
Musée Cernuschi 249
Musée Cognacq-Jay 146
Musée Condé 252
Musée d'Art et d'Histoire du Judaïsme (Museum of Jewish Art and History) 140
Musée d'Art Moderne de la Ville de Paris (Museum of Modern Art of the City of Paris) 249
Musée de Cluny (Musée National du Moyen-Age), Hôtel de Cluny, and Palais des Thermes 49
Musée de la Bataille de Normandie 257
Musée de la Chasse et de la Nature (Museum of the Hunt) 141
Musée de la Contrefaçon (Forgeries Museum) 249
Musée de la Légion d'Honneur et des Ordres de Chevalerie 65
Musée de la Marine 122
Musée de la Musique 248
Musée de la Poupée (Doll Museum) 140
Musée de la Publicité (Poster and Advertising Museum), Musée des Arts Décoratifs (Museum of Decorative Arts) and 178
Musée de l'Armée (Army Museum) 106
Musée de la Serrure (Lock Museum)/Bricard Showrooms 146
Musée de l'Erotisme 242
Musée de l'Histoire de France/Archives Nationales 142
Musée de l'Homme (Museum of Humankind) 122
Musée de Montmartre 238
Musée des Antiquités Nationales 255
Musée des Arts Décoratifs (Museum of Decorative Arts) and Musée de la Publicité (Poster and Advertising Museum) 178
Musée des Collections Historiques de la Préfecture de Police (Police Museum) 45
Musée de Sculpture en Plein Air 61
Musée des Hôpitaux de Paris–Assistance Publique (Museum of Public Health

and Welfare) **44**
Musée des Monnaies/Hôtel des Monnaies (Money Museum/Mint) **90**
Musée d'Orsay **65**
Musée du Débarquement Arromanches **257**
Musée du Louvre **175**
Musée Edith Piaf **247**
Musée Fragonard **216**
Musée-Galerie de la Seita (Tobacco Museum) **110**
Musée Grevin **229**
Musée Guimet **249**
Musée Hermès **206**
Musée Historique de la Ville de Paris (Historical Museum of the City of Paris) **148**
Musée Jacquemart-André **201**
Musée Maillol–Fondation Dina Vierny **68**
Musée Marmottan **250**
Musée National d'Art Moderne/Centre de Création Industrielle (MNAM/CCI) **137**
Musée National de la Coopération Franco-Américaine **257**
Musée National de la Mode et du Textile (Fashion and Textile Museum) **179**
Musée National des Techniques (National Technical Museum) **139**
Musée National du Moyen-Age (Musée de Cluny), Hôtel de Cluny, and Palais des Thermes **49**
Musée National E. Delacroix **87**
Musée Nissim de Camondo **249**
Musée Picasso **144**
Musée Rodin **101**
Musée Victor Hugo **150**
Musée Vivant du Cheval (Living Museum of the Horse) **253**
Museum of Decorative Arts (Musée des Arts Décoratifs) and Poster and Advertising Museum (Musée de la Publicité) **178**
Museum of Humankind (Musée de l'Homme) **122**
Museum of Jewish Art and History (Musée d'Art et d'Histoire du Judaïsme) **140**
Museum of Modern Art of the City of Paris (Musée

d'Art Moderne de la Ville de Paris) **249**
Museum of Natural History **59**
Museum of Public Health and Welfare (Musée des Hôpitaux de Paris–Assistance Publique) **44**
Museum of the Hunt (Musée de la Chasse et de la Nature) **141**
Museum Restaurant ★$ **146**
Museums **13**

N
Naggar, Patrick **100**
Napoléon Courtyard (Cour Napoléon) **177**
National Library of France, François Mitterand/Tolbiac (Bibliothèque Nationale de France, Site François Mitterand/Tolbiac) **246**
National Library of France, Richelieu (Bibliothèque Nationale de France, Site Richelieu) **227**
National Museum of Asian Art (Département des Arts Asiatiques des Musées Nationaux) **249**
National Museum of the Middle Ages (Musée National du Moyen-Age) **49**
National Storehouse (Mobilier National) **58**
National Technical Museum (Musée National des Techniques) **139**
Nervi, Luigi **124**
New Hôtel Roblin $$ **210**
Nina Ricci **189**
North Facade of Place de la Concorde **182**
Nos Ancêtres les Gaulois ★$$ **33**
Notre-Dame-de-l'Assomption **212**
Notre-Dame Gallery **49**
Nouvel, Jean **61**

O
Obelisk of Luxor **182**
Obélisque ★★$$ **183**
Octagonal Fountain and Terraces (Bassin Octagonal et Terrasses) **180**
Office de Tourisme de Paris **195**
Olivier de Sercey **68**
Ombeline **100**
Opéra Bastille **154**

Opéra Garnier(Paris Opera) **218**
Orientation **4**
Orly Airport **7**
Orly Airport, ground transportation **8**
Ott, Carlos **154**

P
Pacific Eiffel ★★$$ **123**
Palais Bourbon/Assemblée Nationale **99**
Palais de Chaillot **122**
Palais de Justice (Law Courts) **24**
Palais de la Cité **23**
Palais de la Découverte **186**
Palais de la Légion d'Honneur **65**
Palais de l'Elysée **204**
Palais des Thermes, Hôtel de Cluny, Musée de Cluny (Musée National du Moyen-Age) and **49**
Palais des Tuileries (Tuileries Palace) **179**
Palais du Luxembourg (Luxembourg Palace) **79**
Palais Royal **223**
Panthéon **54**
Papeterie Moderne **133**
Papeterie Saint Sabin **160**
Parc André Citroën **251**
Parc de la Villette **248**
Parc de Monceau **248**
Parc des Buttes-Chaumont **247**
Parc de St-Cloud **255**
Parc du Champ-de-Mars **118**
Parc Montsouris **246**
Paris 2 (map)
Paris Hilton $$$$ **123**
Paris in Print **120**
Paris Métro *See inside front cover* (map), **9**
Paris Opera (Opéra Garnier) **218**
Paris Seen from Down Below **142**
Paris Seen from on High **29**
Parking **10**
Parlez-Vous Anglais? **124**
Parlez-Vous Français? **40**
Passage des Panoramas **229**
Passage du Chantier **165**
Passage l'Homme **162**
Passage Molière **135**
Passages (Pedestrian arcades) **239**
Passerelle de Solférino **180**
Patchworks du Rouvray **45**
Pâtisserie de la Tour Eiffel ★$ **116**

Pâtisserie de Montmartre (René Raveau) **240**
Pâtisserie St-Germain-l'Auxerrois ★★$$ **174**
Paul Minchelli ★★★$$$ **107**
Pause Café ★★$ **162**
Pavillon de la Reine $$$$ **151**
Pavillon de l'Arsenal **156**
Pedestrian arcades (Passages) **239**
Pei, I.M. **177, 178, 259**
Pencreach, Georges **134**
Peny ★$ **209**
Percier, Charles **175**
Père-Lachaise Cemetery (Cimetière du Père-Lachaise) **247**
Perraudin ★★$ **54**
Perrault, Dominique **246**
Perret, Auguste **58, 190**
Perrette **166**
Perreyve $$ **75**
Personal safety **13**
Petit Hôtel de Villars **104**
Petit Palais **185**
Petit Pont (Ile de la Cité) **26**
Petit Pont (The Latin Quarter) **48**
Petrossian **106**
Peyre, Marie-Josephe **80**
Pharamond ★★$$ **134**
Pharmacie Rapp **117**
Philippo, Jean-Paul **66**
Piano, Renzo **136, 137, 138**
Picard Surgelés **142**
Picassiette's House **254**
Pierre au Palais Royal ★★★$$$ **225**
Pierre Gagnaire ★★★★$$$$ **194**
Pingusson, G.H. **30**
Place André-Malraux **222**
Place Charles-de-Gaulle **196**
Place d'Aligre Market **164**
Place Dauphine **21**
Place de Clichy **242**
Place de Furstemberg **87**
Place de la Bastille **153**
Place de la Concorde **182**
Place de la Contrescarpe **56**
1 Place de la Contrescarpe **56**
Place de la Madeleine **208**
4 Place de la Madeleine **211**
Place de la Madeleine shopping **208** (map)
Place de la Résistance **115**
Place de la Sorbonne **53**
Place de l'Hôtel-de-Ville **171**
Place de l'Opéra **218**
Place des Victoires **129**
Place des Victoires shopping **129** (map)

Place des Vosges **149**
21 Place des Vosges **151**
Place du Carrousel **178**
Place du Châtelet **173**
Place du Louvre **174**
Place du Palais-Bourbon **99**
Place du Parvis-Notre-Dame **26**
Place du Tertre **235**
13 Place Emile-Goudeau **234**
Place Georges-Pompidou **136**
Place Louis-Lépine **25**
Place Maubert **45**
Place Monge **58**
Place Pigalle **243**
Place St-Michel **94**
Place St-Sulpice **82**
Place Vendôme **213**
3–5 Place Vendôme **214**
11–13 Place Vendôme **214**
12 Place Vendôme **215**
16 Place Vendôme **215**
Place Vendôme shopping **213** (map)
Plaza Athénée $$$$ **189**
Pleats Please/Issey Miyake **69**
Poilâne **69**
Point Zéro **27**
Police Museum (Musée des Collections Historiques de la Préfecture de Police) **45**
Polidor ★★$ **80**
Pont Alexandre III **185**
Pont au Change **173**
Pont au Double **46**
Pont de Bir-Hakeim **122**
Pont de la Concorde **182**
Pont de l'Alma **190**
Pont des Arts **89**
Pont-Marie **35**
Pont-Neuf **20**
Pont St-Louis **30**
Porte St-Denis **138**
Porte St-Martin **139**
Poster and Advertising Museum (Musée de la Publicité), Museum of Decorative Arts (Musée des Arts Décoratifs) and **178**
Post offices **13**
Poujauran **110**
Poyet, Bernard **99**
Préfecture de Police **26**
Promenade Plantée **166**
Publications **14**
Public Lavatory **208**
Pub St-Germain-des-Prés ★$$ **91**
Puyricard **117**
Pylones **32**

Q
9–11 Quai aux Fleurs **30**
9 Quai d'Anjou **35**
29 Quai d'Anjou **35**
37 Quai d'Anjou **35**
24 Quai de Béthune **34**
3 Quai de Bourbon **33**
Quai de la Mégisserie **173**
45 Quai de la Tournelle **44**
Quai de Montebello Booksellers **46**
Quai des Grands-Augustins **93**
Quai des Orfèvres (Goldsmiths Quay) **23**
10 Quai d'Orléans **32**
18–20 Quai d'Orléans **32**
53–65, 67–69, and 71–91 Quai d'Orsay **110**
Quai Voltaire **72**
404 ★★$$ **139**

R
Ragut Charcuterie **112**
Raphael $$$$ **195**
Ravi ★★$$$ **67**
The Real McCoy **115**
Régence-Plaza ★★★$$$ **189**
Régine's **193**
Reichen, Bernard **156**
Relais Christine $$$$ **92**
Relais du Massif Central ★★$ **158**
Relais du Parc ★★★$$$ **250**
Relais Hôtel de Vieux Paris $$$ **94**
Relais Plaza ★$$ **189**
Rémy **164**
René-Gérard Saint-Ouen **203**
René Raveau (Pâtisserie de Montmartre) **240**
Rental cars **7, 8**
Résidence Charles-Dullin $$ **243**
Résidence Maxim's $$$$ **186**
Restaurant des Beaux-Arts ★★$ **86**
Restaurant Drouant ★★★$$$$ **228**
Restaurant du Musée d'Orsay ★$$ **66**
Restaurant Laurent ★★★$$$$ **186**
Restaurant Le Champ de Mars ★★$$ **108**
Restaurant Montalembert ★★$$ **72**
Restaurant Paul ★★$$ **22**
Restaurants **14**
Restaurants, rating **6**

Restaurant Véro-Dodat ★★$$ **223**
Rest rooms **14**
Réunion des Musées Nationaux **85**
Rhulmann, Emile **228**
Richelieu Wing **177**
Ristorante Romano ★★$$ **191**
Ritz Espadon ★★★★$$$$ **214**
Ritz Health Club **214**
Robert Capia **223**
Robert, Philippe **156**
Rochon, Pierre-Yves **216, 217**
Rogers, Richard **136**
Roger-Viollet **86**
Roissy–Charles-de-Gaulle Airport **6**
Roissy–Charles-de-Gaulle Airport, ground transportation **6**
Roland Barthélemy Fromager **69**
Roman Arena (Arènes de Lutèce) **58**
Roman Baths **49**
Romanian Church (Eglise Roumaine)/Beauvais College Chapel **50**
Rondelet, Guillaume **54**
Rouge et Noir **76**
Rousseau, Pierre **65**
Royal Monceau $$$$ **197**
Royal Saint-Honoré $$$$ **215**
9 Rue Blainville **56**
8 Rue Bonaparte **86**
24 Rue Bonaparte **85**
28 Rue Boissy-d'Anglas **206**
29 Rue Cambon **212**
2 Rue Cardinale **87**
21 Rue Caulaincourt **241**
5 Rue Christine **93**
16 Rue Christophe-Colomb **192**
Rue Cler **112**
Rue Clovis **55**
Rue Cognacq-Jay **115**
6 Rue Daunou **219**
Rue Dauphine **90**
9 Rue de Beaune **72**
1 Rue de Berri **193**
Rue de Bourgogne **100**
Rue de Buci **88**
Rue de la Bûcherie **47**
Rue de la Colombe **29**
4 Rue de la Colombe **29**
Rue de la Cossonnerie **135**
Rue de la Femme Sans Teste (Street of the Headless Woman) **32**
Rue de la Ferronnerie **133**
27 Rue de Fleurus **76**

Rue de la Harpe **95**
Rue de la Huchette **95**
10 Rue de la Huchette **95**
28 Rue de la Huchette **95**
Rue de la Mire **234**
51 Rue de la Montagne-Ste-Geneviève **51**
Rue de la Parcheminerie **95**
Rue de Lappe **158**
Rue de l'Arbre-Sec **173**
Rue de la Verrerie **136**
Rue de l'Ecole de Médecine **94**
Rue de l'Exposition **113**
12 Rue de l'Odéon **81**
2–4 Rue de l'Université **73**
50 Rue de l'Université **67**
8 Rue de Miromesnil **203**
Rue de Monttessuy **115**
Rue de Nevers **90**
Rue de Paradis **248**
Rue de Rivoli **175**
14 Rue de Tilsitt **197**
Rue des Anglais **45**
Rue des Archives **141**
5 Rue des Beaux-Arts **86**
Rue Descartes **55**
39 Rue Descartes **55**
47 Rue Descartes **55**
Rue des Ciseaux **85**
Rue des Ecoles **50**
Rue des Francs-Bourgeois **144**
7 Rue des Grands-Augustins **93**
5 Rue des Italiens **228**
Rue des Rosiers **144**
19 Rue de Tournon **82**
Rue de Varenne **101**
42–44 Rue de Vaugirard **82**
Rue de Venise **26**
Rue du Bac **67**
110 Rue du Bac **68**
24 Rue du Boccador **192**
2 Rue du Bourbon-le-Château **88**
3 Rue du Champ-de-Mars **112**
Rue du Chat-qui-Pêche **95**
31 Rue du Dragon **70**
Rue du Faubourg-St-Antoine **164**
80 Rue du Faubourg-St-Antoine **164**
15 Rue du Faubourg-St-Honoré **207**
33 Rue du Faubourg-St-Honoré **205**
Rue du Faubourg-St-Honoré shopping **205** (map)
Rue du Fouarre **46**
4 Rue du Mont-Thabor **215**
Rue du Poteau **240**
Rue du Vertbois **139**

7 Rue Edmond-Valentin **117**
Rue Férou **82**
Rue Foyatier **236**
7 Rue François–1er **187**
Rue Galande **47**
Rue Gît-le-Coeur **94**
Rue Jacob **73**
7 Rue Jacob **87**
Rue Jean-Nicot **110**
14 Rue Jacob **87**
27 Rue Jacob **87**
56 Rue Jacob **73**
19 Rue La Boétie **203**
Rue Lepic **241**
54 Rue Lepic **241**
6 Rue Le Regrattier **32**
58 Rue Madame **75**
12 Rue Mazarine **89**
Rue Monsieur-le-Prince **80**
Rue Montorgueil **132**
Rue Mouffetard **56**
12 Rue Mouffetard **56**
51–55 Rue Mouffetard **56**
Rue Mouffetard Market **57**
Rue Pavée **146**
Rue Quincampoix **135**
46 Rue Quincampoix **135**
Rue Robert-Esnault-Pelterie **105**
Rue Soufflot **53**
Rue St-André-des-Arts **92**
28 Rue St-André-des-Arts **94**
46 Rue St-André-des-Arts **93**
5 Rue St-Antoine **156**
Rue St-Denis **135**
Rue St-Dominique **103**
1 Rue St-Dominique **103**
3 Rue St-Dominique **103**
5 Rue St-Dominique **103**
10–12 Rue St-Dominique **104**
14–16 Rue St-Dominique **104**
28 Rue St-Dominique **105**
53 Rue St-Dominique **105**
57 Rue St-Dominique **105**
81 Rue St-Dominique **111**
93 Rue St-Dominique **111**
Rue St-Honoré **211**
163 Rue St-Honoré **222**
Rue St-Jacques **48**
27 Rue St-Jacques **48**
Rue St-Julien-le-Pauvre **47**
5 Rue St-Louis-en-l'Ile **34**
18 Rue Sedillot **117**
Rue Surcouf **109**
10 Rue Vauquelin **57**
26 Rue Vavin **76**
17 Rue Visconti **86**
24 Rue Visconti **86**
49 Rue Vivienne **229**

S

Sabbia Rosa **71**
Safety, personal **13**

St-André-des-Arts $$ **92**
Sainte-Chapelle **24**
St-Etienne-du-Mont **55**
Ste-Ursule-de-la-Sorbonne **52**
St-Eustache **132**
St-Germain **62** (chapter and map)
St-Germain-des-Prés $$ **85**
St-Germain-des-Prés **85**
St-Germain-l'Auxerrois **174**
St-Honoré **198** (chapter and map), **220** (map)
St-James et Albany $$$ **221**
St-Jean **108**
St-Jean-de-Montmartre **233**
St-Julien-le-Pauvre **47**
St-Leu–St-Gilles **135**
St-Louis-des-Invalides **106**
St-Louis-en-l'Ile **34**
St-Médard **57**
St. Jacques Tower (Tour St-Jacques) **172**
St. Michael Fountain (Fontaine St-Michel) **94**
St-Michel Métro **95**
St-Nicolas-des-Champs **139**
St-Nicolas-du-Chardonnet **43**
St-Paul–St-Louis **152**
St-Philippe-du-Roule **201**
St-Pierre-de-Montmartre **235**
St-Pierre du Gros Caillou **112**
St-Roch **221**
St-Séverin **95**
St-Sulpice **82**
St-Vladimir le Grand **73**
Salle Gaveau **201**
San Francisco Book Company **81**
San Régis $$$$ **187**
Sanz-Sans ★★$ **165**
Sauvage, Henri **76**
School of Fine Arts (Ecole des Beaux-Arts) **86**
Sculpture and Fountains **182**
Select Hôtel $$$ **53**
Senlis **253**
Sennelier **73**
Servandoni, Giovanni **82**
Sèvres Porcelain Factory (Manufacture Nationale de Sèvres) **225**
Shakespeare and Company **48**
Shobudo **51**
Shopping **14**
Shu Uemura **74**
Simounet, Roland **145**

Si Tu Veux **227**
Slow Club **173**
Smallhoover, Joseph **35** (bests)
Smoking **15**
Société Théosophique de France **117**
66 Café ★$ **158**
Sorbonne **52**
Soufflot, Jacques-Germain **54, 175, 184**
Spoon Food & Wine ★★$$ **188**
Square Barye **34**
Square Courtyard (Cour Carrée) **177**
Square de Latour-Maubourg **108**
Square du Vert-Galant **20**
Square Jean-XXIII **30**
Square Rapp **117**
3 Square Rapp **117**
Square René-Viviani **46**
Square Suzanne-Buisson **240**
Stained Glass **49**
Starck, Philippe **135**
Statue de Beaumarchais **153**
Statue de Charlemagne **26**
Statue de Clemenceau **185**
Statue de Jeanne d'Arc **222**
Statue de Ste-Geneviève **38**
Steinheil, Louis Charles Auguste **25, 35**
Stock Exchange (Bourse des Valeurs) **229**
Street, George Edmund **192**
Street of the Headless Woman (Rue de la Femme Sans Teste) **32**
Street plan **15**
The Studio ★★$ **140**
Studio Galande **47**
Sukiyaki ★$ **159**
Superlatif **68**

T

Taillevent ★★★★$$$$ **194**
Tan Dinh ★★★$$$ **67**
Tapestries **50**
Taverne Henry IV ★★$ **21**
Taxes **15**
Taxis **7, 8, 10**
The Tea Caddy ★$ **47**
Telephone numbers, essential **16**
Telephones **15**
Temple de Pentémont **103**
Temple de Ste-Marie **153**
Terrasse Fleurie ★★$$ **181**
Terrass Hôtel $$$ **241**
Thaï Elephant ★★★$$ **161**
Than ★★$ **73**
Than Binh **45**

Thanksgiving ★★$$ **152**
Théâtre de la Bastille **161**
Théâtre de la Huchette **95**
Théâtre de l'Atelier **243**
Théâtre de la Ville de Paris **173**
Théâtre de l'Odéon **80**
Théâtre des Champs-Elysées **189**
Théâtre du Châtelet **173**
Théâtre du Rond-Point **186**
Théâtre du Rond-Point Restaurant ★$$ **186**
Théâtre National de Chaillot **122**
Thomas, Albert **185**
Thoumieux ★★$$ **108**
Tickets **15**
Time zone **15**
Tim Hôtel $$ **234**
Tipping **15**
Tobacco Museum (Musée-Galerie de la Seita) **110**
Toraya ★★$$ **211**
Toupary ★★$$ **174**
Tour de l'Horloge (Clock Tower) **24**
Tour Eiffel (Eiffel Tower) **118**
Tours **10**
Tours de Bonbec, d'Argent, and de César (Babble, Money, and César Towers) **23**
Tour St-Jacques (St. Jacques Tower) **172**
Trains **7, 8**
Transportation **6**
Transportation, local **8**
Treasury **49**
Trenta Quattro ★★$$ **101**
Trompe-l'Oeil **203**
Tschumi, Bernard **248**
Tuileries $$$ **221**
Tuileries Bar **181**
Tuileries Gardens (Jardin des Tuileries) **179**
Tuileries Palace (Palais des Tuileries) **179**

U

Underground attractions **142**
UNESCO Secretariat **124**
Upper Level **66**

V

Vagenende ★★$$ **88**
Valentino **189**
Vasconi, Claude **134**
Vaux-le-Vicomte **253**
Vendôme **214**
Vendôme Column **213**
Viaduc des Arts **166**

Via Palissy ★★$$ **70**
Victoire **129**
Vieux Marais $$ **140**
Vignes de Montmartre (Montmartre Vineyards) **238**
Vignon, Pierre **209**
Village St-Paul **152**
Village Voice **84**
Villa Léandre **241**
Villa Savoye **255**
Vin sur Vin ★★★$$$ **116**
Viollet-le-Duc, Eugène-Emmanuel **25, 122, 218**
Virgin Megastore **192**
Visconti, Ludovico **226**
Visitors' information **16**
Vivario ★★$$ **42**
von Spreckelsen, Johan Otto **249**
Vue sur Toi **160**

W

Walking **11**
Wanouchka ★$$ **234**
W.H. Smith and Son **181**
Willi's Wine Bar ★★$$ **226**
Wolfe, Judith **167** (bests)
Wood, Phil **125** (bests)

Y

Yakijapo Mitsuko ★★$$ **70**
Yakitori ★$ **221**
Y's Yohji Yamamoto **71**
Yvan ★★$$$ **187**
Yvan sur Seine ★★$$ **174**
Yveline **87**

Z

Zehrfuss, Bernard **124**
Zoological Park **247**

Restaurants

Only restaurants with star ratings are listed below. All restaurants are listed alphabetically in the main (preceding) index. Always call in advance to ensure a restaurant has not closed, changed its hours, or booked its tables for a private party. The restaurant price ratings are based on the average cost of an entrée for one person, excluding tax and tip.
    ★★★★ An Extraordinary Experience
    ★★★ Excellent
    ★★ Very Good
    ★ Good
    $$$$ Big Bucks ($120 and up)
    $$$ Expensive ($70-$120)

$$ Reasonable ($25-$70)
$ The Price Is Right (less than $25)

★★★★

Alain Ducasse $$$$ **249**
L'Ambrosie $$$$ **151**
L'Arpège $$$$ **101**
La Tour d'Argent $$$$ **39**
Le Grand Véfour $$$$ **224**
Lucas Carton $$$$ **209**
Pierre Gagnaire $$$$ **194**
Ritz Espadon $$$$ **214**
Taillevent $$$$ **194**

★★★

A. Beauvilliers $$$ **237**
Ambassadeurs Restaurant $$$$ **183**
Angélina $$ **180**
Benoit $$$ **136**
Campagne et Provence $$ **42**
Carré des Feuillants $$$$ **215**
Caviar Kaspia $$$ **209**
Chiberta $$$ **196**
Copenhague $$$ **195**
Foc Ly $$ **124**
Goumard $$$ **212**
Guy Savoy $$$$ **197**
Il Cortile $$ **212**
Issé $$$ **228**
Jacques Cagna $$$$ **92**
La Bûcherie $$$ **48**
La Castafiore $$ **32**
Ladurée $ **207**
La Fermette Marbeuf 1900 $$ **191**
L'Affriolé $$ **111**
La Marée Verte $$ **42**
Lapérouse $$$ **93**
La Rôtisserie d'en Face $$ **93**
Lasserre $$$$ **186**
Le Bellecour $$ **109**
Le Bristol $$$$ **202**
Le Carpaccio $$$ **197**
Le Céladon $$$ **216**
Le Divellec $$$ **106**
Ledoyen $$$$ **185**
Le Jardin $$$ **197**
Le Jules Verne $$$ **119**
Le Pré Catelan $$$ **250**
Le Récamier $$$ **70**
Le Restaurant de l'Astor $$$ **204**
Le Restaurant Opéra $$$$ **217**
Les Bookinistes $$$ **93**
Les Bouchons de François Clerc $$ **46**
Les Deux Abeilles $ **115**
Les Muses $$$ **217**

Le Train Bleu $$$ **166**
Macéo $$ **226**
Maison Blanche $$$ **190**
Mariage Frères $$ **143**
Marius et Janette $$$ **190**
Moissonnier $$ **43**
Paul Minchelli $$$ **107**
Pierre au Palais Royal $$$ **225**
Régence-Plaza $$$ **189**
Relais du Parc $$$ **250**
Restaurant Drouant $$$$ **228**
Restaurant Laurent $$$$ **186**
Tan Dinh $$$ **67**
Thaï Elephant $$ **161**
Vin sur Vin $$$ **116**

★★

A La Cloche des Halles $ **131**
A La Cour de Rohan $ **92**
A La Tour de Montlhery $$ **133**
Alcazar $$ **90**
Allard $$ **94**
Altitude 95 $$ **119**
Ambassade d'Auvergne $$ **138**
Androuët $$ **196**
A Priori Thé $ **227**
Auberge d'Chez Eux $$$ **108**
Auberge de Jarente $ **149**
Auberge des Trois Bonheurs $$ **222**
Au Bon Accueil $$ **116**
Au Bon St-Pourçain $$ **82**
Au Clair de la Lune $$ **235**
Au Gourmet de l'Isle $$ **33**
Au Pactole $$ **43**
Au Petit Fer à Cheval $ **143**
Au Petit Marguery $$ **57**
Au Petit Riche $$ **228**
Au Petit Tone $$ **109**
Au Poulbot Gourmet $$ **237**
Aux Charpentiers $$ **83**
Aux Lyonnais $$ **229**
Aux Négociants $$ **237**
Bar Au Sel $$ **110**
Bar des Théâtres $$ **189**
Barfly $$ **194**
Bar St-James $$ **222**
Beato $$ **111**
Bistrot les Sans-Culottes $$ **159**
Bofinger $$ **157**
Bouillon Racine $$ **81**
Boulangerie St-Philippe $ **201**
Brasserie Balzar $$ **53**
Brasserie Bourbon $$ **99**
Brasserie 234 Rivoli $$ **181**
Brasserie Lipp $$ **71**

buddha-bar $$ **206**
Café Beaubourg $$ **136**
Café Bleu $ **207**
Café de Flore $$ **74**
Café de la Paix $$ **217**
Café de l'Industrie $ **160**
Café de Mars $$ **114**
Café du Marché $ **112**
Café Iguana $ **160**
Café Max $ **107**
Café Parisien $ **69**
Casa Bini $$ **91**
Cercle Ledoyen $$ **185**
Charlot, Le Roi des Coquillages $$$ **242**
Charonne Café $ **163**
Chez Agnès $$ **114**
Chez André $ **191**
Chez Francis $$ **190**
Chez Georges (Les Halles) $$ **130**
Chez Henri $ **83**
Chez la Vieille $$ **174**
Chez Maître Paul $$ **81**
Chez Marius $$$ **100**
Chez Paul $ **163**
Chez Pauline $$ **226**
Chez Pento $$ **53**
Chez Ribe $$ **123**
Chez Toutoune $$ **42**
Chez Vong aux Halles $$ **134**
The Chicago Pizza Pie Factory $ **193**
Chieng-Mai $$ **45**
China Club $$ **156**
Christian Constant $ **76**
Claude & Nicole $ **234**
Clementine $$ **229**
Club des Poètes $ **100**
Coffee Parisien $ **84**
Coffee Saint-Germain $$ **73**
Cosi $ **87**
Costes $$$ **215**
Dalloyau (St-Germain) $$ **78**
Dame Tartine $ **155**
Dave $$ **221**
Dominique $$ **77**
Du Côté 7ème $$ **109**
Dynasty $ **225**
Escrouzailles $$ **187**
Flora Danica $$ **194**
Fouquet's $$$ **193**
Gargantua $$ **222**
Gérard Besson $$$ **131**
Hédiard $$ **210**
Hollywood Savoy $$ **229**
Isami $$ **33**
Jo Goldenberg $$ **147**
Juveniles $$ **226**
La Boule d'Or $$ **107**
La Boutique Flora Danica $ **194**

La Brasserie de l'Isle Saint-Louis $$ **31**
La Cafetière $$ **90**
La Charlotte de l'Isle $ **34**
La Closerie des Lilas $$$ **77**
La Coupole $$ **76**
La Crémaillère 1900 $$ **235**
La Distillerie $$ **165**
La Ferme St-Hubert $$ **211**
La Fermette du Sud-Ouest $$ **131**
La Fontaine de Mars $$ **113**
La Fourmi Ailée $ **46**
La Galoche d'Aurillac $$ **159**
La Guirlande de Julie $$ **151**
La Maison de la Lozère $$ **95**
La Maison de la Truffe $$$ **209**
La Maison du Valais $$ **207**
La Méditerranée $$ **81**
La Palette $ **88**
La Poule au Pot $ **110**
La Rose de France $$ **21**
La Rôtisserie du Beaujolais $$ **39**
La Table de Fès $$ **76**
La Tartine $ **147**
La Terrasse $$ **242**
L'Atlas $$ **39**
La Tour de Jade $ **228**
La Truffière $$ **56**
L'Auvergne Gourmande $ **113**
L'Avenue $$ **188**
La Verrière $$ **217**
Le Bar à Huitres (Les Halles, Marais, and The Bastille) $$ **157**
Le Bar à Huitres (The Latin Quarter) $$ **48**
Le Baron Rouge $ **164**
Le Bistrot de Marius $$ **190**
Le Bistrot de Paris $$ **72**
Le Bistrot du Peintre $ **162**
Le Bistrot du 7ème $ **107**
Le Boeuf sur le Toit $$ **187**
Le Café Marly $$ **177**
Le Caméléon $$ **77**
Le Caveau du Palais $$ **21**
Le Chai de l'Abbaye $ **88**
L'Ecluse (Louvre and The Champs Elysées) $$ **192**
L'Ecluse (St-Honoré) $$ **209**
L'Ecluse (St-Germain) $ **94**
Le Cochon à l'Oreille $ **132**
Le Colimaçon $$ **143**
Le Dôme Bastille $$ **157**
Le Duplex $$ **195**
Le Flore en l'Ile $ **31**
Le Garde Manger $$ **101**
Le Golfe de Naples $ **83**
Le Grand Café Capucines $$ **219**
Le Grand Louvre $$ **178**

Le Loir dans la Théière $ **147**
Le Louis d'Or $$$ **191**
Le Maquis $$ **240**
Le Marcande $$$ **203**
Le Maupertu $$ **108**
Le Merisier $$ **202**
Le Monde des Chimères $$ **31**
Le Mouffetard $ **57**
L'Enoteca $$ **153**
Le Pavillon de Montsouris $$ **246**
Le Petit St-Benoît $ **74**
Le Petit Vatel $ **83**
Le Petit Yvan $$ **187**
L'Epi d'Or $$ **223**
Le Poquelin $$ **226**
Le Procope $$ **91**
Le Raccard $$ **51**
Le Restaurant $$ **243**
Le Roi du Pot-au-Feu $$ **211**
Le Sancerre $ **116**
Les Boucholeurs $$ **225**
Les Bourgeoises $$ **149**
L'Escargot Montorgueil $$ **132**
Lescure $$ **182**
Les Deux Magots $$ **75**
Le Sélect $ **77**
Les Fous de l'Ile $ **33**
Les Grandes Marches $$ **155**
Le 6 Bosquet $$ **115**
Le Souk $$ **162**
Le Square Trousseau $$ **164**
Les Taillandiers $ **161**
L'Estaminet Gaya $$ **212**
L'Eté en Pente Douce $ **237**
Le Tire Bouchon Cabaret $ **235**
L'Etoile Verte $$ **197**
Le Toit de Paris $$ **123**
Le 30 (Fauchon) $$ **211**
Le Vaudeville $$ **229**
Le Vieux Bistro $$ **30**
Le Ziryab $$ **61**
L'Impasse $$ **152**
Lina's $ **130**
Lire Entre les Vignes $ **160**
L'Oeillade $$ **67**
L'Orangerie (Ile St-Louis) $$$ **34**
L'Oriental $ **243**
L'Osteria $$ **149**
Ma Bourgogne (Les Halles, Marais, and The Bastille) $$ **151**
Ma Bourgogne (St-Honoré) $$ **201**
Marie & Fils $$ **89**
Maxim's $$$$ **183**
Mirama $ **48**
Obélisque $$ **183**

Pacific Eiffel $$ **123**
Pâtisserie St-Germain-l'Auxerrois $$ **174**
Pause Café $ **162**
Perraudin $ **54**
Pharamond $$ **134**
Polidor $ **80**
404 $$ **139**
Ravi $$$ **67**
Relais du Massif Central $ **158**
Restaurant des Beaux-Arts $ **86**
Restaurant Le Champ de Mars $$ **108**
Restaurant Montalembert $$ **72**
Restaurant Paul $$ **22**
Restaurant Véro-Dodat $$ **223**
Ristorante Romano $$ **191**
Sanz-Sans $ **165**
Spoon Food & Wine $$ **188**
The Studio $ **140**
Taverne Henry IV $ **21**
Terrasse Fleurie $$ **181**
Than $ **73**
Thanksgiving $$ **152**
Thoumieux $$ **108**
Toraya $$ **211**
Toupary $$ **174**
Trenta Quattro $$ **101**
Vagenende $$ **88**
Via Palissy $$ **70**
Vivario $$ **42**
Willi's Wine Bar $$ **226**
Yakijapo Mitsuko $$ **70**
Yvan $$$ **187**
Yvan sur Seine $$ **174**

★

Auberge de la Bonne Franquette $$ **235**
Auberge du Champ de Mars $ **113**
Au Diable des Lombards $ **133**
Au Lys d'Argent $ **31**
Au Père Tranquille $ **135**
Au Pied de Cochon $$ **131**
Au Rendez-Vous des Camionneurs $$ **23**
Au St-Séverin $ **94**
Au Sauvignon $ **70**
Au Savoyard $$ **91**
Aux Anysetiers du Roy $$ **31**
Bar de Jarente $ **149**
Brasserie des Deux Palais $ **25**
Café de Cluny $ **49**
Café de la Cité $ **140**
Café des Hauteurs $ **66**
Café Lunch $ **104**
Café Véry $ **180**

Chartier $ **229**
Chez Claude Sainlouis $ **70**
Chez Germain $ **202**
Chez L'Ami Jean $$ **111**
Chez Nous $ **223**
Chez René $$ **42**
Coconnas $$ **150**
Coyote Café $ **160**
Delices St. Roch $ **221**
The Hairy Lemon $ **152**
Havanita Café $ **159**
Indiana Cafe $$ **157**
Joe Allen $$ **134**
Kniaz Igor $$ **117**
Korean Barbecue $$ **71**
La Bohème du Tertre $$ **235**
La Chaumière en l'Ile $$ **31**
La Chope $ **56**
La Chope des Vosges $$ **150**
La Croque au Sel $ **113**
La Maison Rose $ **238**
La Mandarin de Latour-Maubourg $ **107**
La Mère Catherine $$ **235**
L'Annexe $$ **242**
La Petite Galette $ **241**
La Pirada $ **158**
L'Auberge de la Reine Blanche $$ **34**
Le Bar du Caveau $ **22**
Le Berkeley $$ **187**
Le Bilboquet $$ **74**
Le Bistrot de Bofinger $$ **157**
Le Coupe-Chou $$ **52**
Le Dôme du Marais $$ **143**
Le Gastelier $ **236**
Le Muniche $$ **74**
Le Pavillon Baltard $ **131**
Le Progrès $ **234**
Le Rallye $ **39**
Le Restaurant de la Mosquée $ **59**
Les Colonies du Paradis $ **166**
Les Fontaines $$ **54**
Les Noailles $$ **222**
Les Portes $ **163**
Le Trumilou $ **171**
L'Incroyable Restaurant $ **225**
Matsuri Sushi $$ **226**
Maxoff Restaurant $$ **67**
Museum Restaurant $ **146**
Nos Ancêtres les Gaulois $$ **33**
Pâtisserie de la Tour Eiffel $ **116**
Peny $ **209**
Pub St-Germain-des-Prés $$ **91**
Relais Plaza $$ **189**
Restaurant du Musée d'Orsay $$ **66**

66 Café $ **158**
Sukiyaki $ **159**
The Tea Caddy $ **47**
Théâtre du Rond-Point
Restaurant $$ **186**
Wanouchka $$ **234**
Yakitori $ **221**

Hotels

The hotels listed below are grouped according to their price ratings; they are also listed in the main index. The hotel price ratings reflect the base price of a standard room for two people for one night during the peak season.

$$$$ Big Bucks ($300 and up)
$$$ Expensive ($150–$300)
$$ Reasonable ($75–$150)
$ The Price Is Right (less than $75)

$$$$

Castiglione **206**
Demeure Castille **212**
Four Seasons Hotel George V Paris **192**
Hôtel Costes **215**
Hôtel Crillon **183**
Hôtel de la Trémoille **191**
Hôtel de Vigny **194**
Hôtel François I **192**
Hôtel Inter-Continental Paris **181**
Hôtel Le Bristol **202**
Hôtel Lotti **215**
Hôtel Lutetia **69**
Hôtel Meurice **181**
Hôtel Montalembert **72**
Hôtel Regina **222**
Hôtel Ritz **214**
Hôtel Scribe **217**
Hôtel Westminster **216**
Lancaster **193**
L'Astor Westin Demeure **204**
Le Grand Hôtel Inter-Continental **217**
Le Méridien Etoile **195**
Le Parc **250**
L'Hôtel **86**
Paris Hilton **123**
Pavillon de la Reine **151**
Plaza Athénée **189**

Raphael **195**
Relais Christine **92**
Résidence Maxim's **186**
Royal Monceau **197**
Royal Saint-Honoré **215**
San Régis **187**

$$$

Angleterre **74**
Carlton's **243**
Claridge-Bellman **191**
Colbert **45**
Grand Hôtel de Champagne **173**
Hôtel Beau Manoir **210**
Hôtel Bourgogne et Montana **100**
Hôtel Bradford-Elysées **201**
Hôtel Burgundy **212**
Hôtel de Fleurie **91**
Hôtel de l'Abbaye **75**
Hôtel de l'université **73**
Hôtel de Lutèce **31**
Hôtel des Deux-Iles **32**
Hôtel de Seine **87**
Hôtel des Grands Hommes **54**
Hôtel des Sts-Pères **71**
Hôtel Duc de St-Simon **67**
Hôtel du Jeu de Paume **33**
Hôtel du Louvre **222**
Hôtel Left Bank St-Germain **91**
Hôtel le Régent **91**
Hôtel St-Merri **136**
La Villa **87**
Lenox **73**
Le Sainte-Beuve **76**
Relais Hôtel de Vieux Paris **94**
St-James et Albany **221**
Select Hôtel **53**
Terrass Hôtel **241**
Tuileries **221**

$$

Caravelle **243**
Chopin **229**
Comfort Hotel Louvre Montana **222**
Ducs d'Anjou **133**
Esmeralda **47**
Familia Hôtel **43**
Grand Hôtel des Balcons **81**
Grand Hôtel Jeanne d'Arc **149**
Hotel Bastille Speria **156**

Hôtel Caron de Beaumarchais **143**
Hôtel Colisée **188**
Hôtel de l'Alma **113**
Hôtel de la Place des Vosges **151**
Hôtel de la Tulipe **111**
Hôtel de l'Avenir **75**
Hôtel de Londres Eiffel **114**
Hôtel des Grandes Ecoles **56**
Hôtel de Varenne **101**
Hôtel D'Orsay **65**
Hôtel du Collège de France **50**
Hôtel du Quai Voltaire **72**
Hôtel Jardin des Plantes **59**
Hôtel le Pavillon **109**
Hôtel Muguet **108**
Hôtel Opal **210**
Hôtel Régyn's Montmartre **233**
Hôtel Relais Bosquet **113**
Hôtel Saint Dominique **109**
Hôtel St-Louis **31**
Hôtel St-Louis Marais **153**
Hôtel Thoumieux **109**
La Louisiane **88**
L'Ermitage Hôtel **237**
Montpensier **225**
New Hôtel Roblin **210**
Perreyve **75**
Résidence Charles-Dullin **243**
St-André-des-Arts **92**
St-Germain-des-Prés **85**
Tim Hôtel **234**
Vieux Marais **140**

$

Hôtel Champ-de-Mars **112**
Hôtel Damrémont **240**
Hôtel Daval **160**
Hôtel Henri IV **21**
Hôtel les Sans-Culottes **159**

Features

The Building Baron **22**
Child's Play **102**
The City of Light on the Big Screen **60**
Corridors of Nostalgia **239**
CyberParis **84**
A Festival of Food in Paris's Markets **44**
Fêtes et Foires (Festivals and Fairs) **16**
Metric Conversions **14**

Paris in Print **120**
Paris Seen from Down Below **142**
Paris Seen from on High **29**
Parlez-Vous Anglais? **124**
Parlez-Vous Français? **40**

Bests

Fitch, Noél Riley (Author) **125**
Gaucheron, Eric (Manager, Familia Hotel) **125**
Genty, Françoise (Waiter/Former Editor and Writer, FAO-Rome and OECD-Paris) **167**
Johnston, Mireille (Author) **167**
Smallhoover, Joseph (Attorney, Dechert Price & Rhoads) **35**
Wolfe, Judith (Artist) **167**
Wood, Phil (Co-Owner/Manager, San Francisco Book Co., Paris) **125**

Maps

Additional Highlights **244**
The Bastille **126, 154**
The Champs-Elysées **168**
Day Trips **252**
Eiffel Tower **96**
Ile de la Cité **18**
Ile St-Louis **18**
Invalides **96**
The Islands: Ile de la Cité and Ile St-Louis **18**
The Latin Quarter **36**
Les Halles **126**
Louvre **168, 172**
Map key **8**
Marais **126**
Montmartre **230**
Paris **2**
Paris Métro *See Inside front cover*
Place de la Madeleine shopping **208**
Place des Victoires shopping **129**
Place Vendôme shopping **213**
Rue du Faubourg-St-Honoré shopping **205**
St-Germain **62**
St-Honoré **198, 220**

Credits

Writer
David Burke

ACCESS®PRESS

Editorial Supervisor
Elissa Altman

Managing Editor
Susan Hoffner

Senior Art Director
Robin Arzt

Design Supervisor
Iva Hacker-Delany

Designer
Elizabeth Streit

Map Designer
Patricia Keelin
Mark Stein Studios

Associate Director of
Production
Dianne Pinkowitz

Special Thanks
Stephen Brandon
Jason Lasecki
Doris Ramirez

ACCESS®PRESS does not solicit individuals, organizations, or businesses for inclusion in our books, nor do we accept payment for inclusion. We welcome, however, information from our readers, including comments, criticisms, and suggestions for new listings. Send all correspondence to: ACCESS®PRESS, 10 East 53rd Street, Fifth Floor, New York, NY 10022

Detail from Musée Carnavalet